Arsenal

THE OFFICIAL ILLUSTRATED HISTORY

1886–2011

PHIL SOAR AND MARTIN TYLER

Arsenal

THE OFFICIAL ILLUSTRATED HISTORY

1886–2011

Phil Soar and Martin Tyler

Foreword by Arsène Wenger

125 YEARS
IN THE MAKING

Records and Statistics

Since their foundation in 1886 Arsenal have played over 6,000 first-class matches. We cannot talk about them all but we can at least record them. Throughout the book you will find a complete, match-by-match, week-by-week record (up to June 2011) of every first-class game the Club has played. We have chosen 1970, the year in which the Club won its first European trophy, from which to cover not only all the games and their results, but also all the team line-ups and goalscorers. The statistical sections of the book have been a massive undertaking for all concerned and we should like to thank John Burt, who provided the original material and checked and corrected it; Daniel Feinstein, who prepared the players' records to show every first-class appearance since the Club was founded; Kevin Connolly and Tom Harris for their updates; Roger Walker for his work on the original typography and layout; and Jonathan Culverhouse for his expertise.

NOTE: The records, statistics and history in this publication are as known at 1 June, 2011.

An Hachette UK Company
www.hachette.co.uk

Records by John Burt and Daniel Feinstein with assistance from Jonathan Culverhouse, Kevin Connolly, Rab MacWilliam, Chas Newkey-Burden.

Additional text: Adam Ward, Peter Arnold, Ivan Ponting, Rab MacWilliam, Kevin Connolly, Jem Maidment, Chas Newkey-Burden, Alex Murphy and Tom Harris

2011 edition edited by Cathy Meeus and designed by Schermuly Design Co

This edition published in 2011 by Hamlyn, a division of Octopus Publishing Group Ltd,
Endeavour House
189 Shaftesbury Avenue
London WC2H 8JY
www.octopusbooks.co.uk

First published in 1986
Revised and updated 1994, 1995, 1996, 1997, 1998, 1999, 2000, 2001, 2002, 2003, 2004, 2005, 2007, 2008, 2009, 2010, 2011

ISBN: 978-0-600-62353-3

A CIP catalogue record for this book is available from the British Library

Printed and bound in China

10 9 8 7 6 5 4 3 2 1

TM © THE ARSENAL FOOTBALL CLUB PLC

www.arsenal.com

Photographic acknowledgments

Picture Research: Daffydd Bynon

The photographs in this book have been reproduced with the permission of the following collections:

Arsenal Football Club plc / Stuart MacFarlane, Colorsport, Getty Images, Mirror Syndication International, News International Syndication.

CONTENTS

FOREWORD

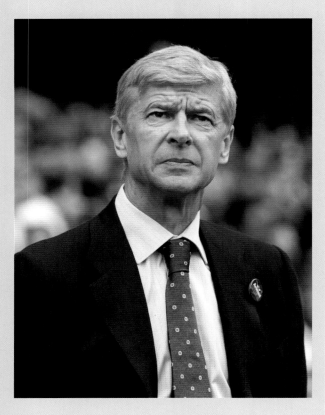

It is an honour to be Manager of Arsenal Football Club on its 125th anniversary. For all of us, it is a time of celebration and reflection. Celebration of all the achievements of this great Club, of what it's achieved on the pitch through the decades and a chance for you, the fans, to celebrate that special bond with your Club. It is also a great time for reflection, for looking back at the incredible history of a football club that started from such modest origins.

Before I arrived at the Club in 1996 I knew that Arsenal had played an important role in English and world football, but it wasn't until I became immersed in day to day life here that I got a full sense of how steeped it was in tradition. From reading this book and talking to those, like Pat Rice – who played in the 'double'-winning team of 1971 – and Don Howe – who gave over 40 years' service to the Club – I got a real understanding of what the Club stands for. The values that every member of staff strives to uphold.

It's fitting that this book should start with the story of Herbert Chapman, as it's Chapman's all-conquering team of the 1930s that set the standard for others to follow, including myself. It wasn't just the trophies his teams won, but the way they pushed boundaries, looking for new ways to improve performance and the style in which they achieved their goals. His team combined skill with self-belief and respect and it's these elements that I try to instill in players at every level. Especially respect. Respect for the game, the fans, for opponents and, most of all, the Club they represent.

When you look back at the history of the Club you will see players that were, and still are, household names. Men such as Alex James, Charlie George, Liam Brady and Thierry Henry, whose skill was admired internationally. You'll also read about games that had an impact on the national game, not least that incredible finish to the 1989 season. You may also be surprised at just how much football innovation started at Arsenal – from white footballs to floodlights. If you consider all this, and look at the stunning, state-of-the-art Emirates Stadium, it's incredible to think that it all started with a simple desire for munitions workers to play the game. From this simple love of the game, and these humblest of beginnings, your football Club emerged and grew into what it is today.

It gives me enormous pride to see my teams and players taking their place in the Arsenal story alongside the legends of the past. It's a huge motivation to think that we might add to the incredible story of this wonderful Club. This is why our history is so important. It shapes our future by inspiring us to live up to the standards of those like Herbert Chapman. I am trying to create my own lasting legacy for the future of Arsenal Football Club. My team and I are trying to build on the successes of the past and trying to create a platform that should see Arsenal maintain its high standards far into the future... maybe even for the next 125 years.

Arsène Wenger

INTRODUCTION

One hundred and twenty five years is a long time. An idea of just how long can perhaps best be given when we realise that 1886, the year of Arsenal's birth, was also the year in which the world's first motor car was built. Even then, the 15 young men who founded Royal Arsenal were probably well into their thirties before they actually saw a motor vehicle.

Much can happen in that time; too much to record fully here. To give our story meaning we must seek out landmarks, find moments through which it is possible to explain much in a short space of time, perhaps even in a single game. That is why we begin our story not with 1886 or even the magical Doubles of 1971, 1998 and 2002, or the incredible unbeaten Premiership campaign of 2003–04, but with the FA Cup final of 1930. The story is more precise even than that. It homes in on the two captains that day, Tom Parker and Tom Wilson, walking on to the field together. In that one innocent gesture they revealed much about the nature of inter-war football and at the heart of Arsenal's story are, essentially, the '20s and '30s.

By some chronological freak, Arsenal's world changed at the turn of the 1930s. The glories that followed can probably be traced to a dramatic few minutes against a team of Second Division nobodies at Elland Road, Leeds United, the first of the games that are the real cornerstones in the Arsenal story. Forty-one years later, on another ground in Yorkshire, those few minutes were to be eerily re-run. If we must pick landmarks, if that is how this history should be told, then those few minutes from those two matches shine like beacons from the dusk of history. It is those two games that will be among the centre-points of our story.

Both were semi-finals. Both games had seen Arsenal, at half-time, 2–0 down and virtually out. Both finished 2–2. The first game eventually led to the 1930 final, the game that defined an era. It was Arsenal's first ever trophy and from it they went on to the glories of the next ten years. Without that FA Cup win and the succeeding events of the 1930s, it is entirely possible the Arsenal of today would be no more significant than a middle-of-the-road club.

The second game was dramatic for its dénouement, a last-minute Peter Storey penalty that was perhaps the second most important goal in the club's long history. It

was to lead to the 1971 FA Cup final and the Double, a feat Herbert Chapman's team of the 1930s could never achieve. This was the second most important goal for one simple reason. Peter Storey's penalty was not so much the moment the Double was won, but it was certainly the moment when it could have been lost. The first Double is a central, vital and highly emotional part of the Arsenal story but it is ultimately not as important as 1930. With or without the Double of 1971, Arsenal would still be Arsenal. The ground, the club and the worldwide reputation were built by Herbert Chapman, Tom Whittaker and the teams of the 1930s. The three Doubles were the icing on an already substantial cake.

All football clubs have their peculiarities; Arsenal's most interesting one is of location and historical accident. Football in England has long been about provincialism, but Arsenal are not a provincial club. Chapman's efforts in the 1930s, coupled with the lack of any alternative, allowed them to become the capital's club, at a time that corresponded with London imposing its economic and political dominance over the rest of a depressed and uncertain nation. It was this historical good fortune that was ultimately to determine the character of Arsenal. A team supported by rich and poor but somehow, then and now, the rich relation. Herbert Chapman chose his time and his location well – but note that even in 2012 London has still to win the ultimate prize – the European Cup.

Numerous people assisted us in our research and talked to us of their own experiences and recollections, including many Arsenal players, past and present, who kindly took time to help. There are simply too many to thank here. Instead we would like to mention just a handful – Don Howe, Don Roper, Billy Wright, Ken Friar, David Miles and, especially, Bob Wilson, who made his own archives available to the authors. At Hamlyn, we would like to mention our art director Chris Pow, editors Sarah Bennison and Peter Arnold, picture researcher Jean Wright, Diana Godwin-Austen and supporters Charles Fowkes and Terence Cross.

Philip Soar & Martin Tyler

CHAPTER 1

HERBERT CHAPMAN

THE ARCHITECT OF SUCCESS

The beginning of everything can really be traced to 2.45 pm on Saturday 26 April 1930. The place was London's vast Empire Stadium. Two men stood together in the Wembley tunnel, tense with just 15 minutes to go before the start of only the eighth FA Cup final to be played there.

Soon they were to emerge into the sunlight together, the first captains ever to lead out their teams side-by-side for a major football match. One of those men was Tom Wilson, captain and centre-half of Huddersfield Town, the dominant team of the age. In the 12 years since the First World War, Huddersfield had won a unique hat-trick of League Championships and reached four FA Cup finals. But, though no one could have believed it that day, the parade had already passed Huddersfield by. They would never again take home a major trophy.

The second man, Tom Parker, captained Arsenal, a north London club of no great distinction, which in nearly 50 years had won absolutely nothing. And yet in the decade that remained between that April day in 1930 and the start of another world war, Arsenal, originally Royal Arsenal, later Woolwich Arsenal and briefly The Arsenal, would win five Championships, match Huddersfield's League hat-trick and reach two more FA Cup finals. By 1939 they would have become the richest, best supported and most successful club side in the world, a bright shining star that has yet to be dimmed in the football firmament.

For that fleeting moment in 1930 the pendulum stood still. Midway between the two world wars the centre of gravity of English football gently moved south. And, as if to mark such a uniquely symbolic game, the teams not only took the field together but crowded into the same dressing room at the end to congratulate the winners and even shared the same celebration dinner that night at the Café Royal.

There had to be more to it than that, of course, much more, certainly another reason for such a peculiarly portentous day. The reason was to be found in the slightly portly, commanding figure of the 52-year-old Arsenal manager, Herbert Chapman. It was he who had earlier led Huddersfield to their hat-trick in the mid-1920s, left that team before the end of it and moved to small, struggling, trophyless Arsenal. When he arrived at Highbury in May 1925 he had said it would take five years to build a winning team. Here he was at Wembley, literally five years to the week later, presumably intending to make good his boast.

In retrospect, with the useful hindsight of half a century, it is easy to see what happened and provide explanations for why it happened. But it was not so clear then. Huddersfield were clearly the better team of the two; Arsenal were in the bottom half of the First Division and had survived several

close shaves on their way to the final. If the Gunners had lost that day it is not unreasonable to argue that the whole history of Arsenal FC might have been very different. There may never have been the 1930s; we may never have had reason to speak of the marble halls of Highbury; Arsenal may have remained, at best, as they had since their 1927 FA Cup final defeat, a middle-of-the-road First Division club. The 1930 FA Cup final might have been remembered primarily for the dramatic appearance of the *Graf Zeppelin*, another peculiarly poignant moment in this symbolic final midway between the two wars. The hopes and fears of years gone by, and of years to come, rested heavily on the shoulders of Tom Parker and Herbert Chapman that day.

It is the measure of this one game, of its remarkable portents, of the future that it promised for one of the two clubs and the past chapter that it closed for the other, that virtually the whole history of inter-war football can be told in its 90 minutes. And, by the same token, the history of Arsenal FC, which remains in essence a tale of the 1930s, can be related in the day's dominant figure – Herbert Chapman. That is why we must start our story of Arsenal Football Club on this one day, with the life of that one man, and with one single, all-encompassing football match.

BIRTH OF THE LEGEND

Saturday 26 April 1930 had begun fine and warm; temperatures were in the sixties, perfect for the 55th FA Cup final. The morning papers had said King George V would not be well enough to attend, but he surprised everyone by arriving to a rousing reception for his first outdoor appearance since an illness 18 months before. The leading story in *The Times* that day had been the arrival home from India of the Prince of Wales, his plane touching down in front of the cameras in Windsor Great Park. But even *The Times* took a more than passing interest in the day's football, pointing out to its readers that: 'The broadcast from Wembley Stadium this afternoon will begin at 2.30 pm with community singing conducted by Mr T. P. Radcliff and accompanied by the band of the Welsh Guards. At 2.45 pm Mr George F. Allison will open the commentary on the Cup final match between The Arsenal and Huddersfield Town, and this is expected to last until about 4.45 pm. The position of the ball in the field of play and the score will be called at intervals by Mr Allison's assistant in the stand.'

George Allison was, as it happened, also an Arsenal director and the club's second biggest shareholder. It was only the fifth time that a game had been broadcast live and the effects of this exciting new medium, wireless, were far from being fully felt. For one thing, the Football League still organised a full programme on Cup final day. The crowds who stayed away to listen to the radio missed some good matches – Wolves drew 4–4 with Bradford Park Avenue, Fred Cheesmuir of Gillingham scored all six goals in his side's 6–0 defeat of Merthyr Town and Lincoln City beat New Brighton 5–3. Sheffield Wednesday stayed five points clear at the top of the First Division with a 1–0 defeat of Grimsby. Arsenal were little concerned about League results. With just two matches left of the season they were in 12th place and the Wembley crowd of 92,488 was understandably only interested in what was

Opposite: Herbert Chapman, the managerial genius who made Arsenal the dominant side of the 1930s and one of the most famous and best-loved clubs in the world. His arrival at Arsenal in 1925 heralded a period of spectacular success, when the Gunners won five League titles and two FA Cup wins – all this at a club that had not won anything since its formation.

Below: Photo-calls and player pools are nothing new; the Arsenal team made a 'talkie' to be shown in news theatres on 16 April 1930 – ten days before the final. Chapman stands between Joe Hulme and Charlie Preedy, with Tom Parker peering over his shoulder.

Above: The 1930 final will be remembered for a remarkable number of reasons, not least the fact that the captains came out side by side for the very first time before a major game. Celebrating Herbert Chapman's association with the two finalists were captains Tom Parker of Arsenal (left) and Tom Wilson of Huddersfield. It was the Yorkshire club's fourth Cup final since the First World War, a period during which they had also won a hat-trick of Championships under Chapman's management.

of subduing Kelly. The defensive plan worked superbly, though it was in no sense a one-sided game. Memories, however, are not made of defensive tactics but of goals, and never more so than in Cup finals.

The Arsenal's first Cup final win remains one of Wembley's most famous. In the team coach on the way from the club's hotel in Harrow, Alex James had spoken to winger Cliff Bastin: 'If we get a free-kick in their half early on, I'll slip it out to you on the wing. You give it me back and I'll have a crack at goal.' Most of the players thought James was joking – since joining the Gunners from Preston he had ceased to be anything other than a very occasional goalscorer. But in the 17th minute just such a free-kick occurred; James was fouled 40 yards from goal, sprang to his feet and looked at referee Tom Crew, who nodded to the Scotsman to take the kick without any ado. Out went the ball to the left-wing, off hared Bastin, drawing Goodall out toward him. At just the right moment Bastin slipped the ball back inside for James, following through, to hit it into the corner of the net. The Huddersfield players protested briefly, but the referee had been quite correct in allowing the instant restart. It was, said *The Times*: 'The skill and bold tactics of James that turned the scale in favour of his side ... to his remarkable control of the ball, he added the craft that both sees and makes openings.'

Some minutes later, in yet another incident redolent with symbolism, the *Graf Zeppelin*, Germany's giant airship and pride of a nation slowly rebuilding its self-confidence, suddenly loomed over the stadium like a massive cloud. Flying at 2,000 feet, well below the legal limit, it dipped its nose in salute to the King and flew on. The players barely noticed; those who did were apparently annoyed at the break in their concentration.

about to happen there and then. Only one London club had won the FA Cup in the 20th century (Spurs) and the capital had still never applauded a League Championship winner.

THE 1930 FA CUP FINAL

As a match, it was one of the better finals. The Arsenal team was Charlie Preedy in goal, Tom Parker and Eddie Hapgood at full-back, Alf Baker, Bill Seddon and Bob John the half-backs, and Joe Hulme, David Jack, Jack Lambert, Alex James and Cliff Bastin the forwards. Nine of the 11 had been brought to Highbury by Chapman himself and, with the substitution of Moss for Preedy, Roberts for Seddon and Charlie Jones for Baker the team was probably close to the greatest one of an era that lives on in the memories of those fans still alive over 80 years later.

Huddersfield were, at the time at least, a rather more distinguished 11. Former England captain Roy Goodall was at full-back, the magnificent centre-half Tom Wilson (a famous Huddersfield surname) remained as stopper, and the right-wing pair of Alex Jackson and Bob Kelly was the best in the country. 'Flying Scotsman' Jackson, scorer of a hat-trick in Scotland's famous 5–1 defeat of England at Wembley two years earlier, had also scored nine of Huddersfield's 11 goals on the way to the final. Eddie Hapgood was given the job of shadowing him wherever he went, Bob John taking the role

ARSENAL WIN THE CUP

Huddersfield attacked for the rest of the game, greatly helped by Arsenal's erratic goalkeeper, Charlie Preedy, who was deputising for the injured Dan Lewis. In the programme pen-notes he had explained how he liked coming out to meet the ball at the earliest opportunity. Unfortunately he appeared not to have explained this to his defence, used to playing in front of a more conservative keeper. Said *The Times* on Monday: '... at times Preedy took risks which hardly deserved to succeed as they did. Three times he let the ball slip from his hands as he was trying to clear.'

The Arsenal goal led something of a charmed life, often unguarded after a Preedy dash had failed to connect with the ball, and the Gunners' centre-forward Jack Lambert spent much of the second half virtually alone on the centre line as his colleagues defended frantically. With just seven minutes left, a sudden long clearance from James found Lambert in the centre circle. Somehow he slipped between Goodall and Spence and the centre-forward hared nearly half the length of the pitch toward the Huddersfield goalkeeper,

Turner, who seemed suddenly dazed by this disastrous turn of events. Lambert shot from the edge of the area past the badly placed keeper, the ball hit the back of the net and Lambert turned, arms outstretched, expecting to greet his onrushing colleagues. But there was no one there; the rest of the side were still in their own half. So Lambert set off alone, applauding himself as he went, to provide one of football's more enduring memories at the end of one of football's most famous matches. It is probably no exaggeration to say that this game, which ended 2–0, along with the FA Cup final and semi-final of 1971 and the end of 1989 are the most memorable in the history of Arsenal Football Club. It was not only the moment when the greatness began, it was also the moment when everything could so easily have slipped away.

The 1930 FA Cup final was the forerunner of two more in the decade that followed – 1932 and 1936 – and of five League Championships, 1931, 1933, 1934, 1935 and 1938. By the time Hitler's war began, Arsenal were without doubt the greatest, the most famous, the most widely supported football club in the world. In the half century since only Liverpool and Manchester United have had a comparable dominance and, even then, it has to be said, without quite the same national prominence or emotional commitment, for and against. One cannot begin to compare, for instance, Liverpool's two defeats by Brighton in the 1983 and 1984 FA Cups with the sensation caused by Walsall when they knocked the Gunners out of the same competition 50 years before. Since the 1930s the glories have inevitably been fewer, the trophies more widely spaced, but the reputation and image that Herbert Chapman built remain essentially as he left them. And so dominant is Chapman in Arsenal's history that, although it was nearly half a century before the club won a major prize, it is surprising to recall that it is also nearly 80 years since Chapman died so tragically in 1934.

The history, status and wealth of the club are so bound up with this one man that it is surely necessary to go back and discover what we can about him, to find what it was that he brought to Highbury which was to generate such an amazing transformation and leave such a lasting legacy. The story of Arsenal Football Club must inevitably begin with the story of Herbert Chapman.

THE HERBERT CHAPMAN STORY

Herbert Chapman was born eight years before Arsenal, on 19 January 1878 in Kiveton Park, a small mining village on the borders of South (then West) Yorkshire and Nottinghamshire. His father was an illiterate miner who had five other sons and one daughter. Herbert was an exceptionally bright child in an age when working class children had virtually no opportunities, so much so that he eventually reached Sheffield Technical College to complete a course in Mining Engineering. He was to use his academic qualifications, and hold down various jobs in industry, for

nearly all of his life. Indeed, it was not until Huddersfield Town first became League Champions, when Chapman was already 46 years old, that he finally turned his back on an engineering career.

He was a moderate footballer, a roly-poly inside forward or wing half, but nothing like as good as his brother Harry, who was a forward with the Sheffield Wednesday Championship winning sides of 1903 and 1904. Herbert remained an amateur through most of his playing career, which took him through a remarkable range of clubs and locations. In the ten years between 1897, when he was 19, and 1907, when he became player-manager of Northampton, he played for Stalybridge Rovers, Rochdale, Grimsby, Swindon, Sheppey United, Worksop, Northampton, Sheffield United and Notts County before heading to north London and Spurs.

In most of these towns he also took an engineering job, which was wise as his playing career could only be described as unmemorable. But ten clubs in as many years also had its advantages. He got to know people in the game throughout the country, he saw numerous styles of management (most of them poor) and he began to develop his own theories about how best to run a football club and win football matches. His longest spell in a single place was two years at White Hart Lane and, though he was usually in the reserves, the potential for a major club in north London (Arsenal were still south of the river) cannot have escaped his attention.

Below: Herbert Chapman (indicated) had joined Spurs as an inside forward in 1905 and finished as their top scorer in the 1905-06 season with 11 goals in 28 games. It was his most successful season in a playing career which spanned ten clubs. Years later, his willingness to join downtrodden Arsenal was partially prompted by a desire to see Spurs' great rivals become a success, for he had generally been poorly treated by Spurs' fans. By a peculiar quirk of fate, his very first game in charge of the Gunners was against Spurs at Highbury – and the visitors won 0-1.

When he took over at Northampton in 1907 they had just finished bottom of the Southern League. In 1908–09 Northampton were Champions. Chapman finished playing the same year and in 1910 Northampton were fourth, in 1911 second and in 1912 third. By that time Chapman had returned to his native Yorkshire as manager of Second Division Leeds City. His first job was to canvass for votes at the League's AGM, where City were facing re-election. The club improved dramatically, just missing out on promotion in 1914 and then, in the rather different atmosphere of wartime football, being good enough to win the unofficial League Championship of 1918. Chapman had taken over the management of a munitions factory in 1916, a move that was probably and paradoxically to save his future career for, in 1919, Leeds were summoned before a League commission to answer allegations of making illegal payments between 1916 and 1918. This had always been, in theory, a major offence in the eyes of the League but was a much more sensitive issue in wartime. The club refused to release their books and were simply thrown out of the League. The club's officials, including their ex-manager, were suspended and Chapman remained in various industrial jobs for the next two years, suffering at least one spell of unemployment.

Chapman probably knew about the payments involved (he had been fined by the League once before, though on something of a technicality, in 1912) but as he was not at the club during the critical period the judgement seemed a little harsh. It was, understandably, to have a lasting effect on him and its echoes were to affect Arsenal in a truly dramatic way a decade later. That part of the story must, however, wait.

SUCCESS AT HUDDERSFIELD

When Leeds City were ejected from the League in 1919, Second Division neighbours Huddersfield Town sensibly decided to move up the road to Elland Road in their place ('From Leeds Road to Leeds City' went the headlines). Town were based in a rugby league stronghold, had little support to speak of and were literally facing collapse. But in a classic instance of 'out of adversity coming strength', meetings of supporters rejected the decision to move towns (though the League had already approved), raised cash and reinvigorated the board. Coincidentally there was a miraculous transformation on the field. Within a year Town were promoted to the First Division and were playing in the first post-war Cup final.

Late in 1920 the Huddersfield secretary-manager, Ambrose Langley (an old playing colleague of Chapman's brother Harry) approached the then unemployed Chapman with an offer of a job as his assistant. Langley had been one of the main advocates of the move to Leeds and he was obviously aware that his own days must be numbered. Chapman had now been out of football for more than four years and as a consequence, the League felt able to cancel his suspension

without further question, but it shows just how far his star had fallen that his new appointment at Huddersfield Town did not receive a single mention even in the local press.

Within a month Langley handed over the reins to Chapman (this must have been agreed in advance), within three years Huddersfield were League Champions and within five they had completed the first League hat-trick in history.

BACK TO LONDON

By that time, however, Chapman had again left Yorkshire and returned to north London. Though Arsenal advertised their manager's job in *The Athletic News* on 11 May 1925, Chapman had already been approached. Arsenal chairman Henry Norris offered him £2,000 a year to take the job, easily the highest salary in the game, and Chapman took little persuading. His days at Tottenham had shown him the potential of London, and when he had visited Highbury before the war he had been particularly struck by the adjacent underground station, only 12 minutes from Piccadilly. In a period of mounting unemployment he was also conscious of the better opportunities his two teenage sons would have in the capital.

THE VISIONARY

So what sort of man was Herbert Chapman? The image that has come down to us over half a century is that of a strict authoritarian, the man who once refused to allow Joe Hulme to spend a weekend at home in Lancashire (though Arsenal

Right: David Jack joined Arsenal in the 1928–29 season, and played in Arsenal's 1930 FA Cup win. Jack was no stranger to success at Wembley having scored the first goal ever at the stadium, for Bolton against West Ham in the 1923 final. He scored again in the 1926 final, and secured winners' medals in both games, before picking up a third medal with Arsenal. In 206 games for the Gunners he scored 123 goals.

were playing at Bolton) because Hulme's two goals on the Saturday were not enough, the man who insisted none of the staff at Highbury left at 6.00 pm before asking whether there was anything more he wanted them to do. But if he was an authoritarian, it was in a far more authoritarian age. Jobs were scarce, jobs at football clubs were good ones, particularly at Highbury. A player earned £8 per week, four times as much as the average working man. To be the most successful club in Britain, you had to have the best. There was no gainsaying that, and it applied across the board. Early on he called the 50 club stewards into his office and told them he was ending the various free perks they received. He wanted everything above board. Though his teams were tough, he never advocated unfair play. There are two celebrated incidents demonstrating this when Chapman immediately transferred players who had been guilty of very bad tackles – Islip from Huddersfield and Black from Arsenal.

He was a committed man. He wanted to build the greatest of all football teams. Bernard Joy said of him: 'There are two kinds of visionary; those that dream of a whole new world, and those who dream of just one thing. Chapman's vision was of the greatest football team in the world. His genius was in actually creating something close to that.'

His players, in their reminiscences, seem to regard him with affection rather than fear; some go even further. Cliff Bastin wrote in 1950: 'There was an aura of greatness about him. He possessed a cheery self-confidence. His power of inspiration and gift of foresight were his greatest attributes. I think his qualities were worthy of an even better reward. He should have been Prime Minister, and might have been but for the lack of opportunities entailed by his position in the social scale.' An extreme view perhaps (and inaccurate as Ramsay MacDonald had been PM at the time), but Chapman believed that his players were worth the very best, hence the tremendous facilities at Highbury, in particular, the medical and physiotherapy side, years before its time, run by Tom Whittaker. He also insisted on his players having part of their earnings saved by the club. 'He was not a bully,' said Bastin, '... he gave few words of praise and fewer of blame.' The signing of Bastin himself also shows other essential elements in Chapman's success as a manager – his absolute commitment to the job and his willingness to back his judgement and take chances.

CHAPMAN SIGNS BASTIN

Chapman had first seen Bastin at Watford, when the manager and George Allison had gone not to watch Bastin at all but to size up a member of the home side named Barnett. Bastin, playing for Exeter in a Third Division South game, was then only 16 but his amazing ball control and composure struck Chapman instantly and Barnett was completely forgotten. In the inter-war period youngsters developed much more slowly and it was very rare to see a teenager even in the

Left: Alex James and Cliff Bastin (right) both joined Arsenal in the 1929–30 season and went on to become two of the great players of Herbert Chapman's side. James both initiated and scored Arsenal's first goal in their 1930 FA Cup win, after linking up cleverly with Bastin. Between them, they made a total of 651 appearances for Arsenal, scoring 203 goals.

Third Division. But Bastin was a natural (when he eventually arrived at Highbury the commissionnaire wouldn't let him in, thinking he was a boy seeking autographs). Chapman set off immediately the following morning for Devon. Bastin, always a phlegmatic man, was unimpressed by Chapman's overtures, even though he had played just a handful of matches for his local club, Exeter City. He was more concerned with a tennis match he was due to play that afternoon. But Chapman persisted. 'I had visions of a lifetime spent sitting there listening to him,' said Bastin a quarter of a century later. Bastin, of course, eventually gave in, signed and became one of the all-time great names in British football, uniquely winning every honour in the game before his 21st birthday.

It was a good example of Chapman personally overseeing Arsenal as a close, family club. He had a very happy home life of his own. His wife was a teacher from the same Yorkshire village, and they had four children. His commitment to his family can be judged by the answer he gave immediately when asked what the proudest moment of such a successful

life had been: 'When my son Ken qualified as a solicitor.' Oddly neither of his sons was to play soccer, but both were accomplished at rugby. Indeed, Ken, the elder, was to become President of the Rugby Football Union. Perhaps the proximity to such tremendous success was a disincentive.

TACTICS FOR SUCCESS

When Chapman joined Arsenal in 1925 he had been playing and managing in the senior game for nearly 30 years, apart from his four-year break. While it would be wrong to say that his conception of the ideal tactical approach was fully formed, it is certainly the case that, over this period, his successes had been based on certain constant themes.

Chapman was, above all else, a believer in great players. He brought Clem Stephenson to Huddersfield as soon as he became manager, and later won the signature of Alex Jackson. At Arsenal he immediately insisted on having Charlie Buchan, and later David Jack and Alex James – among the greatest, if not the greatest, players of their generation. He believed that a great player could fit into any tactical system, and was to prove it, even with the complex Alex James. The fact that a player, like Stephenson or Buchan,

might even be past his best was not in itself important. It is arguable that Chapman was actually not a great tactician – when the offside law was changed from three defenders to two in 1925, Chapman was rather slow to spot the changes required to deal with the extra freedom it gave to attackers. The introduction of a centre-back and midfield link was suggested by Charlie Buchan, who could see the problem from the field, and it took Arsenal some time to settle down to the new system. Where Chapman was obviously magnificent was in fitting the man to the system required; to pursue the example, he found and then developed Herbie Roberts into the definitive stopper centre-back.

If there is another simple key to understanding Chapman's view of the game it is perhaps in the phrase: 'A team can attack for too long.' He is first quoted as saying that while at Northampton in November 1907, after his side had attacked for most of a Cup match but Norwich had stolen a 1–0 victory. Chapman soon instructed his wing halves not to press forward behind the attack quite so readily, and directed the whole team to drop back sometimes, to bring the opposition forward and create the opportunity for a counterattack.

Chapman was to say the same 25 years later: 'You can attack too long, though I do not suggest that the Arsenal go on the defensive even for tactical purposes. I think it may be said that some of their best scoring chances have come when they have been driven back and then have broken away to strike suddenly and swiftly.' That almost sums up a general view of Arsenal in the 1930s, the 'lucky' Arsenal of myth and legend. As with most myths, there is certainly something in it. The speed of Bastin and Hulme, the strength of Lambert and later Drake, the cunning of James, were all essential pieces of a clear plan. But in 1930–31 Arsenal scored 127 First Division goals – three per game. They can't all have come from breakaways.

DEFENCE AND ATTACK

Chapman has been misinterpreted as saying that a team goes on the pitch with one point and, if it doesn't concede a goal, keeps that point. He did indeed say almost exactly that, but not as an advocate. In fact he was criticising the fact that so many teams, particularly in the early 1920s when goalscoring was at an all-time low, were basically defensive, offside orientated tactical units. He once even advocated 11 up and 11 down as a means of forcing teams to look for goals. There is no doubt, nonetheless, that Chapman was one of the first to put to good effect the obvious truth that the best side is the one which scores most goals, not the one which attacks longest or shows most endeavour. This was surprisingly hard for many fans to appreciate in the 1930s, and beyond.

Chapman was never reluctant to admit the necessity of strong defence above all else. As he wrote in 1933: 'I confess I am out to win, and so are my players. It is laid down by law that the team who scores the most goals wins. To accomplish

Below: Eddie Hapgood, Cliff Bastin and Alf Kirchen (right) march down the street as purposefully as the Arsenal side to which they belonged marched on to become the most famous club in the world. Hapgood was a fantastic servant to the club, playing 434 games over 11 seasons at left-back, while Bastin's 17-season service made him a club legend. Kirchen joined from Norwich in 1935 after Herbert Chapman's death, but was still able to secure winners medals in two League Championships and one FA Cup during his four seasons with the Gunners.

this, you must be sure that the defence is sound. All this, I know, is elementary but it is also the rock bottom of football.' Arsenal's system was designed on a pivotal principle, wrote Chapman: 'First, as to the attack, we have ceased to use our wing forwards in the old style, in which they hugged the touchline. Not only is it the aim of Hulme and Bastin to come inside when the Arsenal attack, but also the aim of the wing halves. This gives us seven men going up on goal. Now, as to defence, the team swing the other way, but the same principle applies so we have eight defenders when the goal is challenged. The defence pivots toward the position of attack, the opposite back coming in to support the centre. It is, of course, essential that the two insides should come back and it is on this account that you get what is called the W formation. The two wing halves are therefore the key men, either in defence or attack, and no defence can be sound unless it has the support of two inside forwards.'

All of this is relatively familiar today, going under terms such as 'closing down space' or 'getting behind the ball'. In the 1930s it was genuinely still a mystery. Programmes were always printed with a 5–3–2 formation (five forwards and two full-backs) and crowds continued to believe that this is how teams like Arsenal played right through to the 1950s – despite clear evidence to the contrary in front of their eyes.

THE RIGHT MIX

Because Arsenal so completely dominated English football in the decade after the 1930 Cup final, it is perhaps worth examining exactly what it was about the manager, the club and their tactics that brought such astonishing success.

First of all, it is nonsense to suggest that Chapman arrived at Highbury with a plan in mind and then went out to find the players to fit it. If anything, the reverse was the case. Between his arrival in 1925 and his first game in charge, three months later, the offside law was changed and a whole new era had begun. Chapman had achieved considerable success in refining and exploiting the old system and it would be unrealistic to have expected him, or any other manager, to understand all the implications of the law change overnight. His Leeds and Huddersfield teams had been tight, defensive units, and his roving centre-half at Leeds Road, Tom Wilson, was a key, if now obsolescent figure. When Charlie Buchan forced the third-back tactic on the team (the phrase 'policeman' came in later) the other changes required were reasonably obvious – the full-backs moving out to mark the wingers and one of the inside forwards dropping back to become the midfield link. Arsenal may have adapted to these changes better than most other clubs but there was nothing secret or particularly subtle about them and, by the end of Chapman's first season (1925–26), most of his opponents were using the same formation.

The tactical reason for Chapman's successes definitely lay elsewhere. While it is undeniably true that the use of Alex James as the link-man was the key to Arsenal's success, its essence was further forward. The added dimension in Arsenal's game was actually the use of the wingers Cliff Bastin and Joe Hulme, and the club's relative decline toward the end of the 1930s was due more to the fact that these two could not be replaced than for any other reason.

Chapman did not plan it that way. By the late 1920s it had simply become apparent to him that, in the astonishingly fast Hulme and the cool, clever Bastin, he had two players of very unusual quality. The basic difference in Arsenal's game from that point on was that they generally played only three real front men. There was always a strong centre-forward (Jack Lambert being the most celebrated). Behind him David Jack was a goalscorer of quality but not a true front-runner. The wingers did not play in the manner of their equivalents at other First Division clubs. Their role was not, in other words, to hug the touchline, beat the full-back, get to the goal line and cross for the centre-forward to head home. They were both capable of doing this, but Chapman saw it as essentially wasteful. A normal winger spent too much time waiting. He must be used more extensively and far more effectively.

The result was that both Hulme and Bastin would cut in far more often than they would go outside, that Alex James' most famous pass would become the ball inside the full-back, and that both wingers became goalscorers of importance (in the great era between 1929 and 1935 Bastin scored 116 League goals and Hulme 75; an average between them of almost exactly a goal a game – meaning that Arsenal expected one or other of their wingers to score every week). As long as no other club played this way, it was always likely to work. The opposing full-backs had 40 games a year dealing with conventional wingers going outside; twice a season they met Arsenal and had to deal with a totally different threat. But, and here is the rub, Chapman could only do it because he had Hulme and Bastin and, eventually, Alex James to feed them. His competitors couldn't match his success simply because they didn't have the players.

NEW FORMATIONS

Chapman did not create all of this overnight. Parts of his post-1925 system – the stopper centre-half, the midfield link – were quite straightforward and the manager's strength here was in finding the perfect men for the job. The more subtle development involving the wingers was probably largely chance but, having seen the potential, Chapman worked at the conclusions and maximised them. He didn't just win an odd League Championship, he completely dominated the game. What happened, bluntly, was that he moved one player back through each department of the team. The stopper centre-half actually meant a line of three at the back rather than two. The need to replace the centre-half in midfield meant one of the inside forwards had to fall back to create three in midfield and four up front. This is where most teams

left it – at 3–3–4. As they continued to use conventional wingers they had to have at least two goalscoring forwards. Chapman went further by dropping another man some way back as well, creating a system close to 3–4–3.

The benefit (as was also to be seen in the 1970s when 4–4–2 became the norm) was that the extra man in midfield helped Arsenal gain much more possession of the ball. In purely technical terms, it was a defensive alteration. It moved a man backward. But Arsenal could make it work and scored a lot of goals because they had the genius of James, Hulme and the phenomenal goalscorer Bastin.

Chapman knew it was a scheme perfectly geared for scoring goals on the break. It was arguably the ultimate fulfilment of his old belief that: 'you can attack for too long.' It was, in many ways, an away team's approach (in the six great seasons between 1929–30 and 1934–35 Arsenal won 187 points at home and 147 points away) but, at the same time, it in no way blunted the greatness of the other parts of the team when they wanted to attack and faced opponents who were their inferior. Their goalscoring record was second to none in the 1930s. Nevertheless, one can see the seeds of the tactics of the 1960s (using wingers in such unconventional ways found remarkable echoes in Alf Ramsey's seminal Ipswich side of 1962) and one can understand how the cries of 'Lucky Arsenal' arose from the unsophisticated terraces of the era. Chapman's instinct for fitting the right man to parts of a plan while being able to develop other parts of that plan to the particular skills of the men available was, of course, the mark of footballing genius.

FIRST PROFESSIONAL MANAGER

Another important part of Chapman's philosophy was that the whole club should play to the same system – in other words the first, reserve, third and junior team all tried to play, within their capabilities, to the same pattern. The reasoning was obvious – if a reserve came into the first team he would be familiar with the behaviour of the players around him. This was obviously most important in defence, but was not insignificant in attack. The club's classic moves, the ball from James inside the full-back, or the cutting in of the wingers and the playing of the ground ball sideways, would not have come naturally to any player had they not also played that way in the reserves.

To ensure the tactical messages came across, Chapman turned part of his desk into a plan of the field, with models to represent the players. When players came to see him, it was easy to discuss moves, ideas and developments in a practical way. Chapman introduced weekly team-talks for the whole side; everyone was invited to contribute, and it was from these meetings that many of the best ideas emerged.

To all this in context, this was an era when directors chose the team, whether or not they knew a thing about the game. There was no such animal as a team manager – technically

he was secretary-manager, deputed basically to run the club. Attempts to integrate tactics, combine the best team (as opposed to the 11 players the directors might have thought were best in 11 individual positions) and develop a pattern of consistency were largely outside the control of the average secretary-manager, or were easily frustrated if he tried. Chapman, having seen throughout his playing career how not to run a whole range of clubs, was probably the first real professional in a world of semi-amateurs. These were the days when success was a Cup semi-final here and there, finishing fifth or sixth in the League now and again, and bringing in large enough crowds to balance the books. If further proof is needed, and with the possible exceptions of Wolves' Frank Buckley and Charlton's Jimmy Seed, who now can name any other manager of the inter-war era?

CHAPMAN THE INNOVATOR

What was really remarkable about Chapman was his influence on, or attempts to influence, the game outside the playing area as well. Many of his proposals were firmly opposed by the FA, to whom he must have seemed a constant irritation. He introduced numbering on the Arsenal shirts on 25 August 1928, when the Gunners visited Hillsborough. This was the first time a team had ever been numbered and the FA told him to desist. He had a minor revenge by having the reserves continue to wear the same shirts. He introduced a 45-minute clock and was told to stop that (it was simply turned into the 60-minute clock still standing on the southern terracing), he wanted to start floodlit matches (midweek games then kicked off at 3.00 pm, when very few people could attend, causing the obvious loss of revenue) but was not allowed to, and Arsenal proposed the ten-yard penalty semi-circle ten years before it was finally adopted. Other ideas he put forward have still to come to fruition – goal judges (which he felt very strongly about), two referees rather than one, and far more clubs promoted and relegated.

ENGLAND 'MANAGER'

He was a keen advocate of a single England manager, rather than a selection committee. In 1932 he wrote: 'The idea may be startling, but I would like the England selectors to bring together 20 of the most promising young players for a week under a selector, coach and trainer. The idea would be to practise definite schemes and ... at the end have them hold a conference at which views might frankly be exchanged. I would keep these players together during the season ... if this proposal were carried out, I think the result would be astonishing. I may say that I have no hope of this international building policy being adopted.'

It was, of course, 30 years before these ideas began to be put into practice, and we are still some way from the ultimate conclusion but, surprisingly, the FA did give Chapman a

chance to carry out some of his ideas during an England tour in 1933. He travelled with the England party to Italy and Switzerland and was allowed to act as team manager, giving pre-match talks and trying to decide tactics in advance. With several Arsenal players in the team, this was obviously reasonably practical and the tour was undoubtedly a success – England drawing 1–1 with future World Champions Italy in Rome and beating a strong Switzerland side 4–0.

Though the idea was not repeated, there is no reason to suppose it might not have been eventually, largely because Stanley Rous, Secretary of the FA from 1934 and later, of course, President of Arsenal, was very much in favour of giving the responsibility for coaching and selecting the side to a single manager. It is arguable that, had Chapman lived longer, and applied all his persistence to the project, his ideas for managing the England team might have been accepted and the whole history of post-war English international football could therefore have been very different.

TUBE STATION RENAMED

The exploits of Arsenal as a team are covered elsewhere in this history, but to end a celebration of Herbert Chapman, the man who made the team and the club we know today, we should perhaps mention the most symbolic and yet most visible of all the man's achievements. When he took Leeds City to Highbury for the first time (on 6 December 1913) he had been particularly struck by the fact that the club had an underground station virtually in the ground. It was minutes from Piccadilly on the quickest and most direct of all the tube lines. The station, on what was then the Great Northern, Piccadilly and Brompton Railway, had been opened in December 1906. There was only one problem, the

station was called Gillespie Road. This was obviously a major advertising opportunity missed; what if all of the millions of people who travelled by the Piccadilly Line or looked at maps of the underground could see the name Arsenal right in front of their eyes? There was not much Chapman could do about it when he first arrived at Highbury, but by 1932 the influence of the club had grown so much, through its success on the field and the support it was drawing, that he could invite the managers of the London Electric Railway (as it was by then called) to discuss the matter.

Changing the name was not as simple as it sounds. In those days the destination was printed on each ticket, not to mention on all of the maps, in all of the timetables, and in all of the carriages. The LER was also no doubt wary of numerous other clubs requesting similar things. On the other hand, Arsenal drew so many supporters, Chapman argued, that actually promoting the name might bring more passengers for the LER. Initially the railway proposed a compromise name of Highbury Hill, but Chapman was not satisfied with this. Eventually, his persistence paid off, and on 5 November 1932, the name Arsenal became a fixture on maps throughout London. It remains a tribute to Chapman's skill, persuasion and perseverance and Arsenal celebrated the honour with a 7–1 win at Molineux on the same day.

By the time Arsenal's half century came around Chapman was gone, dying from pneumonia at the age of 55. His bust, by the famous sculptor Jacob Epstein, was later placed in the magnificent entrance hall of the new East Stand, from where he watched over the club he raised to greatness. There are few clubs who can say with any certainty that they have already had their greatest manager and most influential era. It may not even be true of Arsenal, but it seems unlikely that there will ever be another manager like Herbert Chapman.

Above: Herbert Chapman at a football lesson for schoolboys in 1933. Chapman's approach to the game was as distinctive off the pitch as on it, proposing a host of innovations, ranging from floodlit matches to appointing a single manager to select the England team.

CHAPTER 2

ROYAL ARSENAL

All in all, 1886 was a memorable year for football. Blackburn Rovers completed a hat-trick of FA Cup wins, winning a replay against West Bromwich Albion 2–0 on Derby Racecourse in the first final played outside London. It was the initial year of professionalism and, though the Scots banned their clubs and players from any involvement with English professional teams, there did not seem to be any obvious ill-effects south of the border. But when James Forrest, a professional with Blackburn Rovers, played at half-back for England in Glasgow, the Scots objected and the England selectors made Forrest wear a different shirt to distinguish him from the England amateurs.

The Football Association was already 23 years old, but the game was still very different from the one we know today. Apart from the centre line, there were no pitch markings; there was no need to provide a crossbar; there were no nets or penalties; a goalkeeper could handle the ball anywhere on the pitch, and the referee had no power to award a free-kick or even a goal unless the players appealed to him. There was not even any requirement that all members of a team wear the same coloured shirts.

In the wider world, 1886 was not particularly momentous. Prime Minister William Gladstone introduced his first Irish Home Rule Bill, saw it defeated in the Commons and was replaced by Lord Salisbury, after whom the new capital of Rhodesia was to be named. Great Britain extended her African empire even further by annexing Zanzibar, and the Severn railway tunnel, then the longest in the world, was opened. Frances Hodgson Burnett wrote Little Lord Fauntleroy, Robert Louis Stevenson published Dr Jekyll and Mr Hyde and, on the sporting front, the foundation of the Lawn Tennis Association remains the most significant fact that the history books record. But, tucked away in a backwater on the borders of rural Kent and the southern sprawl of the largest city in the world, other events were taking place of which the newspapers and public at large were, understandably, totally ignorant.

FOUNDING FATHERS

It was a small group of Scotsmen that was really behind what happened at the Woolwich Arsenal toward the end of 1886, first among them one David Danskin from Kirkcaldy in Fife. What he actually did was to found a works football team. At

that time Kent was firmly rugby and cricket country, both alien games to a Scot like Danskin. The only local clubs which can claim a prior place in football history are Blackheath and Blackheath School, both attenders at the historic first meeting of the Football Association in 1863. Both defected to play rugby and Blackheath are, oddly, the only founder members of the FA still in existence. The local cricketers were no more sympathetic to Danskin – earlier in 1886 one Joseph Smith had tried to persuade the cricket club at the Woolwich Arsenal to allow part of their pitch to be used for football, but they would not hear of it. None of this was perhaps too surprising. The Arsenal, one of the government's main munitions factories, was rather out of place in both Kent and the Home Counties, as were many of the men who came to work there.

The real spur came with the arrival in Woolwich of two Nottingham Forest players, Fred Beardsley and Morris Bates. Forest were already one of the leading sides in the country, having been the first northern club to reach the semi-finals of the FA Cup, which they did in 1879, 1880 and 1885. On that last occasion they had forced the great Queen's Park to two matches with Fred Beardsley as their goalkeeper. Nottingham also had an ordnance factory next door to the old Forest ground at Trent Bridge, and no doubt this was where Beardsley and Bates had worked before they moved to similar jobs in Woolwich. Their arrival pushed Danskin and three friends, Elijah Watkins, John Humble and Richard Pearce, into action. They asked around to see who might be interested and 15 men were prepared to pay sixpence (2½p) each to start up a club. Danskin added three shillings (15p) out of his own pocket (a tenth of the weekly wages of a man at the Arsenal at that time) and the club bought a football with the money. Apparently they had threepence (1½p) change.

It is interesting to relate that Fred Beardsley had worked for a previous spell at Woolwich Arsenal, back in 1884, and had helped form another team then. Beardsley told his grandson, R. A. Beardsley-Colmer, many years later that this club had been called Woolwich Union and had played on 'Piggy' Walton's field in Plumstead. Beardsley was always a football fanatic – he changed jobs in 1887, going to work for Siemens Engineering, but they quickly dismissed him because he took too much time off to play the game. Although it is possible that many of the same men who played for Woolwich Union also joined the new club, it would not be accurate to say that

the one was the forerunner of the other, particularly as David Danskin and John Humble were apparently not involved in the Woolwich team.

The likelihood is that there was more than one football team comprised of men from the Arsenal at that time, and the team that eventually became Royal Arsenal was no doubt a composite of some or all of these teams. The reason we today regard Danskin's Dial Square as the forerunner is that John Humble (and, to a lesser extent, Danskin himself) became the club's unofficial historian by virtue of eventually being associated with Arsenal longer than anyone else. Humble and Danskin naturally related their own experiences, the story of their earliest involvement with organised football in the Arsenal as they knew it.

HUMBLE BEGINNINGS

It is important to try and put ourselves in the position of those 15 founding fathers over a century ago. As far as they were concerned, the team was a means of providing themselves with a little fun, exercise and, no doubt, a convivial social circle. They gave no thought to the future, of what their team might become. This was entirely sensible, for how could men who had yet to see a motor car and who would be grandfathers before they saw an aeroplane, possibly envisage an FA Cup final watched by 30 million people?

There were, to be sure, thousands of similar groups of young men dotted around the country whose identical efforts would never reach a history such as this. The closest date we have for the initial subscriptions to Danskin's new club is October 1886, but the founding of the Arsenal cannot be accurately attributed to a single day. Apart from the seven names mentioned earlier, others who paid at that point were

Opposite, far left: Above: Arsenal returned to the Manor Ground in 1893. Very few pictures exist of matches there and unless you lived very locally it took so long to get to the ground, either by rail to Plumstead station or by tram.

Left: The first badge adopted by Royal Arsenal FC, probably around 1888. It was essentially the Borough of Woolwich's coat of arms. The vertical columns are not chimneys but cannons. Until the end of the 19th century Woolwich was a separate town and not part of London. It was mentioned in the 'Domesday Book' in 1086 and the first known reference to the famous ferry (for centuries the lowest public crossing point of the Thames) was as early as 1308, when the rights to operate it were sold for £10. The military connections began with the Royal Dockyard (thriving by Henry VIII's time), and then developed with the Arsenal, the Royal Military Academy, the Royal Artillery Regiment and the various military hospitals which still dot the local landscape. At the time of the club's foundation there were no fewer than 28 military units based in the area. It is easy nowadays to forget that the club is called Arsenal because it was an offshoot of the single most important military town in England at the end of the last century.

Left: Dial Square a century after the formation of the team; for the first few weeks of its existence it had no name and was later referred to by Danskin as Dial Square simply because many of the 15 founders worked there.

A NAME, A KIT AND A PITCH

The players met in the Royal Oak, next to Woolwich Arsenal station, on Christmas Day 1886 full of enthusiasm. They immediately set about solving what they saw as their three major problems; a shortage of name, kit and somewhere to play. The name was easy – Dial Square was clearly far too unprepossessing and nothing less than Royal Arsenal would satisfy their ambitions. The name probably came from simply combining that of the pub they were sitting in with their place of work, though that was also referred to on occasions as the Royal Arsenal. It was to remain Royal until 1891, when Woolwich Arsenal was formally adopted though, strangely, the Football League insisted on calling the club Royal Arsenal until 1896.

The kit was almost as easy. Red was adopted because Beardsley and Bates already had shirts of that colour (first-class goalkeepers, like Beardsley, wore the same shirts as their colleagues until 1909), and in future players were supposed to provide their own shorts (several continued to wear knickerbockers) and real boots, as opposed to working boots with bars nailed across them. As the regal Royal Arsenal could not actually afford any of this kit, Fred Beardsley wrote to Nottingham Forest asking if they could help. Forest, who were the first team in the country to adopt uniform red when they began wearing caps of that colour in 1865, generously sent a complete set of red shirts and a ball and Arsenal have worn red and white, like Forest, ever since in consequence. The white sleeves, to add just a little extra distinction, were added before a match against Liverpool on 4 March 1933.

Forest's ball was also useful for the club didn't have one of those either, having lost the original somewhere along the line, now all they lacked was somewhere to kick it. The only option was to use any convenient public land nearby and the obvious choice was Plumstead Common. This is not the flat, pleasant recreation area that the name conjures up. Not only is it uneven and hilly, it was then also stony and rutted owing to it being used by the Royal Horse Artillery. While part of the old Common still exists, housing has been built on much of it in the intervening century and it is no longer possible to determine exactly where Royal Arsenal raised their goalposts. One thing we do know, however, is that the said goalposts were kept nearby in Fred Beardsley's back garden during the week. Many current League clubs started the same way. Spurs played on the Tottenham Marshes for five years before they were able to fence off an enclosure, being forced to do so by a combination of unruly spectators throwing mud at the players, their inability to take money and finding, on more than one occasion, that their carefully marked pitch had simply been usurped by another pair of teams.

The Reds (as they were then nicknamed) invited nearby Erith to Plumstead Common for a match on 8 January 1887, the first under the name Royal Arsenal, and their first formal 'fixture'. The first team ever to play under the name Arsenal was: Beardsley in goal, Danskin and Porteous at

named Price, Whitehead, Porteous, Gellatly, Ratcliffe and Brown (the other two must remain unrecorded by history). Danskin, Humble, Beardsley and Brown all lived to see Arsenal's first honour, the FA Cup victory in 1930. David Danskin himself was fortunate enough to witness all the successes of the decade that followed, writing to manager George Allison from his hospital bed after listening to the 1936 Cup final on the radio, an arrangement surely not even vaguely imagined by his colleagues exactly half a century before when he put the whole thing in motion.

FIRST SUCCESS

The first competitive game of the new club was arranged against a team called Eastern Wanderers on 11 December 1886. There were one or two problems, such as the lack of a name, a pitch and any kit. For the time being the side simply used the name of one of the workshops within the Arsenal in which many of the players were employed – Dial Square. Dial Square itself had been erected as long ago as 1717, and acquired its name when a sundial was built over its entrance in 1764. The building is actually situated between Woolwich and Plumstead, which in part explains why Woolwich Arsenal never played a single match in Woolwich itself.

Sadly, the historic first game of the club did not take place anywhere near the Arsenal or Woolwich. The players crossed the Thames by the famous ferry to a piece of open ground someone had found on the Isle of Dogs. Elijah Watkins, whom Danskin had asked to be the first secretary, described it as follows: 'It eclipsed any pitch I ever heard of or saw; I could not venture to say what shape it was, but it was bounded by back-yards for two thirds of the area and the other portion was ... I was going to say a ditch, but an open sewer would be more appropriate. We had to pay handsomely to have ... the mud cleaned out of our dressing room afterward!'

After the game, there was some dispute about the result, as there were no crossbars, hardly any pitch markings and the ball apparently spent a fair amount of its time in either the back gardens or the sewer. Nonetheless, Dial Square decided they had won 6–0.

full-back, Gregory, Price and Wells at half-back, and Smith, Moy, Whitehead, Crighton and Bee as forwards. Another eight fixtures had been completed by end of the season. The strength of Beardsley and Bates (who became known as the 'iron-headed man' because he regularly used his forehead, rare in an era of solid, heavy balls) was at the core of the team's early success, and they lost only two of their 10 matches that season.

RAPID RISE

Progress from here onward was more than steady. Despite their humble origins, Arsenal actually had one of the fastest rises of all the early League clubs (Chelsea and Bradford City later went straight into the Football League without having kicked a ball, but that's another story). Within seven years of their foundation, Woolwich Arsenal were members of the Football League, a tribute to their entrepreneurial foresight rather, it must be said, than to their playing record.

The first few seasons, nonetheless, had their fair share of local success. As early as 1889 the club reached the semi-final of the London Senior Cup, where they were beaten 0–2 by Clapton. The following season they won the Kent Senior Cup, the Kent Junior Cup and, more significantly, the London Charity Cup. The latter was concluded with a 3–1 win over Old Westminsters (the old boys of Westminster School) at the Manor Ground in front of 10,000 people. The team was Beardsley, McBean and Connolly (both full backs were from Kirkcaldy, Danskin's home town), Howatt, Bates (the captain) and Julian, Offer, Christmas, Robertson, Barbour and Fry. The Old Westminsters had their revenge in the London Senior Cup final, winning 1–0 in what was then the premier competition for clubs in the capital. These four competitions were no easy option, although it must be remembered that the London Football Association at this time was fiercely amateur in nature and that Arsenal had the advantage of being a works team. Good players who they wanted to join them were found jobs at the Woolwich Arsenal by a sympathetic management and, on occasion, the club even bought out the contracts of footballing soldiers who they discovered stationed at the nearby barracks or enlisted with the Horse Artillery.

The next season, 1890–91, the Gunners won the London Senior Cup for the first time, beating Casuals 3–2 in the quarter-finals, Clapton 3–2 at the Oval in the semis (having been 2–0 down 25 minutes from the end) and St Bartholomew's Hospital 6–0 in the final, also at the Oval. This was the first really important success for the club and, as the *Kentish Independent* reported: 'Excitement is a mild description for the scenes in Woolwich and Plumstead on the return of the football champions on Saturday night. A host of admirers met them at the Dockyard Station and drove them in open carriages, shouting and singing. There were celebrations everywhere all evening and, we fear, a good deal of drinking was mixed with the rejoicing and exultation.'

It was when they came up against the professionals, or even the leading amateur sides, that Royal Arsenal were made aware of their status. The club first entered the FA Cup, by far and away the most prestigious competition throughout the country, as early as 1889–90. Their first three ties were relatively easy, against Lyndhurst (an 11–0 victory in their first ever FA Cup match), Thorpe (who could not afford to come to London from Norwich for a replay after a 2–2 draw) and Crusaders. But Swifts beat them easily 5–1 in the next round and Derby County won 2–1 at the club's new Invicta Ground in the first tie of the next season. Two Arsenal players, Peter Connolly and Bobby Buist, played so well in that game that John Goodall, the Derby acting secretary-manager, offered them contracts. They did not go, but the event set off alarm bells in the Arsenal committee and was to begin the train of events which took Arsenal into the Football League and also led to the foundation of the Southern League.

ON THE MOVE AGAIN

By this stage the club had settled at a formal address, the Invicta Ground (Invicta is the motto of the county of Kent). After playing on the Common in 1886–87, for the 1887–88 season they had occupied the Sportsman Ground in Plumstead, an old pig farm situated on the edge of Plumstead Marshes, but because of its site this pitch had a predictable tendency to become waterlogged. On the morning of their first home game against prime local rivals Millwall (to be precise on 11 February 1888), the committee arrived at the Sportsman Ground to find that it was under water.

Looking up Manor Road toward Plumstead Station, they noticed that the field next door, which was used as pastureland, appeared dry. Jack Humble rushed round to the owner, a Mr Cavey, and asked permission to use it. He agreed, Woolwich Arsenal drew 3–3, and for the next two years (1888–90) they played on the Manor Field, which they rather grandly called the Manor Ground. After the Cup successes of 1889 and 1890, they decided to move just across Plumstead High Street, to a new ground, which already had a stand, terraces and dressing rooms – the Invicta. At the Manor Ground, they had to rope off the pitch and bring in wagons (borrowed from the nearby barracks) if they expected a big crowd, which would mean around 500 to 1,000. The players usually changed at the Green Man in Plumstead High Street or at the Railway Tavern beside the station (neither exists

Above: The Arsenal line-up in the summer of 1890. The trophies are the Kent Senior Cup, the Kent Junior Cup, the London Charity Cup (probably the Shield in fact) and a cup won in a six-a-side competition at the Agricultural Hall, Islington. The picture seems to have been taken at their new ground, the Invicta, to which they moved that summer. Founder David Danskin is second left on the bottom row.

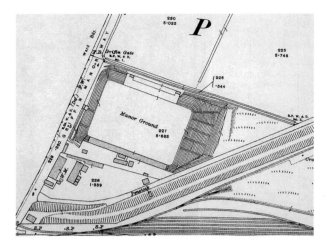

today), and often had to help with collecting the money. All this seemed behind them at the Invicta, particularly when, on Easter Monday 1891, they attracted 12,000 fans to see a game against Scottish Champions Hearts. But when the landlord put a massive increase on the rent (from £200 to £350 per annum) hoping to exploit the club's election to the Football League in 1893, they could not pay and had to move again. The Invicta's owner was one George Weaver, of the Weaver Mineral Water Company, and after Arsenal left, two rows of houses were built on the site named Mineral and Hector Streets. The old Manor Ground was repurchased and club and supporters worked through the summer of 1893 to get it ready for the Second Division. The club stayed there, opposite Plumstead Station, for 20 years until a move far further afield than anyone could have envisaged.

THE MOVE TOWARD LEAGUE STATUS

Back in 1891, committee member and occasional goalkeeper John Humble was shaken by the ease with which his better players could be lured away by a Football League club. As Royal Arsenal were nominally amateur (although their players were undoubtedly paid 'expenses') there was nothing to stop any of them accepting offers from professional clubs. The next step was bold, for everyone knew the obsessive hatred the London FA had of that evil northern virus, professionalism, and few had yet dared challenge it. This was to be a problem for another decade and a half, eventually ending in an almost complete break when the London, Surrey and Middlesex FAs formed the Amateur Football Association as an separate body from the official FA in 1907.

Jack (as he was usually known) Humble deserves something of a diversion for, apart from being the most important influence on the club's history after Herbert Chapman and his chairman Henry Norris, he seems to typify the men who worked at the Arsenal and who founded the football club. He was born in a village called East Hartburn in County Durham in 1862. His father and mother died within three months of

each other in 1880 and Jack and his elder bother decided to leave the relatively depressed north-east. Not being able to afford the train fare, they walked from Durham to London and had both found jobs as engine fitters at the Arsenal by the time of the 1881 census. Theirs was a hard but common story of the times. The Arsenal drew large numbers of poor men from the Midlands, the north and Scotland, of whom Danskin, Beardsley and Humble were unusual probably only in their devotion to, and skill at, football. Humble was to remain connected with the club for four decades, for much of that time the last link with the real working men who had founded the club.

At the 1891 AGM, held in the Windsor Castle Music Hall, Humble proposed taking the chance of going professional to ensure they kept their best players and this was carried by a large majority. Jack Humble declared at this meeting that: 'The club (has been) carried on by working men and it is my ambition to see it carried on by them.' This was in objection to an additional proposal that a limited liability company should be formed simultaneously. Although this proposal was to be adopted two years later, in 1893, it seems to have been regarded as a retrograde step, against the sporting ethos of the club and (rightly as it proved) endangering the control of the working men who had founded it. Humble, nonetheless, remained a director until a scandal in 1927 forced him, though wholly innocent, to resign.

EXILE FROM THE LONDON FA

The London FA were apoplectic about professionals in any form, and immediately banned Arsenal, their previous Cup winners, from all competitions under their auspices and expelled them into the bargain. But for Woolwich Arsenal (there is some dispute whether the name change was in 1891 or 1893 – but it was because of the use of Royal in a limited company) the arguments were not as arcane as they are today; the problems were very practical and very real.

They were effectively banned from playing in all competitions except the FA Cup or in friendlies against professional clubs. The FA Cup was therefore financially critical, but their first round tie in January 1892 took them to Small Heath (later renamed Birmingham) and they went down ignominiously 5–1. The following year was even worse – a first round proper 6–0 defeat by Sunderland. There seemed only one solution – to form a southern version of the Football League, providing real competitive fixtures, and thus staunching the ebb of support that the club was experiencing.

In February 1892 Woolwich Arsenal called a meeting of possible southern members and, initially at least, there was real enthusiasm. Twelve sides were elected: Chatham, Chiswick Park, Crouch End, Ilford, Luton, Marlow, Millwall, Old St Mark's, Reading, Swindon, West Herts (forerunners of Watford) and Arsenal. If the inclusion of Old St Mark's and Crouch End suggests that the meeting was not particularly

Far left: In April 1948 the Gunners invited the only three living members of their first professional team of 1891 to a game versus Chelsea. The three are (left to right) Bill Julian, Gavin Crawford and John McBean. Julian had gone to work at the Arsenal in 1889 and became the first professional captain two years later. Gavin Crawford was a Scot who became the first professional imported by the club in 1891.

Left: The Manor Ground was Arsenal's main home south of the river until 1913. They moved there on 11 February 1888. The game pictured was against Liverpool on 2 September 1905 (Arsenal won 3–1).

prescient, then this is further confirmed by the fact that Spurs came bottom of the poll, unelected with just one vote (presumably their own). Nine years later Tottenham were to become the first southern professional club to win a major honour, the FA Cup. The meeting was held on 24 February 1892 in Anderton's Hotel, Fleet Street. There was an obvious symbolic significance in the location, for it was in the very same hotel that the Football League itself had been formed four years before.

ELECTION TO THE FOOTBALL LEAGUE

The London FA predictably exploded again, threatening to ban the other 11 clubs as well as Arsenal. Surprisingly, the other clubs all backed down, although the idea was successfully revived a year later by Millwall. Arsenal, with no one local to play against, were now desperate. There seemed only one gamble they could make. This was to apply for membership of the Football League, although the Woolwich club had never previously played in any league competition.

At the end of the 1892–93 season the Second Division was extended from 12 to 15 clubs. This created three vacancies, and two more surprisingly yawned when Bootle resigned and Accrington (a different club from the later, ill-fated, Stanley) refused to play in the Second Division after being relegated from the First. Newcastle United and Rotherham Town were given places without a vote, and Liverpool, Arsenal and Middlesbrough Ironopolis were elected at a later meeting. The other recorded new candidates for membership were Doncaster Rovers and Loughborough Town.

The simultaneous addition of Liverpool, Newcastle and Arsenal, who were to win an astonishing 26 of the next 80 Championships of the organisation they joined together, must surely be the most distinguished of all the League's annual elections. It was also clearly Arsenal's good fortune to have applied at a time when there were so many vacancies. In a typical year they would have stood no chance, and even in a year with two new vacancies (the most at any normal time) they could have had little hope of success.

As there were no League clubs south of Birmingham and Burton, it was a considerable step for the League to take. Most journeys would be overnight, costs would be high. Moreover, Woolwich Arsenal had no record of massive crowd support. On the playing front, the FA Cup was usually the acid test for new applicants. Arsenal had never progressed beyond the first round proper and, oddly, were never to achieve even that small distinction in the remainder of the nineteenth century. Nonetheless, someone on the League Management Committee had the foresight to recognise the benefits. Firstly, if the League was ever to become a national institution, it must have members in London, the capital and the country's dominant city. Secondly, travel was becoming less onerous. Cities like Manchester and Liverpool were now only four-and-a-half hours from London by the fastest trains (even if Plumstead was nearly another hour on the other side). And thirdly, and perhaps the telling point in the end, to admit Arsenal would be to reward the club's brave stand on professionalism and to encourage others to do the same.

The summer of 1893 was a critical moment for the future of football. The Scottish FA finally accepted professionalism at their AGM in the same month as Arsenal's admittance to the League, and 16 southern clubs were also persuaded to form the Southern League, though only half were professional at the time. In creating a general acceptance of professionalism, all three decisions were major stepping-stones on the road to legitimacy for the League and the FA and, a mere seven years old, Arsenal were playing a major part.

RAISING FUNDS

It was Arsenal's first significant contribution to the history of British football. For the club and its board, however, one rather more immediate consequence of the club's arrival in the League, and the raising of the rent at the Invicta ground, was the decision to try to buy a ground of their own. The only way to raise enough money was to form a limited liability company, and this happened in the summer of 1893.

The new company had a nominal capital of 4,000 £1 shares. In all, 860 people subscribed for 1,552 shares (the rest were left unissued) and most of the shareholders were workers at the Arsenal who lived locally. There were only three holdings of over 20 shares, the highest being 50 by a coffee house proprietor. The first board of directors contained a surgeon, a builder and six engineers from the Arsenal. At that moment, without a ground, large crowds, or obvious playing resources, the problems were only just beginning.

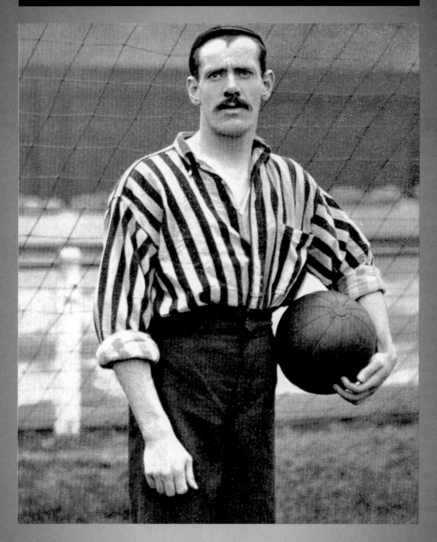

CHAPTER 3

WOOLWICH ARSENAL

1893–1915

The 20 years between Woolwich Arsenal joining the Football League in 1893 and their departure for Highbury in 1913 could not exactly be described as a period of unqualified success. Indeed, apart from the six-year spell following Harry Bradshaw's arrival as manager in 1899, it could better be termed one of financial struggle and footballing mediocrity. The Gunners were never a bad Second Division side. They chuntered along in mid-table until Bradshaw's arrival resulted in a fourth, third and second in successive seasons, the last gaining them promotion to the top division for the first time, in 1904. They stayed there nine years, but never finished better than sixth and even that performance was not as outstanding as it sounds for they won 14, lost 14 and drew 10.

The FA Cup is perhaps a better guide to their real status, for Arsenal went beyond the second round (the equivalent of today's fourth) only twice between 1893 and the First World War. Admittedly, these years, 1906 and 1907, were the highlight of the whole era, for Arsenal reached the semi-final in both seasons, but that proved the last gasp of the team Bradshaw built. He had already left, being lured away to Fulham in 1904.

PROBLEMS OF GEOGRAPHY

So, 1904 to 1907 apart, the era was really the story of a struggle against geography. Despite seeming to be relatively close to the middle of London, Woolwich is actually something of a backwater. No one passes through; it is difficult to reach from the eastern side, and the river effectively cut Arsenal's geographical circle of support by half. It was also a good 20- to 30-minute tram ride further out than the nearest major club (at the time Millwall Athletic).

The young George Allison, who was later to succeed Herbert Chapman as manager, was a junior sports reporter with Hulton's before the First World War and was given Woolwich Arsenal as his regular team to report on. He told more than a few amusing stories about trying to get there: 'From Fleet Street to Plumstead was heavy going. Other sports writers were more than happy when I offered to undertake all the reporting of Arsenal's home games. The payment I received softened the monotony of the long and tedious journey. One could travel on the South Eastern and Chatham Railway from London Bridge, Cannon Street or Charing Cross.

The trains stopped at every station. There were the same halts on the return journey, with the added difficulty that no one knew where the trains were going.'

NO LONGER THE BIG GUNS

When Woolwich Arsenal joined the Football League in 1893, they were London's only professional club. Some 15 years later, there were five in the Football League alone (Chelsea, Fulham, Spurs and Clapton Orient were the others), and a range of Southern League sides like Millwall Athletic and Crystal Palace. Arsenal's unique position was eroded quickly.

Additionally, there was the Boer War between 1899 and 1902, an enormous blow to a club whose dependence on the military, in its earlier days, cannot be overestimated. This took both players and support out of the area, particularly as the Arsenal itself introduced a Saturday afternoon shift. The tradition throughout the country at that time was for men to knock off at Saturday lunch time, have a drink and go to the game. The war was to prove almost as much a disaster for Arsenal as it was for the British troops in South Africa.

By the turn of the century the Reds had so far managed to hold their own in the Second Division. The long distances were something of a help to them, for they rarely lost at home (only 13 defeats in the first five seasons). On the other side of the coin, they never won more than three games on the road in a single season until 1897–98.

There were occasional highlights – the very first game of their League career was on Saturday 2 September 1893 against another newly elected club, Newcastle. It ended 2–2, Shaw and Elliott being the scorers. Arsenal's first League win did not come until 11 September, at home to Walsall Town Swifts, when John Heath scored a hat-trick in a 4–0 home victory. Newcastle scored six against the Gunners at the end of the month, and Burton Swifts did the same in November, but Arsenal returned the compliment twice during the season – against opponents Middlesbrough Ironopolis (away from home) and Northwich Victoria, both long since gone from the Football League. All in all, ninth place out of 15 in their first season, with 28 points from 28 games, was acceptable, though Liverpool took all the attention by winning the division undefeated.

ARSENAL'S CAESAR CAPPED

The next few seasons were similarly unspectacular, though the club soon gained its first representative honours. Goalkeeper Harry Storer was chosen between the posts for the Football League against the Scottish League in April 1895 and the gloriously named Caesar Llewellyn Jenkyns became the first current full international when he represented Wales against Scotland on 21 March 1896. Typically, both men were too good for the club and had been transferred within a year. Also too good were, surprisingly, Loughborough Town, who beat the Gunners 8–0 away in a Second Division game on 12 December 1896.

The Loughborough defeat came during a peculiar spell that has never been surpassed before or since by the club. Between October 17 and Christmas Day 1896, their League results went as follows: a 3–5 defeat at Walsall, a 6–1 win over Gainsborough Trinity, a 4–7 defeat by Notts County, a 2–5 defeat by Small Heath, a 4–2 win over Grimsby, a 3–2 victory over Lincoln, the 0–8 defeat at Loughborough, a 4–2 win over Blackpool and a 6–2 Christmas Day romp past Lincoln. In nine games they had scored 32 goals and conceded 34.

The result at Loughborough remains Arsenal's record defeat, but the compliment was quickly returned on 12 March 1900 when Loughborough came to the Manor Ground and were themselves beaten 12–0. This is still Arsenal's record victory and is one of only 18 occasions when a side has scored a dozen goals in a Football League fixture.

Sadly, these talking points only serve to brighten an essentially dour period. A disastrous FA Cup defeat by non-League Millwall (2–4 away) on 16 January 1896 proved one turning point for the committee. They decided to appoint a secretary-manager, one T. B. Mitchell from Blackburn, who was quickly succeeded by George Elcoat from Stockton. When Harry Bradshaw took over at the turn of the century the club were going nowhere very fast.

Bradshaw soon brought in the two most notable players of the period, an Australian left-back, Jimmy Jackson, who became club captain, and a new goalkeeper from Sheppey United, Jimmy Ashcroft. When Ashcroft played in all three internationals in 1905–06, he became the first Arsenal player to be capped for England.

Results and support improved slowly. By February 1903, over 25,000 were prepared to turn out to see Cup holders Sheffield United win a first round FA Cup tie 3–1 in Plumstead. The receipts were a healthy £1,000, the first time the club had reached the four-figure mark.

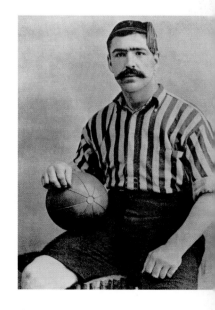

GUNNERS PROMOTED

The following season, 1903–04, led to promotion to the First Division. This was almost entirely the result of an excellent home record, with an astonishing goal ratio of 67 to 5. Not a match was lost at home (all were won but the last two) and there were 8–0 wins over Burton United and Leicester Fosse. The away record was not so impressive, with just six wins, but the overall goal tally of 91–22 remained impressive. Proud Preston won the division a point ahead of Arsenal, with Manchester United another point behind in third. The team which gained promotion was Jimmy Ashcroft (who played in every game), Archie Cross (a local lad from Dartford), captain Jimmy Jackson, John Dick, Percy Sands (an schoolteacher who taught in Woolwich), Roddy McEachrane (a neat Inverness-born schemer who played left-half), Tommy Briercliffe (signed from Blackburn), 'Tim' Coleman, Bill Gooing (the centre forward, who was another ever-present player), Tommy Shanks (the leading scorer with 25 League goals) and Bill Linward (signed from West Ham). Of the 20 players to appear in the promotion season, only two had been with the club before Bradshaw's arrival as manager.

Woolwich Arsenal's success quickly brought problems in its wake. Bradshaw was lured away to Fulham for a large salary before the next season had even begun and his Woolwich successor, Phil Kelso, was to follow him to Craven Cottage five years later. Fulham have a strange affinity for Arsenal when choosing their managers – no fewer than nine of the first 14 managers at Craven Cottage either played for or managed the Gunners.

Kelso was a Scotsman, previously manager of Hibernian, and he reinforced the side, as many have done before and since, with his countrymen. Initially gates were good (averaging over 10,000) and the club made a particular point of encouraging season-ticket holders, one result being that for a time they had more than any other club in the country.

CUP FORM IMPROVES

Those supporters were well rewarded in 1906 when the club managed to get past the second round for the first time in their 20-year history and reach the semi-finals of the FA Cup. Nor was it an easy run: West Ham were beaten away after a home

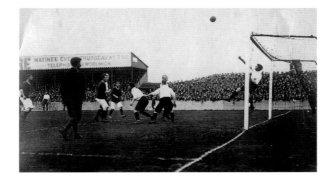

draw, then Watford 3–0, Sunderland (already having been League Champions four times) 5–0, which was a sensational result at the time, and then Manchester United 3–2 away in the quarter final.

The semi-final was at Stoke, against the all-conquering might of Newcastle. Between 1905 and 1911 the Magpies were to reach five FA Cup finals and Arsenal did not really stand in their way. Newcastle won 2–0 with goals from the great Colin Veitch and Jimmy Howie, although they then lost the final 1–0 to Everton. Arsenal had fielded one of their best ever forward lines and, early on, centre-forward Bert Freeman hit the bar before Newcastle had scored. Arsenal could not hold onto Freeman for more than a couple of years, and eventually had to sell him to Everton. He was to lead the Football League's goalscorers three times between 1908 and 1913 and finally won an FA Cup winners' medal when he scored the only goal of the game for Burnley against Liverpool in 1914. The two wingers were also internationals – Bill Garbutt on the right (capped for England later when he was with Blackburn) and the unpredictable Scot Bobby Templeton on the left. Templeton had won caps when with Aston Villa and Newcastle.

Considering that they had never before gone beyond the second round, it was a great surprise to see Arsenal pop up in the semi-final again the following year. This time their progress was easier, past Grimsby, Bristol City (at the time lying second in the First Division), Bristol Rovers and Barnsley. They met mighty Wednesday at St Andrew's in the semi-final and Arsenal went one up after only ten minutes when Garbutt headed in a Satterthwaite cross.

Then came tragedy; keeper Ashcroft was injured in a collison with centre-forward David Wilson when coming outside his area to collect a loose ball (at this time keepers could handle anywhere in their own half) and Wilson scored from the free-kick which referee Jack Howcroft had controversially awarded Wednesday. The incident turned the game and Wednesday scored twice more (making it 3–1) to reach Crystal Palace for the final, which they won by beating Everton 2–1.

Nonetheless, it had been a very successful season for the Reds, perhaps a sign of things to come. They were seventh in the First Division, the reserves had won the London League and the South Eastern League, inside right John 'Tim' Coleman had played for England and full-back Jimmy Sharp for Scotland. As it happened, it was actually the top of the

roller-coaster, not part of a careful ascent. The club's support and finances were not strong enough to survive a decline in results, and, once things started to go wrong, they accelerated virtually out of control.

FINANCIAL PROBLEMS MOUNT

The problems were initially much more acute off the field than on it, where the side finished 15th, 6th and 18th between 1907–08 and 1909–10. Phil Kelso resigned, initially to run a hotel in Scotland, but almost immediately joined Fulham instead, replacing Harry Bradshaw. The new Arsenal manager, George Morrell, found himself having to sell to survive. Within 12 months virtually all of the important names had gone – Coleman, Freeman, Sharp, Ashcroft and Garbutt. After leaving Woolwich Arsenal for Blackburn, Bill Garbutt moved further and further afield. In 1914 he went to Genoa as coach, where his team won the Italian League the following year. By 1927 he was in Rome, and two years later he went on to Naples. In the 1935–36 season he coached the Spanish champions Athletic Bilbao, but the Spanish Civil War drove him back to Italy. During the Second World War he was hidden there by friends and in 1946 emerged from hiding to take up his old post again at Genoa.

Morrell's first full season in charge began on 2 September 1908. The first programme of the season was not shy about discussing the fact that the best players had all gone: 'Here we go again,' began the editor 'and the followers of Arsenal look forward to the advent of another season with a great number of the players on whom we rely practically unknown quantities. The "Reds" will look somewhat strange without such faces as Ashcroft, Sharp, Coleman, Freeman, Kyle and Garbutt but we believe capable men have been engaged to replace them and we look forward to a successful season.'

The hope was misplaced for it was to be nearly two decades before the 'Reds' had another genuinely successful year. Even the greatest of all the pre-war Gunners, Andy Ducat, eventually had to be transferred to Villa. Right-half Ducat appeared for England in all three internationals in 1909–10, when he was only 23. He had scored a hat-trick in his first ever game for Arsenal, on Christmas Day 1905, versus the mighty Newcastle United. It was particularly sad that his best playing days were lost to the First World War. For their part Woolwich Arsenal never recovered from those sudden sales of their best players in 1908, particularly missing keeper Ashcroft. The crowds melted away, as did the results, and by 1910 the club was effectively bankrupt and up for sale.

GUNNERS TO GO WEST?

For the next decade the Arsenal story is really to be told off the field rather than on it. The main reason for this was one Henry Norris, the chairman of Fulham. As we have seen, the links between the two clubs were already close, if not

necessarily friendly, and in 1910 Norris, a wily businessman, was able to use the Woolwich club's problems to effect a takeover of Arsenal as well.

Fulham had experienced a remarkably rapid rise since Henry Norris became chairman. In 1902 and 1903 they won the Second Division of the Southern League, were then elected to the First and, under Bradshaw, won that Division in 1906 and 1907, upon which they applied to join the Football League and were immediately accepted. This was the first concrete evidence of Henry Norris' remarkable powers of political persuasion where the Football League was concerned. At the 1907 election Fulham easily received the highest number of votes (28) and replaced Burton United.

Henry Norris was a self-made man, his fortune based on property development in south-west London. He was Mayor of Fulham for seven years, was knighted in 1917 and represented Fulham East in Parliament from 1918 until 1922. A dictatorial man, he ran his football clubs like his businesses. A thin autocrat with a walrus moustache, he welcomed neither criticism nor advice; nonetheless, he was influential and persuasive. Over the years he developed close friendships with members of the League Management Committee, particularly the president, John McKenna.

Leslie Knighton, Arsenal manager to Norris' chairman between 1919 and 1925, has left us perhaps the best descriptions of Norris. Knighton said in his autobiography: 'I soon found out that everyone was afraid of Sir Henry. And no wonder! I have never met his equal for logic, invective and ruthlessness against all who opposed him. When I disagreed with him at board meetings and had to stand up for what I knew was best for the club, he used to flay me with words until I was reduced to fuming, helpless silence. Then, as I sat not knowing what to say, and trying to bottle up what I was tempted to say, he would whip round and shout: "Well Knighton, we pay you a great deal of money to advise us and all you do is sit there as if you were dumb".' But afterwards, says Knighton: 'Sir Henry would ask my advice, smile, wheedle and I was falling over myself to help him again. He did it with everyone. Those board meetings took years off my life.'

Like many influential Londoners with lower-class roots in the Edwardian era, Norris was sensitive to the fact that London appeared to be unable to compete with the provinces in what had become the national winter sport. For whatever personal reasons, he became determined to create a side capable of competing with the best from the north and Birmingham. His attention first turned to his local club, Fulham, but by 1908 he had obviously become convinced that they would never have a strong enough base for the success he sought.

Although Fulham had not been unsuccessful on the field, they, like Arsenal, were quite poorly supported. By 1910 the Cottagers had an accumulated overdraft of over £3,000 – an enormous sum in those days – while the Woolwich club were to all intents and purposes completely bankrupt.

Above: The 1907 Arsenal Cup squad, who got as far as the semi-final for the second successive year. They lost 3–1 to Wednesday.

Above: Advertising in match programmes is nothing new: the official programme for the match on 4 December 1906 carried details about forthcoming concerts at the Royal Artillery Theatre and Opera House, Woolwich.

Although this was the year in which Norris took over Arsenal, he remained a Fulham director until the war. His co-director at Woolwich, William Hall, was also Fulham chairman until the same date and the two men obviously controlled both clubs. It was partially because of this possible conflict of interests that the League later insisted no one could have a controlling interest in two League members.

NORRIS TAKES CHARGE

Norris had no doubt been putting out feelers for some time, but it was not until the summer of 1910, with the Gunners having escaped relegation by only a couple of points, that he was able to take control. His initial plan was very simple – he wanted to amalgamate Woolwich Arsenal with Fulham, move them to Craven Cottage and have a First Division team play there. When the League said no, he proposed an even more financially attractive solution – Arsenal and Fulham could play at Craven Cottage on alternative Saturdays. The other London clubs objected and that was turned down as well. The League also pointed out the obvious disadvantages of having one man controlling two clubs and Norris was in the position, having failed to achieve either of his objectives, of being informally forced to choose one club or the other.

In the end he came down in favour of the Woolwich club, no doubt because they were still in the First Division. Sadly, this was not to be the case for much longer. After a couple more years of mid-table insignificance, 1912–13 was a disaster. Arsenal finished bottom with only 18 points, 26 goals scored and three wins. The points, goals and wins were all the lowest ever recorded in the First Division and remained records, though equalled, until the end of the two point-system.

ARSENAL IN DIRE STRAITS

By the end of the 1912–13 season, the club was reported as having only £19 in the bank. The size of the disaster had been clear from the first few matches and Henry Norris and William Hall had been looking for some rapid solution to their plight throughout the year.

Their conclusion was as dramatic as it was simple. If the club was to have any chance of becoming the power in the land that Norris desired, then it would simply have to move.

There were four necessary guidelines for a new location for the club. It should be within greater London so as not to lose the backbone of the support which the club had relied upon over the years; it should be in a heavily populated area, preferably not bounded by the river or any other restriction to access; thirdly, it should not be too close to another major club; and, most important of all, it should be very easy to reach by public transport such as the underground or railway. In 1913 the last point was a prerequisite for any side that hoped to attract really big crowds. Among the open spaces that Hall and Norris negotiated for were ones in Battersea

and Harringay, but they found nothing that met all of their requirements. Nor were they to, in the end, accepting that they would probably have to be in the north or west and therefore inevitably close to either Spurs or Chelsea.

A NEW HOME AT HIGHBURY

When and how Highbury came into the reckoning is unknown. The land in question was the site of St John's College of Divinity, but relatively little of it was built upon. Most was taken up by the two football pitches, two cricket pitches and tennis courts used by the students. The keys to the site, for Hall and Norris, were its availability and its proximity to Gillespie Road underground station. Negotiations were not exactly easy and went on for several months, Norris bringing all his considerable influence to bear on the Ecclesistical Commissioners. In the end, Arsenal paid a massive £20,000 for a 21-year lease and agreed not to stage matches on Good Friday and Christmas Day (this restriction was eventually lifted in 1925 when the club paid another £64,000 to buy the whole site outright).

The actual deed of transfer was signed by the Archbishop of Canterbury, but if Norris thought that this implied heavenly blessing for his plans then he was quickly to discover that others disagreed. The objections to Arsenal moving to Highbury came from three main sources. The most predictable was from the other clubs, particularly Tottenham and Clapton Orient, then playing at Homerton. Both were within four miles of Highbury but Arsenal would be closer to the centre and, with that vital underground station, much easier to reach. Spurs had only joined the League five years before and had just spent enormous sums (around £50,000) on improving their ground.

Local residents joined in the outcry – it was one thing having a college of divinity on the doorstep, quite another to see it turn into a football ground. It is impossible to imagine such a transfer being approved today, but at that time there was very little in the way of planning permission required.

Tottenham, Orient, the local residents and even Chelsea appealed to the League Management Committee and a special meeting was called in March 1913. It went on until two in the morning, a not too friendly and highly argumentative debate. To cut a long story short, Arsenal won the day. This was less because the Management Committee agreed with their plans than because: '... of the opinion that under the rules and practice of the League (we) have no right to interfere.'

Many clubs had moved in the past but no one had ever objected before and the transfers had usually been local and to everyone's benefit. Arsenal's case was, by any standards, different. It is only 10 miles as the crow flies from Woolwich to Highbury, but in terms of travelling times within greater London that is very different from Blackburn Rovers or Sunderland moving a mile up the road. Never before had there been a clear incursion into a competitor's catchment area.

Left: The 1912–13 squad at the start of the season. It was a disastrous time for Woolwich Arsenal as they were relegated to the Second Division of the Football League.

FAREWELL TO WOOLWICH

The last first-class game at the Manor Ground took place on Saturday 26 April 1913 against Middlesbrough, and Woolwich Arsenal said goodbye to their name, their home and south-east London with a 1–1 draw, a rather better result than most of that season for they had won only two games in all first-class competitions at the Manor Ground in the previous 12 months. Woolwich was dropped from the name and the club was called The Arsenal from 1914 to 1919 and unofficially, well beyond 1919. Chapman particularly asked for the 'The' to be dropped in 1927, but it is still heard a century later. The official Football League Fiftieth Anniversary History said: 'Thus the new Arsenal club was reborn and, on 3rd April of the following year (1914) it was given permission to drop the Woolwich from the name and was henceforth known as "The Arsenal".'

Now the spending really began. In four months the new pitch was levelled (the north end had to be raised 11 feet and the south end lowered five feet), a new grandstand partly built and turnstiles and terracing installed. It cost Norris another £80,000. Including bank guarantees and loans, by the time the first match was played at Highbury on 6 September 1913 he had found an astonishing £125,000 to put into the club. Cash was so short that the builder of the stand agreed to take a percentage of the weekly gate to pay for its construction.

All Norris had to show for this investment at that time, of course, was a Second Division football team. The first game was against Leicester Fosse and the Reds won 2–1. Scottish international Andy Devine scored the first goal, but it is centre-forward George Jobey whose contribution that day has gone down in history. He sprained an ankle during the game and was helped off by trainer George Hardy. As there were no dressing rooms, Hardy decided to take Jobey to the player's lodgings nearby. To do so he borrowed a cart from the local milkman David Lewis, who lived in Gillespie Road.

All in all, the team did quite well in that Second Division season – finishing third and failing to go up only on goal average behind Bradford Park Avenue. The critical game was the last home match of the season, on 18 April against Clapton Orient, who were sixth in the division. In a bitter

hangover from the controversy over Arsenal's move a year before, Orient fought like tigers to draw 2–2. The following week, though Arsenal won 2–0 at Glossop (the Hill-Wood family club), Bradford beat Blackpool 4–1 and were up.

THE IMPACT OF WAR

But a far greater shock was about to face Norris. He desperately needed First Division football and seemed to have a team that might achieve it but, within a year of that first game at Highbury, Europe was at war. The result was disaster. Players, particularly the many with Woolwich Arsenal connections, went back to munitions work, others joined the forces, the crowds declined and the League, though it was contested in 1914–15, was something of an irrelevance.

The most notable players of the era were right-back Joe Shaw, who was to stay with the club during and beyond the inter-war period as assistant manager, and his full-back partner Bob Benson. Benson was one of the many players who went back into munitions work and therefore lost his match fitness. Having gone to watch the club play at Reading in February 1916, Benson volunteered to take Joe Shaw's place as Shaw himself could not get away from his own job. Benson was clearly unfit, had to leave the field and, having gone to the dressing room, died a few minutes later in the arms of George Hardy. In a fitting tribute he was buried in an Arsenal shirt.

There were many more tragedies in that 'war to end wars'. For the club, having taken such a gamble only a year before, the war was a source of despair. At the end of the 1914–15 season manager George Morrell was unceremoniously sacked to save money. By 1918 the club was £60,000 overdrawn and Norris was, not surprisingly, again desperate.

On Saturday 24 April 1915 Arsenal had played their last game of the season against Forest at Highbury. The programme detailed Morrell's departure and the club's plight. It was, nonetheless, their best display of the year, a 7–0 win with Harry King scoring four goals, Jock Rutherford one, and Bob Benson, less than a year before his death, playing up front and getting two. What no one knew at the time was that it was to be Arsenal's last game in the Second Division.

ALEC. GRAHAM.

Above: Half-back Alec Graham joined Arsenal for their disastrous final season before the move to Highbury, scoring 20 goals in his 179 matches for the 'Reds.'

Above: Highbury as it was at the in the mid-1920s, with original East Stand at the right of the picture and the grounds of St John's College of Divinity visible at the bottom.

PEACETIME PROBLEMS

When the long, terrible conflict known then as the 'War to End All Wars' reached its exhausted conclusion in the November of 1918, first-class football had effectively ceased to exist. Three quarters of a million young British men had been killed, and of those no small number had been professional footballers.

Amid all this, The Arsenal's problems were clearly relatively small ones, but to the club's owner and bankroller, Sir Henry Norris, they were real enough. When the war began the club had been fielding a side which should have quickly fought its way back into the First Division and hence helped with the £60,000 standing debt and Norris' immense investment of £125,000. But those players who had survived the traumas of the war were all five years older and there was absolutely no telling how any club would perform in the season that was to begin in September 1919.

POLITICAL GAMES BEGIN

It was at this point that Henry Norris set out on the single most outrageous enterprise ever to be conceived in the history of English football. There is still no convincing explanation of how Norris achieved his object and it is almost inconceivable that any other individual, before or since, could have carried it off at all. Norris' aim, very simply, was to talk The Arsenal back into the First Division.

In 1914–15 the team had finished fifth in the Second Division. Above Arsenal were Derby, Preston, Barnsley and Wolves. In 1919 it was decided to extend the First Division from 20 to 22 clubs. Extensions of the divisions had happened on several occasions since the League was founded in 1888 and the almost invariable procedure when extending the

First Division was to re-elect automatically the bottom clubs from the previous season and promote the top clubs from the Second Division. Given the unfortunate intervention of the war, there seemed every reason to suppose that this is exactly what would happen.

By chance, two other London clubs, Chelsea and Spurs, had finished 19th and 20th in the First Division in 1915. Showing remarkable stealth and political judgement, Norris used the eight intervening months between the end of the war and the AGM of the Football League in mid-1919 to canvass the other major clubs and various influential friends in the game. He had received his knighthood in 1917 and became a Tory MP in 1918, and one must assume that many were flattered by the attentions of this successful luminary in a game which then had few figures of note outside its own confines.

Norris seemed to have little material to work on with which to prove his case. But there was just one small chink of hope. At the end of the 1914–15 season it had become obvious that the League would have to be abandoned completely for the duration of the war. There had been some allegations of match fixing by one or two players (who had apparently bet on the results) and, in one instance, this accusation was proven after a number of lengthy court cases. That particular game was Manchester United versus Liverpool, and United had won it 2–0 to finish 18th, just one point ahead of Chelsea. Although United would have dropped below Chelsea if Liverpool had beaten them, they would still have finished ahead of bottom-placed Spurs, but the whole business did serve to create an understandable uneasiness that something about the 1914–15 season was not quite as it should have been. It should be said immediately for the record that there was never the slightest suggestion that either Tottenham or Chelsea were ever involved in any wrongdoing.

NORRIS MAKES CLAIM FOR PROMOTION

What Norris said to the other chairmen has never been revealed, but his desperation for First Division status and the size of the investment at risk clearly persuaded enough of them that he had a worthwhile case. Leslie Knighton described his Chairman's technique at the time thus: 'His influence was enormous. (He would) speak to an important person there, suggesting a favour, remind a certain financier who was interested that he had once done him a good turn and been promised something in return.'

When the AGM was convened, Norris' strategy became clear. It must have been agreed with League President 'Honest' John McKenna, a close friend of Norris and the owner of Liverpool, in advance. Firstly, Chelsea were detached from Spurs and their position taken separately. There was no vote, and the fact that Chelsea would have finished third from bottom in 1915 rather than only one place above Spurs had Liverpool beaten United in the fixed match undoubtedly influenced the meeting. McKenna proposed they they be

re-elected on the nod and this was accepted. Then Derby and Preston, first and second in the Second Division in 1914–15, were elected to the First Division without debate.

Then came the bombshell. McKenna, who might have been more reticent given that he was the force behind Liverpool FC, made a brief speech recommending that Arsenal be given the remaining First Division place because of their service to the League and their longevity, particularly pointing out that Arsenal had been in the League 15 years longer than Spurs.

The arguments used were, of course, complete and utter nonsense. The League is not (and never has been) run on the basis of the most experienced clubs being given the higher places, and, in any event, Wolves, who finished fourth, had been members of the League four years longer than Arsenal. Spurs chairman Charlie Roberts found it (not surprisingly) very difficult to counter the illogicalities of this Alice in Wonderland meeting in which he had suddenly, unexpectedly and inexplicably become entrapped. The vote was taken; Arsenal got 18, Spurs got 8, Barnsley (who finished third) 5, Wolves 4, Forest (who finished 19th and had no claim to a place whatsoever) got 3, Birmingham 2 and Hull 1. Hence Arsenal were elected and Sir Henry Norris had his First Division club again.

A MYSTERIOUS DECISION

To this day it is impossible to explain what went on at that AGM. The most plausible explanation is actually the most irrational; the individual representatives assumed that, if McKenna was prepared to support so unlikely a cause, then he must have some very good, if well-hidden, reason for doing so. If there was such a reason, it has remained very well hidden indeed, though it would clearly have been assumed to be something to do with the results at the end of the 1914–15 season. For the sake of completeness, it should be mentioned that for many years there were rumours of the involvement of significant sums of money.

Paradoxically, it was a conclusion that probably favoured Spurs more than Arsenal. Tottenham response to the perceived injustice of it all was on the field. In 1919–20 they scored 102 goals and broke all the records for points (70) and wins (32). Straight back in the First Division, they finished sixth, and won the FA Cup at Stamford Bridge. Until Chapman was bedded in at Highbury, Spurs were clearly north London's leading club. There was, not surprisingly, a heavy residue of bitterness between the clubs, thankfully unparalleled before or since in the English game. In September 1922 the bitterness led to a particularly vicious match, two sendings off, censures, suspensions and an FA Commission of Inquiry.

BITTER NORTH LONDON RIVALS

As late as 1928, Arsenal were accused of throwing games at the end of the season to ensure Spurs went down. The games concerned in that 1927–28 season were both at home – a 0–2 defeat by Portsmouth (who themselves finished 20th) on 28 March and, more relevantly, a 0–1 defeat by Manchester United (who finished 18th) on 28 April, the last week of the season. Both of those clubs finished one point above Spurs, who had finished their programme earlier, and if Arsenal had managed even a draw with either Portsmouth or United then Spurs would have stayed up.

On the other hand, the table in 1927–28 was astonishingly tight. Seven points covered Derby, who finished fourth, and Middlesbrough, who finished bottom. Arsenal, in 19th place, were only three points ahead of Spurs themselves and would therefore, one must assume, have endangered their own position by such unlikely behaviour. The Gunners only very rarely got the better of Spurs in the inter-war period anyway; between Chapman's arrival in 1925 and October 1934 Spurs did not once lose at Highbury.

The Arsenal did not exactly enjoy a successful spell for the few seasons after 1919, but at least they stayed where they were. It was a happy coincidence that the centenary was also the point that Arsenal equalled the record for the longest unbroken spell of First Division membership. Sunderland stayed there from 1890 to 1958, a run of 68 years. Arsenal's 68th year arrived in the second half of the season 1986–87.

MISSION IMPOSSIBLE

Norris had appointed Leslie Knighton as manager in June 1919. Knighton, who had previously had quite successful spells with Huddersfield and Manchester City, was, however, rarely allowed to manage. Among Norris' other edicts, Knighton was not allowed to sign players smaller than 5ft 8in, was not allowed to spend more than £1,000 on anyone (Norris was either not prepared to spend any more money or, more likely, was running short of it), was expected to sign and create a team of purely local players and, to compound all these problems, had to save money by abandoning the scouting system. The task tended to verge on the impossible and the playing record reflects this.

The best position between 1919 and Chapman's arrival six years later was ninth in 1921, the only time the club won more games than they lost. In the Cup The Arsenal got beyond the second round just once, in 1922, when they lost to Preston in the quarter finals after a replay. Knighton's last FA Cup game as manager (and probably one of the reasons behind his dismissal soon afterward) actually provides one of the funniest stories in football history.

KNIGHTON'S 'PLUCK PILLS'

The Arsenal were drawn against West Ham in the first round in January 1925 and Knighton told how he was surprised to be approached by a Harley Street doctor who was also an Arsenal fan: 'I trust you agree that we have a poor chance

Above: Joe Shaw's playing career with Arsenal began in 1907 and went on until 1923. Apart from a short spell at Chelsea, his distinguished career as part of the management team was to continue until the mid-1950s.

of survival against West Ham, Mr Knighton,' said the doctor. 'What the boys require is something in the nature of a courage pill. They do no harm, but tone up the nerves to produce the maximum effort.' Knighton investigated the doctor, who was genuine, and his remedy, which did not appear poisonous or illegal, and decided to go ahead. The team were, naturally enough, reluctant. Knighton tried to reassure them by promising to take one of the pills himself. At 2 pm on the Saturday of the match they all took their pills. At 2.50 pm the referee came into the dressing room and told them he'd called the game off because of fog. 'Getting the boys back to Highbury that afternoon was like trying to drive a flock of lively lions,' said Knighton. 'The pills not only left us raring to go but also developed the most red-hot, soul-destroying thirst I've ever known.'

On the following Monday Arsenal went to Upton Park again and went through the same routine. Down went the pills ... and down came the fog. The game was called off again. The after-effects were the same.

On the Thursday the game finally began, the Arsenal team and their manager having taken their pills for a third time. By half time the Gunners were running around like maniacs. 'They were giants suddenly supercharged. They tore away with the ball and put in shots like leather thunderbolts. They monopolised the play – and yet they couldn't score ... For West Ham there was no defence against the pluck pills. The ball crashed and bounced against the West Ham goal. The Arsenal players ran like Olympic sprinters, jumped like rockets to reach the high ones and crashed in shots from all angles and distances. It is no disparagement to West Ham to say that they had the most incredible luck that half.' The game ended as a goalless draw. But Knighton's troubles were only just beginning. 'I forgot my frightful thirst,' he recounts, 'croaking out congratulations and sympathy to the team. But you should have heard them! Running about had made their thirst and bitter throats a thousand times worse. That night those pills created a riot.'

An hour before the replay at Highbury Knighton took out his box of pills. The team refused point-blank to go through it all again. They drew 2–2. The fifth attempt was at Stamford Bridge. There were no pills and no goals for Arsenal. With the last kick of the game, George Kay scored from a Jimmy Ruffell corner and West Ham won 1–0. The doctor never told Knighton what was in the pills, nor ever offered them again.

TALENTED BUT UNDERACHIEVING

Knighton's team had its strengths, despite the poor playing record. Joe Shaw was still at full-back, Scot Billy Blyth was used everywhere and Tom Whittaker was a very reliable, intelligent, wing half- or full-back until a knee injury in Woolongong, Australia, while on tour with the FA party, ended his playing career and directed him to becoming the most famous trainer/physiotherapist soccer has known.

Above: The 'utility' player and England international Alf Baker joined Arsenal in the 1919–20 season, and remained with the club for 12 seasons, scoring 26 goals in 351 games.

Knighton also made one or two clever signings. Alf Baker, later an England international at right-half, signed for Arsenal after Knighton met him at the pithead in Ilkeston (near Nottingham) to forestall other clubs waiting at Baker's home. Baker was to play in all eleven positions for the club during his career.

Another international who was whisked away for nothing from under the noses of others was Bob John. He came from Caerphilly, where Knighton painted a glowing picture of the glories of the capital (which John was, indeed, later to enjoy with the club) compared with Cardiff, to whom John was pledged. He was in the Welsh national side within six months. Also from south Wales (though he was born in Bristol) came Jimmy Brain, who was to lead the attack for several seasons. Both Knighton and Peter McWilliam, manager of Spurs, reputedly had to disguise themselves when they visited south Wales because of the anger expressed when the two London clubs had stolen away Jimmy Seed, Cecil Poynton and Bob John, and Spurs were at a crucial disadvantage because all their negotiations for Brain had to be carried out in secret.

Because of Norris' transfer edicts (he tried in both 1922 and 1924 to get the League to impose a limit on fees of £1,650 – rarely for a League AGM, they chose to ignore Norris' wishes), Knighton also had to indulge in some rather unusual transfers. Dr Jimmy Paterson was an amateur winger with Queen's Park in Glasgow, when his sister happened to marry the Arsenal club doctor, J. L. Scott. Paterson joined Scott's practice (based in Clapton) and also started to play for the club.

MIDGET MOFFAT SIGNS

A more celebrated transfer was that of the famous 'Midget' Moffat of Workington. Again, this is a story worth telling largely in Leslie Knighton's words.

Knighton had been told about Midget Moffat, the 5 ft tall Workington winger, by an old Huddersfield colleague, who had also warned him that other sides were beginning to take an interest. But chairman Norris had recently imposed one of his absolute edicts – no small men, all new signings had to be at least 5 ft 8 in tall and weigh in at a minimum of 11 stones. Nonetheless, Knighton trusted his source enough to go to Workington by an overnight train and watch the player.

The manager was as mesmerised as the opposing full-back: '... a tiny footballer spinning rings around two perfectly competent full-backs, a midget with a kick like a horse,' Knighton said later. He immediately offered the player a job but Moffat strangely failed to turn up at Highbury the following day. Knighton arrived at the ground the subsequent morning to find the groundsman waiting for him. 'I've got a little tiny chap waiting for you. Says he's come to play for Arsenal. He's asleep in the dressing room.' And, said Knighton: 'There was Moffat, fast asleep on some kit in a corner, his shock of hair sticking out like a squirrel's tail.'

Moffat had arrived at Euston and gone straight to Woolwich, thinking the club still played there (they had moved 12 years earlier). When he arrived it was dark. A road sweeper explained things, and offered Moffat a lift on his cart all the way to Highbury.

Knighton took Moffat straight off on a continental tour to Scandinavia, where the winger was apparently a great success. Norris, who had been on a summer holiday in Nice, returned at the start of the new season to find a midget in his midst. 'Norris smiled and said nothing,' wrote Knighton, 'but, as always, he got his way. Moffat had to go, to Luton and thence on to Everton.'

NORRIS GROWS IMPATIENT

Sadly, Midget Moffat rather sums up Knighton's career at Highbury – clever, thoughtful, but unfortunately bound hand and foot by Norris' peculiar restraints. Whether Knighton would have been a more successful manager for Arsenal in different circumstances is difficult to assess; it certainly seems possible, for he went on to achieve a fair deal with Chelsea and Birmingham.

For his part, it appears that Norris could not work out what was going wrong. As far as we can tell, it doesn't seem to have occurred to him that his restriction on transfers could be affecting the team's potential. He saw the game with an outsider's eye – each of the players seemed good enough, why wouldn't they knit together properly, why did they keep losing by the odd goal? There were other pressures on Norris. As we have seen, Spurs had recovered well from the shenanigans of 1919 and were established as the leading, and best supported, club in the area.

And Henry Norris wasn't getting any younger. If he was ever to do it, to realise the dreams of the past two decades for his club, it would have to be soon. He was no longer an MP, no longer the Mayor of Fulham. Highbury had become his career and, in his own eyes perhaps, the remaining symbol to crown a very successful life.

KNIGHTON SACKED

Knighton was dismissed toward the end of the 1924–25 season. In his autobiography, the manager gives his own explanation of the event. Early on in his Highbury days, he had decided to get married. As his future wife lived in Manchester, and a house was available there, Knighton decided to move back north. Norris, according to Knighton, persuaded him to stay by offering his own apartment for Knighton's use (which Knighton accepted) and the promise of a benefit game in 1925–26, specifically the Arsenal versus Spurs match that season. This game could be expected to bring in perhaps £3,000 to £4,000 for Knighton. At that period a benefit game meant that the player or manager simply kept the takings of a regular season fixture.

Above: The view from the terraces of the North Bank to the Main Stand on a dull grey day during the 1927–28 season.

As it happened, the Arsenal-Spurs match proved to be the first of the 1925–26 season. Knighton believed that Norris fired him simply to avoid paying over the gate receipts of this game. Knighton actually wrote: 'I believe Norris sacked me to get round offering me the big benefit he promised ... when I tackled him about it, he made it clear I had nothing but a verbal promise, but he offered me £500 "without prejudice".' It is worth mentioning that Norris remembered Knighton in his will nine years later, by which time Knighton appears to have forgiven him.

It is certainly an interesting story, but matters are rarely so simple and it does not ring entirely true. A more likely explanation surely lies in the fact that The Arsenal had been knocked out of the Cup by West Ham in the first round, and had finished 20th in the League.

Norris probably approached Chapman in April 1925. The chairman managed one final dig at everything he had railed against with a superfluous advertisement in the Athletic News on 11 May 1925. It read: 'Arsenal Football Club is open to receive applications for the position of TEAM MANAGER. He must be experienced and possess the highest qualifications for the post, both as to ability and personal character. Gentlemen whose sole ability to build up a good side depends on the payment of heavy and exhorbitant (sic) transfer fees need not apply.'

It was a final, forceful restatement of at least one of his beliefs before they were allowed to rest in peace. From this point on, Arsenal and Sir Henry Norris were in the hands of the first football professional.

ARSENAL PLAYERS

Over twelve decades, legions of superb players have thrilled Arsenal loyalists down the years, and among them are those who brought exceptional glory, honour and excitement to the club. Each of them have possessed that extra special ingredient that set them apart from the rest, ensuring that they will always be remembered as Arsenal heroes. From Scouser Jimmy Ashcroft – an indomitable presence in goal when Woolwich Arsenal first played in Division One – through to modern favourites, such as Thierry Henry, they all earned the devotion and affection of Gunners everywhere. Here is a selection of those greats, but every fan will have their own favourites:

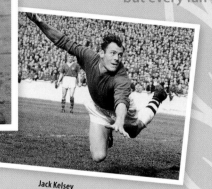

Alex James

Jack Kelsey

Charlie George

Jimmy Ashcroft
Arsenal career: 1900–08;
Appearances: 303;
Position: Goalkeeper
The first Gunner to play for England (he won three caps), Ashcroft was born in Liverpool and signed for the Gunners in June 1900. He played every game for more than four years until October 1904 (154 consecutive games).

Eddie Hapgood
Arsenal career: 1927–1944; Appearances: 393; Position: Full back
Hapgood was one of Herbert Chapman's most successful signings. He went on to captain Arsenal and England, making 393 League appearances and winning five league titles, two FA Cups and 30 international caps.

David Jack
Arsenal career: 1928–1934;
Appearances: 208; Position: Forward
The first player ever to score at Wembley Stadium, Jack was a vital element in Chapman's trophy-winning team. Jack was the Club's top scorer for the 1928–29 season. He recorded 34 goals in the First Division-winning season of 1930–31.

Alex James
Arsenal career: 1929–1937;
Appearances: 261;
Position: Inside-forward
James famously opened the scoring in the 1930 FA Cup final. He played as an inside-forward, providing openings for his striker team-mates. His accurate passing was key to Arsenal's successes in the 1930s. He left after another FA Cup win in 1936.

Cliff Bastin
Arsenal career: 1929–1946;
Appearances: 396;
Position: Outside-left
Signed by Herbert Chapman at the age of 17, Bastin spent the rest of his career at Highbury, ending his first season with an FA Cup winner's medal. By the age of 19, Bastin had won a League title, the FA Cup and an England cap. In total, he scooped five League titles with Arsenal and two FA Cup winner's medals.

Ted Drake
Arsenal Career: 1934–39; Appearances: 184; Position: Forward
Drake netted a breathtaking 42 goals in the title-winning campaign of 1934–35. His most memorable achievement was against Aston Villa, who were defeated by an emphatic 7–1, all the Arsenal goals courtesy of Drake.

Jack Kelsey
Arsenal career: 1949–62; Appearances: 352; Position: Goalkeeper
Widely acknowledged as the greatest goalie of his era, Jack was a world-class player. Kelsey won 41 caps for Wales and played for Great Britain against the Rest of Europe in 1955. He won the League with Arsenal in 1953.

George Graham
Arsenal career: 1966–72; Appearances: 308; Position: Midfielder
A key member of the 1971 Double-winning team, Graham arrived at Highbury in 1966 as a striker, and in his first two seasons he was the Club's top scorer. Bertie Mee moved him to a central midfield role, where his relaxed approach earned him the nickname 'Stroller'. He left the Club as a player in 1972.

Charlie George
Arsenal Career: 1969–75; Appearances: 179; Position: Inside-forward
An insprirational attacking player - the 'darling of the North Bank' helped the Gunners to European Fairs Cup glory in 1970. Upon his return from injury the following season, he assumed a new role as an attacking midfielder, giving the team an added dimension. His thunderous 20-yard drive at the 1971 FA Cup Final secured Arsenal's first Double.

George Armstrong
Arsenal Career: 1961–77; Appearances: 621; Position: Midfielder
Armstrong was an asset on both flanks. His precision crossing and creativity led to

Liam Brady

David Rocastle

scored in the Double season of 1971.

Frank McLintock

Arsenal career: 1964–73; Appearances: 403; Goals: 32; Position: Wing-half/centre-half

Frank McLintock was at the heart of the Double-winning team of 1971. He started at Arsenal as a wing-half, but five years later Don Howe moved him into the defence. His commanding presence as captain and ability to read the game made him an outstanding captain. McLintock ended the Double-winning season Footballer of the Year.

Bob Wilson

Arsenal career: 1964–73; Appearances: 308; Position: Goalkeeper

Wilson's first-team debut came in March 1968 and in 1970 he was in the team that won the Inter-Cities Fairs Cup. Ever-present in the 1971 Double-winning side. Two years later injury forced Wilson out of the Arsenal side but he recovered to claim back his No 1 spot until he retired as a player.

Liam Brady

Arsenal career: 1973–80; Appearances: 307; Position: Midfielder

A wily playmaker, Liam Brady was central to the team of the 1970s with his skill, vision, balance and strength. Brady joined Arsenal as a schoolboy in 1970. The prolific Malcolm Macdonald and Frank Stapleton benefited from the wealth of goalscoring chances conjured up by Brady. He was voted PFA Player of the Year

in 1979.

Kenny Sansom

Arsenal career: 1980-1988; Appearances: 394; Position: Full-back

One of the finest full-backs England has ever produced, Sansom came to Highbury an established international. His attacking runs set a new standard for the modern full-back. In 1987 he led the side in the League Cup victory over Liverpool.

David O'Leary

Arsenal career: 1975–93; Appearances: 722; Position: Centre-Half

A comanding and deceptively powerful, centre-half, O'Leary was also surprisingly quick. Through his long playing career at the Club, O'Leary was a lynch-pin of the Arsenal defence.

David Rocastle

Arsenal career: 1985–92; Appearances: 277; Position: Midfielder

'Rocky' Rocastle brought panache to the Arsenal midfield. He was awarded the Supporter's Player of the Year award in 1986 and picked up his first major honour in the 1987 League Cup, and a League winners medal in 989. A versatile player, he could operate equally well in a central or a wide-right position.

Alan Smith

Arsenal career: 1987–95; Appearances: 347; Position: Centre-forward

Smith' s ability to read the game made him a lethal strike partner. In 1989 as Arsenal pursued the title, Smith continued his own campaign for the Golden Boot. Both targets were achieved. He was the provider for Thomas's historic strike in that year's League-winning match and scored the decisive goal in the Cup Winners Cup Final in 1994.

Tony Adams

Arsenal career: 1983–2002; Appearances: 669; Position: Centre-back

One of the Gunners' greatest ever players, Adams was the ultimate one-club man. The leader of the famous Back Four, Adams was a supreme defender, whose timing of his tackles, his reading of the game and his ability in the air ability made him a defensive colossus for club and country.

Ian Wright

Arsenal career: 1991–98; Appearances: 288; Position: Centre-forward

A predatory striker and a great showman, Wright was an instant favourite at Highbury. He found the net three times in his League debut at Southampton and on the final day of that season, he produced another hat-trick to win the Golden Boot. 1997–98, Wright's last season at the Club, was the pinnacle of a trophy-laden career with the Gunners.

David Seaman

Arsenal career: 1990–2003; Appearances: 564; Position: Goalkeeper

Seaman was the cornerstone of the trophy-winning Arsenal defence. Seaman had fast reflexes, sound judgement and a great sense of positioning. His reassuring presence in goal provided a springboard for the attack for both Arsenal and England.

Dennis Bergkamp

Arsenal career: 1995–2006; Appearances: 423; Position: Centre-forward

Dutchman, Dennis Bergkamp was a world-class player, who was indispensible in the Arsenal successes under Wenger. In the 1997–98 Double-winning season he also won both major Player of Year awards. Bergkamp was the hub of Arsenal creativity for a decade including the 'invincibles' season.

Patrick Vieira

Arsenal career: 1996–2005; Appearances: 406; Position: Central midfielder

A relative unknown when he arrived at Highbury in late 1996, Vieira became one of the world's most authoritative midfielders, a remarkable athlete who could both win the ball and distribute it effectively. Eventually succeeding Adams as captain, his contribution to the Club was immense.

Thierry Henry

Arsenal Career: 1999–2007; Appearances: 380; Position: Striker

France's leading scorer at the 1998 World Cup, Henry was generally regarded as a winger. Wenger transformed him into the Premiership's (and perhaps the world's) leading striker. Henry's goals produced a string of trophies for himself and the Club, and he contributed 39 goals in the 'Invincible', season. He finished his Arsenal career as captain.

Tony Adams and Patrick Viera

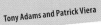

CHAPTER 4

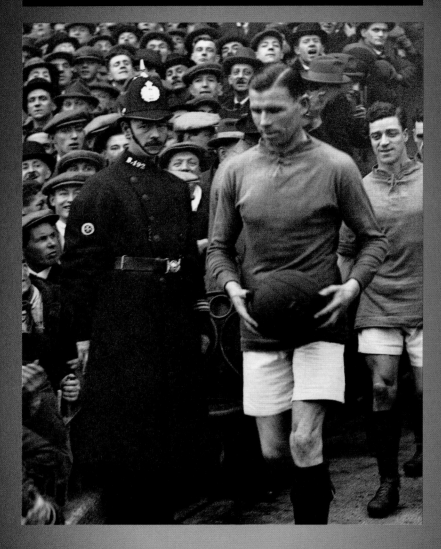

LEGENDARY ARSENAL

1925–1934

Herbert Chapman's first few months at Highbury were not exactly uneventful. Before the start of the 1925–26 season, the old offside law had been changed. Previously, to remain onside required three defenders between the foremost attacker and the goal, and now this requirement was reduced to two. This was in response to the deadening effect of the offside game, refined during the early 1920s by teams such as Newcastle and Notts County. The immediate effect was a flood of goals and a change in tactics which allowed far more goalscoring in the English game until around the late 1960s.

To take one good example of the effect of the change, Huddersfield's first two Championships (1923–24 and 1924–25) under Chapman had been achieved with 60 and 69 goals scored. Chapman's two Championships with Arsenal saw the Gunners score 127 in 1930–31 and 118 in 1932–33. Chapman does not appear to have developed any immediate tactical variations in the light of the new law. His first season started relatively poorly – the very first game was a 1–0 home defeat by Tottenham though this was followed by 1–0 away wins at Manchester United and Leicester.

On 3 October 1925 came a truly critical match, a resounding 7–0 defeat at Newcastle. This defeat so upset Arsenal new man Charlie Buchan that he demanded a tactical change by dropping the centre-half (previously the free-ranging link between defence and attack) back between the full-backs. The centre-half could thus cut out forwards coming through the middle who hoped to exploit having to be behind only one defender rather than two. Apparently Newcastle, with Charlie Spencer at centre-half, played this very system during their 7–0 win and Buchan, who had suggested the tactic at every Arsenal team meeting since the opening day of the season, clearly thought himself thoroughly vindicated.

BUCHAN PROMPTS TACTICAL SWITCH

Charlie Buchan was a player Chapman would always listen to, and was a good example of Chapman's determination to bring the very best players, irrespective of age or price, to his clubs. He had used Clem Stephenson at Huddersfield in the same way in 1920 and Chapman also took the great Alex Jackson to Leeds Road. At Highbury he paid a record fee for David Jack and captured Alex James, the outstanding schemer of the inter-war period.

A SIGNIFICANT SIGNING

Charlie Buchan was Chapman's first purchase at Highbury, and one that was to reverberate round the club for many years. Buchan had actually been born in Plumstead, had watched Arsenal as a boy, studied at Woolwich Polytechnic, and had played four games for Arsenal Reserves. He walked out on the club in 1909 when the notoriously mean George Morrell turned down an expense claim for 11 shillings (55p). He joined Northfleet, then Leyton, and was transferred to Sunderland (after turning down Norris and Fulham) for a massive £1,200 when aged only 18. He played in their Championship side of 1913 and in the Cup final that year, became captain of England and, after his retirement, became a very well known journalist and broadcaster. He was nearly 34 years old when he came to Highbury, and had, a couple of months before, already been the subject of an approach by Leslie Knighton, who had clearly decided to go out with a bang by (unbeknown to Norris) offering £7,000 for Buchan's signature. Buchan's main concern was his sports shop in Sunderland, from which he took a great deal of income. The maximum wage at the time was only £8 per week and the need for sweeteners and compensations was not uncommon in persuading very good players to move.

Chapman was presumably a much more persuasive negotiator than Knighton, for Sunderland were eventually prepared to consider and accept a much lower fee. The signing has, of course, gone down as one of the most celebrated in football history and is worth recounting. Buchan was serving in his shop in May 1925 when in walked Chapman. 'I've come to sign you for Arsenal,' he told Buchan immediately, and the player assumed he was joking. On being told that Chapman had spoken to the club, Buchan telephoned Sunderland manager Bob Kyle, finding it difficult to believe that the club would release him so easily. It was to be another ten weeks before he finally put pen to paper and in the meantime the deal had been thrashed out. It was actually Norris, and not Chapman, who had insisted on handling the financial negotiations. Sunderland had asked for £4,000, but Norris was not prepared to pay that for a 33-year-old player. Kyle argued that Buchan might now be 33 but that he would still score 20 goals in his first season with Arsenal. Norris asked Kyle to put his money where his mouth was – £2,000 down and £100 for every goal scored. Kyle agreed and Buchan scored 19 League goals and two in the Cup. So Kyle got his £4,000 and £100 interest on top. For Arsenal the deal turned out to be great publicity, a ready-made headline every time Buchan scored and the crowd would chant, 'There goes another £100,' whenever Buchan got near goal.

FINANCIAL IRREGULARITIES

Norris must already have given Chapman carte blanche on transfer fees, for within a few weeks the manager had also bought the Scottish international keeper Bill Harper from Hibs for £5,000. The Buchan transfer dragged on for those ten weeks because of the player's insistence that he must somehow be compensated for the likely loss of revenue from his shop if he moved.

Chapman, no doubt remembering only too clearly what had happened when Leeds City were suspended in 1919 and how difficult it had been for him to find work afterward, would not get involved in any illegal payments but, according to Norris, pleaded for the chairman to meet Buchan's demands. The chairman later claimed that Chapman left the room when this delicate point was reached. The payments involved came to light as part of a much wider League commission two years later, which found Norris and William Hall guilty of various financial irregularities. Though the hearing was supposedly secret, the Daily Mail published the details and Norris sued the FA for libel in suggesting he had acted dishonestly.

Norris had a reputation for being quick to take legal action, which he usually won, but in February 1929, the case having gone as high as the Lord Chief Justice, the FA were vindicated and were able to exclude Norris from any further involvement in football.

The significant findings of the commission were that between 1921 and 1924 Norris' chauffeur had been paid by the club, and that in 1926 the club had paid for his motor car. During the case, Norris and Chapman clashed, the chairman saying that the manager and club had known about various payments and Chapman (perhaps again with his mind on 1919) denying it. Norris called Chapman a liar and particularly mentioned that £125 for the team bus was the sum he had given to Buchan, under the counter, to come to Highbury. It should be said that Buchan, in his autobiography, disputed this – though only in general terms: 'Let me say here that I made nothing out of my transfer ... In fact, I lost rather a lot of money through changing quarters like that.' One is, nonetheless, struck by Buchan's careful choice of words, which seem chosen to cloud rather than clarify.

When asked why he had done it, Norris replied very simply and obviously: 'Because (otherwise) we would not have got the players.' It all sounds desperately petty now, but at the time there were many scores to be settled and, in the fashion of a true Greek tragedy, the opportunity was not regretted by some. It was a genuine tragedy for Norris; since 1910, in addition to the money he had found for the club via various business ventures and from his own companies, he had sunk over £15,000 directly from his own pocket and no one could seriously claim that he was alone or unique in his supposed mis-demeanours. Most of the leading clubs were doing the same thing one way or another.

During the case Norris declared that: 'I only made one mistake in my career, and that was sacking Knighton.' Leslie Knighton took this as a signal compliment, but in its context one is tempted to believe that it was more a none-too-subtle jab at Herbert Chapman than praise for Knighton. Nonetheless, as a final epitaph to the man who, almost as

much as Herbert Chapman, built the modern Arsenal, we should return to the manager he had fired, Leslie Knighton: 'Despite everything,' said Knighton in his autobiography, 'I still say he was the best Chairman I ever had (Knighton managed eight clubs). He did miles more for football and for footballers than the public will ever know. If he had not been (such) a rebel against petty authority he would have risen to the greatest position in the game.'

A financial genius, football was his hobby and delight, even though only a bagatelle compared with some of his business dealings. The game was immensely the poorer for his passing out of it, and it was a tragedy indeed that such a man should have gone under a cloud.' In a sense the greater regret was that the dreams were about to come true – the year after his exclusion saw the first major trophy arrive at Highbury. Norris lived to see the FA Cup and League won before dying, an outcast from the game, just six months after Chapman on 30 July 1934.

HILL-WOOD TAKES CONTROL

The new Chairman was Sir Samuel Hill-Wood, whose family had run Glossop North End before the war as a sort of works team, and with some success. Glossop, in Derbyshire, remains by far the smallest town ever to have hosted a top Division club. Hill-Wood had his own place in the sporting record books already. Playing for Derbyshire versus the MCC at Lord's in May 1900, he had scored 10 runs off a single ball, the highest ever recorded before or since from a single hit. He was content to leave the running of the club to Herbert Chapman, who was no doubt greatly shaken by the court case but mightily relieved at its outcome.

But back to October 1925 and to the team meeting after that appalling 7–0 thrashing by Newcastle; it was here Buchan persuaded Chapman that centre-half Jack Butler had to drop back. The meeting was in the Royal Station Hotel in Newcastle and Buchan had started the debate by refusing to catch the train back to London. 'Oh no,' said Chapman. 'You're playing at West Ham on Monday. I know what you want so let's discuss it. Buchan outlined his ideas to the team. He didn't actually want a centre-half 'policing' the centre-forward, rather a man given a geographical 'beat' on the edge of the area. The rest of the defence would wheel around him to provide support. Buchan then pitched hard to be given the now necessary roving inside forward job needed to replace the centre-half's attacking role (he described it as being like the fly half in rugby) but Chapman refused, wanting Buchan to continue as a goalscorer up front. There was no other obvious candidate for the job, so Chapman apparently put it to Buchan: 'It's your plan Charlie, do you have any suggestions?' Buchan suggested occasional inside forward Scotsman Andy Neil, who, though not fast could kill the ball instantly and distribute it quickly and accurately with either foot. After some argument the plan was accepted and Neil took on the

role for the following day's match at West Ham. The plan worked perfectly, Arsenal won 4–0 and, for a year at least, they barely looked back. Jimmy Ramsey and then Billy Blyth later took over the link-man's job from Neil.

THE WM FORMATION

It would not be true to say that the new system was in any sense invented by Buchan and Chapman. As we have seen, Newcastle were already experimenting, as were Queen's Park and several other sides, including Spurs. What Chapman did do, of course, was to refine it and find the players to fit the positions as perfectly as was ever likely to be possible.

He quickly moved his full-backs out to mark the wingers (that job had regularly been done by the half-backs), dropped a second inside forward back half-way between the midfield line and the forwards, and decided that three very fast-moving and adaptable forwards were probably the best attacking answer to the new defensive formations and the revised offside law. This was not developed overnight, but over a period of years, ending with the 3–4–3 or WM formation of the great Arsenal teams. The key was never the scheme itself, but the players whom Chapman fitted into it.

Chapman had retained relatively few of the men he inherited from Knighton. Alf Baker continued at right-half, Bob John for a time at left-back and then at wing half. Bernard Joy said of John that: '... next to Joe Mercer, he is

Right: A handshake begins one of the most symbolic games ever played at Highbury. The date was 29 August 1925, the captains Charlie Buchan of Arsenal and Arthur Grimsdell of Spurs. It was Chapman's first game as Arsenal manager, Buchan's first as an Arsenal player and the first day of the revolutionary offside law.

the finest wing half Arsenal have had and I have played alongside giants like Jack Crayston, Wilf Copping and Archie Macaulay. There was nobody like him for plucking the ball out of the air with his foot, whatever its height or pace, and bringing it to the ground. He did his job quietly, efficiently and unobtrusively, and there lay his strength.' Charlie Buchan was equally unstinting in his praise of John, whom he regarded as the core of the Arsenal side: 'He deserves a place in any list of famous players ... yet one rarely hears him mentioned nowadays (this was in 1955). You could depend on Bob in every game but this dapper player was not showy. He just got on with the job.' Bob John eventually played 421 First Division matches (a club record until surpassed by George Armstrong) over 16 seasons, won three Cup medals, three Championship medals and 16 caps. If there was a cornerstone of the great teams, it was surely Bob John.

Chapman moved Jimmy Brain, who had recently been playing as an inside forward, to centre-forward and Brain immediately established a new club scoring record with 33 goals in 1925-26. By February 1926 another of the critical influences had arrived – right-winger Joe Hulme. Reputed to be the fastest winger in British football, Hulme had previously played for York and Blackburn and eventually won nine England caps, a lot for a winger at the time.

Left: Joe Hulme was another Chapman acquisition for Arsenal. An outside right, he scored 124 goals in 372 games for the Gunners.

FALSE DAWN FOR CHAPMAN'S GUNNERS

All in all, 1925–26 proved to be a successful first season for Chapman. The results were not spectacular, but kept going the right way and Arsenal finished with 52 points, which took them to second place in the League. They never really challenged Huddersfield, who took their third consecutive Championship and the first ever hat-trick. Arsenal's 52 points was the most they had ever achieved in the First Division (eight more than in 1920–21) and the greatest number ever achieved by a London club. Second place was also the highest ever reached by a club from the capital, equalling Spurs' performance of 1922.

But if anyone at Highbury thought that here was the brave new world, then they were wrong. Chapman said it would take five years to win a trophy and he was right, though quite why he was right remains elusive despite the speculations about the gathering legal storm clouds over Norris and his manager. The next four years in the League were almost a definition of mediocre – 11th, 10th, 9th and 14th. Perhaps it was because the team was always in a state of flux as Chapman added to it, or tried to incorporate the skills of a Jack or a James. Certainly it was to continue to be a period of team-building.

The next significant purchase was Tom Parker, Southampton's right-back. He was relatively slow but very good positionally, and Chapman particularly wanted him as a steadying, intelligent captain. He played 155 consecutive League games and was easy to pick out (there were no

numbers in the League until 1939) because of his bald head. Chapman always had a penchant for miners, not surprisingly given his own mining background, and there were over a dozen on the staff during his regime. One of the most popular was the ungainly but highly effective Jack Lambert, acquired as an inside forward for £2,000 from Doncaster Rovers. Chapman was always trying to find the perfect centre-forward and constantly seemed to be buying, or trying to buy, Lambert's replacement. But he always returned to the big fellow and the quest for the ideal was not actually satisfied until after the manager's death, with the arrival of Ted Drake. Lambert stayed with the club after his playing career had finished, going down to Margate to manage Arsenal's nursery club in that town. Tragically the big centre forward was to be killed in a road accident at the start of the Second World War.

For the other side of the field from Hulme, Chapman bought Welsh international Charlie Jones from Nottingham Forest. Jones was a very intelligent, worrying type of player, but an odd choice in the long term for outside left as he lacked speed. Chapman later moved him to right-half, where he became a permanent fixture in the great team of the early 1930s. Jack Butler, on the other hand, failed to adapt to his new stopper centre-half role, all too often venturing upfield and being caught out of position. In December 1926 Chapman somehow found a tall 21-year-old redhead playing for Oswestry on the Welsh borders and bought him for just £200. Roberts became such a feature of Arsenal's success

that he has remained identified forever as the basic mould for the stopper, policeman, centre-half. Rarely moving upfield, he performed his central defensive role consistently and effectively season after season.

POLICEMAN ROBERTS CALLED IN

Roberts was never a particularly skilful player, but he became an essential part of the tactical formation. As Cliff Bastin said: 'As an all-round player he may have had his failings, but he fitted in perfectly with the Arsenal scheme of things. Seldom was it that he wasted a ball ... Alex James picked up ball after ball from him in midfield.' Roberts rarely scored a goal, though he won the 1932 FA Cup quarter final at Huddersfield with a totally unexpected header from a corner right at the start of the match. He is also remembered for scoring two identical own goals in the same game for Derby at Highbury. His case is an interesting one for, by everyone's admission, not only was he not a skilful player, he was a relatively poor kicker of the ball.

Whittaker said that: 'Roberts' genius came from his intelligence and, even more important, that he did what he was told.' His orders were to stay in the centre of the defence, to intercept all the balls down the middle and either head them clear or pass them short to a team-mate. 'Because he carried out his orders,' said Whittaker, 'his inability to kick a ball hard or far was camouflaged.'

While 1926–27 was not a notable year in the League, it did end on a high note. After 40 years, Arsenal made their first appearance in an FA Cup final. It was, incidentally, Chapman who at this time insisted on changing the common name from The Arsenal to plain Arsenal, arguing that it would

mean the club always came first in any alphabetical list – a point which remained valid only until 1932, when Aldershot joined the Third Division South.

In 40 years the club had only gone beyond the second round/fourth round stage (i.e., last 32) on four occasions, frankly a dreadful record for a first-class club. The run to the final was a tough one. Sheffield United were beaten 3–2 at Bramall Lane, then Port Vale 1–0 in a replay. Liverpool were beaten 2–0 at Highbury in the fifth round with both goals coming from headers at free-kicks. Wolves also came to Highbury for the quarter final. Arsenal won the game 2–1, the winning goal being a remarkable one. A Joe Hulme centre was headed straight into the net from around 25 yards by centre-half Jack Butler, who was yet to be replaced by Roberts.

Arsenal were in the semi-finals for the first time in 20 years and were lucky enough not to have to leave London as they were drawn against Southampton, then in the middle of the Second Division, and the game was played at Stamford Bridge. Southampton pressed for much of the match but could only score once, late in the match, through their centre-forward Rawlings. By that time Hulme and Buchan had made the game safe.

FA CUP SURRENDERED TO WELSHMEN

The final is remembered for three things. One is the very first Cup final radio commentary, the second is Cardiff City taking the Cup out of England for the only time. The third is the tragic goal, the only one of the match, that, in truth, lost it for Arsenal rather than won it for Cardiff. Keeper Dan Lewis, a Welshman himself, had only come into the side for the third round tie at Sheffield. He replaced Bill Harper, who immediately set off for the States in search of fame and fortune (and returned to the club slightly disillusioned four years later). Lewis was also to find fame in the final, but not the kind he would have sought.

It had not been a very good game, played on a greasy pitch with much commitment but little skill. Arsenal had been the better side, winning all of the game's eight corners. With just 16 minutes left, Cardiff skipper Fred Keenor took a throw and found his Scots centre-forward Hugh Ferguson around 25 yards out. Ferguson advanced and tried a half-hearted, weak ground shot which should have given Lewis no trouble. The keeper did indeed stop the ball but, turning away slightly to avoid the oncoming Ferguson, it slid out of his grasp and under his left arm. Even now the situation was not lost but, in an attempt to gather the ball up again, Lewis turned and simply knocked it with his elbow so that it trickled gently over the line. The film of the incident is appalling to behold – the whole thing happens in slow motion, as if the projector was running at half speed.

Even then the game was not over: Arsenal were offered the best chance of the match. Sid Hoar put in a long, high centre. Cardiff keeper Tom Farquharson misjudged the

Right: At Stamford Bridge on 26 March 1927, Arsenal finally won an FA Cup semi-final. Their opponents were Southampton and the goals in a 2–1 success were scored by Joe Hulme and Charlie Buchan.

flight, it bounced once and passed over his head. Brain and Buchan both rushed into nod the ball into the empty net. But as Buchan then describes it: '... at the last moment Jimmy left it to me; I unfortunately left it to him.' The ball bounced harmlessly away past a post and, with it, Arsenal's last remaining hopes.

After the presentations, Lewis threw his losers' medal to the turf, from where it was retrieved by fellow Welshman Bob John. 'Never mind, you'll have another chance,' said John, but he was wrong and Lewis was to be injured just before the 1930 final. The Arsenal team in 1927 was Lewis, Parker, Andy Kennedy, Baker, Butler, John, Hulme, Buchan, Brain, Billy Blyth and Sid Hoar. Grease on Lewis' new jersey was partly blamed for the disaster, and when Arsenal reached the 1930 final Tom Whittaker told Charlie Preedy to wear an old, unwashed jersey rather than a new one. The ritual was observed in all the subsequent finals through the Chapman, Allison and Whittaker eras.

CHAPMAN CONTINUES TO BUILD

Chapman was not discouraged. He had lost important matches before. The team-building continued. The left full-back position was something of a weakness, the current incumbents being Horace Cope and Andy Kennedy. To fill the slot, Chapman showed another of his strengths, that of finding rare talents in unlikely places. He had shown this with Roberts and was to show it again with Bastin. Eddie (actually Edris Albert) Hapgood was particularly special because he had played only 12 games for non-League Kettering and in no way looked the part. A 19-year-old milkman who had not been signed at the crucial moment by his home town club, Bristol Rovers, he weighed only 9 stones 6 pounds. Although he was, and remained, a physical fitness fanatic, he was relatively weak and was often literally knocked out when

heading the wet, heavy, leather ball of the period. Arsenal invested heavily in their £750 signing, Tom Whittaker forcing the ex-vegetarian to eat steaks and build up both his strength and weight. A few years later, after an accident in which Hapgood had been burned quite badly, Tom Whittaker built a special leather harness for his body so that he could play without the burns rubbing the whole time, proof of Hapgood's remarkable physical courage and unswerving commitment to the game and to the club.

It was sad that Hapgood eventually became estranged from the game. His relations with Allison were never as good as with Chapman, and between him and Whittaker strains gradually developed as they appeared rivals for future senior roles at the club. This was a great pity, as Hapgood had written in 1944 (before Whittaker took over from Allison as manager) that: 'Tom Whittaker has, perhaps of all the people who helped me at Highbury, been my closest friend.' Hapgood was later manager at Blackburn, Watford and Bath but, after losing the Bath job in 1956, he asked Arsenal for a retrospective benefit and was very upset when the club was unable to agree.

GUNNERS TARGET JACK AND JAMES

Whatever else he now had, by 1927 Chapman clearly felt he lacked the great names and, with the exception of perhaps Buchan and Hulme, the great players. His two great transfer coups were still to come – David Jack and Alex James. The David Jack story has been told so often that it has become part of soccer folklore, but no doubt it bears repetition.

Above: Joe Hulme cuts in to score from the right wing past Sheffield United full-back Green on 3 September 1927. Note that the letters have been removed from the stand. Arsenal won the game 6–1. Hulme was the fastest winger in the game in the 1920s and it was the use Chapman made of his two outstanding wingers (Bastin was the other) which was really the key to Arsenal's unstoppable style in the 1930s.

Left: The Arsenal first team pictured behind Highbury's southern terracing two days before the 1927 FA Cup final. Left to right: Billy Blyth, Bob John, Horace Cope, Andy Kennedy, Tom Parker, Dan Lewis, Bill Seddon, Jack Butler, Alf Baker, Joe Hulme, Jimmy Brain, Syd Hoar and Charlie Buchan.

By 1928 David Jack was one of the great names known in English football. A cultured, stylish inside forward (he used to arrive at the ground in spats), he was one of those always rare animals, an automatic choice for England. He had scored the first ever goal at Wembley, in the 1923 Cup final, and won winners' medals with Bolton in that year and again in 1926. Bolton were one of the handful of top teams at the time, but in the close season of 1928 informed other clubs that they would consider offers for any player, excepting only David Jack. Chapman and George Allison went to Bolton to see their board, initially meeting a blank refusal. Eventually, however, the question was asked: 'How much would we have to offer for you to change your minds?' Bolton, probably to get Chapman and Allison to go away, said £13,000 – almost double the existing record transfer fee.

Allison and Chapman returned to the Midland Hotel in Manchester for dinner, eventually invited the Bolton chairman and secretary to join them and haggled until the small hours. In the end an offer of £11,500 plus the accrued benefit to be paid to Jack was accepted (players then received a benefit after five years, but if they left a club after, say, three years, they could be given a sum to represent three-fifths of what they might have expected to receive). David Jack was roused from his bed and belatedly asked his opinion. After talking to his father (then the Plymouth manager) he agreed to come to London the following day to sign for Arsenal.

That day was coincidentally the first time Bob Wall had ever been involved in the transfer of a player. He had just been taken on at the club as secretary/assistant to Herbert Chapman. Wall takes up the story as he and Chapman headed off for the Euston Hotel to meet the Bolton party off the Manchester train: 'We arrived at the hotel half-an-hour early. Chapman immediately went into the lounge bar. He called the waiter, placed two pound notes in his hand and said: "George, this is Mr Wall, my assistant. He will drink whisky and dry ginger. I will drink gin and tonic. We shall be joined by guests. They will drink whatever they like. See that our guests are given double of everything but Mr Wall's whisky and dry ginger will contain no whisky and my gin and tonic will contain no gin".' According to Bob Wall, their guests were in a very cheerful mood by the time the deal was finalised and were not inclined to question anything further.

Charlie Buchan had by now retired, his last game being the famous 3–3 draw at Everton on 5 May 1928 when Dixie Dean got a hat-trick and broke the League scoring record with 60 goals in a single season. Without Buchan, Chapman lacked a commander on the field. There was actually no obvious candidate whom Chapman could pay the earth for. David Jack was Buchan's counterpart in goalscoring ability, but not as a leader. As Bernard Joy rightly pointed out, the way the Arsenal system had developed, the key man had become the foraging inside forward, the centre of the W, the man who picks up clearances from the defenders and sends the forwards away. Clem Stephenson had done a similar job for Chapman at Huddersfield, but there were very few players in the game with either the technical or strategic skills, never mind both.

One player who did have the vision was Alex James, the creator behind the Scots Wembley Wizards of 1928, infamous 5–1 humiliators of England. He had gone from Raith to Preston, where he was less a schemer than an attacking inside forward. In four years there (admittedly in the Second Division) he had scored 60 goals. In June 1929 Preston, surprisingly, put him up for sale and Chapman beat most of the big clubs – including Villa, Liverpool and Manchester City – for his signature.

BARGAIN FEE SPARKS INQUIRY

George Allison said of James: 'No one like him ever kicked a ball. He had a most uncanny and wonderful control, but because this was allied to a split-second thinking apparatus, he simply left the opposition looking on his departing figure with amazement.' The small size of the transfer fee (£8,750) was such a surprise that the Football League held an inquiry before Arsenal were allowed to register James. With so many clubs interested it had naturally been assumed that the transfer fee would break the David Jack record, and the Lancashire clubs, possibly with the recent Norris case in mind, were muttering about financial inducements. The inquiry showed that Arsenal were completely clean – all they had done was to help find James a job in Selfridges, the famous London store. But even the inquiry had more to it than met the eye. Chapman knew that he would face rumours about the impending transfer (he had already secretly obtained James' signature) and it was actually the manager himself who quietly asked the League to set up the inquiry into the deal. He then publicly insisted he would not sign James (something of a deceit) until after such an investigation had taken place.

It could not be said that James was the perfect club man. It took a season for him to settle in to his new role, after which he virtually gave up scoring goals. Chapman always treated

him slightly differently from the other players (he was allowed to stay in bed until noon on matchdays, for instance). Alex was the key, that was the message; and it is certainly true that the side did not win anything before James arrived but started winning everything soon afterward.

Herbert Chapman's patience was, nonetheless, sorely tested. In the summer of 1931 James refused to re-sign, presumably looking for some sort of extra inducements. In August the club sent him on holiday, then Chapman called him back saying the club had decided to despatch him on a cruise instead. He hurried back to London Docks, only to find that Chapman had booked him into a berth on a banana and general cargo boat. John Peters, the assistant secretary, somehow persuaded James to go on board and he was finally released in Bordeaux. He always claimed to have quite enjoyed it. James eventually signed his new contract the week before the season began. When the team, who were training, heard the news they raided the Arsenal band room and serenaded James into the ground by murdering 'See the Conquering Hero Comes.' More serious was James' failure to turn up at the celebration banquet after the Championship success of 1933. He had refused to go to Belfast to play Cliftonville in the last week of the season and was dropped. As club captain he should have received the trophy from League President John McKenna. James' place was left empty and Charlie Jones accepted the award as vice-captain.

Arsenal were the team of the era, and James was the heart of the team, the definition of football success. Without him the style, the system and the successes would probably never have been achieved. Whether James would have done as much in another era is an interesting point. Some of the greats would arguably not have achieved as much at a different time – Stanley Matthews in the 1970s, for instance – but James was probably a player for any age and every era.

THE JAMES-HULME-BASTIN TRIANGLE

All of this is probably rather peripheral to the essential truth about Alex James – that at the critical time he was the hub of the whole team. He foraged so far back that he was no longer an inside forward, and Bastin therefore had no one inside him for most of the time. For many teams this would have caused problems, but for Arsenal it was an encouragement to develop different moves. The classic was the James-Hulme-Bastin triangle. James, often facing his own goal, would hit a long pass up the right wing. Hulme would race past the defence, and hit his centre way over to the left for Bastin either to shoot or dribble in on goal. Up the middle would steam Lambert, looking for any crumbs that might fall from the table.

In 1932–33 Bastin and Hulme scored 53 goals between them, perfect evidence that Arsenal did play the game very differently from their contemporaries, who tended to continue to rely on the wingers making goals for the centre-forward, rather than scoring themselves. By playing the wingers this

way, Chapman was able to have one more man in midfield, and thus control the supply of the ball, primarily through James. But it was only possible because both wingers were exceptional footballers – Hulme because of his speed and Bastin because of his tactical brain and coolness. Bastin's calm was legendary. Tom Whittaker said of him in 1950: 'Coupled with his sincerity and his loyalty to all his bosses, he had a trait few of us are blessed with – that is, he had an ice-cold temperament.'

Bastin was the last of the major signings, coming a couple of weeks after James. Bastin is very amusing on his first meeting with the Scotsman. James was already a star, while Bastin was hoping just to play for the reserves. James came up and introduced himself to Bastin in an accent which, Bastin says: 'I have never heard rivalled, before or since. I must confess,' Bastin goes on, 'that my chief reaction, apart from feeling rather more at home than I had a few moments earlier, was of trying to understand just what Alex was saying. Alex and I may have developed a well-nigh perfect understanding on the field, but off it I always found him a trifle incomprehensible.' Bastin knew him well of course, and had enormous admiration for the man, particularly for his

Below: The fourth round FA Cup tie against Birmingham at Highbury on 25 January 1930. The match ended 2–2 with Jack and Bastin scoring goals. The next morning Chapman went to see Alex James – who had earlier been dropped and sent to bed for a complete rest – to tell him that Arsenal could not succeed without him, in the hope that James would respond to the responsibility. Many people felt that this was the turning point that led to all of Arsenal's success of the following decade.

self-confidence. 'Nobody had greater faith in the qualities of Alex James than Alex James himself – not even Herbert Chapman, and that is saying something. Alex needed all his self-confidence during his first few months at Highbury, for he was very slow to settle down.'

As part of the settling down process, James established his own trademark – the baggy shorts. They were apparently not his idea at all. Cartoonist Tom Webster drew him playing for Preston in the Daily Mail one Monday with rather long shorts, possibly to emphasise James' small stature. James liked the idea, and insisted on going out to buy a pair to fit the cartoon. They kept his knees warm, he would tell admirers.

NO SIGN OF IMPROVEMENT

By 1930 James was beginning to fit, but there must have been frustration in the boardroom as well as on the terraces. In five years under Chapman, Arsenal had spent a fortune but the world remembered them only for an excruciating goal in the 1927 Cup final and a chairman banned from the game.

It is interesting to speculate what would have happened if Chapman had died exactly four years earlier, in January 1930. Certainly his own reputation would have been dramatically lessened, his days at Huddersfield perhaps questioned as a peculiar fluke or the work of Clem Stephenson. But would the team have gone on to greatness in the 1930s? Who can say, but in the last month of the 1920s no one would have predicted anything very much for the club, Chapman or not.

The season had begun so badly that relegation looked the only sort of news Arsenal were likely to make. The forward line had cost £34,000, by a mile the most expensive in football history, and yet it couldn't score goals. But perhaps there was something magic in that new decade, in the rather-less-than celebrated 1930s. For it was the turn of the year, the passing of the 'roaring twenties', that was the turning point for Arsenal. In the League they achieved no more than respectability (finishing 14th), but in the Cup they truly achieved glory.

GLORY YEARS COMMENCE

The second week of the new decade saw the third round of the FA Cup. Arsenal drew Chelsea at Highbury, never an easy game. Chapman made a courageous decision, possibly the most difficult in his career, and dropped James. If the team wasn't scoring with the class of forward they had, then it had to be the provider who was at fault. David Halliday was also dropped, in came John, Thompson and Lambert. Arsenal won 2–0 in a rainstorm. Two weeks later Chapman simply ordered James to bed. The Scotsman had always suffered from a form of rheumatism in the ankles, which made it difficult for him to play golf, and Chapman felt James needed a complete rest. In the fourth round Birmingham (who reached the final the following year) came to Highbury and went away with a 2–2

draw. Leslie Knighton was now their manager and Chapman knew the replay would be a tough one. If Arsenal lost it, then the whole season would have gone.

Bernard Joy, who was with the team in the 1930s and whose opinion has always been highly respected, argued in 1952 that Chapman's decision after the first Birmingham game that Saturday night, 25 January 1930, was the turning point in the modern history of the club.

Chapman had to win the replay at St Andrew's the following Wednesday. On the Sunday morning he went round to Alex James' home, got him out of bed and took him off to Highbury for training. Chapman gambled that James would react to the crisis, to the obvious placing of responsibility on his shoulders. It worked, not spectacularly, but it worked. Alf Baker scored from the penalty spot, the only goal of a hard game. The fifth and six rounds were no easier – a 2–0 win away at Ayresome Park and a convincing 3–0 win at West Ham, banishing the uncomfortable memories of the pep-pill farce of five years before.

GUNNERS EVADE MCCRACKEN'S TRAP

The semi-final looked easy – Hull City at Elland Road. Hull were at the bottom of the Second Division and were relegated to the Third a month later. It was also their first semi-final. Quite what they were doing there was anyone's guess, but most knowing observers put it down to the wily management of Bill McCracken, the full-back who had perfected the offside game ten years before. All the interest was in the other semi-final between the two Yorkshire giants, Huddersfield and League Champions Wednesday.

This was indeed to be a famous match; with Huddersfield leading 2–1 a Wednesday shot entered the net just as the whistle blew for full time. The referee disallowed the goal but many of the crowd went home not knowing whether there would be a replay or not.

Back at the supposedly less interesting semi-final at Elland Road, shocks were in store. After 15 minutes keeper Dan Lewis cleared a ball from the edge of his area. It was a poor kick, travelling only 30 yards or so, and it went straight to the Hull inside left Howieson. He lobbed it straight back on the volley and it flew over Lewis' head into the net from a full 45 yards out. After 30 minutes Eddie Hapgood sliced a Duncan shot into his own net and Arsenal were 2–0 down at half-time. In the second half, the goals just wouldn't come. And it was not until 20 minutes from the end that whichever gods control football ended their little joke.

Those last few minutes are among the most important in the club's history, and they bear a remarkable similarity to the last minutes of the 1971 semi-final against Stoke at Hillsborough, when the Gunners also came back from a 2–0 deficit. In both 1930 and 1971, the semi-final result was vital to the history of the club, arguably just as vital as the finals themselves.

Firstly Alf Baker got Joe Hulme away on the wing, he crossed and David Jack finally defeated McCracken's offside trap and converted the centre. Just 12 minutes later Cliff Bastin picked up a ball from Alex James, took on the defenders in a solo run and hit the ball into the top right-hand corner. Arsenal were unlucky not to get a third, but the teams met again for a midweek replay at Villa Park. Hull seemed bitter about being robbed so late in the first game and the tackling was fierce. So much so that, in the second half, the Hull centre-half Arthur Childs became the first (and for another 50 years the only) man to be sent off in a semi-final. He was despatched for taking a kick at Jack Lambert. That was the end for Hull. Soon afterward Joey Williams (taking the place of the injured Hulme) hared off down the right wing, pulled the ball back from the goal line and David Jack connected with a right-foot volley to score the game's only goal. Arsenal were at Wembley for the second time in four years, Huddersfield were there for the fourth time in a decade.

SUCCESS BREEDS CONFIDENCE

The defeat of Hull seemed to lift a great weight from the Arsenal attack. Two weeks before the Cup final the Gunners ran up their biggest First Division win to date, 8–1 over Sheffield United. And five days before the final they set yet another record when, having been 3–1 down at half-time, they eventually drew 6–6 at Leicester. It remains the highest scoring draw in any English first-class game, having only been equalled by Charlton v Middlesbrough in 1960. Oddly, Lambert's deputy, David Halliday, had an excellent game at Leicester, scoring four times. But the centre-forward spot was firmly Jack Lambert's by now, a decision that was to be fully justified five days later at Wembley.

A RECORD-BREAKING SEASON

The final against Huddersfield (see Chapter One) was formally the start of the great decade, but it was the following year that has always been known as the great season. 1930-31 saw the establishment of the record points total for a Championship side (66 – later to be surpassed by Leeds United under the now defunct two-point system), and the remarkable total of 127 goals scored would have then been, and remained for all time, a First Division record had Aston Villa not, incredibly, scored 128 the same year. In London, Birmingham and elsewhere it was a wonderful season for spectators.

The season was a massive success for the Gunners from start to finish. The first two games were away, at Blackpool and Bolton. They were both won 4–1. Arsenal were not defeated until their tenth game, at the Baseball Ground against one of the best sides of the 1930s, Derby County. Despite Arsenal's tremendous performance through the whole season, strangely they were never clear of challengers and were not sure of the trophy until two weeks before the

end of the contest, when Liverpool went down 3–1. Villa were, of course, the biggest threat, countering a 5–2 defeat by the Gunners at Highbury with a 5–1 win at Villa Park and the friendly rivalry between the clubs was marked by Villa's attendance at the season's end celebration banquet. Villa were also the first opponents in the Cup, and went 2–0 up at Highbury before Lambert and Jack forced a draw. Arsenal played well to win the replay 3–1 but surprisingly went out 2–1 at Stamford Bridge. Though a disappointment, it did not upset the team. Four days later they beat Grimsby 9–1 at Highbury, their biggest ever First Division win and, a week later, won 7–2 at Leicester, to make it 13 goals in consecutive appearances at Filbert Street.

THE TEAM OF THE THIRTIES

The Gunners lost only four games in all, and, coincidentally, their home and away records were identical – 14 wins, 5 draws and 2 defeats. The team for the final game of the season is probably the one that is best remembered as the great team of the whole era – Ted Harper in goal, Tom Parker and Eddie Hapgood at full-back, Herbie Roberts at centre-half, Charlie Jones and Bob John at half-back, Joe Hulme and Cliff Bastin on the wings, Alex James, as the provider, and David Jack and Jack Lambert up front.

Harper had just returned from his four-year sojourn in the United States, and was re-signed. He replaced Dutchman Gerry Keyser, a wholesale fruiterer who was an amateur with both Arsenal and Charlton.

With Jack Lambert now established as Chapman's first choice forwad the manager let David Halliday go to Manchester City in November. The first of the two meetings

Above: Arguably the most important goal in the history of Arsenal Football Club. The only goal of the game, it was scored by David Jack in the second half of the semi-final replay against Hull at Villa Park on Wednesday 26 March 1930.

between Arsenal and Villa at Villa Park in the 1930–31 season was the celebrated occasion when the Midlanders' magnificent England international centre-forward Pongo Waring cheerfully taunted Chapman with his obsession for buying centre-forwards: 'I bet you'd like to get me Herbert, wouldn't you?' said Waring. And Chapman would have, for Waring was the best in the country until Drake came along, but he was also one of the few players Chapman could never manage to get his hands on. Underrated Jack Lambert actually set up an Arsenal record in 1930–31 with his 38 League goals, although this was soon to be beaten by Drake.

MALE SENT BACK

Those 11 names for that last game of 1930–31, against Aston Villa, would certainly have to be supplemented by one or two others to complete the real first-class roll of honour for the era. The three obvious omissions are George Male, Wilf Copping and Frank Moss.

Male became Hapgood's full-back partner late in 1932 before Tom Parker went to Norwich as manager. Male actually played in the 1932 Cup final in his normal position, left-half, but with Parker ready to retire Chapman needed a replacement and selected Male, who already had a reputation for all-round skill, strength and steadiness.

Male told how Chapman called him into his office and astonished him by explaining how Male was about to become a right-back. Chapman was so convincing about Male's skills that, said Male: 'I wasn't only convinced I was a right-back, I knew I was the best right-back in the country!' And so it proved, Male eventually taking over the England captaincy

Right: George Male was Arsenal's right-back during the 30s. Male, whom Chapman had converted from a left-half role, made 316 first-class appearances in an 18-year playing career before joining the coaching staff. He never scored a goal for the senior side, but was capped 19 times for England.

from Hapgood. He played his first game at right-back on 15 October 1932 and within months he had been chosen for an international trial.

Bernard Joy argued that the success of the Male-Hapgood combination was a matter of contrasts: 'Hapgood was enthusiastic, volatile and poised, the born captain. Male was determined, rugged and fast in recovery; as a person quiet, retiring and modest, the ideal first mate.' Not only did both of them captain England, they also played together for their country 14 times.

Wilf Copping was already an international when he came from Leeds in 1934, he and Jack Crayston (from Bradford) effectively replacing Charlie Jones and Bob John. Copping is probably best remembered for his remarkable display in the 'Battle of Highbury' against Italy on 14 November 1934 when Arsenal provided seven of the England team and the World Cup holders were beaten, in a bitter game, 3–2.

Frank Moss was actually only the reserve keeper at Second Division Oldham when Chapman signed him. Apparently Chapman pretended to be pursuing the first-team keeper Jack Hacking and, when Oldham wouldn't release him, switched his interest to the reserve as an apparent afterthought (this particular story has been told about several of Chapman's signings). He was another agile keeper, totally fearless and a natural for the England jersey. His career was sadly cut short because of a recurrent shoulder injury. His last effective game for the club was at Everton on 16 March 1935, when he was injured, dislocating his troubled shoulder early on and playing the rest of the match on the wing. He was always a very good forward and scored an excellent goal, cutting in past his defender and shooting into the corner for a peculiarly unfitting end to a goalkeeper's career. He did try to come back for a few games the following season, but the shoulder and collarbone were continually causing problems and he was forced to give up the game completely.

WHITTAKER KEEPS GUNNERS PRIMED

The team that brought the League Championship to the south of England for the very first time in 1931 was hardly anonymous, but it was unusual in that its back-up was far more sophisticated than at any other club of the period. The cornerstone was Tom Whittaker, who eventually became manager in 1947. It is almost impossible to do full justice to Whittaker either as coach, physiotherapist or inspiration. The stories about him are legion, almost invariably extremely complimentary. Bernard Joy said that: 'Chapman's success would have been impossible without Whittaker,' but Allison reaches the essential Whittaker more succinctly. Allison was once asked: 'Is it true, what Tom Whittaker says?' 'Of course it is,' was Allison's reply. 'What did Tom say?'

Cliff Bastin was as effusive: 'I can never thank him enough for the care and expert treatment he lavished on me whilst I was at Highbury. Perhaps "expert" is a badly chosen word, for

Tom was something more than an expert. There was about him a touch of genius.' Bastin explained how men who would have remained on the injured list for three or four weeks at another club would be fit at Highbury within three or four days. Bastin, on one occasion, scalded his foot in a boiling hot bath and couldn't stand on it. The foot was agony, but Whittaker built a special soft cast inside Bastin's boot so that the winger felt no pain. His only sensation when he ran, as he explained, was the water inside the blister running up and down his foot. Whittaker also used regularly to snap Bastin's cartilage back into place on the field, doing this on at least a dozen occasions, and when Bastin eventually had to have an operation, Whittaker attended and assisted.

'THE GREATEST TRAINER IN THE GAME'

Tom Whittaker was born in Aldershot in 1898. His father was a sergeant major and Tom also had a military career, studying as a marine engineer and joining the Royal Artillery as, very appropriately, an ordnance engineer. It was while he was playing for the Army that Arsenal spotted him and brought him to Highbury, where he played as a wing half and later full-back until his injury in Australia in 1925. His arrival at Highbury, on 11 November 1919, has a touch of the times about it – Leslie Knighton, newly installed as manager, met him off the tube!

The surgeon who told Whittaker he would never play again in 1925, Sir Robert Jones, was so impressed by the player that he arranged a year's course in anatomy, massage and electrical treatment of injuries, particularly associated with muscles. Whittaker returned to Highbury after that injury unsure about his future. Arsenal had apparently been intending to let him go in 1925, but he was retained so that he could go on the FA tour (players without clubs were not allowed to represent the FA). For six months Whittaker was unable to train and helped in the treatment room. Officially, he was just a player under treatment. One day in February 1926, Chapman called Whittaker up to the top of the stand. For a few moments there was silence, says Whittaker, then Chapman turned and, with his arm stretched out toward the pitch and emphasising every word, said: 'I am going to make this the greatest club ground in the world, and I am going to make you the greatest trainer in the game. What do you say to that?'

Whittaker later built the most modern treatment room in football, and possibly in the country, at Highbury. It was full of sunlamps, heating and electrical apparatus and attracted all sorts of sportsmen who had no association with Highbury. Whittaker was, for instance, also the official trainer for Britain's highly successful Davis Cup tennis team in the 1930s, as well as the regular England soccer team trainer.

He worked seven days a week and his ability to get players back quickly was a crucial element in the club's consistent pattern of success between 1930 and 1936. The other great

contribution Whittaker made to Chapman's personal success was relieving the manager of day-to-day control of the players. This was vitally important for it allowed Chapman time to watch new players, negotiate transfers and consider other essential matters for the club.

Whittaker actually became first-team trainer in February 1927. George Hardy, who had held the job since before the First World War, shouted a tactical switch to the players from the bench during a Cup match against Port Vale on 2 February 1927. Chapman said he wouldn't tolerate the trainer

Above: Frank Moss kept a clean sheet against Manchester City in the 1932 semi-final at Villa Park on 12 March 1932. Cliff Bastin scored the only goal of the game. Moss was the club's most celebrated keeper in the 1930s, but his career was effectively ended by a double dislocation of the collar bone at Everton on 16 March 1935.

Left: Planning department. Bob John, Herbert Chapman and Alex James discuss the aspects of the forthcoming FA Cup final against Newcastle in early 1932.

influencing tactics and relegated Hardy to the reserves, giving the 29-year-old Whittaker the job. Straight after that Port Vale game Chapman marched into the dressing room and, in front of everyone, told Whittaker to take over the first team immediately. Whittaker, who lodged with Hardy, was shocked, but he and Hardy remained friends. Chapman's action was only an excuse. Hardy was of the old school, whereas Whittaker was obviously the man Chapman wanted and he remained as trainer, apart from a spell during the Second World War, for 20 years. He finally took over as manager from Allison in 1947.

DOUBLE DISAPPOINTMENT

Before the 1931–32 season began, the talk was of the chances of the Double, a feat not performed since Aston Villa in 1896–97 and not to be performed again for another three decades. After a month the talk was what happened to the League Champions? Arsenal lost their opener at home to West Bromwich and didn't take both points until their fifth match. They never made up the gap and, although it was a good season, eventually finishing second was something of an anticlimax. Everton were Champions, two points ahead. Bernard Joy says the team was overconfident, pushing forward too eagerly, leaving too many holes for the counterattack. It was a lesson that was certainly learned for subsequent seasons.

The Cup should have provided compensation for the League disappointment, but failed to do so after the most controversial goal in British domestic football.

The run to the 1932 final was straightforward but hard work, and there were to be no replays. Lancashire Combination side Darwen provided an 11–1 walkover in the third round, then Plymouth, with Ted Harper in goal, were removed 4–2. After a 2–0 away win against gradually improving Portsmouth (they reached the final in 1929 and 1934) the quarter final brought Arsenal back to old adversaries Huddersfield at Leeds Road. After only two minutes Hulme won a corner; the winger held the ball until Herbie Roberts came up on a rare (but obviously pre-planned) foray, placed it right on Roberts' forehead and Arsenal had scored the only goal of the game.

The semi-final at St Andrew's also saw just one goal, this time at the end of the game rather than the beginning. The opponents were Manchester City, who were to reach the next two Cup finals as compensation. The 1932 semi-final was already in time added on, with City frantically attacking. But they left their defence undermanned and as a final clearance came out from the Arsenal penalty area Bastin picked it up and hopefully knocked it toward the right-hand corner. The defender let the ball go, thinking it would go over the line, but Jack Lambert suddenly appeared, hooked it back and there was Bastin to touch it home with what was to be the last kick of the match.

JAMES A FINAL DOUBT

The final was to be against Newcastle. The preparations were dominated by whether or not Alex James would be fit as he had damaged knee ligaments in a match against West Ham a couple of weeks earlier.

Three days before the Cup final Chapman announced his team – James and Hulme were not fit enough so in came George Male and Pat Beasley. The news was a surprise, and L. V. Manning, sports editor of the Daily Sketch, got James and Hulme to jog around the Highbury pitch and published a picture captioned: 'The two fittest men in football.' Chapman was furious, and ordered the pair down to Brighton, where the team were staying. Tom Whittaker gave them both a tough try-out the following morning on the Brighton ground, in front of 40 or so photographers. Both came through and were reinstated in the team for Saturday's final. Then, as everyone was making their way back to the dressing room, another photographer, whose car had broken down, came rushing into the ground to plead with Whittaker for a final shot. Whittaker agreed, tackled James once more and, suddenly, James fell to the ground clutching his knee. He was carried to the dressing-room where, says Whittaker: '... almost crying with pain and disappointment, he would not let the doctor touch him and shouted at me to get everyone out of the room. Even Chapman had to go.' George Male, signed from the London amateur side Clapton earlier that season, had been in, out, and back in a Cup final side within the space of an hour. Male played left-half, and it was on that side that the critical moment was to occur.

REF'S MISTAKE COSTS GUNNERS THE CUP

It was almost half-time (with Arsenal 1–0 up after Bob John had headed the ball home when United had made a hash of a clearance) when Newcastle centre-half Davison overhit a long pass up the right wing for inside forward Jimmy Richardson to chase. The ball appeared to cross the goalline and the

Arsenal defenders relaxed, but Richardson carried on and hooked the ball into the centre. Eddie Hapgood could probably have intercepted it, but didn't bother. Centre-forward Jack Allen did bother, flicking it neatly into the net. Referee Bill Harper gave a goal, the Arsenal players were incredulous but did not argue. L. V. Manning said in the Sunday Graphic the next day: 'One cannot praise too highly the restraint of the Arsenal players when the first Newcastle goal was scored. Every man must have known what was so clear to the onlookers– that the ball had crossed the line – but there was not the slightest attempt at a demonstration or protest.' Tom Parker got their minds back on the game but the timing was perfect for Newcastle, who came out for the second half a different team and Allen scored again for United to win 2–1. Arsenal had thus finished runners-up in both major competitions, only the second time this had ever happened.

Though it has always been claimed that the ball was over the line, in fairness it must be said that no convincing photograph exists and the angle of the most reproduced photograph is not necessarily a good one. Newcastle were the first team to win the final at Wembley after being behind in the match, and the first to come from behind in any final since they did the same thing themselves in 1910.

ARSENAL DOMINATE THE LEAGUE

The disappointment of 1932 was to be only short-lived. For many years afterward regret was expressed that, despite their dominance of the decade, the Arsenal of the 1930s were never able to achieve the the Double, winning the Cup and the League. 1931–32 was to be the nearest they came for they did not seem to be able to concentrate on the FA Cup when they were leading the League. And for the next three seasons Arsenal were to do exactly that, equalling Huddersfield's hat-trick with an impeccable period of dominance covering 1932–33, 1933–34 and 1934–35.

Most clubs which have such a successful spell do so with a very settled side. Indeed, it is almost a truism of the game that a great side lasts for no more than three good seasons. The Arsenal of the first half of the 1930s were almost exactly the

opposite. By 1935 no more than three of the regulars of 1932 were still in the team – Hapgood, Roberts and Bastin. Most of the missing had simply succumbed to age, though Frank Moss was an exception. Much more significantly, Herbert Chapman was dead and had been replaced by George Allison. Yet the period was one of remarkably consistent results, with only 24 League games lost and a points average of 58. By Championship standards, none of the three seasons was particularly outstanding, certainly not to be compared with the record breaking efforts of 1930–31, and their number of defeats (9, 8 and 7 in the three seasons) was no better than average for a Championship side. On the other hand, the pattern of consistency during a period of when the team was being rebuilt was most certainly outstanding. If this sounds like grudging praise, it is only so in the context of the heady two years which followed the 1930 Cup win.

Many of the individual replacements proved to be the match of their predecessors. George Male was already a Highbury stalwart when he replaced Parker in 1932, Eddie Coleman and an ageing Jimmy Dunne appeared in Lambert's shirt, although neither of them truly became a fixture, and the great David Jack played only 14 games in 1933–34 and then went to Southend as manager. He was replaced by Ray Bowden, who arrived from Plymouth in March 1933. Cliff Bastin was still a youngster, although he suffered from periods of injury and his deafness was beginning to be a worry, but Joe Hulme proved very difficult to duplicate.

Above: The 1932 semi-final success took the Gunners to Wembley for the infamous 'over-the-line' final against Newcastle. Although Arsenal went 1–0 ahead through Bob John, the over-the-line goal by Jack Allen changed the pattern of the game and his second goal settled it.

Left: The Prince of Wales meets the teams at the inauguration of the new West Stand. The opening of the two new stands (the West on 10 December 1932 and the East on 24 October 1936) was football's equivalent of the unveiling of the Taj Mahal. There was nothing like them anywhere in the country.

ALLISON SEEKS REPLACEMENTS

The Arsenal wingers had performed very different jobs compared with men in the number 7 and 11 shirts at other clubs and it was not easy to slot new men into Arsenal's unique system. They had not only to be very fast in the conventional sense, but also significant goalscorers as well. Only Alex James was allowed the liberty of not appearing on the scoresheet. As has been said before, it was the role of Hulme and Bastin, more than any other aspect of their style, which marked the Arsenal of the early 1930s apart from their competitors. That meant the club's wingers could, and would, often also double up as inside forwards. Pat Beasley, who arrived from Stourbridge, would play in either Bastin or Hulme's place if they were injured, or act as Bastin's inside forward. He would have played in the 1932 Cup final if Hulme had not recovered from that injury but, ironically, he and Hulme then played on opposite wings for Huddersfield in the 1938 Cup final. Ralph Birkett, who later won an England cap while with Middlesbrough, was bought from Torquay specifically to take over from Hulme, but was never an adequate replacement, and by 1935 Alf Kirchen from Norwich was on the right wing.

The midfield men were more easily replaced, Jack Crayston from Bradford and Wilf Copping from Leeds coming in for Charlie Jones and Bob John with remarkably little disruption in the summer of 1934. When Alex James was unavailable the remarkable Peter Dougall would take his place. By all accounts he was an even cleverer player, but could never consistently harness his fabulous ball skills to the team effort, but then it was perhaps unfair to expect anyone to replace the hub of the wheel. In goal Alex Wilson replaced Moss in a quiet, competent way. He had come from Morton in May 1933. When Moss was injured at Goodison in March 1935, however, Wilson was also hurt and George Allison had no other first-class keeper. That day also happened to be the transfer deadline, so he asked Everton if Arsenal could sign their reserve keeper George Bradshaw there and then. Bradshaw was a little bemused by this sudden turn of events, but eventually agreed to the transfer and came to Highbury for a number of years.

A TRIO OF TITLES

The first year of the hat-trick, 1932–33, did not start well. Charlie Jones was injured and, in their first home match, Arsenal lost to West Brom for the second consecutive year. But this season was to be different, with 32 of the next 36 points finding their way back to Highbury. Yet again, though, Villa managed to score five goals in Birmingham and the 5–3 defeat was Arsenal's only setback in that 18-game run. The final match in the sequence was the Christmas Eve 9–2 thrashing of Sheffield United at Highbury. Jack Lambert scored five, his best ever for the club, in what was virtually his valedictory performance. That particular game is often recalled as the height of Arsenal's powers in the whole inter-war period, though, oddly, two days later they went down 1–2 at home to Leeds.

Villa and Wednesday continued to press until April when, though Arsenal were ahead, both their challengers had games in hand. By chance both came to Highbury in April, where Arsenal finished things off in fine style. Villa went down 5–0 and ended four points behind, Wednesday lost 4–2 and were eventually three points further back. The month saw five wins in a row and the last, 3–1 versus Chelsea at Stamford Bridge, confirmed the Gunners' second title in three years. The forwards had been magnificent all season, and the total of 118 goals was the club's second highest ever and included one 9, two 8s and one 7. Cliff Bastin's 33 goals still remain a Football League record for a winger.

The next season, 1933–34, was a strangely subdued one compared with those before and after. It was marred, of course, by Herbert Chapman's death, but, though it saw one more point won (59 rather than 58) the goalscoring record was completely different. Only 75 were scored compared with 118 the season before and 115 the season after. One major reason was Alex James' injury against Birmingham in the first match of the season. He was out for half of the campaign, as was Joe Hulme. However, Arsenal quickly went to the head of the table, putting together a spell of 27 points out of a possible 32. Derby and Huddersfield both took the lead briefly, but they had to play the Gunners in consecutive matches in Easter week. Arsenal beat Derby 4–2 at the Baseball Ground and followed up with a 3–1 defeat of Huddersfield at Highbury. In the end only Huddersfield kept up the challenge, eventually finishing three points in arrears.

It was actually one of those strangely quiet seasons when not a lot seems to happen and no team can really impose its authority. Both Villa and Wednesday had lost their sparkle, finishing mid-table, and Arsenal, despite the loss of Chapman, were able to hold their ground by virtue of their established patterns of play and their consistency. Even so, they had to survive a number of poor results – home defeats by Everton and Spurs within the space of four days, a 4–1 crushing at Leicester and a 3–0 defeat at Sunderland – and were perhaps lucky that their crisis season coincided with a corporate lethargy among their competitors.

NEW BOY DRAKE IS THE HERO

The third year of the hat-trick saw a genuine new star in the making. He was Ted Drake, George Allison's first signing (from Southampton) in March 1934. Drake was to score a record 42 goals with the Gunners in this, his first season. That total included four matches in which he scored four goals and three in which he notched mere hat-tricks. The newcomer almost carried the team. There were numerous major injuries – Dunne, Copping and Bastin all had cartilage operations and even the two trainers, Tom Whittaker and Billy Milne, both

had to be hospitalised during the season. Most of the reserves had fair spells in the first team, but still went on to win the Football Combination for the seventh time in nine seasons. Had Chapman lived, he would have seen it as the perfect validation of his insistence that the reserves play to the same patterns and tactics as their seniors.

The 1934–35 season had started well with an 8–1 crushing of Liverpool and the first four home games produced 21 Arsenal goals. Away from home, matters did not give rise for similar congratulations, with only a single victory prior to the New Year. But none of their regular challengers could put together anything like a convincing set of results and Arsenal headed the table until March when Sunderland, inspired by the young Raich Carter, went a point ahead. Arsenal had games in hand, however, and though Sunderland held them to a goalless draw at Highbury, Arsenal made Sunderland's task almost impossible with a 2–0 win at Everton on 16 March 1935. This was the game in which Frank Moss scored Arsenal's second, magnificent goal as a highly inappropriate finale to his mainstream goalkeeping career. Sunderland ended the season four points behind Arsenal.

CUP SUCCESS PROVES ELUSIVE

Chapman was always surprised, and perhaps a little distressed, that Huddersfield could not get to a Cup final during their hat-trick years. The Yorkshiremen were there in 1920 and 1922, and again in 1928 and 1930, but in the middle years, 1924 to 1926, when they should by rights have made it, they were nowhere to be seen. Arsenal had an oddly similar record. They reached the final in 1930, 1932 and 1936, but missed out in 1933, 1934 and 1935. Oddly, they never even reached a semi-final during those seasons.

We need to skirt around what happened on 14 January 1933. It is not usual in the history of a great club, when there is so much to tell, to dwell for very long on a game that was lost, particularly in the third round of the Cup, but this one is an exception. Exactly 50 years later, when Walsall came to Highbury, still as a Third Division side, and surprisingly won again (this time in the Milk Cup) no one tried to make any serious comparison between the two matches. There was no way they could. Walsall's 2–0 defeat of Arsenal in 1933 remains, very simply, the greatest act of giant-killing in English club history. This is vaguely peculiar. There have been giant-killers whose performances have seemed far more praiseworthy since, there have been non-League clubs knocking out First Division sides, but whenever a giant-killer arises, the comparison is automatically made, above all other games, with Walsall 2 Arsenal 0.

We need to stand back a little to judge the real significance of this result. Arsenal, it should be remembered, had just gone through a run obtaining 32 points from 18 matches. Three weeks before meeting Walsall, they had crushed Sheffield United 9–2. They were well clear at the head of the First Division and were, in a sense, at their very peak, for they had no obvious rivals. In the three previous seasons Arsenal had won the Cup, then the League, then been runners-up in both. The Double in 1932–33 seemed a very strong possibility.

A POPULAR RESULT

The game must also be put in a social and economic context. This was the height of the depression. Three million were out of work, a far higher percentage of the work force then than 50 years later, and benefits were far less generous where they existed at all. As in the 1980s, there was real resentment in the provinces against London, Westminster, 'them' as opposed to 'us'. Walsall may not have corresponded with Lancashire or Tyneside today, but it was a moderate-sized provincial town with problems enough of its own. Arsenal, in its way, was a very visible representative of London, a symbol of the richness of life there compared with the provinces. The fact that this was unfair, that most of the players were from the north and many had been miners, was not the point. What mattered were the symbols, what people wanted to believe was true.

It is also realistic to point out that Arsenal were not a popular club outside London, compared with, say, the Spurs side of the early 1960s. This was a difficult attitude to analyse, for it was a feeling abroad without any rational base, rather than a justifiable dislike. In part it was due to the 'Bank of England' reputation, Chapman's and later Allison's apparent desire to buy success at almost any price, though many clubs had gone the same route and failed dismally. In part it was also the tactical style; the holding back, occupying midfield space, the numerous goals which came from quick breaks from James to Bastin and Hulme, rather than the constant attacking pressure which was the traditional approach of the day. Spectators, having come to expect fast dribbling wingers crossing from the goal line for thundering centre-forwards in the Dixie Dean or Pongo Waring mould, found Arsenal's style odd and, therefore, somehow 'lucky'.

Fans had yet to realise the simplest of all football truths, that the winning team is, by definition, the one which scores most goals. Perhaps 85 minutes of unrewarded but naive pressure may seem more valuable than a single breakaway goal, but that isn't what the laws of the game say. Actually, such perceptions as they related to Arsenal were not only extremely unfair but, very simply, wrong – Arsenal scored 127 League goals in 1931, 118 in 1933 and 115 in 1935, overall considerably more than any of their competitors, and, to repeat the obvious, they couldn't all have come from lucky breakaways. What is true is that, like all teams, Arsenal tended to play differently away from Highbury than at home. Equally, other sides would attack them more on their own grounds, forcing Arsenal toward the use of their 'smash and grab' style. It is very difficult for the generation of fans born after the Second World War to imagine how little exposure

Above: The shield which hung outside the boardroom at Highbury commemorating the hat-trick of Championships between 1932 and 1935. Huddersfield and Liverpool have almost identical trophies. The bust is of Denis Hill-Wood.

pre-war crowds had to the big clubs, north London fans could watch Arsenal every other week but a Liverpudlian or a Mancunian was only able to see this dominating force once or twice a year – thus his views about the sort of team they were, and the way they played, could only be based on very limited evidence. He had no opportunity of seeing Arsenal 20 or 25 times a year on television and thus building a more balanced view. Arsenal at Villa, Hillsborough or Roker would always face a hard game, would always be forced to defend, and would probably rely on Hulme and Bastin for a winning goal. It was the fact that they succeeded so often which bred the resentment.

In any event, the key to the Walsall result, the way it was greeted and the reason it has remained the giant-killing feat par excellence, lies as much in the times as in the football. Walsall were the small, underprivileged, provincial David overthrowing the rich, lucky London-based Goliath and the Midland side's success was fêted far and wide, often by people who probably had not the slightest idea where Walsall was.

A SURPRISING SELECTION

Chapman has been accused of underestimating Walsall, but there is little evidence to support this contention. Walsall had been watched, and, though their last four matches comprised three draws and a 5–0 defeat, Chapman was under no illusions as to the kind of game he was facing. His real problem had been influenza, earlier claiming Bob John, Jack Lambert and Tim Coleman. Eddie Hapgood and Joe Hulme had been injured and Chapman therefore had to decide whether to play recently unavailable men or some of his well-prepared reserves.

He chose the reserves – it would be a hard match but here would be a good opportunity for the second-teamers to push their claims for a first-team place. In many respects, they were less likely than the internationals to be upset by rough Third Division tackling. So in came Scot Tommy Black at left-back, Norman Sidey at left-half, Billy Warnes at outside right and Charlie Walsh at centre-forward. The last two had both been recruited from local amateur clubs. Too much has been made of the side's inexperience – it still contained Moss, Male, Roberts, Jack, James and Bastin. Tom Whittaker later dismissed the suggestion that the first-teamers were unavailable, though, afterward, Chapman seems to have encouraged this belief. Everyone travelled to Walsall says Whittaker, in the team's own railway coach the day before. During the journey Chapman announced the team to, in Whittaker's own words: '... murmurs of amazement.'

The newspapers, always loving a David v Goliath story, gave the game the usual build-up and their angles were predictable enough. Said one: 'Arsenal, the Rich, the Confident, the League leaders, the £30,000 aristocrats, against the little Third Division team that cost £69 all-in. Arsenal train on ozone, brine-baths, champagne, gold

and electrical massage in an atmosphere of prima donna preciousness. They own £87 worth of football boots. Walsall men eat fish and chips and drink beer, and the entire running expenses of the club this season have been £75.'

The players didn't quite see it like that. One or two of the reserves were particularly edgy. Just before leaving the dressing room Chapman came over to Charlie Walsh: 'I'm expecting a lot of you today, son, we're relying on you to show us your best.' Walsh, who had been nagging Chapman for a first-team chance for months, replied: 'OK Mr Chapman, I'm ready to play the game of my life.' Chapman answered: 'Good lad, you'll do,' and then, just as he was turning away, paused: 'Oh, and by the way, you'd better put your stockings on or the crowd will laugh at you.' Poor Walsh was so nervous he had put on his boots before his socks.

Walsh's apprehensions were more justified than his team-mates would have guessed. Walsall employed classic cup-tie tactics. Their enthusiasm was overwhelming, their tackling, especially on James, could only be described as grim. Arsenal failed to settle throughout the match, but should still have won it. Walsh, now complete with socks, made a complete hash of the easiest chance of the first half when he missed a simple Bastin centre and the ball came off his shoulder. In the second half the centre-forward's intervention was even more disastrous when he took the ball off David Jack's toe just as Jack seemed certain to score.

WALSALL TAKE THEIR CHANCE

As Arsenal failed to score, Walsall became more confident, the inches of mud which covered the pitch being much more to their liking. After 60 minutes Gilbert Alsop, the home side's centre-forward, headed home a Lee corner-kick to put Walsall a goal up. Even 50 years later Alsop, still marking out the pitches at the age of 73, remembered: 'We had a corner and their full-back (Black) was marking me. He didn't get up. The ball was just a big plum pudding that day and I headed it off my forehead straight into the corner of the net.' Alsop also remembered the foul which, five minutes later, sealed the game for Walsall. He could still point to a scar on his knee which, he claimed, was caused by Tommy Black's violent tackle after 65 minutes. It was in the penalty area and, as a result, Billy Sheppard scored from the spot.

The Arsenal players had been getting increasingly irritated by Walsall's tactics. 'They could not have complained if five of their men had been sent off in the first quarter of an hour,' said Bastin, 'We had ten free-kicks in the first ten minutes.' Black had become particularly irate, the more so after failing to prevent Alsop's goal, and Arsenal paid the penalty.

The Gunners could do nothing to retrieve the two-goal deficit in the last 25 minutes and the packed 11,000 crowd chaired the Walsall players off at the end. For the Arsenal team, retribution was swift. Chapman was apoplectic. He refused to let Black return to Highbury and had transferred

Above: The cover of the programme for the greatest giant-killing feat in English club history. Arsenal came to Walsall on top of the First Division, having reached two of the three previous finals. The guns and reproduction of James confronting the teddy bear are a delight for a Third Division programme of 1933.

him to Plymouth within a week. Whether this was because of Chapman's anger at Black's tackle on Alsop, or because of his all-round performance in the match, was never absolutely clear, though Chapman certainly said the former. Walsh, whose display was almost as wretched as Black's, was sold to Brentford by the end of January, having, despite his ambitions, played just that one first-team match for Arsenal. Warnes went to Norwich at the end of the season. Only Sidey remained in the reserves, a competent back-up for Roberts.

For Walsall the game was something of an inspiration. Though they were knocked out by eventual finalists Manchester City in the next round, they managed to finish the season third in the Third Division North. For Arsenal it was a hiccup, though one that was to echo down the years as, in all probability, the most famous Cup tie the club have ever contested. Exactly 50 years later the fact that it was Walsall, rather than any other Third Division club, who knocked the Gunners out of the Milk Cup at Highbury must have made some small contribution to Terry Neill's departure from the manager's office.

CHAPMAN'S DEATH ROCKS HIGHBURY

Walsall was the last FA Cup defeat Herbert Chapman ever suffered. By the time Villa defeated the Gunners in the quarter final of 1934 Chapman was dead. It was so sudden, so unexpected, that it was almost prosaic. There is somehow very little than can be said about it. On Saturday 30 December 1933 Arsenal had drawn 0–0 at Birmingham. They were a comfortable four points clear at the top of the League. It was to be a typical, perhaps slightly busy, week for Chapman. On the Monday, New Year's Day, he went to see Bury play Notts County, who had someone in whom he was interested. He then crossed the Pennines to watch Sheffield Wednesday play Birmingham on the Tuesday. Wednesday were the visitors at Highbury on the following Saturday and were Chapman's greatest fear as rivals for the title. By the Wednesday he had clearly developed a heavy cold but ignored the advice of Dr Guy Pepper, the club doctor, and went down to Guildford to see the third team play. 'I don't get a chance to see the lads very often,' he commented. On returning home to Hendon he was much worse and went to bed. By the Friday, some 36 hours later, he seemed rather better but the pneumonia, as it presumably was, suddenly worsened and he died at 3 am on the Saturday morning.

The news came as a complete shock. They players arrived at Highbury a few hours later to discover suddenly that the Boss, who was perfectly healthy when they had last seen him in Birmingham, was dead. Bastin told of the terrible blow the players felt: 'As I approached the ground, the newspaper-sellers were shouting out the news of Chapman's death. It seemed just too bad to be true. In the dressing room, nobody had anything to say, yet each of us knew what (the others) were thinking. Herbert Chapman had been loved by us all.'

George Male was walking past a tube station when he saw the newspaper board: 'Herbert Chapman Dead.' ... 'That was the first I knew about it. I couldn't believe it.' Arsenal and Wednesday stood to attention before the game. 'I suppose Arsenal gave quite a good display that day, considering that to the players the game was just an unimportant incident,' said Bastin. 'Even the crowd was practically silent throughout the 90 minutes of a game which seemed to go on for 90 years.' Arsenal and Wednesday drew 1–1, but the team collapsed afterward and lost three consecutive games, including two home matches against Spurs and Everton.

Herbert Chapman was buried at Hendon, where he had attended church regularly, four days later. The pallbearers were among the greatest names in the game's history – David Jack, Eddie Hapgood, Joe Hulme, Jack Lambert, Cliff Bastin and Alex James. The crowds were huge and the Reverend A. Hunt Cooke, a close friend of Chapman's at St Mary's, recalled that the scenes were a little shocking: 'There were people climbing all over the graves with cameras. Mr Chapman would not have approved.'

Bob Wall, then Chapman's secretary, said that, for several years after Chapman's death, he regularly heard his measured footsteps in the Highbury corridors late in the evening, going along the upper landing, through the boardroom and cocktail bar, into the Press Room and on into the stand. He, and other members of the staff, often looked down the corridors to see if there was anyone there – but no one ever was. If there are such things as ghosts, then if Herbert Chapman's still watches over Highbury it would be perfect. In every sense, he has continued to live on in the club and the ground that he raised, just as he promised Tom Whittaker he would, to the very heights of football.

Above: Herbert Chapman, who guided Arsenal through the rocky years of the late 1920s to greatness in the early 1930s until his untimely and tragic death.

Below: 10 January 1934; the saddest day of the glorious 30s. The cortege carrying Herbert Chapman's body moves slowly through the streets of Hendon, where he was buried in the churchyard of what was then still a quiet village.

CHAPTER 5

ALLISON'S ARSENAL

1934–1939

Chapman's death was so unexpected that there was no obvious successor. The players probably favoured Joe Shaw, who was popular and fully versed in Arsenal's ways. Shaw, apparently, was not particularly keen on the glare of publicity that was now an essential part of the job as manager at Highbury and stayed behind the scenes. Whether George Allison, the director in charge, actually formally offered him the job is unclear. The choice of a successor was an almost impossible one for the board – to follow Chapman was the hardest task in football. As it turned out, the problems were not as intractable as the board probably imagined. The club was run on a day-to-day basis by Joe Shaw, Tom Whittaker and John Peters, all of them highly competent, and the fact that between Chapman's death and the outbreak of war Arsenal won three Championships and the FA Cup (more trophies, interestingly, than when he was alive) is largely due to them. It was also true that the club had established a style and approach to the game that could survive even the passing of a Herbert Chapman.

ALLISON FILLS THE BREACH

The solution that the board came up with, while unlikely, proved in the end to be rather clever. George Allison, who had been involved with the club since its Woolwich days and who became a director in the early 1920s, moved from the boardroom to the manager's office. For some months after Chapman's death, Allison had been acting as Managing Director/Secretary. He did not actually become manager until the end of the 1933–34 season. It was a clever move because it avoided any great disruption, it allowed Shaw and Whittaker to continue to manage the team, the training and the tactics, and it saved the club from facing any new broom that an outsider would probably want to bring, even to so successful a club as the Gunners.

Technically Joe Shaw had become team manager, John Peters secretary and Tom Whittaker trainer. The 'official' job of secretary-manager was not advertised, but there were hundreds of applications anyway, to which Allison had to reply. One from Wales claimed the ability to run 14 miles in

an hour, a mile in 3½ minutes and '... to have developed a private system of team control on the field by verbal orders that will break any defence or attack that does not use my methods ...' As Allison said, presumably tongue in cheek, being the only one who saw the applications gave him ample opportunity to put examples like that to one side, lest they endanger his prospects.

Allison was actually three years older than the Arsenal, having been born in Darlington in 1883. He had built a reasonable reputation for himself as a journalist, and had for a time been the manager's assistant at Middlesbrough, but his name came to national attention when he was chosen to be Britain's first ever radio sports commentator. The very first major event to be broadcast live was to be the 1927 Cup final, played on 23 April between Arsenal and Cardiff City. Oddly, no one seemed to think it unreasonable that the commentator for the Cup final should also be a director of one of the teams on the pitch.

A HARD ACT TO FOLLOW

Bernard Joy, who played for Allison, described him as:

'... tactful, friendly and good-hearted. But he fell short in his handling of footballers and lacked the professional's deep knowledge of the game. (Allison) wisely left dressing-room discipline in Tom Whittaker's hands and it was Whittaker and Joe Shaw who took the brunt of the strained relations which occasionally developed between management and players. The two of them were loyalty itself to Allison – they had to be or the club would have fallen apart.' Cliff Bastin, who also played for the next five years under Allison, clearly agreed with Joy, but there is a slight edge to comments in his autobiography. Having pointed out that Joe Shaw was unhappy with the glare of publicity, Bastin comments: 'The man who did take over the position was one to whom the limelight was far from unwelcome ... he was not, however, a successor shaped in the Chapman mould. Indeed, relations between him and Mr Chapman had not always been of the happiest ... He (Allison) had the name of Arsenal splashed across the front pages of the press, but he lacked Herbert Chapman's gift of getting the best out of his players.'

These were commonly held views when Allison took over, and were to be heard often enough through the rest of the decade. But others were prepared to look at the results and accept what was plain to see; few men, if any, could have taken over from Chapman, and there were still plenty of trophies on the boardroom sideboard. Frank Carruthers, one of the leading journalists of the period, wrote in 1937: 'The continuance of Arsenal's power is a wonderful tribute to Mr George Allison, who has borne his office through a period of extreme difficulty which would have taxed the ingenuity of a Herbert Chapman to surmount.' And to sum up his views about George Allison's success he said, simply: 'Well, we have all been wrong.'

For the season-and-a-half after Chapman's death things went as well as they could have done for anyone. No other man has come into a manager's seat and won the Championship in his first two seasons. But while Arsenal clearly remained the team to beat through the rest of the 1930s they were no longer the best. In the last four seasons prior to the outbreak of war in 1939 their record was a creditable sixth, third, first and fifth, though the Championship of 1938 was won with a mere 52 points, the lowest ever in a full 42-match season. The Cup was again highly creditable, but arguably not outstanding compared with the impossibly high standards set by Chapman between 1930 and 1934. There were, nonetheless, three quarter finals and the 1936 final victory over Sheffield United.

When Allison's third season in charge began in August 1935 success had become a habit. It was seven seasons since Arsenal had not won or threatened to win one or both trophies. In 1930 there was the FA Cup, in 1931 the League, in 1932 the runners-up slot in both, in 1933, 1934 and 1935 the Championship. Could they do it again? After seven matches and only two wins it didn't look likely.

All great teams come to the end of their eras. Some settle slowly, as Arsenal did, some rapidly, as Manchester City did after their Championship of 1937. For Arsenal, as we have seen, nearly all the major players had already gone. Alex James and Herbie Roberts were nearing retirement, Frank Moss' shoulder injury recurred in a Cup tie against Blackburn

Above: The most famous of all Arsenal pictures: Alex James leaves a trail of Manchester City defenders, including (left) Matt Busby, behind him during a game at Highbury on 13 October 1934. The view is towards the North Bank, then graced by the famous clock. The FA had recently told the club to change it from a 45-minute timer to a proper clock. It was eventually moved to the southern end when the North Bank stand was built. Arsenal won this particular game against City 3–0 and ended the season as Champions for the third consecutive time (picture by courtesy of *The Sunday Times*).

Opposite: George Allison talking to journalists at Highbury before the 1936 FA Cup final.

and his career was finally over, reserve centre-forward Ronnie Westcott, of whom great things were expected, injured a knee in only his second League match and never played again.

Allison later wrote that, just before the manager's death, Chapman had told him: 'The team's played out Mr Allison, we must rebuild.' At the time the club was top of the First Division and half-way through the hat-trick. In many ways the quote rings untrue. Perhaps it was just Chapman's way of loosening up a director for yet more major expenditures, or perhaps it was a throw-away line after a single poor game. Nonetheless, the team was rebuilt, and not so much because of Allison's desire to buy new players as the ageing of the first-team squad.

DRAKE HITS VILLA FOR SEVEN

Allison's first signing was Ted Drake, the reluctant gas inspector from Southampton, in March 1934. And the highlight of the 1935–36 season was to be one game involving the same Ted Drake.The date was 14 December 1935 and the match was one of the standard classics of the decade – Aston Villa versus Arsenal at Villa Park. About 70,000 were packed inside the ground to see another instalment in a rivalry which had provided a series of highly memorable encounters since 1930. They were not to be disappointed though, for once, neither Arsenal nor Villa were heading the League. The Gunners were already eight points behind Sunderland while Villa, having conceded 52 goals in 18 games were bottom. Founder members of the League in 1888, Villa had never been relegated and, in an attempt to stave off that ignominy, had recently spent so heavily that Chapman's and Allison's earlier behaviour looked like that of paupers by comparison. Villa fielded six internationals, Arsenal were without James and

Hulme. Centre-forward Ted Drake had been in the reserves and was carrying a knee injury, which was heavily strapped for the first time.

For the first quarter hour Villa were better, but at half time were 3–0 down and Drake had a hat-trick. All the goals were classic Arsenal – a long ball from Pat Beasley for Drake to run on to, a long pass from Bastin which Drake picked up and ran with to the edge of the area before scoring, and a rebound from a Pat Beasley shot from the wing. At the end of an hour Drake had a double hat-trick and Arsenal were 6–0 up. This time the goals came from a mistake by Villa's Tommy Griffiths, who assumed a ball was going over the goal line only to see it rebound off the post for Drake, another pass from Bastin to Drake and an instant return from a bad clearance.

Drake was controlling the ball perfectly, beating defenders at will and shooting so accurately that the Villa keeper, Merton, had no chance. It was the exhibition of a complete centre-forward. By this stage the entire Villa half-back line was marking Drake, but it made little difference for his seventh shot actually hit the bar and bounced down to be cleared. It was one of only two goal attempts of the whole afternoon which missed its mark (the other was saved). Villa did score once, but Drake had the last word in the final minute with yet another goal from a Bastin cross-field pass; seven goals away from home with just nine shots.

One reason it was the highlight of the season for Drake was that he was injured for much of it. As the 1936 Cup final approached, in which Arsenal were to play Sheffield United, Allison needed to test Drake's fitness after a cartilage operation. The game before the final was against Villa at Highbury. Ted Drake scored the winning goal and it was the final nail in Villa's relegation coffin.

Drake's seven goals in Birmingham were a League record, equalling Jimmy Ross Junior's alleged total for Preston against Stoke set way back in 1888 (and since found to be incorrect). By one of those peculiar statistical coincidences, however, Drake's was to remain the record for just 12 days, when Bunny Bell of Tranmere scored nine against Oldham in the Third Division North, though Drake's record remains for the First Division. Drake's goals made little difference to the title race – Sunderland beat the Gunners 5–4 in an exciting game at Roker and went on to win the Championship easily. Arsenal finished sixth, their worst position since 1930.

BASTIN STRIKES DECISIVE GOAL

The Cup was to be a different story that season. Bristol Rovers were defeated 5–1 at Eastville, then Liverpool 2–0 at Anfield. 'Recorder' in the Arsenal programme was particularly effusive about that display: 'It will go down in Arsenal history as one of the most glorious performances. The form of our team ... was superb and would probably have accounted for any team in the land.' The next game was again away (their seventh consecutive away draw) at Newcastle, who

Below: Alex James, dressed in unlikely garb, watches the Barnsley keeper, Ellis, during the FA Cup quarter final tie at Highbury on February 29, 1936. Arsenal won 4–1 with goals from Bastin, Bowden and Beasley (2).

had beaten them in the 1932 final. Moss, Roberts and Drake were all out injured, and the Gunners did well to draw 3–3. The replay at Highbury was easier, a 3–0 win including two penalties by Cliff Bastin. The sixth round finally saw a home draw and a 4–1 defeat of Barnsley. The semi-final was at Huddersfield against highly unfashionable Grimsby (but who were then a First Division club) and some concerns were voiced that this might be another hard struggle like the semi-final against Hull of six years before. It was certainly a hard game, Bastin's goal being the only one of the match and taking Arsenal to Wembley for the fourth time in ten years. Cliff Bastin had a useful habit of scoring the critical goal in semi-finals and in this case, he struck from a Bowden through-ball in a move which had been rehearsed repeatedly on the training ground.

GUNNERS BACK AT WEMBLEY

With no chance of winning the Championship, Allison had been resting his injured players (such as Roberts and Drake) between Cup ties. This did not please the League, who fined Arsenal £250 in a show of displeasure which became almost an annual ritual directed at some club or other between the wars. When the final came round Drake, Roberts, James and Hapgood were all unwell. Drake was barely recovered from a cartilage operation and had only played his comeback game one week before. Allison decided he had to risk the centre-forward and reshuffled his attack – putting Ray Bowden at inside forward and moving Bastin back to the left-wing (he had been playing inside). The upshot was that Pat Beasley, who had been in Bastin's spot for much of the season, was dropped before the final, just as he had been hours before the 1932 game. The FA again refused to mint an extra medal for him. The team that therefore took the field was Wilson, Male, Hapgood, Crayston, Roberts, Copping, Hulme, Bowden, Drake, James and Bastin.

Their opponents were Second Division Sheffield United, who had beaten Burnley, Preston, Leeds, Spurs and finally Fulham to get to Wembley. For most of the game United were on top, almost going ahead in the first minute when Alex Wilson dropped the ball in the six-yard box, and later unluckily hitting the bar with a Jock Dodds header after half-an-hour. There were no goals until the 74th minute, when Bastin picked up a clearance and passed the ball through the middle to Ted Drake. Drake side-stepped past United captain Tom Johnson and hit the ball hard, left-footed, past keeper Smith. United attacked for the rest of the match and suffered further wretched luck when Dodds hit the woodwork a second time. Drake, who had been uncomfortable for the whole game, said afterward that when he got the ball from Bastin he knew it was now or never. After he had scored James and Bastin were first to reach him, but he was on his hands and knees in the grass, unable to get up because of the pain in his injured knee. Drake stayed on the field for the rest of the game, but took no

Left: The 1936 FA Cup final against Sheffield United was not to prove the most glittering moment in the club's history, but the demand for tickets never faltered. The Monday after the semi-final the Highbury staff faced this postbag of requests for Cup final tickets.

further part. It was the only goal of the game and Alex James took the trophy. Hapgood had not realised he wouldn't be captain until he read the morning papers, a communication slip by Allison which appears to have rankled with Hapgood afterward.

The captain and the manager never had a particularly close relationship, Hapgood being another who has described Allison as lucky to take over when he did and not possessing the football knowledge of Chapman. Later Hapgood was particularly hurt that Allison was prepared to let him go to Luton at the start of the 1943–44 season, when the player wanted a final year with the Gunners. But the full-back tells a good story about Allison in his autobiography, admitting that the manager was also very amused by it. Shortly after taking over, Allison was running a team-talk preparing for the following day's match: 'The danger man for Wednesday is Charlie Napier,' he told Jack Crayston, 'and you have the job of marking him and not letting him have the ball.' Crayston tried to interrupt but Allison stopped him: 'Wait a moment, let me finish and then give me your views.' When Allison had finished he asked what Crayston wanted to say. 'Napier does play well for Wednesday, Mr Allison,' the half-back commented, 'but we're playing Blackpool tomorrow.'

STILL GOOD BUT NO LONGER GREAT

Having been largely outplayed by a Second Division side in the 1936 final, Arsenal were forced to face the realities of their new position. They were no longer the outstanding side. Others, having watched what Chapman had achieved, had begun to copy many of his methods. Arsenal's tactical game was no longer a surprise, particularly when Bastin, Hulme and James became older, slower and less effective. The strain of a decade with every game played like a Cup tie was taking its toll.

And yet there was still no single club ready to take over the mantle – Sunderland were always in at the kill, Preston often looked good, Huddersfield kept popping up, Wolves and Derby threatened to win everything and eventually won nothing. So, at the end of the day, Arsenal still maintained a better

overall record than any other club – it is just that we are tempted to judge them by the standards not of the Chapman era as a whole, but solely against the 1930–34 period.

The realities of Arsenal's slightly diminished status were clear in the first few games of 1936–37. The Gunners won only two of their initial nine matches and, by the end of October, were 17th. In a now familiar story, though, the side fought back until, by mid-March, they were on top and seemed to be on the way to a seventh trophy in eight years. But, in true fairy story tradition, Manchester City came with an astonishing run of 36 points out of 40 from the New Year onward. The crucial game was at Maine Road on 10 April 1937, when the Gunners went down 2–0 and left City clear to take the title.

ALEX JAMES RETIRES

For Arsenal, the season's most significant event was probably Alex James' retirement. His last League game was against Bolton on 1 May 1937 and was hardly the send-off he might have wished. Bernard Joy, now in the team in place of the injured Herbie Roberts, called the goalless draw 'dismal'.

It is impossible to underestimate James' contribution to the successful Arsenal side of the 1930s. He was simply the key man. Before he arrived, as has often been repeated, they had won nothing, despite the big signings. In the six years after his arrival they won four Championships and reached three FA Cup finals. 'You might have suspected,' wrote Don Davies in his obituary in *The Manchester Guardian*, 'when you saw him shuffle onto the field for the first time that there was one who might lay claim to genius.' Some held that James' slovenly appearance was natural, others said it was a pose. But it

Below: The only goal of the 1936 FA Cup final: Drake picked up a pass from Bastin, side-stepped the Sheffield captain Tom Johnson and hit the ball hard, left-footed past keeper Smith.

was in sharp contrast to one of the tidiest minds in football. James hated waste, particularly wasted effort. To him it was the surest mark of inadequate technique. "Let the ball do the work" was his motto.' After he had begun to heed Chapman's advice to: '... cut out the circus tricks until we're winning 3–0,' James was at the centre of everything. That was why he was always treated differently from the rest. Chapman would not have put up with his antics, his disappearances in the night and lying in bed until noon from any other player.

When James finished playing he took up a job with one of the pools companies. He later became a Sunday paper reporter and eventually returned to Highbury as a coach. He was to die in 1953, aged 51, one of several of the great names of the 1930s to die tragicallm his injury and a bloodclot complication and Joe Hulme was out for virtually a year-and-a-half after injuring his back when he ran into a concrete wall at one end of the Huddersfield pitch. Oddly, it was back there to Leeds Road that Hulme eventually went in January 1938, and within three months he was playing outside right in the famous FA Cup final against Preston. Hulme was the first man to play in five Wembley FA Cup finals, a club record later to be equalled by Pat Rice. The 1938 Cup final was actually Joe Hulme's last ever first-class match, a wonderful way to end any career.

Herbie Roberts had a less happy sequel to his Arsenal career, which ended after that bad injury on 30 October 1937 versus Middlesbrough. He became part of the backroom staff, moving down to train the nursery club at Margate. After only a brief time there, shortly after the outbreak of the war, he tragically died of erysipelas, a rare bacterial infection of the skin which penicillin can cure relatively easily today. He was a great loss to Arsenal and to football and was the second (after Jack Lambert) of the great team to die soon after moving to Margate.

MARGATE: ARSENAL'S NURSERY BY THE SEA

The nursery club idea had been another of Chapman's brain waves. It was much better training to have your young players competing in a real League than against other juniors, he reasoned. His first move was to try to take over Clapton (later Leyton) Orient, then a Third Division South club, who were threatened with expulsion by the FA in 1931 unless they paid off their debts. Chapman effectively took over the club later that year and all of the players were registered with Arsenal. It was a nice, if short-lived, irony as, 20 years before, Clapton Orient had been one of the main objectors to Arsenal's move to Highbury. Needless to say, the League objected strongly and ordered Chapman to desist (they had clearly had enough of Arsenal bosses running two clubs 20 years earlier). The upshot was that Jimmy Seed, Orient manager since April 1931, found himself just a few weeks from the start of the 1932–33 season with no team, no directors and no registered players.

It was not Chapman, but Allison, who later turned to the Southern League, which was not concerned about the two clubs idea, and Arsenal acquired Margate instead. Seed was to have his own revenge on Arsenal – between 1934 and 1936 he took Charlton from the Third Division to the First and in 1936–37 he squeezed into second place between Manchester City and the Gunners.

FIFTH CHAMPIONSHIP IN EIGHT YEARS

So, having finished third in 1936–37 and been knocked out of the Cup in the quarter-finals at the Hawthorns, it did appear that Arsenal were in decline. All the more surprising, then, was their Championship in 1937–38, the fifth in eight years. Their record was almost identical to that of 1936–37, with exactly the same number of points, 52. They lost as many as 11 games (their highest number of defeats in any season in the 1930s to date, with the sole exception of 1935–36 when they lost 12) and scored only 77 goals, their lowest total since 1929–30 apart from the 75 in 1933–34, that peculiarly quiet season containing Chapman's death.

The side was in no sense settled and the season was tough and inconsistent. At the end the Gunners were to just squeeze past Wolves and Brentford, who were performing the surprise Charlton role one season later. George Hunt had been bought from Spurs to partner Drake up front and did so well that it was a surprise when Allison transferred him to Bolton at the end of the season. Joy had replaced Roberts and Bastin and Male were now the only survivors from the great days, making the winning of another Championship both surprising and impressive.

By February, Arsenal and Wolves were favourites for both major competitions and found themselves drawn together in the Cup one week after meeting in the League. Wolves won the League game 3–1 to go ahead of Arsenal in the table, though both were then several points behind Brentford.

In the Cup the roles were reversed, Arsenal winning a very tough game 2–1 with goals from Ted Drake and Alf Kirchen in what Bernard Joy called the most exciting tie he ever played

in. The effort must have exhausted them, for they went out 1–0 to eventual Cup winners Preston in the next round at Highbury.

Brentford, despite having been seven points ahead of Arsenal at one stage, were like many clubs who rise through the divisions quickly. The elements of unfamiliarity and surprise carry them so far for so long, but the lack of strength in depth tells in the end. Brentford walked the tightrope for a long time, but when they fell they fell heavily. In eight games Brentford took only two points and were out of contention.

At Highbury new names were making their mark – Mel Griffiths at outside right, Eddie Carr, a successful centre forward when Drake was injured, as he so often was. A long run of success put Arsenal three points clear of Wolves, at Easter, but then came disaster. Over the holiday period the Gunners could only draw 0–0 at Birmingham and then lost both games against Brentford. The matches against their London rivals, who were back in form now that their chance had virtually gone, were particularly inept, notable for Ted Drake's injury at Griffin Park, where he was knocked out and then came back on the field despite having blood pouring down his face from a head wound. That was the Drake of Arsenal inter-war legend. He ended this game half-conscious and hanging over Tom Whittaker's shoulder.

FINAL-DAY DECIDER

The Easter debacle put Wolves back on top and the contest went to the last match. Preston had made a late run from behind and were being tipped for the Double. Arsenal were perhaps fortunate to go to Deepdale a week before the Cup final (in which Preston defeated Huddersfield) and, with the Preston players no doubt tense and afraid of injury, the Gunners won 3–1. On the very last day Wolves were away to Sunderland. If Wolves won, they were champions no matter what the opposition did, but if they drew, and Arsenal beat Bolton at Highbury, then Arsenal would be champions again.

The Bolton game was easy for a committed Arsenal, who won 5–0. But, though Sunderland had nothing to play for, they threw themselves into their game with Wolves with a vengeance. Such was their determination that, despite having a defender sent off, they still won 1–0. The game at Roker Park had kicked off 15 minutes before the one at Highbury, and when the result came through on the scoreboards and the crowd started cheering Bernard Joy called to Eddie Hapgood: 'They've lost, Eddie.' Hapgood, typically, was so embroiled in the game, though Arsenal were already 4–0 up, that he simply didn't understand what Joy was talking about.

MONEY TALK

The final season before the Second World War proved to be notable for little but the purchase of Bryn Jones. This was really the point at which Allison was accused of taking

Below: Cliff Bastin was one of the few members of the rapidly ageing Cup-winning squad of 1936 to return as a player after the war. During his 396 games for Arsenal he scored an amazing 178 goals, a record that remained unbroken until Ian Wright finally managed it in September 1997.

over Chapman's 'money bags' reputation with a vengeance. Interestingly such criticisms were a source of unusual irritation to Allison, who usually took disagreements and press comment in his stride. He was very quick to point out that, between 1925 and 1934, Chapman spent £101,000 in fees and received £40,000 for those he sold – a balance of around £7,000 per annum. Between Allison taking over and the war, Arsenal spent £81,000 and received £51,000, a net expenditure of £30,000. This was certainly more than manageable when, during the six seasons 1933–39, the total profit amounted to £136,000, a massive sum for any football club or moderate sized company of the period. In 1934–35 the club became the first ever to have gate receipts of over £100,000, and made a profit of £35,000. Of the other clubs only Portsmouth, with £14,961, even got into double figures. The financial reserves were then £60,000 and even programme sales brought in nearly £2,500.

THE GRANDEST OF STANDS

Financially more debatable, as it happened, was the building of the stands. The West Stand cost £45,000 and was opened by the Prince of Wales (later the Duke of Windsor) on 10 December 1932. It had actually been first used on 12 November for a game against Chelsea (Arsenal won 1–0) and was, by a large margin, the grandest and most expensive structure on any League ground at the time. It incorporated three flats, an electric lift, and 4,100 seats, and the lower level, which was originally all standing, could theoretically hold another 20,000. Work had actually begun on redeveloping the ground in 1931, when the club started building up the banking on all four sides. Local inhabitants were encouraged to bring in their rubbish to help the process and, as Simon Inglis mentions in his invaluable *The Football Grounds of England and Wales*, one coal merchant backed up too close to a hole in the North Bank and saw his horse and cart disappear into the cavity. The animal was so badly injured that it had to be destroyed and it is buried where it fell, in the middle of the North Bank terracing.

The North Bank roof was originally built in 1935 (the clock then being moved to the South Bank) but was destroyed by bombs in the war. A new East, or Main, Stand was not planned to be built until 1941, but the original stand was deteriorating so fast, and the finances appeared to be so favourable, that the decision was made to rebuild it in 1935.

As the club had already borrowed quite heavily to erect the other stands, by early 1937 Arsenal had debts of £200,000 and needed average crowds of 40,000 simply to pay the running expenses and finance the debt. The Main Stand, though planned to be identical to the West Stand, finally cost far more (£130,000 to be precise) and when the war came in 1939 the club found themselves in a similar position to that of Henry Norris in 1914. The war years clearly left the problem unsolved but, with the enormous boom in attendances

between 1945 and 1952, and some intelligent management, the problem happily, and perhaps a little fortuitously, solved itself. One reason why the East Stand cost more than the West was that it had an expensive public frontage – the West was built entirely behind a row of houses and was effectively invisible from that side.

GUNNERS BREAK TRANSFER RECORD

When George Allison finally decided he had to buy Bryn Jones in August 1938, the record fee was still the £11,500 he and Chapman had paid out for David Jack ten years before. Eventually Wolves forced Allison up to £14,000, and Jones was left to carry the very distracting tag of 'most expensive player'. Many players before and since have found this difficult, not least Bryn's own nephew Cliff Jones when he came to Spurs for £35,000 two decades later. Bryn started well enough though, scoring in his first game, against Portsmouth, and getting two more in the next three matches. But he never really settled that season, not enjoying the limelight and feeling the crowd and club's expectations weighing very heavily on his light shoulders.

It was the sort of pressure he could never escape from at Highbury – when he and Allison agreed that a run in the relative calm of the reserves might improve his form, 33,000 turned up to see his second-team debut. As they had nearly all come to see Jones, this was even worse than being in the first team and the experiment was never repeated. Allison was understandably unrepentant about his purchase, pointing out that: '... he was not a prolific goalscorer (though he had scored 52 goals in 163 games for Wolves) just like Alex James, because his chief asset was the holding together of the line and the making of openings for the more vigorous of his team-mates.'

Allison said that Jones often asked to be saved from the ever-present, ever-insistent limelight, and believed that, given time to settle down, he would have made the grade: 'My faith

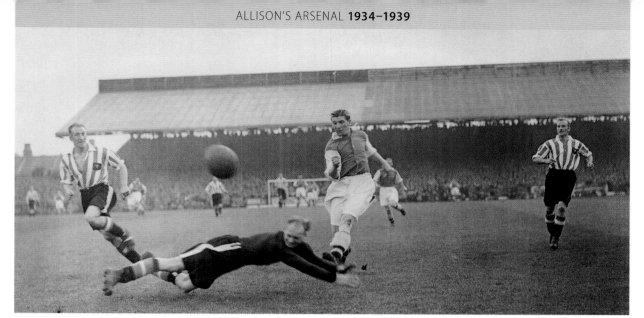

Left: Ted Drake in action again, against bogey team Brentford at Griffin Park on 8 September 1938.

never failed and I have never for a moment considered him a bad buy.' Allison's point seems a fair one. It took Alex James a season to settle down and there was no reason to expect Jones, just as important a buy, to adapt any faster. He played exceptionally well on the team's close-season tour of 1939 but never really had another chance except in the very different atmosphere of wartime football. Like many great players, notably Stan Cullis of Wolves, his best years were inevitably lost to the war.

Interestingly, other members of the club did not share Allison's optimism. Cliff Bastin, in his autobiography, said: 'I thought at the time this was a bad transfer, and subsequent events did nothing to alter my views ... I had played against Bryn in club and international matches and had ample opportunity to size him up. To my mind, he was essentially an attacking player, who was successful at Wolverhampton largely because the rest of the team was playing well.'

Bastin argued that James had a first-class footballing brain and that Jones, while being a first-class footballer, did not. James, whom Bastin, of course, called one of the most self-confident people he had ever met, was able to weather the bad patch of the transition, while Jones, quiet, modest and self-effacing, was not. Bastin was the wing partner of them both, of course, so his judgement is possibly the most reliable available. Sadly, his conclusion is rather dismissive: 'It was his (Jones) natural instinct to play as far upfield as I. Arsenal's attempt to curb that instinct failed...(He) would have been much happier if he had never left Wolverhampton.'

TEENAGE KEEPER DIES

Apart from Jones, the goalkeepers were also in the news in the last season before the war. George Marks, hailing from the non-footballing town of Salisbury, became the first-team keeper and was England's first choice for much of the war, losing his place only after a bad head injury sustained against Wales toward the end of the hostilities. Much more serious was the tragedy that befell the reserve keeper David Ford. Aged only 18, he had played well in a Combination game for the second team against Portsmouth at Highbury. On the way

home, he collapsed in the tube station, was rushed to hospital and found to have a duodenal ulcer. He never recovered and died the following Saturday.

More were to die in the hostilities that followed – of the 42 players on the staff in 1938–39, nine were dead by the end of the war. Nearly all the players joined the forces (Whittaker had served in the First World War and Bastin's deafness disqualified him so the two of them manned the Air Raid post on top of the main stand). The ground was bombed several times – Eddie Hapgood recalled one occasion when the incendiaries missed the stands but managed to set fire to both sets of goalposts. Soon afterward a barrage balloon arrived and was moored on the practice pitch. This did not prevent a 1,000–pound bomb hitting the same pitch, nor various other aerial objects destroying the North Stand and some of the terracing.

THE ARSENAL STADIUM MYSTERY

Arsenal were to conclude their inter-war glories with a flourish in 1939. Though they had never been in the hunt for the League title (Everton won it easily), the Gunners did win five of their last six games to finish, as in 1914–15, fifth. By this time Hitler had already invaded Czechoslovakia and the normality of football already seemed a little unreal.

Although three games were played at the start of the aborted 1939–40 season, it was fitting that the last official pre-Second World War match should have been as peculiar, in its own way, as the last game in 1914–15. That was at Highbury on 6 May 1939, against bogey team Brentford. The game was used to film the playing sequences for a thriller called *The Arsenal Stadium Mystery* by one Leonard Gribble. Brentford wore white shirts and black shorts instead of their usual change strip (to provide better contrast for the black and white cameras) and played the part of the mythical Trojans. Several Arsenal players, as well as the manager George Allison, featured in the film and enlivened the plot. Whether the script called for a 2–0 home win is not clear, but that's the way the game ended. It was to be Arsenal's last official first-class match for over six years.

Above: Denis Compton, like most of the Arsenal players, joined the forces, becoming (appropriately) a gunner in the army.

ARSENAL MANAGERS

It is impossible to compare managers across different eras. But you can say for certain that over the last century-and-a-quarter Arsenal have boasted a string of inspirational figureheads who have each made an enormous contribution to the sport, as well as to the club. From Harry Bradshaw's pioneering tactical savvy at the dawn of the last century, through the years when Herbert Chapman revolutionised football and made Arsenal one of the greatest club sides in the world; and taking in the Double winners, Bertie Mee and Arsène Wenger, the club has always been blessed with leaders of the highest calibre.

Herbert Chapman (centre) with Bob John (left) and Alex James (right)

Harry Bradshaw
1889–1904
Back in the era when Arsenal were still Woolwich Arsenal, Bradshaw quit his playing career at Burnley to manage the emerging London club. He engineered their promotion to the First Division – steering the Gunners to second place in the Second Division in 1904. He left to manage Fulham.

Herbert Chapman
1925–34
The Great, the Immortal, the One and Only Herbert Chapman was the towering genius who presided over Arsenal for a glorious decade in the inter-war years. He made Arsenal a major power in the English game, and the brilliant Yorkshireman also played a big part in revolutionising football, with a tactical acumen that destroyed the traditionally hidebound way of playing the game. The Yorkshireman had been a journeyman professional footballer before finding his true calling as a manager. At Huddersfield Town he built a team that won three consecutive First Division titles. At Arsenal he became the

first modern manager, wresting control of transfers, team selection and tactics from a club committee. His methods were successful on the pitch: under Chapman the Gunners won two League titles and an FA Cup, but he never saw the full fruits of his work. He died in 1934 – and left his successors a team that was just as formidable as Arsène Wenger's invincibles.

George Allison
1934–47
Allison took over from Chapman and maintained the Club's success, but he took a different approach to that of his illustrious predecessor. Where Chapman dominated every aspect of first team activity, Allison was happy to cede influence to senior players, allowing the captain to dictate tactics on the field. Allison managed the team at arm's length, and was more influential in turning Arsenal into one of the best-run clubs in the country – and Highbury into the country's most palatial football stadium. His methods paid off: with the former journalist in charge, Arsenal won two titles and an FA Cup. He provided sterling service during the Second World War, keeping the Club together almost on his own, while younger Gunners did their bit for the war effort.

Tom Whittaker
1947–56
Whittaker, a Geordie, played for Arsenal in the 1920s, and was also the Club's physio before taking the manager's job on George Allison's retirement. Whittaker had already been on the Club's backroom staff for 20 years. Chapman had appointed him to his first training job in 1927 when injury curtailed his playing days. Once he emerged as the boss, he preferred to keep a low profile and let his teams do the talking – which they did to great effect. He brought two League titles and an FA Cup to Highbury.

Bertie Mee
1966–76
Mee, like Whittaker, was another physio-turned-manager who shunned publicity – but nevertheless managed to bring glory to Arsenal. The Club had endured a long fallow spell before Mee took the team to its triumph in the Fairs Cup in 1970. That was followed by one of the greatest seasons in the Club's history – the League-FA Cup Double campaign of 1970–71. Mee's Arsenal were sometimes accused of lacking flair, but he

George Allison (centre)

Bertie Mee (centre) with George Graham (left) and Ray Kennedy (right)

was never the defence-obsessed killjoy he was made out to be. How could he be, with mavericks like Charlie George in the side? He forged a formidable double-act with coach Don Howe, and will live forever in Arsenal legend as the first manager to win a European trophy – and the Double.

George Graham
1986–95
'George knows', claimed the famous Highbury banner. And he did. His peerless organisational ability allowed him to wed a perfectly-drilled back-four with an attack that bristled with threat – and the irresistible combination brought two titles, two League Cups, an FA Cup and the Cup-Winners Cup to Highbury.

Arsène Wenger
1996–
Unknown he may have been when he replaced Bruce Rioch as boss in 1996 – but that state of affairs did not last long. He quickly stamped his unique mark on English football, bringing a professorial intelligence to the game, which was in marked contrast to the traditional blood-and-thunder, up-and-at-'em tradition of British management. His scientific training methods and focus on hitherto arcane areas, such as nutrition, were looked on with suspicion initially. But Wenger's approach to training and nutrition extended the career of many Arsenal players – and paid ample dividends on the field. His first full season brought the Club their second Double, and two further Premier League titles followed in 2002 and 2004. Under his guidance the team won additional FA Cup triumphs in 2002, 2003 and 2005. In 2004 Wenger brought the team through the entire League season unbeaten.

Arsène Wenger

CHAPTER 6

WHITTAKER'S ARSENAL

1945–1966

Altogether, 42 of Arsenal's 44 professionals in September 1939 had gone into the services. The administrators at Highbury followed, and the ground itself played a part in the war effort – Arsenal Stadium was transformed into a stronghold for ARP (Air Raid Precautions). The club was temporarily based at White Hart Lane, although for a time George Allison converted the referees' room at Highbury into a small flat. Amid the confusion of wartime competitions and the difficulties of finding who was able to play when and where, Arsenal's success nonetheless continued.

WARTIME HONOURS

In 1939–40 the South 'A' League was won, and in the following season the club reached another Wembley final in the Football League War Cup. With young Laurie Scott partnering Hapgood at full back and Bernard Joy at centre half, the attack was led by Les Compton, who at Wembley against Preston North End missed a penalty. Brother Denis' goal earned a replay, but with Drake now replacing the elder Compton Arsenal lost at Blackburn 2–1.

The football honours, such as they were in such austere circumstances, continued: Champions of the London League in 1941–42 and the Football League South the following season, when there was also a successful return to Wembley, this time in the Football League South Cup final. Reg Lewis, who was to make his mark at the Empire Stadium in more illustrious peace-time circumstances, contributed four goals in a 7–1 thrashing of Charlton Athletic. The gifted forward whose casual approach and happy knack of scoring was to make him such a popular figure at Highbury in the early post-war years finished the 1942–43 season with a remarkable tally of 53 goals.

Two seasons later Lewis was not available and Arsenal's scoring honours were shared by Drake and Stan Mortensen from Blackpool, one of many guest players. Stanley Matthews was another in one wartime league game – he scored. For Ted Drake, though, a slipped disc proved to be one injury that even that gallant forward could not overcome, and his dramatic career finally ended.

The effort of continuing football in the war years proved extremely costly. Pre-war debts of some £150,000 were a millstone when the 1945–46 season began with regional Leagues retained. The return of the FA Cup was the major concession to normality. White Hart Lane remained the club's home venue and witnessed the most remarkable match of that confused season.

DYNAMO SHINE IN HIGHBURY FOG

Late in 1945 Moscow Dynamo arrived on an unprecedented tour. With regular European football still more than a decade away, the visit was an eagerly anticipated event.

George Allison's own account of the events surrounding the match, played in a peasouper fog, tell of the scurrying around to find a team worthy of the illustrious pre-war standards that Moscow Dynamo would expect and the opposition's misunderstanding of these efforts.

The manager's dealings finally produced six 'guests': goalkeeper Bill Griffiths from Cardiff, left-back Joe Bacuzzi from Fulham, left-half Reg Halton from Bury and three illustrious forwards – Matthews, Mortensen and Ronnie Rooke, whom Allison would sign from Fulham the following season. George Drury, now 31, and Horace Cumner, both survivors from the Arsenal pre-war scene, were the other two forwards, while Joy was at centre-half, 33-year-old Cliff Bastin at right-half and Scott at right-back.

The 54,620 spectators had only sporadic views of the proceedings when the fog occasionally lifted, as did the referee, a Russian, and his two linesmen. Moscow Dynamo

scored in their first attack, through Bobrov, but Rooke equalised and then the ebullient Mortensen struck twice. At half time it was 3–2 but sinister whisperings reached the ears of George Allison that the Russian referee would abandon the match if Dynamo fell further behind. On the other hand, if they were to recapture the lead the match would be played to a finish, however thick the fog.

The Russians scored twice in the second half, and the match ran its allotted span; the suggestion of subterfuge could not disguise the flair and discipline glimpsed through the fog.

LEAGUE FARE RESUMED

First Division football returned to Arsenal Stadium on 4 September 1946 against Blackburn Rovers and Marksman summed up the mood, without forgetting: 'You who talked Arsenal with me over a campfire in Assam and the chap with the Italy Star on the train in India who informed me of Herbert Roberts passing on, the fellow in the Skymaster on the long hop from Ceylon to the Cocos Islands who told me about our Cup Final win and all those who played with or against Tom Whittaker's Arsenal Arps in the very early days of ARP. And the older ones who stuck to the job in London through a bomb and fire and rocket yet still made the long trek up to White Hart Lane to give the boys a cheer. We're home again now!'

On the field the resumption was inauspicious. It began with a defeat at Wolves where six goals and one of Bernard Joy's eyeteeth were lost. Reg Lewis, after scoring, ended up in goal, but his 11 goals in the first ten matches papered over some of the cracks. But others ran deep with little young

talent immediately available; the move to White Hart Lane had deferred the production line at Highbury. Icelander Albert Gudmundsson, an amateur, was one of 31 players used in the League. The charismatic Dr Kevin O'Flanagan, an international at football and rugby, on one occasion on successive weekends, was another. Walley Barnes made his debut early in November, but it was two signings in the subsequent weeks which lifted Arsenal from the bottom of the First Division.

Joe Mercer, who had been in the England team as an attacking wing half at the outbreak of war, was in dispute with Everton. At 32 he had virtually decided to retire to concentrate on a grocery business in Wallasey. Surprise interest from Arsenal reawakened his ambition. He signed on condition that he could live and train in Liverpool. Allison and Whittaker were not worried about his ageing, bandy legs. They had purchased a football brain, and by converting Mercer to a defensive half-back they got full return for an investment of £7,000.

Two weeks after Mercer Arsenal added another bargain. At 35 Ronnie Rooke looked an even more unlikely buy, but the short-term need for goals was critical. Rooke struck 21 in 24 League games and the details of his transfer – a fee of £1,000 plus two players moving from Highbury to Fulham – emphasised again the shrewdness of the Arsenal management. Rooke did not finish top scorer. That honour fell to Lewis with a splendid 29 in 28 First Division matches. From the foot of the table the two lifted Arsenal to the respectability of mid-table; in 13th place they still finished top of the London pecking order, although in the third match of a five-hour FA Cup third round saga Chelsea finally triumphed on 'neutral' soil at White Hart Lane with two goals from Tommy Lawton.

WHITTAKER TAKES CHARGE

For two tremendous servants, however, the road had come to an end. Cliff Bastin had been restricted to just six League matches, and he needed an operation on his middle ear in April 1947. The dreadful winter led to an extension of the season into June. It was too much for George Allison who, after an association with the club of four decades, announced his resignation: 'Now I feel the need for a less strenuous life and I leave the future of Arsenal in other hands.'

Those hands had already cared for so many Arsenal players and other sportsmen of great renown. Tom Whittaker, the master trainer, had modestly stayed in the background, vastly influential on the football side of the club while Allison had shown his considerable talents in the business and publicity departments. Now, for all his personal reluctance to step into the limelight, the time was right for him to accept the demanding post of secretary-manager.

Bob Wall always recalled Whittaker at work in shirtsleeves with a pot of tea never far away. A gentle, kindly man, he had spent the war in the RAF. As a qualified engineer he had

repaired aircraft, sending them out to battle again with the painstaking detail which had aided the recovery of so many Arsenal footballers. Having fought in the First World War, he was awarded the MBE for secret work in connection with the D-Day landings in the Second.

Joe Shaw returned from Chelsea, where he had been assistant manager, to become Tom Whittaker's right-hand man. The 1947–48 season began with a temporary captain. Les Compton still had cricket responsibilities for Middlesex, so Joe Mercer led out Arsenal for the opening League game at home to Sunderland. The pitch had been reseeded, the running track around it resurfaced. There was optimism in the air and it was to be well founded.

The playing strength was augmented by two more signings. Archie Macaulay from Brentford had starred for Scotland at Wembley the previous April and also represented Great Britain against the Rest of Europe.

After much persuading – Whittaker made 11 trips to see him before the deal was done – forward Don Roper arrived from Southampton and a football family. His grandfather played for Chesterfield, his father for Huddersfield Town and Royal Marines, with whom he won an Amateur Cup medal. Rejection by Hampshire County Cricket Club after trials during the summer of 1947 had sharpened Roper's appetite to make a career in football.

GUNNERS' RECORD START

What was to become a historic season began on 23 August with a 3.30 kick-off at Highbury against Sunderland. Three goals, from Ian McPherson, Jimmy Logie and Rooke, all in the opening 15 minutes of the second half, produced a 3–1 victory. Four days later Charlton were swept aside 4–2 at The Valley, with McPherson running riot against the FA Cup holders, scoring one and laying on the other three for Roper, Lewis and Logie. The Scottish winger had returned to football with impressive war-time credentials as an RAF pilot, his bravery winning him the DFC and bar. Though naturally an outside right, his early contributions to Whittaker's bright start to the season were on the opposite flank.

A third successive victory came at Bramall Lane, Rooke levelling the score before Roper's 35-yarder was fumbled by the home goalkeeper Smith with only three minutes remaining. Reg Lewis then took centre stage with four goals – Rooke claimed the other two – in a 6–0 demolition of Charlton in the return match at Highbury; the visitors were handicapped by an eighth-minute injury to defender Peter Croker who went off with knee ligaments damaged trying to curb McPherson.

Manchester United were Highbury's next visitors, and the 10,000 fans locked outside when the gates were closed at 3 pm missed a memorable 2–1 victory, courtesy of goals from Rooke and Lewis. The air of expectation at the club was highlighted even more by the decision of Bryn Jones to turn

Below: Ian McPherson was an RAF pilot of some distinction during the Second World War. The Scottish player was a regular for post-war Arsenal and his wing wizardry was instrumental in bringing the title to Highbury in 1948.

down a move to Newport County. 'I'll stay until they chase me away, first team or not,' was the swift retort of the skilful Welsh international.

For the first time Arsenal extended a sequence of wins at the start of a season to six – Bolton Wanderers, the next victims, were defeated 2–0 at Highbury. McPherson and a Rooke penalty contributed the goals in a match which Arsenal finished with only seven fit men. Tom Whittaker sensed the need for the return of Les Compton, who had been given permission to continue his cricket with Middlesex.

MERCER STILL SKIPPER

The tall wicketkeeper was back in the Arsenal dressing room at Deepdale for match number seven and, as club captain, was given a ball by Whittaker to lead out the team. Modestly Compton passed it to Mercer saying: 'If you don't mind Tom, I think Joe should have this. He's not done too badly with the job so far.' Thus Mercer retained the captaincy which was to bring more than a touch of romance to the twilight days of his career. Without Lewis at the sharp end of the attack the first point was dropped at Preston in a goalless draw, but the following week Stoke City were on the receiving end of a three-goal first-half performance, with Bryn Jones enjoying a rare first-team appearance.

Lewis was back but Mercer missing with food poisoning for a tough trip to Burnley, which brought a hard-fought success, with Barnes making one desperate clearance off the line. The winning goal from Lewis came against the balance of play. With two reserves, Paddy Sloan and the loyal George Male, as wing halves, Arsenal could only draw the next match at home to Portsmouth, but victory had been there for the taking when Rooke's 39th-minute penalty was brilliantly saved by Butler.

Goals remained hard to come by throughout October, a time when the flair of Denis Compton might have added an extra spice to Whittaker's recipe for success. But Britain's most glamorous sports star was confined to a hospital bed for the removal of some floating body from a troublesome knee. Aston Villa's visit to Highbury drew a 61,000 capacity crowd and a 1–0 win, but the goal was disputed with Rooke getting away with a push on centre-half, and ex-Gunner, Frank Moss before racing clear to score. A thumping penalty from Rooke brought a share of the points at Molineux, and it was a penalty against Arsenal, conceded by Leslie Compton and converted by Eddie Wainwright, that cost a point in the next match against Everton at Highbury. The brilliance of visiting goalkeeper Ted Sagar had restricted Arsenal to a solitary score from Lewis in the 65th minute.

ARSENAL PROVE THE BIG DRAW

With football such an attraction after the sacrifices of war, Arsenal, as First Division leaders, had already become the major draw. Stamford Bridge played host to a crowd of

67,277 for Chelsea's clash with the Gunners on 1 November. Astonishingly some 27,000 also watched the reserve game between the two clubs at Highbury on the same afternoon; the appearance of Tommy Lawton in the Chelsea second string heightened the appeal of the fixture.

In the senior match Arsenal came away with a goalless draw, the unbeaten record still intact. It remained so seven days later when Blackpool, with Mortensen and Matthews, were beaten 2–1 at Highbury through another Rooke penalty and a Don Roper goal. Before the Blackpool match Whittaker addressed the Highbury crowd with a request to 'Keep up your reputation for sportsmanship. Don't barrack the referee.'

With more than a third of the season gone Arsenal stood proudly six points clear of Burnley at the top of the tree, with a record of: Played 17, Won 12, Drawn 5, Lost 0, goals for 31, against 8. Yet the tag of 'lucky' was still being pinned on the team. Public opinion held the view that progress had come from efficient organisation and defensive discipline rather than football of a higher level than the opposition.

Thus the inevitable first defeat, on 29 November at Derby County, was not shattering news. The Baseball Ground was packed to the rafters to see the pursuit of a record (22 games unbeaten from the start of a season) held by Preston and Sheffield United collapse to a goal in the 32nd minute.

A goal in the same minute a week later, by Black of Manchester City at Highbury, threatened another defeat, but five minutes from time Les McDowall was penalised for hand-ball. Rooke sent his penalty past Frank Swift, and there was no disputing that, on this occasion, Arsenal were fortunate.

In such circumstances a visit to bottom club, Grimsby Town, could only be viewed as a welcome opportunity to return to the groove of earlier in the season. The Blundell Park club had conceded three goals per match on average over the first half of the season; Arsenal managed four through the reliable Rooke (2), Logie and Roper.

GUNNERS MAINTAIN MOMENTUM

The Saturday before Christmas has now been accepted an an attendance low spot with the demands of shopping for the festivities ahead. It was not so in 1947 when more than 58,000 flocked to Roker Park to watch Arsenal in the flesh. The vast majority of them almost had an early holiday treat when Davis sent Sunderland into the lead with only ten minutes remaining, but five minutes later the limping Barnes, a passenger at centre forward, helped create an equaliser. Bryn Jones was to play only seven times in the Championship season but his Roker Park equaliser, his solitary goal of the campaign, held great significance; a second defeat with the congested holiday fixture list ahead might have badly disturbed the Arsenal momentum.

Instead the two Christmas matches produced typically contrary results. The Football League, with scant regard for the family life of footballers, paired Arsenal home and away

Above: Denis Compton returned to the injury-hit Arsenal first team on 14 February 1948 and was vital to their run-in to the League Championship that year. Here, however, he is seen in the 0–2 defeat by Chelsea on 20 March.

with Liverpool! Only Mercer with his Merseyside base could have relished the Christmas morning start at Anfield, but the team responded to the challenge with two goals from Rooke and another from Roper which ended Liverpool's unbeaten home record. Two days later though, revenge was claimed. Albert Stubbins and Billy Liddell struck to stop Arsenal's invincible run at Highbury; Lewis replied too late to salvage a draw from a match for which touts did a roaring trade, with reports of tickets valued at 7s. 6d. (37p) changing hands at more than four times that price!

On New Year's Day, Arsenal, 4–0 winners at Bolton, stood five points clear at the top. The 37-year-old George Male was pressed into service at Burnden Park and gave a sound performance. Bolton claimed that they had equalised a 32nd-minute goal from Lewis in a late scramble when the ball appeared to have crossed the line before Swindin pulled it clear. The crowd was allowed in only half-an-hour before an early start on a pitch flooded by melted snow and the referee dispensed with the half-time interval.

Arsenal's quest for football honour continued with a 3–2 victory over Sheffield United in the last game of the holiday programme. United were down to ten men when Rooke grabbed an important second goal; the player off the field was Alex Forbes, the flame-haired wing half shortly to return to Highbury as part of Whittaker's team strengthening. Forbes had been concussed and remembered nothing of his return to the pitch, during which time United scored twice in the last five minutes to give the scoreline a rather flattering look.

SHOCK CUP EXIT

With the FA Cup providing a new challenge and a break to the slog for the Championship, Tom Whittaker was not the sort of man to underestimate a kindly draw, a home tie with

Second Division Bradford Park Avenue. Consequently, he took his players to Brighton (shades of pre-war delights) for a few days' preparation in the bracing sea air. It did not have the desired effect. In Billy Elliott, the Yorkshire club possessed a locally born left-winger who would later play for England after a transfer to Burnley; the 22-year-old Elliott knocked in a first-half goal. Bradford also included centre-half Ron Greenwood as the cornerstone of their rearguard action in that third round tie at Highbury, and Arsenal's FA Cup ambitions perished.

There was little time for despondency. The next two First Division opponents also had their eyes on the League title, Manchester United and Preston. United still played their home matches at Maine Road, because of war damage at Old Trafford, and interest in the visit of the leaders was massive. More than 80,000 spectators crammed into the ground for a game that finished level after Lewis had drawn first blood and Jack Rowley equalised.

Lewis was now operating at inside right and he retained the position for the tussle with Preston, striking two more valuable goals. Rooke was also on target, while Don Roper enjoyed an inspired afternoon. With those three important points in the bag since the Cup disappointment, Arsenal continued to set a blistering pace at the top of the League. In February Stoke City took the unusual step of making their home match all-ticket against the leaders, but the 41,000 ticket-holders did not witness a goal, largely due to a succession of saves from Swindin.

For the Valentine's Day fixture against Burnley, the Arsenal team appropriately contained a touch of romance. Denis Compton, who had turned out in only one post-war League match, was called into the senior side in place of the injured McPherson. For such a charismatic performer it was a perfect opportunity against a side which came to Highbury needing a win to close the gap at the top. Compton's return captured the imagination of the paying public; 20,000 arrived too late to get into the packed ground

It took Compton only 14 minutes to play his part. His lob was punched by goalkeeper Strong straight to Roper who drove the ball into the Burnley net. Rooke added two more, with Compton also involved in the move that led to Arsenal's third goal. With 13 matches still to play, the Gunners now held an eight-point advantage over their closest challengers.

A VETERAN LINE-UP

Meanwhile, Tom Whittaker had not grown complacent about the depth of talent at the club. Because of the immediate post-war circumstances Arsenal were fielding one of the oldest sides ever to win the Championship, with Rooke, now 36, Les Compton 35 and Mercer 33 holding three of the key roles. Quietly, Whittaker was adding to his staff. Cliff Holton, an amateur from Oxford City, was signed in November 1947. Peter Goring, eternally to be dubbed as the butcher's boy,

gave up his part-time football with Cheltenham Town to join the Arsenal staff the following January, and the next month a senior player arrived in the shape of Alex Forbes, whose swashbuckling performances for Sheffield United had often caught the eye of the Highbury crowd.

Alex Forbes' Arsenal debut was delayed until after the third defeat of the League campaign, at Aston Villa on 28 February, which should really not have happened at all. An own goal by Frank Moss and another from Rooke gave Arsenal a 2–1 lead when Denis Compton was tripped in the Villa penalty area. Rooke put his penalty wide, and Villa revelled in the second chance they had been given. Leslie Compton had been injured in training and played with one leg strapped from ankle to knee. In Trevor Ford, the fiery Welsh international, the home side had the perfect forward to capitalise on a weak link. Ford roasted his marker completely, and scored twice as Villa raced home to a 4–2 win.

Alex Forbes was chosen at inside left for his debut, with Wolves the opposition on a foggy Highbury afternoon. Many of the crowd were still settling down when Hancocks caught Arsenal cold with a goal after 80 seconds, but Forbes immediately began to justify his £12,000 transfer fee. His equaliser in the eighth minute delighted his new supporters and his dance back to the centre won him a place in their hearts. It was a tremendous start for a player who had once turned his back on football in favour of ice hockey. Whittaker had sent Macaulay to persuade him come to Highbury when Forbes was in hospital recovering from appendicitis.

Wolves led again but with Denis Compton in irrepressible form in the second half Arsenal bounced back to win 5–2. A week later at Goodison Park the cricketing footballer did even better, scoring his first two post-war League goals in a 2-0 triumph over Everton.

UNPREDICTABLE GUNNERS

After only three defeats in 32 games, it came as a surprise that two more followed in the next three matches. The first came at Highbury where Chelsea chalked up a 2–0 victory. John Harris did a magnificent job containing Rooke and Chelsea carried enough venom in their attack to strike through Bobby Campbell and Roy Bentley. The other loss was sustained at Blackpool, where two goals from Stan Mortensen took him to the top of the First Division scorers list, with one more than the 27 of Rooke.

A week earlier fate had not been kind to Bob Anderson, whose misfortune it was to make his League debut in the Middlesbrough goal against Arsenal at Highbury. Smarting from the home defeat by Chelsea, Arsenal confronted the untried keeper in a mean mood. Among the seven goals that flashed past Anderson were two more from Denis Compton, and a hat-trick from Rooke, which was completed when he headed a tentative clearance from the goalkeeper straight back past him. So one-sided was the match that newspaper

reports of the time make reference to several thousand supporters leaving at half time. Poor Bob Anderson never played again in the First Division.

WHITTAKER'S CHAMPS

With fewer and fewer fixtures left available for the chasing pack to close on their prey, Arsenal moved another step nearer to safety by completing the Double over Blackburn Rovers at Highbury, Logie's sixth goal of the season and Rooke's 29th providing a margin of sufficient comfort; on 10 April Arsenal took the field at Huddersfield nine points clear with just five matches left. A win at Leeds Road would see Whittaker's men breasting the tape. The conclusion to the season, however, was not so decisive.

A goal from Don Roper brought only one point, and the players had to bath and change so quickly to catch the London train that they could not discover the day's other results. It was Denis Compton who broke the glad tidings. At Doncaster he ran for a paper which reported defeats for Manchester United, Burnley and Derby County. Arsenal were Champions, and had led from start to finish. George Male, the last of the great pre-war side, played at Huddersfield, and as ever turned in a highly polished performance.

Inevitably anticlimax followed, with Derby winning at Highbury the following Saturday, and two successive goalless draws at Portsmouth and Manchester City. There was, however, a celebration on 1 May though only 35,000, the smallest home gate of the season, were there to see it. Yorkshire-born Lionel Smith was given his League baptism at centre-half, but it was the attack which made the headlines. Arsenal ripped into Grimsby to the tune of 8–0, and four goals for Rooke confirmed him, with 33, as the Football League's leading scorer – and this at the age of 36!

George Swindin had conceded only 32 goals in the full League programme and added a second Championship medal to that gained in 1938. Rooke was the only other ever-present player, though Macaulay, Mercer and Roper missed just two matches and Logie and Laurie Scott three. Les Compton collected a League winners' medal to go with his memento of cricket Championship success the previous September (a rare double). So too did brother Denis, though he had to wait until October to receive his because of doubts as to whether his 14 appearances were sufficient qualification .

THE RETREATING DEFENCE

Undoubtedly the consistency of the big-hearted Rooke proved to be a marvellous attribute throughout the season, but much of Arsenal's success came from the reliability of their defensive method. Joe Mercer labelled it as the 'retreating' defence. The prevailing style of the day was to try to win the ball in midfield with an attempted tackle on the opponent in possession. If that tackle was lost then there was little sophisticated

Above: George Male retired as a player in 1948. His very last first-class game was a perfect ending to a great career; it was on 1 May 1948 at home to Grimsby and Arsenal won 8-0, confirming their status as League Champions. Although Male played two more games on tour that summer, the Grimsby match was the last formal appearance of any of the players from the Chapman era. Like many of his colleagues, Male then went onto the coaching staff and became a tough task-master.

Below: The cover of the official Arsenal yearbook for the 1948–49 season.

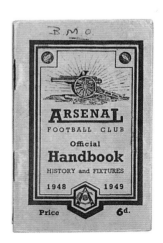

Above: 1950 FA Cup Final souvenir edition of the Sporting Mirror, published the day before the match.

covering. Mercer, with Macaulay as a shrewd ally, preferred Arsenal to leave the ball with the opposition and back off, packing the centre of the defence. Arsenal's captain had noted the success of such manoeuvres in basketball during the war, when he'd played service games with Americans. The crowd did not always like the tactic, newspaper comment denounced it as negative, but most of the First Division, could not fathom out a solution. The seven-point margin at the end of the season was clear testimony to Arsenal's worth as Champions.

The players presented Tom Whittaker with a silver cigarette box inscribed 'To Tom/In Appreciation/From The Boys'. The manager, however, was already aware that the side had not been built to last. Before the end of May 1948 he had acquired the potential of Doug Lishman, a regular scorer for Walsall in the Third Division South. Nevertheless, the 1948–49 season began with the air still full of anticlimax. It took a run of wins in the autumn to lift the club from the bottom half of the table to fifth place, where Arsenal stayed. Derby County again proved to be a bogey team for the Gunners, taking three of the four League points and knocking Whittaker's side out of the FA Cup at the Baseball Ground in the fourth round.

One match did stand out, an extravagant 4–3 victory in the Charity Shield against the Cup holders Manchester United at Highbury. Incredibly Arsenal led 3–0 after just five minutes – Jones, Lewis and Rooke – but United's resolve stood the test. Lewis scored again for Arsenal, a splendid solo goal, but the destiny of the Charity Shield was not finally settled until the last blast of the referee's whistle.

ROOK JOINS PALACE

Rooke's magnificent contribution to the history of Arsenal Football Club ended in June 1949. His 68 goals in 88 First Division games were ample evidence of his contribution. At 37 he refused to contemplate retirement, and moved as player-manager to Crystal Palace, his pre-war club, where he paid his way in goals for two more seasons. A man of iron who never flinched from the physical contact of those who tried to stop him, he left Highbury with the satisfaction of having more than answered the call of George Allison: 'Ronnie, we're in trouble. We've got to get goals, by hook or by Rooke.'

The other half of the duo who turned the tide at Highbury in 1946 remained at the club. Joe Mercer passed his 35th birthday during pre-season training prior to the 1949–50 season, and if one target drove him to continue playing it was a search for the honour which had eluded him, an FA Cup winners' medal. Mercer had been a young reserve at Everton when they had won the most romantic of the game's trophies in 1933. The following day a kindly Albert Geldard, who had played in that final, was cleaning his boots beside Mercer at Goodison Park and offered the youthful Mercer a piece of Wembley turf. 'No thanks, I'll get some myself one day,' was the confident reply. It seemed that those words would haunt him.

Four defeats in the opening five matches of the season may well have concentrated the players' minds on the FA Cup; the only win during that dismal start had come at Chelsea where Peter Goring scored on his debut and Swindin captained the side in the absence of Mercer and Les Compton. Brother Denis had ended speculation that he had played his last for Arsenal by signing for the new season on the eve of the third Test against New Zealand, thus becoming one of 54 professionals on the staff.

THE WEMBLEY TRAIL

League performances improved sufficiently to achieve a respectable sixth place at the end of the season but it was the Cup which cheered all at Highbury. The run began against Sheffield Wednesday on 7 January 1950.

The Yorkshiremen were in-form opponents, unbeaten for three months. Their teamwork almost came to their rescue despite losing right back Vince Kenny, injured in the tie. Reg Lewis finally made the breakthrough with 13 seconds on the referee's watch. The crowd was 10,000 under capacity because publicity suggesting a huge attendance had deterred many from what they believed would be a wasted journey.

The signs remained good in the draw for the fourth round, another home game against Swansea Town, who were labouring in the lower half of the Second Division. On a frosty pitch the underdogs performed gallantly while Arsenal again looked anything but potential winners of the competition. The decisive goal in a fortunate 2–1 win came ironically from a Welshman. Keane handled and Walley Barnes slotted the penalty past the left hand of goalkeeper Jack Parry.

George Swindin, the dry Yorkshireman who had been signed from Bradford City in 1936, had added the role of prophet to his more usual occupation of goalkeeper. Before each round so far he had foretold that Arsenal would be given a home tie. Again his words rang true when Burnley came out of the hat to visit Highbury in round five. In a small way the visitors had contributed to the Cup aspirations of the team they now faced, because on the opening day of the season it had been Burnley who had beaten Arsenal in the capital and thus set the Highbury League campaign off on a flat note.

The lure of the Cup, not for the first or last time, produced an indulgence in preparation. There was no seaside training in the traditional manner; instead the Arsenal squad were treated to sessions under sunray equipment to tone them up. Goals from Lewis and Denis Compton did the trick, though Mercer got away with handball in his own goalmouth.

Swindin forecast another home draw with the added prediction that Leeds United would be the opposition. Incredibly it came true, and it looked as though, in football parlance, Arsenal's 'name was on the FA Cup'. Leeds also languished in the Second Division, but their reaction to a first Cup tie at Highbury produced a creditable display. Lewis, who was to finish behind Goring in the League charts, added to

his catalogue of significant Cup goals by darting between two defenders to score. Arsenal were into the semi-finals and they had not been forced to leave Highbury to get there.

SEMI-FINAL FIGHTBACK

A semi-final with Chelsea meant that they still did not have to leave north London, and the saga of the tie remains as memorable as the final itself. At White Hart Lane Chelsea brought back the former England international Len Goulden; at 37 he had been out of favour for six months. When Chelsea sprinted into a 2–0 lead after 25 minutes, both goals from Bentley, Goulden must have been dreaming of a fairy tale visit to Wembley. Arsenal had other ideas, although it needed an outright stroke of good fortune to make sure those ideas were put into effect.

Outside right Freddie Cox knew White Hart Lane well; he had been signed from Spurs in September 1949 in an attempt to halt the slide at the start of the season. The best years of his footballing life had been sacrificed in wartime when he had flown Dakotas in Transport Command.

In the dying seconds of the first half Cox struck a corner with the outside of his foot. The ball veered in towards the Chelsea goal and was over the line before Harry Medhurst, the goalkeeper, made a vain attempt to keep it out. Cox, who died in 1973 after a career in League management, never claimed any deliberate intent, but Arsenal gratefully accepted the touch of luck, and came out for the second half in an even more determined vein.

A FAMILY AFFAIR

Yet with a quarter-of-an-hour remaining they were still trailing. Another corner, this time from the left wing, came to the rescue. Again the goal had a story behind it. As Denis Compton prepared to take the flag kick he waved forward brother Leslie. Joe Mercer countered by telling the centre-half to stay back, but blood being thicker than water and the need for an equaliser pressing, Compton the elder ignored his captain's instructions. The fraternal pair emphatically won the argument when Denis' corner found the forehead of Les and the ball sped into the Chelsea net. On balance of play Arsenal had been fortunate to earn a replay, but this had been Chelsea's chance and it had gone.

Arsenal's form was much improved in the replay, which also took place at Tottenham, the following Wednesday. George Swindin's ability to predict the future passed, it seemed, to Eileen, the wife of Freddie Cox. On the Tuesday night she dreamed that her husband would score the goal that took Arsenal to Wembley. And so he did, but not until the 14th minute of extra time, with his weaker left foot.

LIVERPOOL IN THE FINAL

The journey to the Empire Stadium, therefore, became the longest Arsenal had had to make in the entire Cup run. By coincidence Liverpool had reached the final without having to leave Lancashire, beating rivals Everton at Maine Road, Manchester in the semi-final. Bob Paisley, later to become a legendary Liverpool manager, had scored the vital goal against Everton, but he was left out of the team for the final.

Below: The first of Reg Lewis' two goals for Arsenal in the 1950 FA Cup final. Both were sharp breaks which left Liverpool keeper Cyril Sidlow with little chance. It had been a good Cup year for Arsenal; they were drawn at home throughout and played both semis against Chelsea at White Hart Lane, and thus never left London.

Most of the country's neutrals hoped that Joe Mercer, one of the game's best-loved characters, would at last complete his collection of medals. Yet unwittingly Arsenal's captain found himself in the midst of what could have been an embarrassing situation. He had continued to train in the north-west of England – with Liverpool! Understandably he was asked not to join the Liverpool first team at Anfield for fear that he would find out too much about their Wembley battle-plan. He was not banned from the ground, but his access was restricted to afternoon sessions.

Liverpool were managed by George Kay, West Ham's captain in the first Wembley final in 1923. Kay had nurtured a team of whom the majority had come through the ranks, notably the Scottish international forward Billy Liddell. Liddell, reckoned the Arsenal players, was the most likely barrier to their winning the Cup. Moreover, Liverpool held an important psychological advantage. They had won both of that season's League meetings with Arsenal, 2–1 at Highbury in September, 2–0 at Anfield on New Year's Eve.

On the eve of the final itself Mercer was hailed Footballer of the Year by the Football Writers' Association. Tom Whittaker had already decided upon his team. Lishman, McPherson, Macaulay and Roper had their merits considered but were passed over; Goring kept his place, the Wembley setting being a perfect ending to his first season at senior level.

Rain fell heavily on 29 April 1950. Wembley was bursting at the seams, although the ticket allocation for each of the two clubs ran to only 11,500 (4,500 seats, 7,000 standing) of the 100,000 capacity stadium.

Below: The victorious 1950 FA Cup squad. From left to right: Reg Lewis, Peter Goring, Freddie Cox, Denis Compton (partly hidden), Walley Barnes, George Swindin, Joe Mercer (with the Cup), Laurie Scott, Alex Forbes, Leslie Compton and Jimmy Logie.

CLASHING REDS

Both teams had to change from their usual red shirts; Liverpool opted for white with black shorts, Arsenal took the field in shirts of old gold with white shorts. Two pre-match decisions helped turn the tide of the battle towards the north London club. Forbes had been given the task of subduing the threat of Liddell, and after some early alarms the forceful wing half, who had been recalled by Scotland two weeks before the final, coped splendidly.

An even more significant decision had been to keep faith with the 30-year-old Reg Lewis. It had not been taken lightly. Lewis undoubtedly scored goals, but at times he could look lazy and lethargic. His skill had not been in question from the moment he had begun his League career with a debut goal against Everton on New Year's Day 1938. Yet Whittaker often dropped him, and Mercer's voice, among others, was heard in defence of Lewis before his place was finally confirmed.

At Wembley he became the match-winner, collecting both goals, coincidentally, at identical times in each half. The first, after 17 minutes, came when Goring moved away, distracting the attention of Liverpool defenders. Jimmy Logie had the ball at his feet; the tiny inside right, who weighed little more than nine stones but was a giant in this match, immediately slotted a pass through a square defence for Lewis to chase.

It was a knife in the heart of Liverpool. Lewis beat their Welsh international goalkeeper Cyril Sidlow. Then, 17 minutes into the second half it was Lewis again, this time assisted by Cox, and from then on there was little doubt that Joe Mercer would at last lay his hands on the FA Cup.

The medal to go with it almost escaped Arsenal's captain. His Majesty King George VI presented the trophy, and the personal memento came from the Queen. Joe was just about to go down the Royal Box steps with a loser's medal when the error was spotted.

COMPTON JNR RETIRES

One Arsenal player did retire a few days later but it was not, in fact, Joe Mercer. Approaching his 32nd birthday Denis Compton realised that the combination of international cricket, top-flight football and a knee that was protesting more and more about wear and tear was no longer viable for him. He had already decided before the Cup final to abdicate from football, a fact used to Arsenal's advantage by Tom Whittaker at half time at Wembley.

Compton's first-half contribution had been unmemorable. 'Now,' said the manager, weighing each word carefully, 'you've got 45 minutes left of your soccer career. I want you to go out there and give it every ounce you possibly can.' Compton rarely lacked confidence, but this time he needed fortification. A glass of whisky was produced, and Arsenal's outside left played a full part in a strong second-half performance. Nor was it quite his football finale. The following week Portsmouth came to Highbury needing

points to win the Championship. Compton gave a brilliant performance; Goring scored twice in a 2–0 victory, though Pompey eventually took the title.

While Denis Compton, after knee surgery, turned his thoughts towards representing England's cricketers in Australia, in 1950–51 football's international selectors sought the services of Les Compton. On 15 November 1950 at the age of 38 Arsenal's veteran centre-half represented his country for the first time, England's oldest international debutant. England beat Wales 4–2 at Sunderland with Lionel Smith also winning his first cap and Ray Daniel, Compton's club deputy, called up for Wales. Compton won his second, and final, cap a week later when Yugoslavia forced a 2–2 draw at Highbury.

Arsenal led the First Division at the half-way mark of the 1950–51 season, but two injuries on Christmas Day against Stoke City turned a Championship sprint into a stumble.

Lishman broke a leg, thus robbing the team of its leading scorer; four of his 16 goals had come in one match against Sunderland in November. Swindin was also hurt, allowing Ted Platt an extended run in goal. Although Whittaker turned again to Lewis – who typically responded with a sequence of four games in each of which he scored twice – and for the first time to the raw Holton, the team unit did not function as smoothly in the second half of the season. Arsenal finished fifth in the League, which was won for the first time by Spurs, and lost their grip on the FA Cup to a Stan Pearson goal for Manchester United in the fifth round.

GUNNERS IN DOUBLE CHANCE

Arsenal's Double of 1970–71 is of course well documented in this history and elsewhere. Less easily recalled are the events of the 1951–52 season when the Gunners stood three games

Below: The crowd rather than the players is the focus of this unusual shot taken on 16 September 1950. Peter Goring completes his hat-trick in a 6–2 thrashing of traditional rivals Huddersfield. Jimmy Logie and Doug Lishman got the others.

away from what would have been the first Double of modern times. Had those three games been won instead of lost the season would have been legendary. Instead it was a bold attempt which foundered in the final analysis on injuries.

Swindin had shrugged aside his injury from the previous year and played a full season in goal, Barnes was absent for just one League game though the fallibility of his knee became a major factor in the last chapter of the story. Mercer, Forbes, Logie and Roper added further threads of continuity. By now Daniel had superseded Compton at centre-half, and the goalscoring department lay at the feet and heads of Lishman and Holton. The cricket connection had not entirely disappeared with the Comptons; Arthur Milton, the Gloucestershire batsman, operated on the right wing on a semi-regular basis.

Progress in the First Division was steady, always in the challenging bunch of clubs, occasionally on top. Lishman enjoyed a golden spell of hat-tricks in three consecutive home games; Fulham, West Bromwich Albion and Bolton were his victims. The League matches were punctuated by occasional prestige friendlies, with floodlights installed at the ground, treating the Highbury faithful to the new experience of watching evening matches. The ground also enclosed the biggest post-war attendance at the club; the visit of Spurs luring 72,164 to see whether the Champions could be toppled.

LEWIS AND COX CLINCH ENSURE CUP PROGRESS

The FA Cup run began at Carrow Road, where Norwich City could not rise up above their Third Division South status. Barnsley in round four provided no more testing opposition;

Lewis, now a weapon to be used only occasionally, added to his store of Cup-tie memories with a first-half hat-trick. Lishman claimed the other in another confident triumph.

On paper the fifth round draw brought a more testing problem. Leyton Orient, who were now in the lower reaches of the Third Division South, were on the giant-killing trail. The homely East London club had already beaten two high-flying Second Division outfits, Birmingham City and Everton, both of whom were slain on their own territory. Now the 'O's' were at home and the prospect of a meeting with Arsenal attracted massive interest.

Whittaker's side, however, did not capitulate, although Lewis was injured scoring the first goal and limped through over half the match; averaging a goal a game in the League at the time plus his four in the FA Cup, he might have forced his way into another Cup final team until this misfortune. Arsenal, however, coped easily with the handicap at Brisbane Road, and Lishman hit two more to kill off the giant-killers.

Arsenal had to travel again in the sixth round, again not very far and the draw against Second Division Luton Town meant that the top clubs were again avoided. After only nine minutes Luton became the first side to put the ball past Swindin in the 1952 FA Cup. Moore headed in a corner taken by Mitchell. Without Jimmy Logie to orchestrate their midfield play, Arsenal were still trailing at the interval, during which Whittaker reshuffled his forward line.

Freddie Cox was switched to the left wing and lived up to his billing as a Cup-tie specialist. Arthur Milton came back to his sparkling best. Cox equalised from a very acute angle and with Luton handicapped by injuries to Davies and Owen the match tilted away from them. Three goals inside five minutes completed the scoring with Cox cutting in again to find the back of the net from an oblique position and then crossing for Milton to collect Arsenal's third. A penalty from Mitchell was Luton's last reply in a riveting match.

The match certainly produced a case of déjà vu for Cox. Again Chelsea provided the opposition. Again White Hart Lane was the venue. And again the first match finished in a draw. In truth it rarely held the imagination of the crowd; no corners in the first hour during which Arsenal scored in the 35th minute. Almost inevitably Cox was the marksman. Chelsea equalised 27 minutes from the final whistle through Billy Gray.

Two days later the teams reassembled at Tottenham, and, as two years earlier, Arsenal won through, this time 3–0. The Cox-Logie combination eased the tensions by conjuring an early goal, and Cox broke the back of the Chelsea resistance with his second 20 minutes from time. Roper, operating at outside left, took his only corner in either game and the diminutive Cox found space to head home. Lishman made sure of Arsenal's return to Wembley with another header.

The final itself offered a showdown between the competition's two most recent superpowers, the holders Newcastle United against the winners from the previous

Below: Leslie, the older of the Compton brothers, carried on playing football for longer than Denis as he did not have the same cricketing demands. He finally gave up professional football a few months before his 40th birthday.

year. It was a match which had statisticians trotting out comparisons with 20 years earlier when Arsenal had been beaten in the 'over-the-line' match.

INJURIES MOUNT

In 1932 Arsenal had also sought the Double, only to fall between the two stools of cliché. They also had to meet Newcastle at home in the League between the semi-final and final just as they had to do in the fixture-congested April of 1952 (drawing 1–1, with Milton – who did not play at Wembley – Arsenal's goalscorer). By then injuries were beginning to damage hopes of bringing the League title back to Highbury.

On Good Friday, 11 April, Ray Daniel broke his arm in a goalless draw at Blackpool. The next day Lionel Smith wrenched a knee at Bolton; Arsenal lost 2–1. Leslie Compton stepped out of the shadows to help out in the crisis.

Three home games brought a fine return of five points, but at the cost of wearying key players. Mercer felt the strain so keenly that Whittaker persuaded his captain to stand down from the crucial visit to West Bromwich Albion, the clubs eighth game in 17 days. Understandably the flesh was weak, even if the spirit was strong and Albion won 3–1 .

That defeat effectively ended the League challenge; only a seven-goal victory at Old Trafford on the Saturday before the Cup final would take the title from Manchester United. Reg Lewis turned out for his last senior appearance and Lionel Smith proved his recovery from injury, but United celebrated their title with a runaway 6–1 victory. Nor did Arsenal escape unscathed physically. Arthur Shaw, who might have pipped Daniel for the centre-half spot in the Wembley line-up, suffered a fractured wrist, a similar injury to his rival. Nevertheless, had the Gunners been victorious in those two last games, against West Bromwich and United, they would have been Champions.

AN AGONISING DEFEAT

Newcastle United's passage over the run-in to the final had been as smooth as Arsenal's had been choppy. Moreover, the holders were able to relax at the seaside while Tom Whittaker and his medical team were checking the casualty list at Highbury. Daniel had not played for more than three weeks, but with a plaster supervised by the manager so that it would pass the scrutiny of the referee the Welsh international was chosen for the fray. So too was Logie, who had been hospitalised earlier in the week leading up to the final.

Lishman, the ex-commando, who had just missed selection two years earlier, tried quickly to make up for lost time with a hooked shot that passed just wide of Newcastle's goal. Arsenal settled quickly and were looking good when fate took a hand. Barnes twisted a knee so painfully that Arsenal faced the prospect of surviving for the last 55 minutes with ten men.

Roper, strong and robust, was immediately switched from outside left to right-back; his heroic display typified Arsenal's tenacity. Smith had to clear a Milburn effort off the line, but the depleted team did not just settle for survival. Cox forayed infield and Forbes added to his usual labour with many attempts to support the undermanned attack. Then 11 minutes from the end Lishman rose to meet a corner from Cox but the ball skimmed the bar. Five minutes later the gallant stand ended. Of the ten Arsenal players remaining Holton and Roper both went down, in urgent need of the trainer's

Above and below: The 1952 Cup Final was not to see a repeat of the success of two years earlier. (Above) Swindin and Smith combine to rob Jackie Milburn of a chance, but (below) Chilean George Robledo beats Lionel Smith to a Mitchell centre and squeezes the ball in off the post to give Newcastle a 1–0 victory.

attention. Daniel's arm was aching; Logie's damaged thigh could no longer be concealed. Mercer yelled at referee Arthur Ellis to stop the game to allow treatment for Holton and Roper. The ball was still in play and Mitchell was allowed to cross into the middle where George Robledo climbed above Smith to send in a header which dropped in off the post. Roper, still on the ground, could only sit and watch it happen. There was still time for Forbes to hit the bar, but Newcastle became the first club in the 20th century to win the FA Cup in consecutive seasons.

Mercer made sure his team left the pitch together to tremendous appreciation from the crowd. Later that night he addressed the guests at the traditional post match banquet, speaking with great emotion: 'I thought football's greatest honour was to captain England. I was wrong. It was to captain Arsenal today.'

A RECORD SEVENTH TITLE

Perhaps some of the resolution forged over those 90 minutes at Wembley brought the players even closer. Certainly those who represented the club in the following 1952–53 First Division campaign proved to be too good for their rivals. The title came to Highbury for the seventh time, setting a new record, but it was to be mighty close.

Walley Barnes was missing for the entire season, though Joe Wade and John Chenhall made light of his absence. Others made meaningful contributions, like Don Oakes, who marked his League debut on the first day of the season at Aston Villa by scoring the winning goal. A tall inside forward from Rhyl, Oakes had waited almost seven years for his chance in the first team. He kept his place for the following match but suffered injury helping in another winning cause at home to Manchester United. He did not reappear at first-team level until the last nine matches of the 1954–55 season. With a regular place beckoning, he contracted a serious illness on tour in the summer of 1955. After protracted treatment, he had to accept medical advice to retire.

With two victories in those first two matches, Arsenal failed to build on such an optimistic start, winning only once in their next six outings. Sunderland and Charlton both plundered two points on visits to Highbury. Only the return of Milton from cricket with Gloucestershire inspired a victory in this dismal spell; the cricketer-winger struck the bigger ball cleanly with one of the goals in a 3–1 home success against Portsmouth.

In November the spotlight turned on Jimmy Logie. His impish genius was recognised at last by Scotland's selectors. The Alex James of his generation, Logie won his first and only cap against Austria at Hampden Park. In the same month as his 33rd birthday the honour came too late for him to make a significant impact for his country. Ten days after Logie's Scotland international appearance, Arsenal put on a display of their own from the very top drawer, demolishing Liverpool

5–1 away at Anfield. Ben Marden struck twice in his first senior match of the season and Cliff Holton weighed in with a hat-trick.

FESTIVE GOAL FEAST

The last match of 1952 deserves special mention, not just because it brought the bonus of an away victory. On Christmas morning the Arsenal players were again a long way from their families, at Burnden Park, Bolton. The first half was above average but not exceptional. Willie Moir sent the home side into the lead but by the interval Milton had equalised and Holton, whose power of shot was formidable, had edged the visitors ahead.

In the second half those who might have had their minds on their Christmas dinners were first able to gorge themselves on a glut of goals. Within the opening five minutes of the half Logie and Roper had increased the Arsenal advantage to 4–1. Then it was Moir making it 4–2 before a Daniel penalty restored the lead to three goals. The action of the final eight minutes was even more frantic. Bolton's defensive generosities extended to the conceding of another goal to Holton, before Nat Lofthouse struck twice for Bolton. Believe it or not there was still time for Bolton to earn a penalty, which could have made it 6–5, but Kelsey, facing a spot kick for the first time in League football, saved Langton's attempt.

TITLE RACE GOES TO THE WIRE

1952–53 was not to be one of the great Championship seasons – it is rightly more remembered for the FA Cup final. Arsenal eventually finished with 54 points, one of the lowest ever for a title-winning team. The excitement was in the finish with Arsenal and Preston neck-and-neck and the Gunners due to travel to Deepdale on the last Saturday of the season.

The points situation meant the Gunners' title ambitions could survive a defeat but not a heavy beating. Preston won 2–0 with goals from their two most revered forwards, Tom Finney and Charlie Wayman. Both clubs now had one match left but not on the same day.

Preston were first into action on the Wednesday before the Cup final. Away to bottom club Derby County, they won 1–0 and left for an end of season tour not knowing their fate. Arsenal's finale was staged before a packed Highbury two days later on Cup final eve; only a win would be enough. Burnley, the opposition, were in the top six of the table. It took only three minutes for the drama to take its first twist.

Roy Stephenson, Burnley's outside right, drove in a crisp, low, centre. Mercer tried to cut out the danger. He succeeded only in diverting the ball into his own net. At that moment the title looked bound for Deepdale.

It was no time for patience. Arsenal threw caution to the winds in a display of forceful attacking football which brought goals for Forbes, in one of his most passionate performances

for the club, Lishman and Logie. Burnley then cut the deficit in the second half, and the all-out policy gave way to the tactics of entrenchment, and what they had Arsenal held. When the sums were done Tom Whittaker's team had won the League on goal average – by less than one-tenth of a goal.

NIGHTMARE ON WEARSIDE

The summer of 1953 was to bring the shock of the sad and premature death, at 51, of Alex James from cancer. It was perhaps a portent – Arsenal's attempt to defend their title began dreadfully. Six of the first eight matches were lost, the other two drawn. The club's predicament reached a crisis point at Sunderland in what turned out to be Swindin's last League match. Lishman had given Arsenal the boost of a goal before the veteran goalkeeper was hurt in a collision with Trevor Ford, with Sunderland by then leading 2–1. Swindin was, in all, beaten seven times.

Barnes, who had not played since his Wembley injury, battled back to sufficient fitness to earn a recall though his problems were to persist. To strengthen his hand in attack Tom Whittaker sought a short-term solution. Tommy Lawton, the nation's pin-up centre-forward throughout the 1940s, was struggling as player-manager of Brentford. At 34 his best years were behind him, but Ronnie Rooke had more than risen to the challenge of a late call to Highbury. Could Lawton do the same? The deal was done in secret and Lawton was unveiled to the Highbury public on 19 September 1953, against Manchester City. He could not, however, in his two-and-a-half seasons with the club sustain a regular place; it was almost seven months before his first League goal against Aston Villa. Yet Lawton loved the glamour attached to being an Arsenal player and recalled that his biggest mistake in football had been in not signing for the club when George Allison wanted him in 1936 (he chose Everton instead).

THE WILDERNESS YEARS

The years that followed were a bleak period for the club that had, by 1953, become the most celebrated in the world. They were to win nothing again until the Fairs Cup all of 17 years later. And between 1954 and 1969 they finished only once above fifth. Between 1930 and 1953 they had finished worse than fifth on only three occasions. Cup performances were, if anything, even worse – including terrible defeats by such lowly sides as Northampton (3–1) in 1958, Rotherham (2–0 after two draws) in 1960, and Peterborough (2–1) in 1965. Tom Whittaker was not there to witness the decline.

HIGHBURY MOURNS DEATH OF WHITTAKER

Tom Whittaker died on Wednesday 24 October 1956 in University College Hospital, London, where he had undergone an operation the previous Easter. Like his great mentor

Herbert Chapman he passed away in harness, which is just as he would have wished. Both had died tragically young (neither reached 60); both in differing ways had been the very heartbeat of Highbury. Tom Whittaker perhaps had a premonition that he would not outlive his job, once admitting: 'Someone has to drive himself too hard for Arsenal. Herbert Chapman worked himself to death for the club, and if it is to be my fate I am happy to accept it.'

MERCER'S TRIBUTE

Joe Mercer had been lured back into football as manager of Sheffield United; his moving tribute to the guardian angel who had extended his career at Highbury to such glorious heights appeared in *The Daily Express*:

'Meeting Tom Whittaker was the best thing that ever happened to me; he was the greatest man I ever met.

As the news of his death goes around the world thousands, perhaps millions, of people will say the same thing. And how so very deeply they will mean it. Arsenal was his kingdom but in every soccer-playing country in the world he was acknowledged as a prince of the game. There never has been a greater man in football. It is a game full of hard knocks. But Tom never hit anybody. He never shirked making a hard decision, like sacking or dropping a player, or any of the other things that can hurt deeply. But the way Tom did it, it never did. Tom made bad sportsmen into good sportsmen. He made good footballers into great footballers.

Tom was responsible for none of the bad things in football. Cynics may smile and say "I wonder". But I know. I know that he never did a bad thing. All problems had only one solution: the one done with kindness.

After Newcastle beat us in the 1952 final, Tom came into the dressing-room, looking as happy as we had ever seen him. He said: "I am really proud of you chaps. You played great football. I am as proud of Arsenal today as ever I have been." Damn it, he made us feel we had won the Cup.

The last time I saw Tom was a couple of months ago. He looked very ill, but he had already started a new phase in Arsenal history. He realised the days of big buying were over. His plans only included youngsters. And every youngster who ever went to Highbury quickly learned one thing. The only thing that mattered was the club.

Tom Whittaker never thought of the chairman, a player or anyone individually when he made a decision. If it was good for the club then it was right.'

Tom Whittaker's reputation had spread way beyond the confines of English football. When Arsenal took on the role of ambassadors on expeditions around the globe, the secretary-manager was the perfect head of the delegation. In 1949, for example, the summer tour took the club to Brazil where in Sao Paulo many supporters of the local team were of Italian extraction; Italy and the rest of the football world had just been stunned by the Superga aircrash which wiped out the

Above: *Gunflash*, the magazine of the Official Arsenal Football Supporters' Club – a far cry from today's glossy magazines and independent fanzines.

Famed for his long throws he was a strapping wing half,
over six feet tall, weighing 13 stones and needing specially
constructed boots for his size 12 feet.

An even longer servant, Joe Shaw, retired. He had been
signed as a player in 1907 from Accrington Stanley, hanging
up his boots in 1923. Following a short spell with Chelsea, he
had resumed his Arsenal connection under the title of Head
Coach and Chief Representative, he was, in effect, Whittaker's
number two.

On 13 March 1957, George Allison passed away; he had
lived with indifferent health over the ten years since he
had resigned from his football career at Highbury. 'George
Arsenal', as he had been widely known, had risen from his
humble start in the club ranks as the writer of the match
programme to secretary-manager. His knowledge of the game
might never have been deep, but he was clever enough to
realise his limitations, not frightened to consult the opinions
of others. Yet as a front person for the prestigious Arsenal
organisation he had been perfect. His rapport with the media
would have been a strength in any era.

The next day another death was recorded, that of J. W.
Julian, club captain in 1890 and the first to lead a professional
side at Woolwich. He had been an enthusiastic and regular
spectator at matches at Highbury up to the time of his demise.

BOARD AND MANAGER CLASH

Jack Crayston's appointment was confirmed in December
1956. The new manager on was not blind to the shortcomings
of his team. He regularly asked the board for money to
strengthen his hand, but it was not forthcoming. Cliff Jones
was just one of a number of players he pursued, but Swansea
realised the value of their winger, who was to play 59 times
for Wales, and were determined not to sell him cheaply. When
he finally became available it was Spurs who struck the deal.

The match programme outlined the Arsenal philosophy
at the time: '... a policy not to bid for a player's transfer. We
always ask the fee required, and having been told make up
our mind whether the player is worth that fee.' Yet with
increasing pressure for success in a market which was
naturally declining after the post-war boom, the ethics of
football business were to change for ever.

Crayston strongly believed that the club did indeed
have the money to invest in the transfer market. At a
board meeting at the end of the season clearly the
frustrations became too much. 'Gentleman Jack' Crayston
resigned, severing a tie with the club that had lasted almost
25 years. He moved back to Yorkshire for a spell as secretary-
manager to Doncaster Rovers, before using his accountancy
skills in a business career. In 1985 he looked back on the
changes in football with a twinkle in his eye: 'In my time
players had short hair, wore long shorts and played in
hob-nailed boots. Now they have long hair, short shorts
and play in slippers.'

brilliant Torino team. Whittaker's sensitivity recognised
that there was a need for a tribute to the dead and before the
match, at his suggestion, the two teams and the crowd stood,
heads bowed, to the music of Ave Maria.

Yet kindness never became weakness. centre-half Bill
Dodgin returned from the 7–1 humiliation at Sunderland in
the dreadful opening to the 1953–54 season feeling that he
had let down the side and wanted to be left out of the team. He
went to see Whittaker: 'I left his office quicker than I entered
it. He told me very firmly that if there was any dropping to be
done, he would do it.'

In February 1956, Arsenal tried to lighten the load on Tom
Whittaker by appointing Leyton Orient manager Alec Stock
as his assistant. Unfortunately, Stock lasted less than two
months before returning to Orient and there was no sign of
Whittaker taking any fewer of the responsibilities.

DOUBLE APPOINTMENT

The obvious stress of the dual role of secretary-manager
persuaded the Arsenal board to split the two jobs. Bob Wall
was promoted to secretary. Jack Crayston, a member of two
League Championship teams and the 1936 FA Cup winning
side, took over as manager. Crayston had been an assistant
to Tom Whittaker, his man 'downstairs at Highbury' helping
particularly with the scouting and at times, because he had
received some training as an accountant, with book-keeping.
Crayston had also won eight England caps before the war.

Although Joe Mercer was clearly the favourite to succeed, it was an Arsenal team-mate, George Swindin, who was actually offered the job. He had brought Peterborough to national prominence with their giant-killing acts and had therefore won his spurs. He was in charge for four seasons but while Arsenal were never relegation candidates, the history of the past 30 years meant that it was trophies or nothing. When Danny Clapton was chosen for England in 1959 he was the first Arsenal player for five years to be capped – an excellent cameo of the decline on the field since the last Championship. Swindin also had to cope with the horrors of Nicholson, Blanchflower and the Tottenham Double of 1960–61.

EASTHAM WINS TEST CASE

More significant in the long run was the Eastham case. George Eastham was England's most skilful creative player. He wanted to leave Newcastle United to join Arsenal, but the Geordies would not let him go. Under the rules of the League at that time (called the 'retain and transfer' system) a player's current club could stop him moving anywhere, and no club could pay any player, from the best to the worst, more than £20 per week. Eastham challenged the system in court and, after a legal battle that began in 1960 and ended in July 1963, he won. By then he had moved to Arsenal for £47,500. Of that fee he got just £20.

George Swindin remained until March 1962 and upon his departure Arsenal broke with tradition by appointing an outsider – the first since Chapman himself had arrived nearly 40 years earlier – Billy Wright. The club's choice had won more caps than any player in the world (105) and held the then record for the most consecutive international appearances (70). He had captained Wolves to three League Championships and one FA Cup. But great players do not necessarily make great football managers. Despite the goalscoring heroics of Geoff Strong and Joe Baker (each scored 31 League and Cup goals in 1963–64) the defence was, surprisingly given Wright's pedigree, the weakness. The same year they conceded 82 goals, worse than one relegated club.

Geoff Strong was to move to Liverpool and, despite the arrival of a then rather raw Frank McLintock from Leicester, the terrible 2–1 defeat to Third Division Peterborough in 1965 was to be the symbol of the period.

WRIGHT PROVES 'TOO NICE'

Season 1965–66 was the last in first-class football for the kindly Billy Wright, whose playing days had been almost devoid of failure, but whose management days were short on success. Maybe the writing was on the wall the previous summer with the change in the club colours to all-red shirts, with the only white being on the collar and the cuffs; white shorts with red seams and red stockings, seen as a return to the style of Nottingham Forest. The change was soon reversed.

As most of football awaited the 1966 World Cup with an increasing sense of anticipation, Arsenal's and Wright's fortunes reached unprecedented depths. A home fixture against Leeds United was misguidedly rearranged for Thursday 5 May 1966, the same evening Liverpool contested the European Cup Winners Cup final against Borussia Dortmund at Hampden Park, shown live on television. That attraction, combined with Arsenal's dismal form, resulted in the Gunners attracting what was then the lowest First Division crowd since the First World War – 4,544 against the second placed club in the League! And they lost 3–0. Only a win over Leicester two days later elevated the club to 14th, their lowest place since 1930.

At the end of the season Billy Wright took a holiday; apart from his responsibilities at Highbury he had also been contracted by BBC Television to take part in their coverage of the World Cup finals. While he was away the board decided that recent results 'justified a change in management'. Denis Hill-Wood broke the news to him on his return. Outwardly it was accepted with the gentlemanly nature with which Wright, the player, had wooed the hearts of the football world. Inwardly it hurt bitterly: 'It was heartbreaking for me. Maybe I was too nice, but that is the way I am. But I wanted so much to make Arsenal great again, and I did feel that with the young players we were moving along the right lines.'

Left: Billy Wright, then England and the world's most capped player, took over the manager's chair from George Swindin (who had held it for four years) in 1962. He, in his turn, was to last another four, by which time directors and fans were becoming restless as the club had not finished higher than seventh since the turn of the 1960s.

CHAPTER 7

ARSENAL'S DOUBLE

1966–1972

Many decisions were involved in the construction of the Double-winning side, which took Arsenal Football Club to the highest of all domestic achievements. Yet surely the most inspired was taken by the board of directors in the summer of 1966. While the media indulged in fruitless speculation about which of the game's big names would be appointed to succeed Billy Wright, the Highbury decision-makers were recognising a quality of leadership within the fold.

Bertie Mee was offered the manager's job at a private meeting with Denis Hill-Wood. The choice of the physiotherapist caught Fleet Street off their guard. It had the majority of the playing staff believing that it could only be a stop-gap appointment, and even surprised the recipient of the offer: 'It was a surprise, but a very pleasant one. I had not planned to become a football club manager. I was very happy in the career of my special interest, and I was enjoying a great deal of job satisfaction from it. But I was used to positions of responsibility. I had run organisations of various types. So my response was that if that's what the board would like, then I would give it a go.'

MEE APPOINTED MANAGER

With two successful careers already behind him – in the military and medical spheres – Bertie Mee was the right man at the right time for a club which needed an urgent injection of authority. Yet though Bertie Mee was by no means a household name, he was very well known inside the game. He had been running the treatment of injuries courses for the Football Association for almost 20 years. At establishments such as Lilleshall he had lectured to all of football's leading managers and coaches, and he had their respect. Such experiences had given the new Arsenal manager a sound working knowledge of the highways and byways of the Football League.

Mee also brought to the job an insight into what was wrong inside the dressing room. After all, it had been his area of operation for six years. The players knew that he stood for no nonsense in the discipline of recovering fitness. Most significant of all, he was not overawed at what he had been chosen to do, but with a characteristic and sensible touch of caution he did make sure that an exit was available if required: 'I asked the chairman if I could initially take the job for 12 months, and that if it didn't work out, I could revert to my previous position. He was most agreeable. So I began by

approaching the task in terms of management, from purely a management point of view. It was my belief that there was nothing radically wrong, but the club had to be more professional from all angles. We needed a general tightening-up. The players were a good crowd, but I felt that they could be more dedicated to the job, and certainly could care more about Arsenal. The danger was that mediocrity was being perpetuated.'

With Les Shannon also leaving the club following the change of management, Mee required a new coach, and successfully sought the services of an old friend, Dave Sexton, then with Fulham. Frank McLintock, in his 1969 autobiography *That's The Way The Ball Bounces*, summed up the players' response to Sexton: 'I haven't come across many people in the game who have his ability to get through to players without shouting the odds and screaming at them. I don't know what it is that Dave has, maybe it's a gift of leadership. That is perhaps simplifying his effect, all I know is that he could have persuaded us to do anything. He thinks deeply about football and pointed out things I wouldn't have dreamed of – and before he came I thought I knew most of it.

LEAGUE CUP DISAPPOINTMENT

At first, relatively little seemed to have changed. Mee's first two seasons saw the side finish 7th and 9th. Arsenal had not entered the League Cup until 1966–67 but 1968 was to see them reach their first final for 16 years. Coventry, Reading, Blackburn and Burnley were the victims on the way, with Huddersfield going down 6–3 on aggregate in the two-legged semi-final. The opponents were Leeds, then still a club without a single trophy in their history. The game was not a classic, rather a forerunner of the titanic games that we were to see between the clubs in the next five years and Terry Cooper scored the only goal.

Frank McLintock was disappointed at yet another losers' medal, but the team was gaining recognition with both Bob McNab and John Radford capped by Alf Ramsey.

The solidity that was binding Arsenal together did not always please the neutrals, but Mee had already established his first priority; his team was never likely to capitulate.

Bob Wilson was making great strides as a goalkeeper, his strength of character growing in the face of regular teasing from his team-mates about his background as a schoolteacher. He was ever-present in the 1968–69 League campaign. So too was the cold-eyed Storey and the resident chatterbox, McNab. Court, who was to be sold to Luton on the eve of the Double, missed only two matches in midfield. Simpson was emerging as a more complete central defender than either Ure or Neill. The options in midfield were increased by experimenting in that area with Graham, who was blessed with a sure touch and sharp football brain, but whose lack of explosive pace was making life up front increasingly difficult for him.

The interest in the FA Cup ended in the fifth round, but hardly in disgrace, a 1–0 defeat away to West Bromwich Albion, First Division rivals. Against a background of such consistency it is unfortunate that the season will ultimately be recalled for another Wembley defeat in the League Cup final.

Unlike the Leeds experience the players could not walk off with heads held high. This time it was a shaming experience.

The two-leg semi-final with Spurs had produced more evidence of the competitive nature of Mee's team. In front of a full house of 55,000 at Highbury, Spurs were only seconds away from a goalless draw when Radford popped up with a crucial goal. Tottenham pinned their hopes of turning the tables at White Hart Lane on the mercurial Jimmy Greaves, who scored in a tough, and at times brutal, encounter, but so did Radford and Arsenal won 2–1 on aggregate.

HUMILIATED BY SWINDON

When Mee and his players learned who their opponents in the final would be, they could have been forgiven for thinking that eliminating Tottenham had been the hard part. Third Division Swindon Town had battled their way to Wembley by beating Burnley over three games.

As expected Arsenal carried the fight to Swindon from the outset, a series of attacks that in treacherous conditions took more energy to mount than to defend against. With eight of the side still touched by the after-effects of a flu virus which had caused the postponement of a League match the week before, such energy was not easily recouped. At this point in their League season Arsenal had let in just 18 goals in 30 matches. But 34 minutes into the League Cup final they allowed Swindon to take the lead with a mix-up between Ure and Wilson which presented Smart with an open goal.

Swindon kept the lead until four minutes from time. Then keeper Downsbrough, a superman on the day, ventured out of his area in an attempt to kick the ball to safety, away from

Above: The great years of 1968–72 were to see no fewer than five major Cup finals, one in each season. The memories are firmly of 1971, but three of the five were lost by tight margins. The 1968 Football League Cup final was decided by a single goal from Leeds United full-back Terry Cooper.

Opposite: Bertie Mee in August 1971, when he had been voted Manager of the Year for his achievement in managing Arsenal to the Double.

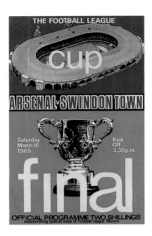

Above: In 1969 Arsenal were back at Wembley for another League Cup final (above) and this time hot favourites to defeat Third Division Swindon Town. The result was a shock 3-1 win by the underdogs. The only Arsenal response was from Bobby Gould, who left the field in tears (right) comforted by John Radford.

the on-rushing Gould. Instead, the ball rebounded off the Arsenal forward, who reacted quickly and headed it into the unguarded net. With extra time beckoning, relieved Arsenal fans believed that they now had a psychological advantage.

At pitch level Don Howe was not so sure. He wanted extra time to be abandoned by Bill Handley to spare the players the slog in the cloying mud. He recognised the weariness in his own players, aggravated by their recent illness. McLintock had cramp in both legs. McNab was also in distress. Graham had already replaced the weary Simpson.

For a team of Swindon's status it would have been forgivable if they had not seized their opportunity. It was a measure of their quality that they did. After 15 minutes of extra time, Don Rogers poked the ball home from a corner and in the second period the Swindon winger etched his trademark onto a Wembley final, running half the length of the pitch for a memorable solo goal.

Stan Harland went up the Wembley steps to collect the League Cup from Princess Margaret. McLintock – now a four-time loser – was stunned. He had not contemplated defeat this time. A good-luck telegram from Don Revie wishing that he could 'be first up the steps this time' was ironic. The Leeds United manager had forgotten that the League Cup final's formalities have the losers collecting their mementoes first.

STIRRED BY DEFEAT

Mee and Howe began the arduous task of reviving morale that had once been so high. Some 16 years later, Bob Wilson, whose pride had been aroused by the humiliation, put the desolation of defeat into perspective: 'I truly believe that the rise of the Double side stemmed from that afternoon at Wembley. We came home to headlines about the "Shame of Arsenal", and a lot of us were determined that it would never happen again. We craved success with even more intensity because of it.'

The one consolation was that fourth place in the League brought them a place in the European Fairs Cup, albeit because Swindon were denied theirs by virtue of being a Third

Division side. Arsenal's progress was convincing against Glentoran, Sporting Portugal, Rouen, Dinamo Bacau and Ajax in the semi-final. In retrospect Arsenal's 3–0 win over Ajax at Highbury looks a lot better now. Within a couple of years their opponents won a hat-trick of European Cups. One week later Arsenal were back in the Low Countries facing Anderlecht. The Belgians chose to play in their away strip in Brussels so that their fans could see the famous red and white shirts. It did not damage Anderlecht's performance – they were ahead 3–0 in the first leg with Jan Mulder scoring twice. It looked as though Frank McLintock was sure to collect his fifth losers' medal. Late in the game Kennedy, still a raw youngster, headed one back and the Gunners returned to Highbury 1–3 in arrears.

Wilson recalled: 'Even with the late goal we were downcast. It looked as though we could be foiled yet again in our efforts to bring the club a trophy. Initially Frank McLintock felt it the most keenly, and he was cursing about being in another losing final. But Frank was always impulsive. If he saw you in a suit he liked he had to get one like it straight away. If you'd been to a great restaurant he'd have to go there the next night. But just as suddenly the mood would change. In Brussels his initial despair turned straight into optimism. He came out of the bath yelling that we were going to win. He lifted everybody, and by the time we left the ground, nobody had their heads down. You could say that the second leg was won at that point.'

EUROPEAN GLORY

McLintock, by his own admission, finds specific matches hard to remember, but his attitude that night remained in his memory: 'Anderlecht were good. Mulder and van Himst were special players. But defensively they had looked vulnerable when we had been able to attack. Their centre-half looked poor in the air. I believed we could do it, and I wanted to make sure the rest of the lads did.'

The second leg of the Fairs Cup final took place at Highbury on Tuesday 28 April 1970. In the match programme Bertie Mee paid tribute to McLintock's new role at centre-half, which earlier in the month had earned him a recall by Scotland after three years out of the international limelight. The manager also wrote of the crop that was being harvested from the youth policy that had been tended by Billy Wright and himself after George Swindin had sown the seeds. George, Kennedy and Kelly were singled out for special mention.

Eddie Kelly repaid the compliment. A stunning early shot brought Anderlecht within reach. But Arsenal tore into their opponents with such frantic commitment that McLintock was asked afterward by one of the Belgians if Mee's players had taken drugs. But the stimulus on the pitch was not artificial; it was the desire for achievement. In the dressing room the talk about Arsenal's past glories had become more than wearisome.

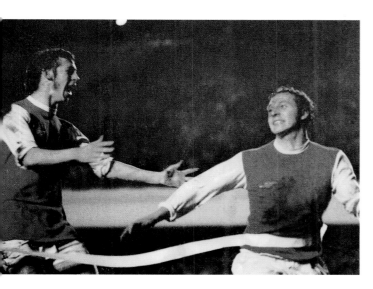

The weakness in the air spotted by McLintock was exploited in the second half, and the muscular Radford found space to head Arsenal's second. Thanks to Kennedy's 'away' goal, Arsenal now led, but were in no position to relax as Mulder hit a post. Sammels, who was to lose his regular place during the Double year, ensured a deserved place on the roll of honour by adding a third. Had Anderlecht managed just one in reply they would have been level on aggregate. Even Bertie Mee's considerable ability to detach himself from the emotion of match action was tested to the limit.

When the final whistle eventually sounded, the floodgates opened. Delirious supporters surged on to the pitch. George for one had his shirt pulled from his back by souvenir hunters. Sir Stanley Rous, then FIFA's President, presented the Fairs Cup, which stayed in England for the third successive year following the victories of Leeds United and Newcastle United. For Arsenal it was the end of 17 barren years. McLintock had his hands on a trophy at last and there they stayed as he was carried shoulder-high around the pitch. Oddly, despite its significance, it was not a much-heralded victory at the time and it is not particularly well remembered now.

The Arsenal Board had never made any secret of the fact that the League was the main priority. It had been nearly 20 years since Highbury had held the prize that once seemed theirs by right. But no one ever mentioned the Double – achieved just once in the 20th century.

DOUBLE TIP

If you were looking for a team on which to stake a few pounds to accomplish such a feat, Arsenal would not have been among the favourites. Finishing 12th in the 1969–70 season, averaging just one point per game with 51 goals scored and 49 conceded, was hardly a confidence-inspiring foundation that would suggest such glories to come. A much better bet would have been Leeds United, runners-up in both

competitions in the previous season, or perhaps Chelsea, FA Cup winners and third in the League, or even Everton, the 1970 League Champions.

With a touch of irony, the Double year began at the home of the defending Champions. On paper it could hardly have been a tougher start, but Bertie Mee's policies of stabilising Arsenal into a side that did not readily concede defeat had already paid dividends. From the outset of his management every goal let in had been put under an analytical microscope.

With the benefit of hindsight the events at Goodison Park on Saturday 15 August 1970 said much about the qualities which were to provide the basis for such an historic campaign and the resilience which was to shine through so many battles in the months ahead.

The manager's selection had already been affected by pre-season injuries. Peter Simpson required a knee operation. Jon Sammels had a leg in plaster. John Roberts, the strong-man from Wales known as Garth, came into the defence alongside McLintock. The strength of Everton's midfield trio of Howard Kendall, Colin Harvey and Alan Ball was recognised in the role given to Peter Storey, who marked Ball throughout; Storey's job at right-back went to Pat Rice, who had played just 13 League games in the previous three seasons.

Royle and Ball were to score for Everton, with Charlie George cracking two bones to provide one equaliser and Graham the second with a floater. It was only a draw, but it was away at the home of the Champions and, as Frank McLintock said afterward: 'This is the best Arsenal side in my six years with the club.'

On 1 September 1970 Arsenal had the honour of ending Leeds' perfect record so far that season. Geoffrey Green in *The Times* encapsulated the tone of the night in the pithy introduction to his match report: 'There were no goals and no broken legs at Highbury last night, and there might well have been one or two of both. Most of the plaudits of heroism went to the home side. Referee Iowerth Jones from Treharris, Glamorgan, quite properly sent off Kelly for kicking Billy Bremner; that senseless episode after 28 minutes seemed to have condemned Arsenal to defeat. The ten men, however, resisted manfully with the raw Rice, in particular, responding to the challenge. Leeds were not allowed to make use of their advantage. Bertie Mee was never given to exaggeration, so his after-match comment deserves recording: "This was the best performance I have ever seen by an Arsenal team against a side of the calibre of Leeds. I am tremendously proud of all of them, and if we can live through an occasion like this we can live through anything."'

BRAWL IN ROME

It was never going to be an easy season for Arsenal, but the toughest evening proved to be in far away Rome, where the Gunners were defending their Fairs Cup. The game was a 2–2 draw but there were no feuds simmering when the two sides

Left: The 1970 Fairs Cup final against Anderlecht was a happier occasion. Arsenal lost the first leg 3–1 in Brussels and were left with a lot to do in the return. No team had ever come back from a two-goal deficit to win a two-legged European final, nor from a three-goal deficit at any point in a final. The goals in the second leg at Highbury were scored by Kelly, Radford and Sammels, and John Radford is seen celebrating his with the help of Charlie George.

attended an after match dinner together. At some point in the evening Ray Kennedy was set upon by a Lazio player and the meal turned into a full scale brawl. UEFA sided with Arsenal and fined the Italians, Arsenal winning the second leg 2–0. Europe rather proved a distraction during the season – victories against Sturm Graz and Beveren Waas leading only to departure on the away goals rule to FC Köln of Germany.

A few days after their Lazio game Arsenal went to Stoke and were hammered 5–0. Bob Wilson was criticised for talking about the goals on television (Bertie Mee felt he was betraying inside information) and the nature of the defeat remains a mystery. It could have had a dramatic effect – but it didn't and the defence only let its shield down once more during the remainder of the season – and that was for another 45 minutes against Stoke. The defeat preceded the run which really laid the foundations for the Championship. After Stoke, Arsenal went 14 games without defeat, drawing just three, until a sticky patch in January when they lost against Huddersfield and Liverpool. Nonetheless, they were still not taken seriously as contenders – the League was clearly there for Leeds to lose rather than anyone else to win, and Leeds were to eventually oblige in dramatic fashion against West Bromwich Albion.

ARSENAL PROGRESS UNNOTICED

In the Cup, wins against Yeovil and Portsmouth were to take Arsenal to the fifth round at Maine Road against a team that was then one of England's best. At the same time the 'high-morale' battle between Leeds United and Liverpool at Elland Road was going in Liverpool's favour – and Arsenal's. The gap was reduced to three points. Charlie George caught the eye of Brian Glanville, *The Sunday Times* correspondent at the match: 'He must surely resemble the late Charlie Buchan; his height, his powerful physique, the delicacy of touch so astonishing in one so large. To see him receive a ball amidst a ruck of defenders and escape them with the skill of a Houdini is delightful.'

They were prophetic words. George was to settle the fifth round FA Cup tie against Manchester City ten days later. The match was put back from the Saturday to the following Wednesday because the Maine Road pitch was flooded, and it remained very heavy. Two goals from George, now operating as a raider from midfield in place of Graham, confirmed Arsenal's superiority in a deserved victory.

The exact date is not important, but it was around this time, in February 1971, that Bertie Mee addressed his players. To a nation which believed that the 20th-century Double could only be achieved by a team with the swagger of the Spurs 1961 side, Arsenal were not contenders. There was speculation about whether they could win the League. The pursuit of Leeds United was becoming one of the season's most fascinating features. But there were no public suggestions that Arsenal could emulate Tottenham and clear all the hurdles.

Inside Highbury it was a different matter. Mee saw the possibilities and had for some time: 'I told the players we could expect two matches a week for the rest of the season: "As this is the case now is the time for you to be really ambitious and to aim for the success which may never be possible for you as players again in your lifetimes." The point was forcibly expressed that all three trophies should be aimed for. They owed it to themselves and their colleagues to accept the challenge of the next three months.' They also owed it to the fans and to the tradition that was Highbury.

Although Leeds were clear favourites; Arsenal just kept winning. Between 6 February and 20 April they played 12 League games and won 11 of them, losing only at Derby (0–2). At the end of that run they had just four League games left to play, and had worked their way through to their first FA Cup final since 1952.

KNOCK-OUT SUCCESS

Leicester City in the quarter final replay had proved to be a tough nut to crack. The match attracted Highbury's biggest crowd of the season, more than 57,000, and they witnessed a match that became the tale of two headers. The first by Fern after 13 minutes was disallowed by the referee. The Leicester forward was adjudged to have pushed Rice as he moved in to connect with Farrington's centre; it was a very close call. Then, with the refereree counting the seconds toward half time, George rose perfectly to meet Armstrong's corner.

Such a blow on the interval did not diminish Leicester's efforts. An absorbing contest continued to the very last kick, and only then were Arsenal sure of their place in the last four.

Right: Charlie George scores the all-important first goal of the fifth round FA Cup tie against Manchester City at Maine Road on 17 February 1971. A free-kick had been given after Joe Corrigan handled the ball outside his area in the 18th minute. George simply shot past the City wall.

SHAKEN BY STOKE

The semi-final draw had paired Everton and Liverpool for a special derby, while Arsenal were drawn against Stoke City, on League form the weakest of the four survivors. The matching of the underdogs and the Arsenal machine produced a riveting contest at Hillsborough. Some 41 years earlier an FA Cup semi-final triumph in Yorkshire in dramatic circumstances provided the impetus to a decade of success. Now, in the frantic pace of a semi-final in the 1970s, the club wrote the most relevant page in the story of the Double season.

Quite simply Arsenal looked as though they had stumbled at the penultimate hurdle. Stoke might have been nervously caught up in a desire to reach their first major final, but Arsenal were at times tentative to the point of distraction in the first half and the London team's players left the field after 45 minutes trailing 2–0.

Semi-finals by nature are cautious, inhibited affairs; the price of defeat is so high that few risks are taken; winning is all-important, the means scarcely matter. Arsenal began the match in that vein, with a greater share of possession in the first 20 minutes but no end product to show for it.

The cautious approach, though, had to be thrown out of the window after a most unusual goal which lifted this semi-final tie out of the rut. Bob Wilson very properly conceded a corner by pushing behind a teasing cross from Greenhoff, Arsenal failed to deal conclusively with the corner-kick, and as Peter Storey booted the ball away, it struck Denis Smith and flew into the Arsenal net.

In the very next attack the flame-haired Conroy played a very effective one-two with Mahoney only to put his shot inches wide. Banks twice put his stamp on the game with sharp saves, foiling Kennedy on both occasions, before Stoke, fortified by their goalkeeper, were boosted further in the 29th minute. It was a gift from George. With time to spare the 20-year-old, stricken perhaps with butterflies in this most draining of matches, sent a dreadfully underhit back pass in the direction of Wilson. Ritchie pounced and reached the ball just before the Arsenal goalkeeper, took it past him and planted it in the yawning goal. It would have been a disaster for any Sunday morning team, let alone one which was pursuing the elusive dream of a League and Cup Double. Stoke should have gone 3–0 ahead when Greenhoff broke clear a few minutes later. But, at a vital moment, he lost his nerve and shot high, wide and anything but handsome. Just like Elland Road in 1930, the tide had turned.

Early in the second half Mahoney charged clear yet again through the constantly square defence. Wilson this time was able to reach the ball. It was a good piece of goalkeeping from a splendid technician, but it carried greater import as Arsenal swept upfield. what might have been 3–0 suddenly became 2–1. Armstrong fed Kennedy, whose chip into the middle caused confusion in the Stoke ranks. Storey unleashed a drive from 20 yards and even Banks could do nothing.

Yet it was Stoke who reacted more positively to the goal. Arsenal were not allowed to dictate the play in their quest for an equaliser, largely because the impressive Greenhoff kept two and even three defenders constantly occupied. Arsenal's momentum was also interrupted by an injury to George, which brought Sammels on for the last 15 minutes. The resultant injury time proved a blessing in disguise.

STOREY STEPS FORWARD

It was in the two minutes that Pat Partridge, the referee, added on, that the salvation came to keep alive Arsenal's appointment with history. Banks was pressed into conceding a corner, angrily protesting after the match that he had been fouled and that the decision should have been a Stoke free-kick. Armstrong took the corner from the Arsenal right, and this time Banks was nowhere. McLintock, a rescuing figure yet again, steered his header toward the left-hand post, where only the hands of John Mahoney prevented a goal. Referee Partridge was perfectly placed to award the penalty.

The thousands of supporters who had made the journey to Sheffield roared but one Gunner was less than thrilled. Peter Storey had made the penalty job his own with a succession of nervelessly executed kicks. Even in the heat of battle he now realised the scale of his task: 'The rest of the lads were all hugging each other as though we'd scored. But I was the one who had to stick it in. And past Gordon Banks too!'

At the other end of the ground Wilson dropped to his knees in prayer. It was one of those moments when the world stops. Had Storey missed, his name, like Waddle's or perhaps Southgate's, would have been engraved forever on the hearts of thousands. But Peter Storey was the man for Arsenal's hour of need. He repaid the faith of colleagues whose celebrations had looked so premature to the penalty taker. As Storey ran up, England's goalkeeper switched his weight on to his right foot and started to move in that direction. Storey sent his shot low, placed with the inside of his right foot, to Banks' left. Stoke City 2 Arsenal 2, the rescue was complete.

If, from the whole season, we are to choose just one moment in which the Double was won but might have been lost, then it was Jimmy Greenhoff's miss in the first half. In a remarkable

display of touch football, Greenhoff had been a giant that day, but, at the vital moment, he had failed and Arsenal were saved. At 3–0 they must have been out.

There can be no doubt that the semi-final was the moment of truth. A League match can be lost (even 1–0 at Elland Road, as we shall see) and the Double still won. But every Cup tie has to end positively. All Cup-winning teams have one match where luck plays its part, when they come through a game they could or even should have lost. This was Arsenal's.

GUNNERS CLAIM FINAL BERTH

Psychologically, after Hillsborough Arsenal were now in the ascendant. Deep down, for all their boasts that they would finish the job at Villa Park, the Stoke squad knew that they had missed their chance. Bertie Mee's players realised that their escape came almost from the pages of schoolboy fiction. There was another omen too. Liverpool had beaten Everton in the other semi-final, and would be waiting at Wembley just as they had been waiting 21 years earlier, the last time Arsenal had won the FA Cup.

Both managers announced unchanged teams, George having recovered from his bruised ankle and spirits, but the match had a very different flavour. Arsenal assumed control from the start and maintained it.

Arsenal's skill at set pieces had kept their tally of goals ticking along for most of the season. In Armstrong the team possessed a master craftsman at corners. Radford, Kennedy, Graham, McLintock and George all relished attacking his accurate crosses. So, in the 13th minute of the FA Cup semi-final replay, Armstrong's service was again a work of precision and Graham's header was so powerful that it completely beat Banks from fully 15 yards.

After the interval Arsenal quickly reaffirmed their grip on the match with a second goal, which held special significance for the provider and the scorer. In terms of scoring the partnership of Radford and Kennedy was undergoing its most fruitless spell of the season. Neither had scored in the previous seven matches. But two minutes into the second half Radford

Right: Bertie Mee celebrating Arsenal's passage through to the 1971 FA Cup final with the goalscorers, George Graham and Ray Kennedy.

darted down the left and as his cross slithered across the goalmouth Kennedy was in exactly the right place to turn the ball into goal. The two danced a jig of relief and triumph. It was the end of the scoring.

McLintock emerged from the dressing room, his own positive nature sharpened by the experience: 'We are going for the Double! There is real character in this Arsenal side, and now we are going to show we can win League and Cup. This will be my fifth time at Wembley and after being on the losing side in four finals the law of averages says I must have a great chance of a winners' medal this year. The way we are playing we can certainly do it.' Bertie Mee sat for the photographers in the dressing room posed between the two goalscorers, a bottle of champagne in hand. It was a night to enjoy, but the manager soon had to restore the concentration. There were ten League games to be fitted in before the Cup final. What happened in those would determine whether Arsenal were going to Wembley simply for the Cup or for the Double.

ARSENAL CLOSE ON LEEDS

While the dramas were unfolding at Hillsborough, Leeds United had been losing at Chelsea. Now they had 54 points from 35 games; Arsenal were on 48 points from three fewer matches. If they won them all, they would be level. Any projected forecasts about the outcome of the race had to take into account that Arsenal had to visit Elland Road.

It brought the set of matches for the clubs on 17 April into even sharper focus. By twenty-to-five that afternoon the lead had changed. Arsenal, seemingly always the more likely losers in the title race, suddenly found themselves topping the table.

The circumstances were in keeping with the story of the season for each contender. Leeds lost at home to West Bromwich Albion in a blaze of controversy. Arsenal beat Newcastle at Highbury with a display which did not easily bring poetic description to mind, but did, at least, bring them two points.

To deal with the events in north London first the two precious points were gathered courtesy of a superb goal from George 19 minutes from the end of a mediocre match. A packed penalty area ahead was not a daunting proposition when the ball dropped to George. He made sufficient inroads to disrupt the massed defence before turning sharply to drive a scorching left-footed shot past McFaul. For the rest of the action George Armstrong provided the perfect postscript: 'I don't suppose anybody will remember the game, but they'll all remember the result.'

Conversely, at Elland Road everybody will remember one particular incident. The turning point of the match concerned a decision by referee Ray Tinkler. He allowed Albion's Tony Brown to burst forward with the ball from just inside the Leeds half on the West Bromwich right. In a more central position his team-mate Colin Suggett was clearly in an offside

position, but not, ruled the referee, interfering with play. Brown ran on with the Leeds defence expecting the whistle, drew goalkeeper Gary Sprake out to meet him, and passed across the goal for Jeff Astle (also in an offside position) to score at will. The crowd invaded the pitch. Chaos ensued.

The Leeds protests carried such venom that the Football Association subsequently fined the club £750 and ordered them to play their opening four home games the following season away from Elland Road. Albion, who had not won away for 16 months, and were to finish the season sixth from bottom, eventually triumphed 2–1. It was a devastating blow for the Leeds' morale, made worse by repeated television showings of the crucial episode which increased their sense of grievance. Leeds were to win their last three League matches and the Fairs Cup, but will always feel that the title was taken from them on a piece of refereeing interpretation.

NINE IN A ROW

If it was a piece of good fortune then Arsenal readily accepted it. Three days later another one-goal victory at Highbury condemned Burnley to the Second Division. With Storey and McNab on international duty for England against Greece in the European Championship, Kelly returned to midfield, and Roberts was given his only League outing over the second half of the season in defence. The absence of Storey in one other respect was covered by George because it was he, in the 26th minute, who accepted the responsibility of taking and scoring the match-winning penalty. The victory was less in doubt than some of Arsenal's one-goal successes during the season, and Wilson's only moment of real anxiety resulted from a careless back pass by Kelly. Paul Fletcher became the latest victim of the bravado of Arsenal's goalkeeper as he sped off his line to take the ball from the toes of the Burnley number nine. From 2 March to 20 April Arsenal had won all their nine League matches; the 18 points were captured with only 16 goals, but in those 13½ hours of First Division hurly-burly the defence was penetrated only once, at Southampton.

It was at The Dell where Leeds returned to winning ways on Saturday 24 April, the day that the Gunners' run of victories was halted, ironically by West Bromwich Albion, at the Hawthorns. It was an unusual match, not least because Asa Hartford scored for both sides. His goal at the right end was the first of the four. For once Wilson's charge off his line could not rescue a square defence. Albion held their lead for only four minutes. Yet again, an Armstrong corner unsettled those defending against it. The ball dropped for George, who was denied a goal by a block on the line. McLintock, however, was first to the rebound to notch his third goal in five games, a fitting celebration of the announcement that he had been chosen as the Footballer of the Year.

Arsenal lost Rice at half time, the legacy of a twisted ankle. Storey moved to right-back but was still prepared to charge forward in the 55th minute in pursuit of a chipped pass from George. Hartford eagerly ran back, aware of the danger, only to increase it with a back pass. Cumbes was caught coming off his line and the ball rolled into goal with a simplicity which would have driven wild any Leeds United fans present. Five minutes from the end, however, Tony Brown, the scourge of the Elland Road supporters a week earlier, earned their gratitude with a thumping equaliser. Arsenal now had 61 points from 39 matches, Leeds were on 60 from 40 games.

Before leaving the Hawthorns, McLintock reflected on the impending clash of the Titans the following Monday: 'It's obviously going to be tough at Leeds, but the odds are still in our favour. I'm sure Leeds would be happy to swap positions with us. Our run of nine League wins had to end sometime.'

SUMMIT MEETING AT ELLAND ROAD

Leeds had just reached the Fairs Cup final and a match with Juventus; against Arsenal they needed nothing less than victory for their Championship dreams to survive. A draw would be very much to Arsenal's liking, and for most of the game it looked the most likely outcome. The Gunners' sense of discipline and tactical organisation, a cornerstone of the season, served them well. Leeds, with Mick Bates deputising for Peter Lorimer, were kept at arm's length throughout a first half in which both teams were kept under excellent control by referee Norman Burtenshaw.

Wilson's main task in the opening 45 minutes was to gather in a succession of crosses, but the pattern altered in the second half. The home side redoubled their efforts; Arsenal partly by design, partly because of Leeds' extra determination, opted to see out the siege rather than to go for the attack. And for all the creativity of Bremner and Johnny Giles, Leeds were continually frustrated by Arsenal's massed defence. It remained a stern, unrelenting battle, and though the prize was so great, the conduct of the players of both teams was more orderly than in other meetings of the period between these two rivals.

It all changed in the dying moments of the game. The ubiquitous Paul Madeley triggered off another Leeds foray. Bremner, who had never ceased in his quest for an opening, played his part, and suddenly the ball broke for Jack Charlton all alone in front of Wilson's goal. England's World Cup centre-half of 1966 directed the ball past the Arsenal goalkeeper as other defenders stood frozen, arms raised in a uniform appeal for offside. Even then the gods, for once, favoured Leeds because the ball struck a post and rebounded out, only for a long Charlton leg to reach it before McNab. Instantly Norman Burtenshaw confirmed the goal.

Arsenal's protests were long on time and short in temper. George booted the ball into the stand and was rightly booked. Wilson and McLintock led the pursuit of the referee, and it was fully five minutes before he could restart the game. The linesman whose flag had stayed down was also turned upon by aggrieved visiting players.

There was still enough time for George Graham to send a back header flying inches over Gary Sprake's crossbar, before even more furious words were directed at the referee when he blew the final whistle.

Many off the pitch queried the goal at the time, though Bertie Mee confined himself to commenting that 'never was a defeat less deserved. Arsenal were fantastic, tremendous.' However, subsequent television re-runs convinced a number of the most bitter Arsenal players at the time that referee and linesman had been absolutely right. McNab, it seemed, had been too slow moving out. Mr Burtenshaw was able to look forward to his next Arsenal match with confidence; he had been appointed the FA Cup final referee.

LEEDS LEAD BUT ARSENAL ARE FAVOURITES

Whatever the actual merits of the offside decision (or not) it meant that Leeds were back on top of the First Division, but William Hill, the bookmakers, still made Arsenal, who had a game in hand, favourites for the Championship at 4–5; Leeds were quoted as even-money.

May Day brought victories for both candidates in the race to be named Champions. Leeds struck twice in the first half at Elland Road, through Bremner and Lorimer, to make sure that their League season ended with a win over Nottingham Forest. Arsenal had to wait longer before gaining a win against their semi-final victims Stoke.

The Gunnners began as though their boots were weighted down with tension until three minutes before half time. George's forward pass caught the Stoke defence in a line, and Radford bore down on the Stoke goal and its guardian, Gordon Banks. He dallied so long that Smith was able to rush back and prevent the shot. It looked a significant miss and Radford later explained: 'Initially I stopped because I thought I was offside. Then I realised I wasn't and tried to lob the ball over Banks. But he started back-pedalling so I had to hold the ball. One of their blokes came in and I've the gash to prove it.'

Early in the second half Arsenal suffered again; Peter Storey limped off with a groin strain and Eddie Kelly entered the congested midfield area. It was the start of a memorable week for the 20-year-old Scot. He had been on the field 12 minutes when he spotted the potential of a long ball into the goalmouth from Armstrong. Graham flicked it on to Radford who skilfully manipulated it into Kelly's path. The substitute blasted in the decisive goal.

DECIDERS AT THE LANE

Arsenal knew exactly what they had to do to win the League for the first time for 18 years. Leeds had finished their League programme: Played 42, Won 27, Drawn 10, Lost 5, Goals For 72, Goals Against 30, Points 64. Arsenal's record read: Played 41, Won 28, Drawn 7, Lost 6, For 70, Against 29, Points 63.

With a wonderful sense of occasion the last fixture was against Tottenham Hotspur at White Hart Lane. The game had been originally scheduled for the day of the FA Cup semi-finals and was now rearranged for the Monday night of Cup final week. Spurs needed three points from the meeting with Arsenal and a trip to Stoke to be sure of qualifying for the next European campaign. Bonuses of £400 per man could depend on beating Arsenal.

The mathematical permutations were even more remarkable. A win would give the title to Arsenal, a defeat would send the trophy to Elland Road. But a goalless draw would mean success for Arsenal while (owing to the goal average system then in force) any scoring draw (even 1–1) would conclude matters in Leeds' favour.

Arsenal's players had only reached this situation through a deep yearning for success. The prospect of crossing another minefield did not alarm them. Frank McLintock rarely lost his sense of optimism: 'I'm sure we can make it. We always give good performances at White Hart Lane.' George Armstrong was equally confident: 'We're playing better away from home because we are not under the same tension, and it's in our favour that Spurs are not a defensive side.'

Alan Mullery, Tottenham's captain, anticipated the mighty clash: 'Arsenal have got as much chance of being handed the title by Spurs as I have of being given the Crown Jewels. They are the last people we want winning the Championship. Everybody is on about the great season Arsenal are having. Well, we're not doing too badly. We have won the League Cup and reached the sixth round of the FA Cup. Now we mean to round off our season by beating Arsenal – and that will put us third in the table. That can't be bad.'

Manager Bill Nicholson recognised that the League title could be the prelude to the Double to which he had guided Spurs ten years earlier: 'We are tremendously proud of our Double achievement. I suppose some other club has got to do it again sometime but we will be doing our best to see that it isn't Arsenal. My instructions to the Tottenham players will be to go out to try to win.'

The Arsenal players rested on the Sunday as usual, but for Storey there was not enough time for recovery. When the players reported for light training on the morning of the match it was clear that Kelly would be in the team from the start. Sammels was chosen as substitute.

KENNEDY THE HERO

The players lunched at their own homes before reconvening at the South Herts Golf Club, the regular pre-match meeting place, at 4.30 pm. Already the football fans of north London were on the march toward White Hart Lane. The gates were locked more than an hour before kick-off with 51,192 spectators inside. Twice that number were on the outside.

The volume of traffic even surprised the police. The Arsenal team coach crawled along. Bertie Mee recalled: 'We gave ourselves an hour for a drive which normally takes 20 minutes. But even then it was a very difficult journey. I have

Left and below: At the final whistle the fans celebrated Arsenal's eighth Championship on the pitch at White Hart Lane, and Frank McLintock was carried aloft, wrapped in a Leeds scarf.

never seen scenes like it. But there was never the pressure that we were going to be late, and seeing those thronging crowds increased the sense of occasion for us. There was no way we were going to be beaten.'

The referee, Kevin Howley, had to abandon his car a mile away to fight his way on foot through the crowds. It was the last League match in a distinguished career, a great occasion on which to bow out. Making his whistle heard in the din which echoed around the ground from start to finish became a problem. The vociferous McLintock bellowed orders to his team-mates which passed largely unheard.

McLintock had his hands full coping with the powerful Martin Chivers. The wise Alan Gilzean continually sought to steal a yard on Simpson. Jimmy Neighbour probed ceaselessly down Tottenham's left and stretched Rice to the full, and all the while Martin Peters hovered menacingly in the Spurs midfield, always likely to time a late run into a scoring position. For all the attacking intent clear-cut chances were few. Peters flicked the top of the Arsenal bar with a swerving shot, and almost scored with a header. Joe Kinnear forced a courageous and painful dive from Wilson at his feet. Gilzean all but connected as the ball flashed across the Arsenal goalmouth.

At the other end George brought an athletic save from Pat Jennings in the opening minute. McLintock saw his goalbound shot bounce clear off the body of Collins. Graham's header curved on to the top of the Spurs goal. Radford and Kennedy hassled at Peter Collins and Phil Beal. Armstrong was everywhere.

For all the energy imparted into the match by both teams, whose conduct had been first class, a goalless draw beckoned. But three minutes from time, Kinnear tried to dribble clear of trouble inside his own penalty area. George recaptured the ball from the Spurs right-back, and twisted instantly to conjure a cross from an angle which would have defeated most players. Even then it seemed as though Arsenal had been denied. Jennings made the save of the night as Radford met the ball provided so cleverly by George.

Tottenham stopped to a man, perhaps in admiration of their goalkeeper, but also because they expected the ball to run behind for a corner. Armstrong had barely stood still all season, and was not going to break the habit now. Rescuing it from near the line his chip back across goal was met by Kennedy's header. The ball sped high to Jennings' left, above the leap of Cyril Knowles behind him. It clipped the underside of the bar and was over the line.

The goal was greeted by instant exhilaration from every Arsenal player. But almost as quickly misgivings followed, particularly from the scorer. In one respect, the goal was irrelevant. A Tottenham goal would still give the Championship to Leeds and there was still time for it. 'That was the longest three minutes I have ever known,' recalled Kennedy. 'I remember thinking to myself as Tottenham came back at us that perhaps it might have been better had

my header not gone into the net.' Spurs hurled themselves forward as the seconds ticked away. One last corner could still have deprived the Gunners, but Wilson's last act in an almost faultless series of performances throughout the 42-game First Division programme was to grasp the ball as though the lives of he and his team-mates depended upon it.

CHAMPIONS ONCE MORE

Moments later Kevin Howley blew a whistle in League football for the last time. The title belonged to Arsenal for a record eighth time. It had been won by a clear point at the last gasp of a marathon that had never been less than compelling. Leeds deserved sympathy for coming so close, but none could deny the magnificence of Arsenal's victory. Like a dog with a bone they had refused to let go right to the end.

Bedlam reigned on the pitch. George, close to the touchline, leapt into the arms of Don Howe. As thousands of fans raced to congratulate their heroes Bob Wilson found himself marooned. Unable to contain his joy he hugged the only participant he could reach – referee Howley! McLintock found a Leeds United scarf wrapped around his neck as he was chaired off shoulder high.

The celebrations became so protracted that Don Howe found his own joy giving way to anxiety: 'My thoughts turned straight to the Cup final and I was worried that the crowd might injure our players. They were ripping at their shirts. Some wanted their boots, which of course they had to wear on Saturday. I was frightened that they would tread on somebody's foot and keep him out of the final.'

Bertie Mee lost his club tie as he returned to the directors' box to acknowledge the crowd's appreciation. Tottenham for their part were most magnanimous in defeat, which the Arsenal manager remembers with great affection: 'We were given champagne in the dressing room by Bill Nicholson. The club could not have done more to help us celebrate our great night. There had been a lot of petty rivalries between the two clubs in past years but in my time we did a lot of work to improve relationships. They must have been very disappointed that they had lost but they didn't let that spoil our evening.'

FINAL PREPARATIONS FOR GUNNERS

The party spirit continued long into the night. The team moved on to the White Hart in Southgate. There were no curfews posted or restrictions made. Tuesday, which had already begun by the time everyone reached home, would be a day for recharging batteries. Wednesday was the time really to begin the concentration on the FA Cup final.

Much of that day was given over to the needs of the media, but not for long. Bertie Mee's medical background gave him strong views about Wembley finals: 'Over the years so much had been said about the problems of playing there,

particularly the victims of cramp. Now cramp is really an emotional problem. It does of course have physical symptoms, but they can often be a result of pressure. I wanted to protect the team from emotional stress, so there was no involvement with the press or television after Thursday.'

Don Howe concentrated on the physical preparation. Amidst the lush acres of the London Colney training ground, the players did their training on a pitch marked to the exact specifications of Wembley. The grass had been allowed to grow to cultivate the feel of the Empire Stadium turf. Two recent League Cup final defeats had raised doubts about the team's ability to win at Wembley. No stone was left unturned in an attempt to create the right atmosphere this time.

For George Wright, the physiotherapist, it was becoming a race against the clock. Peter Storey's presence in midfield was vital to the construction of the side; his injury was only slowly responding to intensive treatment. Bertie Mee had one major decision to make, and Storey was chosen to start the game. It was a risk but the converted full-back had become a fearsome opponent in midfield. Liverpool would not relish the bite in his tackles even if he was less than one hundred per cent fit.

MIND GAMES COMMENCE

There were psychological battles to be won. No one knew that better than Bill Shankly, Liverpool's manager, to whom the old cliché 'a legend in his own life-time' applied. Shankly had

rather surprisingly appeared by the side of the pitch the day before the final when Arsenal were taking a preparatory stroll to acclimatise to the Wembley environment. There was rain about, and Bob Wilson was greeted by one of the masters of gamesmanship with the comment: 'Bob, it'll be a nightmare for goalkeepers out here tomorrow.' It might have induced a sleepless night in a less perceptive character than Wilson.

In fact 8 May 1971 was a stiflingly hot day. The Arsenal ritual did not include the usual lie-in of most Cup final teams. By ten o'clock the players were on the road to familiar

surroundings. At the South Herts Golf Club they took their pre-match lunch with words of encouragement from Dai Rees, the resident golf professional.

The opportunity to gain a spot of revenge on Shankly came 15 minutes before the kick-off. Arsenal had recent memories of the formalities of Wembley finals. FA officials are keen to have the teams standing in the tunnel ready to walk out at the appropriate minute. Often the wait is so protracted that the nervous begin to suffer. So at 2.45pm Bertie Mee politely told the FA representative that he was finishing his team-talk and his players would be out in a moment. A few minutes later the call came again. This time he replied: 'A couple of the players are just tying their boots, we won't be a minute.'

It was only at the third time of asking that Arsenal appeared. Liverpool had come out at the first request and been kept waiting. Shankly scowled, realising that for once he had been outfoxed. There was no delay for Arsenal; immediately they were led out into the sunlight and the wall of sound that was waiting beyond the end of the tunnel.

It had been six weeks since Liverpool had qualified for Wembley. While Arsenal's attentions had been very much elsewhere, at Anfield there had been no escape from the demands of the publicity machine. On the other hand, Arsenal's worries were whether the rigours of the League campaign would now begin to take their toll, and those unhappy memories of League Cup defeats. They were playing their fourth major final in five years under Mee.

GUNNERS GROW IN CONFIDENCE

Liverpool's early promise brought no reward, only the bruises of battle as Storey came in high and late on Heighway. Toshack was then misused by Rice and McLintock. It took a

telling pass from George to switch the balance of the opening minutes toward Arsenal. Kennedy's running was never speedy, and recovering defenders forced him away from the goal and the danger evaporated.

Indeed it was not to be Kennedy's day, and six minutes into the second half he failed with another opportunity much closer to goal. In contrast Radford recaptured the form which had been elusive toward the end of the League season. No one contributed more to Arsenal's eventual victory than the muscular Yorkshireman in the number nine shirt. Though he did not score himself he was the provider of both opportunities which were taken; throughout the match he used the Gunners' possession to excellent effect.

Armstrong was another who could not quite capture his normal excellence, though once, arriving at the far post, he almost beat Clemence for a goal which would surely have spared the players extra time. George Graham, however, strutted his way through the match with an arrogance that set him apart and he was awarded the Man of the Match prize. Just 12 minutes from time he climbed characteristically to direct Radford's long throw beyond Clemence, but it came off the bar. Smith hooked the rebound for a corner which Armstrong planted once more on Graham's head. This time left back Alec Lindsay cleared off the line.

HEIGHWAY NETS OPENER

Both sides used their substitutes. Storey, as expected, gave way to Kelly midway through the second half. Four minutes later Peter Thompson, who was a survivor from the 1965 Cup-winning team, was brought on in an attempt to inject more thrust into Liverpool's performance; the ineffective Alun Evans was replaced. Nevertheless, neither team could

Below: After Heighways' opener for Liverpool and the Kelly/Graham equaliser, it was, almost inevitably, Charlie George who scored the winner for Arsenal nine minutes from the end of extra time.

break the mould of the match in normal time. It had been a highly technical 90 minutes, with both sides cautious in their attempts to seek an advantage. The uncommitted neutrals, however, were seeking a more cavalier approach in the extra 30 minutes.

They had to wait only two minutes. Steve Heighway had rarely freed himself from the shackles imposed on the Arsenal right, but suddenly he slipped past Rice and Armstrong and from a tight angle cut in from the left. Wilson automatically took up position covering his near post. With his usually accurate sense of anticipation already predicting that Heighway should cut the ball back for Toshack arriving in the middle, the goalkeeper slightly overcompensated for the cross. Heighway was nothing if not unorthodox and his shot fizzed into the gap that Wilson had left to his right. Only the beaten goalkeeper heard the nick as the ball glanced the post on its way in; it was no fluke, Heighway had scored from a similar angle in a Merseyside derby earlier that season.

Wilson had little time for self-recrimination. Within moments he had saved Arsenal from certain defeat, plunging to keep out a close-range shot from Hall. On the bench Don Howe was sending George Wright to the touchline with a vital message: 'My first reaction was here we go again, losing at Wembley, but anyway we'd had a tremendous season. But my next thought was that we'd got to change something to pull that goal back. I told George to get to the touchline and tell George Graham to go forward. Charlie George was nearly out on his feet because of the heat and was struggling to make any runs forward, so he was told to drop back into midfield.'

TACTICAL SWITCH BRINGS EQUALISER

There were four minutes left in the first period of extra time when the move paid dividends. Radford hooked the ball over his shoulder into a crowded Liverpool penalty area, where the congestion was perhaps too great for Clemence to risk an intervention. Larry Lloyd, Emlyn Hughes, Smith and Lawler were all between the Liverpool goalkeeper and the ball, which fell for Kelly simply to touch it forward. It certainly could never be called a serious shot.

Yet on it rolled between a tangle of legs as Graham swept in to view. He swung a leg at the ball and Clemence, now very much the last line of defence, could do nothing to prevent its progress into the net. Graham wheeled away in celebration of the goal that everyone in the ground believed to be his. But football had entered a television age. The BBC and ITV were competing on the sporting front and the Cup final was the showpiece for each channel to show off its technical and editorial skills. New camera angles were one area of that competition, and the day after the final the London Weekend Television look-back at the match included a 'revelation', from a camera behind the goal, that Graham had not touched the ball. The last certain touch came from Kelly, declared Brian Moore and Jimmy Hill.

Thus the club credited the scoring of the equalising goal to Eddie Kelly. Years after the event George Graham still believes he made contact with the ball, and is understandably embarrassed at being recalled from time to time as the man who claimed a vital goal which apparently was not his. BBC Television's Barry Davies was stationed that afternoon among the photographers close to Ray Clemence's net. Watching with the eyes of a trained observer, he still believes that the goal should be Graham's. A recent study of the television pictures supports the Kelly theory, but camera angles can be deceptive. It is certainly true that the ball did not change direction whether Graham touched it or not, so Graham's swing might at least have worked like a good dummy on Clemence.

Arsenal, yet again in this astonishing season, had refused to accept second place. But back on the bench the search for victory was not quite so immediate for Don Howe: 'Once we had equalised I settled for the draw. It hadn't really been our day overall, and I felt it would be better to steady ourselves and start out afresh for the replay. I decided to get George Graham back into midfield just to make sure he got behind the ball. Charlie still looked exhausted so I wanted him back up front. Out of the way really. He found his way forward because we were trying to protect our position for the draw.'

CHARLIE NETS FAMOUS WINNER

No one had explained the finer points of this theory to George himself. With the replay nine minutes away he interpassed with the magnificent Radford before letting fly from 20 yards

Above: Bertie Mee with an exhausted George Armstrong.

Below: George Graham and Eddie Kelly at this stage not caring which of them scored the equaliser.

with a right-footed shot which belied his weary appearance. The force in the drive would surely have beaten Clemence even if it had not taken a slight upward deflection off the lunging Lloyd. George marked the moment with a novel salute; his arms were outraised as in more conventional celebration, but he was lying flat on his back at the time! It remains the outstanding image of this unusual character.

How appropriate that Arsenal's Double was sealed by one of north London's own. Charlie George, born in Islington, a product of Holloway School, used to stand on Highbury's North Bank. With his flowing hair and his obvious mocking of convention he acted out the dreams of so many young Arsenal followers. At 20 years old he had earned himself and his team-mates an extra £12,000 a man with that winning goal. The money mattered, but the glory was priceless.

Frank McLintock became a Wembley victor at long last, at the fifth time of asking. Bill Shankly, generous in defeat, was quick to shake his hand. George did handsprings of jubilation. Kennedy embraced Lloyd in consolation. Bob Wilson assured Ray Clemence, a loser on his first Wembley visit, that he would certainly be back.

Wilson later admitted that on a baking afternoon he had gone cold all over at the instant George had struck his momentous goal;. His recollections at the final whistle are also sharp: 'Frank was in so much of a hurry to go up and grab the Cup that I pulled him back. He'd waited so long. I shouted at him that it might never happen again and that he should savour every moment. Not to rush it.' Wilson was right, of course – it never did happen again for McLintock.

Wilson followed McLintock up to the Royal Box, where the second leg of the Double was presented to Arsenal's captain by the Duke of Kent. For some it was too much to take. McLintock relished the ending of his Wembley hoodoo, but years later he confessed that he had no emotion left: 'It may seem strange but I've never been able to feel that supreme thrill of winning the Double. Our Fairs Cup win the year before meant so much. And winning the League was terrific. Maybe I was just too drained at the end of it all.'

About a quarter of a million people still had enough energy to line the route from Highbury to Islington Town Hall the following day. Both trophies were displayed by the team from an open-top bus, along with the FA Youth Cup, the product of more success for the club's prospective stars. Bertie Mee had guided the club to a year of unprecedented achievement. It had taken 51 matches to win the Double, a longer road than that trodden by any of the three previous holders of that accolade. 'I wanted the boys to win the Cup for Frank McLintock. The League Championship was for my chairman Denis Hill-Wood. For myself? I wouldn't mind the European Cup next season. I know we have done the Double, but at the moment it is too much to take in.'

DON HOWE DEPARTS

In any walk of life achieving success is only half the battle. Living with the difficulties it can create is another matter altogether. A month after the Double was won, north London was alive with rumours of the first split in the camp.

No member of the Highbury staff was fuelled with more ambition than Don Howe. It was understandable that other clubs looking to fill managerial positions should be attracted by his superb credentials. None of them knew him better than his old club, West Bromwich Albion and on 8 July Bertie Mee had to respond to the news that Albion had attracted Howe to the Hawthorns: 'There is little need for me to repeat how highly I value Don as a coach – and how sorry I am to see him leaving.'

The popular view at the time was that Don Howe had left because he wanted to step into Mee's shoes. Ten years later he strongly refuted those rumours: 'I did want to manage in my own right. That was only natural. But I wasn't in a hurry. Being manager of Arsenal was still my ambition but I would have been prepared to wait four, five, ten years if necessary. All it would have taken to keep me at Highbury would have been a promise that when Bertie decided to finish I would have been given a go as manager for a year or two. But nobody said that.'

He was speaking then as a Highbury employee, the right-hand man to Terry Neill. Later, when Neill was dismissed, Don Howe finally fulfilled his ambition. After an initial spell as caretaker-manager he was appointed almost 13 years after his departure for West Bromwich Albion. Back in 1971, what would have been a simple sense of loss became

Right: Charlie George, the Gunners' darling, is crowned with appropriate headgear.

more acrimonious when Albion went further and also signed George Wright and the successful youth coach Brian Whitehouse. Denis Hill-Wood was angry enough to go into print. 'Loyalty is a dirty word, these days,' said the Chairman. 'There is nothing I can do about what West Bromwich have done in raiding our staff except just to ignore them.'

A HARD ACT TO FOLLOW

There is always the issue of what comes next. It is a truism that great football sides usually last three years. It seems to have been true of the Arsenal of 1970 to 1972. Somehow the magic goes, other sides watch and learn and the unexpected is now expected. The 1971–72 season, which was started as

Double winners, was eventually to be a disappointment. The first priority was obviously the European Cup. Of the English clubs only Manchester United had ever succeeded, and the competition was still redolent of Real Madrid, of Benfica, and of impossibly long journeys across the steppes of Eastern Europe.

The first two rounds brought easy draws – against Stroemsgodset of Norway and Grasshoppers of Zurich. But the real thing came next in the quarter finals. Ajax of Amsterdam were European Champions, and formed the heart of the Dutch side that should have won the World Cup two years later. In Amsterdam Gerrit Muhren scored twice although Kennedy got one back with a header. At Highbury one goal would have been enough, and Arsenal scored it. Unfortunately it was at

Below: Only the second team to achieve the FA Cup and League Double in the 20th century, the Arsenal players celebrate with a triumphal open-top bus ride through Islington.

the wrong end and George Graham's heartbreaking own-goal ended Arsenal's best chance of winning the world's premier club trophy.

The League was not to prove much kinder, despite the arrival of Alan Ball for a record £220,000. Three losses in a week in August were both a shock and too much to recover from. In the end Arsenal finished fifth, in a season which did not produce an outstanding team and one which went to the wire between Derby, Leeds and Liverpool. None of their totals came near Arsenal's of the season before.

BALL PROVES CUP TALISMAN

Alan Ball's influence was most sharply felt in an FA Cup run, which with a suitable touch of irony started at Swindon. Eight of the Swindon side which had inflicted so much agony on their First Division opponents at Wembley almost three years earlier took part in the match, as did a revered opponent, Dave Mackay, who in his last season as a player at 37 was also managing the Wiltshire club.

Ball was not ravaged by memories of the gloomy day at Wembley, and while the pundits waited for Arsenal to be toppled, the recent signing started to repay some of his transfer fee. He set up the game's first goal for Armstrong before opening his own account.

There was a scare in the fourth round, at Reading of the Fourth Division. Arsenal muddled through 2–1, courtesy of an own goal and Pat Rice bursting forward to strike Arsenal's winner, which was deflected.

DERBY DAYS

The fifth round brought three skirmishes with Derby County. At the Baseball Ground Charlie George netted twice, as he had in the fifth round a year earlier, but Derby matched his two efforts with an Alan Hinton penalty and a goal from Alan Durban. Neither side could break through in the replay, which went to extra time in front of a packed Highbury Stadium, with a crowd of 63,077. Because of Arsenal's European commitments the third match was played two weeks later, only five days before the quarter final. The game took place on neutral soil at Leicester and Ray Kennedy produced the crucial goal.

Away again in the sixth round, for the 18th time in the last 21 draws, Arsenal only had to travel a few miles. Leyton Orient were struggling to avoid relegation to the Third Division, but they had knocked out high-flying Chelsea at Brisbane Road in the last round.

East London was out in force to see whether Arsenal would go the way of Chelsea. With the League title now looking less likely, the Gunners had their hearts set on retaining the Cup. Orient thus met sterner opposition and shortly after half time Ball, resplendent in the white boots which were briefly in fashion, ended Orient's dreams.

RADFORD EARNS WEMBLEY RETURN

By a strange coincidence Arsenal's semi-final opponents were once again Stoke City. Again the venue was Villa Park, where the thrilling saga had ended a year earlier. Arsenal's side showed only one change from the previous semi-final. Ball's inclusion meant Kennedy dropping down to substitute. George wore the number nine shirt, and Radford, recently freed from suspension, partnered him. Storey had briefly been the player to stand down to accommodate Ball, but since March had reclaimed his place in midfield.

Unlike at Hillsborough a year earlier it was Arsenal who received the boost of scoring first. Armstrong received a clearance just outside the penalty area, took the pace off the ball and drove it past Banks.

That might have been the end of the matter but for an injury to Bob Wilson, which left the goalkeeper hobbling in agony. He tore a cartilage, but the decision was made to keep him on the pitch. It made reasonable sense. Wilson's courage was unquestioned. Arsenal would be better with him on one leg than with any fit outfield player.

That judgement, however, was faulty. Defenders suddenly tried to take too much care of the wounded Wilson. In the end Simpson aimed to cut out a cross he would normally have left for the goalkeeper, who moved out to try to gather it but not at sufficient speed. The end product was that Simpson nudged the ball into his own goal. With more than 15 minutes remaining it was time for a re-think. Wilson was pulled off and Kennedy brought into the action. The call for an emergency keeper was answered by Radford, a stern enough character to cope with the task of helping his team stay in the Cup in such an unfamiliar role. He was sufficiently aware of Arsenal's tradition to begin by joking about the famous jersey which was blamed for the slip by Dan Lewis in the 1927 final. Radford coped admirably with the shots that Stoke managed and gave every impression of hugely enjoying the experience. Stoke once again seemed unable to believe their luck.

The final chapter of the Arsenal-Stoke semi-final story was played out at Goodison on Wednesday 19 April 1972 – the perfect setting for Geoff Barnett's return to first team action after more than two years' patience in reserve. Arsenal's other ex-Evertonian, Alan Ball, was invited to lead out the team on his return to the pitch he had graced so often.

The first two goals were penalties: Greenhoff for Stoke, George for Arsenal, with Storey not required this time. It was fitting that Arsenal's winner fell to Radford; he had earned it with his goalkeeping stint at Villa Park. The goal was controversial, however, George breaking away from a seemingly offside position.

LEEDS IN DOUBLE BID

Leeds had already confirmed their place at Wembley with a one-sided 3–0 triumph over Birmingham City at Hillsborough. Arsenal's quest in the final had a double

edge, not just to retain the FA Cup but to end Leeds' strong challenge for the Double, which could take some of the glitter from Arsenal's own glories of 1970–71.

The League insisted that each club should fulfil an outstanding League fixture on the Monday before the Cup final. It was not an unreasonable request although neither manager looked kindly upon it. Arsenal would still be left with two games after the final, Leeds with one.

At Coventry on Monday, 1 May, Arsenal fielded the side which had booked their Wembley places by winning 1–0, McLintock being the scorer with his first goal since August. Barnett would keep goal at Wembley, with the unfortunate Bob Wilson needing surgery. His involvement was restricted to organising the players pool for the perks of the occasion, for which he was the unanimous choice of his team-mates. Kennedy could not force his way back into the attack and was named as substitute.

The bookmakers made Don Revie's team 4–7 to lift the Cup. Arsenal were the underdogs at 6–4. The news that Eddie Gray, who had given a virtuoso Wembley performance in the 1970 Cup final, was fit to play did nothing to shorten the odds against the Gunners.

HOME COLOURS

This year both clubs were able to wear their traditional colours. Both Arsenal's post-war triumphs in the FA Cup had been won in a change strip. Neither team was new to Wembley, but sadly their combined experience did little to raise the tone of the contest.

Referee David Smith from Stonehouse had barely started the game when he was reaching for his notebook. McNab, who had made a splendid return to the senior side for the semi-final after a long absence, cut down Lorimer. From this undistinguished beginning the contest rarely improved. The kindest interpretation of the drab 90 minutes would be to point to the respect that each team clearly felt for the other. Had it been a boxing match the referee would have called for more action.

CUP GOES NORTH

The only abiding memory is of a winning goal of high quality which mercifully spared the frustrated crowd an extra 30 minutes. It did not come from Arsenal, whose attack rarely got out of second gear, even when Kennedy replaced Radford.

Eight minutes into the second half the two Leeds central strikers pieced together a move which deserved to win the match. The foraging Mick Jones tricked McNab on the Leeds right. Allan Clarke met the driven cross with a diving header, stooping to conquer. Barnett and Wilson together would have had difficulty in keeping it out. For Clarke it was a third time lucky affair. He had been voted Man of the Match as a loser for Leicester in 1969; the following year he had been beaten

playing for Leeds against Chelsea. Now he had the decisive goal and another Man of the Match trophy. Jones deserved better than to collect his winners' medal in pain after dislocating an elbow in the dying minutes.

It was a costly injury. With the first leg of the Double in their pockets, Leeds needed only a point from their trip to Wolves two days after Wembley. But they badly needed Jones to respond to a very competitive performance from a team with nothing to play for. Leeds were beaten 2–1, lamenting that they should have had two penalties. It was a surprising result, and meant that for the second consecutive season Leeds missed the title by a point.

So Arsenal had lost the Cup and the League but happily not to the same club. The Gunners also had their say in the destiny of the Championship because, had Liverpool won at Highbury the night Leeds were losing at Molineux, Bill Shankly's men would have been Champions. The game, however, finished goalless, and – to their astonishment – Derby County, on a plane bound for an end-of-season holiday, heard that the League Championship was theirs. Derby finished with 58 points, one more than Leeds, Liverpool and Manchester City. Arsenal had to be content with fifth place with 52 points.

In many ways it had been a satisfactory season, though the placing in the League was not high enough to qualify for a spot in the UEFA Cup. But the standards had been set a year earlier and deep down the players who had discovered capacities for success beyond their wildest dreams knew that they had missed a great opportunity. It would not have taken too much more for the players to have really challenged for a second successive League and Cup combination.

Below: In the second leg of the 1972 Cup semi-final against Aston Villa, Arsenal won 2–1 after a seemingly offside Charlie George put John Radford through for one goal and George scored the other. The key incident was, however, at the other end when a Denis Smith (third left) header was cleared by Bob McNab. Stoke claimed the ball had crossed the line and the photographic evidence seems to support them.

ARSENAL MOMENTS

The word 'magic' is over-used in football. But sometimes, when you are witnessing incredible events which will live in the mind's eye for ever, it is the best one for the job. Fans down the generations will have their own particular favourite Arsenal moment, which they play over and over again in their own private, perpetual action replay. Football is never about dry statistics. It keeps us coming back because the game has the capacity to shock and delight even the most jaded, hard-bitten supporter. You cannot relive the following great Gunners occasions without a surge of pride, or a tingle of recollection …

Herbert Chapman and the Arsenal squad with their silverware in 1931

The brochure for the opening of the West Stand by the Prince of Wales in 1932

First-ever 'Arsenal' match, 11 December 1886

In 1886 a group of pals from the Woolwich munitions works joined together to form a football club, They called it Dial Square, and their first match was an away fixture against Eastern Wanderers from the Isle of Dogs on 11 December 1886. Dial Square won 6-0. On Christmas Day the same year the club changed its name to Royal Arsenal – and 125 years of glorious history was underway.

Bastin's goal against Hull City, FA Cup semi-final, 22 March 1930

Many commentators see this goal as the turning point, not only of that year's Cup campaign, but of the Club's story. With eight minutes remaining and the Gunners trailing 2–1, Cliff Bastin picked up Alex James' pass and rocketed the ball into the top corner of the net. A replay had been secured, which Arsenal won – and the rest is history.

First FA Cup win, 16 April 1930

Arsenal beat Huddersfield Town 2–0 at Wembley to record their first-ever FA Cup triumph. Alex James gave the Gunners the lead in the first-half, and Jack Lambert scored a wonderful solo goal late in the game to win the trophy for the Londoners. The victory parade through Islington was the first of many such celebrations for the Club.

First League title, 18 April 1931

Arsenal clinched their first-ever League Championship – the first by a team from the south of England – with a 3–1 victory against Liverpool at Highbury. It wasn't a last-gasp effort. There were still two matches before the season ended, but the Gunners made sure of the title thanks to the win against the Merseysiders.

The opening of the West Stand, 10 December 1932

After winning the FA Cup and the League, the Club can truly be said to have 'come of age' as a major force in football when the Prince of Wales opened the West Stand at Highbury. At the time, it was the most expensive stand in the country, providing spectators with 'armchair type seating' and a lift to the upper level.

FA Cup win, 29 April 1950

The 2–0 triumph over Liverpool at Wembley marked Arsenal's return to winning ways after the Second World War. The image of iconic captain Joe Mercer cradling the cup was one to raise the spirits of all fans in the years of post-war austerity.

First European trophy, 28 April 1970

Arsenal appeared to have blown their chance in the Final of the Fairs Cup against Anderlecht when they lost the first leg 3–1 in Belgium. But they climbed the mountain to win the return match 3–0 – and capture their first-ever European honour. Eddie Kelly set them on their way, and John Radford made it 2–0 with a header in the second-half. The Gunners made the tie safe thanks to Jon Sammels' goal. The night ended with a

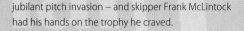
Joe Mercer with the FA Cup in 1950

Arsenal fans at the Premiership-winning match at White Hart Lane on 25 April 2004

Tony Adams celebrates scoring the fourth goal against Everton on 3 May 1998

jubilant pitch invasion – and skipper Frank McLintock had his hands on the trophy he craved.

Peter Storey's penalty in the FA Cup semi-final against Stoke City, 15 April 1971

This was a key moment in the the double-winning campaign of that year. The Gunners had been trailing 2–0 at half time in this critical game at Hillsborough. Storey brought the score back to 2–1 with a 20-yard strike past Banks, the Stoke goalie. And that was how it remained as the match entered the two minutes of added time. A headed ball from Frank McLintock was intercepted by the hands of a Stoke player and a penalty was awarded, which Storey converted perfectly. The Gunners were ecstatic, knowing that the chance to win the Cup was still theirs.

Ray Kennedy's League-title winning goal, 3 May 1971

If you couldn't clinch a League title at Highbury (or now at the Emirates), the next-best place is White Hart Lane. Ray Kennedy scored the only goal of the game with three minutes remaining to bring the Championship back to the club for the eighth time – and the first in 18 years.

The First Double, 8 May 1971

Just five days after winning the title on Spurs' ground, Arsenal went to Wembley in quest of their first-ever League-Cup Double. Liverpool were their opponents in the FA Cup Final, and in a tense match which went to extra time, Charlie George's stunning long-range strike sealed a 2–1 victory and his celebration – lying on the Wembley turf with his arms outstretched – is one of the most memorable Arsenal moments.

The Greatest Cup Finale, 12 May 1979

It wasn't the best FA Cup Final ever, but it was certainly the best last five minutes of any Cup Final. With the match against Manchester United drawing to a close with the Gunners 2–0 up, the Cup was as good as won. But Gordon McQueen scored from a corner to give United hope, and the unthinkable happened when Sammy McIlroy netted an equaliser. With a replay moments away, and Arsenal's hearts in their boots, Liam Brady collected the ball from the re-start and passed to Graham Rix. His cross evaded the United defence, and Alan Sunderland bundled the ball over the line to secure a dramatic 3–2 victory.

Winning the League at Anfield, 26 May 1989

'Thomas, charging through the midfield... it's up for grabs now... Thomas, right at the end! An unbelievable climax to the league season…!' TV commentator Brian Moore found the words to describe the delirious moment when Michael Thomas's late goal won the title at Anfield. It was the final match of the season, and The Gunners needed to win by two goals to seize the title from Liverpool. Arsenal scored early in the second half through Alan Smith, but as time ebbed away the Merseysiders appeared content with a 1-0 defeat which guaranteed them the title. Cue Thomas. Cue the wildest celebrations any Arsenal supporter had ever known.

Tony Adams scoring against Everton, 3 May 1998

No Arsenal supporter will forget the sight of 'Mr Arsenal' striding back down the pitch with his arms aloft, after scoring the fourth, title-clinching goal on the 4–0 win against Everton at Highbury.

The Invincible Season, 30 May 2004

In 2003–04 Arsenal achieved the monumental feat of going through an entire Premier League season without tasting defeat. The Premiership title had been clinched at White Hart Lane on 25 April, amid wild celebrations. The last match of the campaign was against Leicester City at home – and the Midlanders were unable to spoil Arsenal's party. City took the lead, but goals from Thierry Henry and Patrick Vieira kept the unbeaten record safe.

CHAPTER 8

AND SO TO ANFIELD...

1973–1997

At the beginning of 1973 Arsenal had reached five Cup finals in five seasons but Bertie Mee felt the sands of time running out. In what he later described as his greatest mistake, he bought Jeff Blockley from Coventry clearly to be the replacement for Frank McLintock. The mood was turning and, although Arsenal finished the League second to Liverpool, perhaps the final game of the season, a 6–1 defeat against Leeds at Elland Road, was to be the more symbolic. McLintock had been at the core of the Double team but Don Howe's departure had never adequately been dealt with and by the beginning of the 1973–74 season Howe's successor, Steve Burtenshaw, was to be replaced by Bobby Campbell.

CHANGING TIMES

Gradually the Double side drifted away. Ray Kennedy went to greater and unexpected glories at Anfield, Charlie George became an unexpected failure at Derby County. Despite his central role in the Arsenal history, George had played just 169 games for the Gunners. McLintock and Kelly moved, with some success, to QPR while Alan Ball, though not part of the Double team, eventually went to Southampton.

By 1976 Bertie Mee, influenced by the retirement of his friend Bill Nicholson two years earlier, decided that the time had come for him to bow out. It had been a poor season, with the club's 17th place the worst position since Herbert Chapman's arrival in 1925.

Mee's replacement was a surprise, although he followed the tradition of being an Arsenal man. Terry Neill, previously captain of Northern Ireland and manager of Hull, had managed Spurs with no great success for the past two years and became the youngest ever manager at Highbury.

What was to be Neill's most memorable step came almost instantly – the signature of Malcolm Macdonald for £333,333 from Newcastle. Whatever good it did Neill, it effectively ended Gordon Lee's time as manager at St James', so popular was Supermac in Newcastle. He arrived saying he would get 30 goals in his first season and he ended just one short. He also gave a boost to the careers of the then youngsters Liam Brady, David O'Leary and Frank Stapleton. Eventually even John Radford, driest and perhaps the sharpest of the Double team, moved on – after 379 League games and 111 goals – to West Ham. Now only Rice, Nelson and Armstrong remained. Additions came with Alan Hudson from Stoke and, most important of all, the return of the prodigal Don Howe.

CUP SPECIALISTS

The scene was now set for the highlight of the 20-year gap between the Championships of 1971 and 1989 – the hat-trick of Cup finals of 1978, 1979 and 1980. The Gunners contrived to win the one they were expected to lose and to lose the two they were expected to win.

The 1978 game was to be a 0–1 defeat by Ipswich, the 1979 game was to be the 'five-minute final' concluding in the 3–2 victory over Manchester United, and the 1980 final was to be the 0–1 defeat by Second Division West Ham. Arsenal became the first club to reach three successive Wembley FA Cup finals and only the third ever to achieve a hat-trick of finals.

The 1978 FA Cup rounds were impressive – five successive wins (Sheffield United, Wolves, Walsall, Wrexham and Orient) with 17 goals scored, seven from Macdonald who scored in every game except the final. The Wembley confrontation was to be an unhappy experience. Brady was not fit and had to be substituted, Macdonald was to end with a third losers' medal and was never to have another chance – three days later he went into hospital for the first of many knee operations that ended his career at the age of 29. Roger Osborne scored the only goal for Ipswich to win the contest.

THE 'FIVE-MINUTE' FINAL

1979 was more fulfilling for the Gunners, and rather more interesting for everyone. The third round should have been easy – against a Sheffield Wednesday then in the Third

Division. It took five games and 540 minutes for Arsenal to triumph. Immediately afterward Neill acquired Brian Talbot for £400,000 from Ipswich, after Talbot's fine display in the 1978 Cup final. As a result, Talbot was to become only the second player to win Cup winners' medals with different clubs in successive seasons. Notts County were the next victims, then came the key game in the Cup run. Arsenal were drawn at the City Ground, where League Champions Nottingham Forest had not lost in 52 matches. Stapleton scored the only goal with a fine header and, after that, Southampton and Wolves were relatively easy meat. The final brought Manchester United back to London as favourites after their defeat of new Champions Liverpool in the semi-final.

It was to be a hot, stifling day. Talbot was the star again, running his heart out, but Brady and Stapleton looked world-class. In the first 85 minutes there were two goals. The first was unique at Wembley – Sunderland and Talbot arriving simultaneously for the scoring shot, although Talbot later claimed it – and the second was a fine header from Stapleton. Then, in the last five minutes United scored and extra time seemed certain. But Graham Rix set off down the left, swung the ball over for Alan Sunderland, who made it 3–2.

BROOKING'S HEADER

The following year was memorable for the semi-final – a four-game marathon against Liverpool which was finally won by a goal from Brian Talbot. It was the longest ever semi-final

Opposite: In an Arsenal career which lasted from 1973 to 1980, Liam Brady made 307 first-class appearances and scored a creditable 59 goals.

Below left: Tottenham's captain Steve Perryman is no match for a determined combination of Stewart Robson and Brian Talbot (left). Talbot had the distinction of being in the winning side in successive FA Cup finals for different teams — first for Ipswich against Arsenal and second for Arsenal.

Below: Pat Jennings in the 1979 FA Cup final. This was the game which was to become known as 'the five-minute final'. Arsenal were leading 2–0 in the 85th minute, Manchester United then scored twice, and Arsenal netted the winner, all in the final five minutes.

Right: Terry Neill and Don Howe in happier times.

at 420 minutes, and is the only semi-final to be played at Coventry. Unfortunately Arsenal had only nine days between the semi- and the final, against Second Division West Ham, and they still had two League matches to get through in those nine days. The final itself was unmemorable apart from Willie Young's terrible foul on Paul Allen with just three minutes of play left, and Trevor Brooking's stooping header which won the game for West Ham. It was one of only three headed goals that Brooking ever scored.

EUROPEAN FAILURE

Just four days later an exhausted Arsenal had to travel to Brussels for their second ever European final – the Cup Winners Cup against Valencia, the reward for the 3–2 win against Manchester United a year before. Their progress in a quiet year had been against Fenerbahce, Magdeburg, IFK Gothenburg and Juventus. The Turin semi-final, after a 1–1 draw at Highbury, is probably Arsenal's greatest performance in Europe. No British club had ever won there, and Juventus had not lost a European game there in ten years. Paul Vaessen, in his one moment of glory, scored the only goal two minutes from time and two minutes from elimination from the competition. Within two years of the final his playing career was cut short by a serious injury.

The final in Brussels was, like Wembley against West Ham, a poor game and scoreless. It went to a penalty shoot-out with the great Mario Kempas and Liam Brady missing the first two attempts. No one else missed until Graham Rix's shot was guessed right by Valencia keeper Pereira and this exhausting season ended without a trophy. Arsenal ended having played 15 games in 45 days, and 70 in all – the most ever played by a British club in a single season.

Just as the 1970–72 great period had lasted just three years, so had the four-Cup-final team of 1978–80. The decline from here on was as dramatic as in the early 1970s. Apart from a curiously symmetrical pair of semi-finals in both cup competitions against Manchester United in 1983 (Arsenal lost all three games), the news was rarely good. Defeats in Cup games by Middlesbrough and York City were bad enough, but the real moment of truth was the 1–2 home defeat by legendary Walsall in the League Cup on 29 November 1983.

WALSALL SEAL NEILL'S FATE

Defeats by Third Division sides were not that uncommon, but Terry Neill was already under pressure and unlucky that it was Walsall of all clubs and that it was exactly 50 years since 1933. Little else was going right. Charlie Nicholas, who had cost £650,000 in the summer, had scored in just one game and had yet to score in front of his own fans. Neill was phlegmatic under pressure: 'They don't seem to know what it is to hunger for goals and glory. On (some) days I think they just want to pick up their money and go home. But I'll tell you

now; we'll finish in the top six again this season. Whether or not I'll be around to see it is another matter.' They did finish sixth, and Neill was not around to see it.

Walsall was the match that ended the reign of Neill, and after 14 years as a coach Don Howe at last became the Arsenal manager. It was not a happy two-and-a-half-years for Howe. Attendances fell dramatically – regularly to below 20,000 for the first time since Chapman's days. On 22 March 1986, after a 3–0 win over Coventry Don Howe resigned – hurt by media speculation that the club were keen to bring Terry Venables back from Barcelona.

STROLLER RETURNS

And it was to the Double team that the club were to turn for Howe's successor – not just to the Double team, but to the player who was voted Man of the Match at the moment of ultimate triumph – George Graham, 'Stroller'.

Graham's managerial experience to date had been limited. He had done a good job at troubled Millwall, not letting crowd problems deflect from a competent young team. But he was hardly a proven quantity. Nonetheless, 12 months on, the choice seemed no less than inspired. He knew Highbury and the way the board ran things, he had the confidence of the players, the board, the public and even the sponsors, JVC, who had been totally loyal to the club since the first days of real football commercialism.

On the pitch the season was nothing less than a revelation. Firstly Graham did not spend, saying that he needed time to assess the staff and he wasn't going to buy anyone unless he was sure he was good enough. Indeed, it wasn't until season's end that he purchased Alan Smith from Leicester. So he relied on what he had – rehabilitating the impetuous Steve Williams, trusting the imperfect Niall Quinn and showing faith in the young Tony Adams at centre-back with David O'Leary.

The side settled to a steady, if unspectacular, pattern. The rock was, in Arsenal tradition, the defence. By season's end three of the back four (Anderson, Sansom and Adams) were

Below: A dejected Liam Brady walks away after missing a penalty during the shoot-out during the 1980 Cup Winners Cup against Valencia.

England regulars and O'Leary, of course, had been Eire's mainstay for years. After 27 September 1986, when they lost 1–0 at League leaders Forest, the defence locked and defeat was not to be an issue until 24 January 1987, after another 22 games, a club record for Arsenal. In that period they won 17 and drew five, scoring 47 and conceding just 11.

Graham was adamant from the beginning of the run: Arsenal were not good enough to win the title, he insisted, and it was not said simply to generate good press copy. When the side did lose, the disappointment was, nonetheless, intense. The match was at Old Trafford, where United had been struggling all season.

CENTENARY CELEBRATIONS

By the time of the defeat by United, Arsenal were well ahead of the League and going strongly in both Cups. It had been a glorious winter, capped on 27 December 1986 by a wonderful celebration of the club's centenary, which had been two days earlier, on Christmas Day itself. An enormous crowd turned out for the game against Southampton (won 1–0) and so did a great array of stars. Most notable of many notables were, perhaps, Joe Mercer, Ted Drake and, above all others, George Male, the only man present to have played under Herbert Chapman. How appropriate that Arsenal were top of the League that centenary day, how appropriate that Bob Wilson should be the master of ceremonies, how appropriate that the crowd was large, well behaved and appreciative; and, some might say, how appropriate that the defence did not concede a goal against Southampton.

And similar good fortune may have appeared three months later as the Gunners approached the series of games for which the centenary year will surely always be remembered. Having disposed of Huddersfield, Manchester City, Charlton and Forest in the League Cup, Arsenal were drawn to play, and defeated, a newly confident Spurs in the semi-final. Both north London clubs were also in the FA Cup quarter finals.

Frank McLintock, captain of the Double team, watched the match: 'Like us in the 1970s, they've got players who hate to be beaten. I don't remember us losing when we were a goal up.' Spurs arguably didn't remember winning when they were a goal up against Arsenal.

McLintock sympathised with Howe's position: 'I couldn't help feeling a bit sorry for him sitting there. George rightly deserves the credit, but Don encouraged a lot of this success and it's all been forgotten so quickly. He wasn't that far away. The players were all his. George hasn't bought anyone.'

EARLY SUCCESS FOR GRAHAM

Arsenal had drawn the Littlewoods final card no one wanted – Liverpool. After this point any pretensions in the League disappeared completely. Players who might find themselves suspended for the final were rested and, having played seven matches in 21 days, Graham's view on their League chances was realistic. Liverpool came to Highbury in the League. Rush scored and that was that. Was it a portent? Dalglish had done a job, but Graham's young lions contributed to the evening. At least, one no longer felt as one had in the early 1980s that the problem was not the fact that Arsenal did not win anything, but that they did not seem likely to win anything. The game against Liverpool clearly showed that Graham, as he had said, did not have the resources in depth that he really needed to run Liverpool and Everton close over a full season. But, Highbury hoped, that would come. A quarter final defeat (3–1) by Watford ended the team's interest in the FA Cup and all that was left to think about was Wembley and Liverpool.

No matter how good they appeared in day-to-day terms, this was not the great Liverpool side of the early 1980s. They were eventually to win nothing in 1987; shades of 1985 when they not only suffered the Heysel tragedy but (it is easily forgotten) won none of the six trophies they contested. Arsenal were not short of ability. They had their defence, which remained outstanding. Tony Adams was to become Young Player of the Year and a major asset. 'If we had that boy,' said another First Division manager, 'we'd conquer the world.' And there was always the joker, Charlie Nicholas.

Arsenal won the toss for colours and, interestingly, chose to play in their own red shirts. Twice before they had met Liverpool at Wembley. In 1950 they had played in gold shirts, in 1971 in yellow shirts and blue shorts. They had won both times but this time they reverted to the familiar.

The game was on 5 April. The press unfailingly chose Liverpool, who had already won the trophy on four consecutive occasions in the 1980s. Liverpool had, of course, won 1–0 at Highbury a month before. It was to be Ian Rush's last appearance at Wembley before his move to Juventus. Liverpool had even set a record with a 10–0 defeat of Fulham on their way to the final. But this was, perhaps, all a little misleading. Arsenal had lacked Anderson, Rocastle and Williams when they lost 1–0 four weeks before.

NICHOLAS DECIDES FINAL

After 23 minutes Craig Johnston put Ian Rush through to open the scoring. Tediously the football world told itself, yet again, that Liverpool had never lost any of the games (almost 150) in which Ian Rush had scored. But even the oldest records have to go eventually and it was to be the enigmatic Charlie Nicholas who did the damage. The Gunners seemed remarkably unaffected by Rush's goal and took control for the remaining three-quarters of the match. Nicholas poked the ball home after a scramble on the stroke of half time.

Seven minutes from the end Perry Groves, on as a substitute, roared in from the left, depositing a trail of defenders behind him, and pushed the ball to Nicholas. His rather weak shot took a deflection and left Bruce Grobbelaar stranded as it meandered into the net.

The Times offered promise: 'Arsenal had no need to win the Littlewoods Cup at Wembley. Their season has already been lined with enough golden memories. To add a touch of silver as well is not only highly lucrative but it is an unexpected bonus that no one could realistically have foreseen when their centenary season began seven months ago.'

But after that unexpected bonus to conclude their first 100 years, Arsenal and George Graham were quickly brought back to a shuddering start to the second hundred. The very first game of Graham's second season in charge was at home to Liverpool on 15 August. A crowd of 55,000 saw the Gunners lose 2–1 and suffer a goalless draw at Old Trafford four days later. These were to be the sides which finished first and second in the League and which the Gunners only occasionally looked like emulating. Charlie Nicholas played just the first three games of the 1987–88 season and then fell into the reserves. He was later sold to Aberdeen in January 1988 and disappeared into relative obscurity – a classic case of unfulfilled promise.

Graham kept looking for another forward to complement Smith, but made only one serious bid – £2 million for Tony Cottee at the end of the 1987–88 season. Cottee chose to go to Everton, which was perhaps an interesting comment on the perceptions of Arsenal at that time. If Cottee had come to Highbury, his transfer would at last have superseded the nine-year-old club record of £1,250,000 for the non-playing Clive Allen. Graham, perhaps more by necessity than choice, encouraged Paul Merson at the end of the 1987-88 season.

LEAGUE CUP DEFENCE V LUTON

Sunday 24 April 1988 was a delightfully bright, sunny day and an unexpectedly pleasing conclusion to a season that was otherwise disappointing. Back at Wembley for the Littlewoods Cup final, Arsenal were faced with a very different proposition from 1987, when they had defeated hot favourites Liverpool to take the trophy for the first time. In 1988 the positions were reversed. Arsenal's opponents this time were Luton Town, who had never won a trophy in their entire 102-year

history and who arrived at Wembley with morale, injury and selection problems. On the way to the final, Arsenal had scored 15 goals and conceded only one. Their opponents had been Doncaster, Bournemouth, Stoke, Sheffield Wednesday and Everton and the highlight was clearly the first leg of the semi-final at Goodison Park. Perry Groves had scored the only goal to give the Gunners a comfortable lead, which was built on with a pleasing 3–1 win in the second leg at Highbury.

Luton had experienced a considerably more traumatic season. A few weeks before the final all had seemed to be going so well. Luton had reached the final of the Simod Cup, the semi-final of the FA Cup and were in the Mercantile Classic Centenary celebration to be played among 16 clubs at Wembley on 17 April. It all went horribly wrong. They lost the FA Cup semi-final 2–1 to Wimbledon when they really should have done much better. Even worse, they somehow contrived to lose the Simod Cup final 4–1 to lowly Reading. Luton were then knocked out in their first game in the 16-team Mercantile tournament and came back to Wembley for the Littlewoods Cup shell-shocked.

As it happened, it was the Arsenal defence which was shell-shocked after a quarter of an hour at Wembley. After Harford had very nearly put Luton ahead with a powerful header, Foster put Brian Stein through neatly to score well and make it Luton 1 Arsenal 0. Arsenal's first half was no better than poor and Luton started the second half the way they did the first. After just two minutes a superb save by Lukic from a Brian Stein header saved the day.

Smith, Rocastle and Groves were conspicuous by their near absence from proceedings and, indeed, after an hour Groves was replaced by Martin Hayes. This proved an excellent substitution. Hayes gave width and pace and, with a quarter of an hour left, scored after a scramble. Five minutes later Paul Davis put the ball wide to Alan Smith, who shot just between keeper Andy Dibble and the post. It was an excellent goal and, for Smith, only his second in ten games.

WINTERBURN MISSES CRUCIAL PENALTY

Only two minutes later Smith headed against the bar and Martin Hayes contrived to hit the post with the rebound from literally a yard out. Arsenal, after stuttering for an hour, were suddenly totally in charge, surging forward through a tired Luton midfield. Smith went through twice, only to see Dibble save well. Then with eight minutes left Rocastle fell in the area, the referee harshly said he was tripped and Nigel Winterburn, who had scored only once before for Arsenal, took the penalty. Andy Dibble, the Luton reserve keeper dived beautifully and tipped it round the post. It was only the second penalty ever missed in a major Wembley final.

Winterburn and Arsenal were made to pay within seconds. Caesar stumbled and lost the ball in the penalty area. A chaos of bodies ensued, ending with Danny Wilson making it 2–2 with just five minutes left.

Right: The highlight of the centenary season, 1986–87, was a three-part League Cup semi-final tie against Spurs. Arsenal never went ahead in the 300-minute-long tie until two minutes from the end. The key moment was a last-gasp equaliser from Viv Anderson in the second of the three games. Spurs fans were quick to point out that Clive Allen (here in the first leg) scored in all three games against the club that had paid a record fee for him and then never given him a game.

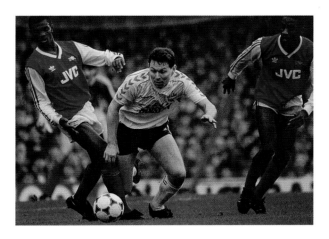

That wasn't the end, for with virtually the last move of the match Ashley Grimes came round the back of Arsenal's left side, hammered the ball with his left foot to Brian Stein and into the net it went: 3–2 to Luton.

Nonetheless, Graham was not short of talent. He had inherited Tony Adams, David Rocastle, Paul Davis and Michael Thomas. All were coming to their peak and all would attract England's attention. The full-back slots had been a problem with the decline of Kenny Sansom and the failure of Gus Caesar to replace Viv Anderson, who headed off to Old Trafford. Graham had already solved the problem by replacing Sansom with Nigel Winterburn (who had cost £400,000) and buying Lee Dixon from Stoke for the same price. Winterburn, still – so early in his Arsenal career – best known for his Wembley penalty miss, had been nervous about replacing Sansom: 'I was worried about being compared with Kenny – after all, he's won more caps than any other England left-back. Then I realised that the comparisons would be made anyway, so I just concentrated on my own game. Highbury's a bit like Wimbledon really. When I was there we were always being criticised, but we drew strength from these attacks. The mood's the same in the Arsenal dressing room. We scored more goals than any other team in 1988–89, yet as soon as we experiment with a sweeper we're called negative.'

GRAHAM PREPARES FOR TITLE TILT

Graham's other signings before the Championship season of 1988–89 were equally modest – Brian Marwood from Sheffield Wednesday for £600,000, third centre-back Steve Bould from Stoke for £390,000 and Kevin Richardson for £200,000 from Watford. It was to be a memorable year for Richardson, who became one of the few players to win a Champions' medal with two different clubs – he also has one from Everton in 1985.

Graham fitted his new players to the existing structure. This led, toward the end of the season, to the three centre-back sweeper system after the offside trap had been battered at Highbury by both Forest and Charlton.

Like the Double side of 1971 the team depended on perspiration rather than inspiration and, in David Lacey's words, was: '... fast, fit and pragmatic. They play the long ball toward the head of Smith and depend on the breakdown of opposition movements as a springboard for counter attack.'

The Arsenal of 1989 were not as resilient as their predecessors of 1971 had proved themselves to be. They lost and drew games that many would say the Double team would have won. Radford, Kennedy, Storey, Simpson and McLintock would force results in games where the team played badly. The 1989 team were not as dependable, particularly at Highbury, where, on occasions, they looked frighteningly frail. Again, the Double team had two clear creative talents – Charlie George and George Graham – who had no real equivalents in 1989. David Rocastle came closest, winning the Barclays 'Young Eagle of the Year' Award.

Future Gunners boss Bruce Rioch said of Arsenal early in the 1988–89 season: 'They work extremely hard to take possession. If you can't stop service into the penalty area, you're in trouble. They have massive midfield strength. Once they get the ball in your half they keep it there. They pressure you on the ball so you make mistakes. It's not easy playing them, and not very pretty either.'

Arsenal were no strangers to the long-ball game, and it was when employing this style that their dependence on the brilliance and consistency of Alan Smith became clear. As the season progressed, he played better and better, ending it as the First Division's top scorer and gaining an international place. His performance at Liverpool in the final game was quite outstanding. 'You could have fired a cannonball at him that day and he'd have controlled it and laid it off to one of the midfielders without a second thought,' said one of the Liverpool defenders afterward.

AWAY FORM THE KEY

The Championship season was, in truth, a patchy one. The Gunners did not reach the top of the League until Boxing Day, and then lost the lead to Liverpool with just 13 days left. They

Above: In 1988 Wembley was not a lucky venue for Arsenal against Luton. Already 2–1 ahead, the Gunners were awarded a penalty in the League Cup final. Andy Dibble made a superb save from Nigel Winterburn's spot kick and the game was turned on its head, with Luton coming through for a 3–2 win.

won more games away from home than at home (12 versus 10), which was very odd indeed for a Championship side. Far more peculiar was that the sides which finished second (Liverpool), third (Forest) and fourth (Norwich) did the same, all having better away than home records. All the top four lost at least three home games during the season.

To some extent Arsenal's League ambitions were helped by early exits in the Cups. Liverpool won a League (Littlewoods) Cup third round tie after two replays while West Ham caused a great surprise in winning an FA Cup third round replay 1–0 at Highbury. Arsenal had managed only to draw 2–2 at Upton Park, despite West Ham's dreadful League form, which eventually led to relegation. Arsenal had some minor consolation in the winning of the Mercantile Credit Trophy, another rather peculiar event which was part of the League's ill-fated centenary celebrations.

SMITH STARTS WITH A TRICK

The League season had begun with a 5–1 victory away at FA Cup holders Wimbledon, with Alan Smith scoring a very welcome hat-trick to provide a perfect foretaste of what the season was to hold for him. It was, however, the only hat-trick that the club were to record during the season – unusual for a Championship side with such a good goalscoring record (73 in the League alone). Unfortunately this was immediately followed by a 3–2 home defeat by Villa and a 2–1 reverse at Sheffield Wednesday. Nonetheless, other results were steady and, with mediocre starts by other contenders, Arsenal found themselves in second place early in November without having had to perform particularly well to get there.

On 6 November they had an outstanding televised win at the City Ground, totally outplaying Forest in a 4–1 crushing which, for the first time, made the press take Arsenal's season

seriously. The goalscorers were Bould, Adams, Smith and Marwood and, although Arsenal were now second behind Norwich, the almost universal view was still that it was a matter of waiting for Liverpool to come good.

The situation, however, had changed completely by the time Arsenal defeated Everton at Goodison Park on 14 January to go five points clear at the top of the table. This was surprising statistically as, between Forest and Everton, Arsenal played 13 first-class games of which they drew four, lost three and won only six. This was not exactly Championship form, but in an open season, it was enough to put them in front.

COMFORTABLE LEAD FOR GUNNERS

They were also, it must be said, playing very well when it mattered. After the 3–1 win at Goodison, Peter Ball said in *The Times*: 'In the best superstitious footballing tradition, George Graham is refusing to count the Championship until it is hatched. No one else at Goodison Park on Saturday harboured any doubts about its destination as Arsenal demolished Everton with a massively authoritative performance.' Obviously Mr Dalglish had not been at Goodison that Saturday and, indeed, Liverpool were now no fewer than 11 points behind. The gap at one time between Arsenal and Liverpool was as great as 19 points, which Liverpool clawed back between January and the ultimate denouement on 26 May. That was an astonishing achievement by Liverpool, but not unprecedented – at Christmas time 1986 Arsenal were seven points clear at the top of the League and by the end of March 1987 Liverpool were nine points ahead – a gain of 16 points in three months. So Liverpool's ability to catch up was not in doubt – it was just that this year it seemed so unlikely that they would, so vulnerable did they look (they had just lost 3–1 at Old Trafford).

Right: David O'Leary against Forest's Neil Webb in a League game in March 1989. Forest won 3–1.

But, above all else, it was Arsenal's performance at Goodison on 14 January which was particularly impressive. Kevin Richardson, who scored one of Arsenal's three goals for his first of the season, was exceptionally enthusiastic. 'It's like history repeating itself,' he said after the game. 'The pattern, team balance and tactics are all very similar to the way Everton played in 1984–85 and that is why I find it so easy to fit in.' Richardson, who won a Championship medal with that Everton team in 1984–85, continued: 'The manager has laid down the same kind of requirements on closing down opponents, denying space and putting quality balls into the box. The Arsenal players are far more experienced now, having had two seasons when they've led the League for a while, and now we have the insurance of a five-point lead. If we don't win it now, it will be the fault of the players and nobody else.'

At Goodison Arsenal brought their impressive away record to eight wins and 29 away goals, true Championship form. This was particularly good as they were troubled by injury at the centre of defence, where O'Leary and Caesar were both only second-choice options, even when available. It was David Rocastle, though, who proved Everton's downfall. The first goal was the result of a fierce cross from the right which Merson finished off with the relish of a forward enjoying his sixth goal in seven games. Just seven minutes later Rocastle went past Sheedy to the by-line, hammered over a cross and Alan Smith flung himself at the ball for goal number two. Richardson scored a clever third against his old club after a neat one-two with the outstanding Smith.

One of the few advantages of Liverpool's dominance of the 1980s was that no one else was expected to win anything, which took the pressure off them. It was only after the Everton game that Arsenal became Championship favourites and it is an interesting comment on what happened in the next four months that the bookmakers gradually changed their quotes from odds-on at the end of January to 7–1 against on 26 May.

PRESSURE STARTS TO TELL

As soon as Arsenal became favourites, the pressure was on. Instead of a steady, if not triumphal, progress toward their rightful prize, the campaign became one of slow attrition, with Liverpool gradually creeping up point by point, week by week, and most people thinking that Liverpool were bound, in the end, to win it as they had done so often. Between the start of the year and that dramatic evening of 26 May Liverpool, in fact, played 24 games undefeated. In a sense, that was irrelevant to Arsenal. All the Gunners had to do was keep winning and the title would be theirs. It was not like that, as we all know.

Of the 17 games between Goodison and Anfield, Arsenal lost three (two at home) and drew five. Those 19 points dropped could have been, and indeed seemed, crucial as Liverpool closed a gap that had been precisely that size.

A 0–1 stutter at Coventry on 21 February was perhaps excusable, but the crisis really struck when Forest destroyed the leaders at Highbury on 11 March. This was the game that everyone attended knowing Arsenal had to win, but Forest scored three times in the first half and made the defence look ponderous, unintelligent and porous. Suddenly the Gunners, though still leading the League, looked anything but Champions. Ten days later lowly Charlton, perennial relegation candidates, drew 2–2 at Highbury and George Graham made a critical move with the change that probably secured the Championship.

TACTICAL SWITCH

Deciding his rearguard was too vulnerable and with three experienced centre-backs now free from injury, he decided to change the pattern. Switching from the traditional four-across-the-back that Forest had so exposed, he switched to the very rare (in England) sweeper system with a third centre-back. By having David O'Leary sweep behind Bould and Adams, Graham reduced the likelihood of fast breaks cutting through a square back four.

In addition, and as important, Graham perceived that, as few opponents played more than two men up front against Arsenal, the sweeper would allow the full-backs Dixon and Winterburn to push upfield to support David Rocastle and Kevin Richardson. This, in turn, released Rocastle from defensive duties and allowed him to go forward. In attack it worked perfectly – the full-backs scored three critical goals in the games that followed and midfielders Thomas and Rocastle two each. As a system it was seen at its best against Liverpool at Anfield, when the full-backs were key elements in the intense system of constant pressure that Arsenal applied to the home club and which, in the end, won them the game and the title.

It was rare for a club leading the League to change its tactics so late in the season but, as Graham said: 'I've always been a good learner and I'm prepared to apply the things I've learned. It's up to me to come up with solutions to the problems that present themselves. The players were no problem at all. I only told them about it a week before we put it into effect (against Manchester United on 2 April), but they were very willing to try it.' Tony Adams agreed: 'In my six years with the club we've always played with four across the back, but when the boss asked us to try it, we just got on with it. Good players adapt. Our usual 4–4–2 was becoming a bit stereotyped. We were all pushing up and getting caught on the break – like we did against Forest.'

The Manchester United game was not the happiest for Adams, for he conceded an unlucky late own goal. This drew a peculiar response from what we must assume was an anti-Arsenal tabloid press, the Mirror in particular attacked Adams in the most puerile and unimaginative way. Happily for Arsenal, the effect was that it bonded the team closer than

Above: On 28 October 1989 David O'Leary made a record-equalling 621st appearance for Arsenal.

Right: Tony Adams towers above Steve Chettle at The City Ground in November of 1988. The Arsenal captain was the backbone of a defence that was becoming recognised as the meanest in the league. The Gunners powered to a 4–1 victory in this match with goals from Adams, Bould, Smith and Marwood.

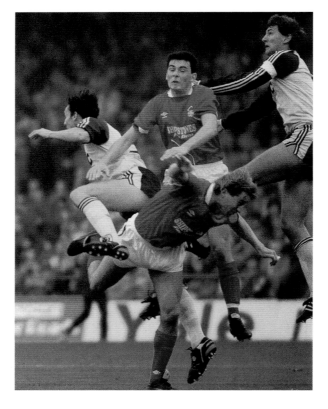

ever and led to Adams' most productive spell of the season. Indeed, the time between the 2–2 draw with Charlton on 21 March and the game against Derby on 13 May was really the period when Arsenal won the Championship. It was their best spell of the season, with five wins and the unlucky draw against United. Coming directly after a run of five matches in which they picked up only four points, it restored belief and set up the most remarkable of pulsating finishes.

GUNNERS OVERTAKEN

On 8 April Arsenal were finally overtaken by Liverpool and lost first place, if only for four hours. Liverpool kicked off at Anfield in the morning that day (because the Grand National was in the afternoon) and so went to the top of the table. Arsenal took the lead back again after a hard-fought win over Everton, but the signs were ominous. The game was hardly a classic, but Chairman Peter Hill-Wood was not downhearted: 'My feeling is that whether we win the League or not, I see no reason why we shouldn't go on to have a great deal of success with this team. I've never been so hopeful about the future.'

A dull 1–0 win over Newcastle on 15 April was totally overshadowed by what happened 200 miles further north, at Hillsborough. Liverpool's sudden surge from 19 points behind, their dramatic unbeaten run since the New Year and the prospect of another Double had generated an astonishing amount of interest in the FA Cup semi-final against Forest. These were the two in-form clubs– having lost just two of 44

fixtures between them in 1989. The crowds at Hillsborough were massive, including thousands without tickets. The consequences are too well known to need repeating here, but the deaths of 96 fans were to cast long, long shadows over the English game for many years.

After the disaster there was considerable confusion as to what would happen next. Liverpool naturally suspended their fixtures, including the vital game against Arsenal at Anfield. Highbury refused the League's thoughtless request to continue as normal and cancelled their next game. Arsenal did not take the football field again for another 16 days.

RIVALS 'OUTCLASSED AND OUTPLAYED'

When they did, on May Day, it was for a fixture which had been expected, several months before, to determine the Championship. Norwich had led the League up to Christmas and had maintained their challenge until the past few weeks. Then their collapse had been far more comprehensive than Arsenal's and this was their last chance to struggle back into the race. The Gunners, however, chose this day for their best display of the season to date. As Stuart Jones said in *The Times*: 'Arsenal withdrew the hand of friendship and sympathy which had been so generously extended to Liverpool. The First Division leaders, whose reaction to Hillsborough was so honourable and dignified, confirmed that now they will show no mercy to opponents or to Merseyside.'

Norwich were completely overrun. Their manager, Dave Stringer, said afterward: 'We were outclassed and outplayed. It was a hammering. We finished as also-rans. On that performance, Arsenal will walk away with the title.'

The display was electric, despite the fact that a key figure in winger Brian Marwood was injured and would be out for the remainder of the season. Dixon and Winterburn pushed up and filled the wide areas. Smith was supported everywhere and played superbly. Norwich were as vulnerable on the wings as in the centre. Winterburn, roaring through, scored the first. Smith volleyed a spectacular second just before the interval. In the second half Thomas got the third and then Smith and Rocastle provided a gala finish. It was Arsenal's biggest win of the season and it seemed to guarantee that the League race would go all the way to the end of the season.

There were now just four matches left for Arsenal. The next was rather more pedestrian – away at Middlesbrough, who were fighting to stay in the First Division.

There was just one goal, the result of what appeared to be an inspired substitution by George Graham. Martin Hayes, who had not scored all season, came on in place of Paul Merson in the 67th minute, was immediately fouled by Parkinson, got up and promptly scored a goal. The rest of the game is perhaps best forgotten, though it certainly bears comparison with the hard, taut game against Stoke City at the end of the Double season, when substitute Eddie Kelly had scored an absolutely essential goal.

FLAGGING AT THE LAST

After Middlesbrough came the stumble. All Arsenal needed to do by then was keep their heads up through the next two matches – at home to Derby and Wimbledon – and then the most they would need was a draw at Anfield in the last game of the season, even assuming Liverpool won all their remaining matches. But the team seemed to crack. On Saturday 13 May, Derby came to Highbury and went away with a 2–1 win. As George Graham said afterward: 'We didn't take our chances and Peter Shilton was in superb form. If anything we were too keen. We hit too many long balls when we needed to build from the back. It's easy to demand patience from the players but it's hard for them to keep showing it when there is so much at stake. We've got to bounce back. We've been written off so many times before that it would be silly to write us off just yet.' But in his programme notes Graham sounded less confident, as if he was going through the motions, saying the right things, that not even he could really believe Liverpool would be beaten now. He declared that he had derived great satisfaction from the progress of the past three seasons and that he wanted Arsenal to take over from Liverpool as the yardstick by which football was measured.

In the still small hours it was hard for anyone really to believe that they could now do it. It was statistically possible, but no longer very likely. Liverpool were back on top. There were two games left. The penultimate match was at home against Wimbledon on Wednesday 17 May. The Dons were never easy opponents, although Arsenal had destroyed them 5–1 at Plough Lane on the opening day of the season.

That was easily Wimbledon's worst defeat of the season and they came looking for revenge. They achieved it of sorts, with a 2–2 draw that seemed to spell the end of any lingering hope for the Gunners. It was a tragedy to the hordes pouring away from Highbury that night; their favourites seemed to have thrown it away by failing to win two home fixtures at the end of the season. Surely these games were the acid tests of Champions? Surely these were the games you won if you were to add your name to the panoply of greats? To take one point out of six when the Championship beckoned – it was as much as flesh and blood could bear.

Liverpool tidied up an emotional but rather stunted occasion by beating Everton 3–2 in yet another Merseyside Cup final. One game left and all Liverpool had to do was avoid defeat by two goals. A 0–1 or 1–2 defeat wouldn't be pretty, but the Double would be theirs.

LIVERPOOL NOW THE FAVOURITES

Arsenal were out of it – that was their great strength. The big bookmakers quoted them at 7–1 against, but you could have got 20–1 and better on any street corner. George Graham seemed relaxed when he was asked about the pressure a few days before: 'I hope we get this sort of pressure every year. Pressure is something the media like to talk about, but I'll tell you what real pressure is – it's being bottom of the Third Division. This is enjoyable pressure.' When asked whether Arsenal would still win the Championship he was more guarded. 'I don't know whether we will win. I know that we can win. Any team can win one game, particularly with an away record like we've got.'

In many respects Graham was right. Arsenal's two advantages were that no one expected them to win and that all the top four sides had played better away than at home. This was not just a statistical freak. It was a reflection of the times. Everyone now tried to build a side which could absorb pressure in defence and then score on the break. The counterattacking game was the order of the day. Liverpool had been playing this way for some time – though with Rush, Aldridge, Barnes and Beardsley their front runners were not exactly understaffed. Graham had developed along these lines with great success during the season to the point where, as a counter-attacking force, Arsenal were perhaps comparable with the James-Bastin-Hulme triangle of the early 1930s.

Alan Smith's role was critical, his growing ability to act as a target man and control long balls forward, as well as score goals, being one of the cornerstones of the season. Brian Marwood was a key supplier, and it was fortunate that Arsenal survived his late injury so well. David Rocastle was the joker, the one man who could provide the trickery and the unexpected on the right, Michael Thomas and Kevin Richardson were the workers in midfield.

To put the task in perspective, consider the following. Only twice since the 1971 Double year had Arsenal won at Anfield – the last time in November 1974. On only nine occasions since Arsenal's Double nearly 20 years before had Liverpool lost at home by two goals, the last time to Everton in 1986. Did it seem likely that Arsenal could perform such an

Below: 17 May 1989 was the final home game of the season. A win would still make Arsenal favourites to take the title, but opponents Wimbledon managed to hold them to a 2–2 draw and the chance appeared to have gone forever. Paul Merson scored one of Arsenal's goals, here volleying past Scales, and Nigel Winterburn the other.

unlikely feat at such an emotional moment? The game was a historian's goldmine. It was only the third time in 101 years of the Football League that the two leading clubs had met on the last day of the season with the fate of the Championship resting on the result. On one other occasion the title race had gone to the final match in slightly similar circumstances when the last game of the season had been the only match that day. Surprisingly, all three occasions had involved either Liverpool or Arsenal.

SHOWDOWN ON MERSEYSIDE

And so to Anfield. The scene was set for a tumultuous end to a deeply emotional season. There were no fences – they had been taken down after Hillsborough and the astonishing sea of scarves and flowers. There would soon be no more Kop, because Liverpool were to install seating throughout the ground. The police appealed to the crowd before the game: 'Many millions are watching. Please do not come onto the pitch at any time. If we can achieve that you will see the presentation.' The crowd obeyed. They did see the presentation, but not the one they expected.

It is impossible to recreate the atmosphere there. Perhaps only United's first game after Munich or Liverpool's replayed semi-final against Forest, both played at Old Trafford, bear comparison. As David Miller said in *The Times*: 'The public came out of Merseyside's mean streets and bleak apartment blocks as the sun disappeared and poured into Anfield for the last game of the season: to share that beautiful illusion which exists inside the stadium, to enjoy the aura of reflected glory which lifts them out of the ordinariness of everyday life ... and the illusion was broken.'

The kick-off was delayed because so many Arsenal fans had been caught in traffic jams on the way to the ground. The tension was palpable, touchable. When Arsenal came out they presented a cheque for £30,000 to the Hillsborough disaster fund. All the players carried bouquets of flowers, which were taken to the supporters around the ground. It was an exceptionally thoughtful gesture, although the kindness ended right there. Here was the crunch, the moment of truth, a time which these players would almost certainly never experience again in their professional lives. Liverpool had gone 24 games undefeated. It did not seem too much to suppose that they would at least manage a draw.

But Arsenal fought; fought harder than perhaps any side representing this famous club has ever fought in its history. They battled, even kicked, Liverpool out of their majestic stride. It was pressure, pressure, pressure. Dixon forced Barnes back toward his own half. Bould prevented Aldridge from controlling the ball in the way he had done all season. Richardson, Thomas and Rocastle fought and harried in midfield and gradually overwhelmed their illustrious opponents. Were Liverpool tired, or did Arsenal just make them seem tired? They were leaden, they couldn't push

forward, they couldn't compete with the fury of Arsenal's fight. It seemed to be sheer willpower which kept driving Arsenal forward. Their supporters seemed to be sucking the ball toward the Liverpool goal. Yet, for all this, Liverpool only had to survive. They didn't have to score themselves, they simply had to stop Arsenal scoring twice. And at half time it was still goalless. There had only been one real chance. Thomas, outpacing the aggressive McMahon, whose spirit had personified Liverpool since Hillsborough, put over a beautiful cross from the right. Grobbelaar missed it but Bould rose beautifully. Somehow, Nicol got to the header and deflected it over the bar.

SMITH GOAL PANICS POOL

In retrospect 0–0 at half time was a good thing. If Arsenal had scored in the first half it would have given Liverpool time to regroup and to come back, to score an equaliser and make the Gunners' task impossible. The ideal scenario had always been two late goals, preferably late enough to stop Liverpool replying or allowing the Arsenal players to relax for a moment.

The second half was as frenetic as the first. Said Patrick Barclay in The Independent: 'The tackling was ferocious. Seldom can English football have been played with such intensity.' The first goal came after 52 minutes. Nicol was punished for a foul on the edge of the Liverpool area. Winterburn went over to take the free-kick. The ball drifted across the goal to the far post, where Alan Smith suddenly appeared, unmarked, to deflect it off the side of his head into the corner of the net. The Liverpool players surrounded the referee, David Hutchinson. The linesman had briefly flagged. Why? Some Liverpool players claimed a foul, others that Smith had not touched the ball from that indirect free-kick. Hutchinson consulted the linesman. Ten million watching caught them in close-up, as their conversation happened in front of the touchline camera. The destination of the Championship rested on that minute. The officials finally agreed: no foul, no reason to disallow the goal. Television replays showed they were right. Liverpool panicked. Rush had gone off in the first half after a distant shot (the best of the night from the home side) had caused him a leg injury. Beardsley was on in Rush's place, but Liverpool could not string their passes together. Everything foundered on the rock of the sweeper and Arsenal's determination and commitment. Never can a football team have expended so much energy in 90 minutes.

CLOCK TICKS FOR GUNNERS

But while Liverpool were panicked, Arsenal were sitting on a depreciating asset – time. The minutes ticked by and it became harder to create a clear chance anywhere. Only one good one was to appear in normal time. After 74 minutes a

pass from Richardson found Thomas with an instant to spare on the penalty spot. He shot quickly, but not hard enough and too predictably and Grobbelaar saved easily going slightly to his right. Grobbelaar had not appeared on the losing side in 28 appearances so far this season. As long as it stayed 1–0, he wouldn't mind losing this one.

The sands of time were running out. The Kop breathed a sigh of relief as Arsenal seemed to have beaten themselves out pounding on the rock of Liverpool, a rock that seemed to be saying: 'Forget tonight, history is ours. This is the season of Hillsborough and the Double. This is what was meant to be.' With the minutes ticking by, there came a lull. Kevin Richardson was injured. Liverpool had stopped pressing completely. They had hardly had an effective attack all night. It was easy to say afterward that they were unlucky knowing that even a one-goal defeat was enough. If they had to win, maybe they would have played differently. Perhaps. But when the referee correctly added two minutes on for Richardson's injury, Liverpool had just five minutes left to hold out.

THE GAME COMPLETED

The Kop whistled frantically for the finish, not just to the match, but to a season and to its place in the history books. The seconds ticked by as Arsenal pressed forward again. Surely one last time. A clearance from Lukic was controlled by Dixon, who pushed a long ball through to the magnificent Alan Smith, 30 yards from goal. Michael Thomas ran into the inside-right slot inside Smith. The centre-forward lobbed the ball on, straight into Thomas' path. The clock said 91 minutes and 26 seconds, 86 seconds overtime. Would there even be time for Thomas to finish the move? Steve Nicol came across to tackle. The ball bounced off the defender, onto Thomas and forward. Thomas was clear. He surged into the penalty area. Nicol and Houghton lung themselves at him in desperation. Grobbelaar, everything at stake, came out and spread himself. Thomas waited, then flicked the ball over Grobbelaar's body into the right-hand corner of the net. 2–0. There was a stunned silence and then, from the Arsenal fans, euphoria. The Double was gone; the Championship surely snatched from the jaws of certain Arsenal failure. Thomas, scorer now of the most famous goal in Arsenal history, ran at the Gunners' fans and took off in a somersault. For the millions watching it was beyond belief. 'Re-run the video, it can't have happened. We've strayed into a film script. Seasons just don't end like this.' It was many minutes before anyone believed it really had happened.

NORTH LONDON CELEBRATES

There were a few seconds left. Long enough for hero Thomas to intercept a Liverpool attack in his own penalty area and put the ball calmly back to Lukic. The whistle went. The most dramatic domestic season in living memory, probably ever,

was at an end. Arsenal were Champions. For the first time the League Championship trophy was presented as if it were the FA Cup. And how ironic that Arsenal received it at Anfield. The Kop applauded them; the dream for Liverpool was over.

The memories were inevitably of another late goal, of another Double. But that goal, from a yellow-and-blue-shirted Charlie George against a similarly red-shirted Liverpool had won a Double, whereas Michael Thomas' had prevented one. George lay down, a never to be forgotten gesture, Thomas took off in his somersault, to give the fans another never to be forgotten moment.

George Graham was understandably euphoric: 'We have laid a foundation of belief at Highbury. If you lose hope, or lose belief, you may as well get out of football. Tonight was the fairy tale, the unpredictable that makes us all love football. There is no doubt that we had a mountain to climb. A lot of people thought we would get carried away and try to play gung-ho football but in fact we were very controlled and content to be 0–0 at half time.' Graham gave the credit to his players, particularly Tony Adams: 'He has suffered a lot of stick which has been very undignified and done little for football. But he has proved his strength and character, and we all did that tonight. At the end of the day it is the players who go on and do it on the pitch, and we're delighted for them. It was nice to see Michael Thomas get the winner. In the first half of the season he was the most effective midfield player in the country. He has had a lapse, but exceptional players don't go bad overnight and he has soldiered on, staying in the side because of Paul Davis' injury. He's had his reward.'

The commentators found analysis almost impossible in the shadow of such unexpected and unlikely events. Rob Hughes probably got closer than anyone else: 'Arsenal looked like nervous wrecks in surrendering home points to Derby and Wimbledon. They were lions at Anfield. The reason, I believe, is that they are better chasing a cause than protecting one.

Below: Anfield, 26 May 1989. Michael Thomas scores the most dramatic goal in the whole history of the Football League – in the final minute of the final match of the season.

If the roles had been reversed, and if Arsenal had been three points ahead with the final game at Highbury, what then would have been the result?' What indeed, but it is difficult enough to explain what happened without speculating on what might have been. What did happen is that Arsenal won the League Championship in circumstances which no fiction writer would have dared to create. It truly was the most remarkable end to a League season ever.

GRAHAM CONTINUES TO BUILD

But as Arsenal had seen before, winning the Championship and retaining it were different propositions. In the previous 108 years it had happened on just 19 occasions, two of them by Arsenal in 1934 and 1935. In the season 1989–90 a final position of fourth was no disgrace, but it was 17 points behind Liverpool and there was no joy in the Cups.

Graham went out to buy, paying a record for a goalkeeper to acquire David Seaman from QPR. John Lukic went back to Leeds. Like Jimmy Rimmer a decade before, he was to be rejected by Arsenal only to win a Championship medal quickly with his new club. Anders Limpar provided variety on the wings, and defender Andy Linighan came from Norwich.

The next season, 1990–91, was to be something of a fairy tale, with Limpar buzzing like a bluebottle, Seaman keeping 29 clean sheets in 50 matches and the season starting with 17 games undefeated. It came to an end in an astonishing

game at Highbury when Manchester United won a League Cup tie 6–2. Young Lee Sharpe scored a hat-trick in what will probably be the game of his career. Seaman had only conceded six goals in the season's previous 17 games.

BRAWL LEADS TO TWO-POINT PENALTY

Four days later the Champions Liverpool were convincingly despatched 2–0 by Merson and Dixon but the Gunners had other worries. An undistinguished fight on the pitch at Old Trafford six weeks before – involving almost all 22 players – had generated an FA Commission, with Arsenal particularly concerned because they had been fined £20,000 for a similar scrap with the unlikeliest of opponents for a fight – Norwich City – the previous season.

On November 13, a five-man FA commission deliberated for three-and-a-half hours on the Old Trafford skirmish and deducted two League points from Arsenal – precisely the punishment the directors' swift censure of their players and manager had sought to avoid. In addition, United were docked one point and both clubs were fined £50,000. To the Gunners, this was a drop in the ocean compared to the potential loss of revenue if they were pipped to the title by one or two points.

The two-point deduction left Liverpool eight points clear at the top. The Arsenal players privately conceded that the commission's verdict was tantamount to handing the Championship to Kenny Dalglish with less than a third of the season gone. But, on the pitch, they showed no signs of a side who believed they were chasing a lost cause. Four days after the FA hearing, Southampton were trounced 4–0 at Highbury and three impressive wins over the Christmas holiday period brought the Gunners back to Liverpool's shoulder. This, in itself, was triumph over adversity after another bodyblow to Graham in the week before Christmas. Tony Adams, convicted of reckless and drunk driving, was sentenced to four months' imprisonment.

The timing of the incarceration of the England defender's could scarcely have been less propitious. A first-team regular since 1986, he had just regained his international place after losing out to Des Walker and Mark Wright for Italia 90. And, for Graham, who regarded Adams as the bedrock of his back line, there was no disguising the disappointment of his captain's extended leave. 'He is my eyes and ears in the dressing room and my sergeant major on the pitch,' said the manager.

GUNNERS BACK JAILED SKIPPER

Arsenal stood four-square behind their captain. Managing director Ken Friar pledged: 'The player has made a mistake and has been punished for it. As far as the club are concerned, he will continue to be an Arsenal player and will receive our full support.' It is to Adams' credit that he maintained a remarkable level of physical fitness; and his unequivocal

refusal to sell his story of 'life on the inside' to national newspapers who were ready to wield six-figure cheques in his direction – allowed him to resume his career with dignity.

Adams was restored to his beloved No 6 shirt in the FA Cup fifth round at Shrewsbury Town's Gay Meadow, where cigar-smoking John Bond's underdogs had already seen off 1988 winners Wimbledon in the previous round. In total, Tony Adams missed 13 games. Four of them comprised the fourth round FA Cup marathon with Leeds, in which Highbury witnessed two goalless draws and Elland Road most of the excitement. Limpar, with a brilliant solo goal, earned the second replay and Seaman's spectacular diversion of Gary McAllister's shot, destined for the top corner, took the sides back up the M1 for a third encore. Finally, and to the relief of both sides, Dixon and Paul Merson settled the issue. By this time, however, Arsenal had sacrificed the unbeaten League run of which they were justifiably proud.

UNBEATEN RUN SHATTERED BY BLUES

The FA Cup arm-wrestle with Leeds was clearly draining the Gunners of sharpness and stamina when, on 2 February 1991, their record perished after 23 games at Stamford Bridge. Chelsea were already 2–0 up and worthy winners by the time Smith snatched a late consolation. Dixon said: 'That defeat hurt. A couple of years earlier, Liverpool had threatened to go unbeaten in the League all season until they came unstuck in the local derby with Everton. I suppose it was inevitable that we would lose our record in a local derby as well. We were beginning to believe that we really could go right through the season unbeaten in the League, even though we knew that was being unrealistic.'

That setback at Stamford Bridge was to be Arsenal's last of an astonishing First Division season. They had coped so well defensively in Adams' absence that it was almost a surprise when he was recalled at Shrewsbury; less startling was the hero's reception he was afforded by the travelling fans from London, and Michael Thomas made the skipper's return a happy one with the decisive goal.

The following week, the Gunners returned to Anfield for what was becoming the annual title decider. Nothing would be cut and dried with 13 games remaining, whatever the result of this proverbial six-pointer, but Merson gave Arsenal a huge psychological advantage with the winner in a thrilling match happily spared the attrition of normal top-of-the-table dogfights. Suddenly the talk around Highbury – though certainly not in George Graham's office – was of another Double.

DREAMING OF THE DOUBLE

The FA Cup quarter final with Third Division Cambridge, before a season's best crowd of 42,960 at Highbury, took them a step nearer the dream. It also capped Adams' rehabilitation

Left: The fly in the ointment. Dennis Wise celebrates one of the unlikeliest goals and unexpected results of the 1990-91 season – Chelsea's 2–1 win over Arsenal on 2 February. It was Arsenal's only League defeat of the season.

after his prison ordeal. Kevin Campbell put the Gunners in front with a typical opportunist effort before Cambridge, whose direct, primitive style had been described by one columnist as that of 'Wimbledon without the frills', hit back through Dion Dublin. The visitors had been galvanised into a stirring Cup run by manager John Beck's innovative methods of motivation, not least of which was pouring buckets of ice-cold water over his players before kick-off. Now, briefly, they threatened Arsenal's passage to the semi-finals before Adams, rising like a jump-jet at the far post, shattered the ambitions of Beck's would-be giant-killers.

Before the small matter of a north London semi-final with Tottenham at Wembley, the Gunners cemented their Championship challenge by taking 15 points from a possible 21, conceding just two goals in the process. Among those seven games was yet another meeting with Leeds; Campbell's double strike preserved the Gunners' unbeaten record against them and condemned Howard Wilkinson to his sixth match without a win in his exhausting personal test series with George Graham.

WEMBLEY SEMI-FINAL V SPURS

All eyes then focused on Wembley. Some 12 months previously 96 Liverpool supporters had died in the disaster at Hillsborough during the Liverpool-Forest semi-final. Up to this point, the FA had never allowed a tie, other than the final, to be played at Wembley, for fear of devaluing the ultimate moment. But, apart from Wembley, no football stadium in the land, and certainly no neutral venue in the south of England, could have coped with ticket demands on such a critical day for both Arsenal and Spurs.

'Common sense prevailed,' said Graham. 'After Hillsborough, staging the tie at Wembley was the only acceptable solution. I don't think it devalues the glamour or pomp of the Cup final just because we're playing the semi-final there as well.'

For both clubs, the match was not only an historic departure from tradition but a watershed. For Arsenal, the equation was simple: lose, and another Double was gone. But for Tottenham, whose financial plight had recently come to

prominence – they were reported to be more than £10 million in the red – defeat threatened their very existence. Gascoigne's express recovery from a hernia operation gave them hope of eclipsing their north London rivals, installed by bookmakers as red-hot favourites ... and although his contribution to the game lasted barely an hour, it was ultimately critical. The dramatic denouement was set to be played out with Alan Sugar and Terry Venables buying the club and it was already clear that Spurs really were in desperate straits.

GAZZA PROVES MATCH-WINNER

Less than five minutes of the semi-final had elapsed when Gascoigne's amazing 30-yard free-kick was too venomous for David Seaman's fingertips to alter its path toward the top left-hand corner. And when, 15 minutes later, Gary Lineker's predatory instincts finished a move inspired by Gascoigne's impudent back-heel, Arsenal's visions of another Double must have seemed like a cruel mirage to a desert explorer. Alan Smith briefly brought the dream back into view with a far-post header, but Lineker restored Spurs' two-goal cushion midway through the second half.

Afterward, there were tears in the Arsenal dressing room. With just five League games left, the title was still there for the taking; but the FA Cup, which had beckoned Arsenal through seven ties, was suddenly gone. It was no consolation, but Gascoigne's goal has remained one of the most startling images of a football generation. Rarely has its like been seen at such a crucial moment.

'There was nothing to choose between the sides after the first 20 minutes. That's where the match was won and lost,' reflected Graham. 'In fact, we probably shaded it from that point onward – but the damage had been done by then. You can't give a highly motivated team a two-goal start in Cup semi-finals because they're going to fight tooth and nail to protect it. It was a bitterly disappointing experience for my players, but the true test of their character is whether they can bounce back from these things.'

LIVERPOOL SUSTAIN CHALLENGE

Arsenal had little time to lick their wounds. Three days later, Manchester City came to Highbury and exposed the frailty of their hosts' confidence. Paul Merson and Campbell hit the target, but a 2–2 draw was by no means the tonic Graham had in mind. Liverpool were clinging to the Gunners' shirt-tails. On the same weekend as Arsenal's Wembley heartbreak, the Mersey men – now under the management of Graeme Souness – waltzed to a 4–0 half-time lead at Leeds. That they required a fifth goal after the break to sneak home 5–4 substantiated the views of those who claimed Dalglish had baled out of a club in decline. The Liverpool of old would surely have put up the shutters and sauntered past the post instead of requiring a desperate dive at the tape.

Graham, with three of the campaign's last four games at home, knew there was no margin for error. Three points separated the sides. Arsenal had held the initiative since late February, the weekend Dalglish quit Anfield, when they thrashed Crystal Palace 4–0 at Highbury and Liverpool's internal disarray was laid bare by an unexpected 3–0 defeat at lowly Luton. Now the Gunners couldn't lose the title – they could only throw it away. Graham felt his task was to ensure that any tension he sensed went undetected among his squad.

GRAHAM TURNS TO FLOWER POWER

Graham told pressmen that his antidote to the despair which forced Dalglish to quit was gardening. 'A bunch of pansies never won the League,' said the *Today* newspaper, 'so green-fingered George grows one in his back garden to escape the managerial pressure trap.

Nigel Winterburn, ever-present during the season and curiously overlooked by England, recalls: 'We could easily have gone unbeaten in the League all the way to February for nothing. Nobody would have remembered us for coming second in the table and going out in the FA Cup semi-finals. Or, at least, they wouldn't have remembered us for the right reasons. If we'd blown the last few games, we'd never have lived it down. People would simply have thought we'd bottled it at Wembley and bottled it on the League run-in, and we deserved better than that for our contribution to the season.'

On April 23, with four games to go, Arsenal's lead could still have been wiped out at a stroke as Queen's Park Rangers came to Highbury. Liverpool had, on paper at least, a comfortable home game against Crystal Palace the same evening. More than 42,000 fans came armed with smelling salts and transistor radios to Highbury for 90 minutes of ritual nail-biting. This, said Graham, was the final countdown. True to Don Howe's word, QPR were obstinate opponents and the match was hardly a classic. But as news filtered through of Liverpool's 3–0 canter against Palace, the Gunners dug deep. Merson scored for the second successive match and Dixon converted his fourth spot-kick of the season to keep the heat on Souness. Three games to go, no change in the cushion: three points.

It is not always easy to pin-point the moment when Championships are won and lost, but Liverpool will always mourn the events of the May Day Bank Holiday weekend in 1991. The demands of live television, becoming increasingly intrusive on the fixture calendar, twice fragmented the First Division programme, on each occasion leaving Arsenal to kick off knowing the result of their closest rivals. On the Saturday, the Gunners were required to commence battle with Sunderland at Roker Park at the curious hour of 5.30 pm – 45 minutes after the final whistle at Stamford Bridge, where Chelsea were entertaining Liverpool.

As the only team to get the better of Arsenal in 38 League games, it was perhaps appropriate that Chelsea should repay the debt by supplying their London neighbours with a giant helping hand toward the winning post. Liverpool's 4–2 demise at Stamford Bridge left the Gunners safe in the knowledge that their leadership would be immune to any Roker Park revival on Wearside. As it transpired, Sunderland had neither the guile nor the firepower to breach Arsenal's dogged rearguard; Graham was far happier with a dour 0–0 draw than opposite number Denis Smith, for whom the result spelled almost certain relegation.

MAY DAY DECIDER

Monday 6 May was, in many ways, an average Bank Holiday: 20-mile traffic jams along coast roads caused by day trippers who wouldn't normally venture into their back gardens in such unspecial weather; the obligatory air traffic control dispute over mainland Europe; and in the pop world, Cher was No 1 with 'the Shoop Shoop Song'. Arsenal's home game with Manchester United, the only team to have beaten them on home soil in 13 months, did not kick off until 8 pm, yet the players congregated at the ground from lunchtime to watch Liverpool's game with Nottingham Forest.

With Arsenal now four points to the good and only 180 minutes of the season left, the algebra was elementary: if Liverpool lost, the title returned to Highbury; a draw gave them only the tiniest mathematical hope of keeping it in the Anfield boardroom. It was the ultimate irony in their season of disruption that Liverpool's flickering hopes were finally snuffed out by a 23-year-old unknown who used to cheer them on from the Kop. Ian Woan's 64th-minute winner at the City Ground made wonderful viewing for Graham's players after Nigel Clough and Jan Molby had exchanged penalties.

HIGHBURY CELEBRATES IN STYLE

The result made Arsenal's fortunes against United academic. For ITV executives, who could not have foreseen Liverpool emerging pointless from their two holiday games, it was an anticlimax. But for the Highbury faithful, it turned a night of potentially unbearable nerve-jangling into a knees-up. No sooner had the Championship been clinched than the order was issued to open up the turnstiles and let 42,229 guests join the party.

Graham, returned to the boardroom from a TV interview in one of the Clock End boxes commandeered by a camera crew, found himself the recipient of a bear-hug and kiss from an East Stand season-ticket holder as he marched up the touchline, his face betraying barely a flicker of emotion. One by one the players emerged for the pre-match kick-in to thunderous acclaim. David Seaman, Lee Dixon and Michael Thomas entered the party spirit by donning a variety of headgear. North Bank fans, who filled the terrace to bursting

point with more than an hour to kick-off, persuaded the players to abandon the normal practice of plying the keeper with shots and crosses; even Seaman happily bludgeoned 25-yarders into the arms of supporters going through their repertoire of victorious refrains.

Dixon conducted the singing, Anders Limpar his own personal side-show – which might have been entitled '20 Things You Never Knew You Could Do With A Football'. But such was the professionalism Graham had instilled in his side that, despite all the pre-match euphoria, there was a manifest determination not to let the party fall flat. As the sun sank reluctantly behind the North Bank, Arsenal set about United as if their medals depended on it. Champions or not, they were in no mood to show their illustrious visitors – soon to defeat mighty Barcelona and lift the European Cup Winners Cup – any clemency.

BORING, BORING ARSENAL

Alan Smith put the Gunners in front after 19 minutes with an accomplished finish to Dixon's right-wing cross and three minutes before the break he confirmed their swaggering superiority. Kevin Campbell's pass exposed United's back line and Smith applied another uncomplicated execution to the move from 18 yards. His night was complete when referee Bob Nixon penalised Steve Bruce for handball and regular penalty-taker Dixon stepped aside for Smith to complete his hat-trick from the spot. Perhaps the only blot on Arsenal's copybook – an eminently forgettable one – was the last-minute consolation Bruce claimed for United, which robbed Seaman of his 30th clean sheet of an outstanding term.

Graham, serenaded by the sarcastic and now ritual chants of 'Boring, boring Arsenal' from his players in the dressing room, modestly stayed in the tunnel while Tony Adams hoisted the trophy and led the team on a lap of honour. 'I didn't think it was important for me to join in ... the players are the ones who have done it. I can enjoy all the reflective glory because of their efforts, but they deserve all the credit and limelight. The fans pay their money every week to watch them play football, not to watch me sit in the dugout. I felt it was appropriate for me to stay in the background this time.' He had, after all, done it all before.

Arsenal were finally in the European Cup. In 1989 they had not entered because of the post-Heysel ban on English clubs. The competition's new format, with seeded teams kept apart in the first two rounds then thrown together in two round-robin groups of four, was thought to favour Arsenal's propensity for durability and compactness. And their chances did not seem unduly diminished by an indifferent start in the League – just three wins from their opening eight games. Graham, ostensibly satisfied with his squad depth, had surprisingly declined to increase it during the close season – a repeat of his apparent inertia after the Championship triumph of 1989.

EUROPEAN CUP DEBUT

There seemed little to concern Graham about his team's quality in a European context in the first round match with Austria Vienna, though. Drawn at home in the first leg, the Gunners secured an abyss between the sides, and 24,424 fans saluted their 6–1 rout. Liverpool trounced Finland's Knusysi by the same score on the night and, like Arsenal, had their own hero. Colin Gibson of *The Daily Telegraph* wrote: 'Alan Smith emulated Liverpool's Dean Saunders with the four goals that must establish Arsenal as one of the most feared sides in this season's European Cup. Smith's goals, his first in Europe, but bringing his total to 20 in the last 20 games, demolished the Austrian challenge.'

The Gunners could even afford the luxury of Dixon's penalty miss as Andy Linighan and Limpar completed the scoring. Vienna's 1–0 victory in the return was hollow, indeed, and by then Graham had left his domestic rivals behind with the crucial record £2.5 million outlay on the young Crystal Palace striker Ian Wright. Although he was ineligible for the early stages of the European Cup, Wright – capped by England seven months earlier – gave Graham an embarrassment of riches in attack.

Wright wasted little time in making an impact, scoring in the 1–1 League Cup draw at Leicester and then, spectacularly, a hat-trick in his first League game for the Gunners, at Southampton. But he had to sit out the next continental expedition, which took Arsenal to Benfica's famous Stadium of Light in Lisbon.

BENFICA CRUSH GUNNERS' EURO HOPES

In front of 84,000 devoted Portuguese, Arsenal acquitted themselves admirably – especially Paul Davis, whose attentive marking job on Brazilian midfield player Isaias clamped the biggest single threat to the Gunners' hopes of progress. The inclusion of Isaias had raised more than a few eyebrows in the Arsenal camp in the first place, particularly when he lined up beside two Soviet internationals and two Swedish imports, an apparent contravention of UEFA's ceiling of four foreigners per team. Dissection of UEFA's small print revealed that Isaias qualified for Portuguese citizenship through marriage.

In the event, the sting was in the tail. Thanks to a disciplined rearguard action and Kevin Campbell's polished equaliser, the teams came to Highbury at 1–1, with the match well balanced. However, Isaias, so well shadowed in the Stadium of Light, found a new sphere of influence in the second leg. Arsenal's barnstorming start yielded an early goal from Colin Pates, making only his tenth appearance in 18 months, a disallowed 'goal' from Merson and Campbell's shot against an upright. But the early optimism among expectant home supporters was to be snuffed out ruthlessly by Isaias. The Brazilian possessed that elusive ability to change the course of a match. Now, he graduated to the ability to turn the course of an entire season – Arsenal's season, that is – with one stunning swing of his boot. The 30-yard volley with which he restored parity in the tie brought all Arsenal's worst fears to the surface: they now had to chase the winner knowing that, if Benfica caught them cold at the back, the European Cup would be wrenched irrevocably from their reach. In extra time that is exactly what happened.

The Soviet, Kulkov, and then – inevitably – Isaias left the Gunners to count the cost of failing to reach the mini-league section of the competition. Conservative estimates put the loss of revenue at £1.5 million. Worse still, another potentially lucrative avenue had been sealed off to Graham between the two games with Benfica. Following the 1–0 League Cup defeat at Coventry, he had said the result 'may yet prove a blessing in disguise' because the club's fixture commitments were already 'frightening'. But elimination from two cup competitions in the space of eight days, sandwiching a home defeat against struggling West Ham, suddenly limited the scope of Arsenal's ambitions for the season.

Right: The 1991–92 season saw the arrival at Highbury of one of football's greatest showmen, Ian Wright.

CHAMPIONS FALL TO LOWLY WREXHAM

Wright's form continued to be irresistible – he scored all four goals in the 4–2 home win against Everton, for example – but Arsenal's, collectively, was erratic. Graham, sensing that his team was off the pace in the First Division, made the FA Cup 'a major priority'. A disastrous Christmas, in which the point gleaned from a 1–1 draw with Wimbledon was their only return from three games, increased the Gunners' sense of urgency in the Cup. The third round draw handed them a trip to Fourth Division Wrexham. It was one of those heads-you-win, tails-I-lose ties that top players hate.

Deprived of the suspended Wright, Graham looked to Smith – just two goals between September 21 and the New Year – for increased productivity, and after 43 minutes of embarrassing superiority the penny finally dropped. Merson burrowed his way to the byline and presented Smith with the kind of opportunity for which all strikers in a lean spell pray. Arsenal preserved their lead without undue alarm until the 82nd minute, when Mickey Thomas, a nomad with 37 years on the clock and 11 previous employers, equalised with a thunderous free-kick. Thomas had barely emerged from the scrummage of delirium when Steve Watkin hooked Gordon Davies' right-wing cross past Seaman for a barely plausible winner. The media predictably feasted on the biggest Cup upset since non-League Sutton's eclipse of Coventry in 1989.

Rob Hughes wrote in *The Sunday Times* 'Oh, what lovely pandemonium, what delightful illogicality the Cup still provides! Who will believe that Arsenal, prime movers of the Premier League (and hustling) through to kill 108 years of League tradition, should fall in a theatre principally of their own making. Arsenal should have won the game by half-time ... but this was hardly the mastery of Super Leaguers.'

Graham admitted bluntly that the calamitous defeat in north Wales was 'the lowest point of my career'. Arsenal had become accustomed to adversity under his management and they were hardened against prejudice. Kicked when they were down, damned with faint praise when they won, Graham found himself yearning for the minor irritants of jealous epithets such as 'Boring, boring Arsenal'. Out of the running for the Cups, his team were also stranded in no-man's land in the Championship they had won so vibrantly seven months earlier. It seemed just like a re-run of 1990.

ENGLISH FOOTBALL'S BRAVE NEW WORLD

But the next season was to bring a more dramatic change – the end of the old First Division and the start of the Premier League. The Premier League's conception owed much to a handful of visionaries, including Gunners' Vice-Chairman David Dein, one of the first modern administrators to realise that aggressive marketing increased clubs' income and, in turn, provided a springboard for extra investment on facilities and players. History will judge the commercial orientation of Arsenal overseen by Dein. In the shorter term, the new,

all-seater North Bank would perhaps be remembered as his personal monument to the club prior to his surprising resignation in 2007.

When the bulldozers moved in to replace the North Bank with a 12,500-seater edifice, brickbats flew over the methods chosen by Arsenal to finance the ground's biggest development in more than half a century. Bond schemes to pay for new facilities were pioneered successfully in the United States, and Glasgow Rangers' Ibrox Stadium was transformed without a murmur of dissent by way of a similar venture. In the face of a fierce recession, borrowing or flotation – the alternatives to a bond scheme – could have been monstrous burdens on Arsenal's finances. The board were very aware of two successive Spurs' boards being deposed as a result of the cost of new stands at White Hart Lane.

The reaction to the rebuilding programme at Highbury was perhaps a reflection of English football's parlous state in the summer of 1992. Graham Taylor's national side belly-flopped alarmingly in the European Championship finals in Sweden and the Premier League kicked off in funereal mood. One of the European Championship's stars, Danish mid-fielder John Jensen, impressed George Graham so much he spent £1 million to bring him to Highbury, while David Rocastle's love affair with Arsenal resulted in an amicable divorce. He joined the new Champions Leeds United for £2 million, but failed to impress at Elland Road and became another of the 1989 Championship stars who seemed to have faded since that glorious night at Anfield.

THE NORTH BANK MURAL

Jensen, a bustling, no-nonsense player, had scored Denmark's first goal against Germany in their unexpected European Championship triumph. His arrival reaffirmed Graham's determination to atone for the previous campaign's disappointments. In the 1992–93 Championship, however, they simply never got going.

Arsenal's performances at Highbury were generally as incomplete as their North Bank. In an effort to camouflage the jungle of cranes and scaffolding, the club spent large sums of money commissioning and erecting an enormous mural, 75 yards wide and 18 yards high, to hang from corner to corner behind the North Bank goal. Thousands of painted faces peered out across Highbury in a commendable initiative to retain some of the atmosphere within the stadium (not to mention its qualities as a safety net which prevented wayward shots sailing into the building site). It was fun and an unusually creative motif at a football ground.

The mural received much good-humoured criticism and became a vehicle for political point-scoring when it came to light that none of its faces was black, an oversight quickly rectified. With ground capacity temporarily reduced to 29,000, home games were virtually sold out every week. To be frank, few provided great entertainment in the Premier

League; one exception was the seven-goal thriller against Southampton. But this was to be a season in which Arsenal discovered a 'home from home', a venue at which they remained unbeaten in four games ... Wembley.

CUP SPECIALISTS AGAIN

Prospects of the Gunners winning the League Cup looked anything but rosy when they trailed 1–0 to Millwall at Highbury in the second round, first leg; Kevin Campbell's late introduction spared Arsenal's blushes, and he worked the miracle again at The Den a fortnight later before the Gunners scraped through on penalties with the tie deadlocked at 2–2. With Millwall moving at season's end, Arsenal were never to play again at their original 'local derby' location.

Arsenal needed two bites at the cherry to see off Derby in the next round (Campbell again scoring in both games) and it required two trips to the seaside for the team to dispose of little Scarborough. The first was a wasted journey because of wintry weather, and conditions were far from ideal for the second when Nigel Winterburn's winner earned the Gunners a quarter final tie against Nottingham Forest. Six days and two Wright goals later, Arsenal were in the League Cup semi-finals.

By now, every other game in Arsenal's tiring schedule was a Cup tie, and Graham was almost prepared to forgive his team for an 11-week barren spell without a League win. Wright scored from the spot against his old club and the resurgent Smith netted twice at Selhurst Park in the first leg as Crystal Palace's bid to throw the Gunners off their inexorable collision course with Wembley was sunk almost before it had begun. The return at Highbury smacked of

going through the motions as Wright, inevitably, and the increasingly assured Andy Linighan completed a 5–1 aggregate rout of Palace.

MERSON PROVES CUP FINAL HERO

Their opponents in the League Cup final were to become frequent imposters on Graham's path to glory this season. Sheffield Wednesday, conquerors of big-spending Blackburn Rovers, arrived at Wembley with a reputation for flowing – if defensively flawed – football, and the teams treated their fans to an enthralling afternoon. Without the injured Smith, the suspended Dixon and the cup-tied Martin Keown – repatriated from Everton for £2 million, ten times the figure Arsenal received when he was sold to Aston Villa in 1986 – the Gunners were forced to shuffle their pack. Paul Davis was recalled, to unanimous amazement, after just one comeback match in the reserves following hamstring trouble. And Northern Ireland defender Stephen Morrow, so often restricted to little more than walk-on parts in previous Arsenal productions, was pressed into service beside Davis in midfield, where he was to command centre stage.

England manager Taylor, under fire from all quarters for his refusal to restore Wednesday's former Tottenham winger Chris Waddle to the international boards, would have drawn some minor, though valueless, comfort from Waddle's familiar retreat toward anonymity after a promising start. He looked worthy of all Fleet Street's platitudes about his enduring skill as the Owls snatched an early lead through American John Harkes. But Waddle was to be upstaged by Paul Merson, not least because of the 20th-minute equaliser which sparked an Arsenal revival.

Rob Hughes said in *The Times*: 'Like Wednesday's goal, Merson's goal came from a free-kick and finished, like Wednesday's, with a right-foot finish of class. When the ball was headed down to Merson just outside the penalty area, he hit across it to induce a kind of swerve that is sometimes mistakenly regarded in this country as the preserve of Brazilians. The ball obeyed his instruction and beat the diving Woods inside his left-hand post.'

HIGHS AND LOWS FOR MORROW

Merson wasn't finished by any means, though. After 68 minutes, with Arsenal's vigour now firmly in the ascendancy, he fashioned the winner. Thrusting deep into Wednesday territory, his low cross from the left flank caught Carlton Palmer off balance and Morrow had the simple but joyous task of thrashing it past Woods – his first senior goal for the club. For Merson, it was the perfect climax to an emotional week in which he had become a father for the second time; but for Morrow, there was to be a painful sting in the tail. On the final whistle, Tony Adams hoisted his match-winner shoulder-high by way of playful celebration, only for Morrow to come

Below: While the North Bank was being rebuilt, Arsenal broke new ground with the now famous Highbury mural. It was intended to represent a crowd and ensure that balls were returned quickly.

crashing to earth and break his arm, ruling him out of action for the last month of the season. Adams was so upset that assistant manager Stewart Houston had to persuade him to climb Wembley's famous steps to accept the trophy.

Poor Morrow required oxygen and was carted out of Wembley by ambulancemen instead of on the shoulders of adoring supporters. He was unable to collect his winners' medal, and Graham said: 'It was silly, really, a freak accident. But you can't tell players not to celebrate when they've just won a major Cup competition. It did, however, remove just a little of the gloss from our victory for me – you couldn't help feeling desperately sorry for the boy.' For the press the story was obvious: 'How did you break your arm?' 'I fell off a donkey', the donkey being the tabloids' less-than-friendly nickname for Tony Adams.

Above: An ecstatic Paul Merson celebrates Arsenal's victory over Sheffield Wednesday in the 1993 League Cup final.

CAMPAIGN ON TWO FRONTS

For Arsenal, the job was only half-done. They had another opportunity to test their Cup-tie expertise against Wednesday in the FA Cup final. Never has he perverse nature of Cup football been so ably demonstrated as in Arsenal's fortunes in successive seasons. After Wrexham, you wouldn't have backed them to knock out a pigeon with a tranquilliser gun, now they were the name everybody wanted to avoid when the numbered balls came out of the bag.

Not that the 1993 FA Cup started out that way. When the Gunners were required to tackle non-League Yeovil Town on their own patch at The Huish, the Press descended on the West Country ready to bury Graham again. But Ian Wright's hat-trick, and the League Cup win at Scarborough four days later, forced them to dispense with the obituaries and instead hail Arsenal's professionalism on two thankless missions. 'Sorry you've had two wasted journeys,' Graham taunted the members of media corps.

Trailing 2–0 to Leeds at Highbury in the fourth round, Arsenal demonstrated their newfound belief by bouncing back to force a replay through Ray Parlour's persistence and a 25-yard Merson special. In the Elland Road encore, the Gunners again had to force the issue when they found themselves 2–1 down with eight minutes left. Smith's first goal for three months was already a symptom of Arsenal's resurgent morale before Wright, returning from suspension to spectacular effect, struck twice to sink Leeds in extra time.

Now Arsenal were through to the quarter finals. Already in the Coca-Cola Cup final, they were 180 minutes from another medal for the mantelpiece. Ipswich, whose defensive blanket had smothered the life out of Arsenal's Boxing Day party, were more enterprising hosts at Portman Road.

Much of the build-up had focused on the gash sustained by Tony Adams in a fall during a night out with friends, which had forced him out of two games. But the resilient skipper returned to inspire those around him and Ipswich were stitched up 4–2. Adams contributed to the scoring spree,

which was an overdue statement of the Gunners' attacking resources. The previous 14 League games had yielded only four goals.

NORTH LONDON GIANTS CLASH AT WEMBLEY

The semi-final draw was, in itself, a mandate for civil strife in Sheffield and north London: Wednesday v United and Arsenal v Tottenham. Mouth-watering prospects, but powder kegs to boot. Falling at the final hurdle before the Cup final is still the most soul-destroying experience in football. Add local pride to the equation and the stakes become even greater. Adams greeted the pairing with Spurs in a cautious, circumspect manner. 'It's one for the fans to get excited about and it obviously gives us a chance to gain revenge for our semi-final defeat in 1991,' he said. 'But semis aren't about revenge or settling old scores – they're all about getting through to the final, and we mustn't lose sight of that.'

Adams' apprehension was entirely justified. Arsenal's League match at White Hart Lane four months earlier had been pock-marked by a series of niggles and unpleasantness. Spurs' 1–0 win was a travesty and their coach, Doug Livermore, was evidently carried away by euphoria when he

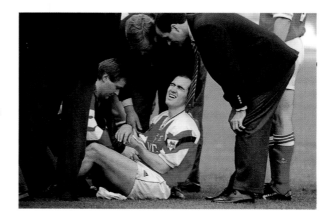

Left: Stephen Morrow, on the other hand, was in agony. He had fallen from Tony Adams' shoulders during a post-final whistle celebration and broke his arm.

declared it 'a great day for football'. In truth, it was nothing of the sort. Referee Alf Buksh seemed to lose his grip as early as the second minute, when Dean Austin's palpably illegal tackle on Ray Parlour warranted a penalty.

Buksh's failure to intervene became a licence for misbehaviour. Graham complained to him in the tunnel at half time that the game was almost out of control – which later earned him a £500 rebuke from he FA. Wright was not among the five names Buksh scribbled in his notebook, but TV cameras caught him aiming a rabbit-punch at Tottenham's David Howells and he was later suspended for three matches.

ADAMS GOALS EARNS PASSAGE TO FINAL

Spurs defender Justin Edinburgh admitted later that he had 'wound up' Adams by using 'the D-word' and warned of no truce in the Cup semi-final. For the Gunners, the ominous promise of more trench warfare was not necessarily as worrying as it was for Spurs. In the end the game was a great anticlimax, not remotely comparable with Gazza's game two years earlier. The only goal was a far post Tony Adams header from a Paul Merson free-kick.

By the time the big day arrived, fatigue was going to be a factor. Arsenal were playing their 48th competitive match of the campaign and their 12th in six weeks. Graham preferred Jensen to Selley in midfield, while Morrow collected his League Cup winners' medal before kick-off. He was the only man to enjoy the privilege on a desperately disappointing day.

If the rise and fall of Paul Morrow whetted the appetite, the sequel was barely palatable viewing. Chris Waddle threatened briefly to ruffle Arsenal's feathers but, after one rasping free-kick was diverted by Seaman, he became more and more anonymous.

Below: Tony Adams scores the only goal in Arsenal's FA Cup semi-final victory over Spurs, leading to another Wembley clash with Sheffield Wednesday.

Wright, playing with a broken toe, struggled for 90 minutes before Graham granted him sanctuary on the bench. But he did at least make the most of his only clear-cut opportunity. After 21 minutes, Paul Davis flighted a right-wing free-kick on to Linighan's head and the big centre-half nodded it across the six-yard box. Wright, lurking with Paul Warhurst on the far post, outjumped his marker to head firmly beyond Chris Woods. Arsenal were one up, and the familiar chorus of 'Ian Wright-Wright-Wright' rang round Wembley. As Emily Bell of *The Observer*, perhaps something of a fan, said: 'Wright is the yeast in the bread, the coke in the cola, the buck in the fizz, the Pardoner in Chaucer's Tales. Without him, there is a void, an impenetrable black hole of uncertain future ...' Wednesday's renowned artistry never surfaced, but they summoned enough strength to conjure David Hirst's 68th-minute equaliser. That only hastened the onset of stalemate and neutrals agreed that parity was the only fair result.

O'LEARY REWARDED FOR 20 YEARS' SERVICE

Two days later, Arsenal put out a full-strength side at Highbury against Manchester United in a testimonial for David O'Leary, granted a free transfer after 20 years' service. O'Leary thought the Cup final would be his last competitive appearance for the Gunners and was hoping all three major domestic trophies would be on display at his benefit game – Arsenal parading the two cups and United the Premier League trophy they had won with such panache. It turned out to be the sandwich filling between the Cup final and its replay, although 24,000 fans paid their respects to him.

O'Leary admitted: 'To be honest, I didn't want my time at Arsenal to end. But I was thrilled to be able to complete 20 full years of service with them. I would have hated to be shown the door after 19. The 20-year landmark kept me going. When I realised it was all over, that I had worn the red shirt for the last time, there was a tear or two in my eye. But I wouldn't have missed it for the world. And one day, if the club ever decide they want me back, I'd love to return to Highbury as a coach or manager. That would be the ideal happy ending to the fairy tale.' And if you're going to go out, an FA Cup final has to be the ideal setting.

Thursday came round and Arsenal found Wednesday waiting for them again. The FA Cup final replay attracted only 62,367 spectators, the lowest crowd ever for the fixture at Wembley and the lowest FA Cup final attendance for 71 years. But at least they saw a climax as dramatic as Anfield '89. This was in contrast with the early portents, it must be said. With the kick-off delayed by 30 minutes and Wednesday fans jamming the BBC switchboard with pleas for more time to reach Wembley after a crash caused tailbacks on the M1, the game started in heavy rain.

But if the quality of the original tie left much to be desired, it was preferable to the brutality which scarred the opening stages of its successor. Adams (on Hirst) and Jensen (on

Waddle) were given the benefit of the doubt by referee Keren Barratt for challenges which looked worse than the damage they inflicted. But Mark Bright's aerial confrontation with Linighan after 19 minutes was clearly unacceptable even to the most lenient officials. Bright appeared to use his right elbow maliciously as he jumped and the yellow card scarcely seemed sufficient punishment for an offence which left Linighan with a broken nose, although he carried on playing.

WRIGHT OPENS THE SCORING

Once football was restored to the top of the agenda, Wright deservedly put the Gunners ahead after 33 minutes. It was his 30th goal of a fragmented season, his 56th in 79 Arsenal appearances and his fourth FA Cup final goal in four Cup final appearances. Two of the goals came as a late substitute for Crystal Palace in 1990. Smith, restored to the starting line-up, provided a judicious through-ball and Wright, galloping clear, belied his excitable nature to chip Woods from 12 yards. Waddle, booed for some apparent play-acting when he hit the ground as if pole-axed by Winterburn, claimed Wednesday's equaliser after 66 minutes with a deflected volley. Now, at last, tired legs were no longer able to compress space so readily and the chances came thick and fast at either end. Mark Bright spurned the best of the lot, shaving the outside of an upright from ten yards, but perhaps this was divine retribution for his earlier offence. The excitement even stirred Mr Barratt, who chose to show yellow cards to Davis and – for the first time in his career – Smith for fouls innocuous compared to those which he allowed to disfigure the first half. Merson, struggling to live up to the high standard of his League Cup heroics, suffered from the same profligacy which afflicted Bright, and the tie was doomed to more extra-time torture when Woods recovered a Merson shot which had squirted under his body inches from the line.

Punch-drunk and dreading the prospect of a penalty shoot-out, the teams traded shots and tackles until, right on time, Arsenal won a left-wing corner. Paul Merson dragged his weary legs across the sodden turf as Mr Barratt checked his watch. Would there be time to take it? Adams and Linighan ventured forward for one last fling. On the bench, Graham was apoplectic. What if Wednesday hoiked the ball clear and raced upfield to score? Who would take the penalties?

O'Leary, who had again been brought on for Ian Wright, must have let his mind wander, back to Genoa with the Republic of Ireland and to the 1980 Cup Winners Cup nightmare against Valencia, when Rix and Brady had missed. Please, God. Not penalties.

AN UNLIKELY HERO

Merson's corner swung in invitingly. Woods stayed rooted to his line and Wednesday's defence followed his lead fatally. Linighan, who had spent years as a million-pound spare part

in the reserves, who had heard his name greeted with groans when it was announced on the Highbury tannoy, sensed Wednesday's collective inertia. He rose like a phoenix above Bright, whose elbows this time remained firmly by his sides, and connected with a thumping header. Its power carried it through the grasp of Woods, arching back on his line, and Nigel Worthington's attempt to hack it clear only confirmed initial impressions: it had crossed the line, Worthington's clearance hit the roof of the net and raised the roof at Arsenal's end of the stadium. Linighan was engulfed by a tide of red-and-white delirium. Just 18 months earlier, he had asked for a transfer because he could not gain regular first-team football at Highbury. Now he will be remembered as the man who scored the latest FA Cup goal of all time.

The significance of Linighan's goal was not lost on Graham, the first man to win all three major domestic trophies as both a player and manager. He said: 'Andy's goal is strange

Left: May 1993 and yet another trip to Wembley, Arsenal's third of the season. This time it was the FA Cup final, in which Ian Wright played with a broken toe but maintained his remarkable goalscoring record for the season, striking with his only clear-cut opportunity. After 21 minutes Wright outjumped Paul Warhurst to give Arsenal the lead after Andy Linighan headed on a Paul Davis free-kick.

Below: Andy Linighan scores one of the most celebrated of all Arsenal goals – the winner in the 2–1 defeat of Wednesday in the 1993 FA Cup Final replay. The goal, from a Merson corner, came in the 120th minute and is the latest ever to have won the final.

Above: Andy Linighan with the FA Cup. His last gasp header was even more remarkable for the fact that his nose had been damaged by Mark Bright's elbow earlier in the match.

Right: Eddie McGoldrick scores the final goal in the 7–0 demolition of Standard Liège in the second leg of the Gunners' tie in the Cup Winners' Cup, on 3 November 1993.

because, like Stephen Morrow, he's scored the winner in a Cup final and has finished with broken bones. But I'm delighted hat our heroes on both occasions have been players who would not normally command such attention.

They are not really the people you think of in these situations. I never thought of taking him off just because he had a broken nose. I tried to get one throughout my career because it adds some character to your face!'

CUP DOUBLE GOES UNNOTICED

Graham's men were, one must admit, largely ignored for their unique double. To the uncommitted, they were not Cup football experts or knockout kings. Just Arsenal. Boring Arsenal. Lucky Arsenal. But two League titles and two cups in four years can't all be down to luck. Think of Arsenal and you think of greatness. The club's very strength is in its name. But it had been an odd season. The denouement had gone on too long. Arsenal and Sheffield Wednesday had come to Wembley too often. To think that there were 18,000 empty seats at a Cup final with two such prominent teams playing is a remarkable comment on the season's end. Despite Manchester United finally winning the League, the new Premier title had seemed to create uncertainty.

As for Arsenal, it is hard to escape the conclusion that they owed it all to Wright. In the League the Gunners scored just 40 goals in 42 games, while in the two Cup competitions they managed 33 in 17 games. To score only 40 League goals and still end the season with two major trophies is an unlikely achievement. Of the season's 73 goals in all, no fewer than 30 were scored by Wright. No other player even reached double figures in all competitions, Campbell scoring just nine in all and Smith a depressing six, despite appearing in much of the Cup campaign and in no fewer than 31 League matches.

CUP WINNERS CUP THE PRIORITY

With Manchester United running away with the League, 1993–94 was to be about the Cup Winners Cup. After Odense and Standard Liège came Torino in the quarter finals. The first leg against Arsenal was no consolation for the Italians. Arsenal were well on top, played a tight formation, and went back to Highbury with a 0–0 draw.

It was not a great night for the fans and it hardly set the pulse racing, but this was Arsenal's last real chance of a trophy in 1994 and caution was the only credible watchword. A 1–0 win, with another goal scored by the captain Tony Adams, was an appropriate reward for a very tight and conservative approach.

Interestingly, George Graham chose to play Campbell rather than Wright. Campbell had been the butt of intense jeering from Arsenal fans after a 3–1 defeat at Highbury by Bolton Wanderers. Certainly Campbell missed a number of chances, but the current Arsenal game remained directed

toward Ian Wright, and Campbell had to fill the roll of foil throughout his career. As Chris Lightbown pointed out in *The Sunday Times*, Arsenal were a team that tended to run deep from defence or knock the ball over the top for Wright to run on to. They have never been a pure, instinctive passing team in the style of Liverpool or Spurs and the Highbury crowd has had a tendency to impatience with a side which doesn't show the tenacity and grit to grind out results.

The passing game was probably an essential for success in Europe – here sweepers are much more capable of plucking off the long through balls that Wright thrives on. Only Merson and Anders Limpar of the contemporary players really exhibited the skills that can turn a game despite its tactical pattern and Limpar continued to be in and out of the team with Merson continuing to look uneasy on the left. Indeed, by the end of March, George Graham had sold Limpar to struggling Everton and, despite a good 1–0 defeat of Liverpool, it was clear that the only thing that counted was the Cup Winners Cup.

On Thursday 29 March the team travelled to Paris for the semi-finals to play the French League leaders, Paris St-Germain, who were unbeaten in 35 first-class matches. For perhaps the first time realistic memories of that shoot-out with Valencia 14 years before entered the head.

Graham surprised everyone by picking Ian Wright and the striker had another outstanding game, leading the line and tirelessly running off the ball to create room for Merson and Smith. Wright had just come off an excellent away hat-trick at Ipswich and was playing as well as he ever had. In the 35th minute Graham's decision paid off, with Wright beating his marker to a Paul Davis free-kick and heading just inside the far post.

After 50 minutes St-Germain equalised from a corner, but Arsenal's organisation was outstanding. At 1–1, with a precious away goal, everything was set up for the return game in London two weeks later.

WRIGHT SUSPENDED FOR EURO FINAL

This task proved not particularly difficult by Arsenal's high standards. One goal, early on in the game, from the previously abused Campbell, proved more than adequate and Arsenal held their ground in reasonable comfort. Paris St Germain were impressed. Said their manager: 'The quality of Arsenal's play surprised us. We knew they would be strong in defence but did not expect quite so much creativity upfront or in midfield.' But there were negatives, in particular a crucial second yellow card for the irreplaceable Ian Wright. George Graham was pleased to have concluded an inconsistent season with a Cup final, the first for the club in Europe for so long. In an interview with Joe Lovejoy he praised Manchester United: 'Everyone's getting out of their prams right now about United, and rightly so, but it took them 25 years to get it right. They've got more gifted individuals than us, but they've not got a Chippy Brady or Glenn Hoddle ... The difference between them and us is that their midfield players are better than ours. I still think that Cantona will let you down at the very highest level ... If Limpar (before he was sold) or Merson would work harder, that would improve our midfield. I'm not saying it would make it right, but it would help. what I really need is a young Peter Reid to be the boss there.'

Graham agrees that, if Manchester United wish to be personified by Cantona, then Tony Adams is the heart of Arsenal. 'We have always been strong defensively,' says Graham, 'and what's wrong with that? What I won't have is all this talk about us being a long-ball team. Sometimes we do bypass the midfield, but not all the time. Without Alan Smith (who was having an excellent end to the season) we don't hit it as long. We play better football ... I don't know anyone who wants to be successful without playing attractive football, and I'm no different from anyone else in that respect.'

GRAHAM REFUTES BORING TAG

On the all-too-familiar subject of boring Arsenal, Graham is direct. 'We won two Championships playing super football. We played great football with a team that had great individuals. We went to Liverpool and won it in the best Championship finale there has ever been. Then we won a second title and lost one game in the whole season. That's the first time anyone's done that in a hundred years. But I agree there was some pretty ropy stuff last season (1992–93) and in the early part of this (1993–94). We were terrible in the League last year, but we still won two Cups. I know we're not right at the moment because I know what it takes to win Championships. We've got a defence as good as any in the country, but we definitely need more quality in midfield, although we've got good forwards.'

Arsenal also proved to be the only English club for three years to have progressed to the final stages of a European competition. As they flew to Copenhagen for the 1994 Cup Winners Cup final against Parma on 4 May their worries revolved around a squad hit by injury and suspension – Wright, Jensen, Hillier and Keown would all be missing. Parma were the reigning Cup Winners Cup holders, having beaten Royal Antwerp 3–1 in the final a year before. Parma were not a grand club, but they had a rich benefactor and the Swede Brolin's outstanding skills playing just behind the front two, Asprilla and Zola.

The absentees meant George Graham had to change the 4–3–3 formation he had introduced after the Cup defeat by Bolton. The traditional 4–4–2 had begun to go stale with too much being expected of Ian Wright, and the switch to Wright, Smith and Campbell upfront allowed Wright more freedom on the flanks to rove around. It was a system hat depended on Alan Smith's ability to hold the ball and it was to be Alan Smith who shocked Parma in the 21st minute of the final with a stunning left-foot volley from 20 yards. Dixon took a throw 40 yards out and Minotti, one of Italy's best sweepers, attempted a totally unnecessary overhead clearance. The ball fell to Alan Smith, who chested it down and struck it on the volley to perfection. The shot flew off the post into the net with keeper Bucci just beaten and Arsenal were 1–0 up in front of a crowded Copenhagen stadium. Just six minutes earlier, an excellent shot from Brolin had hit Seaman's right-hand post and bounced back from the inside along the line. Parma were at this stage much the better team.

SMITH'S VOLLEY PROVES DECISIVE

But that, in a sense, was that. Parma had 80 per cent of the game, Brolin was outstanding, but they could not score. Adams and, in particular, Bould were excellent and both were called up to the England squad a week later. They defended superbly while Alan Smith held the ball up front and frustrated Parma. George Graham said later: 'Once we went a goal in front I knew we had a chance because our strength is keeping clean sheets. We had a team of heroes tonight and none more so than Alan Smith, who worked tirelessly up front.' In the end Brolin's shot against the post was the closest Parma came to scoring and Arsenal had won their first European title in 24 years. Steve Bould won the Man of the Match plaudits and, given their injury problems, it had been a remarkable evening for the Gunners.

Graham was rightly effusive in his praise of Parma after the match: 'They were fitter than us, they were sharper than us. Their forwards, particularly Brolin, were outstanding and it was a marvellous defensive performance by Arsenal. We're a club with marvellous team spirit and everyone– including the guys who couldn't play – was completely involved. You have to remember that around ten of the Parma squad will be in the World Cup in a month's time and, at the end of a long, hard season, they were a very tough proposition for us.'

Parma had passed he ball around well and played the game prettily. But Arsenal, as Joe Lovejoy said, had marked and chased assiduously and kept their opponents at bay. Few

Above: Alan Smith turns away after scoring a stunning volley against Parma in the Cup Winners' Cup final on 4 May 1994 in Copenhagen. It proved to be the only goal of the game as Arsenal practised their 'we hold what we have' approach, so familiar to English fans down the years.

Below: Celebrations at the end of the 1994 Cup Winners Cup final, which Arsenal won 1–0 thanks to an Alan Smith goal.

teams do better than Arsenal when it comes to defending a lead, said Lovejoy, and they slipped comfortably into the familiar 'what we have, we hold' mode. Nevio Scala, the Parma manager, also praised Arsenal: 'Tactically and technically we did not function ... because Arsenal were a better team.'

GUNNERS DEFEND EURO TITLE

The season that followed was to be all about Europe, but it was not to be until the arrival of Sampdoria in the semi-final that Arsenal faced the real test of their strength in the renewed European campaign of 1994–95. The manager of the team from Genoa was Sven Göran Eriksson, one of Europe's most successful chiefs of the decade. He had already won the Swedish title with Gothenburg, three Portuguese titles with Benfica and taken Roma to a European final. The last time Eriksson had been at Highbury, his Benfica team had thoroughly embarrassed Arsenal in the European Cup of 1992.

Perhaps the most surprising pre-match statistic was that Arsenal had now played 24 consecutive European Cup Winners Cup matches undefeated – easily a record for the competition. The run covered a 'who's who' of European names– Fenerbahce, Magdeburg, IFK Gothenburg, Juventus, Valencia, Odense, Standard Liège, Torino, Paris St-Germain, Parma, Omonia, Brondby and Auxerre. Of the 24 games, 13 had been won and 11 drawn. It hardly needs to be added that Arsenal didn't actually win the Cup Winners' Cup of 1980.

Sampdoria were without David Platt and Ruud Gullit at Highbury but most certainly did not come to defend. With a magnificent recent record, they were one of Europe's experienced teams. No fewer than seven of the Sampdoria starting 11 were over 30. The first half was full of excitement. After 28 minutes Bould flicked on a corner and Tony Adams

got a touch to put it into the corner of the net. The goal was disallowed because the referee believed that Wright had jumped into goalkeeper Walter Zenga. It was a sign of things to come.

BOULD STRIKES AGAINST SAMP

After 35 minutes an excellent swerving shot from Lee Dixon was brilliantly tipped away by Zenga. From the resulting corner David Hillier shot from he edge of the area, Zenga saved well but the ball fell to Steve Bould, who carefully steered the ball home with the delicacy of an Ian Wright. It was Bould's first goal of the season. It took him just two minutes to double his total. Yet another corner from Stefan Schwarz was met by Bould at the near post. The ball looped backward, Adams and Wright jumped at the near post but the only touch was a slight one by Walter Zenga and the ball was in the net. Steve Bould had scored again.

Then, 15 minutes into the second half Sampdoria pulled one back through the Yugoslav Jugovic. But with 20 minutes left, Paul Merson drove a beautiful ball from the centre circle for Ian Wright to run onto. There were two defenders around him and Zenga came out fractionally too early, giving Wright he opportunity to flick the ball into the right-hand corner of the net. At 3–1 it all seemed set for Arsenal to reach their second consecutive final, but just eight minutes later Jugovic was again left free in the penalty area and the score was a very different 3–2. Not only that, but Sampdoria were clearly much he more creative side in the second half.

Back on the domestic front, Arsenal were in the unfamiliar throes of a relegation struggle. With four teams to go down at the end of the 1994–95 season, there was a very undignified scramble at the bottom of the Premier League. At Easter, only five points separated nine clubs in danger of ending up in the final two places. Arsenal were one of those nine teams, but two excellent wins (4–1 against Ipswich and 4–0 at Villa Park) made the flight to Genoa more comfortable than it would otherwise have been.

SCHWARZ HITS LATE EQUALISER

Arsenal were facing a much stronger Sampdoria team than at Highbury, with Martin Keown given a marking job on Jugovic. After 13 minutes Mancini broke away with the Arsenal back four appealing for offside. He lobbed the ball over a Seaman stranded in no-man's land and it was 1–0 to Sampdoria. In many ways Arsenal were fortunate that the goal came so early. But it took until the 62nd minute for the Gunners to respond. One of numerous corners from Merson was headed on by Hartson and the ball bounced off Wright's legs into the net; 1–1 and Arsenal were ahead again on aggregate. The game was surprisingly open, if a little aggressive, and Arsenal were openly adventurous with Wright a continual threat until he went off, battered and

bruised, with ten minutes left. He had so far scored in every game. Just as Wright went off, Sampdoria won a free-kick 30 yards out. It was hit against the wall, but the return fortuitously reached substitute Bellucci, who deflected it into the net. Within a minute Lombardo broke away and, with Arsenal concentrating on attack, Bellucci was on hand to slot a third past Seaman.

With just six minutes to go Sampdoria were 3–1 up and 5–4 ahead on aggregate. It had to be all over. But on 87 minutes Stefan Schwarz took a free-kick from fully 35 yards out. He hit it low and not exceptionally hard but somehow it travelled through the wall and into the corner of Zenga's net off the keeper's left hand; 3–2 to Sampdoria, an impossibly unlikely 5–5 on aggregate at 90 minutes.

Sampdoria had much the best of extra time but could not score the all-important sixth goal. The Arsenal attack, in the unlikely shape of Kiwomya, Hartson and McGoldrick made little headway against the Italian defence.

SHOOT-OUT DRAMA

And so to penalties. After 26 games undefeated in Cup Winners Cup matches, it was all down to David Seaman, who a year later would be England's hero at Euro 96, in the Arsenal goal. The keeper, despite conceding three goals, had had a very good night indeed.

Lee Dixon went first and scored easily. Seaman saved from Michaelovic going to his left. Eddie McGoldrick put his shot way over the bar. Seaman then saved from Jugovic low to his right. After four shots, it was 1–0 to Arsenal. Hartson made it 2–0. Aspero scored for Sampdoria; 2–1. Tony Adams made it 3–1 to the Gunners. Then Sampdoria scored; 3–2. So it was left to Paul Merson to score and finish things. He didn't, Zenga saving. But Seaman made his third save out of five to deny Lombardo and Arsenal were through to their third European Cup Winners Cup final.

Real Zaragoza had gone through 4–3 on aggregate against Chelsea, so the final was to be held in Paris. Had Chelsea won their semi-final, the game would have been at Wembley. Arsenal were seeking to become the first team for 35 years to retain the European Cup Winners Cup on May 10.

UNLIKELY EVENTS

A glorious end to an era rather than a new era in itself was Ian Ridley's assessment on 1994–95 for Arsenal. It was a season completely dominated by three events of significance matched only by their sheer unlikelihood. One was the dramatic departure of manager George Graham – winner of more trophies than even the incomparable Herbert Chapman – and the second was an unimaginable 5–5 draw with Sampdoria in the European Cup Winners Cup semi-final. The latter match was even more astonishing because it was the result of three goals in the last ten minutes, extra time and a

truly glorious penalty shoot-out. The third event was to come at the very end. Of the rest of the season, there is arguably little to say. The Gunners scored in only one of their first five League matches, fell immediately to mid-table mediocrity and stayed there throughout the whole season.

GRAHAM SACKED

The news that Arsenal had fired George Graham finally came on 21 February, but circumstances had been moving toward that conclusion for some time. In some regards, the whole affair was the result of a shower of sheer bad luck. In the second leg of the European Cup Winners Cup Arsenal were drawn to play Brondby of Denmark. Arsenal won the tie 4–3 on aggregate in October and November 1994. It was from Brondby that Arsenal had bought the scorer of the winning goal in the 1992 European Championship, John Jensen.

Hamburg, who had transferred Jensen to Brondby, were due 20 per cent of the fee and had recently approached Arsenal for confirmation of the amount involved. Presumably the answers they were getting from Brondby were not entirely satisfactory. Arsenal did not answer Hamburg's enquiry, but it was one reason why David Dein, Arsenal's Vice-Chairman, asked Brondby to confirm what they had received for Jensen when the two clubs met in Denmark. Both sides knew there was an agent, Rune Hauge, involved, and certainly expected him to have taken a cut. But as Peter Hill-Wood told Mihir Bose of *The Daily Telegraph*: 'The Brondby chairman said they had kept £900,000, which did surprise us.' It meant simply that some £676,000 must have gone somewhere else.

Not all the details are clear, and may never be so, but it was established that George Graham had declared to the Inland Revenue that he had received £425,000 as an unsolicited gift or gifts from Rune Hauge. Eventually Graham paid this money back to Arsenal. This happened some time before his eventual departure, and Hill-Wood later told Bose that Graham had also asked to leave Highbury with two years

Above: Ian Wright scores Arsenal's first goal in the second leg of the Cup Winners' Cup semi-final against Sampdoria on 20 April 1995. A Merson corner was headed on by Hartson and the ball virtually bounced off Wright's legs into the far corner. It meant that he had scored in every game of the tournament so far, and if he did so in the final, he would become the first player to score in every game or round of any European competition. In the end, of course, Zaragoza's Esnaider scored in the final and became the record breaker, but the Paris final could have seen two players achieve this scoring feat.

Above: Yet another penalty shoot-out. This time against Sampdoria in the 2nd leg of the 1995 Cup Winners Cup semi-final. Seaman denies Lombardo's kick to put Arsenal through on penalties 3–2 after extra time.

Above right: A rightfully jubilant and relieved David Seaman after his heroics in the Cup Winners Cup semi-final penalty shootout secure Arsenal's place in the final.

of his contract left. He felt he could not motivate the players and he and Hill-Wood agreed he could leave at the end of the 1994-95 season.

But on 17 February Peter Hill-Wood and Ken Friar were asked to meet the Premier League's investigation committee. Rick Parry, Robert Reid, Steve Coppell and John Quinton, the League's chairman, went through their findings of an investigation into transfers of foreign players in detail. They revealed that there had been a similar situation over the transfer of Pal Lydersen from the Norwegian club 1K Start. Although Graham had paid back everything, which he described as unsolicited gifts, and had asked for an open hearing on the whole affair, the Arsenal board felt justified in their decision to dismiss him on 21 February.

REVELATIONS THAT SHOOK FOOTBALL

Despite the fact that many had expected it, the mood was one of intense shock. This was after all Arsenal, the most upright of all English clubs, the bearer of the historical banner for the English game. It was inevitable that many should say that Graham was unlucky and that the allegations against him would prove to be only the tip of the iceberg, and a reflection of a season of similar behaviour elsewhere in the game. There was certainly a great deal of money sloshing about in the game since the arrival of the Premier League and the Sky television deal. Very modest players were receiving signing-on fees which made the wages of the greatest stars of George Graham's day seem like a pittance.

Stewart Houston was to be the new George Allison – taking over from the most successful manager, in terms of silverware won, in the club's history. But Houston inherited a team past its best and one steeped in Graham's trademarks – defensive orientation, the grinding out of results, 1–0 to Arsenal, the acquisition of numerous central defenders but only two forwards, Wright and Smith (before Hartson and Kiwomya in the 1994–95 season).

George Graham was always aware of the attitudes taken toward Arsenal, and clearly cared deeply about them. He was presumably aware of criticisms about the lack of creativity

– the lack of a new Liam Brady. At the start of the 1993–94 season he had said: 'The fans keep on at me about a midfield player. They're telling me nothing I don't already know. Every paper, every radio station, every TV station is saying "George needs to buy a midfield player." In fact I actually had a T-shirt made up which said "I AM TRYING TO BUY A MIDFIELD PLAYER". I was thinking of wearing it at a press conference after a game, but eventually thought better of it ...'

END OF AN ERA

Graham's system changed in his nine years with the club. To begin with, Graham played Brian Marwood wide and his contribution to the 1989 Championship was enormous. And despite a lengthy flirtation with the massively popular Anders Limpar, Marwood was never really replaced and as a result Arsenal changed their formation to a straightforward four-man midfield, with Ian Wright up front partnered by Alan Smith, Kevin Campbell and, latterly, John Hartson. This made life much harder for the second-choice forwards. As Alan Smith said: 'We don't have a crosser anymore. If Paul Merson or Kevin Campbell play wide, they're not exactly wingers, are they? As a result, we play in straight lines. I'm flicking it on, which means I'm out of the game and someone else has to score.'

Arsenal's overdependence upon him was hardly Ian Wright's fault and it has become a truism of the modern game that without a recognised goalscorer no team achieves anything. The 1994–95 Premier League season was as good an example as any. Newcastle fell away dramatically when they lost their supply of goals in the form of Andy Cole. Blackburn won the Championship because they had two sources of goals – Shearer and Sutton. Nottingham Forest came from nowhere because of Stan Collymore and Liverpool lived off the efforts of Robbie Fowler.

Graham had not solved this problem by the time he left. He had created a team and a system which was very much his. As Lee Dixon said: 'The keys to the success have been the manager and the team spirit within the club. If you look at the Anfield team of 89, there is still that nucleus of players

who are at the club. We've done it all. It is something George Graham can take he credit for, he's bought new players but based it around that core – built around defence. And the defence that won the League in '89 and '91 went on to Copenhagen and Paris four years later.'

GRAHAM'S LEGACY

George wants to be remembered as someone who has been successful,' said Brian Marwood, 'and that's definitely how people will view him. They will say he was successful but not a great character. The man [ran] a high-pressure football club and he's won two Championships, two League Cups, an FA Cup and the European Cup Winners Cup. That's good going. Practically something every year ... as time passes he will become a greater and greater figure in Arsenal's history. People's views are always kinder with history. He will be a terribly hard act to follow. I wouldn't like to think I was taking over from him.'

Dixon had insights into Graham's total coaching method. 'On the coach to away games, we'll always have the opposition's last game on the video. But you think "I only played against him a few months ago", plus there's so much football on television that you're seeing the opposition every week. The boss might get very excited watching the video and say: "Look lads, come and watch this", and we'd say: "Right, boss, and just carry on playing cards."'

The striker of strikers was, of course, Ian Wright. No successful Arsenal team had ever been so dependent on one man. Through a season beset with poor form, scandals and crises, Wright had kept scoring. By the time he ran out in the Parc des Princes on 10 May 1995, he had already scored 30 precious goals in the season. He had now scored more than one hundred for Arsenal and had become the club's highest ever scorer in Europe. Between 15 September and 23 November 1994 he had scored at least once in each of his 12 appearances, a record for Arsenal.

NAYIM FROM THE HALFWAY LINE

But there were other records which needed to be achieved. No club had ever retained the Cup Winners Cup and Arsenal were to become no less than the seventh holders to be defeated in the following season's final.

There was a full house of 48,000 at the Parc des Princes, and all of them would leave with one abiding memory. The game went to extra time, Esnaider scoring for Real Zaragoza to become the first man to score in every round of a European competition, and John Hartson equalising for Arsenal. With just 25 seconds left of the 120 minutes, and everyone in the ground convinced it was to be penalties yet again, the truly remarkable happened – a moment which comes rarely in a lifetime of watching football. It was to be the perfect goal, not only in its execution, but also in its total unexpectedness.

Nayim, usually the Zaragoza playmaker, had been policed constantly since the game began – first by Keown, then by Hillier. But everyone had become tired after 120 minutes of chasing back and closing down space and there was now just a little more room on the park.

Nayim picked up a loose ball out on the right. He was 15 yards from the centre line and five yards in from the touchline. Unusually, Hillier was not in attendance, and Nayim had time to look up and see if anyone was making a forward run. There was no apparent danger – no one in the penalty area. Although Nayim had played for Spurs for five years, he had been in Gascoigne's shadow, and the skills which Terry Venables recognised in Barcelona had not been much appreciated in north London. But it was to be the nightmare of the 1991 FA Cup semi-final relived as Nayim, again in white shirt and blue shorts, took aim. With no other long option available, and with time running out, Nayim lofted the ball toward the Zaragoza fans. It looped off his foot in a delicate parabola, dropping finally toward Seaman's goal like a baseball pitcher's slider for a third strike. It seemed to take forever to fall, the whole ground appeared to stop breathing, and from nothing suddenly there was drama.

SEAMAN STRANDED

Seaman, who had been correctly positioned about ten yards out, started back-pedalling at speed. But the ball, by design or pure chance, was perfectly positioned. Another ten centimetres further back and it would have struck the crossbar. Another ten centimetres further forward and Seaman's hands would have pushed it over the bar. As it was the goalkeeper, hero in Genoa, could only help it into the roof of the net. There was silence, and then the sigh that accompanies news of a great disaster from the Arsenal end. Very few had any idea who had scored, or even how.

Had the shot gone over, it would have been the game's last moment. By the time Seaman had taken a goal-kick, the referee would have blown to bring on the penalty shoot-out.

The Zaragoza players and officials rolled around on the ground, completely obscuring Nayim. His shot, carefully judged, had been from all of 50 yards. Seaman later blamed himself, but he was wrong. The goal was neither a freak nor a fluke, but there are always some percentages on a football pitch that no goalkeeper can weigh the odds for. As for Nayim, he had written his epitaph. He will always be remembered for this moment. *The Sun* was astonishingly eloquent: 'In one beautiful moment, he changed the way he will be remembered in Britain for ever more. He will no longer be Nayim the playactor, Nayim the diver, Nayim the fake, the nuisance. He will be Nayim who scored probably the greatest goal ever in any European final.'

Nayim, gave his account of the goal: 'It was the last minute and the last chance. I didn't have any option but to try, really. I saw Esnaider was offside. I saw the goalkeeper was a bit

Above: Stewart Houston took over when George Graham left the club so dramatically on 21 February 1995. Despite winning his first two games in charge, he always seemed to be a stop-gap. Had the team won the final in Paris, the board's position might have been more difficult, but in June they announced the arrival of Bruce Rioch from Bolton.

forward from his line and I tried. I was quite clear in what I was trying and I was really concentrating.' Terry Venables confirmed Nayim's own account: 'I've seen him try the same thing in training and in a match. He and Gazza were always trying to outdo each other in training. If he had just lobbed it, Seaman would probably have got back, but he really whacked it and put a whip on it, and that's what beat David.'

Arsenal had now played a total of 27 games in the European Cup Winners Cup, had reached the final every time they competed, had lost only the last two of their 27 matches, and had still failed in two of their three finals. The crowd may have sung 'We'll win 'cos we're Arsenal' but it was ultimately as empty as it was unimaginative and for years Spurs fans would sing 'Nayim from the halfway line'. A more imaginative banner read 'One life, one game, one club, one nil' and that perhaps summed up the mood of Highbury in the last two seasons. where Spurs had *The Glory Game* as their contribution to football literature, Arsenal had he very personal, anguished Nick Hornby and *Fever Pitch*. It was as good an epitaph to he Graham era as anyone was likely to produce.

RIOCH TAKES CHARGE

A year of transition began on June 15. Ex-Bolton manager Bruce Rioch was named as Arsenal's new boss. Stewart Houston reverted to first team coach. Rioch's arrival promised a positive approach after the dourness of the previous three years. The day after he was appointed, Rioch spent six hours with the coaching staff, dissecting the Gunners squad.

'They told me we probably had only one 20-goals-a-season man, Ian Wright,' remembers Rioch. He moved quickly to boost Arsenal's firepower. The Dutchman, Dennis Bergkamp, arrived from Internazionale for a club record £7.5 million, swiftly followed by England captain David Platt from Sampdoria for £4.75 million. Those signings signalled a radical change of policy for a club hitherto reluctant to spend huge sums in transfer fees or wages.

Meanwhile, Kevin Campbell left for Forest at the end of his contract – and Arsenal soon lost two more experienced players. Stefan Schwarz was one of 1994–95 successes. But the Swedish midfielder and his family never settled in England. On he moved, to Fiorentina in Italy. Then Rioch's plans took another knock when Alan Smith confirmed that a prolonged cartilage injury had ended his career.

Highbury fans saw a new-look team, in style as well as personnel. After the gloom of the months before, smiles were back in fashion. 'We go into training every morning and feel relaxed,' said Tony Adams.

By the end of the season, senior pros were admitting, they'd been through a learning process. Arsenal had gained a UEFA Cup place too, though it was a close-run thing. With eight minutes of the final Premiership Sunday left, Rioch's team were 0–1 down to relegated Bolton at Highbury. A repeat of the fixture at Burnden Park in October – when Arsenal tore Wanderers apart, but lost 0–1 – looked on the cards. Then Platt popped up with the equaliser. Two minutes later Bergkamp drilled home the winner, and another full house crowd celebrated; in relief as much as triumph.

'That's what I bought them for!' smiled Rioch.

BERGKAMP SHOWS HIS SKILLS

The two new signings' fortunes contrasted sharply. After Bergkamp had scored – two corkers in the 4–2 win over Southampton – he settled down to become the fulcrum of the attack. The actor and Arsenal fanatic Tom Watt summed up his impact: 'He's made the season for me. I'd pay to watch him train, he's got that much ability.'

However, injury wrecked David Platt's season. He volleyed a brilliant goal in the fourth game, a 1–1 draw against Forest – then went into hospital for a cartilage operation that kept him out until November. More time on the sidelines followed early in the New Year.

Injuries and suspensions caused the manager all sorts of problems after an impressive start. Ligament injuries ruled out Ray Parlour for two spells. Steve Bould missed the last four months because of a groin problem. Adams was out for nearly as long after a cartilage operation. Suspensions forced Rioch to make changes too. Wright was the most high-profile victim. The manager wanted his top scorer on the pitch, not banned. In March, Wright asked for a transfer, which the club refused.

With his skipper and Bould ('the colossus') injured, Rioch switched to a 3–5–2 formation. Martin Keown, Andy Linighan and Scott Marshall formed the back line – and the Gunners conceded only seven goals in 12 matches.

Keown, in particular, had an outstanding year, ending as captain in Adams' absence. It was a remarkable turn-round for the versatile defender, who'd admitted he was concerned about his future after not playing in the pre-season friendlies.

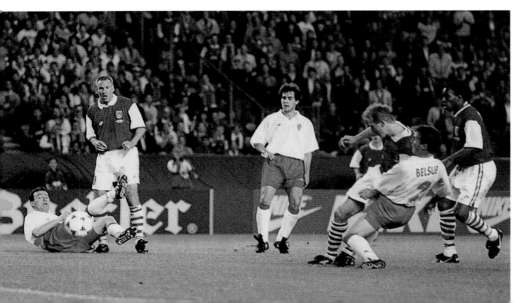

Below: John Hartson stabs home Paul Merson's pass to equalise for Arsenal in the final of the 1995 Cup Winners Cup in Paris. Earlier, Esnaider had put Real Zaragoza ahead the the game went into extra time. With just 25 seconds left, everyone was preparing for penalties, but Nayim lobbed the ball 50 yards and the ball span under the crossbar as Seaman grabbed at air.

Marshall was one of several young players who came into contention. So did lively, fellow Scot Paul Dickov, left-winger Adrian Clarke and midfielder Paul Shaw. There were encouraging signs that the Arsenal youth policy was producing again. Matthew Rose, Stephen Hughes and Gavin McGowan all came through from Pat Rice's 1994 Youth Cup winners to play in the first team.

David Seaman, Lee Dixon and a rejuvenated Paul Merson were ever-present. Merson finished the season with a bumper benefit match against an International Select, with the 1971 'Double' squad in attendance.

The low point was undoubtedly the Coca Cola Cup semi-final against Aston Villa. Bergkamp played superbly against the competition's eventual winners, poaching two memorable goals to put Arsenal 2–0 up in the first leg. Defensive lapses enabled Dwight Yorke to strike twice in reply. The second leg at Villa Park stayed goalless despite extra time, meaning Arsenal were knocked out on the away goal rule. Aston Villa went on to beat Leeds in the final.

RIOCH'S REIGN ENDS ABRUPTLY

So 1995–96 turned out to be a season of 'what might have been'. But it wasn't unsuccessful. A Cup semi-final appearance, fifth in the Premiership and a place in Europe for 1996–97 would have been something the fans would gladly have settled for during the turbulence before Bruch Rioch's arrival.

However, five days before the Premiership season started, Arsenal parted company with their manager Rioch. A statement from Peter Hill-Wood, the Arsenal chairman, announced that the board had decided that it was in the best interest of the club that Bruce Rioch should leave and that accordingly the club had released him from his position as manager. Rioch's 14-month reign was the shortest of any Arsenal manager this century. Mr Hill-Wood announced that the club had a successor in mind but that it was not possible at that stage to identify him. It did not take long for Fleet Street to name the new manager-in-waiting as a Frenchman, Arsène Wenger, who was managing Nagoya Grampus Eight in Japan, with whom he had a contract which would keep him

there until January 1997. Wenger had been thinking over an offer to become the FA's technical director. An intelligent man, he appeared to be a typical Arsenal type, knowledgeable and authoritative without being flamboyant.

While waiting to announce the new appointment, Stewart Houston, assisted by first-team coach Pat Rice, were responsible for team affairs. It was the second time that Houston had stepped into the shoes of the manager, as he had ably filled the gap between the departure of Graham and arrival of Rioch. Two new appointments for the season were old Arsenal men Tom Walley, the new youth team coach, and Liam Brady, head of youth development. Brady, of course, was one of Arsenal's greatest players and since then had experienced big-time management at Celtic.

FRENCH DUO ARRIVE AT HIGHBURY

On the playing side, John Jensen had returned to Brondby in Denmark and two newcomers arrived just in time for the new season. Both had French international honours. Patrick Vieira, a tall midfielder, was an Under-21 international, born in Senegal. He had begun his career with Cannes in France and had been made captain at just 19 years of age. He'd been snapped up by AC Milan, to whom Arsenal paid just over £3 million for him. Although still only 20, he was regarded throughout France as a star of the future. The second signing, Remi Garde, a midfielder/sweeper, was 30, and had played for Lyon and Strasbourg, from whom Arsenal engaged him under the Bosman ruling, his contract having expired.

So Arsenal at the last minute had signed two top players from the continent. The Bosman ruling in the European courts had denied the right of clubs to claim transfer fees on players whose contracts had expired, thus giving players a new freedom of movement. This, together with the Premiership's new wealth, arising out of Sky Television contracts, had led to the import into England of a number of top continental players.

Neither of Arsenal's imports appeared in the opening match of the season. Captain Tony Adams was also missing from the line-up although, along with Seaman, Platt and Bergkamp, he had played in the biggest football event in England for 30 years – Euro 96, the European Championships. He had played, with Bruce Rioch's blessing, despite not having fully recovered from a knee operation in January. He had another operation afterward and did not return until well into September. Ian Wright, too, was not fully fit and was to be a substitute in the first four League games of the season, during which he still scored twice.

GUNNERS START STRONGLY

Arsenal got off to a good start by beating West Ham 2–0 at Highbury. Hartson and Bergkamp, with a penalty, scored the goals. It was the reverse story at Liverpool, where the Gunners

Left: The new order at Highbury: Manager Bruce Rioch, who took over in June 1995, flanked by his expensive signings from the Italian League, England skipper David Platt (left), who was acquired from Sampdoria, and Dutch international forward Dennis Bergkamp (right), who became Arsenal's most expensive player to date when bought from Internazionale for £7.5 million. Bergkamp's subtle brilliance, and his explosively accurate finishing, brought a new dimension to Arsenal's football.

lost 2–0, but an away win at Leicester, again 2–0, had them third in the table already. There was then an exciting game with Chelsea at Highbury, in which Chelsea led 2–0, but Arsenal came back to lead 3–2, only for a last-minute goal from Chelsea's Dennis Wise to restrict the Gunners to a draw. Another 2–2 draw at Villa was a good result and, with Bergkamp, Wright and Merson already on the scoresheet with two apiece, things looked very promising for the first leg of the UEFA Cup, which was a home tie against the German Bundesliga giants Borussia Monchengladbach.

Arsenal's display was disappointing, hampered as it was by Dennis Bergkamp having to go off early in the match with a hamstring injury. Arsenal were 2–0 down soon after half time, staged a rally but finished 3–2 down. It left a big task ahead for the second leg.

Three days later (Friday the 13th) Stewart Houston resigned. He had been offered a post as assistant to George Graham who, after being banned from football management for a year, had taken over at Leeds. However Houston, who said it was clear to him he would never get the no 1 job at Highbury, stated that he was not interested in being no 2 any more. Houston's move was to facilitate him taking over the managership at First Division Queen's Park Rangers. He gave the Loftus Road side a distinctly ex-Arsenal look when he appointed his old boss at Highbury, Bruce Rioch, to be his assistant.

WENGER ARRIVES EARLY

With what appeared to be crisis looming at Highbury, Chairman Peter Hill-Wood revealed he had been in contact with Japan and expected Arsène Wenger to be released from his contract with Grampus Eight and to be able to take over somewhat earlier than had been expected. Meanwhile Pat Rice was the new caretaker manager at Highbury, and in his

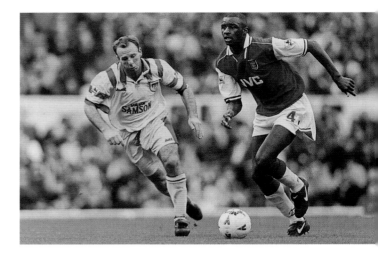

first programme notes he confessed that what he wanted for Arsenal was to get back to some 'boring' 1–0 wins again, the way to win trophies in his view.

Ian Wright emphasised Arsenal's buoyant outlook in the next game by scoring a hat-trick in a 4–1 home win over Sheffield Wednesday and he got another goal in a 2–0 win at Middlesbrough, where Adams returned as a substitute, before Arsenal went to Borussia Monchengladbach to try to win by two goals and keep themselves in Europe. Arsène Wenger flew in to join Arsenal for his first match, although for the time being Pat Rice remained in control. Wenger was encouraged by what he saw. After going one behind, Arsenal equalised just before half time through Wright and went ahead just afterward through Merson. One more might have led to them winning on aggregate but, after Monchengladbach scored again in the 64th minute, Arsenal's pressing need was for a goal to force parity over the two legs, and in pressing they conceded another in injury time to lose the tie by a disappointing six goals to four.

Wenger had flown in to take over before Arsenal's next match, and saw good wins over Sunderland and Blackburn to lift Arsenal to second in the table. Two draws with Midlands teams followed, at home to Coventry and away at Stoke, the second being in the third round of the Coca-Cola Cup – Arsenal, in keeping with some other top clubs, had been given a bye to this stage. Before Arsenal could beat their First Division opponents Stoke in the replay 5–2, George Graham returned to Highbury in charge of Leeds United. Former Arsenal favourite David O'Leary was with Graham as his no 2 at Leeds. The Gunners won 3–0.

GUNNERS GO TOP

Arsenal's interest in the Coca-Cola Cup ended in the fourth round on 27 November when they were well beaten by Liverpool – 4–2 at Anfield, the two coming from Ian Wright penalties. However, three days later it was a different story in a remarkable match at St James' Park against the Premiership

leaders, Newcastle. A minute after a 12th-minute goal by Dixon had been replied to by a 21st-minute Shearer equaliser, Tony Adams brought down Shearer when he was through on goal, and was sent off. It seemed all over for the Gunners, but they withstood the Newcastle siege and, in the 60th minute, an Ian Wright breakaway goal put Arsenal top of the table. 'There is something special about this team', said Wenger. 'They have a good camaraderie because they have been playing together for a long time'.

Arsenal's table-topping didn't last long and a surprise 2–1 defeat at relegation strugglers Nottingham Forest plus a couple of draws began a mini-slide that dropped them to third. In January Arsenal negotiated the third round of the FA Cup by winning a replay 2–0 at Sunderland, this otherwise frenetic encounter was illuminated by an exquisite goal from Dennis Bergkamp. On 4 February at home to Leeds in the fourth round, they crashed 1–0 to a 12th-minute goal by Rod Wallace and inspired goalkeeping by Nigel Martyn. Apart from the UEFA Cup defeat, it was Arsenal's first defeat of the season at home, and the first time Leeds had beaten Arsenal in the Cup in ten encounters since the Cup final of 1972.

So their ejection from their third Cup competition left Arsenal with just the Premiership to fight for, or at worst a place in Europe. But the next home defeat, which quickly followed on 19 February, was a blow. Two first-half goals by leaders Manchester United, only one of which Bergkamp managed to pull back in the second half, left Arsenal trailing five points behind in third place, and with fewer games in hand than any of their rivals. After this match Wenger wrote off Arsenal's title chances.

In March Wenger completed the signing of Nicolas Anelka, a talented French striker days short of his 18th birthday, from Paris St Germain. The tall, slim youngster delighted with appearances as a sub in Arsenal's run-in.

Strangely, because Arsenal strung together some good wins and other title contenders faltered, their mathematical hopes of taking the title continued nearly to the end of the season, and their prospects of a Champions League place right to the last day.

The title hopes disappeared with another home defeat – a vital one to rivals Liverpool. Arsenal's 2–1 defeat was overshadowed by a controversial penalty decision against them. Robbie Fowler stumbled over David Seaman and immediately jumped up, waving his arms to indicate that he did not think a penalty should be awarded. Referee Gerald Ashby had already pointed to the spot, and wasn't inclined to change his mind. Although the referee thought Fowler had been tripped by Seaman he did not send the keeper off. Seaman blocked Fowler's weak spot-kick, but Jason McAteer slammed in the rebound for the vital goal.

On the second-to-last day of the season Arsenal entertained close rivals Newcastle United in another vital home match. And again they lost, 1–0. Wenger noted they had lost at home to all their immediate rivals: Manchester United, Liverpool and Newcastle. Unfortunately, these late-season defeats were to cost them dear.

CHAMPIONS LEAGUE DISAPPOINTMENT

With Manchester United already crowned as Champions of the 1996–97 season, any one of Liverpool, Newcastle or Arsenal could finish in second position in the Premiership and gain a Champions League place on the very last day of the season, with Arsenal and Newcastle starting the day on identical points totals and goal differences.

Arsenal played Derby County at the last match to be played at the Baseball Ground, and things looked black after 11 minutes with Adams sent off and Arsenal one goal down, but they rallied strongly to win the game 3–1. It was all in vain however as Newcastle won 5–0. Arsenal's third place ensured a UEFA Cup place – but things could have been so much better ... .

During a season in which Arsenal's charismatic former player Denis Compton died to worldwide tributes, Arsenal had found young players likely to uphold the reputation of the club for quality in the future. In particular, Patrick Vieira had been a great success in his first season, 20-year-old Stephen Hughes, picked for England's Under-21 side, had impressed in a late run in the team and Nicolas Anelka's promise was obvious to all. The team's 'old-stagers' were also showing no signs of slipping – Nigel Winterburn had a deserved benefit match in a 3–3 draw with Rangers on 13 May. With Arsène Wenger in charge, the future was looking bright for Arsenal.

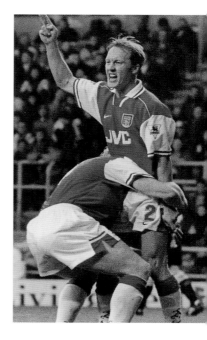

Above: Lee Dixon celebrates his goal against Newcastle at St James'. The long-serving full-back seemed to find a new enthusiasm for the game in 1996–97 and his energetic displays were widely acclaimed.

Left: Martin Keown enjoyed an excellent first season under Arsène Wenger. By the end of the campaign the stylish defender had impressed the new England manager, Glenn Hoddle, enough to be included in the squad for a busy summer schedule.

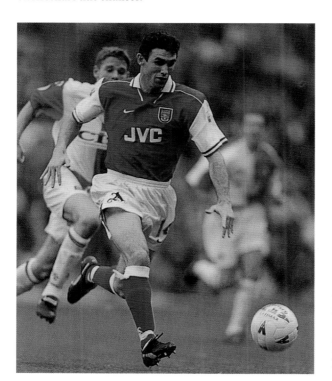

ARSENAL GOALS

On 5 October 1889 a newly-formed association football club, Royal Arsenal, played what could be classed as their first-ever significant match in a senior competition. Those ground-breaking Gunners racked up an 11–0 victory in an early qualifying round of the FA Cup. History doesn't have much to say about the quality of the goals scored on that October day so long ago. We do know that Glaswegian forward Humphrey Barbour and full-back William Scott both scored hat-tricks. They were just the first of the thousands of goals that have poured in over the past 125 years. Here we celebrate some of the best...

Jobey v Leicester Fosse, League Division Two, 6 September 1913

The details of this long-ago goal are not recorded, but George Jobey's equaliser was notable as the first of thousands of Arsenal goals to be scored at their new home at Highbury.

Bastin v Hull City, FA Cup semi-final, 22 March 1930

With just eight minutes remaining in this vital game, Cliff Bastin grabbed an equaliser, picking up Alex James' pass, evading several challenges and firing into the top corner.

Jack v Hull City, FA Cup semi-final replay, 26 March 1930

This historic goal for the Club launched the Gunners on their trophy-winning run of the early 1930s. The only goal of the game was right-foot volley by David Jack from a pass by Joey Williams.

Drake v Aston Villa, League Division One, 14 December 1935

The best of his 7-goal haul, 30 minutes into the game, Ted Drake picked up a pass from Cliff Bastin and after shrugging off two Villa defenders, slammed the ball into the corner of the net.

Drake v Sheffield United, FA Cup Final, 25 April 1936

Drake scored the only goal of the match 16 minutes from the end to clinch the Cup for the Gunners. Cliff Bastin passed the ball to the unmarked Drake, who swiftly swung with his left-foot to send the ball rocketing into the goal.

Lewis v Liverpool, FA Cup Final, 29 April 1950

Reg Lewis scored both goals in this 2–0 victory. With the Liverpool defence distracted by a move by Goring, Lewis's first goal was slotted past the keeper from a pass supplied by Jimmy Logie.

Holton v Liverpool, League Division One, 15 November 1952

A superb drive from centre-forward Cliff Holton that clipped an upright before settling in the far corner.

Lishman v Burnley, League Division One, 1 May 1953

In this critical game, prolific goal-scorer Doug Lishman produced a stunning volley to give Arsenal the lead and put them on their way to the title - which was won on goal difference.

Baker v Staevnet Kobenhaven, Inter-Cities' Fairs Cup, 25 September 1963

Prolific goalscorer Joe Baker evaded a trail of defenders before pounding the ball into the net. Arsenal won 7-1.

George v Liverpool, FA Cup Final, 8 May 1971

Deep into extra time, after an exchange of passes with John Radford, Charlie George fired a fierce shot into the back of Liverpool's net. His celebration has become an iconic image.

Brady v Tottenham, League Division One, 23 December 1978

Following a scramble in the Spurs box, the ball was cleared, only for Brady win it back from a defender with a sliding challenge. Brady advanced to the edge of the box and let loose a fierce swerving shot into the top corner of the goal.

Thomas v Liverpool, League Division One, 26 May 1989

Thomas's run into the penalty area, leaving the opposition defence stranded, and his final touch that took the ball past Grobbelaar into the net will never be forgotten by Arsenal fans.

Rocastle v Manchester United, League Division One, 19 October 1991

After surviving one hefty challenge and evading another with a delicate side step, David Rocastle floated an elegant chip over United goalkeeper Peter Schmeichel from 25 yards. The ball hit the crossbar and bounced into the net off the helpless goalie.

Limpar v Liverpool, League Division One, 20 March 1992

An outrageous goal from the Swedish international Anders Limpar, scored from a perfectly judged lob.

Wright v Everton, Premier League, 28 August 1993

Latching onto a long up field pass from David Seaman, the ever-predatory Ian Wright confounded the Everton defence with some nifty footwork before floating a delicious lob over the Everton goalkeeper Neville Southall.

Smith v Parma, Cup Winners Cup Final, 4 May 1994

Picking up a loose clearance on the edge of the Parma area, Smith chested the ball down and launched a stunning left-footed volley that clipped the post before settling in the net.

Bergkamp v Leicester, Premier League, 27 August 1997

The third goal of an outstanding hat trick, running into the opposition area onto a perfect lofted pass from David Platt, Bergkamp instantly controlled the ball with his right foot, flicked it past the defender with his left, and coolly shot the ball into the top corner.

Kanu v Chelsea, Premier League, 23 October 1999

In the last minute of normal time, Kanu blocked an attempted Chelsea clearance that cannoned off him towards the Chelsea corner. The goalkeeper raced out of his area, but with a clever dummy, Kanu by-passed the goalie and slammed the ball into the top corner of the net from an astonishing angle, sealing his hat-trick.

Bergkamp v Newcastle, Premier League, 2 February 2002

This is undoubtedly one of Bergkamp's most memorable goals. Robert Pires picked out Bergkamp on the edge of the box with a sweet side foot pass. As the ball arrived at his left foot, Bergkamp deftly flicked it one side of his marker and dodged around his other side to collect it and coolly slotted the ball into the bottom corner of the net past the goalie.

Parlour v Chelsea, FA Cup Final, 12 May 2002

With the Final locked at 0–0 with 20 minutes left, Wiltord slid a short pass to Ray Parlour, running through the centre of the pitch. 25 yards out from goal, Parlour paused slightly, slipping the ball onto his right boot before slamming a shot into the top-right hand corner of the net.

Henry v Liverpool Premier League, 9 April 2004

One of Henry's best goals, he received the ball just inside the opposition half, before setting off on a run that saw him slalom in between a flat-footed Liverpool defence and side-foot into the back of the net.

Henry v Real Madrid, Champions League, 21 February 2006

Henry's solo-run from the centre circle, culminated in a calm, left-foot finish, slotted into the far corner of the Real Madrid goal.

Adebayor v Tottenham, Premier League, 15 September 2007

A neat flick and a thunderous volley by Adebayor from 25 yards secured a stunning goal for the Gunners in a 3–1 away victory over Spurs.

Fabregas v Tottenham, Premier League, 31 October 2009

Winning possession immediately from a Spurs kick off, Cesc Fabregas skilfully evaded three challenges before powering the ball home.

Nasri v Porto, Champions League, 9 March 2010

Picking up the ball near the Porto corner flag, Samir Nasri dribbled infield, danced past three opposition defenders and fired a low shot from an improbably narrow angle, across the goalkeeper and in off the far post.

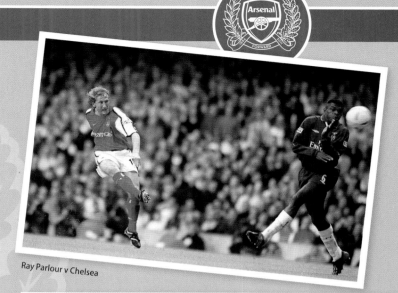

Ray Parlour v Chelsea

Dennis Bergkamp v Newcastle

Emmanuel Adebayor v Spurs

Thierry Henry vs Real Madrid

Samir Nasri v Porto

Cesc Fabregas v Spurs

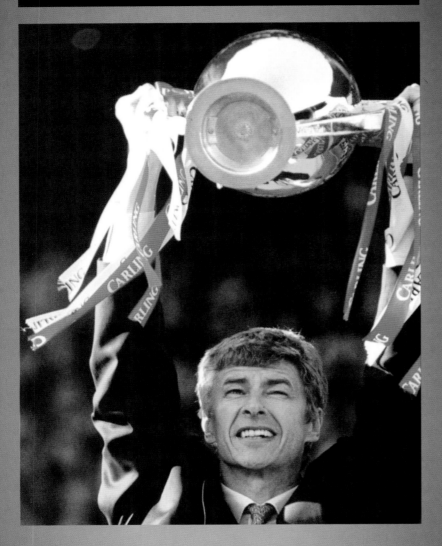

CHAPTER 9

WENGER'S FIRST DOUBLE

1997–2000

As the final whistle was blown at the Baseball Ground to bring a trophyless 1996–97 campaign to a close, Arsène Wenger was already plotting how to improve his team for his first full season in charge. The summer break would be anything but rest. As Keown, Wright, Seaman and Adams travelled to Wenger's homeland to represent England in Le Tournoi, the Arsenal coach also headed to the continent as he sought to strengthen his side.

WENGER RINGS THE CHANGES

An abundance of European talent was available to Premiership managers – particularly those based in the capital – during the summer of 1997. The Bosman ruling and the increased profile of English football, not to mention high wages, had made the Premiership the choice of a multitude of European-based players. The Arsenal coach identified his targets and wasted no time in moving to clinch their signatures.

With Paul Merson departing for Middlesbrough, the first name on Wenger's list was the electric-paced Dutchman Marc Overmars. Some critics had expressed doubts about his fitness after a knee injury had kept him out of the game for eight months. The good news for Wenger was that these doubts had left just two clubs – Arsenal and Real Betis – willing to match the Amsterdam club's £5 million valuation. Wenger was confident that the Dutchman was fit and mentally prepared for the Premiership and later remarked: 'When I did my homework on him I discovered he was upset at the rumours he was not fit and that he could never play to his true ability again. That was a good sign for me, a hurt player. He had something to prove.' Overmars opted for Highbury, leaving Betis to look elsewhere.

Two other experienced players arrived at Arsenal over the summer, both from Wenger's former club Monaco. Gilles Grimandi and Emmanuel Petit crossed the channel in time for pre-season training and reports suggested that they were intended as ready-made replacements for members of Arsenal's veteran-filled defence. Wenger knew Petit well, having handed him his debut as an 18-year-old at Monaco. For much of his career, he had operated as a defender but Wenger had a different assignment in mind for him at Highbury. The Arsenal coach planned to pair Petit with Patrick Vieira in midfield.

Having added experience to his squad, Wenger was keen to inject youth into his first-team pool. With this in mind, two young strikers – Christopher Wreh and Luis Boa Morte – and 23-year-old midfielder, Alberto Mendez, arrived to join 18-year-old defender Matthew Upson, who had made the

short trip from Luton Town in May. All would play some part in first-team affairs during a season that would see Arsenal play 54 matches in all competitions.

WRIGHT CHASES RECORD

Arsenal began their Premiership campaign at Leeds. Predictably Wright grabbed the Gunners' first goal of the season to earn a share of the points. Wright was on the scoresheet two days later when Coventry visited Highbury. His double-strike gave Arsenal a comfortable victory and edged him to within a single goal of Cliff Bastin's record.

The game against a dogged Southampton side at the Dell brought the best out of Bergkamp. With an hour played and the scored at 1–1 the Dutchman made his mark. He picked up the ball in midfield and carried it into the Saints' penalty area and, with the defence fearfully backing-off, drove a precise shot past Paul Jones. Then, 20 minutes later, the Saints opted for a different approach when finding Bergkamp in possession. In an effort to restrain the Arsenal striker, Francis Benali gripped hold of Bergkamp's shirt, but his challenge was in vain. Shrugging the defender aside, the Dutchman unleashed an unstoppable shot into the Saints' goal.

Two draws followed: first there was a trip to Filbert Street to take on Martin O'Neill's Leicester City. In a match full of hard work, enterprise and far too many defensive errors, Bergkamp provided a faultless display of forward play. The Dutchman's three goals were of the highest quality and included the winner of the BBC Match of the Day Goal of the Season. Bergkamp used his left foot deftly to control a cross from the right, moving the ball onto his right foot before despatching it past the on-rushing Leicester keeper. A home draw against Spurs three days later left Arsenal in fifth place, four points behind Blackburn and Manchester United at the end of August.

Bergkamp's domination of Arsenal's scoring had left Ian Wright marooned on 177 goals since the second game of the season. Fortunately for Wright his partner was in generous mood as newly promoted Bolton came to Highbury in September. In the 20th minute, a Bergkamp through-ball gave Wright a sight of goal and the striker made no mistake, sliding the ball past Keith Branagan. The goal that set a new record came just five minutes later and again Bergkamp was at the hub of things. The Dutchman stabbed a shot goalward, but was foiled by Branagan and the loose ball broke to Wright two yards out in front of an unguarded net. Ray Parlour added a third goal, but nobody could gatecrash Ian Wright's party and he completed his hat-trick in the second half.

NON-FLYING DUTCHMAN

Wright barely had time to bask in the glory of his goalscoring achievements before he was on a plane heading for Greece and the first leg of Arsenal's UEFA Cup tie against PAOK

Salonika. One absentee was Bergkamp. His fear of flying forced Wenger to rejig his team, naming 19-year-old Nicolas Anelka alongside the experienced Overmars and Wright.

On a frustrating night for the Gunners, Wenger's attacking approach failed to reap rewards. Several good chances had been squandered by the time Greek international Fratzeskos skipped into the area to put the ball past Seaman. It was little more than the home team deserved and after the game Wenger declared: 'PAOK were more consistent overall. We dropped our level in the second half. The atmosphere was not an excuse and nor was the absence of Dennis Bergkamp. Now we have to win by two goals, which will not be easy.' Wenger's concern was well founded. Despite an early Bergkamp goal, Arsenal failed to score a second and were eliminated from the competition when the Greeks snatched an equaliser.

Between the games against Salonika, the Gunners had beaten Chelsea at Stamford Bridge – courtesy of a rare goal from Nigel Winterburn – had overcome West Ham at home and drawn away at Everton. By the end of September, Arsenal had reached the summit of the League table. Eight goals from nine games for Bergkamp had undoubtedly been the catalyst for the Gunners' storming run to pole position in the Championship.

A RARE DEFEAT

The trip to Pride Park, Derby's new ground, brought Arsenal's first defeat of the season. It was the worst possible preparation for the visit of Manchester United the following Sunday. Despite the absence of the suspended Petit and Bergkamp, Arsenal got off to a sensational start against the Champions, scoring twice in the first half hour. Bergkamp's replacement, Anelka, struck first before fellow Frenchman Vieira sent a superbly angled shot past Peter Schmeichel on 27 minutes.

Above: '179, Just Done it!' Ian Wright finally breaks Cliff Bastin's 81-year-old club scoring record of 178 goals, against Bolton in September 1997. Wright confessed that the record-breaking goal was one of his easiest (tapping into an empty net from close range), but it was typical of Wright to cap the feat by completing a hat-trick as the Gunners ran out 4–1 winners.

Opposite: One down, one to go. Wenger lifts the Championship trophy after the 4–0 win over Everton on 3 May 1998.

United came back strongly and Teddy Sheringham grabbed two goals, but his efforts were in vain, Platt, in the team for Petit, heading a late winner. The triumph against United provided the only addition to Arsenal's points in November and by the end of the month they had slipped to fifth place in the table.

The Coca-Cola Cup was Arsenal's only early season respite from League action. However, this competition lost much of its appeal once UEFA threatened to withdraw its winners' European place. Arsène Wenger had used Arsenal's first game in the competition to field younger squad members, but for the tie against Coventry City in November he selected a strong line-up that included Denis Bergkamp. The Dutchman was eligible despite his League suspension and his extra-time goal decided the tie.

EARLY SEASON FORM DESERTS GUNNERS

Arsenal's indifferent League form continued in December. The low point of this frustrating period coming in a 3–1 reverse at home to Blackburn. Floodlight failure in the next match, away at Wimbledon, denied Wenger's team the chance to get back on course in the title race. The match was abandoned at 0–0 after 46 minutes and rescheduled for March, by which time Wenger hoped to have Arsenal running on full power again.

Christmas brought four points but little festive cheer for Gunners fans. Arsenal were no longer playing the fluent, attacking football that had seen them waltz to the top of the table in the autumn. At New Year, Wenger's team were in sixth place, 12 points adrift of Manchester United. Most pundits considered that Arsenal's chance had gone. Fortunately, the two domestic cup competitions gave a welcome distraction and a chance to get back to form in the early weeks of 1998.

The first Saturday in January brought with it the FA Cup third round, and for Arsenal a primed and armed booby trap in the shape of a home tie against First Division Port Vale. The 37,471 crowd watched as Arsenal laboured to overcome a side that had not won for two months. A 0–0 draw gave Wenger's team a second chance at Vale Park and for the replay they would be able to call upon record goalscorer Ian Wright.

PENALTIES PROVE TURNING POINT

Cup action continued the following Tuesday as Arsenal made the short trip to take on West Ham at Upton Park. The Hammers had a formidable home record, winning 12 of their 13 home games so far in all competitions. The game turned on an incident after just ten minutes. West Ham striker Paul Kitson darted into Seaman's penalty area, only to be met by the out-rushing keeper. The referee pointed to the spot and up stepped former Gunner John Hartson to take the kick. Hartson, the Premiership's top scorer v Seaman, England's top

goalkeeper. It was a contest which had no doubt been played out during numerous Arsenal training sessions. The outcome was strangely inevitable. Seaman comfortably collected the striker's scuffed shot. Hartson bowed his head and Arsenal were buoyed. Goals from Overmars and Wright confirmed victory and put the Gunners into a two-legged semi-final against Chelsea. The following week, Wenger's team made it to the FA Cup fourth round by overcoming Port Vale after a penalty shoot-out. In retrospect, it was perhaps the closest they came to missing the eventual Double.

In the League, a bad-tempered match against Coventry at Highfield Road saw Vieira sent off, but, more worryingly for Wenger, Seaman suffered a finger injury which would keep him out for several weeks. The experienced keeper would be replaced by 20-year-old Austrian Alex Manninger. The blow of losing Seaman was slightly diminished by the return of skipper Adams to first team duty. He had suffered a series of niggling injuries and had lost form in the first half of the season. After the defeat by Blackburn in December he sought much-needed rest and recuperation in the south of France and celebrated his recall with his first goal of the season, heading home from a corner in a 3–0 win over Southampton.

GUNNERS REDISCOVER FORM

Arsenal were beginning to rediscover the fluency and invention that had entertained the Highbury faithful so richly during early season. In the League, Wenger was forced to employ most of his squad members as the Gunners made

Right: Stephen Hughes scores his first goal of the season against Chelsea in the first leg of the Coca-Cola Cup semi-final. Marc Overmars netted for the fifth time in five matches, but Mark Hughes came off the bench to give Chelsea a lifeline. The Gunners were guilty of spurning a hatful of chances and they would pay a heavy price for their profligacy in the return fixture at Stamford Bridge.

their way up the table despite a growing list of injuries and suspensions. Wins over Crystal Palace and Chelsea had arrived courtesy of goals from two players, Gilles Grimandi and Stephen Hughes, who had been largely confined to the bench throughout the season. Despite this upturn, the pundits' view remained that United had all but won the title and that the best Arsenal could achieve was runners-up spot and a Champions League place.

Wenger's squad continued to be stretched and the situation was not helped by increasing cup commitments. In the Coca-Cola Cup, the Gunners had taken a 2–1 lead to Stamford Bridge in the second leg of their semi-final. Arsenal's advantage was not enough. The return match in west London swung in Chelsea's favour when Vieira was shown the red card just after half time. A 3–1 victory gave Chelsea a 4–3 aggregate win.

Arsenal were left to focus their attention on the Premiership and the FA Cup. Wenger's team had little time to nurse their wounds after the bruising battle at Stamford Bridge. An FA Cup fourth round replay against Palace gave the Gunners the perfect opportunity to revive their Wembley ambitions but a striker shortage was worrying Wenger before the trip to Selhurst Park. Wright was struggling to recover from a hamstring injury, Overmars had been in America with the Dutch team and was due back in the UK on the morning of the game, and Bergkamp had flu. Wenger need not have worried. First-half goals from Anelka and Bergkamp – who started the match but was replaced by Overmars in the second half – gave Arsenal a quarter final tie at home against West Ham. Afterward Wenger praised Overmars' commitment: 'It was a big surprise that we could have him playing at all. Last night he was in America playing for Holland but he was able to catch a flight to Paris and was back in London this morning.'

FIXTURE BACKLOG HINDERS PROGRESS

Two London derbies against the Hammers followed. The first in the League was one of three games the Gunners had in hand on leaders United as they attempted to close a 12-point gap. The clash at Upton Park saw the return from injury of Petit. After playing a key role in Arsenal's upturn in form, the former Monaco man was keen to keep the momentum going, declaring: 'I think it will be difficult for us because we have to continue our good run to put pressure on Manchester United and to leave the other clubs like Chelsea, Liverpool and Blackburn behind. We will lose some day. I just don't want it to be the next game.' A 0–0 draw was a good result given the Hammers form at Upton Park, but it was not enough. The Champions' 11-point lead seemed unassailable and several bookmakers stopped taking bets on the title race.

Wenger, however, would not concede that Arsenal's Championship bid was over: 'It's not over yet but, of course, it will be very difficult for us now. A point was a good result

when you look at the tough match we faced at West Ham but in the context of the Championship now draws are not good enough for us.'

The fixture backlog worsened six days later, when a Bergkamp penalty cancelled out a West Ham goal and forced an FA Cup quarter final replay at Upton Park. Before that game, Arsenal faced two critical League matches. First there was a return to Selhurst for the aborted clash with Wimbledon, followed three days later by a summit meeting at Old Trafford.

For both the Wimbledon and United games, Wenger rotated his young strikers. Anelka, whose form had been fitful in the early part of 1998 was replaced by Chris Wreh. The young Liberian bubbled with confidence as he lined up for his first start of the season, against the Dons. A crisp finish from Wreh on 22 minutes gave Arsenal a deserved half-time lead. The second half saw Arsenal doggedly defend their lead in the face of growing Wimbledon pressure. If the first half had belonged to Wreh, then the second went to Alex Manninger, whose faultless display secured Arsenal all three points. The efforts of Arsenal's young stars prompted a glowing testimonial from Wenger after the game. He declared: 'I am very pleased for Chris Wreh. We have not had a chance to see the best of him yet and it has been a difficult year for him. Manninger was also very good. Unfortunately, he has taken a knock on his knee and there is a slight chance he could miss the Manchester United match.'

MANNINGER TAKES HIS CHANCE

Wenger needn't have worried about the fitness of his young keeper. The Austrian was in the midst of a 13-game run in the first team and was not prepared to relinquish his place. His performances would earn him many plaudits, a place in the Austrian full international squad and the Carling Player of the Month award for March. By the end of the season, he was left in no doubt about his future at Highbury. Wenger declared: 'I see Alex as the future Arsenal goalkeeper. He is an excellent prospect and he is willing to learn and be patient.'

Left: Most of Highbury felt that David Seaman was irreplacable, but in Alex Manninger they had a more than adequate stand-in. The 20-year-old Austrian international was the hero of the FA Cup quarter final when ten-man Arsenal beat West Ham in a penalty shoot-out.

The win against Wimbledon had put a new complexion on the title race. As the Gunners were collecting maximum points at Selhurst, Manchester United were settling for a single point at West Ham. The Champions' lead was still significant – nine points – but Arsenal had three games in hand. The game at Old Trafford on 14 March took on a new significance; if Arsenal could leave Manchester with a win, their fate would be in their own hands. Wenger tried to play down the billing of the match: 'There is a bit more pressure on United now, but not enough,' declared the Gunners' coach. 'Even if we go there and win we will still have to win our games in hand to make it worthwhile. But I hear the bookmakers are taking bets again.'

It had seemed that United would romp to their third consecutive Premiership title, but as Arsenal closed the gap, so interest returned to the battle at the top of the table. The match kicked off at 11 am and was screened live on Sky TV. Wenger had kept faith with Wreh after his scoring start at Selhurst, but after 67 minutes he withdrew the young Liberian and sent on the inhumanly quick Anelka to unsettle the United back line. The young Frenchman had been on the field for just 11 minutes when he rose to flick a header into the path of Overmars. The Dutchman sprinted clear and despatched the ball between Schmeichel's legs. Thereafter, chances arrived for both teams but a combination of poor finishing and assured goalkeeping saw the score remain at 1–0 to Arsenal.

The leaders now looked decidedly catchable. Arsenal were in form and looked capable of converting their three games in hand into nine points and a place at the top of the table. Wenger remained circumspect: 'Manchester United have a small advantage because we have to take the points available from the games we have in hand and that won't be easy.'

BERGKAMP SEES RED

Arsenal's punishing schedule continued with another Cup match against West Ham. Wenger, without Wright, Seaman, and Parlour, must have feared the worst when Bergkamp was shown the red card by Mike Reed after 32 minutes for elbowing Steve Lomas. The Gunners had controlled the game until the Dutchman's dismissal and, though they had been thwarted by French international goalkeeper Bernard Lama, an Arsenal goal seemed inevitable. Bergkamp's dismissal visibly lifted the home side as they eagerly strove forward, relieved that their chief tormentor had departed. The Hammers' security was ill-founded and deep into first-half injury time, Anelka pinched the ball from the boot of Vieira, took aim and curled an exquisite shot into the left-hand corner of Lama's goal.

The second half brought a faultless defensive display from Wenger's team in which Manninger and Keown were outstanding. Keown's efforts in stopping Hartson were Herculean, but there was little the stopper could do as the Welshman bludgeoned his way into the penalty area to force

a low drive inside Manninger's near post after 84 minutes. Extra time beckoned. With both teams flagging from an electric-paced 90 minutes, gaps began to appear at both ends, but amazingly the scores remained unaltered. Manninger was once more the Gunners' hero, saving from Eyal Berkovic and watching as Hartson and Samassi Abou placed their kicks against the frame. For the second time in 1998, Arsenal could celebrate a quarter final victory at Upton Park. Arsenal's opponents in the semi-final were to be First Division Wolverhampton Wanderers.

ARSENAL CLOSE THE GAP

There were no Premiership fixtures for the weekend following the Gunners' Cup success in East London and for Bergkamp the break would be extended to two weeks. On the last day of March, Arsenal payed a visit to struggling Bolton, knowing that a win would take them to within three points of Manchester United with two games in hand. For Wenger, the urgent issue was his lack of striking options and the Frenchman stated: 'We will miss Dennis Bergkamp and the target for me is to find someone to replace him for Tuesday's game at Bolton.'

Once more Chris Wreh stepped into the breach, playing alongside fellow rookie Nicolas Anelka. A fourth consecutive Premiership 1–0 win duly arrived courtesy of a sharply taken 20-yarder from the young Liberian on 47 minutes. Then, 15 minutes after taking the lead, Martin Keown was dismissed for a second bookable offence and Steve Bould replaced Wreh, but Bolton rarely troubled the Gunners rearguard. United's lead was now just three points, and the confidence of the Arsenal coach was growing. 'The message for Manchester is that we go from game to game and what is important is that we have another away victory. Now, like always, it is down to the most consistent team.' Arsenal's consistency was awesome.

Right: Patrick Vieira produced a typically dominating performance at Old Trafford in March 1998. The tough-tackling Frenchman had an inspirational season that would take him back home to play in the World Cup for France.

The FA Cup semi-final brought a routine Gunners victory. An early Wreh goal, a tightly locked defence and another win. In truth, Arsenal played well within themselves at Villa Park and though Wolves had tested them in the second half, the thought remained that if Wenger's team had conceded a rare goal – it would have been their first in five matches – they would merely have gone up the other end to restore their lead.

As spring arrived, Arsenal's run of impressive results continued. Newcastle United, who would provide the Gunners' Cup final opposition come May, arrived at Highbury when Premiership action resumed after a two-week break on 11 April. An Anelka brace and a 30-yard drive from Vieira broke a sequence of five 1–0 victories.

BLACKBURN CHASING SHADOWS

Arsenal were back to their fluent form of early season. The peak came on Easter Monday and the trip to Blackburn to face the last team to beat Arsenal in the League. With Dennis Bergkamp back in action the Gunners were untouchable and after 14 minutes the home side were three goals down. Wave after wave of penetrating Arsenal attacks left the Rovers defence stunned. It took Bergkamp just 75 seconds to open the scoring as he burst onto a flick from Nicolas Anelka to fire home. Two more goals from Parlour and a clinical finish from Anelka gave Arsenal an unassailable lead. It was to be their best display of the whole season Arsenal were now favourites to win the League, but Wenger would not be coaxed into offering any sound bites that might inspire Alex Ferguson and his team. 'We didn't listen to anyone when people said we didn't have a chance and we won't listen now that we are favourites. The players were happy in the dressing room, but they were not going crazy,' explained the Arsenal coach to the Ewood Park press room.

The top of the Premiership beckoned. If United failed to beat Newcastle at home and Arsenal could defeat Wimbledon at Highbury, the Gunners would top the League for the first time since October. Nothing could stop Arsenal and the Dons were hit for five without reply. A draw at Old Trafford meant the Gunners were top, their one-point lead reinforced by two games in hand. The win against the Dons saw Arsenal share the goals out among five scorers, but the loudest celebration greeted the fourth goal, from Petit. He had been an immense figure in the Arsenal midfield alongside Vieira and the Highbury faithful took immeasurable pleasure from the former Monaco star's first goal in an Arsenal shirt. The manner of Arsenal's rise to the top had the purists purring.

ONE WIN TO CLINCH TITLE

Another Petit strike, this time against Derby, was enough to leave Arsenal needing just one win from their final three fixtures to clinch the Championship. Between the Wimbledon and Derby games, the Gunners had condemned Barnsley to

relegation with a 2–0 win at Oakwell Park courtesy of goals from Arsenal's Dutch duo. Bergkamp contributed 19 goals, and many more assists, in his 39 games but these impressive statistics fail to reveal the importance of his contribution. He had quite simply been breathtaking. He had scored goals which left his opponents open-mouthed in disbelief, his passing was intuitive and his ball skills fast and faultless. Small wonder that both the football writers and Bergkamp's fellow professionals voted him their player of the season.

Awards meant little, however, if the Gunners failed to deliver the silverware that was in their grasp at the beginning of May. Arsenal's final two League games of the season were away, so if they were to celebrate with their home fans they would need to defeat relegation-threatened Everton. In a match which the visitors could ill-afford to lose, Everton manager Howard Kendall named a defensive line-up – including Croatian defender Slaven Bilic in midfield. After just six minutes his plans were in tatters, as Bilic headed an own goal to give Arsenal the lead. On 28 minutes Arsenal had a crucial second goal, Marc Overmars accelerating past three defenders before sliding the ball underneath the advancing keeper. Overmars added a third goal, but the celebrations leapt into overdrive in the final minute when Adams latched onto a pass from Steve Bould to crash home his third goal of the season.

HIGHBURY APPLAUDS WENGER'S CHAMPS

After seven years, the title had returned to the capital. The importance was not lost on Wenger, who declared: 'This is my greatest ever achievement as a manager and I am proud for the club, my staff, the players and the supporters. We have shown great spirit all season and our last goal typified that as Steve Bould sent Adams through. They have been great players for Arsenal. I am surprised but delighted that we have won the title so soon but this team can get better.'

Arsenal now had a chance to complete their second League and FA Cup Double and emulate Bertie Mee's team of 1970–71. Before the Cup clash with Newcastle United, Wenger's team faced two away matches at Liverpool and Aston Villa. Having won ten consecutive League games to clinch the title, Arsenal could be forgiven for relaxing and recording two defeats. These games were no form guide for Wembley on 16 May.

THE DOUBLE IS RECLAIMED

At Wembley, Wenger employed his tried and tested formula. A back four of Dixon, Winterburn, Adams and Keown was reinforced by the energetic presence of Petit and Vieira in midfield. The flanks were manned by Overmars and Parlour, who were to supply the bulk of service to two strikers, on this occasion, Wreh and Anelka. Wenger's game plan got off to a stunning start with Overmars and Parlour both

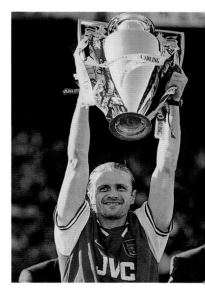

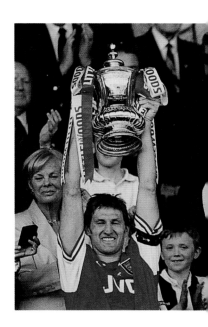

Above and below: Double jubilation. Emmanuel Petit (above) holds aloft the Premiership trophy. Tony Adams (below) raises the FA Cup aloft at Wembley to complete Arsenal's second FA Cup and League Double.

carving out good opportunities for Anelka, but each time the teenager spurned the chance. His moment would come, but before Anelka could redeem himself, Overmars acted. The Dutchman latched onto a Petit chip to race clear of the Newcastle defence and place the ball between Shay Given's legs and into the goal.

Newcastle responded and Seaman was forced into action by a Temuri Ketsbaia effort in the first half. After the interval the Magpies had their best chance when Keown's mistake, on 63 minutes, gave Shearer a clear sight of goal. He struck a post and five minutes later Anelka collected a Parlour pass, and galloped forward to drive a shot into the corner of Given's goal. It may not have provided the drama of Charlie George's late winner against Liverpool in 1971, but Anelka's goal cued celebrations of similar proportions throughout north London.

After the game even the normally restrained Wenger was animated. 'The Championship was our main aim,' said the Highbury boss, 'but it would have been terrible to have lost at Wembley because we really wanted the FA Cup too.'

THE 1998–99 SEASON

The following season proved to be just as dramatic, although not as glorious. The scenes at Highbury on 16 May told their own story. Tearful fans comforted each other, as Manchester United wrested back the Championship from the Gunners. It had been another memorable season. But this time without a trophy to show for it. The mathematics on the last day of the Premiership race were simple. Arsenal had to beat Aston Villa, and hope Spurs – now managed by George Graham – won or drew at Old Trafford.

Les Ferdinand's early goal detonated an explosion of cheers at Highbury. Never before has the old stadium rang to chants of 'Come on, you Spurs'. At least, not from Arsenal fans. But it was a forlorn hope. David Beckham levelled. Andy Cole, ironically an ex-Gunner, scored the goal that took the title back to Manchester.

So near, and yet so far. United, the new Champions of Europe, had been Arsenal's nemesis, in the Premiership, and the FA Cup. TV will replay Ryan Giggs' brilliant winner in the semi-final replay at Villa Park, for years to come. Yet Highbury fans thought the Gunners were on the brink of another trip to Wembley as Dennis Bergkamp stepped up to take that stoppage time penalty with the score at 1–1. Peter Schmeichel guessed right and flung himself to tip the ball away. The rest is history.

United were only doing what they'd promised. Giggs was one of several Old Trafford players who acknowledged the hurt they'd felt when Arsène Wenger's team won the Double. Arsenal's success galvanised United.

In the end, Giggs' strike – and Jimmy Floyd Hasselbaink's late winner in the penultimate Premiership game at Leeds – wrecked Arsenal's season. The Gunners were magnificent in the New Year. But they had left themselves too much to do.

As 1998–99 approached, Alex Ferguson snapped up the towering Dutchman Jaap Stam, to remedy United's problems at centre-back. He signed the Swedish winger Jesper Blomqvist. Then, as the season began, he added a vital ingredient – Dwight Yorke from Aston Villa. At £12.6 million, Yorke was United's record buy. He provided value for money from day one. His Champions League performances marked him as one of Europe's finest forwards.

By contrast, Arsenal signed teenage left back David Grondin, from French Youth Cup winners St Etienne, and the Argentina defender Nelson Vivas from Swiss club Lugano.

Arsenal's first choice line-up probably had a slight edge on United. But Old Trafford's back-up was formidable. United's bench regularly housed the likes of David May, Henning Berg, Wes Brown, Nicky Butt, Teddy Sheringham, Blomqvist and Ole Gunnar Solskjaer.

Wenger admitted as much at the end of the campaign. 'There are several teams in the Premiership with the same financial potential,' he said: 'Then there is Manchester United. They spent £24 million at the start of the season. I can't do that. I have money to spend and I'm looking for three players. But I have to be wise. I have to strengthen without spending too much.'

Such thoughts lead to another comparison between United and Arsenal – the capacity of their grounds. United were guaranteed a full house 55,000 for every home game, a capacity since raised to 75,000. Highbury could then only accommodate 38,000. Every Highbury home match in 1998–99 was packed. Seventy-thousand-plus gates at Wembley for the Champions League games proved Arsenal's potential drawing power.

Discussions continued with Islington Council about enlarging Highbury. Studies were conducted. Meanwhile, rumours abounded, about Arsenal moving to a new site. All sorts of locations were suggested.

Whatever the rumours, United were able to generate more cash than any of their rivals, which Alex Ferguson used to good advantage.

'When you finish one point behind the winners in a 38-game season, it feels like losing a marathon by just one yard,' said Wenger. The Frenchman added: 'No one can say we had a bad season. There were three outstanding teams – United, ourselves and Chelsea. At the end, the difference was very small. But we want to be first, not second.'

Indeed, in five matches against United, the Gunners won two, drew two, and lost only the semi-final replay. That was little consolation at the end of the battle.

AFTER THE WORLD CUP

After the Double triumph, Wenger had identified the problems the Gunners faced. Players coming back from the World Cup finals would be tired. They wouldn't be able to find their best form until later in the season. Wenger also shrewdly realised

that such problems would trouble forwards – like Dennis Bergkamp and Marc Overmars – much more than defenders and midfield players.

David Seaman, Tony Adams, Martin Keown, Patrick Vieira and Manu Petit seemed to suffer little reaction. They were consistent throughout the season. But Bergkamp and Overmars did suffer. And Wenger had few alternatives.

Record goal scorer Ian Wright moved on to West Ham two months after the Gunners beat Newcastle in the FA Cup final.

On the first day of 1998 pre-season training, David Platt announced his retirement. The departure of two such experienced players left big holes. In September, Wenger signed the Swedish international midfielder Freddie Ljungberg to fill one gap. Unfortunately Ljungberg arrived a fortnight too late to play in the Champions League group stage games. Wenger knew the forward he wanted too: Overmars' old Ajax colleague, Nwankwo Kanu, who had moved to Internazionale and missed more than a season because of heart-valve surgery. But Inter Milan would not sell. Not until December. By then the Gunners were out of the Champions League and fifth in the Premiership, four points behind Aston Villa and United.

'Looking back, we lost the Championship in the first half of the season,' said Wenger: 'We dropped too many points at home.' Relegated Charlton and Southampton – who narrowly escaped the drop – both nicked points at Highbury despite Arsenal's massive dominance. Spurs, Middlesbrough and Liverpool escaped with draws too.

With Bergkamp and Overmars searching for their best form in those early months, Nicolas Anelka carried a heavy burden. Anelka had not been included in France's World Cup-winning squad. His form with Arsenal made him one of the first names on new coach Roger Lemerre's team list. Despite his frequent talk of moving on, the French striker produced some memorable performances and goals – like his stunning winner against Everton. He finished Arsenal's top scorer with 17 in the Premiership.

But Chris Wreh, striker of vital goals in the Double campaign, couldn't rediscover that form. Luis Boa Morte, so impressive for Portugal in the Toulon tournament of 1997, found it hard to fulfil his potential. The Argentinian forward Fabian Caballero came on loan from Paraguayan club Cerro Porteno but couldn't break through into Premiership football. France U-21 striker Kaba Diawara arrived from Bordeaux, but didn't score in 12 appearances.

KANU CONTRIBUTES

It wasn't until February, when Kanu was fit and available, that Wenger had the options he wanted in attack. Kanu soon became a Highbury hero. His last minute FA Cup sixth round winner against Derby won the fans over. His second goal at Middlesbrough proved his class. His strike at Tottenham was arguably Arsenal's goal of the season.

'I wish he had joined us earlier,' said Wenger, who used Kanu mainly as a tactical sub. But the Nigerian forward remained optimistic. 'Joining Arsenal was one of the best moves of my career,' he said: 'They have allowed me to play. By the time next season starts, I'll be completely fit – for the first time in years.'

'Almost every time he came on, he changed the game,' said Wenger: 'I expect a lot of him. He will play many more games from the start next season. He can make a huge impact.'

Left: Marc Overmars gets Arsenal off to a flying start as his overhead lob over Dave Beasant secures a 2–1 victory on the opening fixture of the 1998–99 season at home to Forest.

Below: Denis Bergkamp fires Arsenal ahead during a a 3–0 win against Newcastle at Highbury in October. Bergkamp bagged two and Anelka made it three. The win was a welcome lift to morale as it came on the back of a defeat away to Sheffield Wednesday and was only the third of the season.

Suspensions didn't help either. As Bruce Rioch used to say: 'You want your best players on the pitch.' Wenger, ever loyal, defended his players. But the statistics made grim reading. Petit was sent off three times; Keown twice. Lee Dixon, Vivas and Parlour took early baths too. United were at least as aggressive as Arsenal. But they channelled their fighting spirit so that they picked up far fewer cards than the Gunners.

Yet the season started so brightly. In the Charity Shield, at Wembley, Arsenal blasted United 3-0, even though Bergkamp had to retire at half time to rest his hamstring injury. Overmars, Wreh and Anelka scored. It was as if Wenger and his troops had an Indian sign on Fergie's team.

A SLOW START

After all the pre-match presentations, Nationwide League Champions Nottingham Forest proved surprisingly tough opponents in the Gunners opening Premiership game, a Monday night event for Sky Sports. Petit carried on where he'd left off for France, putting Arsenal ahead. Geoff Thomas levelled. The Highbury crowd were growing anxious when Overmars launched an acrobatic shot past Dave Beasant for the winner.

Arsenal had the better of the play in the goalless draw against Liverpool – especially in the first half – but couldn't score. It was to be the start of a trend. Charlton survived a battering at Highbury and escaped with a point after another 0–0 draw. Petit was sent off for a second bookable offence.

Dixon walked 11 days later in a bad-tempered game at Chelsea, after flattening Graeme Le Saux. The score was 0–0, again. Stephen Hughes, in for the suspended Petit, hit a last minute equaliser at Leicester, after Emile Heskey had put the home side in front.

THE CHAMPION'S LEAGUE

Then the Gunners faced their first Champions League match, away to the French Champions Lens. The Champions League campaign was another tale of 'what might have been'.

Arsenal had decided to play their home games at Wembley. Chairman Peter Hill-Wood explained: 'We'd have preferred to play at Highbury. But we couldn't play at Highbury and provide normal service for our supporters. That was the deciding factor. UEFA's regulations on the size of perimeter board advertising would have meant taking up several rows around the stadium with advertising boards. By the time we'd complied with that, we'd have lost many thousands of seats from our capacity, which isn't very big anyway. We'd also have lost the disabled enclosure which is very important to us.

'Then we had to consider the large number of tickets that UEFA required. That would have meant moving whole blocks of East Stand season ticket holders, because UEFA would have needed the areas around the Directors' Box and the press box. That would have caused huge disruption.'

The club tried to keep down the price of Wembley tickets. Season ticket holders could use their cup tie credits to get in. Many of the other tickets cost only £10. The fans – many of whom rarely managed to obtain tickets at Highbury – flocked to Wembley. The Arsenal board had made a wise decision in all the circumstances. In football terms though, might the Gunners have done better in the tight confines of Highbury, where they could close down opponents more quickly than in Wembley's wide open spaces? At Highbury the crowd were on top of the pitch. At Wembley they were yards away. And playing at Wembley seemed to inspire the opposition, especially Dynamo Kiev and Lens.

But back to the start; at Lens' Stade Felix Bollaert. Lens had lost three key players after winning the French title – skipper Jean-Guy Wallemme, midfield playmaker Stephane Ziani, and top scorer Anto Drobnjak. Marc-Vivien Foe, the Cameroon international who later joined West Ham, was out injured. Lens hopes centred on France's Tony Vairelles and the Czech attacker Vladimir Smicer.

Arsenal took charge early on – and missed chance after chance. Overmars ran through to bury a low shot. But one goal wasn't enough. In stoppage time, Vairelles forced home a corner, off Keown. The Gunners would regret their profligacy.

SHEVCHENKO INSPIRES RUSSIANS

The other two teams in the group were the Greek Champions Panathinaikos, and Dynamo Kiev, famous flag bearers for Ukraine. Wenger said all along that Dynamo were favourites, even if they did lose their first game 1–2 in Athens. 'They have so much experience in this competition. They're very good at keeping the ball and Andrei Shevchenko and Sergei Rebrov are such dangerous strikers.'

First, the Gunners saw off Panathinaikos 2–1 at Wembley, thanks to headers by Adams and Keown. Then came Kiev. After losing to Panathinaikos, they had drawn at home to Lens. At Wembley, they were inspired. Shevchenko was majestic, Rebrov a constant irritant. Oleg Luzhny charged up

Right: Andrei Shevchenko of Dynamo Kiev is halted by Tony Adams in the 1–1 draw at Wembley in October. The Russian was one of the stars of the Champions League of 1998–99 and Dynamo went on to reach the semi-finals. This result was to prove costly for the Gunners as they went on to lose in Kiev 3–2 and failed to qualify from the group stage after losing to French club Lens at Wembley.

and down from right-back. Shevchenko had what looked a good goal disallowed. Adams produced a magnificent tackle to dispossess Shevchenko after he'd broken clear. Vieira was suspended, Petit injured. Remi Garde and Hughes in central midfield had a hard job, coping with Dynamo's fast-breaking attacks. But Bergkamp netted a rare header from Dixon's cross. Then, with time running out, came a vital moment. Overmars burst through, rounded the Kiev keeper Olexandr Shovkosky and shot. The 70,000 Arsenal fans screamed 'Goal' Somehow Luzhny raced back to hook the ball off the line. Had that gone in, Dynamo were dead. Instead they won a free-kick. As the ball flashed across the Arsenal box, Rebrov forced it home. The Gunners claimed offside. The linesman's flag stayed down.

A fortnight later, in Kiev, Arsenal crashed 1–3. Adams was out injured. So was Overmars, who'd torn a hamstring at Coventry the previous Saturday. Anelka was sidelined, after picking up a knock in that game too. Bergkamp's refusal to fly kept him out.

Two minutes before half time, Bould added to Arsenal's woe when he limped off with a hamstring injury. Rebrov struck a 27th-minute penalty – for a foul by Keown. That turned the game. Olexandr Golovko headed a second, then Shevchenko curled a free-kick past Seaman, for Kiev's third. Sub Hughes pulled one back. Wreh had a goal disallowed for offside. Suddenly Arsenal were struggling to qualify.

EUROPEAN EXIT

The last game at Wembley, against Lens, was a disaster. Vieira was injured. So was Bergkamp. Petit was suspended. Adams had to go off at half time. Lens won 1–0 with a late goal by Mickael Debeve and Parlour was sent off for a hack at Cyril Rool. Kiev, meanwhile, beat Panathinaikos.

In the final group games, the Gunners beat Panathinaikos 3–1 in Athens, while Dynamo won at Lens to reach the quarter finals. The Ukraine Champions eventually lost to Bayern in the semi-finals. But Arsenal – however fortuitously – had missed the chance to finish them off at Wembley.

The Gunners had slid out of the Worthington Cup as well. That was the least of Wenger's priorities. More a case of give the reserves a chance and see what happens. In the third round at Derby, Hughes ran the game. Arsenal led through an own goal. Vivas headed a second. 2–1 to Arsenal.

MIXED LEAGUE FORM

Wenger fielded another mainly reserve line-up – strengthened by Bergkamp, returning after a back injury, and Ljungberg – for the fourth round tie at home to Chelsea. The Gunners stayed in the game – though a goal down – until Garde was injured. A penalty, awarded against Gilles Grimandi, gave the Blues a 2–0 lead. 'For me, Grimandi took the ball,' said Wenger. But Chelsea ran out 5–0 winners.

Left: Dennis Bergkamp turns away from Ugo Ehiogu during a 3–2 defeat at Villa Park on 13 December 1998. Aston Villa were the early-season pace setters and by Christmas they were still leading the pack.

In the Premiership, Arsenal stuttered. They thrashed Manchester United again, 3–0 at Highbury, when Bergkamp conjured up his finest form. Adams headed Arsenal in front. Anelka converted Bergkamp's pass for the second. Ljungberg, coming on as a sub, managed to score and collect a yellow card in the space of a few minutes.

Then the Gunners went down at Sheffield Wednesday, who were rapidly becoming a bogey team. Owls striker Paolo Di Canio was sent off, after flooring the referee, Paul Alcock. Keown followed him, though the FA wiped out the defender's ban on appeal.

Kevin Pressman pulled off flying saves from Bergkamp, Anelka and Parlour, before Lee Briscoe's long shot beat Alex Manninger to send the Gunners home 0–1 losers. Said Adams: 'I was disappointed with the result because I felt we should have finished the game long before Briscoe scored. We have to kill off opponents when we're on top. Otherwise we run the risk of what happened at Hillsborough. It's a bit like killing a snake. You can chop off the tail, but unless you cut off the head, it can always bite you.'

Eight days later, Arsenal hammered Newcastle 3–0 at home. Adams was outstanding. Bergkamp netted twice. Anelka hit the other. The happy Gunners fans taunted Geordie Alan Shearer with chants of 'There's only one England captain.'

The Gunners couldn't press home their advantage against Southampton 13 days later. Anelka made it 1–0. Then the Gunners spurned chance after chance – until ex-Spur David Howells grabbed a 67th-minute equaliser.

Petit's deflected free-kick and Anelka's finish earned a 2–1 win at Blackburn, who had Chris Sutton sent off. Overmars' run set up the winner at Coventry. Magnus Hedman palmed out his shot and Anelka tucked away the rebound.

Anelka's goal beat Everton in a game the Gunners could have won by a hatful, rather than 1–0. Enter Tottenham and George Graham. Watching Spurs that derby day was like watching so many of the Gunners' backs-to-the-wall performances under George. It wasn't pretty, but Tottenham departed with a goalless draw. A 0–1 defeat against Wimbledon at Selhurst Park followed. There was, allegedly, a heated debate in the dressing room afterward. Middlesbrough

Below: Left-back Nigel Winterburn secures the ball from Everton striker Ibrahim Bakayoko. A 2–0 win in March was part of a sequence that saw the Gunners record eight wins out of nine and have many fans reminiscing about the 1997–98 charge to the title.

left Highbury with a 1–1 draw. Arsenal, with Garde and Grimandi in midfield because of injuries, then escaped with a goalless draw at Derby.

Bergkamp, injured against Wimbledon, returned at Villa Park the following Sunday – and scored twice. Two up at half time, the Gunners seemed to be coasting to victory against the leaders. But Joachim pulled one back after 61 minutes. Dublin levelled three minutes later, then grabbed Villa's winner seven minutes from time. Villa won 3–2 and marched on, if only for another few weeks. It was the low point of Arsenal's season.

GUNNERS' WINNING STREAK

By now the Gunners were trailing Villa, United and Chelsea. Wenger virtually conceded the title. Who would take it – Chelsea or Manchester United? But 13 December 1997 had been a crucial date. That home defeat by Blackburn was the last Arsenal suffered before they won the 1998 Championship. The date of the defeat at Villa was ... 13 December 1998. As if on cue, the Gunners embarked on another long unbeaten run.

They beat Leeds 3–1, with goals by Bergkamp, Vieira and Petit, then edged Wright, John Hartson and West Ham 1–0 on Boxing Day, thanks to Overmars. The Dutch winger, this time from the penalty spot, scored the only goal at Charlton two days later. Liverpool bucked the trend. Now run by Wenger's old friend Gerard Houillier, they defended in depth and left Highbury with a goalless draw.

In the FA Cup third round, five days earlier, Arsenal found themselves two down at Preston. It was a bruising contest. Boa Morte replied just before half time. Petit scored twice in the second. Overmars, coming back to his best, made it 4–2.

HONOURABLE WENGER REPLAYS TIE

Bergkamp from a deflection, and Overmars, scored to beat Wolves at Molineux – after Havard Flo had equalised Bergkamp's goal. But Petit said too many words to a linesman – and got himself sent off.

The fifth round tie against Sheffield United has passed into history. The score was 1–1. A Blades player had been injured and the visitors kicked the ball into touch so he could receive treatment. By the game's conventions, a Gunner should have returned it to United. Ray Parlour threw the ball to Kanu. Instead of kicking it back to United, Kanu fed Overmars who scored. The Sheffield players were incensed. So was manager Steve Bruce. At one point, he looked like calling his team off the field.

Wenger solved the problem. He was embarassed about the 'winning' goal – and immediately offered Sheffield a replay. The FA agreed. UEFA, at the last minute, tried to block the game. They were worried about future legal arguments. But they bowed to the strength of feeling in England. Overmars and Bergkamp won the tie 2–1 for Arsenal.

As the Highbury fanzines pointed out, would other clubs have been as generous to the Gunners? In 1996, for instance, Tottenham scored an equaliser when they didn't throw the ball back to Arsenal after such a stoppage. The Gunners won that game 3–1. Later in the season though, Arsenal's generosity deprived them of a Champion's League place. Blackburn should have thrown the ball back to Arsenal again. Instead, Chris Sutton went on to net an equaliser that cost the Gunners the runners-up position.

In the quarter final, sub Kanu's late strike saw off Derby's combative resistance. So Arsenal met Manchester United at Villa Park in the semi-final. Petit was suspended, the result of another dismissal, this time against Everton.

CUP EXIT

Vivas took his place. He was sent off for a second yellow card offence, after elbowing Nicky Butt. David Beckham clattered into Nigel Winterburn, who needed treatment for cuts and bruises. Roy Keane had a goal controversially disallowed for offside. Ljungberg and Bergkamp had chances for the ten-man Gunners in extra time. 0–0. On to a replay.

After 17 minutes, Beckham lashed a 20-yarder past Seaman. It took Arsenal 51 minutes to level, with an all-Dutch goal. Bergkamp shot, the ball hit Stam and flew past Schmeichel. The tide was running the Gunners' way. Anelka had a goal disallowed after rounding Schmeichel. Keane was sent off for a second bookable offence, à la Vivas. In stoppage time, Phil Neville tripped Parlour. Penalty. Up stepped Bergkamp. Schmeichel guessed right and saved. Giggs pounced on Vieira's misplaced pass, ran, and on, then lashed a thunderous shot past Seaman. Arsenal were out.

In the Premiership, Arsenal's famous defenders had kept them in the hunt while the forwards weren't scoring. 'The mob at the back,' Leeds manager and ex-Highbury hero David O'Leary called them, with a smile on his face and huge respect. Now they had found their goal touch again.

Keown, who makes a habit of scoring at the City Ground, headed the winner against Forest. Bergkamp struck against Chelsea, and the Gunners stayed rock solid to clinch the points. As Wenger acknowledged, not many teams could have withstood Chelsea's second-half onslaught. That afternoon summed up the calibre of Arsenal's defence. They conceded just 17 goals in 38 league games.

Parlour, Overmars, Bergkamp and Anelka scored in a 4–0 romp at West Ham. Then it was on to Old Trafford. Anelka gave Arsenal the lead, but Gunners couldn't conjure up a second. Cole levelled 20 minutes from the end. That 1–1 scoreline proved crucial for United at the end of the season.

O'LEARY'S LEEDS SCUPPER ARSENAL'S HOPES

Anelka celebrated a hat-trick as the Gunners hammered Leicester 5–0. Eight days later, they needed to win at St

Below: A breath of fresh air. The tall Nigerian Nwankwo Kanu arrived at Highbury in December 1998 for £4 million and breathed new life into Arsenal's title challenge with some crucial goals. His exquisite touches belied his giant frame, and Gunners fans took him to their hearts immediately.

James'. Anelka scored again. But Didi Hamann slipped through four layers of defensive cover to hit Newcastle's equaliser. A brilliant solo goal, but a serious blow to Arsenal's hopes.

Bergkamp inspired a 3–0 win over Sheffield Wednesday and a 2–0 victory at Everton. At Goodison though, Petit was sent off again. Parlour was magnificent – on the right flank, then as a stand-in right-back – as Arsenal beat Coventry 2–0. He scored a vital goal too.

The goalless draw at Southampton was another setback. Arsenal – still without Petit – were lucky to escape with a point. Mark Hughes hit a post, then forced a blinding save from Seaman. At the other end, Francis Benali cleared off the line from Kanu.

Bergkamp again orchestrated victory over Blackburn, whose goalkeeper John Filan pulled off some marvellous saves to stop the Gunners boosting their goal difference.

ALL GUNS BLAZING

Then Arsenal went on the rampage. Parlour, Vieira, Kanu, Bergkamp and an own goal contributed to a 5–1 rout of Wimbledon. At Middlesbrough, Anelka and Kanu struck twice, Overmars and Vieira once each, as the Gunners defended solidly throughout the first half, then broke out to overwhelm Bryan Robson's team.

Anelka struck again, to beat Derby at Highbury. Now Tottenham – and George Graham – beckoned. Arsenal turned on the style. Bergkamp pulled off the Spurs defenders and no-one went with him. His passes set up goals for Petit and Anelka. Darren Anderton pulled one back from a free-kick. But Kanu's magificent lob over Luke Young and deadly shot past Ian Walker killed the contest.

Suddenly Arsenal were in the driving seat. Alex Ferguson, ever the pyschologist, was ready to make the Gunners title favourites. Wenger didn't accept the role. The title turned on two midweek results.

Arsenal faced a tough trip to Leeds, while United travelled to relegation-haunted Blackburn, who were managed by ex-United star Brian Kidd.

Leeds fans wanted anyone but United to win the title. Leeds manager O'Leary was a Highbury playing legend. But dedicated as ever, he did the Gunners no favours: 'It's a big game for us. We're not going to dream about our summer holidays already. I'd never let the players think that way,' said O'Leary.

Leeds piled into Arsenal from the start. Seaman saved a penalty from Jimmy Floyd Hasselbaink. Leeds' leading scorer admitted: 'When Seaman saved the spot-kick, I thought they were going to win.' Seaman was at his best. So was Nigel Martyn – three times thwarting sub Diawara.

Vivas replaced the injured Winterburn at left-back. While the Gunners regrouped, Hasselbaink bundled in Leeds' late winner. Arsenal's season was on the brink.

On that final Premiership Sunday, Arsenal duly beat Aston Villa 1–0, thanks to Kanu. But United beat Spurs and chants of 'Champions' rang round Old Trafford. At Wembley six days later, United defeated Newcastle 2–0 to win the FA Cup. In Barcelona, they pulled out an astonishing comeback to pip Bayern 2–1 and bring home the European Cup. The first English club to do the 'treble', they had ensured their place in history. The Gunners had been shaded by remarkable opponents. Yet Highbury fans could still wonder: 'What might have been?'

ANELKA TO GO

After an exhausting 53-match season, Arsenal's players looked forward to a relaxing break, free from the interruption of major tournament football, during the summer of 1999. However, for Arsène Wenger, like all Premiership managers, the close season meant transfer dealings, and in the Frenchman's case one transfer deal in particular. Throughout the summer, Wenger would have to contend with intense media speculation over the future of star striker Nicolas Anelka, a player who had frequently made plain his discontent with life and football in England. Anelka's summer, it seemed, would not be spent on a beach but in residency on the back pages of Britain's tabloid newspapers.

Wenger was fully aware of Anelka's 'situation' by the end of the 1998-99 season, but, publicly at least, the manager remained optimistic that his goalscoring prodigy would remain at the club. 'Something crazy can always happen, but I'm 95 per cent certain that he will be at Arsenal next season,' proclaimed Wenger in May 1999. Alas, the craziness soon began, with Anelka linked first with Real Madrid, then Lazio, then Juventus and, most bizarrely, with a joint deal

Above: Bergkamp's penalty is saved by Peter Schmeichel during the FA Cup semi-final. Despite the numerical disadvantage of having Roy Keane sent off, the penalty miss seemed to give United impetus and a Ryan Giggs wonder-goal meant the Gunners ended the season trophyless.

Above: Marc Overmars celebrates scoring Arsenal's first goal in the 1998 FA Cup Final against Newcastle United.

Above: Arsenal's commitment to buying the best was underlined with the £11-million signing of Thierry Henry from Juventus in August 1999. Henry had been part of the French World Cup-winning squad and proved a revelation in his first season with the Gunners, scoring 17 League goals.

Above: Davor Suker arrived at Arsenal with an impressive pedigree. The left-footed Croatian striker, who was signed from Real Madrid in August 1999, had scored 41 goals in 49 internationals and was the Golden boot winner at France 98. However, Suker would struggle to establish himself in Wenger's line up and after eight goals and 22 appearances in the league his one-year contract was not renewed.

to both Lazio and Juventus. Endless stories emerged about Anelka's suffering, about purported wages and transfer fees, about illegal approaches and about the player's brothers-cum-agents. By July, the situation seemed to have reached an impasse, although, in truth, many supporters had grown so tired of the rumours that they wanted the situation resolved one way or another.

The Anelka case would rumble throughout Arsenal's pre-season's preparations but did not prevent Arsène Wenger from making several constructive moves in the transfer market. Predictably, the Gunners' aged-defence was again targeted as an area in need of new blood. To this end, Wenger recruited the Ukraine captain and right-back, Oleg Luzhny, from Dynamo Kiev for a fee of £1.8m, and Corinthians' Brazil international left-back, Silvinho (full name Sylvio Mendes Campos Junior), for £4m. Luzhny, a versatile performer who can play at either full-back or central defence, was well known to Arsenal fans, having played against the Gunners in their Champions League encounters with Dynamo in 1998. Silvinho, however, was something of an unknown, and Wenger informed the media that his new Brazilian was: 'quick, strong, versatile and can also play in midfield'.

Silvinho's ability to play on the left of midfield was particularly significant, given the departure of Stephen Hughes to Fulham on a three-month loan deal. Another of Arsenal's home-grown players would also leave the club during the close season, Jason Crowe joining First Division Portsmouth for around £600,000. Highbury's most expensive summer departee was Kaba Diawara, whose short stay in London N5 was brought to a close with a £2.5m move to Marseille. However, the most significant exit was that of Steve Bould, the veteran defender ending an 11-year association with Arsenal by moving to newly promoted Sunderland for £500,000.

PRE-SEASON INJURY PROBLEMS

With the European Championships looming at season's end, the 1999–2000 Premiership campaign was scheduled for an early start. Arsenal's first fixture was at home to Leicester City on 7 August, but before the Gunners could focus upon this match, there was the small matter of a Charity Shield meeting with Manchester United at Wembley. A game against Monaco on 26 July would be Arsène Wenger's final opportunity to assess his key players in a pre-season fixture. The match ended in a 1–1 draw but proved something of a disaster for goalkeeper David Seaman, who injured a calf when attempting a clearance in the final minute. Seaman joined a worrying injury list that already included the names of captain Tony Adams, and Dutch forwards Dennis Bergkamp and Marc Overmars. Wenger was also still wrestling to resolve the Nicolas Anelka affair in time to sign a replacement ahead of UEFA's Champions League deadline.

Neither Arsenal's injury crisis nor Anelka's transfer had

been resolved by 1 August, the day of the Charity Shield, so it was a somewhat makeshift Gunners line-up that took the field at Wembley against champions Manchester United. Freddie Ljungberg and Nwankwo Kanu led the Arsenal attack, with Silvinho, Gilles Grimandi and Alex Manninger, deputising for, respectively, Overmars, Adams and Seaman. It was nothing like the team that Arsène Wenger had envisaged would start the campaign, but it was a side that produced a committed and skilful performance and, on a humid day, deservedly ran out 2-1 victors. A Kanu penalty had cancelled out David Beckham's opener, and a goal from Ray Parlour 13 minutes from time proved decisive, but nobody was reading too much into the result. After all, the Gunners had also won the previous season's Charity Shield against the same opponents, and had then watched as their rivals collected the 'treble'.

A NEW STRIKE FORCE

Arsène Wenger may not have allowed himself any great celebration after Arsenal's Wembley victory over Manchester United, but he undoubtedly enjoyed a well-earned sigh of relief when, the following day, Nicolas Anelka completed a £23m move to Real Madrid. There was no doubting that Highbury had lost a player of immense potential, but the size of the transfer fee, which represented a £22.5m profit on a player signed in 1997, gave Wenger every chance of finding an adequate replacement. The Arsenal manager opted to spread his risk by signing two players, both of whom had starred at the 1998 World Cup finals. First to sign was Real Madrid's Croatian international striker Davor Suker, winner of the Golden Boot at France 98 and a player of proven pedigree. Suker, whose international record read, 'played 43, scored 40', arrived for a fee of around £3m. Wenger said: 'I am delighted to get Suker, he is an Ian Wright-type of player,' but when asked whether the Croatian would be an automatic selection for his team, the manager replied: 'Nobody has that guarantee'.

Twenty-four hours after the signing of Suker, a second new striker arrived. Frenchman Thierry Henry had begun his career under Arsène Wenger at Monaco and, still only 21 years old, joined Arsenal from Juventus for a club-record fee of £11m. Henry had played mainly as a winger for Juve, but Wenger had a more central role in mind for the member of the French World Cup-winning squad and told the press: 'Thierry has the ability to do as well as Nicolas... he has all the qualities, best of all is his pace and power dribbling.' The Arsenal manager added, 'We have given ourselves the experience of a player like Suker and the promise of a young man like Henry... our ambition is there for everyone to see.'

Wenger's immediate 'ambition' was to ensure that his team got off to a better start than that of the previous season, when four draws in the first five games had proved costly in the title race. The opening day clash with Leicester City, a team who had been beaten 5-0 on their last visit to Highbury,

provided the perfect opportunity for the Gunners to kick off the campaign with a win. However, the game arrived too early for the rehabilitating duo of David Seaman and Tony Adams, while Marc Overmars was considered only fit enough to merit a place on the bench. The good news was that Dennis Bergkamp, who had not managed to play 90 minutes during pre-season, was included in the starting line-up. For Arsenal supporters, however, there was the disappointing news that only two of Wenger's latest signings, Silvinho and Henry, had made the bench, while none of the newcomers were included in the starting 11.

OG SECURES WINNING START

The match against Leicester proved more difficult than many had anticipated and, with the score at 0–0, Thierry Henry was introduced for the second half. The debutant made an impressive start, getting in behind the Leicester defence on several occasions, but each time his finishing proved wayward. Then, after 57 minutes, former West Ham striker Tony Cottee opened the scoring for the visitors. The game briefly opened up, and seven minutes later Bergkamp struck an equaliser to lift the Highbury crowd. The game returned to a more frustrating pattern for the closing stages, but in the final minute Arsenal won a corner. Emmanuel Petit swung the ball over, Henry glanced it goalwards and Foxes defender Frank Sinclair did the rest, putting the ball into his own net and giving Arsenal an opening day victory. Wenger was relieved: 'It would have been a nightmare to lose at home on the opening day. The psychological effect would have been terrible.'

A second Premiership victory followed three days later, Arsenal defeating Jim Smith's Derby County 2–1 at Pride Park with a performance that Wenger described as 'more resilient than brilliant'. Petit and Bergkamp were the Gunners scorers, and the Dutchman had looked particularly sharp. At the start of the previous season, Bergkamp had returned still exhausted from the World Cup in France, and throughout the campaign he had struggled to contend with a series of niggling injuries and a growing sense of fatigue. This time, however, Bergkamp, appeared well-rested and focused. Alongside Bergkamp in the Gunners forward line, Thierry Henry, who began the season playing on the wing, was also showing glimpses of the form that had seen Arsenal and Juventus pay combined fees of £19m for the young Frenchman. Henry's finishing remained somewhat erratic, but the player, at least, was not unduly worried: 'I have to get fitter and find my best form. I still haven't adjusted to the Premiership and a different style of football, it takes time.'

A 0–0 draw against Sunderland at the Stadium of Light meant that Arsenal, with seven points from their first three games, had achieved the good start that Wenger had called for, and, with Adams, Overmars, Seaman and Suker recovering from injuries, the signs were that things could

only get better. Unfortunately, Petit had injured his knee ligaments in the Sunderland match and would be out for more than two months. More bad news lay in the fact that Manchester United had made an equally impressive start, and it was the champions who were next on the Gunners' Premiership agenda for a Sunday meeting at Highbury. The match was to be the first screened on Sky TV's new interactive channel, which gave viewers the chance to watch the game from their chosen camera angle. Arsenal fans would, no doubt, have enjoyed Sky's new service for most of the first hour, during which the Gunners were the game's dominant force. The home team's superiority was eventually rewarded when, three minutes before the interval, Freddie Ljungberg galloped onto Bergkamp's through ball to beat United keeper Raimond Van Der Gouw. A 1–0 lead, however, proved too fragile, and when Roy Keane struck twice for the visitors in the last 30 minutes, Arsenal's 20-month League unbeaten home record reached an end.

LOOKING FOR A WINNING FORMULA

Arsenal's gloom at the defeat against Manchester United was lifted, three days later, by the tonic supplied by a 2–0 home win against newly-promoted Bradford City. A sterner test, however, came in the shape of a trip to Liverpool the following weekend. It was Arsenal's third game in seven days, a fact that did not impress Arsène Wenger, and the Gunners, though buoyed by the returning Tony Adams and Marc Overmars, produced a leg-weary display to lose 2–0. The season was just three weeks old, but already Arsenal had played six Premiership matches. A tally of ten points from the season's opening exchanges was a respectable haul, but it left the Gunners six points adrift of Manchester United. Arsenal

Below: Thierry Henry scores Arsenal's second goal in a 3–1 Champions League victory against Swedish side AIK Solna. Henry's goal came in injury time, but there was still time for Suker to add a third in a rare Wembley victory for Arsenal.

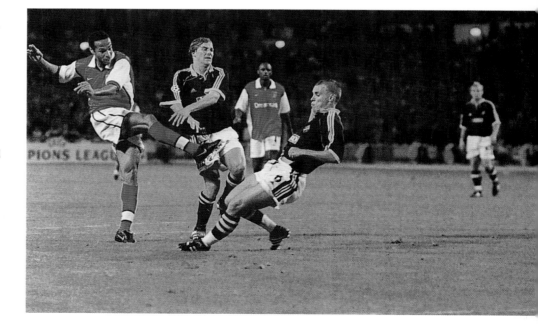

Above: Gabriele Batistuta celebrates the goal that ended the Gunners chances of progressing to the second phase of the Champions League. Fiorentina won 1–0 at Wembley.

Above: Kanu slams home his and Arsenal's second goal in a thrilling victory against Gianluca Vialli's Chelsea at Stamford Bridge in October 1999. The Nigerian's hat-trick was rounded off in style with a goal from an improbable angle that left two World Cup winning defenders baffled.

Right: In a home game against Leeds United in December 1999, Thierry Henry shrugs off a tackle from Lucas Radebe to score the second Arsenal goal, securing a 2–0 win.

had also lost two matches, a worrying statistic given Wenger's assertion that it was unlikely that a team could lose more than four games and still win the Premiership. There was, however, clearly much more to come from Arsenal. Wenger's selections remained affected by injuries to key players, and the manager was still tinkering with his forward line to find the right blend of pace and invention. Wenger was clearly keen to combine the high velocity of Henry with the transcendental skill of Bergkamp, but the young Frenchman was still without a goal.

September began with a break from domestic football, the international game taking centre stage for a round of Euro 2000 qualifiers, but Arsenal's gruelling schedule soon resumed. This time the Gunners faced three Premiership fixtures and three Champions League matches in the space of just 18 days, and this time they coped with the workload in impressive style. In the Premiership, Wenger's team recorded three straight victories; the most memorable of which was a 3–1 home success against Aston Villa. Davor Suker, making his first appearance in the starting line-up, scored twice against Villa, while Thierry Henry at last opened his account with the only goal against Southampton at The Dell. By the end of September the Gunners were just three points behind United in the Premiership table.

CHAMPIONS LEAGUE KICK-OFF

In the Champions League, Arsenal would again play their home matches at Wembley, but it was in Florence that Wenger's team began its European campaign with a 0–0 draw against Fiorentina. It could have been even better had Francesco Toldo not saved an 80th minute Kanu penalty. This was followed by a dramatic victory against Swedish champions AIK Solna, who were beaten by a late Gunners rally at Wembley. The match against AIK had looked to be heading for a 1–1 draw after Krister Nordin had cancelled out Freddie Ljungberg's opener, but as the game entered injury time Arsenal struck twice through Henry and Suker to earn the three points that took them into second place in Group B. Spanish champions Barcelona topped the group, and a trip to the Nou Camp beckoned next for the Gunners.

Arsène Wenger, still without the injured David Seaman as well as influential midfielder Emmanuel Petit, operated a rotation policy with his strikers throughout the Champions League campaign, and for the match at the Nou Camp the chosen men were Kanu and Bergkamp. Both strikers, however, saw little of the ball in the first 45 minutes. Barça, urged on by the majority of the 98,000 crowd, produced a first-half display that Wenger described as 'technically perfect', although it took a mistake from Patrick Vieira to gift the Catalans the goal their football merited.

The half-time break gave Arsenal the opportunity to regroup and, spurred on by some well chosen words from their manager and captain, the Gunners produced a much

improved display in the second half. On 73 minutes Wenger, with his team now enjoying an improved share of possession, played his trump card, bringing on Henry and Suker for Parlour and Bergkamp. The introduction of Suker, a former Real Madrid player, was greeted with boos from the Barça fans, but the Croat would soon silence the home supporters. It seemed Barcelona had done enough to earn victory, particularly when Gilles Grimandi was sent off for violent conduct after 80 minutes, but within seconds Arsenal had struck an equaliser. To the annoyance of the Barça supporters Suker was the architect of the Gunners' goal, hitting a shot that Ruud Hesp could only parry into the path of Kanu. The Nigerian made no mistake and the game ended 1–1. Arsenal now had five points from their opening three Champions League matches. 'The two most difficult away matches are out of the way,' said Wenger. 'Fate is in our hands. It's at Wembley that we have to perform now.'

Alas for the second year in succession it was at Wembley that Arsenal's Champions League dreams evaporated. First came a disappointing 4–2 reverse against Barça, then a 1–0 defeat at the hands of Fiorentina. Qualification for the competition's second phase was now out of reach. 'We'll never feel at home at Wembley as we do at Highbury,' said Wenger. 'It's a psychological thing.' The only consolation for Arsenal was that, because of UEFA's radical restructuring of its two club competitions, the Gunners were now handed a place in the UEFA Cup. Home matches in Europe for the remainder of the season would, thankfully, be played in the more intimidating atmosphere of Highbury.

VIEIRA HAMMERED BY FA

The decline of Arsenal's Champions League campaign was accompanied by an equally dramatic series of games in the Premiership during October. The month began with

the Gunners making the trip to Upton Park for the latest instalment of a London derby that had been a reliable source of high jinks over the past few seasons. The match itself ended 2–1 to West Ham, but will be remembered most for the sending-off of Patrick Vieira and the midfielder's subsequent confrontation with West Ham's Neil Ruddock. Vieira, who was dismissed after collecting a second yellow card for a foul on Paolo Di Canio, reacted angrily after a verbal exchange with Ruddock and, as he was departing the pitch, the Frenchman spat at his adversary. Vieira was quick to apologise for his moment of madness, which seemed wholly out of character, but the FA found no significant mitigation in either his apology or the provocation he had been exposed to. Three weeks later Vieira was fined £45,000 and banned for six games. Wenger was understandably disappointed and defended his player: 'I think the punishment is very severe... Patrick is not a dirty player. His attitude is right and I don't think this will affect his aggression on the field.'

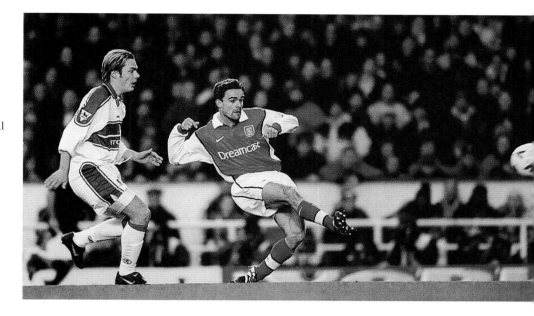

CHEERS AT CHELSEA

The Vieira incident aside, October was also notable for two of Arsenal's best performances of the season. First came a 4–1 home victory over Everton, Davor Suker scoring twice and Lee Dixon and Kanu grabbing the other goals in a game that saw Arsenal hit 28 shots to Everton's seven. A week later, Arsenal were at Stamford Bridge to take on Gianluca Vialli's highly fancied Chelsea in, what would prove to be, a match of rare excitement. Despite the disappointment of the Barcelona defeat just four days earlier, the Gunners started the game in positive mood, but after 52 minutes found themselves two goals down. Chelsea had not conceded a goal at home all season and, even when Kanu scored after 74 minutes, there seemed little prospect of Arsenal getting a result. The Nigerian striker, however, had failed to read the script and after 83 minutes struck an equaliser. Then, in injury time, the game took its final twist. Kanu pounced on a mistake by Albert Ferrer and took possession on the left wing, side-stepped the on-rushing Chelsea goalkeeper Ed de Goey, and with Frank Leboeuf and Marcel Desailly guarding the goal, chipped the ball into the net from the most acute angle. It was Kanu at his extravagant best. When asked whether he thought he should have crossed the ball, he replied: 'I was never going to cross. Immediately I beat the keeper my mind was on how to score. At 2–2 there was nothing else for it.'

Victory against Chelsea pushed Arsenal into second place, just a point behind David O'Leary's Leeds at the end of October. However, during the next two months the Gunners' League form became inconsistent. The season's first North London derby provided an undoubted low point; Arsenal losing 2–1 at White Hart Lane and having both Ljungberg and Keown sent off in a bad tempered match. A better result came, two weeks later, with a 5–1 victory over Middlesbrough at Highbury. Dennis Bergkamp (2) and Marc Overmars (3)

were the Gunners' goalscorers against Boro, and the same players were joined on the scoresheet by Nigel Winterburn five days later when Arsenal opened their UEFA Cup campaign with a 3–0 victory over FC Nantes. Two weeks later the Gunners drew 3–3 with the French team to book their passage into the last 16 of the competition.

In the Worthington Cup Arsenal defeated Preston 2–1 en route to a tie against Middlesbrough at the Riverside. However, the competition was low on Arsène Wenger's list of priorities, and his team for the match against Boro comprised a handful of first-teamers and a mixture of squad players and youngsters. The most notable of Arsenal's fledglings was

Above: Marc Overmars slots home the first of this three goals against Middlesbrough in Arsenal's biggest league win of the season. The Gunners won the match 5–1, with Overmars' compatriot Dennis Bergkamp also scoring twice.

Left: Freddie Ljungberg nips in to profit from Jaap Stam's hesitation in the game at Old Trafford in January 2000. Ljungberg, playing as a makeshift striker, went on to score and put Arsenal 1–0 up, however, a Teddy Sheringham goal gave the champions a share of the points.

Above: Gilles Grimandi holds his head in his hands after missing the vital penalty in the shoot-out against Leicester City in the fourth round of the FA Cup at Filbert Street.

substitute Jermaine Pennant who, at 16 years and 319 days, became the youngest first team player in the club's history. The game was eventually decided on penalties, Arsenal losing 3–1.

FESTIVE FUN FOR THE GUNNERS

Arsenal were unbeaten during December 1999, claiming ten Premiership points from a possible 12 and progressing to the fourth round of the FA Cup with a 3–1 victory over Second Division Blackpool. The most impressive feature of this run of good form, which included a 2–0 home victory over top-of-the-table Leeds at Highbury, was that it was achieved despite the unavailability of several key players. Most notable among December's absentees were Seaman, Adams, Bergkamp, Parlour and, of course, Patrick Vieira, who was left inactive courtesy of his six-match ban. Arsène Wenger's squad was stretched to the limit, but in Gilles Grimandi, Freddie Ljungberg and Oleg Luzhny the manager found able deputies for his more established stars. Grimandi, a player who had suffered his share of brickbats from supporters and critics since arriving from Monaco in 1997, proved himself a particularly versatile performer, filling in for Vieira in midfield and producing a series of accomplished displays.

One fringe player, however, who was unable to benefit from the seasonal vacancies in Arsène Wenger's line-up was Matthew Upson. The 20-year-old central defender had spent more than a year waiting for an extended run in the first team, but, just as it seemed his chance had come, he suffered a cruciate ligament injury to his left knee in the 3–0 victory over Leicester at Filbert Street. Upson's season was over, and Wenger was left with just three first-team centre-backs.

RIVALS HEAD FOR BRAZIL

Assistant manager Pat Rice bemoaned his club's poor luck with injuries: 'From the start of the season, I wouldn't think we've put out what people consider to be our best 11.' Nevertheless, at the turn of the year, Arsenal were well placed in third position in the Premiership. The Gunners were five points behind top club Leeds, and four points behind Manchester United, who had a game in hand. United, however, would kick off the new year in Brazil, playing in the Club World Championships. The pundits said that Arsenal and Leeds now had the opportunity to open up a lead at the top of the table; a lead which the champions, who would apparently return leg weary from their exertions in South America, would be unable to make up. Arsène Wenger, however, would pay little attention to such suggestions and instead focused on his own team's problems. 'We have 39 points from 20 games which is not too bad, but compared to previous seasons, we have conceded more goals [20] than before' said Wenger. 'We now have to prove to be more consistent and have to work on being much stronger defensively.'

Alas, consistency was one quality Arsenal would would find elusive during the first two months of 2000. The year began with a draw at Sheffield Wednesday but, despite a 4–1 victory over Sunderland, the Gunners remained in third place when they travelled to Old Trafford to play Manchester United on 24 January. Alex Ferguson's team had returned from Brazil level on points with Arsenal, still just a point behind Leeds and with games in hand on both. Arsenal could not afford to lose to the champions, but with Adams, Bergkamp, Kanu, Suker and Overmars all absent, avoiding defeat seemed a tall order. Wenger's chosen 11 rose to the challenge and United struggled to contend with the makeshift strike-partnership of Ljungberg and Henry. After 11 minutes Arsenal took the lead, Ljungberg scoring against the champions for the second time in one season. It was a lead that Arsenal should have added to, with good chances coming to Henry either side of the break, but the second goal did not arrive and with 17 minutes to go, Teddy Sheringham struck an equaliser. The match ended 1–1, but Wenger felt it was a point gained rather than two dropped: 'I have to give credit to the team. They showed outstanding character. Our target was to show how strong our spirit is,' said Wenger. 'One-one is a fair result.'

The draw with Manchester United was followed by a weekend of inactivity for Arsenal, who were left with no game due to their fourth round exit from the FA Cup. The Gunners had lost out 6–5 to Leicester City on penalties after a somewhat dire contest had ended goalless after 210 minutes of football. Wenger was disappointed by Leicester's defensive approach and said: 'They tried to play for a draw and in the end we were punished because we did not score a goal... It wasn't like a cup tie atmosphere. It lacked passion mainly because Leicester did not come out. They decided to defend and, to be fair, they did that well.'

TITLE HOPES RECEDE

Arsenal's injury list had eased little by the time the Gunners made the trip to Bradford on 5 February, but Wenger remained sanguine: 'We have shown that, even with lots of players out, we are still a good team. The problem is more of belief than in our physical abilities.' All optimism, however, would ebb away from Arsenal's Championship challenge when Dean Saunders struck the winning goal for Bradford after 57 minutes. Manchester United now had a nine-point lead at the top of the table, together with their seemingly omnipresent game in hand. Barring the most spectacular series of results, the Premiership was now out of the Gunners' reach. A top-three finish and, thereby, a Champions League place now became the priority.

Liverpool, who like Arsenal had 44 points from 24 games, appeared to be the Gunners' most likely rivals for a Champions League place, and it was the Merseysiders who were next on the Highbury guest list. Arsenal had not beaten Liverpool since August 1994 and, despite the return to the

first-team line up of Dennis Bergkamp, the Gunners could not break the sequence and lost 1-0. Wenger was rightly concerned by his team's falling League position, and the manager was no less worried by the ascendancy of Liverpool, who had climbed from 12th to third in just 14 games. Patrick Vieira put it succinctly: 'We have to improve or we could end up with nothing.'

Vieira's words were heeded, and during March Arsenal produced the improved run required to maintain their position in the hunt for Champions League places. Consecutive victories against Middlesbrough, Spurs and Coventry were at the core of this good run, and it was, of course, the win against George Graham's Spurs that was most celebrated. March had also seen Arsenal return to UEFA Cup action with a tie against Spain's champions-elect, Deportivo La Coruña. The tie against Deportivo provided a keen test of Arsenal's quality, and Wenger's team passed with flying colours. The first leg was played at Highbury, and a far-post header from Lee Dixon after five minutes settled the nerves before Thierry Henry added a second on the half-hour mark. After the interval Deportivo enjoyed their best period of the game, scoring a penalty through Brazilian midfielder Djalminha, but the same player would immediately undo his good work by getting himself sent off for a clash with Grimandi. Arsenal seized the moment and added three goals before the end of the game to give themselves an insurmountable 5–1 lead for the second leg. Henry scored twice and was named man of the match, but the pick of Arsenal's goals came from Kanu, who produced a sublime dummy to perplex the Deportivo keeper before slotting the ball home.

The second leg against Deportivo proved an intriguing affair, with Arsenal travelling to the Riazor Stadium without a recognised centre-back among their squad. Emmanuel Petit and Oleg Luzhny were deployed at the heart of the Gunners defence and performed with great composure against one of Spain's most attacking teams. It was not until the 69th

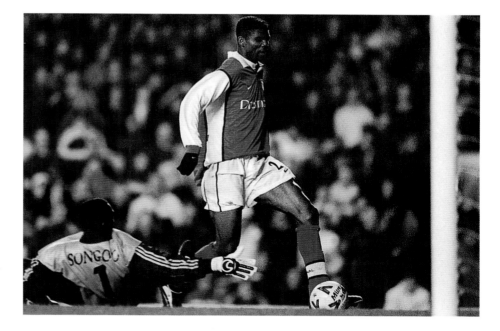

minute that Arsenal's goal was breached, but by then the Gunners had already taken the lead through Henry. The match finished in a 2–1 victory for Deportivo, but it was Arsenal – 6–3 aggregate victors – who celebrated progress to a quarter-final meeting with Werder Bremen.

After the high jinks of the Deportivo match at Highbury, Arsenal's fans were treated to rather different fare against Werder Bremen. The Germans arrived at Highbury with no intention of attacking, and seemed content when they departed London N5 with a two goal deficit after conceding goals from Henry and Ljungberg. The second leg, however, proved as controversial as the first leg was frustrating. After 25 minutes, Arsenal found themselves two goals in front and, with a 4-0 aggregate lead, the tie seemed all but over. Both Gunners goals had been scored by Ray Parlour and the midfielder would complete a deserved hat-trick in the second half, however, by then his contribution had been overshadowed by the dismissal of Thierry Henry for a trip on Mike Barten. Henry's challenge was neither dangerous nor cynical and hardly seemed to warrant a yellow card, much less a red one. Wenger's disappointment at referee Kim Nielsen's decision was compounded by the fact that the manager had been attempting to substitute Henry, but had been refused permission to make two changes simultaneously. Henry, who had scored the third goal in Arsenal's 4–2 victory over Bremen, would now miss the first leg of a semi-final against Lens.

HENRY THE HERO

Thierry Henry's suspension was a huge blow to Arsenal's plans. The young striker had enjoyed a run of breathtaking form during March, scoring seven goals and earning a recall

Above: Nwankwo Kanu sends Deportivo's Cameroon international goalkeeper, Jacques Songo'o, to ground with a sublime dummy before scoring in the 5-1 UEFA Cup victory over the Spaniards at Highbury.

Left: Kanu scores his third European goal of the season to help Arsenal beat Lens in the quarter final of the UEFA Cup.

Above: Martin Keown celebrates scoring the second goal in Arsenal's 4–0 away win against David O'Leary's young Leeds United team at Elland Road in April 2000. Victory against Leeds put the the Gunners back in contention for a Champions League place.

Above: Galatasaray's veteran forward Gheorghe Hagi clashes with Tony Adams during the UEFA Cup final. The Romanian was shown the red card for his indiscretion, however, his dismissal had little effect upon the result of a match that was decided by a penalty shoot-out.

to the blue shirt of France. Henry, who was rewarded with the *Evening Standard* Footballer of the Month award, said: 'I am feeling more confident in myself, in my play and I am developing a good understanding with the players around me.' It was a view shared by Arsène Wenger, who also believed that, good as Henry's form had been, there was still more to come from the young striker.

Arsenal's number 14 did not disappoint and duly delivered his 20th goal of the season after coming on as a substitute in the 3–1 win against Wimbledon at Selhurst Park on 2 April. Victory against the Dons had been secured despite the sending off of Oleg Luzhny, and kept Arsenal in fourth place. The Gunners were now two points behind Liverpool and three behind second placed Leeds. The chase for a Champions League place was undoubtedly Arsenal's main aim, but their only chance of silverware remained the UEFA Cup. However, to reach the final, the Gunners would have to overcome Racing Club de Lens, a team that had defeated them in the previous season's Champions League and that had already knocked out Kaiserslautern, Celta Vigo and Atletico Madrid in the UEFA Cup. The first leg of the semi-final was played at Highbury and, although Dennis Bergkamp's second-minute goal earned Arsenal a 1–0 victory, the match was overshadowed by the deaths of two Leeds United fans in Istanbul ahead of the other semi-final between Leeds and Galatasaray.

Between the two legs of the UEFA Cup semi-final, Arsenal returned to their Champions League chase with a match against Leeds United at Elland Road. The Yorkshire side were still three points ahead of Arsenal, but were in the midst of a disastrous run that had seen them lose five games in succession. The match against Leeds was preceded by a moving tribute to the supporters who had died in Istanbul, with the Arsenal players each handing a bouquet of flowers to a member of the opposition. However, Arsenal's compassion ceased once referee Steve Dunn had blown his whistle to start the game, and after 21 minutes Arsenal took the lead when Henry prodded home from Parlour's cross. The Gunners squandered a string of good chances during the remainder of the first half, but two minutes before the break their cause was aided by the dismissal of Ian Harte for an off-the-ball kick on Dennis Bergkamp. The second half saw Arsenal dominate the game, and three goals in the final 20 minutes secured a victory that took the Gunners back into the top three. Arsenal were now five points behind second-placed Liverpool but had a game in hand over the Merseysiders.

INJURY PROBLEMS RELENT

For the remainder of the season, injuries ceased to be the determining factor in Arsène Wenger's team selections, and at last the Gunners began to reveal their true calibre. For the second leg of the UEFA Cup semi-final against Lens, the manager even enjoyed the luxury of naming a line-up

unchanged from that which had taken the field against Leeds. However, eight of Wenger's players were just one booking away from a UEFA suspension that would rule them out of the final, so a degree of caution would need to be employed along with the usual Arsenal competitive spirit. The red-shirted Gunners heeded their manager's instructions and produced a disciplined performance that saw them keep the game scoreless for the first 43 minutes. When the breakthrough did eventually arrive, it was via the right boot of Thierry Henry. Lens did equalise midway through the second half, but it proved no more than a consolation, with Kanu scoring a second for the Londoners to ensure a 3-1 aggregate victory.

A PLACE IN EUROPE

Arsenal had booked a place at their third European final in six years and would travel to Copenhagen, venue of their victory against Parma in the 1994 Cup Winners Cup, as favourites for a match against Galatasaray. However, before focusing upon the UEFA Cup final, Arsène Wenger and his team still had the small matter of Champions League qualification with which to concern themselves. According to the pundits, Arsenal's run-in was more difficult than that of their chief rivals, Liverpool and Leeds, but the experts had failed to appreciate that the Gunners had found form at the perfect time. In their final 11 matches, Arsenal dropped just five points and won nine consecutive matches. Liverpool, meanwhile, took just two points from their final five fixtures and, with a 3–3 draw in their penultimate fixture at home to Sheffield Wednesday, Arsenal clinched runners-up spot and a valuable place in the 2000–2001 Champions League.

Arsenal's final League fixture of 1999–2000 came against Newcastle United at St James' Park and was to be played just three days before the UEFA Cup final. Arsène Wenger, who had appealed unsuccessfully to have the game moved forward by 24 hours, fielded a weakened line-up for the clash with Newcastle and was unconcerned by his team's 4–2 defeat. One result that Wenger would have paid more attention to, however, came in the FA Youth Cup, where Don Howe's side claimed an impressive 5–1 aggregate victory over Coventry City. Arsenal would establish themselves as the pre-eminent youth team in England during 1999–2000, progressing to the finals of both the Under-17 and Under-19 Premier Youth Leagues. This unprecedented record of junior success represented a huge achievement for Liam Brady (head of the Gunners' youth section) and his coaching staff.

A DARK DAY IN THE 'WONDERFUL' CITY

All that was left now was for Arsenal to claim the UEFA Cup and provide their supporters with the silverware that they craved. It mattered little to either players or fans that the Gunners' only chance of a trophy now rested with a competition that neither they, nor their opponents, had

Left: Theirry Henry chips the ball over a prostrate Chelsea defence to score his sixth goal in seven games. The match, played in May 2000, ended in a 2–1 victory for Arsenal and secured the club's passage into the Champions League.

entered at the start of the season. 'We want to win and it's essential that the players are focused on the game and nothing else', said Wenger.

Fighting between Arsenal and Galatasaray supporters in Copenhagen's City Hall Square, however, would overshadow the build up to the UEFA Cup final. Five supporters were injured and more than 20 arrests were made. Politicians and journalists immediately began an inquest into how such trouble had been allowed to flare. Arsenal quickly condemned the hooligans and pledged to ban them from Highbury.

The Gunners, who were 10/11 favourites to lift the Cup, had no significant injury problems, and a full strength line-up took the field in Copenhagen. Arsenal, however, struggled to live up to their star billing and, in a cagey first half that brought few clear cut chances, were well below their best. The game opened up a little after the interval, but Galatasaray remained slightly in the ascendant, although the best chance of the match fell to a Gunner.

Alas, Martin Keown, who popped up in an unfamiliar position inside the opposition penalty area, crashed his close range shot over the bar. For the remainder of the second half, the better of the chances fell to the Turks, but neither side could break the deadlock and, with a certain inevitability, the game entered extra time. A goal would now be enough to win the Cup for either team and, when Galatasaray's inspirational Romanian Gheorghe Hagi was sent off four minutes into extra time, the most likely winners appeared to be Arsenal.

Once down to ten men, Galatasaray's ambition diminished. Fatih Terim's team now set their sights on a penalty shoot-out and, after 30 minutes of extra time, the Turks got their wish. For Arsenal fans, however, thoughts immediately returned to the shoot-out defeats against Middlesbrough and Leicester earlier on in the season and to the Cup Winners Cup defeat against Valencia in 1980.

PENALTY JINX RETURNS

Arsenal's concerns, unlike their penalties, were well-placed. First Suker and then Vieira struck their shots against the frame of the goal and, although Parlour's effort found the net, it proved not to be enough. Former Spurs player Gheorghe Popescu was left to take the decisive spot-kick, and made no mistake. It was a bitter pill for Arsenal supporters to swallow, and Wenger was equally despondent about his team's performance: 'We did not play well in the first half, but we were much better afterwards. It is very disappointing... if we had won the shoot-out it would not have made any difference to the quality of our game and so of course I want to strengthen for next season.'

It had been a season of great drama for Arsenal. From the Anelka saga in pre-season to the defeat in Copenhagen, the Gunners had never been far from the headlines. The season's undoubted highlights had been the form of Thierry Henry and the nine-game winning sequence that had taken the club into runners-up position in the final Premiership table. In contrast, Arsenal's away form had been disappointing, and had prevented a sustained title challenge. The summer of 2000 would, no doubt, see Wenger busy himself in the transfer market once more, and, with the most accomplished youth team in England to provide further reinforcement, the disappointment of Copenhagen will soon recede to allow thoughts to drift to happier times.

CHAPTER 10

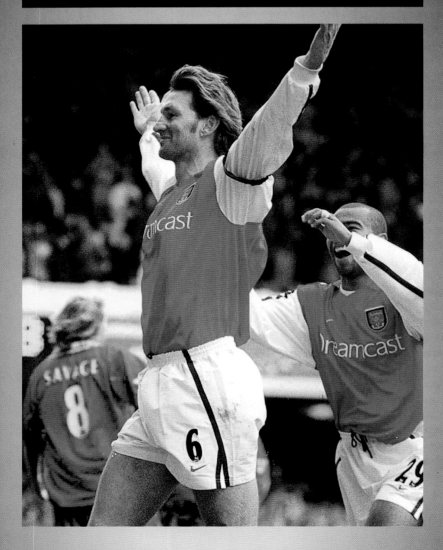

INTO THE NEW MILLENNIUM

2000-2006

The dawn of the new millennium may have coincided with football's commercial revolution and the imminent arrival of a European Super League, but for Arsène Wenger the thorny and perennial problem of team restructuring dominated the summer of 2000. Just like every manager in Arsenal's 104-year League history, Wenger would spend the close season buying and selling, however, his job had become somewhat more difficult than his predecessors' following a shift in the balance of power from clubs to players.

The sale of Nicolas Anelka in 1999 had provided ample illustration of football's new order, and a year later two more members of Wenger's Double team opted to wield their new found power. Following intense media speculation, both Marc Overmars and Emmanuel Petit made it clear that their ambitions lay away from Highbury. A £30m joint sale to Barcelona was duly agreed, leaving the Arsenal manager to fill a considerable gap in his midfield.

The departures did not end with Overmars and Petit, and in June veteran full-back Nigel Winterburn severed his ties with the Gunners after 13 years, signing for West Ham in an effort to increase his chances of first team football. However, with both Silvinho and the emergent Ashley Cole offering adequate cover at left-back, Wenger turned his attention to bolstering his midfield.

Real Mallorca's versatile Cameroon international Lauren Mayer was first to arrive, signing in a £7.2m deal in May. The remainder of Wenger's transfer business was conducted after the European Championships, a tournament at which several players with Arsenal connections would take centre stage. Patrick Vieira and Thierry Henry both starred for the victorious France team, which beat Italy in the final, while transfer targets Robert Pires and Sylvain Wiltord also made significant contributions to Les Bleus Euro 2000 success.

Marseille winger Pires, who supplied the cross for France's winning goal (scored by Wiltord), eventually signed for a bargain £6m fee in July. Pires was seen as a direct replacement for the outgoing Overmars. The final piece in Arsenal's midfield reconstruction was Brazilian Edu, a former team-mate of Silvinho's at Corinthians. However, a passport fiasco would delay Edu's arrival until January, leaving Vieira without an obvious central midfield partner. Nevertheless, Wenger decided against making a stop-gap signing and waited instead for Edu to gain the necessary international clearance. The Gunners boss would also show commendable patience over delays in the signing of Bordeaux striker Sylvain Wiltord.

Wiltord's protracted transfer extended beyond the summer close season and was only finalised after Bordeaux agreed to accept a £13m offer for the 26-year-old toward the end of August. Arsenal's record signing would complete an impressive attacking quartet of strikers along with Henry, Dennis Bergkamp and Kanu. Wenger's team-building efforts had cost in the region of £32m, but with the departures of Overmars, Petit and several fringe players, the manager had financed his purchases entirely through sales.

VIEIRA DISMISSALS MAR GOOD START

The season's opening fixture saw the Gunners travel to the Stadium of Light to take on Peter Reid's highly rated Sunderland team. Arsenal dominated the game but could not convert their superior possession into goals, spurning several good chances. Sunderland eventually made the visitors pay for their profligacy when former Gunner Niall Quinn headed into an empty net after David Seaman had misjudged a cross from Michael Gray. Worse was to follow for Wenger, with Patrick Vieira sent off late in the game for an altercation with Darren Williams. Even Reid admitted that Vieira's sending off had been harsh, commenting: 'The referee's job is very difficult but I think Vieira's a fantastic player and I thought he was unlucky to go.'

Referees and sendings-off were again the chief topic of conversation after Arsenal's next match, against Liverpool at Highbury. The Gunners hadn't beaten Liverpool for over six years, so a 2–0 victory courtesy of a home-debut goal from Lauren and a late effort from Henry, would normally have been worthy of celebration. However, the result was overshadowed by the sending-off of Vieira for the second match in succession. The France international was clearly distraught and was left pondering his future in the Premiership. 'It's a sad night,' said Wenger, "Patrick is very

upset... I don't want to repeat what he said to me. Maybe I am wrong, but after what happened against Sunderland, this may be too much.'

Fortunately, for Arsenal fans, Wenger was wrong for once and Vieira neither spoke out nor walked out on English football. The midfielder would recover from his early season setbacks to become the Premiership's most consistent performer, and he showed his professionalism with a polished display against Charlton at Highbury in Arsenal's next match. Vieira scored twice in the 5–3 win over the Addicks and had Wenger purring: 'He is committed to the club and committed to the fans... he was less aggressive today but he was playing against a team that also wanted to play football and not just antagonise him.'

After three games Arsenal sat on top of the Premiership table, two points ahead of reigning champions Manchester United. Alex Ferguson's team remained 4–6 odds-on favourites to retain their title, but according to the bookmakers, Wenger's new look Gunners were their most likely challengers, at 5–1 to take United's crown. However, to stand any real chance, Arsenal would need to keep up with the leaders in the early weeks of the campaign, something they had failed to do in recent seasons.

The task was made all the more difficult by Vieira's suspension, a series of niggling injuries to skipper Tony Adams, and Lauren's call up to Cameroon's Olympic team. Despite these difficulties, Wenger's team remained unbeaten in the 12 games following the defeat at Sunderland and kept United in their sights throughout the autumn.

The highlight of this impressive run, was a dogged 1–0 victory over the champions Manchester United at Highbury on 1 October. The game was decided by a sublime goal from the boot of Thierry Henry, who flicked the ball up before turning to hit an unstoppable, swerving volley into the corner of the net, past his former Monaco team-mate, Fabien Barthez. It was Henry's first goal for seven weeks, and the Frenchman confessed, 'I was a bit down because I haven't scored recently,' and the World Cup winner added, 'This is an important result because last year there was a big gap between us and Manchester United... Now it is going to be interesting for the rest of the season.'

Leicester City moved top of the Premiership after Arsenal's victory over United, but Alex Ferguson was in no doubt as to who his main rivals were: 'Arsenal are alongside us now and I think they will be our biggest rivals for the title,' but the Old Trafford boss added, 'We are not worried, it's only October.'

Progress on the pitch was mirrored by developments behind the scenes, and in September, Arsenal announced that they had signed a strategic partnership agreement with Granada Media. The deal involved the investment by Granada of £47m into the partnership, which would be used to finance a new joint venture media company called AFC Broadband and the development of the proposed 60,000 stadium at Ashburton Grove.

Left: Patrick Vieira protests his innocence but is still shown the red card for a clash with Sunderland's Darren Williams on the opening day of the 2000–01 season. The French midfielder was sent off in each of Arsenal's first two games but recovered to collect the Carling Player of the Season award in May.

Opposite: Tony Adams, one of the steadiest defenders of his generation, celebrates his goal against Leicester with the hottest young prospect of that particular moment – Ashley Cole.

Above: Summer signing Lauren celebrates scoring Arsenal's first goal of the season in the 2–0 victory over Liverpool at Highbury, August 2000.

Above: Thierry Henry was in top form during the 1–0 home win over Manchester United at Highbury, October 2000.

According to chairman, Peter Hill-Wood, the Granada deal would help the club to 'develop the Arsenal brand on a global basis by extending our fan base around the world.'

EUROPEAN CHALLENGE COMMENCES

UEFA Champions League football would also do much to increase Arsenal's global profile. The first group phase began with a 1–0 away victory over Sparta Prague, courtesy of Silvinho's stunning goal, but Wenger was not getting too carried away by the Gunners' winning start. A 3–2 triumph over Shakhtar Donetsk at Highbury in the next match secured another three points, but the manner of the victory was far from convincing. The Ukrainians scored twice in the first half hour and, although Wiltord pulled back a vital goal just before half time, with five minutes remaining the Gunners were still trailing. Arsenal's eventual salvation came from the unlikely figure of Martin Keown, who scored twice in the closing minutes to earn victory. Wenger was clearly grateful to his match-winning centre-half. 'We felt that Martin was a threat for them in the air. He has a high motivation and his body language also shows his desire.'

Arsenal followed the victory over Donetsk with a disappointing 1–1 draw against Ipswich, earned via a late equaliser from Dennis Bergkamp. The unbeaten run continued but the results were no longer as convincing, and the Gunners forward line was beginning to display a worrying profligacy. The next Champions League fixture would offer a stern test of Arsenal's progress, with Italian double-winners Lazio providing the visiting opposition for a Group B match.

After two campaigns at Wembley, where the Gunners won just once in six 'home' fixtures, they were back at Highbury for European games. The match against Lazio vindicated the club's decision to come home, although it was the performance of Dennis Bergkamp that proved most decisive.

The Dutchman was at his creative best and was the architect of both Arsenal goals; each scored by fellow midfielder Freddie Ljungberg. Lazio manager Sven Goran Eriksson was fulsome in his praise of the Gunners: 'Arsenal could win it [the Champions League]... They have been a very good team for some time. They are good technically and are physically very strong.'

The Gunners proved that their result against Lazio had been no fluke by holding the Italians to a 1–1 draw in Rome three weeks later. Robert Pires's late goal had earned Arsenal the single point they needed to guarantee qualification for the second phase of the Champions League, but it was veteran goalkeeper John Lukic who received the post-match plaudits. The 39-year-old was given a round of applause by his team-mates at the end and commented, 'It might sound a bit soppy, but that really touched me.' However, it was tales of racism rather than sentimentalism that dominated the following day's papers when it was revealed that Patrick Vieira had been the target of alleged racial abuse from Lazio's Sinisa Mihajlovic. The Yugoslav would later apologise for his actions, reading out an anti-racism statement before his club's next European match a week later.

Arsenal lost one of their two remaining first phase Champions League games, but still finished top of Group B. A 4–2 home win over Sparta Prague had guaranteed the Gunners qualified as group winners for the second phase, and this time they had not lost a game at 'home'. However, Arsenal's early season momentum had begun to wane, and they won just once in seven matches during November.

GOODBYE TO GEORDIE

The month began with a Worthington Cup defeat to Ipswich Town at Highbury, but the result of this match was overshadowed by the sad news that reserve team coach George Armstrong had died of a brain haemorrhage the previous night. Many of the players Armstrong had coached and nurtured were given the opportunity of a first team appearance against Ipswich, and several were clearly affected on an emotional night at Highbury. Arsène Wenger summed up the occasion perfectly: 'Many of those players out there tonight worked on a daily basis with Geordie and this was a very difficult day and night for them. Losing him has been a massive blow to everybody. But they showed the same spirit that made him a true Arsenal man, a real symbol of the club who played over 600 matches and helped win the Double.'

Worthington Cup elimination was of no great consequence to Arsenal, but their failing Premiership form had become worrying by the start of December. Although still in second

place in the table, a run of three games without scoring had seen the Gunners collect just a single point and enabled Manchester United to establish an eight-point lead. Wenger refused to admit defeat, 'Manchester United keep on winning, but we are not going to concede the Championship in November.' For Arsenal to mount a serious challenge, however, they would have to remedy their Jeckyll and Hyde home and away form. At Highbury, the Gunners seemed invincible, but on their travels they were an altogether different proposition.

SPARTAK AND BAYERN FRUSTRATE GUNNERS

The second phase of the Champions League began with a trip to Russia and a meeting with Spartak Moscow and, true to their away form, Arsenal lost the game 4–1. It was not a disastrous result, as there was time to recover from this early set back, and the manager remained optimistic, 'we are in a difficult period but I believe we still have the mental strength to come back and show our true form.'

It seemed that Wenger's prediction was about to come true when Henry and Kanu collaborated to give Arsenal a 2–0 lead after 55 minutes of the next Champions League match, at home to Bayern Munich. Alas, it was to be the German side who showed the greater 'mental strength' coming back to earn a 2–2 draw and leave Arsenal in a precarious position. However, with Lyon beating Spartak Moscow in the other Group C match,

Bayern coach Ottmar Hitzfield believed Arsenal were still in with a chance of qualification, 'It now looks like this will be a very tight group, which will not be decided until the very last round of matches. You cannot rule Arsenal out at this stage.'

After the Bayern game, the Champions League went into hibernation for two months, leaving Arsenal to concentrate on domestic matters. A 5–0 victory over Newcastle United at Highbury, in which Ray Parlour scored a hat-trick, hinted at a renewed title challenge and cut Manchester United's lead to six points. The differential was reduced by a further point the following week by the combined effect of Vieira's late equaliser against Spurs at White Hart Lane, and Liverpool's victory over the Champions at Old Trafford. Liverpool would provide the opposition for Arsenal's next Premiership fixture, but Wenger had still not found a cure for his team's away day affliction and they were beaten 4–0 at Anfield. The lead was back up to eight points, and when the Gunners failed to win any of their first three league games of the New Year, they found themselves 15 points off the pace.

DEFENSIVE HOLES

By the 25 February, Arsenal trailed by 13 points, and to maintain any hopes of a title challenge they required not only a victory from their away match against United but also a run of form to equal the ten successive wins of the Double

season. It was not to be. A weakened Gunners team, which was without key defenders Dixon, Keown and Adams, were crushed 6–1. Latvian centre-back Igor Stepanovs was singled out for blame, but in truth the whole team defended badly. 'Everything went wrong for us today,' declared Wenger. Even the usually enigmatic Alex Ferguson had no need for mind games and his appraisal of the situation at the top of the Premiership was undoubtedly accurate, though painful

Above: A shaven-headed Freddie Ljungberg sends the ball goalwards and braces himself for the challenge of Lazio goalkeeper Luca Marchegiani in Arsenal's 2–0 victory over the Italian Champions, September 2000. The Swedish midfielder scored both Gunners goals on a memorable night of Champions League football at Highbury.

Left: White Hart Lane is silenced. Patrick Vieira wheels away after heading a late equaliser in a hard-fought North London derby.

Right: Arsenal and Tottenham Hotspur players observe a minute's silence for the late David Rocastle, who died of cancer at the tragically young age of 33, March 2001.

for Gunners fans. 'If we had lost or drawn today Arsenal would have still had thoughts of catching us,' said the United manager, 'But 16 points ahead and the goal difference we have makes it impossible for them to catch us.'

CUP FOOTBALL THE PRIORITY

Arsenal may have had to concede defeat in the title race, but the season was far from over. Premiership points were still vital to the Gunners, as a top-three finish offered the most straightforward route back into the Champions League. Wenger's team were also still in with a chance of qualifying for the quarter-finals of the current Champions League after taking four points from their two games against Lyon during February. In addition, almost unnoticed, they had made impressive progress in the FA Cup.

Victories over Carlisle, QPR and Chelsea had seen the Gunners move stealthily into the last eight of the cup, and it was only once the draw for the quarter-finals offered up a home tie against First Division Blackburn Rovers, that the fans began to anticipate a glorious cup run. Arsenal's progress owed most to the form of striker Sylvain Wiltord, who had taken an instant liking to the FA Cup, scoring five times in his first three appearances in the competition.

Wiltord's fine cup form began to carry over into the Premiership, and he struck a hat-trick against West Ham at Highbury to lift the gloom six days after the 6–1 debacle at Old Trafford. However, the Frenchman found himself back on the bench alongside Kanu for the crucial Champions League match against Spartak Moscow at Highbury. But if the night began with disappointment for Wiltord it ended in frustration for Bergkamp. The Dutchman toiled tirelessly as the Gunners struggled to find a way past Spartak's massed defence. With 18 minutes remaining, Wenger took the bold decision to substitute Bergkamp. Boos echoed around Highbury as the former Inter Milan striker trudged off the pitch. The manager,

however, was proved right and with eight minutes remaining Henry struck the game's only goal to keep alive Arsenal's Champions League hopes.

The win over Spartak had left the Gunners needing to win their final Champions League group game, away to Bayern Munich, to be sure of qualification for the quarter-finals. The Champions League would dominate thoughts for the next eight days, but the Gunners did at least have the small matter of an FA Cup quarter-final against Blackburn to distract them. With Rovers chasing promotion, and Arsenal resting both Vieira and Henry ahead of the trip to Munich, it was to be no blood-and-thunder cup tie. The Gunners took an early lead through the predictable source of Wiltord, were three goals up at half-time and cruised into the last four with relative ease. A semi-final against Tottenham Hotspur would, however, offer a sterner test of Arsenal's commitment to the competition.

BAYERN BLUES

The match against Bayern proved a cagey affair, made no easier when the Germans took the lead after just ten minutes. It was to be the only goal of the game, however Arsenal would still qualify providing Lyon did not beat Spartak. When the final whistle blew in Munich there were still four minutes remaining in Moscow and the score was 1–1. 'It was like 90 minutes for me,' confessed Wenger. But Spartak held out for the draw and Arsenal progressed into the last eight. Valencia, beaten finalists in 2000, would provide the opposition for a two-legged quarter-final in April.

The Gunners warmed up for the first leg of the Valencia tie with a Premiership clash against North London rivals Spurs. Second half goals from Pires and Henry secured a 2–0 win, but Highbury was in no mood to celebrate victory in this dress rehearsal of the forthcoming FA Cup semi-final. On the morning of the game, former Arsenal midfielder David Rocastle had lost his battle against cancer and had

passed away at the heartbreakingly young age of 33. Rocastle had played in both of George Graham's championship winning teams before moving on to Leeds United in 1992, and a minute's silence was perfectly observed by both sets of supporters before the kick-off of what was to be an unusually subdued North London derby.

Against Valencia four days later, it was one of Rocastle's former team-mates, Ray Parlour, who scored the goal that completed a dramatic comeback and gave the Gunners a narrow lead to take into the second leg. At half-time Arsenal were a goal down after a disappointing showing, but after the interval they played with greater urgency and began to create chances. Henry eventually struck a seemingly inevitable equaliser on 58 minutes and two minutes later Parlour fired home to put Wenger's team into the lead. However, Henry's later failure to score when one-vs-one with the keeper, denied Arsenal a two-goal cushion and left Valencia needing only a 1–0 victory in the second leg to progress. 'We scored two goals but I felt the third and fourth goals were really possible,' declared Wenger, 'We missed some clear cut chances.'

SPURS IN THE SEMIS

Arsenal's inability to convert territorial advantage into goals would dominate the remainder of the season. The FA Cup semi-final against Spurs provided further illustration of this worrying tendency. Tottenham took an early lead at Old Trafford, but despite dominating the game, Arsenal struggled to score. After 33 minutes Patrick Vieira, strode forward and showed them the route to goal. It took another 41 minutes of painfully one-sided football before Robert Pires finally put Spurs out of their misery. 'We did it the hard way because we were creating chance after chance,' said Wenger, 'Unfortunately we missed chance after chance but we scored a second goal and then it was all over.' Arsenal had made it to the FA Cup final and would meet Liverpool at the Millennium Stadium, Cardiff in May.

In the Champions League, Arsenal's dreams finally came to an end in Valencia's Mestalla stadium. On an evening of heartache for Gunners fans, Wenger's team defended their lead doggedly for 75 minutes. But with the game entering its final quarter hour, Norwegian striker John Carew rose above Tony Adams to send a header past the despairing dive of David Seaman. The Gunners, who had been just 15 minutes away from a semi-final against David O'Leary's Leeds United, were out of the competition on away goals.

Arsenal would now have to rely on their Premiership position to qualify for a place in the 2001–02 Champions League. The Gunners' cause had, however, been handicapped by a bizarre home defeat to relegation-threatened Middlesbrough the week before the Valencia game. Wenger's team had not lost at home in the league all season, but a brace of own goals from Brazilians Silvinho and Edu, had given Boro the platform for a most unlikely 3–0 victory.

Fortunately, the Middlesbrough result proved to be no more than an incomprehensible blip, and Arsenal soon recovered their form with victories over Everton and Derby. With three Premiership games to play, the Gunners took on Leeds United at Highbury knowing that victory would guarantee another season of Champions League football. The previous meeting between the two clubs, at Elland Road, had proved a bad tempered affair and this time the football was no less competitive. However, assured defending from Adams and Keown, and goals from Ljungberg and Wiltord secured a 2–1 victory along with Arsenal's continued presence among Europe's elite.

All thoughts could now turn toward the FA Cup final. The Gunners were slight favourites for the Millennium Stadium showpiece, although Liverpool were fast developing a reputation as cup specialists, having already won the Worthington Cup and progressed to the UEFA Cup final. Gerard Houllier's team were also renowned for their counter-attacking style, so it came as no surprise that they were content to defend for much of the first half of the final.

Arsenal's attacking play gradually gathered momentum, and in the 17th minute Henry rounded goalkeeper Sander Westerveld and struck a shot goalward, only to see it repelled by the arm of Reds centre-back Stephane Henchoz. Henry appealed for a penalty, but the referee had failed to notice Henchoz's handball, and the adjacent linesman considered it to be unintentional.

At half-time the game remained goalless and, although Liverpool became slightly more adventurous after the interval, the Gunners deservedly took the lead through Freddie Ljungberg 18 minutes from time. Arsenal's advantage was a narrow one, but their goal had rarely been threatened and they seemed destined to complete a hat-trick of Cup final victories over Liverpool. However, on 83 minutes the Gunners failed to deal with a Gary McAllister free-kick and Michael Owen pounced to smash the ball home and bring the scores level. Six minutes later Owen completed the most unlikely of comebacks when he outpaced Lee Dixon to reach a pass from Patrick Berger, before eluding Tony Adams and guiding a left-footed shot past the outstretched arm of David Seaman.

Just as they had against Valencia, Arsenal were left to rue missed chances and late defensive mistakes. Henry took the defeat somewhat personally and admitted, 'We should have won the game... I missed the chance to score the second goal and we missed so many chances.'

Arsène Wenger was clearly distressed at the way his team had lost the final and was frustrated by the injustice of the Henchoz penalty incident. Wenger complained: 'The linesman said it was not on purpose, but it's the first time I've seen anyone handle on the line and it was not deliberate.' However, despite the disappointment, Wenger retained a constructive sense of perspective and offered an accurate and succinct analysis of the match: 'It was a little bit an image of our season. We look like we should win but can't finish.'

Above: Lee Dixon embraces Ryan Rocastle, son of the late David Rocastle, who was made Arsenal mascot for the 2001 FA Cup final at the Millennium Stadium.

Above: Ray Parlour celebrates
his goal in Arsenal's 2–1 victory
over Valencia at Highbury, April
2001. Parlour's long-range strike
completed a memorable comeback
for the Gunners who had been 1–0
down to the Spaniards at half-time.

Left: 'My decision was based on
football... I felt this was the place
to be.' Sol Campbell, who was to
be a goliath in the Arsenal defence
in 2001–02, explains his move to
Highbury.

A POINT STILL NEEDED

In a break with tradition, the FA Cup final had not been the
last domestic match of the season. Arsenal still had two
Premiership games to play, and they needed a point from
one of them to guarantee runners-up spot and thereby avoid
having to play an early-season Champions League qualifier.
The necessary point was achieved at the first attempt, via
a goalless draw away to Newcastle United just three days
after the Cup final. 'The players have shown a great mental
strength,' enthused Wenger, 'We were in the quarter-finals of
the Champions League and we were in the final of the FA Cup
and we finished runners-up, and that shows the huge quality
of my team.'

THE PROMISE OF YOUTH

Wenger's positive attitude was not without foundation. For
the second year running Don Howe's youth team had swept
all before them in the FA Youth Cup, beating Blackburn
Rovers 6–3 in the final, and with Ashley Cole already making
the breakthrough from junior to senior ranks there is good
reason for optimism. Cole's progress during 2000–01 was
startling. He had made his Arsenal debut in the final game
of the previous season, and quickly took his chance when
Wenger was denied the services of first choice left-back
Silvinho in the autumn of 2000. The Stepney-born defender
proved himself an able deputy and his attacking instincts
soon brought him to the attention of England manager Sven-
Goran Eriksson, who handed him a first cap in the World Cup
qualifier against Albania in March.

With young stars like Cole, Ljungberg and Henry at
Highbury, there was every reason to believe that Arsenal
would make a significant impact upon both the Premiership
and Champions League in 2001–02, and for many years to
come. However, Arsène Wenger was not ready to rest on his
laurels yet, declaring: 'This team has huge potential but we
need some extra quality to take us that step further. I know
who I want and we have enough time to sort it all out.' Few
would bet against Wenger signing the players that he needed
to take Arsenal on to even greater glories and indeed he
quickly busied himself on the transfer market.

SOL BRIGHTENS WENGER'S SUMMER

The need for a predatory striker to complement the talents
of Bergkamp and Henry had been made apparent by the
frustrating Cup final defeat to Liverpool. Henry himself had
even spoken about the need for a 'fox in the box' who could
snaffle up the chances created by the Arsenal midfield.
Everton's 20-year-old centre-forward Francis Jeffers was
the player targeted to fill this role by Wenger and he became
the first new arrival at Highbury in the summer of 2001.
Jeffers would be joined by the versatile Holland international
Giovanni van Bronckhorst, who signed from Rangers after a

successful three-year spell with the Glasgow club. However,
it was the signing of a new defender on 1 July 2001 that
dominated the back pages.

Spurs captain Sol Campbell became a free agent at the end
of June and speculation had been rife about which club would
sign him. Barcelona, Manchester United, Real Madrid, Roma
and Liverpool had all registered their interest in the Newham-
born defender, but few pundits considered Arsenal among the
front runners for his signature. On 1 July a press conference
was called at the club's London Colney training ground. The
journalists were expecting Arsenal to announce the signing
of Ipswich goalkeeper Richard Wright, and there was a fair
degree of surprise when the formidable figure of Campbell was
brought forward. Wenger continued his squad-strengthening
with the long-anticipated signing of Richard Wright before
making Japan international midfielder Junichi Inamoto his
final summer addition.

AUTUMNAL INCONSISTENCY

Arsenal kicked off the new campaign away to Middlesbrough
and fielded a familiar-looking line-up. The new trio of van
Bronckhorst, Jeffers and Wright were all on the bench, with

Campbell the only one of the summer signings making it into the starting eleven. Wenger had tweaked his selection somewhat, deploying Parlour alongside Vieira in central midfield, switching Lauren to right-back and giving Wiltord a central striking role.

The tactical changes got the desired result at The Riverside, where Arsenal won 4–0. Henry had opened the scoring on 43 minutes against the Teessiders, but in a worrying reminder of the previous season, it took Arsenal until the final four minutes to make the game safe with a goal from Robert Pires, which was duly followed by a brace from substitute Dennis Bergkamp.

A frustrating clash with Leeds United at Highbury ended in a 2–1 defeat for the Gunners in their first home game of the season. Arsenal would struggle for consistency throughout the early weeks of the season, and it was not until 13 October that they won back-to-back Premiership games. It was a similar story in the first group phase of the Champions League. Defeat in the opening fixture, away to Real Mallorca, had come after Ashley Cole conceded a penalty that brought the game's only goal. A home victory against Shalke 04 followed, but Arsenal lived dangerously en route to a 3–2 win over the Germans.

It seemed that Wenger's team were unable to move up a gear during the autumn of 2001, although there were occasional glimpses of the slick, incisive attacking play that would come to characterise their football later in the season. There were mitigating factors for this, most notably a succession of injuries to defenders that required Wenger to name six different centre-back pairings in the first eight Premiership games.

GOAL FEST

Fit defenders may have been in short supply at Highbury, but Wenger had a positive surfeit of in-form attacking players in the early weeks of 2001–02. Pires, Ljungberg, Bergkamp and Wiltord had all impressed, however, none could rival the form of the rampant Thierry Henry, who scored 14 goals in the first 15 games.

Despite the wealth of goals from Henry, Arsenal's capacity to frustrate remained, as illustrated by an enthralling 3–3 draw against Blackburn Rovers at Highbury, in which the visitors clinched a point with an 89th-minute equaliser. Worse followed in the next home game in the Premiership against Charlton Athletic.

The South Londoners hadn't won at Highbury for 46 years, and when Henry opened the scoring after six minutes there seemed little hope for Charlton, who had already been spared by a post and a goal-line clearance. A procession of chances followed for the rampant Gunners but each was missed and on 35 minutes the visitors equalised when Steve Brown headed in Paul Konchesky's free kick. Richard Wright then punched another deadball delivery from Konchesky into his own net

to give Charlton a barely plausible interval lead, and shortly after the resumption there were two more quick-fire goals from the Addicks. Henry's penalty reduced the deficit but it proved no more than a consolation.

Arsenal had created 25 scoring attempts, 12 on target, while Charlton had fashioned just five shots on goal and had scored four times. It was a defeat that meant the Gunners had dropped more points from their first five home games of the season than throughout the whole of the previous season's campaign.

The good news, although of course Wenger did not know it at the time, was that Arsenal's season had reached its nadir, and despite their inconsistent form the Gunners were still in a respectable fifth place in the Premiership, just four points behind leaders Leeds United.

REVIVING THE TITLE CHALLENGE

In the Champions League, home wins in successive weeks against Panathinaikos and Real Mallorca secured progress to the second phase; although the draw, which placed Arsenal in Group D along with Juventus, Deportivo La Coruña and Bayer Leverkusen, could not have been tougher. The programme began with a tricky away fixture against Deportivo, who had already beaten Manchester United home and away in the competition's first phase. The Gunners' European curse struck again and the Spaniards won the game 2–0. This game came just four days after Arsenal had contested a typically fierce

Right: Thierry Henry seizes on Barthez's second mistake to score Arsenal's 85th-minute winner at Highbury in November. The 3–1 victory lifted Arsenal above United to third in the table and sent Henry well on the road to the Golden Boot.

Above: Freddie Ljungberg sprints away from Alessio Tacchinardi during Arsenal's magnificent 3–1 victory over Juventus. Ljungberg scored twice against the Turin giants and underlined his value to Arsenal's attacking options.

and hard-fought North London derby at White Hart Lane. The match had ended in a 1–1 draw, with Spurs equalising in injury time. While the fans were devastated at the loss against Deportivo, for Arsène Wenger the performance of his players against Tottenham had given cause for optimism. Pires had illuminated the game with a stunning 25-yard curler and had been the most creative player on show, but, it was Sol Campbell who had impressed Wenger most. The England defender had given his most commanding display yet in an Arsenal jersey.

Campbell was again at his best when Manchester United were the visitors for a clash at Highbury. After 14 minutes and against the run of play United took the lead when Paul Scholes fired past Stuart Taylor, who was making his Premiership debut in place of the injured duo of Seaman and Wright. Arsenal surged forward in formidable fashion as they attempted to restore parity, and three minutes after half-time Ljungberg struck with an exquisite chip over Fabien Barthez from the edge of the box. Arsenal pressed for the winner and in the 80th minute they gained the lead. Up until then Barthez had been a contender for man of the match, but twice in quick succession his mistakes let in Henry to score.

Wenger was delighted with his team's 3–1 victory over the reigning champions and was also pleased when Arsenal won their next two games and were up to second place in the table by mid-December.

All was going well at home, but of more immediate concern to the Arsenal manager was a Champions League match against Juventus at Highbury. It was the first time the two

clubs had met since the Gunners' victory over the Italian giants in a UEFA Cup semi-final in 1980 . On the night, Henry was just one of a clutch of Arsenal players who starred in a fantastic performance that saw the Gunners win 3–1. A goal in each half from Ljungberg and a 25-yard Henry free kick clinched a victory that also owed much to Taylor in goal.

Wenger also had good reason to applaud his young charges five days later when they overturned a 2–0 half-time deficit to beat Aston Villa 3–2. An injury-time goal from the prolific Henry – his 20th of the season – had earned the Gunners a victory that took them to within three points of leaders Liverpool. Arsenal's season had come alive and they now looked like serious contenders for the Premiership.

On 18 December Arsenal had the chance to climb to the top of the table when fellow title challengers Newcastle United visited Highbury. Just when it seemed the Gunners' Premiership assault was gathering momentum, the team were left stunned by defeat. Pires had opened the scoring after 20 minutes and Arsenal remained in control of the game. Newcastle grew in confidence after the interval but, though they equalised on the hour, Arsenal still looked like taking a point until the visitors were awarded a penalty, which Shearer duly converted. Then Robert increased Newcastle's margin of victory.

It was the third time Arsenal had lost a home game during 2001–02 and, as on both previous occasions, the result was somewhat freakish. There was all to play for, though, as Arsenal's next match saw them face title rivals Liverpool away at Anfield.

TEN GUNNERS TRIUMPH AT ANFIELD

As was becoming customary, the Gunners began the match the stronger of the two teams. All could have changed, though, when Giovanni van Bronckhorst slipped and fell in the Liverpool penalty area. Although there were no theatrics nor appeals for a penalty from the Arsenal midfielder, the referee interpreted the Dutchman's fall as a dive and showed him a red card for his second bookable offence. Despite this setback Arsenal responded in impressive fashion and three minutes later Ljungberg was brought down by Liverpool goalkeeper Jerzy Dudek as he was about to score. This time the Gunners did appeal for a penalty and this time the referee pointed to the spot, from where Henry opened the scoring to put Arsenal ahead at the interval.

Wenger, showing commendable ambition, resisted the temptation to take off one of his attacking players for the second half and Pires, Ljungberg, Henry and Kanu all immediately took the fight to Liverpool. Seven minutes after the break Pires set up Ljungberg who scored what proved to be the game's decisive goal. The hosts halved the deficit three minutes later, but Arsenal held out for a deserved victory that took them ahead of Liverpool and into second place in the table.

Arsenal's resurgence had, however, coincided with a parallel improvement in the form of Manchester United and, by the time Arsenal met Liverpool in their return match at Highbury on 13 January, Sir Alex Ferguson's team had moved ahead of both their main rivals for the Premiership title. Arsenal trailed by a point but had a game in hand. It would be nip and tuck for the remainder of the season between these two great rivals.

REDS DOMINATE TITLE RACE

After eight successive victories United finally lost a Premiership game when Liverpool's Danny Murphy struck the only goal of a tense encounter at Old Trafford on 22 January. Arsenal themselves dropped two points in a disappointing 1–1 home draw against Southampton. At the end of the first week in February just three points separated four teams (Manchester United, Newcastle United, Liverpool and Arsenal) at the top of the table.

Arsenal won their next game, away to Everton, with a somewhat fortuitous goal from Sylvain Wiltord who miscued a shot that looped over the Toffees keeper and into the corner of the net. However, fortune would rarely be required for the remainder of Arsenal's Premiership campaign. In Robert Pires the Gunners had the competition's most creative player, while in Henry they had the most potent striker, and in Ljungberg an elusive and equally predatory midfielder.

However, the most significant factor in Arsenal's progress was undeniably manager Arsène Wenger. He had long been noted for his objectivity and calm, but in the early spring of 2002 he began to speak with an assurance and an authority that bred confidence not only in the players but also the fans. There was depth in the squad, too, and when Henry was unavailable for the Premiership match against Newcastle at St James' Park, his absence gave Dennis Bergkamp the opportunity to take centre stage. The Dutchman did not disappoint and he struck with a goal of sublime quality. With his back to goal Bergkamp met a pass from Pires with a delicious first touch that spun the ball round one side of his marker, while he ran round the other. With a minimum of fuss the ball was duly collected and calmly dispatched past the Newcastle keeper.

Bergkamp's goal against Newcastle helped secure a 2–0 win that cemented Arsenal's position in second place in the Premiership. It was a third successive victory for the Gunners, who were still chasing silverware on three fronts.

In the Champions League they were in a strong position to qualify for the competition's knock-out stage after drawing with Bayer Leverkusen away. What is more, they had also made good progress in the FA Cup; beating both Watford and Gillingham but most notably Liverpool – Bergkamp was the scorer of the game's only goal in the tie against the Merseysiders – en route to a sixth-round showdown with Newcastle at St James' Park.

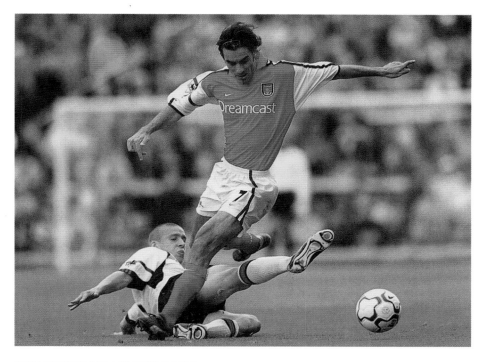

CUP FOOTBALL TO THE FORE

March would be a month dominated by cup football for Arsenal, and the action commenced with the FA Cup tie at St James' Park. For once, however, Arsenal failed to dominate and it was they who were grateful for a goal against the run of play scored by Edu. The match ended in a 1–1 draw.

However, three days later the Gunners would lose a game on a frustrating night of Champions League misery against Deportivo at Highbury. A 2–0 defeat left Arsenal no longer in control of their Champions League fate ahead of the final fixtures of the second group phase.

Arsenal's European woe continued as they lost their game against Juventus, going down to a header from Uruguayan-born Marcelo Zalayeta. Arsenal had created sufficient chances to win the game but the result mattered little as Deportivo lost 3–1 at home to Bayer Leverkusen in the other Group D game, leaving Arsenal to go no further in the competion.

However, Wenger was in no mood for pessimism and rallied his team, and it was a refreshingly vibrant Arsenal team that swept aside Newcastle at Highbury to reach the FA Cup semi-final with goals from Pires, Campbell and Bergkamp. The Gunners' championship challenge had also been aided by an Alen Boksic goal that gave Middlesbrough a crucial and unexpected victory at Old Trafford.

Wenger's team had won five Premiership games in succession and were just two points behind Premiership leaders Liverpool with two games in hand as the Easter fixtures approached. However, on 25 March, Arsenal were hit by the news that Pires's season was over due to a cruciate ligament injury sustained in the game against Newcastle.

Right: Robert Pires was a revelation in 2001/02. His touch and vision were underlined by the fact he won the Football Writers' Player of the Year despite missing the last ten games of the season.

Above: Just days after scoring with a deft chip against Bayer Leverkusen, Dennis Bergkamp scored 'goal of the season' against Newcastle United.

Better news for Wenger came from Pires's compatriot Patrick Vieira who reaffirmed his commitment to Arsenal with a commanding, goalscoring display in the 3–0 victory over Sunderland at Highbury on Easter Saturday. However, for the remainder of the season another Gunners midfielder would take the limelight. Freddie Ljungberg had long been a popular figure with the Highbury faithful but his status was about to take a leap into the stratosphere with a prolific run of goalscoring that could not have been better timed.

Ljungberg's impressive scoring sequence, which would extend to seven goals in seven games, began in Arsenal's emphatic 3–0 victory over Charlton at The Valley. It was a result that took Arsenal back to the top of the table.

Rivals Liverpool and Manchester United, who were now one and two points behind Arsenal respectively, had each played a game more and were no doubt hoping that the Gunners next fixture, a North London derby at Highbury, might be the occasion on which the seemingly unstoppable league leaders dropped some points. It proved a dramatic encounter, and with the score at 1–0 to Arsenal – courtesy of a goal from the irrepressible Ljungberg – Spurs won a penalty, which was duly converted by Teddy Sheringham in the 81st minute. Just when it seemed that Tottenham might take a share of the spoils, Thierry Henry was fouled and, with the Frenchman temporarily off the pitch receiving treatment, Lauren took the penalty, coolly rolling the ball into the centre of the goal. All three points were safe and Arsenal remained top of the table.

DOUBLE CHANCE

With only five Premiership games left to play and an FA Cup semi-final against Middlesbrough to contend with, whispered talk of a third Double began to be heard. The whispers grew in volume after the Gunners won their FA Cup semi-final against Middlesbrough at Old Trafford, and they soon escalated to a cacophony when further progress was made in the League.

Arsenal's seemingly ubiquitous game in hand, which was against West Ham at Highbury, was finally scheduled for 24 April. If they beat the Hammers, Wenger's team would extend their lead to four points over second-placed Liverpool with only three games to play. The tension was palpable and the atmosphere inside Highbury grew in intensity throughout a difficult first half that saw Glenn Roeder's West Ham enjoy the better chances. The Hammers even had claims for a goal waved away after Ashley Cole cleared Frederic Kanoute's shot from the goal line. Arsenal produced an improved performance in the second half but it was not until the 77th minute that they got the goal Highbury craved. Predictably it was Ljungberg who scored the decisive opener against the Hammers. Kanu added a second shortly before the final whistle to settle the nerves of the Gunners faithful.

A TWO-WAY FIGHT

Three days later the title race effectively became a two-way fight between Arsenal and Manchester United after Liverpool lost to Spurs at White Hart Lane. United were desperate to keep the pressure on Wenger's team in the hope that they might lose their nerve; particularly since the two rivals would meet in the penultimate fixture at Old Trafford. The Champions maintained their challenge with a 1–0 win against relegation-threatened Ipswich at Portman Road, courtesy of a penalty.

Arsenal knew that if they could win their next game, away to Bolton Wanderers, they would find themselves needing just one victory from their final two fixtures to guarantee the Premiership crown. Like most of the Gunners' recent matches the game at Bolton's Reebok Stadium proved a tense encounter and with equal predictability it was Freddie Ljungberg who opened the scoring. Sylvain Wiltord added a second. Arsenal were now only two victories away from the Double.

RETURN TO CARDIFF

The victory over Bolton had also been notable for the return to fitness of Sol Campbell, who made a brief substitute appearance, after making an extraordinarily quick recovery from a hamstring injury sustained in the FA Cup semi-final.

Campbell's recovery created a defensive selection dilemma for Wenger ahead of the FA Cup final against Chelsea. The manager would have to decide which two of his three centre-halves – Adams, Keown and Campbell – would be given the task of marking the formidable strikeforce of Hasselbaink and Gudjohnsen. He would also have to choose between his two senior goalkeepers. David Seaman had been in exceptional

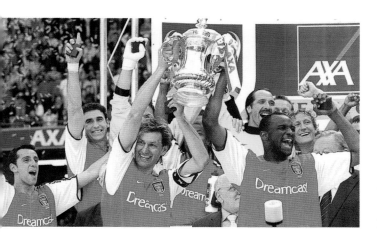

AND SO TO OLD TRAFFORD

Comparisons with 1989 were obvious and, although the 2002 showdown did not have the same finality as the game at Anfield, since the title would not necessarily be decided on the night, it was unquestionably the most dramatic and significant fixture in the history of the Premiership. The Gunners, who had won 12 successive League games since drawing with Southampton at the start of February 2002, were in confident mood.

The match itself proved a predictably dogged encounter with chances at a premium. The deadlock was eventually broken when, after 57 minutes, Sylvain Wiltord gave Arsenal a deserved lead by profiting from a shot on goal by Freddie Ljungberg that Manchester United goalkeeper Fabien Barthez could only palm into the path of his compatriot. It was the end of the scoring and the end of the title race. Not for the first time, 1–0 was enough for Arsenal and the celebrations began in earnest.

A triumphant Arsène Wenger was quick to praise the spirit of Arsenal's third Double-winning team. 'We have 84 points, completed the Double, not lost away from home and won 14 away games, and scored in every League game this season,' beamed the Frenchman. 'It is absolutely tremendous. The character in this side is great.'

The official presentation of the Premiership trophy took place at Highbury three days later when Everton were the visitors for the season's final game. A much-changed Arsenal line-up took the field against the Toffees as Wenger attempted to give several of his fringe players a taste of glory and, in some cases, the chance to qualify for a Championship medal. However, even with the carnival atmosphere and some questionable defending, Arsenal retained the competitive spirit that had swept them to the Double. Winning had become a habit and an entertaining 4–3 victory extended the sequence of successive Premiership wins to a record-breaking 13 games.

A BURNING AMBITION

Despite his team's success and the adulation heaped upon him, Wenger was already mentally preparing himself for the next campaign. 'I want to maintain this success now,' declared the Arsenal manager, 'The best way to fail the season after is to celebrate and relax too much because while you are doing that, everyone else tries to strengthen and catch up... The Champions League is our next challenge and I believe we have the quality in our squad to win it one day.' Few would argue about that after a season of incredible achievement at Highbury.

The summer of 2002 offered little prospect of an extended vacation in the sun for many of Arsenal's players. For 11 members of the current Arsenal squad, the World Cup finals in Japan and South Korea beckoned rather than any much-needed recuperation after their Double-winning exertions.

Above: Tony Adams holds aloft the Barclaycard Premiership trophy to round off a glorious season for Arsène Wenger's record-breaking team.

Above left: Arsenal lift the 2002 FA Cup.

form since returning from injury in February, but Richard Wright had played in five of Arsenal's six FA Cup ties and appeared to be Arsenal's first choice FA Cup keeper. However, Wenger denied that Wright had any guarantee that he would play in the final. 'There is no pact or agreement to play him in every game no matter what happens. Every individual only has one agreement with the club – to do everything to win trophies.'

Wenger was as good as his word and named the in-form Seaman in goal, with Adams and Campbell getting the nod at centre-half in preference to Keown. The Gunners were slight favourites to lift the Cup. However, Claudio Ranieri's talented team were not to be underestimated.

PARLOUR PROVIDES

The first half of the final proved a rather disjointed affair and although chances came and went for both sides, it was not until the 70th minute that Arsenal took the lead. Ironically, the goal, which was scored by Ray Parlour, came at a time when Chelsea were enjoying their best spell of the game. A move involving Adams and Wiltord presented Parlour with the ball 40 yards from goal and, after assessing his options, the midfielder crashed home a 25-yard shot that Carlo Cudicini was powerless to keep out.

Not to be outdone, Ljungberg then scored an even more impressive goal ten minutes later. The Swede picked up the ball on the left-hand side and surged forward, resisting a challenge from Chelsea defender John Terry, to break into the box and curl a fine shot beyond Cudicini.

Arsenal had won their first trophy for four years, but, while the fans were delighted with the FA Cup, Wenger was desperate to repeat the Double success of 1998. If the Gunners were to do so, they would need to win one of their remaining two games (away to Manchester United and at home to Everton). The supporters were desperate to see Arsenal clinch the title at Old Trafford so that they could celebrate inside the ground of their rivals, just as they had after that famous victory at Anfield in 1989.

Above: Gilberto fires home the winning goal against Liverpool in the 2002 Community Shield. The Brazilian had arrived at Highbury from Atletico Mineiro just weeks after helping his country to success in the World Cup finals. He would make 51 appearances in his first season at Arsenal, scoring three goals.

For the Arsenal manager, the tournament provided the opportunity to assess potential new signings, although even at the World Cup it would not be easy to find players who were, firstly, available and, secondly, who would improve a team that had swept all before it in 2001–02.

In any case, there was growing concern that transfer fees were set to fall following the game's much-discussed, impending financial crisis. Aside from Manchester United – who signed England defender Rio Ferdinand from Leeds for a record sum – there was a degree of caution among Premiership clubs with regard to their summer spending in 2002. Arsène Wenger was as usual circumspect when discussing potential targets during the early months of the close season, but in July the Arsenal manager clinched his number one target. Brazil's World Cup-winning midfielder Gilberto Silva was the man in question, and the 25-year-old arrived at Highbury from Atletico Mineiro with a reputation as a skilful and energetic performer.

The only other major signing ahead of the 2002–03 season was French centre-back Pascal Cygan, who joined from Lille and would compete with Sol Campbell and Martin Keown for a place at the heart of Arsenal's defence following the retirement of Arsenal legend Tony Adams. Both Cygan and Gilberto were left on the bench when the Gunners kicked off the domestic season against Liverpool in the Community Shield at the Millennium Stadium. The match proved a full-blooded encounter and both newcomers must surely have been wincing at the ferocity of some of the tackling. At half-time Gilberto swapped his seat on the bench for a more active

role, replacing his compatriot Edu to partner Patrick Vieira in midfield. It proved an inspired substitution, as midway through the second half Dennis Bergkamp provided an inch-perfect cut-back from the deadball line for Arsenal's Brazilian debutant to fire home the game's only goal.

'I'm happy for him,' declared a jubilant Wenger. 'He's an intelligent boy, makes things simple and gets into the box at the right time. Maybe he was still a bit surprised by the physical side of the fight but he will adapt quickly to that and I believe he will be a very strong player for us.'

BLUES BEATEN BUT HAMMERS HELD

The Gunners began their Premiership defence with a relatively straightforward 2–0 victory over Birmingham City, but a week later the Champions faced a much sterner test of their character when they travelled to Upton Park for their first London derby of the season. The Hammers had enjoyed a formidable home record throughout the previous campaign and were clearly in confident mood on a hot afternoon in the East End.

A minute before half-time the home side made the breakthrough when Joe Cole curled the ball home from the edge of the box, and within ten minutes the hosts had doubled their lead. The Gunners had not lost an away game in the Premiership since May 2001 but their record now looked in grave danger. Wenger urged his team on with an uncharacteristically animated display from his technical area and his players, who were visibly buoyed by their manager's encouragement, wrested the initiative from the Hammers as the second half reached its midway point.

Thierry Henry's frustrations were as obvious as Wenger's and on 65 minutes he received a pass from Patrick Vieira, span and lashed in an unstoppable half-volley from the edge of the box. It was an expression of defiance as much as anything and it was celebrated lustily. But just as it seemed as though Arsenal were on the verge of completing a notable comeback, referee Neale Barry awarded West Ham a penalty for Ashley Cole's innocuous looking push on namesake Joe. Defiance, however, was clearly infectious. Freddie Kanoute stepped up, struck the ball unconvincingly and David Seaman dived to his right to save. The stage was set for a dramatic finale and with two minutes remaining Wiltord guided a side-footed shot through a crowded penalty area and past James to snatch a deserved point for the Champions.

'When you come back from 2–0 down to 2–2 – and it could have been 3–2 – it feels a bit like a victory', explained Wenger after the game. 'When it went to 2–0, we needed special, exceptional strength to come back. We found our game after an hour and showed talent to save a penalty and get two great goals.' The Arsenal manager reserved special praise for Henry's goal: 'It was amazing, like a missile. There wasn't even time to realise it was in and it wouldn't surprise me if it is one of the goals of the season.'

MEMORIES...

RECORDS AND AWARDS 2001–02

As Arsenal closed in on their third Double in the spring of 2002, it became virtually impossible to keep track of the achievements of Arsène Wenger's phenomenal team. A host of club and Premiership records fell to the rampant Gunners, while both Wenger and his players collected a variety of individual awards for their part in a historic season.

INDIVIDUAL AWARDS

Arsène Wenger – Voted manager of the season by both the League Managers' Association and Premiership sponsors Barclaycard

Thierry Henry – Opta Player of the Season and Golden Boot winner

Robert Pires – Football Writers' Player of the Year

RECORDS

The New Invincibles – Arsenal became the first team since Preston in 1888–89 to remain unbeaten away from home throughout an entire top-flight season. It is also worth noting that Preston's 'Invincibles' played eight fewer away games than the Gunners.

Arsenal's winning run – Victory over Manchester United at Old Trafford on 8 May equalled United's record of 12 successive Premiership wins. The victory over Everton three days later established a new record for the Gunners.

One–nil to the Arsenal – In 28 of their 38 Premiership games Arsenal scored first, thereby setting a new record. Consistent entertainers – Arsenal scored in each of their 38 Premiership games.

Away-day specialists – Victory over Manchester United at Old Trafford established a new club record for successive away wins. The Gunners had won eight in a row.

WILTORD'S WINNERS

Henry would, indeed, score the Goal of the Season, according to watchers of ITV's 'The Premiership', but that would not be until mid-November, and in between the Frenchman provided several other highlights. However, in the early weeks of the season it was Thierry's compatriot Sylvain Wiltord who was arguably the club's most potent striker. After six games Wiltord topped the Premiership's scoring chart, and his six goals had also played a major part in Arsenal's concurrent rise to the top of the table. It was a significant achievement for a player who was frequently deployed on the right flank.

Wiltord's presence on the wing was, in part, prompted by the continued absence of both Robert Pires and Freddie Ljungberg during the opening weeks of the season. However, the good news for Wenger was that – aside from his two wide

Top: David Seaman dives to his right to save a penalty from West Ham's Freddie Kanoute at Upton Park in August 2002. Had Kanoute's spot-kick found the net, the score would have been 3–1 to the Hammers. However, Seaman's save kept Arsenal in the game and with two minutes remaining Sylvain Wiltord equalised.

Above: Freddie Ljungberg marks his return from injury with a neatly taken goal against Borussia Dortmund in the Champions League at Highbury in September 2002.

men – he had few injury problems and was able to select from a strong squad. Nevertheless, the manager made every effort to utilise fully the playing staff at his disposal and younger, less established players like Jermaine Pennant, Jeremie Aliadiere and Kolo Toure frequently featured in the first team during the autumn.

In both the Premiership and the Champions League things were going to plan. Eight consecutive victories followed the 1–1 draw with Chelsea at Stamford Bridge on 1 September and by mid-October Arsenal's campaigns in Europe and at home were gathering momentum.

In the Premiership, Liverpool were emerging as Arsenal's most likely challengers, with Manchester United enduring an uncharacteristically stuttering start to the season, but in Champions League Group A, Arsène Wenger's men appeared to be without significant rivals. Arsenal won their first three games in Europe, scoring seven goals without reply. Arsenal fans were also delighted to see the return to the pitch of Freddie Ljungberg, who marked his recovery from injury with a goal against Borussia Dortmund in the 2–0 home win.

AUTUMNAL STRUGGLES

As summer turned to autumn the Champions' apparently unstoppable progress unexpectedly stalled. After 24 games without defeat, Arsenal lost four games in succession as October turned into a month to forget for Arsène Wenger's men. Goodison Park was to be the stage for the first of this quartet of reverses. David Moyes' Everton were rapidly becoming the Premiership's surprise package and at home they were proving themselves formidable opponents. The Toffees also boasted English football's latest wonder-kid, Wayne Rooney, and it was the 16-year-old who stole the show and the three points with a stunning last-minute winner. The game had looked to be heading for a 1–1 draw after Tomasz Radzinski had equalised Freddie Ljungberg's eighth-minute opener, but Rooney's introduction ten minutes from time proved decisive. With only time added on for stoppages still to play, the powerfully-built youngster controlled an awkward dropping ball, span and struck a devastating 30-yard drive that crashed past David Seaman via the crossbar.

Despite his obvious disappointment, Wenger was magnanimous in defeat. 'We were beaten by a special goal from a very special talent. I've seen a bit of him [Rooney] in recent months... you do not need to be an expert to see that he is a special talent, very special.' Of his own team's performance, the Arsenal manager commented: 'This was our first league defeat in seven months and I would like to congratulate my team for that and offer them my utmost respect. We fought hard, but Everton also did for the full 90 minutes. They wanted to win with strength and power and not technique, but they were excellent. We always looked like scoring in the second half, except that our final ball wasn't good enough.'

It was a similar story against both Auxerre and Blackburn Rovers in Arsenal's next two games. Both ended in 2–1 defeats and on each occasion Arsenal could point to a host of missed chances and a territorial domination that belied the final scoreline. There was rather less to complain about when Arsenal's fourth successive game ended in yet another 2–1 reverse, this time against Borussia Dortmund in the Westfalenstadion. Despite their defeat, Arsenal clinched a place in the last 16 courtesy of results elsewhere.

CONFIDENCE BUILDS

After such a disappointing sequence of results, Arsène Wenger would have been delighted to turn over his calendar at the end of October, and it appeared that Arsenal's luck had changed when they began November with a 1–0 win away to Fulham. Victory over the Cottagers was secured via an own goal from Steve Marlet, but for Wenger the only important issue was the game's result. 'We were very resilient,' explained the delighted Arsenal manager. 'We wanted three points and got them. We were strong and I'm delighted to win the match no matter what it took. I would have preferred to have won with a different goal but I'll take that one. If you lose four [games] you have to be concerned. We're not used to it and it's how the team responds. The response was there today. 'Confidence drops when you have lost four in a row and we felt luck had turned against us against Everton and Blackburn. We had to dig deeper and that's what we have done. This team will fight for the future.'

Arsenal's immediate future was on display at Highbury three days later when the Gunners fielded a team that included several young, emergent stars against Sunderland in the Worthington Cup. Arsenal lost the game 3–2 but it had provided an opportunity for the likes of Ryan Garry, Moritz Volz and Sebastian Svard to enjoy a taste of first-team action.

The game was also notable for Robert Pires' first goal since recovering from the serious knee injury he had sustained against Newcastle United the previous March. The Frenchman had returned to first-team duty two weeks previously, coming on as a substitute in the 2–1 defeat from Auxerre. Pires would later speak passionately about his comeback game. 'When I came on against Auxerre, 20 minutes from the end, I had goosebumps. What I experienced then was a very intense moment – it was magical, unforgettable. The fans have been fantastic to me. It seemed that they had been waiting for this instant, just like I had. I saw them standing up as I was running in the middle of the field to take my position. My heart was full of happiness... I was running all over the place and my heart was pounding and I said to myself, "Calm down, Robert!" We lost but I personally felt better and better with my body.'

By 12 November Pires' fitness had improved sufficiently for him to play the full 90 minutes against PSV Eindhoven at Highbury. The match ended in a goalless draw and was

most notable for the debut performance of goalkeeper Rami Shaaban, who had arrived from Djurgardens in August. Shaaban's clean sheet brought Arsenal the point they needed to top their qualifying group and ensure seeding for the second phase of the Champions League.

HENRY POWERS THROUGH

Buoyed by their progress in Europe, Arsenal were at their scintillating best for the first north London derby of the season at Highbury four days later. The Arsenal faithful had to wait just 13 minutes to witness the game's first goal and it was a goal that they would never forget. Thierry Henry collected the ball just outside the Arsenal penalty area, turned and galloped forward. His jinking run carried him over 70 yards and past challenges from Matthew Etherington, Ledley King and Stephen Carr before he sold goalkeeper Kasey Keller a dummy and fired the ball into the net. Two more Arsenal goals followed without reply, but it was Henry's opener that dominated the post-match coverage and which was later voted Goal of the Season.

'Thierry scored a world-class goal,' said Wenger. 'It is a very special goal when you take the ball from the edge of your box and score. At this level you need special powers and special strengths. He needed that goal because although he did not have a dip in his performances recently he had a dip in his goalscoring record. But I expect so much from him, and he makes the pitch look small when he has the ball.'
Wenger was also encouraged by his team's overall display, telling reporters: 'Our confidence is back. It takes two or three games but we are back to our best. It is important to be up there at the top of the Premiership because two weeks ago before the Fulham game we were seven points behind Liverpool. But it is a long race.'

Arsenal's progress, however, hit a glitch a week later at Southampton's St Mary's Stadium, where the hosts triumphed in an entertaining 3–2 thriller. The Gunners' disappointment at defeat was accentuated by the sending-off of Sol Campbell for an honest attempt to win the ball against Saints' Ecuadorian striker Agustin Delgado. Of no less concern, was the fact that the England defender would now be suspended for the vital showdown with Manchester United at Old Trafford on 7 December.

In the interim, Campbell played a full role in a brace of impressive 3–1 victories against Roma and Aston Villa, which saw Thierry Henry once more take centre stage, scoring five goals in the process. Against Roma the Frenchman was simply unstoppable, completing a deserved hat-trick with a breathtaking, curling free-kick from the edge of the box. As if to prove that it had been no fluke, he repeated the feat against Villa three days later.

Henry might have wished he'd saved one of his goals and a little good fortune for the meeting with United a week later. Arsenal certainly appeared to be all out of luck in a match

that ended in a 2–0 defeat for the Champions. Ruud van Nistelrooy had clearly handled the ball in the build-up to United's first goal, while the second had deflected off Keown. To compound Arsenal's misery Rami Shaaban had been forced out of the game through injury just before half-time.

United were now just three points behind Arsenal and had put their stuttering start to the season behind them with an exceptional run of form. Arsène Wenger was in candid mood after the game, declaring: 'We have been given a good warning as to how much the other teams want to beat us. The title race is now open again for Manchester United. We knew that before but the reality is there after this game, although it will not only be them, it will be Liverpool and maybe Chelsea as well. However, it is our title still to win as we are still in front and it depends on us.' They would prove prophetic words.

Initially, at least, it seemed that Arsenal had heeded the warning offered by the defeat at Old Trafford. They remained unbeaten for the remainder of the year and began 2003 with a five-point lead in the Premiership. They also were

Above: Thierry Henry breaks forward en route to scoring the 2002–03 Goal of the Season against Spurs at Highbury in November. The Frenchman carried the ball 70 yards and past a succession of defenders before depositing it in the net with a measured finish past Kasey Keller.

Left: Patrick Vieira challenges for midfield possession in the Champions League showdown with Valencia in March 2003. A draw would have been enough to take Arsenal through to the quarter-finals but two goals from John Carew provided a 2–1 reverse for Arsène Wenger's men.

at the top of their Champions League group, having drawn 0–0 with Valencia at Highbury in the final match before the competition's winter break.

HAPPY NEW YEAR

Arsenal's good form continued and after a 3–2 win against second-placed Chelsea on New Year's Day, they won each of their next four games, scoring 14 goals in the process. It was a sequence of results that not only cemented the Gunners' position at the top of the Premiership but also secured their progress to the fifth round of the FA Cup and a mouth-watering tie against Manchester United at Old Trafford. However, ahead of the trip to Manchester, there was the small matter of League games to consider against title rivals Liverpool and Newcastle United either side of a London derby against Fulham. It was a trio of games that would prove somewhat frustrating despite yielding a respectable five points for Arsenal.

Against Liverpool at Anfield, Arsenal had unquestionably enjoyed the better chances and played the better football, but a last-minute goal from Emile Heskey, which had come from a hotly disputed corner, earned the hosts a 2–2 draw and a share of the points. Against Fulham, too, the Gunners had struggled to convert their territorial advantage into goals and required a last-minute strike of their own to secure all three points. It was the same story against Newcastle United at St James' Park. For the third game in succession, Arsène Wenger's team had taken the lead only to see their advantage undermined by an opposition equaliser. The game finished in a 1–1 draw that ended Newcastle's run of 11 straight Premiership victories at home, but which also denied Arsenal the chance to re-establish a five-point lead at the top of the Premiership.

There was, however, no reason to panic, and Arsenal arrived at Old Trafford for their FA Cup meeting with United in confident mood. Aside from Freddie Ljungberg, who was injured, Arsène Wenger had a full squad to choose from, though his decision to rest Thierry Henry and Dennis Bergkamp was, to say the least, surprising. Thankfully, and for neither the first nor last time, Arsène knew what he was doing. Francis Jeffers and Sylvain Wiltord played in attack and their effervescent forward play proved a constant menace to the United defence. Brazilian Edu was also promoted to the starting line-up in place of his jet-lagged compatriot Gilberto, who had been away on international duty, and it was former Corinthians midfielder Edu who scored the game's first goal with a deflected free-kick after 35 minutes. This time, it seemed, fortune would favour Arsenal, who had already seen Ryan Giggs blaze over the bar when faced with an open goal. Shortly after half-time the Cup holders extended their lead with a neatly taken goal from Wiltord that concluded the scoring.

'It was a composed performance,' said Wenger. 'We controlled the game from the first minute to the last. This win will give us confidence and belief for the rest of the season.' It was a view echoed by Sol Campbell who added, 'It's not easy coming here. The boss wanted to rest Dennis Bergkamp and Thierry Henry for Ajax [in the Champions League] in midweek. The fans were unbelievable but it's up to us to keep it going.'

EUROPEAN FOOTBALL RESUMES

Arsenal's Champions League campaign resumed on 26 February 2003, and, as anticipated, Bergkamp and Henry were back in harness against Dutch Champions Ajax at Highbury. Sylvain Wiltord, despite his goal against United, was moved out to the wing to make way for the duo, but it was the former Bordeaux striker who opened the scoring after five minutes, cutting in from the right to collect Bergkamp's pass and drive home venomously. Ajax responded 12 minutes later with an equaliser from Nigel De Jong and, though both sides played with great enterprise, there were no further goals.

It was a disappointing result for Arsenal, who had only one more home game left in a Champions League group that was looking extremely tight. The return against Ajax was Arsenal's next European fixture and Arsène Wenger's team warmed up for the showdown in the Amsterdam ArenA with a punishing 5–1 victory over Manchester City. The Champions were simply too strong for Kevin Keegan's City side who found themselves

4–0 down after just 19 minutes. However, four days later in Amsterdam, Wenger's team were unable to reproduce the momentum and attacking fluency that they had displayed at Maine Road. Nevertheless, the point gleaned from a goalless draw against Ajax did at least give the two teams joint leadership of Champions League Group B as February came to an end. The group would, though, take on a rather different complexion when Arsenal drew their next game 1–1 against 10-man Roma on a night of immense frustration at Highbury. It was a result that left Arsenal needing to win their final match – away to Valencia – to be sure of qualification for the competition's knock-out phase.

INJURY WOES

To make matters worse for Arsenal, injuries were beginning to take their toll. Patrick Vieira, David Seaman, Ashley Cole and Sol Campbell were all absent for the Premiership trip to Blackburn Rovers that immediately preceded the showdown with Valencia in the Mestalla Stadium. Arsène Wenger's problems, however, did not end there and after 18 minutes in the match at Blackburn Martin Keown limped out of the action with a hamstring strain. The ever-willing Gilberto stepped into the breach, filling in alongside Pascal Cygan at centre-half, but Arsenal's depleted defence could not withstand the pressure of Rovers' attack, and conceded a goal in each half en route to a disappointing 2–0 defeat. March, like October, was rapidly turning into a month to forget.

The good news for Wenger was that Sol Campbell was fit enough to return to action against Valencia. However, Valencia's Norwegian striker John Carew would be lining up against Arsenal. The giant frontman had been Arsenal's Champions League nemesis in 2001 and two years later he was again the architect of their downfall.

Carew scored the game's opening goal with a shot from the edge of the box after 34 minutes but when Henry equalised with an adroit, curling finish around Santiago Canizares shortly after half-time, the situation looked promising. With Ajax and Roma drawing in Italy, a point would have been enough for the Gunners.

Disaster and Carew, however, were lurking around the corner, and when possession was conceded cheaply to Vicente Rodriguez out on the Valencia left, the Norwegian completed the resultant Valencia attack by delivering the killer blow with a powerful headed goal on 57 minutes. Wiltord and Henry both went close to snatching an equaliser in the dying

moments, but neither could find a way past Canizares. The season had reached its pivotal moment. Arsenal's Champions League campaign was at an end and their lead at the top of the Premiership table had all but disappeared, eaten up by a voracious Manchester United team that was closing in ominously. Nevertheless, the 'Double-Double' was still on.

It was simply a question of perspective. Sure, the lead had dwindled and the European dream was over, but Arsenal were still in pole position in the league while, following a 2–2 draw with Chelsea at Highbury, they were only a replay victory away from the FA Cup semi-finals.

THE ROAD TO CARDIFF

An own-goal from John Terry gave the Gunners the perfect start to their FA Cup excursion to Stamford Bridge. Terry's goal not only settled the nerves but also provided the platform for a confident performance that fully merited the 3–1 final scoreline in Arsenal's favour. March may have been a difficult month but it had at least ended on a high note. Arsenal would now face Sheffield United in the semi-finals as they attempted to reach a third successive Cup final.

Arsène Wenger was in buoyant mood after the victory at Stamford Bridge: 'I'm very proud of the whole team and what they've given in the last week,' said the Arsenal manager. 'We played well in Valencia but needed to keep the energy to beat Everton [in the Premiership three days later] – and tonight is just fantastic. I'd like to say how great the spirit is. The team just want to win every game – and the players give everything in every game and fight for each other.'

Arsenal's spirit was undoubted, but their fortune throughout the season had been variable and confidence appeared to be wearing thin. An immensely frustrating 1–1 draw against Aston Villa at Villa Park did not help matters.

Above: Paul Peschisolido (right) and Peter Ndlovu (centre) look on aghast as David Seaman claws the ball back off the line to prevent a seemingly certain equaliser for Sheffield United in the FA Cup semi-final at Old Trafford in April 2003. Seaman's save was hailed as one of the greatest of all time and was a fitting way for the affable Yorkshireman to mark his 1,000th career appearance.

The home side's equaliser had come wholly against the run of play via a freakish own goal scored by Kolo Toure and with six games to go in the Premiership, the Champions' lead at the top of the table was down to goal difference. It was a scenario that made Arsenal's next Premiership match – at home to Manchester United – take on huge significance. However, ahead of the summit meeting with United at Highbury, there was the small matter of an FA Cup semi-final to contest.

Arsenal were, of course, favourites for the meeting with Sheffield United at Old Trafford. Neil Warnock's Blades with their committed and well-organised display belied their underdog status. It took a controversial goal for Arsenal to secure victory, with Freddie Ljungberg netting after a challenge from Sol Campbell had won possession in the build-up to the goal. An inadvertent body-check by referee Graham Poll on United's Michael Tonge had added to the controversy, and it had also taken a world-class save from David Seaman to prevent a late equaliser for the Blades.

The long-serving goalkeeper had been forced to dive backwards and claw back a point-blank header from Paul Peschisolido with just six minutes remaining. It was a save that defied belief and which prompted England legend Gordon Banks to compare it to his own great save against Pele in the 1970 Mexico World Cup:

'You would have to put this one by David in the same category as mine against Pele in 1970,' said the World Cup-winning keeper. 'The great thing with David's save is that he had his weight all on the wrong foot. He had to shift all his weight on to the other foot and then get right across his goal. Then he didn't just block the ball with his arm, he scooped it away, which was crucial... For any goalkeeper it would have been an outstanding save but at the age of 39 it is quite remarkable.'

Below: On 4 May 2003 Arsenal's Championship defence came to an end with a dramatic 3–2 defeat against Leeds United at Highbury. Here Sylvain Wiltord takes the fight to the Leeds defence.

HIGHBURY SHOWDOWN

Controversy would resonate after Arsenal's next game, though this time both teams would find themselves feeling hard-done-by after Arsenal's eagerly awaited showdown with Manchester United ended in a 2–2 draw. United could point to a degree of fortune in both of Arsenal's goals – the first of which came when Henry unwittingly deflected Ashley Cole's shot past Fabien Barthez while there was a suggestion of offside about the Frenchman's second – but the sending-off of Sol Campbell was perhaps of greater significance. The England defender would be suspended for four games as the title race reached its climax.

Arsène Wenger, however, was in sanguine mood after the game: 'The Championship is open for everybody to take,' began the Arsenal manager. 'At half-time I thought if we lost it would be over but now I think we have a very good chance. You can't say anyone is in the driving seat – we go from game to game now because it changes so quickly. We want to win it and the only way to do that is to give everything to try and win the next game.'

BLOCKED BY BOLTON

Arsenal did win their next game – 2–0 at Middlesbrough – but it was to be their last significant Premiership victory of the season. On 26 April, in the unlikely environs of Bolton's Reebok Stadium, Arsenal saw their title challenge falter in agonising fashion. Victory against a struggling Bolton Wanderers would have taken the Champions back to the top of the table and when Wiltord and Pires gave them a 2–0 lead shortly after the interval, no other result seemed likely. However, with Bolton fighting for their Premiership status, Arsenal faced determined opponents who were willing to fight to the last. With a quarter of an hour remaining, Youri Djorkaeff halved the deficit, and seven minutes later Arsenal were left stunned when the ball glanced off Martin Keown's head and past David Seaman for an equalising goal that was greeted with a collective groan in London N5. Manchester United now had a two-point lead at the top of the table and the ultimate destination of the 2002–03 Premiership crown was in their hands.

'At the moment we lack a bit of freshness,' offered Arsène Wenger after the game. 'Maybe we just want to do the minimum to win games. It is not in our hands and we need some good results. I think we want to focus on us. It is still open but it is not in our hands. I don't think the pressure is telling. It was a lack of concentration on the first and second goals. We should not have conceded those goals.'

Eight days later Arsenal faced a make-or-break Highbury meeting with Leeds United – another team fighting to stay in the Premiership. Manchester United had stretched their lead at the top with victory against Charlton Athletic the day before, leaving Arsenal needing to win their remaining games to have any chance of retaining their crown. However, Arsène

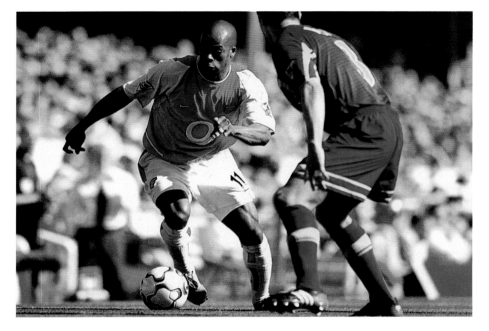

Left: Robert Pires scores the winning goal in the 2003 FA Cup final against Southampton at the Millennium Stadium. It was fitting that Pires should strike the game's decisive goal, as the Frenchman had been forced to sit out the previous season's final after sustaining a serious knee injury just weeks earlier.

Wenger's team, which was without both Patrick Vieira and Sol Campbell, got off to the worst possible start against Leeds when the impressive Harry Kewell opened the scoring with a raking 25-yard shot after just five minutes.

Arsenal responded well enough, equalising through Henry after half an hour, but Leeds again took the lead shortly after half-time courtesy of Ian Harte's deflected free-kick. Arsenal were unperturbed, and when Bergkamp scored a deserved leveller, they surged forward in search of a late winner with Henry going close through a curling shot that struck the foot of the post. Arsenal's pressure was incessant, but as is so often the case in these situations, they were vulnerable to the counter-attack. With just two minutes remaining, Arsenal lost possession and Dominic Matteo released Mark Viduka from a seemingly offside position. The Australian charged forward and struck his shot past Seaman before checking to see that the linesman's flag was still down. It was. Leeds were safe and Arsenal's hopes of defending their title were at an end. Four years later Leeds were in the third tier of football.

Arsène Wenger was quick to congratulate Manchester United on winning the Premiership but he also explained that he believed his team were still the best in the country. 'Over the whole season, if you look at the FA Cup and the Premier League, then we were certainly the best team in England,' said Wenger. 'But in the Championship, United found their form at the right moment and had a consistent run recently. United have won the Championship and we can just congratulate them and say they were the best in the Premiership this season.'

Wenger was in no doubt that the draw at Bolton had been a match of great significance: 'If we had won at Bolton, we would certainly have won the Championship, I can guarantee you that. We had things in our hands at 2–0 up with 15 minutes to go before we lost three players injured and then conceded two goals. It was as close as that. You lose or win on a little thing and, afterwards, you have to accept that everyone will say the difference was big... I feel that we've been unlucky and badly done by recently. We've had difficult games and played against teams who had a real go every time we played them.'

CUP CHALLENGE

The challenge now for Arsenal was to pick themselves up for the remaining two Premiership fixtures and gather some momentum ahead of the FA Cup final against Southampton in Cardiff. The response from Wenger's players was perfect and despite the manager giving several fringe players a taste of first-team action, the Gunners were at their devastating best in both the 6–1 win against Southampton and the 4–0 win at Sunderland. Perhaps the most surprising feature of these two games was that Thierry Henry scored only one of Arsenal's ten goals. The other nine came in the shape of hat-tricks for Robert Pires and Jermaine Pennant (against Southampton) and Freddie Ljungberg (against Sunderland). If nothing else, Henry could at least console himself with the knowledge that he was the undisputed Player of the Season after picking up both the PFA and Football Writers' awards for 2002–03.

After their impressive end-of-season form, Arsenal were unsurprisingly installed as favourites to beat Southampton in the Cup final. The Gunners made a vibrant start to the final, with Henry going close to scoring the fastest goal in Cup final history after good work from Ljungberg. The Swede was himself bidding to become the first Arsenal player to score in three successive Cup finals, but he too would be denied a place in the record books. He would, though, play a major role in the game's only goal, as it was his blocked shot that fell invitingly at the feet of Robert Pires for the Frenchman to fire home neatly after 38 minutes. Chances came and went at both ends thereafter, with the most notable falling to Southampton in the dying minutes. However, Seaman saved impressively from Brett Ormerod and then Cole cleared off the line from James Beattie's header.

The Arsenal goalkeeper spoke candidly after the game, telling reporters: 'We were so determined to win the game today after our disappointment in the League and we knew we would be under pressure until the last minute from Southampton. It may not have been a great final, but we are lifting the trophy and that's all that matters.' It was Seaman himself who raised the trophy as stand-in captain, together with Club captain Patrick Vieira. It was a very touching moment in what had been a long season.

Right: David Seaman shares the honour of lifting the FA Cup with injured club captain Patrick Vieira. Seaman had given a faultless display against the Saints.

THE UNBEATEN RUN BEGINS

For Wenger, the hard work was only just beginning. After the League title disappointment, he had to maintain the players' morale, and strengthen and prepare his squad for the challenges of the coming season. 'The Three Musketeers' – Henry, Pires and Vieira – all signed new contracts, with Vieira, the subject of the usual ill-informed press speculation concerning his future, commenting: 'I've always said I'm very happy at Arsenal.'

Dennis Bergkamp also signed a new, one-year contract. David Seaman, after 13 illustrious and popular years of service with the club, joined Kevin Keegan's Manchester City while Oleg Luzhny moved to Wolves. To replace the iconic Seaman, Wenger bought 6 ft 3 in goalkeeper Jens Lehmann from Borussia Dortmund.

In what was a relatively modest summer of expenditure for the manager – particularly in relation to the many millions spent by rivals Chelsea and Manchester United – he also acquired the services of Philippe Senderos, an 18-year-old Swiss central defender from Servette Geneva; Gael Clichy, an 18-year-old left-back, who had impressed in trials, from Cannes; and Francesc Fabregas, a hugely talented 16-year-old from Barcelona. Clearly, Arsène Wenger was looking to the future.

Below: Van Nistelrooy's penalty strikes the bar and Arsenal come away from Old Trafford with a hard-earned point. It was a gritty display that would emphasise a growing belief that Arsenal was a side that refused to be beaten.

TOURE STEPS UP

The 2003–04 season began with the Community Shield at the Millennium Stadium, Cardiff, where a 1–1 draw was settled 4–3 on penalties in favour of Manchester United. The Premiership kicked off with a 2–1 home win over Everton. The goals came from an Henry penalty and from Pires. Wiltord and Henry shared the attacking role, while Kolo Toure, who had originally joined the club as a midfielder, took over at centre-back in preference to Keown, a role in which the young Ivory Coast player would blossom during the coming campaign.

Pires and the inspirational Vieira were outstanding in the next match, an emphatic and deserved 4–0 demolition of Middlesbrough at the Riverside. Arsenal were 3–0 ahead by the 22nd minute through Henry, Gilberto (the Brazilian's first League goal for the club) and Wiltord, who went on to score his second later in the game.

They kept their 100 per cent record intact three days later against David O'Leary's Aston Villa at Highbury where Campbell, with a second-half header, and Henry, in injury time, scored in the 2–0 victory. 'The side showed maturity,' said Wenger.

They then came away with a 2–1 win at Manchester City despite Lauren scoring an unfortunate early own goal. The three points had been secured in the second half through a Wiltord strike and a Seaman error, on which Ljungberg had capitalised gratefully. Newly promoted Portsmouth visited Highbury in the next game and achieved a deserved draw. A retaken Henry penalty cancelled out Teddy Sheringham's opening goal.

BACK IN EUROPE

Four days later, Arsenal met Inter Milan at Highbury in their opening Champions League game of the 2003–04 season. Although Inter were under strength – missing two key players in Christian Vieri and Alvaro Recoba and fielding Julio Cruz and promising youngster Obafemi Martins – the visitors were 3–0 ahead by half-time. Arsenal's defence had been deftly penetrated by an inventive and mobile Inter side and, to rub salt into the wound, Francesco Toldo had saved Henry a first-half penalty. The final 3–0 defeat was the biggest at home in a European game since Arsenal had lost 5–2 to Spartak Moscow in September 1982. 'We have to stick together and concentrate on our next game,' said Wenger. The 'next game' was against Manchester United at Old Trafford.

A solid, defensive performance by Arsenal, matched by speedy counter-attacking, held out United and the game finished 0–0. Vieira, however, was dismissed by referee Steve Bennett for a second yellow card, following an alleged foul on van Nistelrooy. The Dutchman missed a penalty in the last minute, the ball smacking against the crossbar and, when the game ended, an unseemly mêlée involving several players ensued on the pitch.

The tough fixtures continued with Newcastle United visiting Highbury a week later. A 3–2 win saw Henry scoring his second and the winner with a nonchalantly chipped penalty with 11 minutes remaining. That saw Arsenal move four points ahead at the top of the Premiership.

Lokomotiv Moscow hosted Arsenal in the London club's first away Champions League match of the season and without the injured Vieira, Ljungberg and Campbell, Arsenal achieved a creditable 0–0 draw.

MAKING LIGHT OF THE LEAGUE

Three critical League games awaited in October. With Aliadiere supporting Henry in attack and Vieira absent, Arsenal were 1–0 down to Liverpool at Anfield early in the first half but a Sami Hyypia own goal and a splendid strike from Pires from 25 yards gave them the three points. Chelsea at Highbury were next and, in an open, attacking game, Hernan Crespo scored superbly from 25 yards for Chelsea to equalise Edu's fourth-minute deflected free kick. With 15 minutes remaining, a weak cross from Pires was fumbled by the Blues' goalkeeper Carlo Cudicini and Henry bundled the ball into the net for the winner. Arsenal were now the only unbeaten side in the Premiership.

In the Champions League, however, the situation appeared to be deteriorating. Maksim Shatskikh volleyed the opener for Dynamo Kiev at the Olympic Stadium in the Ukraine in the 27th minute and Valentin Belkevich added another after Shatskikh had taken advantage of a miskicked clearance from Lehmann to feed his fellow striker for a tight-angled but open goal. Henry replied in the 79th minute, converting a Pires pass, but the match ended 2–1 to Dynamo Kiev. Although

Left: An error by Carlo Cudicini gifted Henry a winning goal at home against Chelsea in October. This was a vital result for Wenger's men as the west Londoners were emerging as Arsenal's main contenders for the Championship. It also completed a difficult run that saw a draw against Manchester United and wins against Newcastle United and Liverpool.

Right: Henry leaps for joy as he celebrates his first goal in the San Siro during Arsenal's 5–1 demolition of Inter Milan.

Above: At 16 years 177 days, midfield playmaker Francesc Fabregas became the youngest player to represent Arsenal at a senior level. He played in the Carling Cup game against Rotherham and in the next round he became Arsenal's youngest ever goal scorer during the 5–1 victory over Wolves.

they had played well against Dynamo and had been unlucky to lose, Arsenal now had only one point from their first three European games and were bottom of their group. Arsenal had not won in Europe for eight games.

TRIUMPH IN MILAN

Early in November at Highbury, Arsenal had ten shots on target in their fourth Champions League group game, against Dynamo Kiev, but had to wait until the 88th minute for their diligence to be rewarded when Ashley Cole dived to head the winner from a Wiltord cross. On 25 November Arsenal more than redeemed themselves in the Champions League with one of their finest ever performances in Europe. They destroyed Inter Milan at the San Siro, inflicting a crushing 5–1 defeat on the Italian side. Although Vieri equalised Henry's opening goal in the 32nd minute, courtesy of a Campbell deflection, the second half was all Arsenal. Ljungberg made the score

2–1 on 49 minutes and Inter collapsed in the last five minutes of the game, with Henry and Edu scoring before Pires, capitalising on a fine run and pass from substitute Aliadiere, made it five. No English team had beaten Inter at the San Siro since Birmingham City in the 1960–61 season and this was Arsenal's biggest win in the Champions League. They were now second in Group B with seven points.

In Arsenal's final Champions League game – against Lokomotiv Moscow at Highbury on 10 December – they needed to win to be certain of going through. In a skilful display of attacking football, Pires put Arsenal ahead in the first half from a sweet Henry pass and Ljungberg lobbed the keeper, again from a Henry assist, midway through the second half to give Arsenal a 2–0 victory that won the group for them. Favourites Inter Milan failed to qualify, dropping into the UEFA Cup after drawing with Kiev.

In common with other leading Premiership managers, Wenger saw the League (Carling) Cup as an opportunity to blood and assess some of the younger players. A 9–8 penalty win over Rotherham in the third round at the end of October, after a 1–1 draw, had been notable for the appearance of Fabregas, who became the youngest player – at the age of 16 years, 177 days – ever to represent Arsenal in a first-class game. Then, in the fourth-round 5–1 crushing of Wolves at Highbury in early December, Fabregas became the club's youngest-ever goal scorer.

THE FA CUP RUN

On 4 January Arsenal met Leeds in the third round of the FA Cup and beat the luckless Yorkshire side 4–1; it was the third game in succession between the sides at Elland Road that had ended with Arsenal winning by that scoreline. Aiming for a fourth consecutive appearance in the FA Cup final, Arsenal swept Leeds aside, although an error by Lehmann allowed Mark Viduka to open the scoring for Leeds in the eighth minute. By half time, however, the Gunners were 2–1 ahead, through a beautifully executed volley from Henry and an Edu goal from a Henry centre.

Goals from Pires and Toure, his first of the season, cemented the victory. The increasingly assured Toure, swift into the tackle and elegant in his distribution, was forming a formidable centre-back partnership with Sol Campbell. Vieira was in typically magisterial form in front of the back four. And the attack were not doing too badly, either. 'Some of our passing today was brilliant and the goals were brilliant. We just love to win,' commented Wenger.

By the end of 2003 Arsenal had slipped to second place in the League, one point behind Manchester United – but the Gunners had remained unbeaten and it had only been through dropping points in draws that they had lost their League lead. That unbeaten League run continued in January and by the end of the month the Gunners led the League, two points clear of Manchester United.

Left: Quick off the mark, Henry's alertness pays dividends as his free kick catches David O'Leary's in-form Villa unawares. Arsenal won the match 2–0, a result that saw them go two points clear at the top of the table.

The impressive FA Cup form at Highbury in the fourth round continued with another 4–1 win, on 24 January, this time against Middlesbrough, the highlight being a precocious chip over goalkeeper Mark Schwartzer by substitute David Bentley from the edge of the box. The 19-year-old England youth international came on for the last five minutes and scored his first goal for the club. 'I believe he's a bit characteristic of Bergkamp,' said Wenger.

At the end of January Wenger acquired José Antonio Reyes, a 20-year-old forward, from Spanish club Sevilla. His electric pace, tight control and tactical awareness immediately alerted the Highbury faithful to his potential, although he was unlucky to slice the ball into his own net on his first full appearance, the second leg of the Carling Cup semi-final against Middlesbrough in early February. The 3–1 aggregate defeat was probably not a major concern for the manager, who was focused on more substantial and lucrative tournaments.

Arsenal's winning ways – and unbeaten streak in the League – continued in early February, with three straight victories – over Manchester City, Wolves and Southampton – in ten days. The apparently unstoppable Thierry Henry scored four out of the seven goals in the fixtures and, after the Wolves game, Arsenal had set a new club record of 24 games unbeaten in the top division. By the end of the month they were nine points ahead of both Manchester United and Chelsea.

Arsenal had also disposed of Chelsea in the fifth round of the FA Cup at Highbury. Henry had been injured and Bergkamp had partnered Reyes in attack. Adrian Mutu had put Chelsea ahead with a well-taken, left-footed shot late in the first half but ten minutes into the second period Reyes accelerated from the right side of the Chelsea box to send a brilliant 25-yard drive into the top corner of the Blues' net. Seven minutes later, with Cudicini having been substituted for Neil Sullivan, the young Spaniard scored again, anticipating a clever through ball from Vieira and sending a left-foot shot from the edge of the six-yard box

past the Scottish keeper. Reyes was substituted near the end and received a standing ovation from the home support in recognition of a special talent.

A TALE OF TWO EDUS

Arsenal's late resurgence in the Champions League had taken them into the knockout phase of the competition; a welcome return to tradition by UEFA that meant the last 16 took their chances home and away. Spanish side Celta Vigo, toiling in La Liga, were Arsenal's opponents on 24 February at the Estadio de Balaidos. With Reyes on for absent Bergkamp, Arsenal took the lead early on when Edu scored with the help of a close-range deflection. Ten minutes later, ex-Arsenal player Silvinho sent over a free kick and Celta's Edu headed in the equaliser. In the 58th minute, Arsenal's Edu, perhaps annoyed by his namesake's impertinence, collected the ball on the edge of the area, dribbled past three Vigo defenders and curled an inch-perfect shot with his normally under-used right foot into the corner of the net, with keeper Pablo Cavallero a spectator. It was a magnificent goal by the Brazilian midfielder who had adapted admirably to the hurly-burly and pace of the Premiership and had now demonstrated his talents in European competition. Although Ignacio equalised a few minutes later, a nifty one-two, with ten minutes remaining, between Pires and Henry, resulted in Pires stroking home the winner. Arsenal had won in Spain at last. A relieved Wenger said: 'We found the resources. We never panicked when they came back.'

THE NEW STADIUM

Shortly before the Celta Vigo game, there was good news off the pitch. Not only had Wenger signed a one-year extension to his contract that would keep the manager at the club until 2006 ('Arsène can stay for as long as he wants,' said chairman Peter Hill-Wood), but also the club had finally secured funding for a new £357m stadium. Hill-Wood commented: 'Today is

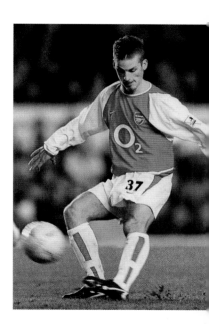

Above: During the FA Cup 4th Round 4–1 win against Middlesbrough a fresh, English talent emerged from the bench to excite the fans. David Bentley scored the final goal, an inch-perfect chip over Mark Schwartzer with his unfavoured left foot.

an historic day for Arsenal Football Club.' Wenger concurred, saying: 'I love the fact that the new stadium is so close to Highbury. It's where our heart is and from a personal point of view I am hopeful of being the Arsenal manager when we move to the new stadium. '

The FA Cup run continued on 6 March with a visit to Portsmouth for the quarter finals that ended in a 5-0 Arsenal victory. Arsenal played some sublime passing football, a fact appreciated by the generous Pompey support. Vieira, Ljungberg and Henry were substituted in the 70th minute and, incredibly, given a standing ovation by Portsmouth fans who, long before the final whistle, were singing: 'Can we watch you every week?'

Celta Vigo came to Highbury for the return game in the Champions League and a silky, assured performance by the Gunners gave them a 2–0 victory that saw them progress into the quarter finals. The draw for that stage of the Champions League paired Arsenal with Chelsea, who had not beaten the Gunners in their previous 16 games. At Stamford Bridge, Eidur Gudjohnsen put Chelsea ahead with an opportunistic shot but, on the hour, Pires timed his jump perfectly to beat John Terry to the ball from a Cole cross and equalise with a header. The game ended 1–1 and although Arsenal had the advantage of the away goal, the return match at Highbury was going to be a nervy one.

In an increasingly crowded schedule, Arsenal next faced Manchester United, now trailing Arsenal in the Premiership by 12 points, at Highbury. Early in the second half, Henry smashed an unstoppable swerving shot past goalkeeper Roy Carroll and although Louis Saha scored in the closing minutes for United, at the final whistle Arsenal had set a new League record of 30 successive games unbeaten in a season; an extraordinary achievement in the current era.

United were again Arsenal's opponents a week later in the FA Cup semi-final at Villa Park. Curiously, in the light of the importance of the game, Henry was on the bench and was replaced by young Aliadiere, making only the seventh start of his Arsenal career. The Gunners nearly scored twice in the first three minutes, Bergkamp curling a shot in from the edge of the box and Edu chipping against the crossbar with Toure not quite able to convert the rebound. However, Ronaldo began to cause Gael Clichy all sorts of problems down the right and it was from the right wing that United scored, Giggs crossing for Paul Scholes to lash in from ten yards in the 32nd minute. Early in the second half Henry and Reyes came on for Aliadiere and Pires, then Kanu replaced Edu with 15 minutes to go. Now playing a 4-3-3 formation, Arsenal made a desperate but ultimately futile attempt to equalise in the dying minutes. It was their first defeat in the FA Cup in 19 straight ties.

In that crucial week for Arsenal, they lined up against Chelsea at Highbury on 6 April for the second leg of their Champions League quarter final, with Henry on from the start alongside Reyes. In a fast, attacking first half,

Arsenal were denied an opener by the Chelsea defence, well marshalled by John Terry, until the last minute when a Lauren cross was headed back by Henry to Reyes who shot home from five yards. In the second half Chelsea's Scott Parker was replaced by Jespar Gronkjaer and Chelsea took up the attacking initiative. In the 51st minute Lehmann parried a fierce Claude Makelele drive but Frank Lampard buried the rebound and, with three minutes to go, Wayne Bridge struck Chelsea's winner. 'We were very good in the first half but we dropped too deep in the second,' said Wenger.

The Treble dream had evaporated within four days but the Premiership was still Arsenal's for the taking. The Gunners met Leeds at Highbury on 16 April and Thierry Henry scored four goals – the first time an Arsenal player had achieved this feat since Ian Wright in December 1991. The highlight was a scorching run from near the centre circle past two defenders to place the ball wide of Paul Robinson for Arsenal's fifth on the night, his 38th of the season and his 150th for Arsenal. He passed John Radford's tally of 149 and became Arsenal's third highest-ever scorer behind Ian Wright and Cliff Bastin. Wenger commented: 'It's difficult each time to find new words for Thierry. Rather than talking about him, it's better watching him'. The unbeaten League run was now an astonishing 33 games with just five left to play.

Right: Henry celebrates scoring his second goal and would later claim his hat-trick as Arsenal come back from twice being behind to beat Liverpool 4–2 at Highbury. The result put them seven points clear at the top of the Premiership.

THE CHAMPIONSHIP AGAIN

By the time Arsenal met Spurs at White Hart Lane on 25 April they were nine points ahead of second-placed Chelsea with five games remaining. Earlier in the day, Chelsea had been defeated 2–1 by Newcastle and the Stamford Bridge club had only three games left in their League season. Older fans cast their minds back to the match between Spurs and Arsenal in 1971, when Ray Kennedy's 87th minute header from a Geordie Armstrong cross secured the League title and the first leg of the Double at the Lane. Three minutes into the 2004 encounter, a clever ball from Henry to Bergkamp on the left was crossed by the Dutchman to Vieira, sprinting through the middle, and the captain slid the ball into the net. Just before half time, Pires sidefooted in his 19th goal of the season. Jamie Redknapp pulled one back for Spurs in the 61st minute with a fine drive from 25 yards and the home team equalised in the fourth minute of added time when, following a tangle between Lehmann and Robbie Keane on the Arsenal goal line, the Irish striker scored from the resultant penalty. But there was never any doubt that this was going to be Arsenal's day and, when the final whistle went, the Gunners had claimed the 13th League title in their history.

Sol Campbell, a stalwart for both clubs in his career, commented: 'This team is fantastic and we can play some great football. But we can dig in as well. There have been times in the season when it was going against us and we dug it out. It has been tremendous.' Wenger said: 'We have won the title without losing a single game. That for me is a tremendous achievement.' To cap the day, Thierry Henry was voted PFA Player of the Year, the first player in the history of the award to retain the honour.

THE NEW INVINCIBLES

It was party time at Highbury for the remainder of the season and in the early summer sunshine on 15 May, relegated visitors Leicester City provided the opposition for the final League match of the season. Leicester lined up in a defensive formation, the sole attacker being ex-Gunner Paul Dickov. Nonetheless, by half time the Foxes were 1–0 ahead, Dickov heading past Lehmann late in the first half. Shortly after the restart, it was 1–1, Henry confidently converting a penalty after Frank Sinclair had tripped Ashley Cole in the box. Twenty minutes later, with Arsenal dominating possession, Bergkamp sent a superb pass through to the overlapping Vieira who skipped past Ian Walker and sidefooted in the winner. It was appropriate that Vieira, the captain and heartbeat of the team throughout the campaign, should seal Arsenal's historic victory.

Arsenal had become the first team since Preston North End in 1888–89 to finish a season unbeaten in the top division and had done it over 38 games against Preston's 22. 'Immortal' and 'Invincibles' were the next day's headlines and the streets around Highbury and Islington the following

ARSENAL LADIES

Established in 1987, Arsenal Ladies FC are the most successful side in the history of English Women's Football.

Under the stewardship of General Manager, Vic Akers, who also doubles as kit man for the men's first team, the Arsenal Ladies team have accrued 34 major trophies, including 12 Premier League titles, 11 FA Cups and a landmark victory in the Women's UEFA Cup in 2007.

Their victory, in April 2007, over Swedish outfit Umeå IK – who were ranked the number one women's club side in world football – in the Women's UEFA Cup final was the culmination of 20 years' hard work by manager Vic Akers, and as the first European trophy won by an English women's team in Europe, a major breakthrough for English football.

The 2006–07 season saw the team sweep all before them, completing an unprecedented quadruple, winning all 22 league matches, plundering 119 goals in the process and only conceding 10.

An emotional Akers, after seeing his side beat Charlton Athletic 4–1 in the FA Cup Final to complete a clean sweep of trophies, described the season as a 'personal landmark', and shortly afterwards it was announced that the entire squad was to be awarded the freedom of the London Borough of Islington for their extraordinary efforts.

John Buckley, manager of Doncaster Belles, admitted: 'I have the coaching badges and everything, but I just don't know how to stop them. They come at you from all angles – I've not seen a women's team as good as them, they are just a different class.'

Their dominance has seen them attract the cream of British talent. 50 cap veteran Jayne Ludlow is captain of the Welsh national side, Julie Fleeting is Scotland's all-time top goalscorer, goalkeeper Emma Byrne is a Republic of Ireland stalwart and Faye White, Katie Chapman and Rachel Yankey are three of England's most capped players.

The Gunners' success is built on a professional approach to training, education and youth development. They are one of the few clubs to run a Ladies Academy and operate a Centre for Excellence for Under 16, 14, 12 and Under 10 levels. They also run soccer schools for 7–14 year olds.

Akers relinquished his role of Ladies First Team Manager in 2009. Now managed by former Birmingham City Ladies Manager, Laura Harvey, the 2009–10 season saw the Arsenal Ladies Team win their seventh consecutive Women's Premier League title.

In 2010–11 the Arsenal Ladies cemented their position as one of the country's leading women's teams with a 2–0 win over Bristol Academy to secure the FA Women's Cup.

The 2010–11 season has also seen the ladies' team take part in the newly formed FA Women's Super League, which runs from April to August.

morning were a blaze of red and yellow as hundreds of thousands of fans celebrated the epic triumph and saluted the team at Islington Town Hall. Wenger said it was, 'The biggest moment since I've been here... I'm very happy and proud of the players.'

It was a hugely satisfying end to a season in which Arsenal had dominated English football. To go through a League campaign unbeaten is the sign of a unique team. It was an achievement that bore testimony to the consistency, flair, efficiency and breathtaking brilliance of the team that Arsène Wenger had constructed.

THE LAST OF THE OLD GUARD

The pre-season of 2004–05 saw two popular long-serving Gunners move on to pastures new. Martin Keown said goodbye to Highbury for a second time when he joined Championship side Leicester City. The defender had left the Club once before, in 1986, as a rookie defender, going to Aston Villa and returning via Everton seven years later. A dyed-in-the-wool Arsenal man, he had served the Club with distinction in his second spell in north London, which ended with a star-studded testimonial in May and his third title medal. Midfielder Ray Parlour was also to leave, heading north to Middlesbrough after thirteen-and-a-half successful years at Arsenal. His wholehearted style and consistent performances had been a large factor in Arsenal's successes during his time at the Club, and his departure finally severed all links on the playing side with the George Graham era.

The significant additions to the Invincibles squad were Robin van Persie and Mathieu Flamini. Rotterdam-born van Persie was the Dutch Young Player Of The Year in 2002. His talents on the pitch were not to be questioned, and Arsenal beat off the attentions of several other clubs – including Eredivisie rivals PSV Eindhoven – to secure his signature in May. France Under-21 midfielder Mathieu Flamini was another highly regarded youngster and arrived from Marseilles with glowing reviews, as Wenger continued to reduce the average age of the squad.

Other squad additions included Spaniard Manuel Almunia, brought in from Celta Vigo as cover for Jens Lehmann because Stuart Taylor's injury problems were leaving the goalkeeping backup in a precarious state at times, and 17-year-old Italian striker Arturo Lupoli from Parma. Francis Jeffers' spell at the Club ended with a move across London to Charlton Athletic on 10 August, but the player who was expected to leave Highbury that week was skipper Patrick Vieira. Real Madrid had courted the France international for the fourth successive close season and on this occasion it had appeared they had done enough to lure him to the Spanish capital. Money – he and Arsenal would both maintain – was not a consideration and after pondering the chance to become the latest Galactico long and hard, he delighted the Champions by deciding to stay. 'This is one of the few occasions in our

sport when money has played no part,' said a relieved and delighted Arsène Wenger, who admitted that he had been resigned to losing his captain, the manager's second signing after he arrived in north London in 1996. 'We did not put any extra pressure on him. He just changed his mind.' Popular Dutchman Giovanni Van Bronckhorst did finally make his loan move to Barcelona permanent, however, resigned to the fact he was fighting a losing battle to get into the starting line-up at Arsenal.

CARDIFF, HERE WE COME

Arsenal's season would begin as it was to end, winning a trophy by beating Manchester United in Cardiff. In August the Gunners put on a vibrant display in the Welsh capital to take the Community Shield, the twelfth time they had won the traditional curtain-raiser, thanks to goals from Gilberto, Jose Antonio Reyes and Ashley Cole, the latter's cross-cum-shot taking a wicked deflection off United defender Mikael Silvestre. Wenger played several youngsters, with 17-year-old Cesc Fabregas catching the eye, in particular, with a remarkably mature 87 minutes before making way for Dane Sebastian Svard. Few could have expected just how big a part the talented Spaniard would play in the forthcoming campaign. In fact, he was to make his League bow – becoming Arsenal's youngest ever Premiership debutant at 17 years and 103 days – seven days later in the season opener at Goodison Park, when Arsenal steamrollered Everton 4–1 as David Moyes' hard-working side looked set for another relegation battle. Like Fabregas, they were to be another surprise package over the coming nine months.

A RECORD-BREAKING START

A week later Arsenal were just 90 minutes from equalling Nottingham Forest's 42-game unbeaten League record but they looked to have blown it when Middlesbrough struck three times in ten minutes either side of the break to go 3–1 up and stun Highbury. Goals from Joseph-Desire Job, Jimmy Floyd Hasselbaink and then a stunning strike by Franck Queudrue had put Boro in the driving seat by the 53rd minute, but right from the restart after Boro's third, Dennis Bergkamp's spectacular strike reduced the lead to a single goal before two in 60 seconds from Jose Antonio Reyes and Robert Pires turned it around in the Gunners' favour. Thierry Henry added to his opener in injury time to put the result beyond doubt.

A comfortable 3–0 midweek win over Blackburn Rovers set a new English League record (beating the long-standing record previously held by Nottingham Forest) of 43 unbeaten games for Arsenal – with Fabregas diverting Gilberto's header in for the second to become the Club's youngest ever League scorer – as they won their first six Premiership games to head the table by the second week of September.

Left: The 3–0 win against Blackburn gave Arsenal a new record of 43 unbeaten games in the Premiership.

By then the Champions League campaign had kicked off with a 1–0 home win over eventual semi-finalists PSV Eindhoven. A 42nd-minute own goal from Brazilian defender Alex settled a scrappy affair at Highbury for Arsenal's first home win over Dutch opposition since they beat Ajax in 1970.

Fabregas, in the meantime, was rewarded with a long-term contract, but the Gunners' 100 per cent record was halted the following Saturday when Bolton took a point from Highbury, thanks to Danish substitute Henrik Pedersen's toe poke five minutes from the end of a pulsating match, and the score ended at 2–2. 'It was frustrating for us because we were twice in the lead,' said a despondent Wenger afterwards.

It was a bad day at the office all round, with Brazilian Gilberto coming off injured with a recurrence of a back injury picked up in the opening day win at Everton. Later it would emerge he had a broken vertebra in his back that would keep him out until April – and at one stage even threaten the popular midfielder's career. Arsenal returned to winning ways a week later at the City of Manchester Stadium when Ashley Cole's smartly taken goal earned them all three points against Kevin Keegan's Manchester City. They also remained top of Champions League Group E, despite Rosenborg snatching a draw in Norway thanks to the magnificently named Roar Strand's 52nd-minute strike cancelling out Freddie Ljungberg's opener.

EMIRATES SPONSORSHIP DEAL

Arsenal rediscovered their fluency when Charlton visited north London on 2 October: Thierry Henry scored two goals, the first an outrageous backheel that bamboozled the Addicks' defence. A fortnight later Arsenal went five points clear at the top of the League with a 3–1 home win over Aston Villa, Lee Hendrie having given David O'Leary's side a third-minute lead before a Robert Pires double and Thierry Henry's goal on

the stroke of half time rewarded Arsenal for a mouthwatering display of attacking football. The unbeaten League run now stood at 49, and the magic half century could be achieved so long as they could avoid defeat at Manchester United eight days later.

In the meantime, Arsenal had signed the biggest club sponsorship deal in English football history with Emirates Airline, in an agreement worth £100m. The Dubai-based company purchased the naming rights of the rising £357m 60,000-seat stadium at Ashburton Grove until 2019. The agreement also included a kit sponsorship deal for eight years from the beginning of the 2006–07 season.

Below: Champions Arsenal beat Manchester United at the beginning and end of 2003–04, a season dominated by Arsenal's astonishing unbeaten League run.

Arsenal's Managing Director, Keith Edelman, was in no doubt of the importance of the deal. 'The sheer size and scale of this is an amazing opportunity for Arsenal – we are delighted,' he said. Emirates chairman HH Sheikh Ahmed bin Saeed Al-Maktoum described the deal as a 'once-in-a-lifetime opportunity ... a win-win partnership.' The deal would see Arsenal receive £72m in instalments before 2012 – vital revenues with the Club's financial commitments at their highest because of construction costs for the new stadium – with the rest coming afterwards.

ALL GOOD THINGS MUST END...

Back on the pitch, Arsène Wenger's side had again blown the lead twice as they could only draw at Panathinaikos in the Champions League, with Ljungberg and Henry – who was skipper for the evening in the absence of the injured Vieira – on target at the intimate Apostolos Nikolaidis stadium in Athens. And so on to Old Trafford, where United were expected to provide the sternest test of the season yet. And so it proved as Arsenal's unbeaten run was finally ended – and, unsurprisingly, it came in controversial circumstances.

Arsenal had started well and Freddie Ljungberg was denied a clear goalscoring opportunity just 18 minutes into the game. Dennis Bergkamp sent him scuttling away with a trademark throughball and as the Swede bore down on Roy Carroll's goal, he appeared to be clumsily bundled over by Rio Ferdinand. Referee Mike Riley saw nothing wrong with the challenge and waved play on. Thierry Henry then saw Carroll deny him with an excellent save but as the game wore on, United's belief grew, and there was more debate when they finally took the lead with just 17 minutes left. Wayne Rooney wove his way into the area and went down under Sol Campbell's challenge. Riley showed no hesitation as he pointed to the spot. Campbell protested long and hard that

he had not touched his England colleague – television replays later backed his claim – but Ruud van Nistelrooy, who had missed a last-minute penalty in the corresponding fixture a year before, placed the ball on the spot and sent Jens Lehmann the wrong way and the majority of the 67,862 crowd wild.

Arsenal had scored in every game of the season so far and needed to keep that run going to earn a point, but as they pushed forward the hosts took full advantage and Rooney settled it in injury time when he slotted the ball home from Alan Smith's low cross. So after 542 days, Arsenal had finally tasted defeat in the Premiership, but having remained unbeaten for an entire season the players could look back with huge pride on a feat that may not be equalled for decades.

The blow was cushioned by the news that Arsène Wenger had agreed a new three-year contract which would see him stay at the Club until 2008. 'I love this Club and I am very happy here,' he said after signing the deal. 'I still have so much to achieve and my target is to drive this Club on, not only by sustaining our recent success but building upon it. These are exciting times for Arsenal and I am proud to be the manager.'

Arsenal did not have long to wait for their return to Manchester, with a side made up of youth and reserve team players showing the future is bright at the Club with Robin van Persie and Daniel Karbassiyoon scoring in a 2–1 win over Manchester City at the City of Manchester Stadium in the Carling Cup.

Arsenal stumbled through the next League game when van Persie curled a fantastic injury-time leveller at home to Southampton to make it 2–2 when Rory Delap's late double had appeared to set the relegation-haunted Saints up for a shock victory after Thierry Henry had given Arsenal the lead. The Gunners' confidence had appeared to be knocked after the defeat at Old Trafford and Panathinaikos came away from Highbury with a 1–1 draw in the Champions League before Crystal Palace earned the same result at Selhurst Park in a game they dominated for long stretches. That draw in south London also saw Arsenal relinquish the leadership of the Premiership as Chelsea moved two points clear at the top.

The young guns offered some light in a dark patch with a thrilling 3–1 win over a full-strength Everton, who were third in the table at the time, in the Carling Cup. A vociferous Highbury audience of 27,791 was treated to a wonderful display. Dutch striker Quincy Owusu-Abeyie was in scintillating form as he scored the equaliser after Thomas Gravesen's eighth-minute opener for the Toffees. Arturo Lupoli hit a second-half double to show his credentials and Everton were well beaten, as they would be again later in the season.

The older Arsenal hands were back in the side for the tricky visit to Spurs, who had a new head coach in Dutchman Martin Jol, and the two sides served up an absolute cracker. The first 45 minutes ended with Thierry Henry neatly slotting home to cancel out Noureddine Naybet's 37th-minute volley –

but the real fireworks came after the break. Lauren's penalty, after Noe Pamarot up-ended Ljungberg, and a sweeping Patrick Vieira finish put Arsenal 3–1 up on the hour, but within a minute Jermain Defoe's superb wriggle, run and shot kept Spurs in the game. Ljungberg made it 4–2 only for Ledley King to head another for Spurs, but Pires seemed to wrap things up with nine minutes to go when he tucked his shot under Paul Robinson from an acute angle. The home side pushed Arsenal all the way and Mali striker Frederic Kanoute set up a grandstand finish with two minutes left on the clock, sliding the ball home after Henry had needlessly conceded possession. The Gunners were mightily relieved to hear referee Steve Bennett blow for time at the end of a game of sloppy defending and breathtaking attacking from both sides.

However, the win against Spurs was papering over defensive cracks and when relegation contenders West Brom left Highbury with a point a week later – courtesy of a late equaliser from sub Robert Earnshaw – serious questions were being asked of the normally solid defence. Many fans had begun to rue the absence of the 'Invisible Wall' that Gilberto had provided before his injury.

Back in the Champions League Arsenal needed all their resilience to scrap for a 1–1 draw at an impressive PSV Eindhoven. André Ooijer gave the Dutch side an eighth-minute lead but Thierry Henry drilled home the equaliser on the half hour, after a cute backheel from Freddie Ljungberg, to restore parity. But things deteriorated for the English side after the break as they finished the game with just nine men. Lauren picked up a second yellow for a foul on Korean Young-Pyo Lee and with twelve minutes remaining ten became nine when skipper Vieira was also shown a second yellow. The remaining men in blue defended stoutly to earn a draw – but PSV didn't care as the result confirmed their qualification to the next phase.

Arsenal suffered their second League defeat of the season at Anfield four days later when Neil Mellor's spectacular 90th-minute strike earned Liverpool a 2–1 win after Xabi Alonso had put them in front before Patrick Vieira's well-worked 57th-minute equaliser. The Carling Cup bid ended at

Old Trafford as David Bellion scored after just 20 seconds to earn the Red Devils a 1–0 win over an Arsenal side with an average age of just 19.

BACK ON TRACK

A run of three home games in early December began with a 3–0 win over Birmingham to stay in touch after League leaders Chelsea had beaten Newcastle 4–0 earlier in the day. The Gunners then sealed qualification to the next stage of the Champions League when they annihilated Rosenborg 5–1 with Jose Antonio Reyes, Cesc Fabregas, Thierry Henry, Robert Pires and Robin van Persie all on target as they leapfrogged PSV to finish top of Group E. Fabregas became Arsenal's youngest ever scorer in Europe at the age of 17 years 217 days – 95 days younger than Stewart Robson when the latter netted in a UEFA Cup defeat at Spartak Moscow in September 1982. Rosenborg manager Per Joar Hansen admitted, 'Arsenal showed us a level tonight we could not really reach.' Arsenal had the opportunity to eat into Chelsea's lead at the top of the Premiership a few days later when the Blues made the short trip to north London. Henry fired Arsenal into a second-minute lead with an immaculate volley but John Terry's header drew Chelsea level. Arsenal regained the lead in the most opportunistic fashion when Henry casually sidefooted a 30-yard free-kick into the corner of the net while Chelsea were still organising their defensive wall. Eidur Gudjohnsen netted Chelsea's second equaliser a minute after the restart but Henry should have won it for Arsenal late on when he blazed over from close range. The performance heartened Arsenal and they went on a four-game winning run, beating Portsmouth, Fulham, Newcastle and Charlton, before an impressive Manchester City drew 1–1 at the first Highbury game of 2005 when Ljungberg's goal cancelled out a wonderful Shaun Wright-Phillips strike that even had the home fans applauding in admiration.

Highly rated Ivorian defender Emmanuel Eboue signed on 5 January and made his debut four days later as the FA Cup campaign opened with a 2–1 win over Stoke, who scored first before goals by Jose Antonio Reyes and Robin van Persie put Arsenal through to the next round. The Gunners suffered their third defeat in 14 League games next – and slipped farther behind Chelsea in the title race – when Stelios' header gave Bolton their first win over Arsenal in 11 attempts, at a chilly Reebok Stadium.

In the meantime, the Club gave a sneak preview of their new home jersey for the final season at Highbury – an unusual 'redcurrant' strip inspired by the kit Arsenal wore when they moved from Plumstead to north London in August 1913. 'This is the proper colour, right from the start of our time here and I'm sure people will like it,' opined Thierry Henry as he modelled the shirt. Dennis Bergkamp's solitary strike gave Arsenal a League double over Newcastle on Sunday 23 January when the Dutchman slipped the ball

under Shay Given for his first goal since August. Kolo Toure would later be suspended for three games after the video disciplinary panel found him guilty of – uncharacteristically – elbowing Newcastle legend Alan Shearer. That week, Jermaine Pennant left Highbury on loan to Birmingham City until the end of the season, a move that would be made permanent in the summer.

SETTLING FOR SECOND PLACE

Back in the FA Cup, goals from Patrick Vieira and Freddie Ljungberg saw off Championship side Wolves before Manchester United's League visit to Highbury the following Tuesday. Whoever lost, it was widely agreed, would be out of the title race. Arsenal opened the game with real zest and took an eighth-minute lead when skipper Vieira rose to head past Roy Carroll. Ryan Giggs levelled ten minutes later with a deflected effort, but Arsenal went into the break leading 2–1 thanks to Dennis Bergkamp's fiercely struck goal. Arsenal's inability to hold on to a lead was to cost them dear, as Cristiano Ronaldo levelled after the break and then, just four minutes later, made it 3–2 to United when he slid home Giggs' cross. Arsenal piled forward for an equaliser and were given further hope when United defender Mikael Silvestre was sent off for head-butting Freddie Ljungberg. They couldn't make the most of their numerical advantage, though, and United condemned Arsenal to their first home defeat in 33 games when John O'Shea hit a fourth from a well-timed Paul Scholes pass with two minutes to go. Arsenal's misery was further compounded as Sol Campbell hobbled off the pitch with an ankle injury that would keep him out of action for two months.

Wenger conceded the title was as good as gone after this game but his side responded by remaining unbeaten from then until the final day of the season, bouncing back with

a 3–1 win at Aston Villa and then a 5–1 St Valentine's Day defeat of Crystal Palace at Highbury, with Henry hitting two on his 200th appearance for the Club.

END OF THE EUROPEAN DREAM

In the FA Cup Arsenal were taken to a Bramall Lane replay after Sheffield United striker Andy Gray's injury-time penalty cancelled out a Robert Pires goal. Arsenal would go through in Yorkshire on penalties after a 0–0 draw. How they would settle for a result like that if they reached the final...

Their European ambitions were dealt a blow with what Arsène Wenger described as their 'worst performance ever in the Champions League' in Bavaria. Bayern Munich won 3–1, but it could have been 6–1, as German keeper Jens Lehmann – up against his international goalkeeping rival Oliver Kahn – was picking the ball out of the back of his net as early as the third minute. Kolo Toure smashed home a late consolation to give Arsenal hope for the second leg but a perplexed Wenger said, 'I'm not satisfied – I am disappointed with the quality of our performance.'

Robin van Persie saw red in the next League match as Arsenal again failed to hold on to a lead given to them by Ljungberg to draw 1–1 at Southampton. Thierry Henry hit a hat-trick – his sixth for the Club – in a 3–0 win over Portsmouth on 5 March as he closed in on Ian Wright's Arsenal goalscoring record. He also netted the winner in the next home match as Bayern were beaten 1–0. The slender win – courtesy of a fine late goal from the France international – was not enough for Arsenal to progress as they went out of the Champions League 2–3 on aggregate and again left many questions about their inability to progress in Europe. 'For me Bayern are the best team we have played in a long time,' said Arsène Wenger graciously.

The FA Cup's importance was growing by the week and Arsenal kept the season alive with a 1–0 win at Bolton in the sixth round. Arsenal discovered their semi-final opponents would be Blackburn, who were slowly turning around a poor season under the guidance of Mark Hughes. Rovers were Arsenal's next League opponents, too, and Robin van Persie's goal just before half time earned the Gunners three more points in the chase for second spot, as they also found some solidity at the back with a fourth successive clean sheet.

CARDIFF, HERE WE COME, AGAIN

An English Heritage blue plaque was unveiled at the former home of legendary Gunners manager Herbert Chapman in Hendon and the great man would have approved the following Saturday as Norwich were steamrollered 4–1 at Highbury, with Thierry Henry returning from injury to fire a hat-trick – his second in successive outings – as Arsenal regained second place in the table from Manchester United. It also saw the welcome return of Gilberto – the largest cheer of

Below: Arsenal's most emphatic result of the season was the 7–0 home win over Everton, which gave them an added boost of confidence for the FA Cup final ten days later.

the afternoon – as he played his first competitive game since September. The Club's 500th Premiership game ended in a slightly fortunate 1–0 win at Middlesbrough, with Robert Pires calmly scoring the goal, before they made the journey to Cardiff for the Cup semi-final. Pires was again on target to give the Gunners the lead and Robin van Persie came off the bench to score a couple of beauties in the final four minutes, sustaining a fat lip from the flailing arm of Rovers defender Andy Todd as he fired home his second and Arsenal's third. Arsène Wenger was not happy with the Lancastrians' rough-house tactics and said, 'Blackburn decided to stop us at any cost – I'm proud we didn't respond.'

... AND AGAIN

Significantly, Arsenal were through to their fourth final in five years and would play Manchester United, 4–1 victors over Newcastle United in the other semi-final. In the Premiership Stamford Bridge was next up as Arsenal took on Champions-elect Chelsea, emerging with a creditable 0–0 draw to give the Blues a timely reminder that Arsenal were not giving up their title without a fight.

Arsenal completed the double over Spurs in the north London derby on 25 April with a goal made in Spain, as in-form Jose Antonio Reyes netted after a great ball from compatriot Cesc Fabregas. Van Persie and Edu – who had announced he was quitting Highbury at the end of the season – scored in a 2–0 win at West Bromwich Albion and second place was secured with a dazzling 3–1 home win over Champions League finalists Liverpool on Sunday 8 May. The Merseysiders would go on to win a thrilling final on penalties against AC Milan having come back from a 3–0 deficit.

But Arsenal were to produce their best performance of the season – and their biggest win under Wenger's stewardship – with a magnificent 7–0 demolition of the other Merseyside club, Everton, who had sealed the fourth spot just the previous week. Van Persie started the rout after eight minutes as Arsenal ran riot with a perfect display of one-touch attacking football. The goal of the game was the third, and came from skipper Patrick Vieira, who clipped the ball over former Gunner Richard Wright after a deliciously weighted pass from Dennis Bergkamp. It was a perfect way for Arsenal to play in red and white for the very last time at Highbury. The League campaign ended with a disappointing 2–1 defeat at Birmingham. Bergkamp netted his eighth of the season, but thoughts were already turning to Cardiff and the eagerly awaited Cup final.

THE KINGS OF CARDIFF

Arsenal were dealt a blow on the Monday before the final when Thierry Henry was ruled out with a double Achilles injury. Arsène Wenger was forced to adopt a new formation, crowding the midfield to deny United space, but it appeared

to backfire as the Mancunians dominated throughout. Paul Scholes spurned an early opportunity when he headed over and Ruud van Nistelrooy did likewise as Arsenal struggled to get to grips with Cristiano Ronaldo and Wayne Rooney. Jens Lehmann, playing his best game in an Arsenal shirt, brilliantly denied Scholes and later tipped Rooney's audacious effort on to the post. Then van Nistelrooy totally missed Ronaldo's pullback with only Lehmann to beat and, with the clock ticking down, Ljungberg stretched his head just enough to deflect the Dutchman's header on to the post.

Van Persie replaced Bergkamp up front and Edu, in his last game for the Club, came on in place of Fabregas. After 120 minutes it was down to penalties, with the drama unfolding at the end of the stadium exclusively populated by United fans. The first two penalties were despatched by either side before Scholes saw his low effort beaten away by Lehmann – surely the first time a German saving an Englishman's penalty was greeted with glee by the Highbury faithful. Arsenal and United traded successful penalties until skipper Patrick Vieira was presented with the opportunity to bring the cup back to Highbury for the tenth time. He placed the ball past Roy Carroll with consummate ease to leave United deflated and Arsenal elated. Arsenal had ended the season with a trophy – and the news got even better as Bergkamp revealed that he was staying on for another year.

THE GOLDEN SHOE

Thierry Henry's remarkable 25 League-goal haul in a season blighted by injury saw him share the Eurosport Golden Shoe with former Manchester United striker Diego Forlan, now of Athletico Madrid. It was the first time a player had won the title in two successive seasons.

PATRICK DEPARTS

Arsenal's final season at Highbury, before moving to the stunning Emirates Stadium less than half a mile away, would be played without the hero of Cardiff and their inspirational skipper, Patrick Vieira. For several seasons media speculation linked the tall Frenchman with a move to Serie A or La Liga, but Arsenal had resisted the temptation to cash in. So it came as a surprise on 14 July 2005, when the Club confirmed it had sanctioned the sale of Vieira to Juventus.

'It was a common decision,' explained Wenger. 'Patrick's and ours. I made up my mind last year that from now on that I would not close the door anymore if he got the right opportunity. There is never a good moment to sell Patrick Vieira. The real reason is that he had given nine years to the Club and you could not stand in his way of a five-year contract at Juventus. That is it.

'We have faced this sort of problem before and every player in the squad respects Patrick's decision. Not everyone in our squad can say he has given nine years of that quality.'

Above: In the first FA Cup final to go to penalties, Lehmann's save of Paul Scholes' kick ensured that Arsenal took the trophy home to Highbury for their last season before the move to Ashburton Grove.

Above: After an exhausting 120 minutes, followed by the tense penalty shoot-out, Patrick Vieira finally gets to show off the FA Cup to the Arsenal fans in the Millennium Stadium.

Above: A striking new look. Robin van Persie's and Thierry Henry's shirts hang in the dressing room ahead of the first game of the last season at Highbury. The redcurrant-coloured tops were designed to simulate those worn by the first Arsenal team to play in north London in 1913. The modern kit proved extremely popular with the fans.

'I'd like to thank the Arsenal fans,' said Vieira, who won three Premierships and three FA Cups in his time at Highbury. 'They have been fabulous. Even recently in the street they were saying "if you are going, then thanks for the last nine years." That is really touching and it makes me feel that I gave my best for the Club.'

Edu also left for pastures new – a sizeable contract offer attracting him to Valencia, while understudy goalkeeper Stuart Taylor moved to Aston Villa and David Bentley departed for Blackburn Rovers.

On a brighter note, Alexander Hleb joined the Club from VfB Stuttgart. The Belarus international arrived with a burgeoning reputation as one of the finest attacking midfielders in the Bundesliga. The only other arrival was former Derby goalkeeper Mart Poom to provide cover for Jens Lehmann.

As the FA Cup holders, the new era without Vieira kicked off with a 2–1 loss to Jose Mourinho's Chelsea in the Community Shield at the Millenium Stadium in Cardiff. Didier Drogba, who would become a nemesis for Arsenal as time wore on, netted twice for the Blues before Cesc Fabregas pulled one back.

Wenger put on a brave face afterwards: 'I am happy because we were consistent, our technical quality was good and our spirit was strong. The result is not too important. The most important thing is not to have any injuries.'

The 58,014 fans who had made their way to Cardiff for the match had seen an entertaining encounter – but it was merely a taster for the two sides' Premiership clash at Stamford Bridge a fortnight later.

THE BEGINNING OF THE END

The last ever season at Highbury, home for 93 years, began with a routine 2–0 home win over Newcastle United, Henry and van Persie netting late on. The game was notable for the distinctive 'redcurrant' jerseys worn by the Gunners, a special shirt to commemorate the last season at the majestic stadium.

Chelsea was next team to be faced in the League in a match that was Wenger's 500th in charge of the Club. Drogba's lucky goal – the ball deflecting off his shin – gave the west Londoners their second win over their city rivals in less than a fortnight. It was Chelsea's first League win over Arsenal for ten years.

Fulham was quickly dispatched 4–1 back in north London, but a second successive away defeat came at Middlesbrough, 2–1 on Teesside. In between Henry picked up a groin strain while playing for France that would mean that he was sidelined for several weeks.

The Champions League campaign kicked off in stuttery fashion with a 2–1 home win over Swiss minnows FC Thun. Gilberto headed the Gunners in front after van Persie had been harshly shown a straight red but Thun levelled within two minutes through Nelson Ferriera.

Time was almost up when ice man Dennis Bergkamp slotted home to hand Arsenal victory – amazingly, it was his first European goal for three years.

Arsenal made it three wins out of three in the League at home with a 2–0 defeat of Everton the following Monday – a rare double for defender Sol Campbell – and drew 0–0 at West Ham to get the title charge back on track.

The most impressive result of the season so far came at Ajax on 27 September, when goals from Fredrik Ljungberg and Robert Pires saw off the Amsterdammers 2–1 and put Arsenal top of their group, ahead of Thun who were surprise 1–0 winners over Sparta Prague.

The unbeaten home run was extended to 13 when Stephen Clemence deflected Robin van Persie's shot, an 81st-minute effort past Maik Taylor, who was outstanding in repelling Arsenal's rampant attack, as newly promoted Birmingham were beaten 1–0.

Meanwhile, despite scepticism from some fans, the brave decision to replace the familiar red-and-white jerseys with the new redcurrant kit for one season was proving a stunning success, smashing all Club sales records. 'We are 30 to 40 per cent up year-on-year in the figures from our Club shop, retail and internet sales,' said managing director Keith Edelman.

'We felt we should do something for this grand old stadium. There are a lot of celebrations going on this season and the shirt is a part of that.'

HENRY BREAKS RECORD

Away from our old home, Premiership form was wretched. Philippe Senderos smashed home his first goal for the Club at West Brom, but the Baggies won 2–1 courtesy of goals from former Gunner Kanu and Darren Carter. 'Arsenal artists fall to artisans,' bellowed *The Times*. But it was all forgotten in the Czech capital three days later when Thierry Henry returned to the bench and wrote himself into the history books.

Jose Antonio Reyes, who was finding his form in a Gunners jersey, lasted just 16 minutes before injury put paid to his night against Sparta, and Henry was thrown into the fray. Chasing Ian Wright's Club record of 185 goals, Henry pulled level and gave Arsenal the lead within six minutes of his arrival when he turned beautifully to send a stunning, swirling drive into the far corner.

But his work was not done, and the ancient central European city was to witness a little piece of north London history when he dummied two defenders and fired past Jaromir Blazek. It was his 186th strike in just 303 games since arriving from Juventus in August 1999. In true English footballing parlance, the Frenchman declared: 'I'm over the moon. Wright is a legend – to beat his record is tremendous!'

Manchester City were beaten at Highbury, 1–0, in the next League game and Henry played his part in a farcical penalty. Robert Pires had already netted from the spot when the Gunners were awarded another penalty.

Pires stepped up again, but at the last minute tried to touch the ball to Henry. The pass was ineffective and was booted away by a desperate City defender's boot, and the two Gallic Gunners were left with egg on their faces!

'Pires was not trying to be disrespectful,' said Wenger, in light of accusations from certain sections of the media. Henry, in a television interview afterwards, simply burst out laughing!

A crowd of 47,366 – attracted by £5 ticket prices – saw a youthful Arsenal side win 3–0 at Sunderland in the Carling Cup, Emmanuel Eboue smashing home the first before a Robin van Persie double. The Dutchman certainly impressed Henry, who was watching from the stands at the Stadium of Light.

'Robin is really confident,' said the Frenchman. 'Without going too far he has everything a footballer would dream to have. Robin can play anywhere he wants. I am not joking, it is up to him and his desire.'

A 1–1 draw at White Hart Lane in the first north London derby was followed by a 3–0 home win over Sparta to confirm the Gunners' place in the last 16 of the Champions League, van Persie again scoring twice late on after replacing Henry. Europe could now take a backseat until the New Year.

November continued with four more wins a 3–2 victory at Wigan being the first three points earned in the League away from home.

Reading was roundly beaten in the Carling Cup, 3–0, while a League win over Blackburn by the same scoreline produced Henry's 100th Premiership goal at Highbury. It was preceded by a minute's silence for Northern Ireland legend George Best, who had died earlier in the week aged 59. There was more sad news with the announcement that former Gunners skipper Joe Wade passed away, aged 84.

December began with a 2–0 loss at Bolton – the first loss in 11 matches – while Wenger rested five regulars as the Club finished top of their Champions League group with a goalless home draw with Ajax as Henry uncharacteristically missed a first half spot kick.

CHELSEA COMPLETES HAT-TRICK

Gilberto was sent off in the next League match for two bookings as Newcastle's Nobby Solano scored the only goal of the game, eight minutes from time, at St James's Park.

And a poor December continued with champions Chelsea securing a mightily impressive 2–0 Highbury triumph, Arjen Robben and Camden-born Joe Cole netting for the Blues, who had now beaten the Gunners three times this season.

Progress was made in the Carling Cup with a 3–1 penalty shoot-out win at Doncaster after a 2–2 full-time scoreline, Gilberto levelling in the last minute of extra time to send the game to penalties.

In the meantime, Arsenal announced a technical partnership with Spanish outfit Celta de Vigo while van Persie was named Barclay's Player of the Month for November.

HENRY NETS NEW RECORD

A return to winning ways came at Charlton on Boxing Day thanks to Jose Reyes netting the only goal of the game, and a 4–0 win over Portsmouth, followed by a goalless draw at Aston Villa, giving the Gunners three clean sheets and seven points from nine going into 2006, which would be a milestone year for the Club.

It began with a lame 0–0 Highbury stalemate with their old foes, Manchester United, while the FA Cup campaign began with a 2–1 win over Cardiff City.

Wigan led 1–0 after the first leg of a disappointing Carling Cup semi-final at the JJB Stadium but back in the League a young Middlesbrough side were ripped apart 7–0. Thierry Henry's hat-trick helped him beat Cliff Bastin's record of 150 League goals for the Club, while Alexander Hleb scored his very first goal for the Club with the seventh goal of the day. Senderos, Gilberto and Pires also netted.

TEEN IDOL ARRIVES

In the meantime there had been several new additions to the playing staff. France Under-21 midfielder Abou Diaby and Togo striker Emmanuel Adebayor both excited interest, but the big news concerned Southampton's highly rated forward Theo Walcott. He was handed the number 32 shirt and said: 'I'm so pleased to be joining Arsenal, a club I have admired for a long time. Coming to Arsenal will give me the opportunity to work with world-class players every day and play football at the highest possible level.'

On the pitch, it was not so good. James Beattie's 13-minute strike gave Everton a 1–0 Goodison Park win while FA Cup interest ended at Bolton with a 0–1 reverse. In the Carling Cup, the Gunners looked to be heading to a Cardiff final on a bitterly cold night after Henry and van Persie put Arsenal 2–0 up against Wigan in the second leg of their semi-final.

But Jason Roberts bundled the ball home in the 120th minute after a defensive mix-up to send the Latics to their first major final. They would face Manchester United. And it got

Above: Emmanuel Eboue (partially obscured) and Cesc Fabregas rush to congratulate Thierry Henry after the Frenchman's goal at Sparta Prague beat Ian Wright's Club goalscoring record.

Above: Cesc Fabregas (right) gets the better of former Gunners skipper Patrick Vieira, in the black and white of Juventus, in Arsenal's 2–0 home win in the quarter-final, first leg.

worse, a 3–2 home loss to West Ham on 1 February. Thierry Henry brightened the mood with his 200th Arsenal goal in a 2–0 win at struggling Birmingham while Adebayor also made his mark with a debut goal.

'It was the kind of performance we needed,' said Wenger, whose side then limped through a 1–1 home draw with Bolton and a narrow defeat at Liverpool.

GALATICOS HUMBLED

But Europe offered a ray of light in a deteriorating domestic campaign. The Gunners had been paired with nine-times winners Real Madrid in the last 16 and travelled to Spain with many journalists expecting a large home win.

Thierry Henry broke Madrid hearts and earned a first competitive win for any English side in the Bernabeu with a stunning individual effort after 47 minutes, skipping past several tackles before producing an outstanding finish past Ilker Casillas for the game's only goal.

'We were not scared,' he said defiantly afterwards, after his goal set up a thrilling second leg at Highbury. Madrid, with 10 wins in 11 matches, was shellshocked.

Arsenal warmed up for the return with a 4–0 Premiership win at Fulham and then finished the job off with one of the most entertaining 0–0 draws that Highbury, or indeed, any English stadium had seen for many a year. Madrid pushed hard throughout and Jens Lehmann made several outstanding saves, but the Gunners hung on for a famous 1–0 aggregate win to set up a quarter-final against Juventus.

HIGHBURY SQUARE

In the meantime Liverpool and Charlton were both beaten at Highbury as the chase for fourth place hotted up – and Wenger revealed he wished to buy an apartment at Highbury when it is turned into a housing development, due for completion in 2009. The Club revealed that 80 per cent of the apartments at the soon-to-be-built 'Highbury Square' development had already been sold. MD Keith Edelman said: 'We have been overwhelmed by the success of the development and would emphasise to those looking to invest in the property market, that this is an opportunity not to be missed.'

Back in Europe, Juve was next to feel the force of the resurgent Gunners; Cesc Fabregas outshone Highbury legend Patrick Vieira on his return to north London with a man-of-the-match display and a goal, as the Italians were beaten 2–0, Henry netting the other. Juve also finished the game with nine men as their suspect temperament surfaced in front of a baying Highbury audience.

'This is what the boys do – and they can get better,' purred Arsène Wenger, who watched his side finish the job with ease with a 0–0 draw in Turin in early April. A semi-final with Villarreal beckoned.

Above: Thierry Henry accepts the adulation of the North Bank and team-mate Jose Antonio Reyes, after scoring one of his three goals in the last ever competitive match at Highbury, a 4–2 win over Wigan.

ARSENAL HONOURS ITS GREATS

Meanwhile, Arsenal fans remembered David Rocastle on 1 April – almost five years to the day he died – by designating the home match with Aston Villa 'Rocastle Day' as part of the Charity of the Season events.

Wenger even admitted he would have made the current side, and the class of '06 did Rocky proud with a thumping 5–0 win against Aston Villa, keeping 67.5 per cent possession into the bargain – a new Premiership record.

Before the Villarreal match, the 3–1 home win over WBA was designated 'Bergkamp Day' in homage to the Dutch legend. Many fans wore orange – the colour of the Netherlands – and the man of the moment, Bergkamp, obliged with a late goal at the Clock End in front of his family who were watching from an executive box. It would be his last goal for the Club.

One banner read: 'Bergkamp doesn't fly – he walks on water!' Meanwhile plans for his testimonial had been drawn up – Arsenal's first game at their new Emirates Stadium would be against his former club Ajax in July.

But before any of that, Villarreal was to be Arsenal's last ever European opponent at Highbury. Kolo Toure, the unlikeliest of scorers, netted the only goal of the game 41 minutes into the contest. It appeared to excite members of north London's wildlife community; a squirrel later appeared on the Highbury pitch to much amusement and a cry of 'Sign Him Up!' from the North Bank, before he scuttled back anonymously into the night...

Arsenal were still in a battle with rivals Spurs for fourth spot and the Lilywhites took the lead at Highbury in the very next match through Robbie Keane, the Irishman controversially scoring after two Arsenal players lay injured on the ground after colliding with each other.

JENS SENDS GUNNERS TO PARIS

But the Gunners were thrown a lifeline six minutes from the end with a neat Henry finish to earn a point and keep Arsenal in close proximity to their old enemy in the League table.

A place in the Champions League final was earned with a 0–0 draw at Villarreal – but it almost went to extra time when the hosts were awarded a last gasp penalty.

Up stepped Juan Riquelme – but Jens Lehmann beat away the Argentine's effort and the Gunners were through. 'I just thank God Jens did it,' said Henry, who in the meantime had been named Football Writers' Player of the Year for a third time. Before a Paris final with Barcelona, Arsenal had to finish the job off in the League – fourth place was a necessity.

A THRILLING FAREWELL

It was all set up for a stunning finale in the last-ever game to be played at Highbury. A win – coupled with a defeat for Spurs at West Ham – would secure Champions League football for

Arsenal the next season, regardless of the result in Paris. Pires fired Arsenal ahead before Paul Scharner and David Thompson put Wigan 2–1 up.

Spurs, meanwhile, were 1–0 down at Upton Park.

Over to Henry, who showed his class with a fairytale hat-trick to earn the Gunners a memorable 4–2 win. West Ham, meanwhile, had scored a second, so the Highbury farewell party could really begin.

A parade of ex-players and a huge fireworks display saw off the old stadium in style – a day none of the 38,359 fans present will ever forget.

As for the hat-trick hero, he was the epitome of professionalism while fans partied long into the night: 'Party? No. I'm going to go home, to chill – and now I'm definitely starting to think about the Champions League Final,' he said.

It even eclipsed the astonishing news that Theo Walcott had been chosen for England's World Cup squad, despite the fact that he had yet to appear in the Premiership for Arsenal.

A NOBLE DEFEAT

An armada of 50,000 Arsenal fans – many who didn't have tickets – headed to Paris for the Club's first ever Champions League final.

On a rain-soaked night, Arsenal's dream looked to be dead after Lehmann was shown a straight red for hauling down Samuel Eto'o. But with Manuel Almunia in goal, and Pires sacrificed, Sol Campbell headed Arsenal into the lead as the Gunners settled.

Now they had to hold out against the on-form side in Europe. It was not to be.

Sub Henrik Larsson's introduction changed the game and he played in Eto'o for a 77th minute equalizer.

Now Arsenal's shattered ten men were on the backfoot and Julien Belletti beat Almunia again four minutes later to kill off the Gunners' stubborn resistance.

Above: Arsenal fans wear either red or white on the last day at Highbury.

Left: Sol Campbell rises to head ten-man Arsenal into a shock lead against Barcelona in the Champions League final in Paris. The Spanish champions fought back to win 2–1.

Arsenal's heart was broken, but the fans and players left Paris with their heads held high after a display of pure grit.

It was so near, yet so far...

'We can be proud,' said skipper Henry. 'We can be so proud. But some of the refereeing was horrendous. We will take this on the chin and come back stronger.'

But would Henry, whose contract was winding down, return for the Emirates move?

After several days of rumour and counter-rumour, the Frenchman opted to sign a new four-year deal and lead Arsenal into a new era.

His reason? The supporters who idolize his every touch:

'We lost on Wednesday [in the Champions League Final] but when I turned to clap the fans they were still there and they clapped us,' he explained.

'In some other countries they would have left or been upset with the team but they understood that on the day we gave everything.'

ARSENAL INNOVATIONS

If they handed out cups for ideas in football, Arsenal would need an extension on their trophy room. The Gunners have been among the most forward-thinking and imaginative of clubs through their history, notably when Herbert Chapman was the manager. Among the many innovations which poured from his fertile mind in those ground-breaking inter-War years: floodlights, numbered shirts, clocks inside grounds, white footballs, physiotherapy and the three-man defence. The ingenuity has carried on through to the modern era, where Arsène Wenger was credited with revolutionising training methods and players' nutrition in British football. The game would be the poorer if it were not for the imagination and foresight dispayed at Highbury and the Emirates down the years.

Arsenal players in numbered shirts in a friendly against a Vienna IX in 1933

Numbered shirts

On 25 August 1928 Arsenal took to the field at Highbury to play Sheffield Wednesday, and they looked like no other football team ever had in the history of the game. Each player wore a number on his shirt. It was the idea of Herbert Chapman, who thought it would make it easier for the paying spectator to recognise the players. The FA did not like the change and ordered Arsenal to cease and desist. They did so – for the first team, at least, but Chapman continued the experiment with the reserve team and in friendlies. But it didn't take long for the idea to catch on. By 1939 the FA had made them compulsory.

White footballs

Ahead of his time, Chapman thought that white footballs would be easier for spectators and players to see, especially on miserable winter afternoons long before floodlights had been invented. His plea fell on deaf ears. White footballs weren't officially sanctioned for use until 1951.

Stadium and pitch improvements

Chapman is credited with numerous stadium improvements, including clocks inside grounds and the 10-yard crescent around the area to help the referee spot encroachment at penalties. Many of his brainwaves had the interests of the paying supporter in mind. Chapman promoted the installation of electronic turnstiles to count supporters coming in, keeping crowd numbers at safe levels. Thanks to Chapman, the club also introduced a public address system, so the ground authorities could pass on information to fans. That kind of communication is taken for granted now, but it was ground-breaking in its day. In the modern era, Highbury groundsmen won numerous awards for the quality of the pitch, and this tradition has been carried forward to the

Emirates, where innovative UV lighting systems and pitch aeration brought the 2009 Groundsmen of the Year award to Arsenal.

Dual referees

Chapman championed the concept of two referees to control a match – one for each half of the pitch. His idea was not followed up in his lifetime, although the FA did sanction an experiment in the mid-1930s. The concept was stillborn – but the notion has gained new support in modern times. Football has become so fast at the top level that some observers claim it has become impossible for one referee to cover the entire field. Chapman's idea has been dusted off for closer examination – nearly a century further on. Little wonder Chapman has been hailed as a visionary ahead of his time.

Sports medicine

Arsenal's first great post-World War Two manager, Tom Whittaker, had been the club's physio, and he brought a new scientific rigour to the treatment of injured players. His medical room at Highbury was more advanced than many hospitals, and it helped earn Arsenal the reputation for treating its players like elite sportsmen. That couldn't be said of every club in an era when the level of sports science at most clubs was rudimentary at best. The tradition for leading the way on the use of science and technology in the conditioning of athletes lives on. Arsenal's training ground at Colney features state-of-the-art equipment and facilities for taking care of injured players.

Broadcasting

Highbury hosted the first-ever live radio broadcast of a football match on 22 January 1927, when Arsenal played Sheffield United. Ten years later, in September 1937, under George Allison, a former journalist, Arsenal staged the first-ever television broadcast of live football – a practice match between Arsenal's first team and reserves. George Allison supplied the commentary. Arsenal, however, had no part to play in these decisions –

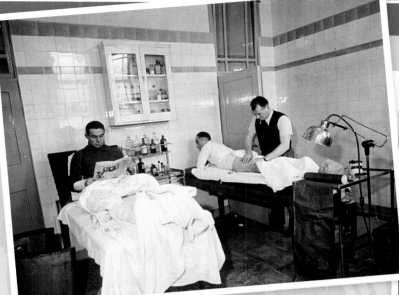

Tom Whittaker treats Wilf Copping in Highbury's up-to-the minute facilities in 1936

The first televised football at an Arsenal training session at Highbury in 1937

their ground was chosen for the test transmissions for no reason other than that it was the closest League ground to the BBC Studios at Alexandra Palace.

Floodlights

Long before their use was agreed by the game's rulers, Arsenal experimented with floodlighting to permit evening football. The move came in the 1930s, when greyhound racing and speedway were attracting large audiences to stadiums in big cities. In the 21st-century football stands alone as the principal spectator sport in Britain. But in the inter-war years, the dogs and speedway were real rivals for the support of the working man. Although Arsenal erected lights at Highbury before the War, they weren't seen by paying spectators until 1951. The first floodlit match was a Boxers v Jockeys exhibition game, followed by a friendly against Hapoel of Tel Aviv.

Continental competition

Highbury Stadium had a long tradition of hosting foreign visitors, often providing the venue for England matches such as one against Spain in December 1931. Long before the European Cup was launched, Arsenal embraced continental competition. In November 1930 Arsenal travelled to Paris to play the first in a series of friendlies against Racing Club. In the process. The Gunners also became the first British club to use air travel regularly.

GPS tracking for players

Arsenal has introduced GPS technology to track the movement of players on the pitch. Although this technology is relatively well-established for matches, the Club is now using GPS tracking in training to provide a scientific analysis of the work-rate of each player as a means of reducing injury problems.

Floodlights at the Emirates: Arsenal pioneered artificially lit football at Highbury

The modern successor at the Emirates to Chapman's famous Highbury clock

CHAPTER 11

ARSENAL AT THE EMIRATES

2006–2011

Highbury, such a proud monument to the achievements of the remarkable Herbert Chapman and his all-conquering 1930s side, was now but a memory as Arsenal prepared for a new era at a new home.

The 60,432-seater Emirates Stadium had risen slowly just east of the old ground and was now ready to house the Club. Highbury, or Arsenal Stadium, to give it its correct title, was now to be stripped and almost virtually flattened to make way for a stunning housing development.

All that would remain to remind future generations of its presence in the borough would be the stunning façade of the old East Stand, along with sections of the West Stand structure.

But on the pitch the rebuilding job would not be quite so extreme. Arsène Wenger was, by and large, happy with his talented squad.

For 17-year-old starlet Theo Walcott – yet to appear in a Premiership game for the Gunners – it had been an unforgettable summer, travelling to Germany as part of England's World Cup squad even though he failed to make an appearance on Sven-Goran Eriksson's misfiring side.

BOBBY LEAVES

Robert Pires, after six years with the Club, departed for pastures new. The Frenchman accepted an offer to play in north-east Spain with Villarreal CF. Arsenal manager Arsène Wenger said: 'He is not only a great footballer but a good man, so of course, we are sad to see him go.

'It's difficult to pick out one or two highlights, but he was superb in our Double-winning season during the 2001–02 campaign and contributed hugely to our unbeaten season with 19 goals.'

Czech international Tomas Rosicky – a Wenger target for more than six years – was finally enticed to Highbury from German giants Borussia Dortmund.

'This is the best club in Europe and I will give everything for Arsenal,' Rosicky said as he surveyed his, and the Club's, new home.

Sol Campbell, looking for a fresh challenge, was also granted a free transfer from the Club and joined Harry Redknapp's Portsmouth.

DENNIS' DAY

The first match at the Emirates, watched by a 54,000-strong crowd of committed Arsenal fans, saw the cream of world football – past and present – join forces to celebrate the career of the legendary Dennis Bergkamp, who had retired in May after 11 years with the Club. Johan Cruyff, Marco van Basten,

Frank Rijkaard, Thierry Henry and Ian Wright were just some of the stars who put in an appearance as Ajax, his first love, was beaten 2–1 by the Gunners. Both sides were allowed unlimited substitutions and it was a special treat for the crowds to see some of the Arsenal and other greats of yesteryear don their boots again.

'It is people like Cruyff and Van Basten who truly love football,' said Bergkamp. 'Apart from being there for me they love the game too, so they want to show that with every opportunity.

'We asked them and they were ready to come over and be here. I showed them a lot of respect down the years and this is how they have paid it back.'

Arsenal returned from their pre-season tour of Austria to kick off the competitive season with a Champions League qualifier against Dinamo Zagreb.

A 3–0 win in Croatia was followed by a nervy 2–1 home victory in the return as the Gunners qualified for their ninth successive Champions League campaign.

The League campaign stuttered into life with a 1–1 home draw with Aston Villa in front of 60,023, Arsenal's largest home crowd for nearly three decades. Olof Mellberg gave Villa the lead before Gilberto saved his side's blushes with an 83rd minute leveller. It would prove to be a taste of things to come at the new stadium.

Joey Barton then netted from the spot as the Gunners went down 1–0 at Manchester City despite missing a host of chances to bury the Blues.

BUSY TRANSFER TIME

Then came a flurry of transfer activity. Notably Ashley Cole, whose actions in talking to Chelsea had alienated Arsenal followers the previous year, finally got his move across London.

William Gallas, the France defender, moved in the opposite direction while Wenger did a straight loan swap with Real Madrid, trading a discontented Jose Reyes with Julio Baptista.

Defender Pascal Cygan, 32, also joined Robert Pires at Villarreal, when he secured a two-year contract with the 'Yellow Submarine' after four successful years at Highbury.

As things settled down off the pitch, on it Arsenal were still struggling to find their best form, only scraping a 1–1 home draw with Middlesbrough, Thierry Henry levelling matters after James Morrison neatly swept the Teessiders into a first half lead.

ADEBAYOR COMES TO THE FORE

As in the previous season, it was the Champions League that finally kickstarted Arsenal's season. A 2–1 win at big-spending SV Hamburg – Tomas Rosicky netting his first goal in red and white – was a huge confidence boost going into the first meeting with a title rival, Manchester United away.

Thierry Henry's foot injury ruled him out so it was down to Emmanuel Adebayor to shoulder the attacking burden. Adebayor won the Gunners a 13th minute penalty after he was hauled down by United's stand-in goalkeeper Tomasz

Right: Brazilian midfielder Gilberto is flanked by Kolo Toure and Alexander Hleb after scoring the equaliser against Aston Villa in the first ever League match at the new stadium.

Kuszczak but Gilberto, skipper in Henry's absence, saw his spot-kick saved by the rookie custodian. Arsenal, however, were dominating with Cesc Fabregas enjoying the freedom of the midfield and with just four minutes remaining he forced an error from Cristiano Ronaldo and found Adebayor who found space to squeeze the ball home. 1–0 to the Arsenal!

ARSÈNE CELEBRATES A DECADE

New boy Gallas netted the opener as Sheffield United succumbed 3–0 at the Emirates in a week that saw Wenger celebrate ten years at the helm.

It had been a decade since newspapers asked 'Arsène who?' on their back pages, but after three titles and three FA Cups, his impact on English football has been mighty. And there was surely more to come.

Fredrik Ljungberg paid tribute to his boss: 'I wasn't here when he joined, but if I remember rightly, when he arrived Arsenal weren't doing that great and they were not at the top

Below: Emmanuel Adebayor escapes the attentions of Wes Brown to poke the ball past Tomasz Kuszczak for the only goal at Old Trafford.

of the table but in his first full season in charge they won the Double. So he turned it around quickly and since then we've had great success. He's done brilliantly.'

Three more wins followed as the Gunners cemented their place at the top of Champions League G.

Charlton were beaten 2–1 away while newly promoted Watford had no answer at Emirates, losing 3–0.

MIXED EUROPEAN FORTUNES

Champions League 2004 winners Porto were also beaten in between, 2–0 in north London, thanks to goals either side of the break from Thierry Henry and Alex Hleb. For Henry, his neat far-post header was his 50th European goal for the Club.

'It's quite a haul and really he doesn't play only to score goals,' commented Wenger on Henry's achievement.

'It was a tremendous performance tonight and the numbers don't lie.'

Henry was not so happy in his next European encounter, a 1–0 loss at CSKA Moscow. Trailing to Daniel Carvalho's first-half free-kick, Henry looked to have equalized late in the second half only for the referee to rule the goal out for handball. To add to Henry's anger – clearly he had not handled the ball – he was booked for his 'actions'.

'If anyone sees me handle the ball on the TV replay then they should come and tell me,' stated Henry.

ROYAL VICTORIES AND APPOINTMENTS

It ended a six-match victorious run but the Gunners would get back to winning ways in the next game with a 4–0 thumping of Reading in Berkshire and followed that up with a 2–0 defeat of West Brom at the Hawthorns in the Carling Cup thanks to a Jeremie Aliadiere brace. After the Reading win, a contented Cesc Fabregas said: 'Our type of game makes me feel so happy, and when I go home I can relax and enjoy it on the television because all of our goals today were great goals.'

On 26 October 2006 Prince Philip, the Duke of Edinburgh, officially opened the new Emirates Stadium, deputising for the Queen who was not well enough to attend.

STARS SHOW COMMITMENT

Further good news came when Kolo Toure, Johan Djourou and Cesc Fabregas all revealed they had committed their long-term futures to the Club. Fabregas signed a new eight-year deal – the longest in Premiership history – while Djourou and Toure put pen to paper on six-year contracts.

Two home draws followed: 1–1 with Everton and 0–0 to CSKA Moscow in a game which Arsenal should have scored six goals.

'Sometimes you can try as hard as you like and the ball will just not go in,' lamented Gael Clichy after the Moscow match.

A bad-tempered match at West Ham was settled by Marlon Harewood as the Hammers won 1–0. A touchline spat with home manager Alan Pardew would later cost Wenger a £10,000 FA fine.

Emmanuel Adebayor sent the Gunners through to the Carling Cup quarter-finals with the winner at Everton and the other Merseyside giants, Liverpool, were then beaten 3–0 at Emirates in the Premiership after goals from the French-speaking triumvirate Mathieu Flamini, Kolo Toure and William Gallas.

Meanwhile, Arsenal legend Liam Brady was, finally, inducted into the National Football Museum Hall of Fame, while another Irish Arsenal player, young Dubliner Anthony Stokes, shot to the top of the Scottish Premier League scoring charts with a flurry of goals on loan at Falkirk. He would later move to Roy Keane's Sunderland in the transfer window for £2m.

November ended poorly, with League losses at Fulham and Bolton, although a 3–1 home win over Hamburg meant a point in the final game at Porto would seal qualification to the Champions League last 16.

DERBY DELIGHT

Directly before the trip to Portugal, Tottenham made their first ever visit to the Emirates and were steamrollered 3–0. A sciatic nerve injury sidelined Henry but his replacement, Adebayor, was in mischievous mood and slotted home a 20th minute opener before a pair of Gilberto penalties either side of the interval earned a welcome three points.

'It was vital for us to win, because we were a little bit backs-to-the-wall,' said Wenger. 'If you lose at home today against Tottenham, you couldn't have a worse preparation before you go to a game like Porto.'

Porto were hoping for revenge for their defeat by the Gunners the previous month but Arsenal ditched the beautiful game for some ugly defending and earned the point that put them through.

Left: Julio Baptista wheels away in delight after scoring in the 6–3 Carling Cup win over Liverpool on 9 January 2007. The Brazilian netted four times – and missed a penalty! – on a stunning night at Anfield.

A 0–0 draw was welcomed by even a purist such as Arsène Wenger, and after finishing top of Group G ahead of Porto the relieved Frenchman commented: 'Now we can put the Champions League into the cupboard until February and focus on the Premiership.'

In their next league game, Arsenal were just six minutes from smashing Chelsea's unbeaten home record, courtesy of Mathieu Flamini's opener, before Michael Essien curled a stunner past Jens Lehmann at Stamford Bridge to earn the champions a point.

The draw meant Arsenal had lost just five times in the previous 50 London derbies.

Arsenal, though, had shown more of that mental toughness displayed in Portugal and took four points from their next two games – against Wigan and Portsmouth – before hammering Blackburn 6–2 at Emirates.

YOUNG GUNS FIRE

The year 2006 ended with contrasting away results. A 2–1 Boxing Day win away at Watford was followed on 30 December with a 1–0 loss at Sheffield United, after Christian Nade turned Kolo Toure with ease and curled the ball past Jens Lehmann.

The early weeks of 2007 would bring a series of stunning results with the Young Guns taking centre stage. Thierry Henry returned from injury to score the first in a 4–0 thumping of relegation-haunted Charlton. That was followed by a 3–1 FA Cup win at Liverpool, with Tomas Rosicky netting two as his confidence visibly soared.

Above: Julio Baptiste was a revelation in the Carling Cup run. After scoring four at Liverpool he netted twice at Tottenham in the semi-final, including this strike.

Arsenal were rattled, but responded magnificently with Aliadiere restoring the advantage on 105 minutes and Pascal Chimbonda putting through his own net to seal a 5–3 aggregate win for the Gunners – and a place in the final where they would meet Chelsea.

BRAZIL BETTERED

The international spotlight fell on the Emirates on 6 February when Brazil and Portugal locked horns. A 60,000 sell-out crowd saw the Portuguese triumph 2–0. Wenger also took time to defend his multi-national selection policy. 'Whenever England do not win it is always my fault,' he joked, 'even when I am not at the game.'

'To put players in my team who are not good enough would not strengthen the England team but weaken the Arsenal team. We are in a world where you have to be good enough. If England want to beat Brazil then an English player who comes to Arsenal has to be stronger than the Brazilian. If you are not good enough you won't beat Brazil!'

The Gunners, with youngsters Alex Song, Theo Walcott and Denilson starting, then returned to Anfield three days later in the Carling Cup – and came out on top in a nine-goal thriller.

Julio Baptista, also making a rare start, was rampant with a four-goal haul and could even afford a penalty miss as the Kop was stunned by Arsenal's astonishing 6–3 win.

It was the Gunner's first League Cup win at Anfield and Liverpool's heaviest home defeat since the 1929/30 season, when Sunderland scored six without reply.

Wenger said: 'It is a very satisfying night. I feel there is a continuity there inside the Club. We feel we have worked very, very hard and we feel the future of the Club is very promising. If we keep the players together and the spirit is right there is a chance for the future.'

Another win in the north-east arrived shortly after, 2–0 at Blackburn Rovers in the Premiership, before the visit of table-topping Manchester United. Wayne Rooney headed the visitors into a second half lead but Robin van Persie levelled – breaking his foot in the process, an injury that would sideline him for the rest of the season – and then, in a grandstand finish, Henry headed a super winner past Edwin van der Sar in stoppage time.

Lauren, the long-serving Cameroon defender, was granted permission to join Portsmouth with Wenger admitting he had lost a 'fantastic player'.

In the Carling Cup, the Gunners fought back from 2–0 down to earn a draw at Spurs, with Anfield hero Baptista netting three times – including an own goal for the homeside.

A 1–1 home draw in the FA Cup with Bolton – Arsenal would win the replay 3–1 – was followed by the Carling Cup return. Adebayor slotted the ball under Paul Robinson for the opening goal but Mido took the tie to extra time with a close-range header.

CARLING FINAL LEAVES A BITTER TASTE

Theo Walcott gave Arsenal the lead in the Carling Cup final with his first goal for the Club, but a Didier Drogba double gave Chelsea the trophy. Wenger opted to leave out many of his experienced players, a policy he defended rigorously.

A mass brawl at the end of the match saw Emmanuel Eboue, Kolo Toure and Chelsea's John Obi Mikel all shown red cards. But the Gunners had, for many, been the better side playing some really wonderful football – but the Blues took the silverware.

DUTCH DISASTER

FA Cup interest ended the next week with a 1–0 replay defeat at Blackburn, following a 0–0 home draw earlier in the month, before PSV came to north London. The Dutch side had already won their Champions League first leg 1–0 in the Netherlands but the tie was levelled after 58 minutes of the return when Brazilian defender Alex put through his own net. Arsenal poured forward for a second, but seven minutes from the end Alex went up the other end and headed a stunning equalizer to send Arsenal out. To compound matters, groin and stomach strains were to end Henry's season – his least productive for the Club.

'All credit to PSV,' said Fredrik Ljungberg. 'They are a good side but we should still have won the game and gone through.

'We had opportunities to kill off the game and had them on the brink of defeat. But we didn't and eased off a bit. When they equalized with five minutes to go, it killed the game.'

Arsenal's season was all but over in the middle of March. A surprise 1–0 win at Aston Villa was followed by defeats at Everton and Liverpool.

The poor form continued when West Ham became the first visiting side to win at Emirates. Bobby Zamora netted the only goal (despite Arsenal having 30 shots to the visitor's 2), a neat lob over Lehmann, to add impetus to the Hammers relegation escape – and secure the Double over their London neighbours.

LADIES FLY THE FLAG

Arsenal's Ladies, however, were having the season to end all seasons. Already winners of the League Cup, they regained the title – for the fourth successive season – winning all 22 games and then won the FA Cup for a domestic treble.

But, most impressively, they also became the first English side to win the coveted Uefa Womens' Cup. A 1–0 first leg win at Swedes Umea IK, courtesy of a late Alex Scott strike, set up a thrilling second leg in Boreham Wood.

The Gunners held on 0–0 in the return to secure the trophy to help manager Vic Akers celebrate 20 years at the helm.

ARSENAL END SEASON ON A HIGH

The men were finally finding their form in the League as they looked to hold on to fourth place. Successive April home wins over Bolton and Manchester City – Cesc Fabregas scoring in both games – virtually assured fourth spot, while they came close to winning at Spurs before Jermaine Jenas levelled in injury time to end the game 2–2.

There was one final day of drama at Emirates when Chelsea visited north London needing victory to stay in touch with leaders Manchester United. Gilberto gave Arsenal the lead with a 43rd minute penalty after Khalid Bhoularouz hauled down Julio Baptista. The Chelsea defender was shown a red card and, with it, his side's title hopes were left in tatters.

The ten Chelsea men fought back well and Michael Essien levelled 20 minutes from the end, but it was too little, too late, and the title had gone north to Manchester.

For Arsenal, a fourth place finish meant a second successive trophyless season – but qualification for a tenth successive Champions League campaign went some way to alleviating the fans' frustrations at a lack of silverware.

OFF TO A FLIER

The League campaign began spectacularly. Inside the first minute of the opener against Fulham at the Emirates, Gael Clichy sent a seemingly straightforward back-pass to Jens Lehmann. However, the German slipped as he attempted to return the ball to Clichy, and David Healy pounced to put the visitors ahead. The season was less than a minute old.

In the final 10 minutes of the match, goals from van Persie and Hleb sealed a deserved victory for the Gunners who were in battling spirit. The team entered into a celebratory huddle at full time, and a powerful sense of self-belief and invincibility filled the air.

Another van Persie goal secured a point at Ewood Park after a scrappy encounter with Blackburn Rovers. By this time, the team's Champions League campaign had kicked off in the shape of a qualifying tie away to Sparta Prague. After a testing opening half, the visitors won thanks to goals from Cesc Fabregas and Alexander Hleb. The Gunners sailed through to the Group stages after winning the return leg 3–0 in front of an appreciative home audience.

Back in the Premier League, Wenger's boys were proving formidable, with commentators noting a new-found confidence among the youngsters. This was apparent in none more than Fabregas. The Spaniard was in fine form, scoring in four consecutive Arsenal league victories.

Among these wins were a 10-man home triumph over Portsmouth after Philippe Senderos had seen red, and a storming performance at White Hart Lane. At half-time, Tottenham were 1–0 ahead and looked set to record their first

Left: Theo Walcott, the most expensive teenager in British football, finally broke his duck in red-and-white when he gave the Gunners a first-half lead against Chelsea in the Carling Cup final. Chelsea eventually ground out a 2-1 after extra time – but not before Arsène Wenger's youngsters had dominated large swathes of an entertaining match.

Below: A late goal from Henry secured a win over Premiership leaders Manchester United. Eboue sent in a cross and Henry was free to header a super winner past Edwin van der Sar to the delight of Arsenal fans.

Above: Cesc Fabregas reels away after scoring a stunning goal in the 3–1 victory over Spurs at White Hart Lane. The Spanish midfield star had a blistering start to the 2007–08 season, netting seven times in his first nine matches.

Right: Eduardo nets during an impressive 3–0 victory over Sevilla in the Champions League. The Croatian forward began to command a regular first team place in 2007–08 as well as plaudits from the Emirates faithful before his season was painfully curtailed by a nasty injury.

victory against Arsenal for eight years. However, Fabregas's long-range pile-driver and a brace from Emmanuel Adebayor turned the tide for Arsenal.

ABSOLUTELY FABREGAS

Four days later on 19 September, Arsenal faced Sevilla in a game billed as a clash between European football's two most fluid sides. After a tame start, Arsenal won the 'battle of the breathtakers' 3–0 with van Persie and Eduardo joining the newly prolific Fabregas on the scoresheet.

The young Spaniard was winning widespread plaudits for his goal-scoring run, and his influential performances in general. Arsène Wenger offered a particularly gratifying comparison: 'His vision is comparable to Michel Platini, and that is a compliment. He is at the start of his career and we know that Platini has finished his. Cesc has it all in front of him, but he has a vision and he will develop still more.'

The visionary Fabregas was again among the goalscorers as Arsenal thrashed Derby County 5–0 at the Emirates. However, it was Adebayor's hat-trick that was the story of an afternoon that saw the Gunners go four points clear at the top of the table.

Life without Henry was not proving as hopeless as many commentators had predicted. Having brushed aside Derby, the Gunners had to fight tooth and nail in their next Premiership tie at West Ham, but emerged 1–0 victors, their first win at Upton Park for seven years.

Arsenal Holdings plc then announced their financial results for the year ending 31 May 2007. It made highly satisfactory reading, with Group turnover and operating profit at record levels.

Non-executive chairman Peter Hill-Wood welcomed the results. 'The best way that Arsenal can continue to deliver success is by maintaining a business that pays its own way,' he said. 'This philosophy helped establish our objectives for the Club's move away from Highbury, and Emirates Stadium now provides Arsenal with the increased income, profitability, cash generation and firm financial foundations from which we will continue to build trophy winning Arsenal teams for many years to come.'

This good news for the Gunners was quickly complemented by signs of a rosy future on the pitch, when an Arsenal side with eight changes from the Derby County line-up beat a more-or-less full-strength Newcastle United side in the Carling Cup. Could a second-string Arsenal team go all the way to the competition's final once again?

SEVEN AGAINST SLAVIA

The first action in October came in the Champions League with a visit to Steaua Bucharest. It was a somewhat fraught tie, but van Persie's fifth goal of the season secured the side's ninth straight victory in all competitions. As at West Ham, Wenger's side showed they could scrap, as well as sail to victory. They were sitting pretty at the top of both the Premier League and Group H tables.

In the same month, newly promoted Sunderland were beaten 3–2 at the Emirates, and the Gunners also prevailed in front of their own fans over Bolton Wanderers, with Kolo Toure and Tomas Rosicky on the scoresheet.

Then came one of the season's most memorable nights. The Gunners demolished Slavia Prague 7–0 in a tie that saw Theo Walcott truly come of age as an Arsenal player. He scored twice, and was only prevented from completing a deserved hat-trick due to an extraordinary save by Martin Vaniak. Fabregas also netted twice.

The supporters had thoroughly enjoyed the evening. So, too, had Arsène Wenger: 'It is a joy to watch. Overall there is a happiness in the team to play together, to play a mobile, technical game and we certainly did that well tonight.' The result was just the confidence boost the Gunners needed, as next on the horizon for them were Premier League ties with Liverpool and Manchester United.

Both matches were inevitably seen as the biggest tests to date for Arsenal's title ambitions. At Anfield on 28 October, Steven Gerrard's early free-kick looked to have won the game, but in the 80th minute Fabregas levelled for the visitors.

That draw saw Arsenal return to the top of the table, thanks to their superior 'goals scored' tally over their next Premier League opponents – Manchester United.

In that clash, Arsenal again finished level with their opponents and once more left it late to do so. United took the lead on half-time, when Gallas accidentally converted a Ronaldo cross. Then, in injury time – after Fabregas and Ronaldo had scored for their respective teams – Gallas was on target at the right end, slamming a volley home to secure a 2–2 draw.

In the same week, the Gunners continued to make progress in the Carling Cup, with Eduardo scoring twice in a 3–0 victory over Sheffield United. However, when the Gunners returned to Champions League action, it was another draw, a goalless one at Slavia Prague. Nonetheless, this was enough to guarantee their progress into the knockout stages of the competition. A reverse against Sevilla and a victory over Steaua Bucharest at home completed the group phase.

DIVERGING DERBIES

Domestically, the Gunners returned to their fine league form with three successive victories. The first was over Reading – where Adebayor scored the Club's 1,000th goal in Premier League football – followed by wins against Wigan Athletic and Aston Villa. Adebayor's goal against Reading came after some fine interplay between Fabregas and Rosicky, drawing praise from the manager: 'It's a special one because it's the 1,000th one, but also because it's a special quality one,' said Wenger. 'It's how we like to play the game and it was certainly the best moment of the game.'

Then came two matches in four days in the north-east, where Arsenal drew 1–1 with Newcastle United but then suffered their first league loss of the season, at Middlesbrough.

Another encounter seen as a signpost for Arsenal's league ambitions was the visit of Chelsea. William Gallas capitalised on a Petr Cech error and slammed home a header on the stroke of half-time.

Six days later came another London derby at Emirates, this time against Tottenham Hotspur. With the score at 1–1, Almunia saved a Robbie Keane penalty. Wenger then sent on Nicklas Bendtner for Emmanuel Eboue, and the substitute duly scored the winner with his first touch.

That completed the league double over Tottenham, but the Gunners had not seen the last of them. Thanks to their 10-man, extra-time win at Blackburn Rovers in the Carling Cup, they would face their rivals again in the semi-final of that competition. A goalless draw with Portsmouth and a 4–1 victory over Everton – with Eduardo scoring twice to cap a fine comeback after the Gunners had fallen behind – completed 2007's Premier League business for Arsenal.

With January came the FA Cup third round, and Wenger's side won comfortably at Burnley thanks to goals from Bendtner and Eduardo, who notched his sixth goal in four starts for the Club. Later in the month, Newcastle United were dispatched 3–0 in the fourth round with Adebayor finding the net twice.

Between these FA Cup ties, the Gunners had faced Tottenham in the two legs of the Carling Cup semi-final. Theo Walcott was on target in the first leg at the Emirates, which ended tantalisingly at 1–1. However, two weeks later at White Hart Lane, the Gunners lost 5–1 and missed the chance to reach the final for the second successive season. It was the first time Spurs had beaten Arsenal in the 21st Century.

ADEBAYOR KEEPS ON SCORING

In the Premier League, Arsenal were experiencing far more joy. West Ham United had proved to be a bogey side of late. They were the last team to beat Arsenal at Highbury, and were the first visitors to prevail at the Emirates, too. However, in January the Hammers found themselves on the wrong end of a 2–0 defeat.

At Craven Cottage, Rosicky was among the scorers as Fulham were beaten 3–0, and Newcastle United were beaten by the same scoreline. The only blot on an otherwise perfect Premiership month was a draw with Birmingham City at the Emirates. A subsequent encounter with the Midlanders would soon cast another shadow over the Gunners' league ambitions.

Above: Arsenal equalled the highest margin of score for a Champions League game by thrashing Slavia Prague 7–0. Both Walcott and Fabregas netted twice with Bendtner, Hleb and an own goal making up the record result. It also equalled Arsenal's own highest score in Europe – Standard Liège had suffered a similar fate at the start of Arsenal's successful 1993–94 Cup Winners Cup campaign.

Above: Nicklas Bendtner steps off the bench to head home the winner from close range in a pulsating North London Derby. It was the Dane's first touch of the ball and gave Arsenal the double over Spurs.

Below: The most impressive result of the 2007–08 season was the 2–0 win at the San Siro against AC Milan. It was the Italians' first ever defeat at home by English opposition. This goal by Adebayor, following a Fabregas strike eight minutes earlier, rounded off a well-deserved win.

A brace of Adebayor goals helped Arsenal to a resounding victory at Manchester City and back to the top of the Premier League. Asked what was behind the Togolese striker's fine form, Wenger said that a special spirit at the Club was partially responsible.

'But it is down to his talent and dedication as well,' added the Frenchman. 'Before he signed for us there was a question mark about Adebayor – his attitude and his spirit. Did we change him or did he realise he had wasted enough time already? I don't know.'

Adebayor was again on target in the hard-fought 2–0 home victory over Blackburn Rovers. The visitors' resilience had been immense, and the fact the Gunners overcame it had the fans dreaming that this could be a title-winning campaign once more.

In February, with the team's exit from the FA Cup following a disappointing 4–0 fifth-round defeat at Old Trafford, the league fortunes assumed even greater significance. Then came a match that would prove to be one of the season's most memorable – for all the wrong reasons. Just three minutes into the Premier League clash at Birmingham City, Eduardo was caught on his left ankle by Martin Taylor. After nine minutes of treatment on the pitch, he was stretchered off with an oxygen mask on his face. It was later confirmed he had broken his leg.

EDUARDO'S INJURY HAS AN IMPACT

Asked if Eduardo's injury affected his team's performance on the day, Wenger was unequivocal: 'Yes 100 per cent. You could see that straight away it had a big effect.' Despite Theo Walcott netting twice – the first strike being his debut Premier League goal – the Gunners had to settle for a single point due to a controversial injury-time penalty from James McFadden. The team's disappointment at the final whistle was palpable to all observers.

As for Eduardo, he remained positive. 'All I remember is that when I fell, I looked down at my foot and it had turned the other way,' he said. 'The rest is just a blank. It was an unfortunate situation but these things can happen in football. I am determined to overcome this injury.' The Croatian international had suffered a horrific injury, and the Gunners' title bid was also to suffer in the wake of this tie. It would be 35 days before they next tasted Premier League victory.

Could the Champions League prove happier terrain? With holders AC Milan their opponents in the second round, this would be a telling test for Arsenal's European ambitions. The first leg at the Emirates was as cagey as European football comes, with Adebayor's last-ditch header against the bar the closest the deadlock came to being broken. However, Arsenal had been dominant on the night and so there was plenty of optimism going into the second leg.

At the San Siro, Arsenal showed poise, patience and class. Six minutes from time, Fabregas scored from 30 yards. The travelling fans erupted with joy as the Spaniard slid to his knees in front of the bench in celebration. Adebayor doubled the lead in injury time to confirm Arsenal's passage to the quarter finals, and AC Milan's first defeat at home to English opposition.

Naturally, Wenger was fulsome in his praise of his team's performance. 'I have big respect for Milan, but my team deserves a lot of credit – having come here and beaten a team like them. We have given the performance we wanted. We played with organisation and never dropped off. We did not give them time and went forward every time we could. We played with authority, maturity, talent and intelligence.'

A COMEBACK AT BOLTON

Arsenal found it hard to perform as spectacularly in the Premier League as they had in Milan. They drew three times, and injury-time headers from Nicklas Bendtner and Kolo Toure were required to prevent defeats against Aston Villa

and Middlesbrough respectively. The clash at Wigan Athletic ended goalless. Worse was to come at Stamford Bridge, where Didier Drogba struck twice in the second half to cancel out Bacary Sagna's opener and put a major dent into Arsenal's title hopes.

However, at the Reebok Stadium a 10-man Arsenal side put in a stunning, resilient performance against Bolton Wanderers that once again filled the side with confidence. At half-time, the Gunners were two goals down and one man down after Abou Diaby was sent off. However, 45 minutes later the visitors had secured their first win in six Premier League games thanks to a volley from Gallas, a van Persie penalty and an own goal by Jlloyd Samuel in the dying seconds of the match. A hard-fought 3–2 to the Arsenal.

This win gave the Gunners a lifeline in the title race. April would prove a make-or-break month. Arsenal would face Liverpool in the Champions League quarter final, and among their Premier League opponents would be league leaders Manchester United.

The first leg against Liverpool was played at the Emirates and the home side were ahead for just three minutes after Adebayor netted with a thunderous header. Dirk Kuyt equalised to give the Merseysiders the away-goal advantage going into the second leg at Anfield. Before that tie, the sides met again at Emirates, this time in the Premier League.

Arsenal went into the game in third place, six points behind league leaders Manchester United, so victory was vital. However, again the sides finished level at 1–1.

So to Anfield. It proved to be a dramatic but heartbreaking night. Abou Diaby opened the scoring, but goals from Hyypia and Torres put Liverpool ahead. Then came a glorious, 60-yard run from Theo Walcott which set up Emmanuel Adebayor to tap home and level the aggregate score at 3–3.

With Arsenal ahead on away goals, the visitors were just seven minutes from a place in the semi-finals. However, a penalty from Steven Gerrard and a Ryan Babel strike sent the home side through.

THE LEAGUE RUN-IN

Wenger's side were back in the north-west just five days later where nothing short of victory at Old Trafford would be enough if they were to stand a realistic chance of winning the Premier League. The visitors dominated the first half of the game and took the lead just three minutes after the half-time break, when Adebayor bundled home a van Persie cross.

Five minutes later, Cristiano Ronaldo levelled from the penalty spot and Owen Hargreaves netted the winner on 73 minutes. The Gunners battled to get back into the tie, with Nicklas Bendtner hitting the post, but the match ended 2–1 to the home side.

Back at the Emirates in front of a record attendance of 60,132, Arsenal beat relegation-threatened Reading comfortably, with the 2–0 scoreline scarcely doing justice

to a masterful performance, spearheaded by a rampant Theo Walcott. 'It was his most complete game,' said Wenger of the youngster's performance. 'One where he looked most "the man", the most mature. Theo is not a monster, but he has great body power. When he starts on the first five yards, it is like you throw him away. You do not see him, he is gone. That is more important than just more power.'

Walcott was on target in the next game, away to Derby County. Bendtner and Van Persie also scored, but it was Adebayor's three goals in the second-half that truly stole the show. It was the Togolese man's second hat-trick of the season against the Rams.

The Gunners' 6–2 win left them with a mathematical but implausible chance of winning the title, but most were already looking ahead to next season's chances of success. Hope was given for the next campaign by Arsenal's two final games of the season, against Everton and Sunderland, both of which ended 1–0 to the north Londoners.

The Gunners ended the season in third place, four points behind Premiership champions Manchester United. Compared with the pessimistic predictions made on the eve of the season, this constituted a surprisingly good season. Having topped the table regularly during the first six months of the season, the side had showed their pedigree.

REASONS TO BE CHEERFUL

The Gunners had amassed 83 points during the campaign, and Wenger pointed out that he had won titles with fewer points. 'You have to be reasonable – when you get 83 points and you call that failure, what would the other teams say?'

'I feel quality-wise we have been remarkable the whole season. I have never had a team that has consistently produced quality games like this team. We lost a 100 metres race by a fraction of a second. We were on the same line and somebody has put their chest in front of us just at the end.'

A number of key players also suffered injuries. In addition to the loss of Eduardo, Tomas Rosicky was injured in the FA Cup tie with Newcastle in January and did not reappear for the rest of the season. Robin van Persie, too, was out injured for much of the season, making just 13 Premier League starts.

At the season's conclusion, Cesc Fabregas was named PFA Young Player of the Year, reflecting a remarkable season for the midfield ace. He joined three other Arsenal stars – Emmanuel Adebayor, Gael Clichy and Bacary Sagna – in the PFA's team of the year. Although The Gunners had not won a trophy, they had won admirers aplenty.

NASRI ON-BOARD

The Gunners wanted to win trophies as well as admirers in the season ahead and with this in mind some lively additions were made to the squad. Samir Nasri was the main summer signing. The skilful 20-year-old midfielder, widely seen as

Above: Walcott skips past challenge after challenge from desperate Liverpool defenders before squaring the ball to Adebayor to make it 2–2 on the night. It was the moment every Arsenal fan thought they would be in the semi-final of the Champions League. It was, by a considerable distance, the best goal scored by an English club in the whole of the 2007–08 season and it deserved a better fate. One minute later their dreams were dashed thanks to a controversial penalty.

Below: Emmanuel Adebayor claims another match ball as he scores his second hat-trick of the season, both of which were against Derby County.

the future of French football, joined on a long-term contract. 'I really hope everything will go well for me here,' he said. 'I will give my best for Arsenal and its fans, and I am honoured to be part of such a great football club.' Another Frenchman, Mikael Silvestre, who had already won a host of trophies with Manchester United, arrived at the end of August, while 17-year-old Welshman Aaron Ramsey and Mexican striker Carlos Vela were also signed.

NEW SEASON OPTIMISM

Pre-season friendlies included the annual Emirates Cup, in which an Emmanuel Adebayor penalty secured victory over Spanish giants Real Madrid. The Gunners then beat Ajax in the Amsterdam Tournament, coming back from a 2–0 half time deficit to win 3–2. But the important question was how Arsenal would fare once competitive action began. Manager Arsène Wenger predicted difficult challenges ahead, with more teams competing for a top-four finish, including Aston Villa: 'What we want, though, is to focus on ourselves, express our own beliefs, strengths and ambition.'

On the opening weekend of the season, new signing Nasri took just three minutes and 44 seconds to make an impact, scoring against West Bromwich Albion at Emirates Stadium. This turned out to be the only goal of a disappointing game, but it was a promising start from the Frenchman, who continued to impress throughout August and was voted Player of the Month by visitors to the official Club website. However, there were mixed League performances that month, the 1–0 loss at Fulham foreshadowing a frustratingly inconsistent Premiership campaign.

By the end of August, though, a 6–0 aggregate win over FC Twente had secured UEFA Champions League football for an 11th successive season. A classy performance against FC

Porto saw the Gunners emerge 4–0 victors in September, a month in which they also beat Blackburn Rovers 4–0 and Bolton Wanderers 3–1 in the Premiership. The victory at the Reebok Stadium was the first of several great comebacks this season: after going 1–0 down, goals from Emmanuel Eboue, Nicklas Bendtner and Denilson secured the eventual win.

Meanwhile, in the Carling Cup the second string were also in fine form, brushing aside Sheffield United 6–0, with Vela scoring a hat-trick. An unexpected 2–1 home defeat by Hull in the Premiership – only the second defeat in 60 games at Emirates Stadium – put a dampener on an otherwise fine month. Brutally honest about his disappointment, Wenger said, 'There were certainly enough ingredients in the game to make me physically sick.'

A BRIGHT FUTURE

The manager will have found it easier to digest the financial results for the year ending 31 May 2008. Group turnover increased from £200.8 million to £223 million, broadcasting income from £44.3 million to £68.4 million, and match-day income from £90.6 million to £94.6 million. Chairman Peter Hill-Wood said, 'I believe that the strong financial position which the Group has established, as confirmed by the results for the year, provides the best possible platform from which to deliver that success for the long term.'

There was further cause for optimism when Theo Walcott put in an extraordinary performance for his country on 10 September. In England's 4–1 victory over Croatia in Zagreb, Walcott netted three of the goals, making him the third Gunner to score an England hat-trick (the others were Ted Drake against Hungary in 1936 and Ian Wright against San Marino in 1993).

Although October began quietly with a 1–1 draw at Sunderland, it turned out to be another month rich in goals and drama. Leon Osman gave Everton an early lead at the Emirates but a second-half comeback spearheaded by substitute Walcott saw Arsenal win 3–1. Just three days later the team travelled to Turkey to face Fenerbahce. An imperious performance saw them win 5–2, with Cesc Fabregas creating two goals (for the on-song Walcott and Adebayor) in a glorious 70-second period.

The following weekend, while both Manchester United and Chelsea showed signs of post-Champions League weariness, Arsenal won 2–0 at London rivals West Ham United. However, the most memorable derby of the month was against Tottenham Hotspur at the Emirates. Arsenal recovered from an opening wonder goal scored by former Gunner David Bentley to lead 4–2 with just two minutes left. But in their first match under Harry Redknapp, Tottenham were not prepared to give up and they scored again twice to grab an unlikely draw. 'I think my players are intelligent and they will learn from their mistakes,' mused Wenger in the aftermath. 'In life you must make the maximum with what you have.'

Right: With an assured touch and an eye for the goal, Samir Nasri (right) arrived in the summer of 2008 as a ready-made replacement for Hleb. It didn't take long for the France international to make an impact scoring within the first four minutes of his League debut.

BIG SCALPS AND SLIP-UPS

November was a mixed month that in many ways told the story of the entire season. In the Premiership the Gunners beat Manchester United and Chelsea, but lost to Stoke City, Aston Villa and Manchester City. Meanwhile, a late winner from Nicklas Bendtner against Dynamo Kiev secured passage to the knockout stages of the Champions League.

The defeat at Manchester City was the fifth of the season and came amid much speculation about the future of captain William Gallas, who did not attend the match. With injuries mounting and winter setting in, it was a dark weekend for the Club. However, eight days later Robin van Persie lightened the mood at the Club with two goals in three minutes to win the tie against Chelsea.

Frustration was the order of the day for December. A 2–0 defeat in the quarter-final at Burnley saw Arsenal exit the Carling Cup. Premiership victories over Wigan Athletic and Portsmouth were welcome, but sandwiched in between were draws with Middlesbrough, Liverpool and Aston Villa. The draw with Villa, who were in fine form under Martin O'Neill and proving to be Arsenal's main challengers for a top-four place, as Wenger had predicted, left the Gunners ten points behind League leaders Liverpool. The disappointment of drawing with Liverpool was compounded by an injury to Fabregas, who suffered a partial rupture of his medial knee ligaments, ruling him out for months. 'That is a massive blow for Cesc, because he is a competitor who wants to play every day,' said Wenger. It was a massive blow for the team too. More happily, though, that month the manager reached a milestone in his Arsenal career with the tie against FC Porto. It was his 700th match in charge and his record was admirable: 408 wins, 163 draws and just 129 defeats.

DEBUTS AND RETURNS

With no Champions League matches in January, Arsenal could focus on domestic affairs. Substitute Bendtner slid home a late winner against Bolton Wanderers, capping an afternoon of relentless pressure from the Gunners. The resurgent Dane was again among the goals as Arsenal won 3–1 at Hull City. Van Persie was also on form and his late equalizer at Everton meant he had scored or created every Arsenal goal in January. The Dutchman also captained Arsenal for the first time in the 3–1 FA Cup victory over Plymouth Argyle, when he celebrated by scoring a brace. At 16 years and 256 days, Jack Wilshere became the youngest player to appear for the Club in the FA Cup that afternoon. He signed professional terms the same day.

January closed with a 0–0 draw against West Ham United and all three Premiership ties the next month finished goalless as Arsenal's scoring touch deserted them. In September they had scored 19 times in all competitions, but in February they scored only in cup matches. Eduardo made an emotional return to competitive action in February, 358 days

after being stretchered off at Birmingham. He scored twice as Wenger's team dismissed Cardiff City 4–0 in the FA Cup, celebrating emotionally with physio Tony Colbert, who had worked so hard to ease him back to fitness. 'This guy is small but has the mental strength of a mountain,' said an approving Wenger of Eduardo.

On 3 February, in the last moments of the transfer window, talented Russian striker Andrey Arshavin joined the Club from Zenit St Petersburg on a long-term contract. 'He is a player I have admired for a long time,' said Wenger. 'Andrey is an exciting impact player with a huge amount of ability and has been an influential force with both Zenit St Petersburg and the Russian national team in recent seasons.' Arshavin shared the manager's joy. 'I am so happy to be joining Arsenal,' he said.

'I am looking forward to making the Arsenal supporters happy and helping this great Club win trophies.'

GUNNING FOR TOP FOUR

It was now Champions League knockout time. Wenger had urged his team to 'take the handbrake off' and a first-half van Persie penalty at home to Roma gave Arsenal the advantage going into the second leg in Italy. However, Juan's tenth-minute goal levelled the tie, which meant it went to penalties. Eduardo missed the first spot-kick, but Almunia saved from Mirko Vučinić to level matters. At 7–6, Max Tonetto sent the ball sailing over the bar and The Gunners romped into the quarter-finals.

European success seemed to have a positive effect on domestic games as Arsenal rediscovered their scoring form, with Arshavin opening his account in an impressive 4–0

Above: Theo Walcott skips past Fenerbahce's keeper Volkan Demirel to score Arsenal's second in their 5–2 victory over the Turkish side. The Gunners only suffered one defeat in the group stages as they qualified comfortably behind Porto.

Below: After 12 years and just under 2 months, a smiling Arsène Wenger faced the press ahead of his 700th game in charge of Arsenal. During that time he'd overseen victories in an impressive 58 per cent of games.

Above: Eduardo returned to first team action following his horrific injury the previous season in dramatic fashion. He scored a brace against Cardiff City and poignantly celebrated the second goal with Tony Colbert, the fitness coach who had worked with him during his 12-month rehabilitation.

Below: Manuel Almunia is mobbed by his teammates following Arsenal's dramatic penalty shootout win over AS Roma in the Champions League. Max Tonetto's penalty cleared the bar and the Gunners won the spotkicks 7–6 following a nervous, but entertaining two ties that were won 1–0 by the home team.

victory over Blackburn Rovers, while the next week another Almunia penalty save contributed to a 3–1 win at St James's Park. Walcott returned after a four-month absence through shoulder injury for the FA Cup tie against Burnley. Eduardo captained the side in his second game back and scored a wonder goal as Arsenal triumphed 3–0. In the quarter-final against Hull City, they went behind to a goal from former Tottenham ace Nicky Barmby, but van Persie and Gallas scored in the final 16 minutes to earn the Gunners a Wembley semi-final.

As April arrived, Arsenal's task was clear: to finish in the top four and to reach the Champions League and FA Cup finals. The first match of the month – against Manchester City – gave grounds for optimism. Fabregas returned after three and a half months out, while two goals from Adebayor confirmed victory and took the Club's unbeaten Premiership run to 17 games. The Gunners were back on Premiership form as players returned from injury in style, Silvestre netting in his comeback against Wigan Athletic.

Arshavin had increasingly been showing his class and nowhere was this more apparent than at Anfield on 21 April. The Russian scored four times against Liverpool, but these strikes were not enough to secure victory. Yossi Benayoun scored with virtually the last kick of the match to grab a 4–4 draw in front of a stunned crowd. Prior to the clash with Middlesbrough five days later, Fabregas had scored only once all season, but against Gareth Southgate's side he netted twice. That victory as good as confirmed a fourth-place finish for Arsenal: with four games left, they were ten points ahead of nearest rivals Aston Villa.

A FINAL WITHIN TOUCHING DISTANCE

The Champions League quarter-finals paired Arsenal with Villarreal, the side they had dispatched in the semi-final of 2006. In the first leg in Spain the home side took a deserved first-half lead. However, in the second half Adebayor controlled a Fabregas pass on his chest and equalized with an exquisite overhead kick. In the second leg at the Emirates the Togan striker was joined on the scoresheet by Walcott and van Persie as The Gunners strode into the semi-finals.

Things were looking promising, as Walcott confirmed: 'Everyone is buzzing and that's the feeling we want to get on the pitch. As soon as we walk on the pitch we want teams to be scared of us. That's what we're getting at the moment.' The manager was confident his team could perform well against their opponents, Manchester United: 'I believe that both teams produce always very exciting games. Both teams like to go forward, so it will be a promising semi-final. We are up for the challenge and it will be very interesting.'

In the middle of April the Gunners faced London rivals Chelsea in the FA Cup semi-final at Wembley. Walcott shot them ahead, as he had when the sides met two years earlier in the Carling Cup Final, but once again the west Londoners fought back to a 2–1 victory, thanks to a later winner from Didier Drogba. With Arsenal's interest in the FA Cup over, the two-legged Champions League semi-final now took on even greater significance, as it held the last remaining hope of silverware for the season.

In the first leg at Old Trafford the Gunners were lucky to escape with a scoreline of 0–1. The first-ever European tie between the two teams turned out to be a one-sided affair and only some heroics in goal from Almunia prevented a heavier defeat. The Gunners would need to perform much better in the second leg at home six days later.

To help them along, special souvenir flags had been placed on each seat and the atmosphere in Emirates Stadium was electric when the game began. But after 11 minutes the contest was as good as over. Ji-Sung Park scored on eight minutes and was joined on the scoresheet by Ronaldo three minutes later. The Portuguese ace scored again on 61 minutes to put his team 4–0 ahead on aggregate, with three crucial away goals to make the Gunners' task impossible. Van Persie's 75th-minute penalty was scant consolation.

All that remained for Arsenal was to achieve maximum points and pride from their remaining Premiership ties against Chelsea, Manchester United and Stoke City. The Blues inflicted a 4–1 thrashing on Arsenal, their biggest defeat to date at Emirates Stadium. There was more to be proud of when Arsenal travelled to Old Trafford on the penultimate weekend of the season. Manchester United required just a point to win the title and were in confident form, while the Gunners had conceded seven goals in their previous two games. The match ended goalless, which was enough to guarantee the title for United, but this was no walkover, as the Gunners put on a brave and determined display.

Left: One of the matches of the 2008–09 season was Arsenal's 4–4 draw at Anfield. The Gunners' fourth was scored by Andrey Arshavin. The talented Russian arrived from Zenit St Petersburg in February and his ability was plain to see with impressive displays against West Brom, Burnley and Blackburn. The 27-year-old, former Russian Player of the Year, managed to score 6 goals from only 12 starts.

The season ended on a note of victory and optimism. When the Gunners travelled to Stoke City back in November, their 2–1 defeat marked a low point in a difficult campaign. The return fixture on the closing day pointed to a brighter future. Van Persie, in irresistible form, was involved in all four Arsenal goals. He helped set up James Beattie's own goal that opened the scoring and Abou Diaby nodded home his free-kick. The Dutchman also scored two himself, including a penalty. The Arsenal crowd performed Mexican waves and sang passionately in praise of the manager as the season came to an end. Wenger returned the compliment, saying, 'It makes me feel appreciated and even more regretful that we couldn't give them what they wanted this season. I am very respectful for their faith in me. It's very warming and it makes me even more determined to pay them back.'

LOOKING FORWARD

True, it had not been a particularly memorable League season, but the youthful squad could take great satisfaction from Champions League qualification and their continued reputation for playing attractive, flowing football. Arsenal had amassed 72 points, which left them in fourth place and a considerable way behind Manchester United, on 90 points. However, they had been on great form in front of goal, netting the same number of Premiership goals as the champions: 68. While another trophyless season was naturally disappointing for players, coaches and fans alike, on a positive note the Club had reached the semi-finals of both the Champions League and FA Cup.

Captain Cesc Fabregas was clear in his assessment of the season: 'We have to look at where we can improve, and make sure we do that for next season. We haven't been in any Finals and perhaps that's because of something. We've gone 21 games without losing in the League, so we know we are good, but when we've played in the semi-finals of the FA Cup and Champions League we haven't been at the level everyone expected us to reach.' Meanwhile, Wenger was keen to

highlight the positive end to a mixed campaign: 'The difficult thing for a manager is feeling that the team has stood still. I feel that we had to refind a balance after the departures of Hleb and Flamini and the injury to Rosicky. We had a little bit of a dodgy start but in the last 23 games we only lost once, against Chelsea, here.'

YOUNG GUNS ABLAZE

Further cause for hope came when Arsenal beat Liverpool in the final of the FA Youth Cup. The youngsters' professional 2–1 victory at Anfield secured a 6–2 aggregate win after a fine first leg at the Emirates. The venue and the date of the second leg were both rich in symbolism, being 20 years to the day since Arsenal won the League championship at Anfield with that famous last-gasp goal from Mickey Thomas. Steve Bould, who coached the youth team to their victory, played on that night in 1989. 'It doesn't seem like 20 years,' he said, grinning. 'It's an awful long time. The place has changed quite a bit. When we won the title at Anfield it was the old Kop and all the fans were standing and swaying. It's a slightly different place, but what an anniversary to have. It couldn't have fallen on a better day for me, it's fabulous.'

STARTING AT THE TOP

For a while now, Arsenal had been hinting at a glorious future, with a fine new stadium and a squad brimming with youthful talent. The long-term approach of the Club was sensible and admirable, given the unwise tendency of many in the game to concentrate solely upon immediate gain. However, all concerned with Arsenal were of course keen to see promise and potential turn into tangible success as soon as possible. For the 2009–10 season the team would have to chase that without the services of Togan striker Emmanuel Adebayor and Ivorian defender Kolo Toure, both of whom signed for Manchester City during the summer. The ambition of City foreshadowed a highly competitive campaign ahead.

Right: When Thomas Vermaelan arrived from Ajax most fans thought they were getting an athletic centre back to fill the hole left by Kolo Toure. What they didn't expect was goals. But here he is celebrating one on his debut against Everton, which was followed by a brace against Wigan the following month and a further four in the rest of the 2009–10 campaign.

The major Arsenal signing of the summer was centre back Thomas Vermaelen. The Belgian international arrived from Dutch side Ajax, where he had worn the captain's armband. Doubts were voiced in some quarters about whether he was tall enough to thrive in the face of the often direct tactics of Premier League teams, but his impressive aerial ability at both ends of the field was soon on show.

'I'm just so happy to be joining Arsenal,' said the Belgian after signing. 'Everything is set up for Arsenal to be very successful for years to come and I joined this Club because I know Arsenal will be challenging for trophies.'

In July the team capped a fine, free-scoring pre-season by retaining the Emirates Cup with a 3–0 victory over Rangers, but it was more prestigious trophies that they would be seeking once the real business began in August.

SIX OF THE BEST

The Gunners entered the campaign with renewed experience and the additional prospect of Russian playmaker Andrey Arshavin's first full season for the Club. He lined up in attack alongside Robin van Persie and Nicklas Bendtner for the Premier League opener at Everton. Many commentators had already written off Arsenal's chances for the campaign, but

they were hurriedly revising their opinions after the Gunners thrashed their first opponents 6–1. Among the goals was a curling 25-yard shot from Denilson, a thumping header from Thomas Vermaelen and a Fabregas-capped counter-attack. 'We are top of the League,' chanted the jubilant visiting fans. On this evidence, the Gunners looked a good bet to remain there for a while.

INTO THE GROUP STAGE AGAIN

So to Europe, and just three days later it was time to begin the quest for Champions League glory. A frantic first leg at Celtic Park was dominated by Wenger's men, though it was two moments of luck that separated the sides in this battle of Britain. William Gallas deflected a Fabregas effort to take the lead just before the break and Celtic's Gary Caldwell accidentally turned a Gael Clichy cross past his own keeper in the second half. In the second leg at the Emirates, goals from Eduardo, Eboue and Arshavin saw Arsenal cruise past the Scottish giants and into the group stage of the competition, their 12th successive presence there. The Club is now a fixture in Europe's elite competition and hopes are high that one day the trophy will come to north London.

Meanwhile, the Club's explosive start in the League continued with an emphatic 4–1 victory over Portsmouth, a win spearheaded by two goals in four first-half minutes from the lively Abou Diaby. The game was also notable for witnessing the first Premier League start by Eduardo since he was injured at Birmingham in February 2008 and the Gunners faithful naturally cheered him back into the fold. However, Diaby put through his own net in the final match of the month, which saw Manchester United beat Arsenal 2–1.

September started as August had ended for Arsenal – with defeat in Manchester. There was plenty of edge for the clash with City, who lined up with two Arsenal old boys in the shape of Toure and Adebayor. The Togan hit man was among the home side's goals as they dispatched Arsenal 4–2. The goals from van Persie and Rosicky were scant consolation as the Gunners' Premier League quest hit its second successive buffer. However, it was soon back on track with a 4–0 home victory against Wigan Athletic.

Vermaelen had accepted the Club website's Player of the Month award for August prior to kick-off and by the end of the game he had scored twice and helped keep a clean sheet at the back. In securing the latter he blocked a close-range shot on the line in the dying minutes. It had been a heroic performance from the Belgian, who was proving another inspired Wenger signing.

Goalkeeper Vito Mannone was the hero a week later when he pulled off a string of spectacular saves against Fulham, thus preserving the lead given by van Persie's 52nd-minute strike. The Gunners were also progressing in the Carling Cup, with a fledgling line-up seeing off Championship leaders West Bromwich Albion at Emirates Stadium.

COMEBACK KINGS

September had been a successful month in the Champions League. Arsenal won both their ties and scored five goals in so doing. The first came against Standard Liège in Belgium. Arsenal had won 7–0 here in a European Cup Winners' Cup tie in the 1990s, but were two goals down after just five minutes this time. The visitors needed a dramatic comeback and they made one. Just before the half-time whistle Nicklas Bendtner, in his 100th appearance for Arsenal, pulled a goal back. Second-half strikes from Vermaelen and Eduardo grabbed the points for the visitors. At home to Olympiacos the Gunners left it late, with goals from van Persie and Arshavin in the final 12 minutes confirming the victory. The month included a good result off the pitch as well. Arsenal Holdings announced a record profit for the year ending 31 May 2009. The Club was in good shape on and off the pitch, increasing optimism in the red half of north London.

October began explosively when, after falling behind in the third minute, Arsenal walloped Blackburn Rovers 6–2. After Vermaelen equalised on 17 minutes, Rovers took the lead again, but goals from van Persie, Arshavin, Fabregas, Walcott and Bendtner completed a rout of a comeback in a season that was to be replete with them. It was a great start to the month that saw the team remain in the capital for all its Premier League and Carling Cup business. Van Persie, Diaby and Arshavin were on target in the 3–0 victory over Birmingham City and the Gunners moved to third in the table after a 2–2 draw at West Ham United. It was disappointing to end that lively London derby all square, as the visitors had been 2–0 up, but they failed to capitalize on their lead and their numerical advantage after Scott Parker was sent off for the East Enders.

QUICKFIRING AGAINST SPURS

The highlight of the month came with the first north London derby of the season. A fairly tame match exploded into life when the Gunners scored twice in 60 seconds. First, van Persie turned in a Bacary Sagna cross to give his side the lead. Straight from the resulting kick-off, the Dutch striker captured the ball and unleashed it to Fabregas, who eased past a few challenges to score his sixth goal of the campaign. On the hour mark van Persie converted another Sagna cross and the Gunners played out the remainder of the match with confidence.

Arsenal had comfortably claimed north London bragging rights on the day, but Tottenham would snap at their heels until the very end of the campaign.

Above: Captain Fabregas celebrates the second goal against Spurs in a 3–0 win at the Emirates. The goal came 11 seconds after van Persie had put the Gunners in front and was the result of an electrifying run past stranded defenders.

Left: During the campaign Nicklas Bendtner had come under unfair criticism from the media for his goal-scoring tally. But this season he proved that he could score crucial goals in pressure games. Here he is celebrating his 100th Arsenal appearance with a goal in a 3–2 away win at Standard Liège.

Above: One of the most exciting young talents to emerge in 2009 was Aaron Ramsey. Signed from Cardiff in the summer of 2008, the midfielder had an amazingly assured touch for someone so young. Here he celebrates a goal against Stoke in a 3–0 win. Unfortunately, during the return fixture in February, Aaron's season was cut short due to a double fracture of the leg following a challenge by Stoke's Ryan Shawcross.

Just as the Gunners surrendered the lead to finish all square at West Ham United, the same thing had happened five days earlier at AZ Alkmaar in the Champions League. Fabregas's first-half goal looked good enough to maintain the Club's 100 per cent record in the competition, but deep into injury time Mendes da Silva volleyed into the top corner. However, in the return leg two goals from Fabregas, plus one each from Nasri and Diaby, saw Arsenal comfortable 4–1 winners. Towards the end of November, goals from Nasri and – in his 100th appearance for Arsenal – Denilson were enough to beat Standard Liège at Emirates Stadium and guarantee the Club top spot in Group H.

The Gunners were absolutely cruising in Europe, but the rigours of the Premier League would prove a greater challenge all season, particularly after Robin van Persie was injured during international duty in November.

WENGER REACHES 500 AND EMIRATES 100

The harsh reality of the challenge that faced Arsenal was already clear by the end of November. Chelsea convincingly beat the Gunners 3–0, with a brace from Drogba among the goals. Wenger's team had been dominant for much of the match, but, unlike their opponents, they failed to take their chances. The defeat left them 11 points adrift of the leaders. The Gunners needed a quick and strong recovery. They got it in December, with five wins and a draw in the League. The glory began with a home clash against Stoke City. It was the Club's 100th match at Emirates Stadium and Arsène Wenger's 500th League game in charge. The team marked Wenger's milestone by notching up the 293rd victory of his glorious reign. So to Anfield, where Arshavin proved the master of the Merseysiders, contributing a goal to the visitors' 2–1 victory, which took Arsenal third in the Premier League.

An early Fabregas goal at Burnley was cancelled out from the spot by Graham Alexander. The result at Turf Moor was particularly disappointing, since Wenger had said in the build-up to the match that if Arsenal wanted to finish top of the League they must go to Burnley and win. However, they were to win their next three Premier League ties as the title race became more interesting. A Denilson free-kick was the pick of the goals as the Gunners beat Hull City 3–0. A brace from Fabregas provided a fine foundation for another 3–0 victory, this time over Aston Villa.

Since the Gunners had been widely written out of Premier League contention, they had grabbed 13 from a possible 15 points. Then a 4–1 win at Portsmouth moved them to just four points behind leaders Chelsea. A wonderful solo effort from Aaron Ramsey was the pick of the goals in a match that ended 2009 on a fine note for the Club.

Having been dispatched from the Carling Cup at the hands of Manchester City, the Gunners were still fighting on three fronts as 2010 dawned. Two goals in five second-half minutes were enough to seal victory over West Ham United in the

third round of the FA Cup, but a tough fourth round at Stoke City saw the Club exit the competition after a 3–1 win by the home side. So Wenger's team were left with the Champions League and the Premier League in their sights. It was the latter competition that was to be the focus in January. A last-minute Rosicky strike on a freezing day earned a 2–2 draw against Everton. Arsenal then won 2–0 at the Reebok Stadium in the first of two successive League clashes with Bolton Wanderers.

TOUGH AT THE TOP

Three days later at Emirates, the Gunners fell behind to two first-half Bolton goals, but a Rosicky strike just before the break hinted at a second-half comeback. That comeback was completed in style as goals from Fabregas, Vermaelen and Arshavin saw the home side 4–2 winners. The victory took them back to the top of the table, where they had not been since the end of August. But remaining there was to prove difficult in a Premier League season low on drama but strong on competition. In January Sol Campbell made a surprise return to the Club. The 35-year-old had been a free agent since parting company with Notts County the previous month. Campbell, capped 73 times by England and a Double-winner in 2002, was welcomed back by Arsène Wenger: 'He is a hugely experienced and intelligent footballer, who will bring a great amount of quality and knowledge to our squad. Sol as a player and a person will be an enormous asset to us.'

The wisdom of the signing became immediately apparent when Campbell was sent on to replace the injured Vermaelen at Villa Park. He quickly showed that he had lost none of his composure and ability. Campbell was key in keeping a clean-sheet in the 0–0 draw. The fixture list dictated that the next three opponents for Arsenal were Manchester United, Chelsea and Liverpool. How the Gunners fared against these leading lights would go a long way to determining how likely the Club was to win its first Premier League title for six years.

The first two matches of this trio made depressing watching for the Gunners faithful. By the time the recovered Thomas Vermaelen struck against Manchester United the Gunners had already conceded three goals. This reverse made victory against leaders Chelsea imperative.

The Gunners were undone for the second time in the campaign by a brace from Drogba. This time, the Ivorian nearly claimed a hat-trick but was denied by the crossbar. The Gunners had plenty of chances but failed to convert any. The 2–0 defeat left Wenger's side nine points adrift of the leaders with just 13 games left to play. They would need to be on top form for the remainder of the campaign and hope that Chelsea and Manchester United slipped up. It seemed a tall order and so it proved. The 450th win of Arsène Wenger's Arsenal career came against Liverpool courtesy of a late far-post header from Abou Diaby. The relief of his team-mates was clear from the rapturous celebrations that saw half of

them leap on top of the goalscorer. News that Chelsea had lost and United had dropped two points renewed confidence in the Arsenal dressing room.

BENDTNER'S CRUCIAL STRIKES

No team member needed an injection of confidence more than Nicklas Bendtner, who had thus far scored just one Premier League goal during a campaign disrupted by injury. He opened the scoring in the next match against Sunderland and was joined on the scoresheet by captain Fabregas, who netted a late penalty. United had lost at Everton and the Gunners continued to believe.

Their next league opponents were Stoke City at the Britannia Stadium. Goals from Bendtner, Fabregas and Vermaelen won the three points for Wenger's men, who moved within three points of leaders Chelsea. However, the tie was most memorable for the injury suffered by Aaron Ramsey. In the 65th minute Stoke's Ryan Shawcross and Ramsey challenged for the ball. The young Welshman was left in a crumpled heap on the field. The reactions of his team-mates quickly suggested Ramsey had suffered a very serious injury and it was later confirmed as a double leg break.

'I remember what happened clearly and after the tackle went in I saw that my leg was broken and hanging at an angle,' he said, recalling the horror of the incident. For the supporters Ramsey's experience brought back memories of the dramatic injuries suffered by Abou Diaby and Eduardo in recent years.

During the first half of the campaign Arsenal had simultaneously excelled in Europe and struggled in the Premier League. The reverse was the case in February and March: three Premier League victories followed hot on the heels of defeat in Europe, at the Estádio do Dragão. Sol Campbell scored the first goal of his second Arsenal career against Porto, but the hosts were to emerge victorious. Their winner was controversial. A quickly taken free-kick from Falcao beat Fabianski and Wenger led the protests that play had restarted too quickly. Still, thanks to the away goal secured by Arsenal in Portugal, a simple 1–0 victory back at Emirates Stadium would see the Gunners through to the next round. They were to do much better than that, sending a warning across Europe in the process.

PORTO PULVERISED

A hat-trick from Bendtner was the most memorable part of a magnificent performance against Porto, which saw Arsenal emerge 5–0 winners. His first two were both set up by Arshavin, who was himself on fine form, and Bendtner completed his treble from the spot at the death. In between Nasri and Eboue had also netted. In truth, the scoreline scarcely did justice to Arsenal's dominant brilliance. Walcott was just one of the Gunners who nearly added to the scoreline. This win in Europe was sandwiched between two Premier League victories, against Burnley and Hull City. The latter saw Bendtner again in decisive form, netting the winner in injury time. Walcott, too, had been crucial to the victory,

Above: Remember him? Arsenal hero Sol Campbell returned to the Club in January at the age of 35. Arsène Wenger revealed, 'Sol has been training with us since September and during this time he has shown he still has the required fitness, hunger and passion to compete at the top level.'

Left: A Fabregas penalty may not seem an unusual or remarkable thing. However, not only was this against Barcelona in a pulsating Champions League quarter final first leg, but it later emerged that he took the penalty with a fractured fibula, a result of the challenge that brought the penalty. The match ended 2–2, but Fabregas was out for the rest of the season.

which was just the type enjoyed by those who are going to be making a serious challenge for the title come May.

That battling brilliance was carried into the next match, a home clash with West Ham United. Vermaelen was sent off – the first Arsenal red card in 68 matches – after conceding a controversial penalty. Almunia saved that spot-kick and goals from Denilson and Fabregas sealed another three points for Arsenal. Denilson's strike had been his sixth in 20 games, a fine return for a defensive midfielder. He celebrated with a samba dance and Gunners fans dared to dream once more that they might be celebrating the arrival of silverware soon. However, a last-minute equalizer from Kevin Phillips at Birmingham City put a huge question mark over the Gunners' title ambitions. Chelsea had simultaneously beaten Aston Villa 7–1, leaving Wenger's team hoping for better fortunes in the Champions League. All season, while Arsenal had been in and out of title contention domestically, they had been far more consistent in Europe and hoped for silverware there.

THE BARÇA GAMES

Their next opponents in the competition were none other than the mighty Barcelona, European giants and the side that had beaten the Gunners in the 2006 Final. They were also the childhood team of Arsenal captain Cesc Fabregas. The young Spaniard's involvement was doubtful right up until kick-off because of an injury he had picked up in a previous tie. However, he did appear on the night and made a heroic contribution to a dramatic and memorable match. The first half saw the visitors in absolutely irresistible form. They

dominated proceedings and only a combination of fine saves by Manuel Almunia and a large slice of luck prevented the Spanish giants from taking the lead. The Gunners returned to the dressing room relieved to have survived the opening half intact.

A mere 25 seconds into the second half, Zlatan Ibrahimovic chipped a stranded Almunia and Arsenal were a goal down. Just before the hour the Swedish striker doubled Barcelona's lead. Given the sheer imperious class of their performance on the night, few could begrudge them the scoreline at this stage of the tie. Seven minutes after the second goal, Wenger sent Walcott on in place of Bacary Sagna with the aim of igniting some Arsenal attacks. His hopes were fulfilled when, only two minutes after his introduction, the Englishman thumped home after a fine run. Then, with six minutes left, Fabregas was fouled in the box. The Spaniard – who had earlier picked up a booking, which would heartbreakingly rule him out of the second leg – stood up and whacked the spot-kick home. He had been injured during the penalty drama and hobbled for the rest of the game. 'Cesc is a soldier,' said Walcott afterwards. It was something of a miracle that the Gunners had managed to end on equal terms with their opponents.

Former Arsenal captain Thierry Henry had received a standing ovation when he left the field at Emirates Stadium. The Gunners legend was to remain on the substitutes' bench for the second leg at the Nou Camp. It would be a tough task for Wenger's men, but the Arsenal fans took hope when Bendtner scored following a fine run by Walcott. The initiative was now with the visitors, but their new-found spring was compromised when Lionel Messi equalised just three minutes later. It was a goal worthy of his billing as he fired into the top right-hand corner from just outside the box. The Argentine magician had been fairly subdued in north London but was at the centre of much in Spain. He scored four in total on the night – including a cheeky chip to complete his hat-trick – as Arsenal lost 6–3 on aggregate. In truth they had been well beaten over the two legs.

THE TITLE CHALLENGE ENDS

All that remained for the season was the possibility of a title charge. Back in the Premier League, Bendtner struck another late winner, this time at home to Wolverhampton Wanderers. There were only seconds left when he converted Sagna's cross. The three points thus secured took Arsenal to within three points of the top with five games left. It had been one-way traffic throughout the afternoon and the Gunners, showing character galore, were well worth their win.

Hopes remained that they could go on to challenge for the title in the closing games of the campaign, particularly as their fixtures meant they had a relatively easy run-in. However, at this point their title charge came to an abrupt end. They were not to taste victory in any of the following four League games.

Left: A 0–0 draw against Manchester City edged Arsenal closer to securing third place and another Champions League spot for next season. It was notable though for the return of a fan's hero. 'Vieira' rang out around the Emirates before kick off, and Patrick acknowledged the crowd and the affection they held for him.

What made this late blip all the more painful was that it began at White Hart Lane. Goals from debutant Danny Rose and Gareth Bale gave Harry Redknapp's side the lead and Bendtner's 85th-minute strike was not enough to prevent Arsenal's first Premier League reverse to their old rivals since 1999. With the Gunners now six points off the leaders with just four games left, the priority was to secure as high a runners-up position as they could. Tottenham would chase them all the way there too. With goals from Walcott and Silvestre either side of half time at Wigan Athletic, the Gunners seemed to be cruising to victory. However, in the last 10 minutes the home side stunningly scored three times to take the points.

Arsenal took only one point from their next two matches. First came a 0–0 home draw against Manchester City in a game most memorable for the return to the Club of former captain Patrick Vieira, who was naturally cheered to the hilt by the home fans. The Gunners then left Ewood Park with no points after a 2–1 defeat to Blackburn Rovers. A goal from the returning Robin van Persie was scant consolation.

Results elsewhere conspired to put the Gunners under pressure in the race for third place from – of all teams – Tottenham Hotspur. Their final opponents of the campaign were Fulham. Arshavin, van Persie and Vela were on target for Arsenal and a Chris Baird own goal sealed the 4–0 win for the Gunners and with it third place in the Premier League, securing Champions League football the following season.

Wenger summed up the season 'For us if you look a long way back we have done beyond expectations,' he said. 'But of course we are still frustrated, because one month ago we were in touch with the title but didn't win it. Overall, we had a

season with a good attitude, strong character – the team has improved a lot on that front. Overall we conceded too many goals to win the title.'

The Arsenal Ladies' team won a seventh successive Premier League title the following day, but for the men's team another campaign had ended without a trophy.

A SEASON OF HIGHS AND LOWS

Arsène Wenger is not by nature a revolutionary. In the aftermath of another trophyless season, his instinct in the summer of 2010 was not to splurge his club's money on expensive new buys. There was only one significant addition to his squad – the defender Sebastien Squillaci from Sevilla. He cost precisely no money, in transfer fees. On the other side of the ledger, the luckless Eduardo moved on to Shakhtar Donetsk for £6m, and almost an entire back-four – Sol Campbell, William Gallas and Mikael Silvestre – left the club on free transfers.

The coach had applied the gentlest of touches to the tiller, rather than a violent lurch. He was prepared to back the youngsters coming through, the talented kids that had been nurtured in Arsenal's prolific nursery, and been brought up to play the Arsenal way. This approach set Arsenal apart from their elite Premier League rivals. Chelsea and especially Manchester City were willing to spend vast amounts on cornering the market in established footballing talent. Wenger, though, wasn't interested in joining the transfer arms race, by bidding ever-escalating amounts of cash for proven performers. As always, he preferred to invest Arsenal's money in the stars of tomorrow.

Right: A regular first-team starter in 2010–11, Theo Walcott netted 13 goals in all competitions that season. Here, he shoots past the Blackpool goalkeeper to score the fifth Arsenal goal in the 6–0 home win on 21 August 2011 – a game in which he secured a hat-trick.

WALCOTT ON FIRE

As the the 2010–11 season kicked off, The Gunners looked in perfect shape to challenge for a long overdue title. They began solidly with a 1–1 draw at Anfield, and their first home fixture gave the fans cause for optimism. Premier League new boys Blackpool suffered a 6–0 chasing, with Walcott, grabbing a hat-trick. He scored again in the next game – a 2–1 win at Blackburn, and the goals kept flowing as Bolton were dispatched 4–1 at the Emirates.

The whirlwind start to the season continued when the Gunners launched their Champions League campaign. Portuguese outfit, Braga, were blown off the park as Arsenal chalked up another 6–0 victory. By now Arsenal had established themselves as early Premier League pace-setters, and had also thrown down a marker in Europe. The club's sunny mood wasn't harmed by a 4–1 win at Tottenham in the Carling Cup.

With the team in ebullient form, the visit of West Bromwich Albion at the end of September should have given the Gunners a chance to keep the pressure on Chelsea at the top of the table. But inexplicably Arsenal were off the pace for much of the match, and were beaten 3–2. Wenger commented: 'What is the most frustrating is that there was no electricity there.'

It was the kind of aggravating result, coming after a string of stellar displays, that was to be a trademark of the team's season. It was only the first time of many occasions in 2010–11 when Gunners fans left the Emirates bemoaning a host of if-onlys.

The summer optimism faded a little more when Arsenal lost 2–0 at Stamford Bridge the following weekend. The hope of overhauling the West Londoners at the top of the table any time soon was for the time being put to one side. But in Europe Arsenal were still showing that they were live contenders for club football's greatest prize.

Wenger's men took control of Group H by winning their second match almost as easily as they had their first: they travelled to Partizan Belgrade and beat the Serbian side 3–1. In the third game the Gunners went a long way to confirming their place in the knockout stages as Shakhtar were thumped 5–1 at the Emirates. Defeats in the return games with Shakhtar and Braga caused some moments of concern, but the team removed any doubts about their further progress by their 3–1 home win over Partizan.

Arsenal could not have come up against tougher opponents in the last 16: Barcelona who were universally acknowledged as the outstanding team in the competition. Their squad was studded with world-beating stars such as Messi, Villa and Iniesta. Nobody could really understand how they had managed to lose to Internazionale in the previous season's Final, and everyone recalled that Arsenal had been among their victims on the way to that match. Yet the Gunners were not over-awed at the size of the challenge. Walcott, with all the precocity of youth, said: 'I would love to go back there and show them what we are all about this season.'

The story of how the two-legged tie unfolded summed up the story of Arsenal's season. It featured moments of supreme

elation and passages of golden football, interlaced with episodes of gut-wrenching disappointment.

BARCELONA: TRIUMPH...

The first leg at the Emirates will live long in the memory as one of Arsenal's great European nights. The club had done their bit to create a festival atmosphere by distributing flags inside the stadium, and the ground was a seething ocean of colour as the teams walked out. The match began with Arsenal in command, but the first half ended with Barcelona in the ascendancy. Where Arsenal had been all about pace, passion and thrust down the flanks in the opening spell, Barca took the initiative as the game wore on, weaving intricate passing patterns across the pitch. In defence, Barça's disciplined pressing game choked Arsenal's attacks at the outset. The Gunners chased shadows as Barça kept the ball at will. When the visitors took the lead half-way through the first period through Villa it was thoroughly deserved.

If Arsenal were as brittle as their critics would have them, the home team would have crumbled in the face of Barca's dominance. But they bounced back with a second-half display that showed reservoirs of character as well as bundles of ability. The Gunners stayed in the tie and matched Barcelona throughout the second period, until with 12 minutes left Robin Van Persie scored one of the goals of the season with a sublime shot from a daunting angle. Five minutes later, with the momentum behind them, Arsenal took the lead when substitute Andrey Arshavin netted.

It was a night of wonder on so many levels. Firstly, The Gunners had beaten a team widely recognised as the finest in club football anywhere in the world. Individually, too, many players had proved their class at the highest level. None more so than young Englishman, Jack Wilshere, who was many fans' choice of Arsenal's best player on the night. He didn't look out of place alongside Barça's cast of world-beaters.

Wenger, as always, treated a famous victory as coolly as he might have done a defeat. But despite his balanced words, you could sense his pleasure – with the result, the performance and the occasion. 'There are few nights in football where everywhere clicks well from the first to the last minute,' he told the world's press in the afterglow of victory.'With the fans, the vibes, the quality of the game and the quality of the behaviour. The commitment, talent and quality on both sides

Left: Robin van Persie celebrates scoring the first Arsenal goal in Arsenal's memorable 2–1 win in the UEFA Champions League on 16 February 2011.

Above: A stunning new talent to emerge in the 2010–11 season was young midfielder Jack Wilshere. Here, he powers past Adriano in the second leg of the Champions League tie against Barcelona the Camp Nou on 8 March 2011.

effort to set Arsenal on the counter-attack. A less ambitious player might have kept possession, or even cleared the decks with a long ball down-field. But Fabregas, a perfectionist to his toe-nails, ignored the ugly alternative, preferring guile over grit. Alas, the ball was intercepted by Iniesta, who played an astute pass through to Messi. The Argentinian star still had a lot to do – but his genius on the ball, deft touch and unerring instinct for a goal was enough to put Barca up on the night – and send them ahead in the tie on away goals. It was a hammer-blow from which Arsenal never really recovered.

The tide wasn't even turned when Arsenal notched up an unlikely equaliser, as Busquets headed past his own keeper from a corner in the early minutes of the second half. If Arsenal could have held the aggregate lead for a while longer and kept a foothold in the match, they might yet have made it through. But their hopes were cruelly dashed when Van Persie received a second yellow card for kicking the ball scant moments after the referee's whistle had blown for a stoppage. In vain did the Dutchman explain that he hadn't heard the whistle amid the fervour and din created by a packed Nou Camp. He trooped off the field, and with him went Arsenal's chance of progress.

Xavi scored after the hour, and Messi converted a penalty mid-way through the second half. Even now, Arsenal would still have gone through on away goals if they could conjure up an opening – and at one point Bendtner did sniff the ghost of an opportunity. But Barça rode out the late squall, and the Arsenal's Champions League involvement was over for another year.

Wenger was certain that his team would have been in the quarter-finals if Van Persie hadn't received his freakish sending off. 'You want to be given a chance to play a normal football match,' he said. 'Everybody has the same regret in our dressing room.'

was exceptional. Emotionally for us it finished on a high so of course it is a great night to be involved in.

"When you are down 1–0 against such a quality team you need something special to win the game and that's what I liked in my team. They always had the right mental resilience and stamina not to give in because you can quickly collapse against a team of that quality.'

... AND DESPAIR

Needless to say, Arsenal had only done half a job – with a formidable second leg to follow in Barca's Nou Camp fortress. For the first 45 minutes of the re-match in Catalonia, Arsenal's travelling legions dared to dream that they might make it through to the quarter finals at Barça's expense. For all the home team's creative threat and domination of possession, they had failed to make many goal-scoring chances. Arsenal looked comfortable with their one-goal aggregate lead. They did not even appear to be unduly worried when they lost their keeper, Szczesny, to injury after a quarter of an hour, bringing Almunia off the bench as substitute. But then they were undone by a moment which encapsulated so much of their season.

With the seconds counting down to half-time a Barça move broke down on the edge of the Arsenal area. The ball fell to Cesc Fabregas, who attempted a speculative back-heel in an

CUP EXITS

The defeat in Catalonia cast a gloomy pall over the club. Dreams of a glorious Quadruple, which optimistic supporters had nurtured throughout the winter, were dashed in a miserable spring. A week after the Champions League exit Arsenal lost 2–1 against Birmingham City in the Carling Cup Final. In March they lost 2–0 at Manchester United in the FA Cup quarter finals. That left them with only the Premier League to play for, and prospects of challenging for that title appeared bleak.

Arsenal had been threatening to challenge for the top spot all season, but their efforts were thwarted by inexplicable lapses along the way. In the most extreme example, away to Newcastle in February, they allowed a 4–0 lead to finish as a 4–4 draw. Immediately after the FA Cup exit at Old Trafford, their mission to overhaul United at the top stalled as they drew 2–2 at West Brom, and then endured a 0–0 home draw with Blackburn. Despite all the frustrations of an in-and-out

season, the Gunners were still in second place with eight matches to play, seven points behind United who had played a game more. The title was a long-shot, but still feasible.

But even those slim hopes disappeared as the run of victories the Gunners needed to pile pressure on the leaders failed to materialise. Frustratingly, there were moments when Arsenal showed that they could be just as good – even better – than the best teams in the land.

Champions-in-waiting Manchester United came to the Emirates in May seeking the win that would all-but wrap up the title for them. But in one of the classiest – and gutsiest – displays of the season, Arsenal won the match 1–0. The highlight of the afternoon was Aaron Ramsey's second-half goal, but all over the pitch there were reasons to rejoice. The young English duo, Walcott and Wilshere, were to the fore once again as Arsenal outplayed United. After the final whistle the mood around the Emirates was jubilant, but there were also plenty of 'if onlys'. If only the team could have achieved that level of performance more frequently, the Premier League trophy would be on its way back to Arsenal.

IN THE BOARD ROOM

There was newsworthy activity in the boardroom as the season drew to a close, as Stan Kroenke increased his stake in the club and became the majority shareholder. The activity indicated a new direction for the ownership of the club, but

Left: Arsenal defender Laurent Koscielny tangles with Nikola Zigic of Birmingham City in the 2011 Carling Cup Final.

Below left: Gunners captain, Cesc Fabregas evades Tottenham's Luka Modric in a Premier League meeting at White Hart Lane on 20 April 2011. The game was drawn 3–3.

Below: Aaron Ramsey side foots the ball past Michael Carrick to score the winning goal in Arsenal's 1–0 victory over the eventual Premier League champions Manchester United at the Emirates Stadium, 1 May 2011.

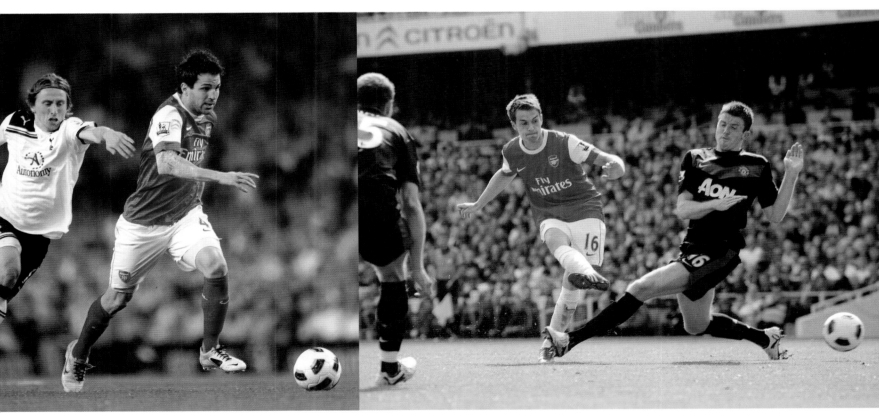

Above: Regularly filled to its capacity of over 60,000, the Emirates Stadium continues to provide a fitting venue for the best of English and European football.

Above: Manager Arsène Wenger and the Club's new majority shareholder Stan Kroenke at the AGM in 2011.

there was little sign of revolution around the Emirates. It was a typically low-key move for a club that has prided itself on keeping boardroom drama to a minimum. Loyal Gunners only had to recall the executive upheavals that had taken place at other big clubs, and breathe a sigh of relief that Arsenal had escaped such traumas.

The curtain finally fell on the season at Fulham, with a 2–2 draw that summed up the Gunners' campaign. Arsenal showed flashes of their best, but did not boss the action sufficiently to take all the points. The results confirmed a final Premier League position of fourth. Amid the disappointment of a season that had promised so much only to end sourly, Wenger was in the mood for looking ahead, not back. He set his sights on re-engineering the defence during the summer, and finding a winning mentality that had been absent in the closing stretch:

'We have shown that we have the technical quality to win the League but certainly not the defensive solidity to do it,' he said. 'We have learned that we have the quality, despite what everybody is saying, but of course we need to gain some strength in some areas of the team. Mentally I hope that the team has learned a lot this season because we could not cope with the number of games nor the pressure in the important moments of the season.'

The manager shared the same frustration as the supporters. Amid the inexplicable lapses, these young players had turned in some virtuoso performances. Wenger knew his job: to keep the standard of football high, while instilling the mental toughness required to compete consistently at the highest level. It was a quality that seemed to be lacking in the early spring of 2011, when Arsenal had four trophies in their sights.

'This was, as well, the season that we produced our best games ever,' said Wenger. 'But in the end it was difficult to get over the line.'

A PROUD HISTORY

In spite of the disappointments of recent seasons, there can be no denying the Club's incredible achievements in the 125 years since that Christmas Day in 1886 when 15 men met in

the Royal Oak, a pub next to Woolwich Arsenal Station, and decided they should take their kickabouts more seriously.

Few, if any, can be left alive who remember standing watching the team play in its days south of the river, on the long-gone terraces of Plumstead or the original Spion Kop at the Manor Ground, and who witnessed the woebegone Woolwich Arsenal of that disastrous season, which ended with relegation in 1913. No brick or pillar of the ground remains, no film exists of those games.

When Highbury and Emirates Stadium are quiet and the underground closed on Christmas Day, they still echo to memories of the thousands of people who have walked up those dank, ill-lit Edwardian tunnels. That's around 40 million, equivalent to two-thirds of the population of Great Britain. What dreams did they have, why did they come, what drew them to Gillespie Road, what did Arsenal mean to each and every one of them?

A quiet day is a good time to think of Bastin, of James, of Drake, of Jack, of Hapgood and Male; and, more recently, of a happier, demobbed and optimistic generation in crowds of 60,000 who would come every other week to see Reg Lewis and Ronnie Rooke, the immortal Joe Mercer and the golden 'Brylcreem Boy' Denis Compton, to live the two Championships and Cup Finals of Tom Whittaker's tragically brief Highbury reign.

Think of the intensity, of the hopes and fears, imagine if you can the mood on 1 May 1971, the last home game of the Double season. The tension was unbearable, and nothing but a win was conceivable. It would be easy to go on, but each generation has its own memories. The next will have its own, and they will be just as glorious. It is the great-grandchildren of the men who cheered Lambert and Hulme who now pin pictures of Fabregas and Walcott to their walls. Arsenal are different from any other football club. Why? Because the history of English football can be told through their story, because they did dominate a crucial generation and a vital decade, because they are Herbert Chapman's legacy and because they won the Double in 1971, 1998 and 2002.

So if you can, spare the time to think of the old Highbury, a repository of memories. Think of 24 April 1915, of that same Nottingham Forest who donated the red shirts over a century ago, coming to Highbury to lose a Second Division game 7–0, the last match fifth-placed Arsenal ever played outside top company. Think of a new, shiny Wembley, almost exactly 15 years to the day later, on 26 April 1930, the moment when the pendulum swung from north to south, the day Arsenal first won the FA Cup, the day the Graf Zeppelin hovered above the pitch.

Think of 40 years further on, of 27 March 1971 at far away Hillsborough, of a clock that read 4.44 pm, of the dreams of a Double which paused an instant from consignment to the dustbin of football history. That was perhaps the most unforgettable moment, a perfect illustration that football can, and should, be about the emotion such set-piece dramas can evoke. Think what we would say now about the game had

McLintock's header hit the post rather than Mahoney's hand, or if Banks had guessed correctly at Storey's penalty. Think of where you were during the fevered excitement of that match at Anfield in 1989 – the most intense, glorious and inspiring 90 minutes of all. Think, at the end of the Double of 1997–98, when Arsenal won the Championship after being so far behind that the bookmakers had ceased taking bets on the result.

Think about the astonishing achievements of the Unbeaten season of 2004–05. No matter how long we watch League football we will never live such moments again. If the next 125 years can bring just moments like the last few seconds at Anfield in 1989, the Doubles in 1998 and 2002, or the style and flair of the 2004 team, then we will all have much with which to justify our enthusiasm and anticipation.

Below: The heart of the Club will always be the fans, who follow their side through thick and thin and have witnessed some of the most seminal moments in the game. They can rightly be proud of their club's history.

SEASON 1886-1887
FRIENDLIES

11 Dec	Eastern W	A	W	6-0
8 Jan	Erith	H	W	6-1
15 Jan	Alexandria U	H	W	11-0
22 Jan	Eastern W	H	W	1-0
29 Jan	Erith	A	W	3-2
5 Feb	Millwall Rov	A	L	0-4
12 Feb	Alexandria U	A	W	6-0
25 Feb	2nd Rifle Brigade	H	D	0-0
12 Mar	Millwall Rov	H	W	3-0
26 Mar	2nd Rifle Brigade	A	L	0-1

	P	W	L	D	F:A
Arsenal	10	7	2	1	36:8

SEASON 1887-1888
FRIENDLIES

30 Sep	Alexandria U	H	W	5-1
15 Oct	Clapton Pilgrims		D	2-2
22 Oct	St Lukes			
5 Nov	Grange Institute		W	4-0
12 Nov	Iona Deptford		D	1-1
19 Nov	Tottenham H	A	L	1-2
26 Nov	Millwall Rov	A	L	0-3
2 Dec	Grange Park		H	
10 Dec	Brixton Rangers	H	L	1-2
16 Dec	Shrewsbury Park		W	4-0
31 Dec	Forest Gate Alliance	A	L	1-2
14 Jan	Iona Deptford	A	W	3-2
28 Jan	Champion Hill		W	6-0
3 Feb	Tottenham H	H	W	6-2
11 Feb	Millwall Rov	H	D	3-3
17 Feb	Erith		W	2-1
24 Feb	Forest Gate Alliance	H	D	1-1
2 Mar	Grange Institute		W	2-1
9 Mar	Brixton Ran		W	9-3
16 Mar	Ascham		W	5-0
30 Mar	Millwall Rov	H	W	3-0
6 Apr	Alexandria U	A	W	3-1

London Senior Cup

8 Oct	Grove House	H	W	3-1
29 Oct	Barnes		L	0-4

Junior Matches

10 Nov	Woolwich Pupils & Teachers	H	W	1-0
26 Nov	Erith	A	L	0-1
24 Feb	Thistle		L	1-2

	P	W	L	D	F:A
Arsenal	24	14	6	4	66:33

SEASON 1888-1889
FRIENDLIES

15 Sep	London Scottish		D	3-3
22 Sep	Tottenham H		L	0-1
29 Sep	Old St Pauls		W	7-3
6 Oct	Grove House		W	2-0
13 Oct	London Scottish		W	4-0
20 Oct	2nd Rifle Brigade		L	1-2
27 Oct	Brixton Ran		L	1-3
10 Nov	Millwall Rov			
17 Nov	St Lukes		D	1-1
1 Dec	Phoenix		D	0-0
22 Dec	St Brides			
5 Jan	Vulcan		D	1-1
12 Jan	Unity		D	0-0
26 Jan	St Lukes			
2 Feb	Ilford		L	1-2
16 Feb	Millwall Rov			
23 Feb	Ilford		L	0-1
2 Mar	London Caledonians		L	1-2
9 Mar	Tottenham H		W	1-0
16 Mar	South Eastern Ran		L	1-2
23 Mar	Royal Artillery		W	9-0
30 Mar	2nd Rifle Brigade		W	2-0
1 Apr	2nd Rifle Brigade		W	6-1
6 Apr	Old St Pauls		W	1-0
13 Apr	Millwall Rov		W	3-0
19 Oct	Boston T		L	1-4
20 Apr	Spartan Rov		W	6-0
23 Apr	Scots Guards		W	7-2
27 Apr	London Caledonians		L	0-1

London Association Cup

3 Nov	Phoenix		W	3-0
24 Nov	Dulwich		W	4-2
8 Dec	Old St Pauls		W	3-1
19 Jan	Clapton (Semi-Final)		L	0-2

Kent County Challenge Cup

10 Nov	Horton Kirby		W	6-2
29 Dec	Iona		W	5-1
9 Feb	Gravesend		D	3-3*

*Arsenal disqualified for refusing to play extra time.

	P	W	L	D	F:A
Arsenal	32	16	10	6	83:40

SEASON 1889-1890
FRIENDLIES

7 Sep	London Caledonians	H	D	2-2
14 Sep	Casuals	H	W	6-0
21 Sep	Tottenham H	H	W	10-1
28 Sep	Unity	H	W	8-0
19 Oct	St Old Marks College	A	W	2-1
30 Nov	Marlow	A	L	0-2
21 Dec	Ilford	A	W	2-0
25 Dec	Preston Hornets	H	W	5-0
26 Dec	Chatham	A	D	2-2
27 Dec	Reading T	H	W	5-1
4 Jan	Windsor Phoenix	H	W	3-1
18 Jan	Old Harrovlans	H	W	2-1
25 Jan	Foxes	H	W	7-2
8 Feb	Chiswick Park	H	D	1-1
1 Mar	Birmingham St George	H	L	1-4
15 Mar	Ilford	A	W	4-1
28 Mar	Clapton	A	L	0-2
31 Mar	W. H. Loraine XI	H	W	3-1
7 Apr	1st Lincs. Regt.	H	W	2-1
12 Apr	Marlow	H	W	3-1
19 Apr	Chatham	H	W	1-0
26 Apr	Clapton	H	W	6-1
3 May	London Cal/Clapton Comb	H	W	3-2
10 May	Millwall Athletic	A	D	3-3

FA Cup

5 Oct	Lyndhurst (Q1)	H	W	11-0
26 Oct	Thorpe (Q2)	A	D	2-2*
16 Nov	Crusaders (Q3)	H	W	5-2
7 Dec	Swifts (Q4)	H	L	1-5

*Thorpe withdrew

London Cup

2 Nov	Unity	H	W	4-1
23 Nov	Foxes	H	W	4-1
14 Dec	St Martins Ath	H	W	6-0
11 Jan	London Caledonians	H	W	3-1
8 Mar	Old Westminster (Final)		L	0-1

London Charity Cup

1 Feb	Marlow	H	W	4-1
22 Feb	2nd Batt Scots Guards	H	W	3-0
5 Apr	Old Westminster (Final)	H	W	3-1

Kent Senior Cup

12 Oct	5th Northern Fusilliers	H	W	6-1
9 Nov	West Kent	H	W	10-1
14 Dec	Gravesend	H	W	7-2
15 Feb	Chatham	H	W	5-0
22 Mar	Thanet W (Final)		W	3-0

Six-a-Side Competition
Run by National Physical Recreation Society at Agricultural Hall

31 May	London Caledonians		W	15-7

	P	W	L	D	F:A
Arsenal	41	31	5	5	158:49

SEASON 1890-1891
FRIENDLIES

6 Sep	93rd Highlanders	H	D	1-1
13 Sep	Casuals	H	W	5-4
20 Sep	Ilford	H	W	6-0
27 Sep	London Caledonians	H	W	3-1
4 Oct	Chiswick Park	A	W	4-0
11 Oct	93rd Highlanders	H	W	4-1
18 Oct	Old St Marks	A	W	4-0
25 Oct	St Bartholomews Hospital	H	W	1-0
1 Nov	South Shore (Blackpool)	H	D	2-2
8 Nov	Ilford	A	W	3-0
15 Nov	Clapton	A	L	1-2
22 Nov	Gainsborough Trinity	H	W	2-1
1 Dec	Cambridge Univ	H	W	5-1
6 Dec	Casuals	H	D	0-0
24 Jan	Millwall Athletic	A	W	1-0
26 Jan	Everton	H	L	0-5
7 Feb	St Bartholomews Hospital	H	W	5-4
14 Mar	Old Harrovians	H	W	5-1
21 Mar	Sheffield U	H	D	1-1
27 Mar	Highland Light Infantry	H	W	3-1
28 Mar	Old Harrovians	H	W	5-0
30 Mar	Heart of Midlothians	H	L	1-5
31 Mar	Nottingham F	H	L	0-5
18 Apr	Clapton	H	W	3-1
25 Apr	Sunderland	H	L	1-3
30 Apr	London Caledonians	H	D	1-1
2 May	1st Highland Light Infantry	H	W	5-1
3 Jan	London Caledonians (abandoned)			

FA Cup

17 Jan	Derby Co (1)	H	L	1-2

London Cup

13 Dec	Old Westminster	A	W	4-1
31 Jan	Old Westminster	A	L	4-5
21 Feb	Casuals	H	W	3-2
28 Feb	Clapton	A	W	3-2
7 Mar	St Barts Hosp (Final)		W	6-0

London Charity Cup

14 Feb	Crusaders	H	W	1-0
4 Apr	Old Carthusians	A	D	1-1
8 Apr	Old Carthusians	A	D	2-2
11 Apr	Old Carthusians	A	L	1-2

	P	W	L	D	F:A
Arsenal	37	22	6	7	98:58

SEASON 1891-1892
FRIENDLIES

5 Sep	Sheffield U	H	L	0-2
12 Sep	Casuals	H	W	2-1
19 Sep	Gainsborough Trinity	H	L	1-4
26 Sep	W B A	H	D	1-1
3 Oct	St George Birmingham	H	L	1-5
8 Oct	Royal Engineers	H	W	8-0
10 Oct	Crusaders	H	W4-1	
17 Oct	Bootle	A	D	2-2
19 Oct	Sheffield Wed	H	L	1-8
24 Oct	Long Eaton Rangers	H	W	3-1
29 Oct	Royal Artillery	H	W	10-0
31 Oct	Clapton	A	W	7-0
5 Nov	Notts Co	A	L	3-4
7 Nov	London Caledonians	A	W	4-3
12 Nov	Erith	H	W	7-0
14 Nov	Cambridge University	H	W	5-1
19 Nov	Woolwich League	H	W	6-1
21 Nov	St Bartholomews Hospital	H	W	9-0
23 Nov	2nd Scots Guards	H	W	6-0
28 Nov	Canadians	H	D	1-1
30 Nov	Sheffield W	A	L	1-5
3 Dec	Canadians	H	W	4-0
5 Dec	Lincoln C	H	W	3-1
10 Dec	2nd Royal West Kent Reg	H	L	1-2
12 Dec	Chiswick Park	H	W	5-1
19 Dec	Preston N E	H	L	0-3
25 Dec	Sheffield U	A	D	3-3
26 Dec	1st Lincolnshire Reg	H	W	6-0
2 Jan	Cowlairs (Glasgow)	H	L	1-2
7 Jan	City Ramblers	H	W	3-0
9 Jan	Crusaders	H	W	4-1
21 Jan	Windsor Phoenix	H	W	3-1
23 Jan	Grimsby T	H	W	4-1
30 Jan	Burton W	H	W	3-1
4 Feb	Sheffield U	H	L	1-4
6 Feb	Cambridge University	H	W	2-1
13 Feb	Chatham	H	W	3-2
20 Feb	Burton Swifts	H	W	3-1
25 Feb	Windsor Phoenix	A	W	5-0
27 Feb	Derby Co	H	L	3-4
3 Mar	Borough Road College	H	W	5-1
5 Mar	Wolverhampton W	H	L	1-4
10 Mar	Casuals	H	W	3-1
12 Mar	Marlow	A	W	5-2
14 Mar	3rd Lanark Rovers	H	L	0-1
19 Mar	Highland Light Infantry	H	W	3-2
22 Mar	Preston N E	H	D	3-3
26 Mar	Everton	H	D	2-2
31 Mar	Notts Co	H	L	2-4
2 Apr	Chatham	H	W	5-3
9 Apr	South Shore Blackpool	H	D	1-1
15 Apr	Small Heath	H	L	1-2
16 Apr	Crewe Alexandra	H	W	2-1
18 Apr	Bootle	H	D	1-1
23 Apr	Clapton	H	W	4-1
26 Apr	Bolton W	H	W	3-2
30 Apr	Glasgow Ran	H	L	2-3

FA Cup

16 Jan	Small Heath (1)	A	L	1-5

	P	W	L	D	F:A
Arsenal	58	33	17	8	183:107

SEASON 1892-1893
FRIENDLIES

2 Sep	Highland Light Infantry		W	9-0
7 Sep	Gainsborough T		W	4-2
8 Sep	Scots Guards		W	5-1
10 Sep	Casuals		W	4-0
12 Sep	Sheffield U	A	L	0-1
16 Sep	Darlington		W	3-2
24 Sep	Crusaders		W	4-0
1 Oct	Marlow		W	4-0
6 Oct	3rd West Kent Rangers		W	3-0
8 Oct	Clapton		W	4-1
20 Oct	Sheffield U	H	W	1-0
22 Oct	Staffordshire Reg		W	1-0
27 Oct	Oxford University		L	0-4
5 Nov	Lincoln C	H	W	4-0
7 Oct	Fleetwood Rangers		L	1-2
12 Nov	Cambridge University		D	6-6
14 Nov	Sunderland	H	L	0-4
23 Nov	Ipswich T		W	5-0
25 Nov	Norfolk County		W	4-1
26 Nov	Clapton		W	5-0
3 Dec	W B A	H	W	3-1
12 Dec	Mr Armitage XI		W	3-1
17 Dec	Nottingham F	H	L	2-3
23 Dec	Leith Athletic	H	W	1-0
25 Dec	Burslem P V		L	1-3
26 Dec	Stockton		W	1-0
27 Dec	Blackpool	H	D	1-1
2 Jan	Glasgow Thistle	H	L	1-2
7 Jan	Middlesbrough		L	0-2
11 Jan	Sussex Martelos		W	2-0
12 Jan	Brighton		W	2-0
14 Jan	Wolverhampton W	H	L	1-3
25 Jan	Oxford University		L	0-1
28 Jan	Chatham		L	1-3
31 Jan	1st Batt Sherwood Foresters	W	3-0	
3 Feb	Casuals		W	4-1
6 Feb	Royal Lancaster Regiment		W	2-0
9 Feb	Cambridge University		L	2-4
11 Feb	Small Heath	H	W	3-1
13 Feb	3rd Lanark	H	W	3-0
18 Feb	Millwall		W	5-0
25 Feb	Walsall Town Swifts	H	W	4-0
27 Feb	Notts Greenhalgh		L	1-3
3 Mar	Middlesbrough		L	0-2
11 Mar	Dumbarton	H	W	3-1
13 Mar	Aston Villa	H	L	0-1
18 Mar	Middlesbrough		W	4-2
25 Mar	Millwall		W	1-0
31 Mar	Middlesbrough		W	4-1
1 Apr	Accrington St	H	W	3-1
3 Apr	Grimsby T	H	L	3-5
8 Apr	Casuals		W	2-0
15 Apr	Crusaders		W	3-0
22 Apr	Derby Co	H	D	0-0
24 Apr	London Welsh		W	4-0
26 Apr	Sevenoaks		W	11-0
29 Apr	Stoke	H	L	0-1

FA Cup

15 Oct	Highland Light Infantry (Q1)	H	W	3-0
29 Oct	City Ramblers (Q2)	H	W	10-1
19 Nov	Millwall (Q3)	H	W	3-2
10 Dec	Clapton (Q4)	H	W	5-0
21 Jan	Sunderland (1)	A	L	0-1

	P	W	L	D	F:A
Arsenal	62	41	18	3	172:76

SEASON 1893-1894
FOOTBALL LEAGUE (DIVISION 2)

2 Sep	Newcastle U	H	D	2-2
9 Sep	Notts Co	A	L	2-3
11 Sep	Walsall	H	W	4-0
25 Sep	Grimsby T	H	W	3-1
30 Sep	Newcastle U	A	L	0-6
21 Oct	Small Heath	A	L	1-4
28 Oct	Liverpool	H	L	0-5
11 Nov	Aldwick	H	W	1-0
13 Nov	Rotherham	H	W	3-0
18 Nov	Burton Swifts	A	L	2-6
9 Dec	Northwich Victoria	A	D	2-2
25 Dec	Burslem	H	W	4-1
26 Dec	Grimsby T	A	L	1-3
30 Dec	Ardwick	A	W	1-0
1 Jan	Liverpool	A	L	0-2
6 Jan	Burslem	A	L	1-2
3 Feb	Lincoln C	A	L	0-3
6 Feb	Rotherham	A	D	1-1
10 Feb	Crewe Alexandra	H	W	3-2
12 Feb	Walsall	A	W	2-1
17 Feb	Lincoln C	H	W	4-0
24 Feb	Middlesbrough Ironopolis	A	W	6-3
3 Mar	Crewe Alexandra	A	D	0-0
10 Mar	Middlesbrough Ironopolis	H	W	1-0
23 Mar	Northwich Victoria	H	W	6-0
24 Mar	Notts Co	H	L	1-2
31 Mar	Small Heath	H	L	1-4
14 Apr	Burton Swifts	H	L	0-2

FA Cup

14 Oct	Ashford University (Q1)	H	W	12-0
4 Nov	Clapton (Q2)	H	W	6-2
25 Nov	Millwall (Q3)	H	W	2-0
16 Dec	2nd Scots Guards (Q4)	A	W	2-1
27 Jan	Sheffield W (1)	H	L	1-2

Friendlies

4 Sep	Doncaster Rov		W	4-1
16 Sep	Charlton		W	5-0
23 Sep	Middlesbrough	H	W	3-1
7 Oct	Casuals		W	5-1
9 Oct	Sunderland	H	L	1-4
12 Oct	London Caledonians		W	10-3
23 Oct	Mr Roston Bourkes XI		W	4-3
30 Oct	Wolverhampton W	H	W	1-0
30 Nov	London Caledonians		D	1-1
2 Dec	W B A	A	W	5-0
11 Dec	Preston N E		D	1-1
23 Dec	Crusaders		W	7-0
13 Jan	Accrington Stanley		W	2-0
15 Jan	Aston Villa	H	L	1-3
20 Jan	Chatham		W	4-0
29 Jan	Blackpool		W	5-2
1 Mar	London Caledonians		W	1-0
5 Mar	Luton T		W	2-0
12 Mar	Sheffield U	A	W	2-0
17 Mar	Millwall		D	2-2
26 Mar	St Mirren		L	1-3
2 Apr	Nottingham F	H	L	1-3
7 Apr	Millwall		W	4-1
9 Apr	Sheffield U	H	L	0-1
11 Apr	New Brompton		W	4-1
12 Apr	Westerham District XI		W	6-3
16 Apr	Luton T		D	3-3
21 Apr	Burnley	H	W	2-0
25 Apr	Corinthians	A	L	3-4
28 Apr	Stoke	H	D	3-3

Position in Football League Table

	P	W	L	D	F:A	Pts	
Liverpool	28	22	0	6	77:18	50	1st
Arsenal	28	12	12	4	52:55	28	9th

SEASON 1894-1895
FOOTBALL LEAGUE (DIVISION 2)

1 Sep	Lincoln C	A	L	2-5
10 Sep	Grimsby T	H	L	1-3
15 Sep	Burton Swifts	A	L	0-3
22 Sep	Bury	H	W	4-2
29 Sep	Manchester C	H	W	4-2
6 Oct	Lincoln C	H	W	5-2
13 Oct	Newton Heath	A	D	3-3
20 Oct	Rotherham	A	W	2-1
27 Oct	Notts Co	A	D	2-2
3 Nov	Notts Co	H	W	2-1
10 Nov	Walsall	A	L	1-4
24 Nov	Newcastle U	A	W	4-2
8 Dec	Darwen	H	W	4-0
15 Dec	Manchester C	A	L	1-4
25 Dec	Burslem Port Vale	H	W	7-0
26 Dec	Grimsby T	A	L	2-4
1 Jan	Darwen	A	L	1-3
7 Jan	Leicester Fosse	A	L	1-3
12 Jan	Newcastle U	H	W	3-2
19 Jan	Burslem P V	A	W	1-0
26 Jan	Burton Wanderers	H	D	1-1
9 Feb	Rotherham	H	D	1-1
23 Feb	Burton Swifts	H	W	3-0
2 Mar	Bury	A	L	0-2
9 Mar	Leicester Fosse	H	D	3-3
23 Mar	Crewe Alexandra	A	D	0-0
30 Mar	Newton Heath	H	W	3-2
6 Apr	Crewe Alexandra	H	W	7-0
12 Apr	Walsall	H	W	6-1
20 Apr	Burton W	A	L	1-2

FA Cup

2 Feb	Bolton W (1)	A	L	0-1

Friendlies

3 Sep	Nottingham F	H	W	3-2
8 Sep	Fleetwood Rovers		W	4-0
17 Sep	W B A		L	0-1
24 Sep	Renton		W	6-1
4 Oct	Casuals		W	8-0
15 Oct	Sunderland	H	W	2-1
29 Oct	Luton T		W	5-0
12 Nov	R. Bourkes XI		W	6-2
17 Nov	Casuals		W	4-1
21 Nov	Marlow		W	4-2
1 Dec	Stoke C	H	W	3-1
3 Dec	St Bernards	H	L	1-2
24 Dec	New Brompton		L	0-5
29 Dec	Dresden University		W	1-0
5 Jan	Sheppey University		W	6-1
11 Feb	Luton T		W	2-1
16 Feb	Chatham		W	6-0
25 Feb	Liverpool	H	W	4-3
6 Mar	Eastbourne		W	5-1
13 Mar	Bromley & District		W	4-1
16 Mar	Gainsborough Trinity	H	W	2-0
20 Mar	Home Park Plymouth		W	2-1
21 Mar	Weymouth		W	5-0
25 Mar	Millwall	H	D	1-1
1 Apr	Blackburn Rov	H	D	2-2
8 Apr	Millwall	A	D	0-0
13 Apr	Dumbarton		W	5-1
15 Apr	Small Heath	H	L	3-4
25 Apr	Royal Ordnance		L	0-1
27 Apr	Millwall	A	W	3-1
30 Apr	Grimsby T		L	0-2

Position in Football League Table

	P	W	L	D	F:A	Pts	
Bury	30	23	5	2	78:33	48	1st
Arsenal	30	14	10	6	75:58	34	8th

SEASON 1895-1896
FOOTBALL LEAGUE (DIVISION 2)

2 Sep	Grimsby T	H	W	3-1
7 Sep	Manchester C	H	L	0-1
14 Sep	Lincoln C	A	D	1-1
21 Sep	Lincoln C	H	W	4-0
28 Sep	Manchester C	A	L	0-1
5 Oct	Rotherham	H	W	5-0
12 Oct	Burton W	H	W	3-0
19 Oct	Burton Swifts	H	W	5-0
26 Oct	Rotherham	A	L	0-3
2 Oct	Notts Co	A	W	4-3
9 Nov	Newton Heath	H	W	2-1
16 Nov	Liverpool	H	L	0-2
30 Nov	Newton Heath	A	L	1-5
7 Dec	Leicester Fosse	H	D	1-1
14 Dec	Burton W	A	L	1-4
21 Dec	Burton Swifts	A	L	2-3
23 Dec	Crewe Alexandra	A	W	1-0
25 Dec	Burslem Port Vale	H	W	2-1
4 Jan	Loughborough	H	W	6-0
11 Jan	Liverpool	A	L	0-3
18 Jan	Newcastle U	A	L	1-3
25 Jan	Leicester Fosse	A	L	0-1
15 Feb	Burslem Port Vale	A	W	2-0
29 Feb	Loughborough	A	L	1-2
7 Mar	Notts Co	H	W	2-0
14 Mar	Darwen	A	D	1-1
21 Mar	Crewe Alexandra	H	W	7-0
4 Mar	Grimsby T	A	D	1-1
6 Apr	Newcastle U	H	W	2-1
18 Apr	Darwen	H	L	1-3

FA Cup

2 Feb	Burnley (1)	A	L	1-6

Friendlies

9 Sep	Millwall	A	W	3-1
23 Sep	Sheffield W	H	W	2-1
14 Oct	Everton	H	L	0-2
4 Nov	Royal Ordnance		W	3-1
21 Nov	Casuals		W	3-0
23 Nov	Barnsley St Peters		W	4-1
9 Dec	Sunderland	H	L	1-2
26 Dec	Cliftonville	H	W	10-1
28 Dec	Darlington		W	6-2
1 Jan	Hastings		W	12-0
20 Jan	Cambridge University	H	W	7-1
10 Feb	Royal Ordnance		W	6-0
22 Feb	Stirlingshire		W	5-0
24 Feb	Newton Heath	H	W	6-1
2 Mar	Casuals		W	4-1
16 Mar	Tottenham H		L	1-3
23 Mar	Sheffield U	H	W	3-1
26 Mar	Tottenham H		W	3-1
28 Mar	Millwall	A	W	3-1
2 Apr	Stockton		W	2-0
3 Apr	Dundee		W	3-1
7 Apr	Gravesend		W	4-0
11 Apr	Millwall	H	D	2-2
13 Apr	Everton	H	W	2-1
20 Apr	Whittaker XI		W	3-2
25 Apr	Luton T	H	W	5-2
27 Apr	Luton T	A	L	0-2
29 Apr	Chatham		W	1-0
30 Apr	Tottenham H		L	2-3

Position in Football League Table

	P	W	L	D	F:A	Pts	
Liverpool	30	22	6	2	108:32	46	1st
Arsenal	30	14	12	4	59:42	32	7th

SEASON 1896-1897
FOOTBALL LEAGUE (DIVISION 2)

5 Sep	Manchester C	A	D	1-1
12 Sep	Walsall	H	D	1-1
14 Sep	Burton Wanderers	A	W	3-0
19 Sep	Loughborough	H	W	2-0
26 Sep	Notts Co	H	L	2-3
12 Oct	Burton Wanderers	H	W	3-0
17 Oct	Walsall	A	L	3-5
24 Oct	Gainsborough	H	W	6-1
7 Nov	Notts Co	A	L	4-7
14 Nov	Small Heath	A	L	2-5
28 Nov	Grimsby T	H	W	4-2
5 Dec	Lincoln C	A	W	3-2
12 Dec	Loughborough	A	L	0-8
19 Dec	Blackpool	H	W	4-2
25 Dec	Lincoln C	H	W	6-2
26 Dec	Gainsborough	A	L	1-4
1 Jan	Darwen	A	L	1-4
4 Jan	Blackpool	A	D	1-1
23 Jan	Newcastle U	A	L	0-2
13 Feb	Leicester Fosse	A	L	3-6
20 Feb	Burton Swifts	H	W	3-0
13 Mar	Burton Swifts	A	W	2-1
22 Mar	Newton Heath	A	D	1-1
29 Mar	Small Heath	H	L	2-3
3 Apr	Newton Heath	H	L	0-2
8 Apr	Grimsby T	A	L	1-3
16 Apr	Newcastle U	H	W	5-1
17 Apr	Leicester Fosse	H	W	2-1
19 Apr	Darwen	H	W	1-0
28 Apr	Manchester C	H	L	1-2

FA Cup

12 Dec	Leyton (Q)	H	W	5-2
2 Jan	Chatham (Q)	H	W	4-0
16 Jan	Millwall (Q)	A	L	2-4

United League

7 Sep	Rushden		W	3-2
3 Oct	Luton T		D	2-2
5 Oct	Rushden		L	3-5
19 Oct	Wellingborough		W	2-1
2 Nov	Kettering		D	1-1
9 Nov	Tottenham H		W	2-1
23 Nov	Kettering		W	1-0
30 Nov	Wellingbrough		L	1-4
9 Jan	Loughborough		W	5-3
25 Feb	Tottenham H		D	2-2
27 Feb	Millwall		W	3-1
20 Mar	Luton T		L	2-5
7 Apr	Loughborough		L	0-4
24 Apr	Millwall		L	1-3

Friendlies

1 Sep	Rossendale		W	4-0
10 Sep	Millwall		W	2-1
10 Oct	Millwall		L	1-5
26 Oct	Luton		L	1-3
31 Oct	Clyde		L	2-3
21 Nov	Millwall		D	2-2
7 Dec	Aston Villa		L	1-3
30 Jan	Ilkeston		W	7-0
8 Feb	Luton		W	5-1
15 Feb	Celtic		L	4-5
1 Mar	Reading		W	6-2
6 Mar	Casuals		L	3-5
10 Mar	Reading		W	2-1
15 Mar	St Mary's, Southampton		W	2-1
27 Mar	Nottingham F		W	1-0
20 Apr	Norfolk		L	3-4
28 Apr	Sheffield U		D	1-1

Position in Football League Table

	P	W	L	D	F:A	Pts	
Notts Co	30	19	7	4	92:43	42	1st
Arsenal	30	13	13	4	68:70	30	10th

Position in United League Table

	P	W	L	D	F:A	Pts	
Millwall	14	11	2	1	43:22	23	1st
Arsenal	14	6	5	3	28:34	15	3rd

SEASON 1897-1898
FOOTBALL LEAGUE (DIVISION 2)

1 Sep	Grimsby T	H	W	4-1
4 Sep	Newcastle U	A	L	1-4
6 Sep	Burnley	A	L	0-5
11 Sep	Lincoln C	H	D	2-2
18 Sep	Gainsborough	H	W	4-0
25 Sep	Manchester C	A	L	1-4
2 Oct	Luton T	A	W	2-0
9 Oct	Luton T	H	W	3-0
16 Oct	Newcastle U	H	D	0-0
23 Oct	Leicester Fosse	H	L	0-3
6 Nov	Walsall	A	L	2-3
13 Nov	Walsall	H	W	4-0
27 Nov	Blackpool	H	W	2-1
4 Dec	Leicester Fosse	A	L	1-2
18 Dec	Loughborough	A	W	3-1
27 Dec	Lincoln C	A	W	3-2
1 Jan	Blackpool	A	D	3-3
8 Jan	Newton Heath	H	W	5-1
15 Jan	Burton Swifts	A	W	2-1
5 Feb	Manchester C	H	D	2-2

(Season continued)

12 Feb Grimsby T A W 4-1
26 Feb Newton Heath A L 1-5
5 Mar Small Heath H W 4-0
12 Mar Darwen A W 4-1
19 Mar Loughborough H W 4-0
26 Mar Gainsborough A L 0-1
2 Apr Burnley H D 1-1
9 Apr Darwen H W 3-1
11 Apr Burton Swifts H W 3-0
23 Apr Small Heath A L 1-2

FA Cup
30 Oct St Albans (Q) H W 9-0
20 Nov Sheppey United (Q) H W 3-0
11 Dec New Brompton (Q) H W 4-2
29 Jan Burnley (Q) A L 1-3

United League
22 Sep Loughborough A W 3-1
4 Oct Kettering H W 4-0
11 Oct Wellingborough A W 3-2
13 Dec Rushden H W 3-1
20 Dec Southampton H D 1-1
25 Dec Tottenham H H L 2-3
10 Jan Wellingborough H W 3-1
22 Jan Millwall A D 2-2
19 Feb Millwall H D 2-2
21 Feb Luton T H D 2-2
28 Mar Rushden A W 3-2
1 Apr Loughborough H W 4-1
4 Apr Kettering A W 2-1
8 Apr Tottenham H A D 0-0
13 Apr Southampton A L 0-3
16 Apr Luton T A L 1-2

Friendlies
15 Sep Gravesend A W 3-1
1 Nov Reading H W 3-0
8 Nov Blackburn Rov H W 3-0
15 Nov Bristol C A L 2-4
9 Feb Maidstone A W 3-0
21 Mar Bristol C H W 3-1
26 Apr Thames Iron Works A D 2-2
28 Apr Tottenham H H W 5-0
30 Apr Millwall A L 0-2

Position in Football League Table

	P	W	L	D	F:A	Pts	
Burnley	30	20	2	8	80:24	48	1st
Arsenal	30	16	9	5	69:49	37	5th

Position in United League Table

	P	W	L	D	F:A	Pts	
Luton	16	13	1	2	49:11	28	1st
Arsenal	16	8	3	5	35:24	21	3rd

SEASON 1898-1899
FOOTBALL LEAGUE (DIVISION 2)

3 Sep Luton T A W 1-0
5 Sep Burslem PV A L 0-3
10 Sep Leicester Fosse H W 4-0
17 Sep Darwen A W 4-1
24 Sep Gainsborough H W 5-1
1 Oct Manchester C A L 1-4
15 Oct Walsall A L 1-4
22 Oct Burton Swifts H W 2-1
5 Nov Small Heath H W 2-0
12 Nov Loughborough A D 0-0
26 Nov New Brighton H W 5-1
3 Dec Newton Heath H W 5-1
10 Dec New Brighton A L 1-3
17 Dec Lincoln C H W 4-2
24 Dec Barnsley A L 1-2
31 Dec Luton T H W 6-2
7 Jan Leicester Fosse A L 1-2
14 Jan Darwen H W 6-0
21 Jan Gainsborough A W 1-0
4 Feb Glossop A L 0-2
11 Feb Walsall H D 0-0
13 Feb Glossop H W 3-0
18 Feb Burton Swifts A W 2-1
25 Feb Burslem PV H W 1-0
4 Mar Small Heath A L 1-4
13 Mar Loughborough H W 3-1
18 Mar Blackpool H W 6-0
22 Mar Blackpool A D 1-1
25 Mar Grimsby T H D 1-1
1 Apr Newton Heath A D 2-2
3 Apr Manchester C H L 0-1
8 Apr New Brighton H W 4-0
15 Apr Lincoln C A L 0-2
22 Apr Barnsley H W 3-0

FA Cup
28 Jan Derby Co (1) H L 0-6

Chatham Charity Cup
18 Jan Chatham A D 1-1
20 Feb Chatham H D 3-3
6 Mar Chatham A L 1-2

United League
14 Sep Reading A D 1-1
3 Oct Reading H W 2-0
8 Oct Millwall A W 2-1
10 Oct Luton T H W 3-2
17 Oct Rushden A L 1-5
24 Oct Kettering A L 1-5
29 Oct Southampton A L 1-5
31 Oct Brighton & HA H W 5-2
9 Nov Bristol C A W 2-1
14 Nov Wellingborough A L 0-3

---

19 Nov Southampton H W 2-1
21 Nov Rushden A W 6-0
12 Dec Bristol C H L 1-3
26 Dec Millwall H L 0-1
27 Dec Luton T A D 1-1
4 Jan Brighton & HA A D 1-1
6 Feb Kettering H W 4-2
11 Mar Tottenham H H W 3-1
31 Mar Wellingborough A W 3-0
29 Apr Tottenham H A L 2-3

Friendlies
1 Sep Gravesend H L 0-1
19 Sep Thames Iron Works H W 4-0
25 Oct Gravesend W 1-0
23 Nov Corinthians A L 1-4
28 Nov Chatham A L 1-3
8 Dec Thames Iron Works A W 3-1
25 Jan Sevenoaks A W 7-1
30 Jan Millwall H L 1-4
15 Feb Gravesend A L 2-3
23 Feb Clapton A W 3-0
9 Mar Casuals A W 3-1
23 Mar Past XI v Present XI Present won 3-1
4 Apr Millwall A D 0-0
24 Apr Notts Co A W 3-1
26 Apr Woolwich Locals W 3-0

Position in Football League Table

	P	W	L	D	F:A	Pts	
Manchester C	34	23	5	6	92:35	52	1st
Arsenal	34	18	11	5	72:41	41	7th

Position in United League Table

	P	W	L	D	F:A	Pts	
Millwall	20	14	3	3	42:19	31	1st
Arsenal	20	10	6	4	40:30	24	4th

SEASON 1899-1900
FOOTBALL LEAGUE (DIVISION 2)

2 Sep Leicester Fosse H L 0-2
9 Sep Luton T A W 2-1
16 Sep Burslem PV H W 1-0
23 Sep Walsall A L 0-2
30 Sep Middlesbrough H W 3-0
7 Oct Chesterfield A L 1-3
14 Oct Gainsborough H W 2-1
21 Oct Bolton W A L 0-1
4 Nov Newton Heath A L 0-2
11 Nov Sheffield Wed H L 1-2
25 Nov Small Heath H W 3-0
2 Dec New Brighton A W 2-0
16 Dec Burton Swifts H D 1-1
25 Dec Lincoln C A L 0-5
30 Dec Leicester Fosse A D 0-0
6 Jan Luton T H W 3-1
13 Jan Burslem PV A D 1-1
20 Jan Walsall H W 2-0
3 Feb Middlesbrough A L 0-1
10 Feb Chesterfield H W 2-0
17 Feb Gainsborough A D 1-1
24 Feb Bolton W H W 1-0
3 Mar Loughborough A W 3-2
10 Mar Newton Heath H W 2-1
12 Mar Loughborough H W 12-0
17 Mar Sheffield Wed A L 1-3
24 Mar Lincoln C H W 2-1
31 Mar Small Heath A L 1-3
7 Apr New Brighton H W 5-0
14 Apr Grimsby T H W 2-0
16 Apr Grimsby T H W 2-0
21 Apr Burton Swifts A L 0-2
23 Apr Barnsley A L 2-3
28 Apr Barnsley H W 5-1

FA Cup
28 Oct New Brompton (Q) H D 1-1
1 Nov New Brompton (QR) A D 0-0
6 Nov New Brompton (QR) A D 2-2
8 Nov New Brompton (QR) H W 1-0
14 Nov New Brompton (QR) A L 0-1

Southern District Combination
11 Sep Millwall L 0-1
27 Sep Reading W 3-0
11 Oct Southampton L 0-3
23 Oct Portsmouth L 0-2
30 Oct Bristol C W 3-0
10 Jan Bristol C W 3-1
29 Jan Chatham W 4-0
7 Feb Portsmouth L 1-3
26 Feb Chatham W 2-1
5 Mar Southampton L 0-1
19 Mar Q P R W 5-1
26 Mar Reading D 1-1
2 Apr Millwall L 0-1
9 Apr Q P R L 0-1
17 Apr Tottenham H L 2-4
24 Apr Tottenham H W 2-1*
*unfinished

Friendlies
4 Sep Stoke W 5-3
2 Oct Aston Villa W 2-1
29 Nov Eastbourne W 2-1
9 Dec Southampton D 1-1
23 Dec Swindon T W 3-0
27 Jan Bedminster W 3-0
19 Feb Derby Co L 0-1
13 Apr Burnley W 2-0

Position in Football League Table

	P	W	L	D	F:A	Pts	
Sheffield Wed	34	25	5	4	84:22	54	1st
Arsenal	34	16	14	4	61:43	36	8th

Position in Southern District Combination League

	P	W	L	D	F:A	Pts	
Millwall	16	12	2	2	30:10	26	1st
Arsenal	15	7	7	1	61:21	15	4th

(Exclusive of match unfinished 24 April, against Tottenham H, Arsenal leading 2-1)

SEASON 1900-1901
FOOTBALL LEAGUE (DIVISION 2)

1 Sep Gainsborough H W 2-1
8 Sep Walsall H D 1-1
15 Sep Burton Swifts A L 0-1
22 Sep Barnsley A L 1-2
29 Sep Chesterfield H W 1-0
6 Oct Blackpool A D 1-1
13 Oct Stockport Co H W 2-0
20 Oct Small Heath A L 1-2
27 Oct Grimsby H D 1-1
3 Nov Leicester H W 2-1
10 Nov Newton Heath A W 1-0
17 Nov Glossop H W 1-0
24 Nov Middlesbrough A D 1-1
1 Dec Burnley A L 0-3
8 Dec Burslem PV H W 1-0
15 Dec Leicester A L 0-1
22 Dec New Brighton H W 2-1
24 Dec Walsall A L 0-1
29 Dec Gainsborough A L 0-3
12 Jan Burton Swifts H W 1-0
19 Jan Barnsley A L 0-3
26 Jan Lincoln C A D 3-3
16 Feb Chesterfield A W 1-0
19 Feb Grimsby T A L 0-1
9 Mar Lincoln C H D 0-0
16 Mar Newton Heath A L 0-1
23 Mar Glossop A W 2-0
30 Mar Middlesbrough A D 1-1
6 Apr Burnley H W 3-1
8 Apr Blackpool H W 3-1
12 Apr Burslem PV A D 1-1
27 Apr New Brighton A L 0-1

FA Cup
5 Jan Darwen (Q) A W 2-0
2 Feb Blackburn Rov (1) A W 2-0
23 Feb W B A (2) H L 0-1

Friendlies
1 Oct Aston Villa H W 3-0
1 Nov Southampton L 1-4
25 Nov West Ham U W 1-0
26 Dec Newcastle U H D 1-1
1 Jan Newcastle U L 1-5
4 Mar Southern League XI W 2-1
1 Apr Millwall D 1-1
5 Apr Nottingham F H D 1-1
20 Apr Notts Co H W 3-0
25 Apr West Ham U D 0-0

Position in Football League Table

	P	W	L	D	F:A	Pts	
Grimsby T	34	20	5	9	60:33	49	1st
Arsenal	34	15	13	6	39:35	36	7th

SEASON 1901-1902
FOOTBALL LEAGUE (DIVISION 2)

2 Sep Barnsley H W 2-1
4 Sep Leicester H W 2-0
14 Sep Preston NE A L 2-0
21 Sep Burnley H W 4-0
28 Sep Burslem PV A L 0-1
5 Oct Chesterfield H W 3-2
12 Oct Gainsborough A D 2-2
19 Oct Middlesbrough H L 0-3
26 Oct Bristol C A W 3-0
9 Nov Stockport Co A D 0-0
16 Nov Newton Heath H W 2-0
23 Nov Glossop A W 1-0
30 Nov Doncaster Rov H W 1-0
7 Dec Lincoln C A D 0-0
21 Dec Burton Un H L 0-1
26 Dec Blackpool H D 0-0
26 Dec Burslem PV H W 3-1
28 Dec Barnsley A L 0-2
4 Jan Leicester A L 1-2
11 Jan Preston NE H D 0-0
18 Jan Burnley A W 1-0
1 Feb Chesterfield H W 1-0
8 Feb Gainsborough H W 5-0
15 Feb Middlesbrough A L 0-1
22 Feb Bristol C H L 0-1
1 Mar Blackpool A W 2-0
8 Mar Stockport Co A W 2-0
15 Mar Newton Heath A W 1-0
22 Mar Glossop H W 4-0
29 Mar Doncaster Rov A W 1-0
31 Mar W B A H W 2-1
5 Apr Lincoln C H W 2-0
12 Apr W B A A L 1-2
19 Apr Burton Un A L 0-2

FA Cup
13 Dec Brentford A D 1-1
17 Dec Brentford (QR) H W 5-0
7 Feb Sheffield U (1) H L 1-3

Southern Charity Cup
9 Feb Millwall H L 2-3

London League
1 Sep West Ham U A W 3-1
15 Sep Q P R A W 2-0
27 Oct Q P R A W 2-0
10 Nov Brentford H W 2-0
17 Nov Tottenham H H W 1-0
1 Dec Tottenham H A L 0-3
26 Dec Millwall H D 0-0
21 Feb West Ham U H L 0-1
23 Mar Brentford A W 1-0
18 Apr Millwall H L 0-2

Friendlies
8 Sep New Brompton A W 3-2
18 Mar Brighton & HA A W 3-1
14 Apr Northampton T A D 1-1
20 Apr Bristol C A W 2-0
25 Apr Chesterfield H W 1-0

Position in Football League Table

	P	W	L	D	F:A	Pts	
Manchester C	34	25	5	4	95:29	54	1st
Arsenal	34	20	6	8	66:30	48	3rd

Position in London League Table

	P	W	L	D	F:A	Pts	
Tottenham H	10	7	2	1	19:4	15	1st
Arsenal	10	6	4	0	14:10	12	3rd

FA Cup
14 Dec Luton T (Q) H D 1-1
18 Dec Luton T (QR) A W 2-0
25 Jan Newcastle U H L 0-2

Southern Charity Cup
7 Apr Portsmouth A W 2-1
23 Apr Tottenham H (Semi Final) H D 0-0
29 Apr Tottenham H (Semi Final) A L 1-2

London League
16 Sep Tottenham H L 0-2
30 Sep Millwall D 1-1
21 Oct West Ham U L 0-5
4 Nov Tottenham H L 0-2
3 Feb Q P R D 2-2
17 Feb Q P R W 3-0
24 Apr Millwall W 2-0
28 Mar West Ham U W 2-0

Friendlies
2 Nov Reading H W 1-0
18 Nov Southampton H L 0-1
1 Apr Blackburn Rov H W 2-0
25 Apr Plymouth Arg A W 4-1
26 Apr W B A H L 0-1

Position in Football League Table

	P	W	L	D	F:A	Pts	
W B A	34	25	4	5	82:29	55	1st
Arsenal	34	18	10	6	50:26	42	4th

Position in London League Table

	P	W	L	D	F:A	Pts	
West Ham U	8	5	2	1	19:9	11	1st
Arsenal	8	2	4	2	9:13	6	5th

SEASON 1902-1903
FOOTBALL LEAGUE (DIVISION 2)

6 Sep Preston NE A D 2-2
13 Sep Burslem PV H W 3-0
20 Sep Barnsley A D 1-1
27 Sep Gainsborough H W 6-1
4 Oct Bristol C A L 0-1
11 Oct Glossop H W 2-0
18 Oct Glossop A W 2-1
25 Oct Manchester U H L 0-1
1 Nov Manchester C H W 1-0
8 Nov Blackpool A W 3-0
15 Nov Burnley A W 3-0
22 Nov Doncaster Rov H W 3-0
29 Nov Lincoln C H W 2-1
6 Dec Small Heath A L 0-2
20 Dec Manchester C A L 1-2
25 Dec Burton Un H L 1-2
27 Dec Burnley H W 5-1
1 Jan Stockport Co H W 3-0
3 Jan Preston NE H D 1-1
10 Jan Burslem PV A D 1-1
17 Jan Barnsley H W 4-0
24 Jan Gainsborough A W 2-0
31 Jan Burton Un A L 0-1
14 Feb Glossop NE H D 0-0
28 Feb Stockport Co H D 0-0
7 Mar Blackpool A D 0-0
9 Mar Manchester U A L 0-3
14 Mar Chesterfield H W 3-0
21 Mar Doncaster Rov H W 3-0
28 Mar Lincoln C A D 2-2
4 Apr Small Heath H W 6-1
10 Apr Chesterfield A W 2-0
11 Apr Leicester A W 2-0
13 Apr Leicester H D 0-0

FA Cup
13 Dec Brentford A D 1-1
17 Dec Brentford (QR) H W 5-0
7 Feb Sheffield U (1) H L 1-3

Southern Charity Cup
9 Feb Millwall H L 2-3

London League
1 Sep Tottenham H W 1-0
7 Sep Tottenham H W 2-0
14 Sep West Ham U W 4-1
14 Nov Tottenham H D 1-1
23 Nov Brentford D 1-1
7 Dec Millwall L 1-3
11 Jan Q P R W 6-2
8 Feb Brentford W 3-2
22 Feb West Ham U W 4-2
7 Mar Millwall L 0-3
21 Mar Q P R L 1-3
30 Apr Fulham L 0-1

Friendlies
17 Oct Luton D 2-2
30 Nov Army W 4-0

Position in Football League Table

	P	W	L	D	F:A	Pts	
Preston NE	34	20	4	10	62:24	50	1st
Arsenal	34	21	6	7	91:22	49	2nd

Position in London League Table

	P	W	L	D	F:A	Pts	
Millwall	12	11	0	1	38:8	23	1st
Arsenal	12	6	4	2	24:19	14	3rd

SEASON 1904-1905
FOOTBALL LEAGUE (DIVISION 1)

3 Sep Newcastle U A L 0-3
10 Sep Preston NE A L 0-1
17 Sep Middlesbrough A L 0-1
24 Sep Wolverhampton W H W 2-0
1 Oct Bury A D 1-1
8 Oct Aston Villa H W 1-0
15 Oct Blackburn Rov H W 3-1
22 Oct Nottingham F A L 0-3
29 Oct Sheffield Wed H L 1-3
5 Nov Sunderland H D 0-0
12 Nov Stoke H W 5-1
19 Nov Derby Co A D 0-0
26 Nov Small Heath A L 0-1
10 Dec Manchester C H W 1-0
17 Dec Notts Co A W 5-1
24 Dec Aston Villa A L 1-3
26 Dec Sheffield U H W 3-1
28 Dec Sheffield U A L 0-4
31 Dec Newcastle U H L 0-2
7 Jan Preston NE A L 0-3
14 Jan Middlesbrough H D 1-1
21 Jan Wolverhampton W A L 1-4
28 Jan Bury A W 3-1
11 Feb Blackburn Rov H W 2-0
25 Feb Sheffield Wed A L 1-2
4 Mar Sunderland A D 0-0
11 Mar Stoke H W 2-1
18 Mar Derby Co A D 0-0
1 Apr Small Heath H W 2-0
5 Apr Everton A L 0-1
8 Apr Manchester C A L 0-1

SEASON 1903-1904
FOOTBALL LEAGUE (DIVISION 2)

5 Sep Blackpool H W 3-0
12 Sep Gainsborough A W 2-0
19 Sep Burton Un A W 8-0
26 Sep Bristol C A W 4-0
3 Oct Manchester U A W 4-0
10 Oct Glossop A W 3-0
24 Oct Burslem PV A W 3-2
31 Oct Leicester A L 4-0
7 Nov Lincoln C H W 4-0
14 Nov Chesterfield H W 6-0
28 Nov Bolton W A L 1-2
19 Dec Gainsborough H W 5-1
25 Dec Bradford C H W 4-1
26 Dec Leicester A D 0-0
1 Jan Stockport Co A D 2-2
2 Jan Blackpool A D 2-2
9 Jan Gainsborough H W 6-0
16 Jan Burton Un A L 0-1
30 Jan Manchester U A L 0-1
27 Feb Barnsley H W 4-0
29 Feb Burnley H W 4-0
5 Mar Lincoln C A W 2-0
12 Mar Stockport Co H W 5-2
14 Mar Bristol C A L 0-1
19 Mar Chesterfield A L 0-1
26 Mar Bolton W A D 0-0
1 Apr Preston NE A D 0-0
2 Apr Burnley A L 0-2
4 Apr Glossop A W 2-1
9 Apr Preston NE H D 0-0
16 Apr Grimsby T H D 2-2
19 Apr Bradford C A D 0-0
25 Apr Burslem PV H D 0-0

FA Cup
12 Dec Bristol Rov (Q) A D 1-1
15 Dec Bristol Rov (QR) H D 1-1
21 Dec Bristol Rov (QR) A* W 1-0
6 Feb Fulham (1) H L 0-1
20 Feb Manchester C (2) H L 0-1
*at Tottenham

Southern Charity Cup
12 Oct West Ham U W 1-0
18 Jan Reading (Semi-Final) W 3-1
28 Apr Millwall (Final) L 1-2

London League
1 Sep Tottenham H W 1-0
7 Sep Tottenham H W 2-0
14 Sep West Ham U W 4-1
14 Nov Tottenham H D 1-1
23 Nov Brentford D 1-1
7 Dec Millwall L 1-3
11 Jan Q P R W 6-2
8 Feb Brentford W 3-2
22 Feb West Ham U W 4-2
7 Mar Millwall L 0-3
21 Mar Q P R L 1-3
30 Apr Fulham L 0-1

Friendlies
17 Oct Luton D 2-2
30 Nov Army W 4-0

Position in Football League Table

	P	W	L	D	F:A	Pts	
Preston NE	34	20	4	10	62:24	50	1st
Arsenal	34	21	6	7	91:22	49	2nd

Position in London League Table

	P	W	L	D	F:A	Pts	
Millwall	12	11	0	1	38:8	23	1st
Arsenal	12	6	4	2	24:19	14	3rd

SEASON 1904-1905
FOOTBALL LEAGUE (DIVISION 1)

3 Sep Newcastle U A L 0-3
10 Sep Preston NE A L 0-1
17 Sep Middlesbrough A L 0-1
24 Sep Wolverhampton W H W 2-0
1 Oct Bury A D 1-1
8 Oct Aston Villa H W 1-0
15 Oct Blackburn Rov A L 1-3
17 Sep Middlesbrough A L 0-1
1 Nov Tottenham H W 1-0
26 Dec Manchester C H W 2-1
29 Dec Sheffield Wed A L 1-3
5 Nov Sunderland H D 0-0
12 Nov Stoke A L 0-1
19 Nov Derby Co A D 0-0
3 Dec Small Heath A L 0-1
10 Dec Manchester C H W 1-0
17 Dec Notts Co A W 5-1
24 Dec Aston Villa A L 1-3
26 Dec Sheffield U H W 1-0
28 Dec Sheffield U A L 0-4
31 Dec Newcastle U H L 0-3
7 Jan Preston NE A L 0-3
14 Jan Middlesbrough H D 1-1
21 Jan Wolverhampton W A L 1-4
28 Jan Bury A W 1-0
11 Feb Blackburn Rov H W 2-0
25 Feb Sheffield Wed A L 1-3
4 Mar Sunderland A D 0-0
11 Mar Stoke H W 1-0
18 Mar Derby Co A D 0-0
1 Apr Small Heath H W 2-0
5 Apr Everton A L 0-1
8 Apr Manchester C A L 0-1

---

15 Apr Notts Co H L 1-2
22 Apr Everton H W 2-1

FA Cup
4 Feb Bristol C (1) H D 0-0
8 Feb Bristol C (1R) A L 0-1

Southern Charity Cup
10 Oct Tottenham H H L 1-3

Friendlies
1 Sep Bristol C A W 1-0
12 Sep West Ham U A D 1-1
31 Oct Cambridge Univ H W 3-0
22 Nov Cambridge Univ A W 4-3
5 Dec French International Team H W 26-1
18 Feb Corinthians A L 1-2
27 Feb Queens Park (Glasgow) H W 6-1
25 Mar Burnley A W 2-0
12 Apr Southend U A W 4-0
21 Apr New Brompton H W 3-1
24 Apr Dundee A W 2-0
26 Apr Ipswich T A W 3-1
27 Apr Norwich C A L 1-2
29 Apr Sheffield U A L 2-3

Position in Football League Table

	P	W	L	D	F:A	Pts	
Newcastle U	34	23	9	2	72:33	48	1st
Arsenal	34	12	13	9	36:40	33	10th

SEASON 1905-1906
FOOTBALL LEAGUE (DIVISION 1)

2 Sep Liverpool H W 3-1
9 Sep Sheffield U A L 1-3
16 Sep Notts Co H D 1-1
18 Sep Preston NE H D 2-2
23 Sep Stoke A L 1-2
30 Sep Bolton W H D 0-0
7 Oct Wolverhampton W A W 2-0
14 Oct Blackburn Rov A L 1-2
21 Oct Sunderland H W 2-0
28 Oct Birmingham A L 1-2
4 Nov Everton H L 1-5
11 Nov Derby Co A L 1-5
18 Nov Sheffield Wed H L 1-3
25 Nov Nottingham F H L 1-3
2 Dec Manchester C A L 0-2
9 Dec Bury A L 0-2
16 Dec Middlesbrough H D 2-2
23 Dec Preston NE A D 2-2
25 Dec Newcastle U H W 4-3
27 Dec Aston Villa A L 1-2
30 Dec Liverpool A L 1-6
1 Jan Bolton W H W 5-1
6 Jan Sheffield U H W 5-1
20 Jan Notts Co A L 1-2
27 Jan Stoke H W 2-1
10 Feb Wolverhampton W H W 2-1
17 Feb Blackburn Rov H W 5-0
3 Mar Birmingham A L 3-2
17 Mar Derby Co H W 1-0
24 Mar Everton A L 1-0
2 Apr Nottingham F A L 1-2
7 Apr Manchester C H W 2-1
13 Apr Aston Villa A L 0-1
14 Apr Bury H W 4-2
16 Apr Newcastle U A D 1-1
21 Apr Middlesbrough A L 0-2
25 Apr Sunderland A D 2-2

FA Cup
13 Jan West Ham U (1) H D 1-1
18 Jan West Ham U (1R) A W 3-2
3 Feb Watford (2) H W 3-0
24 Feb Sunderland (3) H W 5-0
10 Mar Manchester U (4) H W 3-2
31 Mar Newcastle U (Semi-Final)* L 0-2
*at Stoke

Southern Charity Cup
9 Oct West Ham U H W 3-2
9 Apr Tottenham H A D 0-0
28 Apr Tottenham H H W 5-0
30 Apr Reading (Final) A W 1-0

Friendlies
21 Sep Faversham Rangers A W 9-0
18 Oct Corinthians A L 1-2
30 Oct Oxford Univ H W 3-0
26 Dec Corinthians H D 1-1
15 Jan Cambridge Univ H W 4-2
22 Jan Oxford Univ A W 4-0
18 Apr West Hartlepool A W 4-0

Position in Football League Table

	P	W	L	D	F:A	Pts	
Liverpool	38	23	10	5	79:46	51	1st
Arsenal	38	15	16	7	62:64	37	12th

SEASON 1906-1907
FOOTBALL LEAGUE (DIVISION 1)

1 Sep Manchester C A W 4-1
3 Sep Bury A L 1-4
8 Sep Middlesbrough H W 2-0
15 Sep Preston NE H W 2-0
22 Sep Newcastle U H W 2-0
29 Sep Aston Villa A D 2-2
6 Oct Liverpool H W 2-1

13 Oct	Bristol C	A	W	3-1
20 Oct	Notts Co	H	W	1-0
27 Oct	Sheffield U	A	L	2-4
3 Nov	Bolton W	H	D	2-2
10 Nov	Manchester U	A	L	0-1
17 Nov	Stoke	H	W	2-1
24 Nov	Blackburn Rov	A	W	3-2
1 Dec	Sunderland	H	L	0-1
8 Dec	Birmingham	A	L	1-5
15 Dec	Everton	H	W	3-1
22 Dec	Derby Co	A	D	0-0
26 Dec	Bury	H	W	3-1
29 Dec	Manchester C	H	W	4-1
1 Jan	Sheffield Wed	A	D	1-1
5 Jan	Middlesbrough	A	L	3-5
19 Jan	Preston NE	H	W	1-0
26 Jan	Newcastle U	A	L	0-1
9 Feb	Liverpool	A	L	0-4
16 Feb	Bristol City	H	L	1-2
2 Mar	Sheffield U	H	L	0-1
16 Mar	Manchester U	H	W	4-0
27 Mar	Bolton W	A	L	0-3
28 Mar	Sheffield Wed	H	W	1-0
30 Mar	Blackburn Rov	H	W	2-0
1 Apr	Aston Villa	H	W	3-1
6 Apr	Sunderland	A	W	3-2
10 Apr	Everton	A	L	1-2
13 Apr	Birmingham	H	W	2-1
15 Apr	Stoke	A	L	0-2
17 Apr	Notts Co	A	L	1-4
27 Apr	Derby	H	W	3-2

FA Cup

12 Jan	Grimsby T (1)	A	D	1-1
16 Jan	Grimsby T (1R)	H	W	3-0
2 Feb	Bristol C (2)	H	W	2-1
23 Feb	Bristol Rov (3)	H	W	1-0
9 Mar	Barnsley (4)	A	W	2-1
23 Mar	Sheffield Wed (Semi-Final)*		L	1-3

*at Birmingham

Southern Charity Cup

10 Dec	Millwall	H	L	1-2

Friendlies

12 Sep	Reading	A	W	1-0
19 Sep	West Norwood	A	W	1-0
5 Nov	Oxford Univ	H	W	7-1
19 Nov	Clapton Orient	A	W	3-1
3 Dec	Cambridge Univ	A	W	3-1
25 Dec	Celtic	H	L	0-2
14 Jan	Cambridge Univ	H	W	6-3

On Tour

5 May	Racing Club, Brussels	W	2-1
7 May	The Hague	W	6-3
9 May	BFC Pressen, Berlin	W	9-1
12 May	SP Sportorina, Prague	W	7-5
16 May	Klub Slavia, Prague	W	4-2
18 May	Combined Vienna Team	W	4-2
19 May	Magyaren Buda Pesth	W	9-0
20 May	Buda Pesth	D	2-2

Position in Football League Table

	P	W	L	D	F:A	Pts	
Newcastle U	38	22	9	7	74:46	51	1st
Arsenal	38	20	14	4	66:59	44	7th

SEASON 1907-1908
FOOTBALL LEAGUE (DIVISION 1)

2 Sep	Notts Co	H	D	1-1
7 Sep	Bristol C	H	L	0-4
9 Sep	Bury	A	L	2-3
14 Sep	Notts Co	A	L	0-2
21 Sep	Manchester C	H	W	2-1
28 Sep	Preston NE	A	L	0-3
5 Oct	Bury	H	D	0-0
12 Oct	Aston Villa	A	W	1-0
19 Oct	Liverpool	H	W	2-1
26 Oct	Middlesbrough	A	D	0-0
2 Nov	Sheffield U	H	W	5-1
9 Nov	Chelsea	A	L	1-2
16 Nov	Nottingham F	H	W	3-1
23 Nov	Manchester U	A	L	2-4
30 Nov	Blackburn Rov	H	W	2-0
7 Dec	Bolton W	A	L	1-3
14 Dec	Birmingham	H	D	1-1
21 Dec	Everton	A	D	1-1
25 Dec	Newcastle U	H	D	2-2
28 Dec	Sunderland	H	W	4-0
31 Dec	Sheffield Wed	A	L	0-6
1 Jan	Sunderland	A	L	2-5
4 Jan	Bristol C	A	W	2-1
18 Jan	Manchester C	A	L	0-4
25 Jan	Preston NE	H	D	1-1
8 Feb	Aston Villa	H	L	0-1
15 Feb	Liverpool	A	L	1-4
22 Feb	Middlesbrough	H	W	4-1
29 Feb	Sheffield U	A	D	2-2
7 Mar	Chelsea	H	D	0-0
14 Mar	Nottingham F	A	L	0-1
21 Mar	Manchester U	H	W	1-0
28 Mar	Blackburn Rov	A	D	1-1
4 Apr	Bolton W	H	D	1-1
11 Apr	Birmingham	A	W	2-1
17 Apr	Newcastle U	A	L	1-2
18 Apr	Everton	H	W	2-1
20 Apr	Sheffield Wed	H	D	1-1

FA Cup

11 Jan	Hull C (1)	H	D	0-0
16 Jan	Hull C (1R)	A	L	1-4

Southern Charity Cup

23 Sep	Reading	H	L	0-1

Friendlies

16 Sep	Barnsley	H	W	1-0
14 Oct	Rest of Kent	A	W	3-1
26 Dec	Liverpool	H	D	2-2
1 Feb	Tottenham H	A	W	1-0

On Tour

21 Apr	Hearts	L	1-3
22 Apr	Raith Rovers	L	0-1
23 Apr	Aberdeen	L	1-4
25 Apr	Dundee	L	1-2
27 Apr	Motherwell	D	1-1
28 Apr	Glasgow Rangers	D	1-1
29 Apr	Greenock Morton	L	0-1
30 Apr	Kilmarnock	W	2-1

Position in Football League Table

	P	W	L	D	F:A	Pts	
Manchester C	38	23	9	6	81:48	52	1st
Arsenal	38	12	14	12	51:63	36	15th

SEASON 1908-1909
FOOTBALL LEAGUE (DIVISION 1)

2 Sep	Everton	H	L	0-4
5 Sep	Notts Co	A	L	1-2
7 Sep	Everton	A	W	3-0
12 Sep	Newcastle U	H	L	1-2
19 Sep	Bristol C	A	L	1-2
26 Sep	Preston NE	H	W	1-0
3 Oct	Middlesbrough	A	D	1-1
10 Oct	Manchester C	H	W	3-0
17 Oct	Liverpool	A	D	2-2
24 Oct	Bury	H	W	4-0
28 Oct	Chelsea	A	W	2-1
31 Oct	Sheffield U	A	D	1-1
7 Nov	Aston Villa	H	L	0-1
14 Nov	Nottingham F	A	W	1-0
21 Nov	Sunderland	H	L	0-4
5 Dec	Blackburn Rov	H	L	0-1
12 Dec	Bradford C	A	L	1-4
19 Dec	Manchester U	H	L	0-1
25 Dec	Leicester	A	D	1-1
26 Dec	Leicester	H	W	2-1
28 Dec	Sheffield Wed	A	L	2-6
2 Jan	Notts Co	H	W	1-0
9 Jan	Newcastle U	H	L	1-3
23 Jan	Bristol C	H	D	1-1
30 Jan	Preston NE	A	D	0-0
13 Feb	Manchester C	A	D	2-2
20 Feb	Liverpool	H	W	5-0
27 Feb	Bury	A	D	1-1
13 Mar	Aston Villa	A	L	1-2
17 Mar	Middlesbrough	H	D	1-1
20 Mar	Nottingham F	H	L	1-2
27 Mar	Sunderland	A	L	0-1
1 Apr	Sheffield U	H	W	1-0
3 Apr	Chelsea	H	D	0-0
10 Apr	Blackburn Rov	A	W	3-1
12 Apr	Sheffield Wed	H	W	2-0
17 Apr	Bradford C	H	W	1-0
27 Apr	Manchester U	A	W	4-1

FA Cup

16 Jan	Croydon Common (1)*		D	1-1
20 Jan	Croydon Common (1R)	H	W	2-0
6 Feb	Millwall (2)	H	D	1-1
10 Feb	Millwall (2R)	A	L	0-1

*at Crystal Palace

London FA Challenge Cup

28 Sep	Fulham	A	W	1-0
9 Nov	Crystal Place	H	W	2-1
22 Feb	Clapton Orient (Semi-Final)	A	L	1-2

London Professional Charity Fund

7 Dec	Chelsea	H	W	1-0

Friendlies

7 Oct	Rest of Kent	A	W	3-0
22 Oct	Ryde	A	W	2-0
10 Mar	Hastings	A	W	3-1
9 Apr	Exeter	A	L	2-3

Position in Football League Table

	P	W	L	D	F:A	Pts	
Newcastle U	38	24	9	5	65:41	53	1st
Arsenal	38	14	14	10	52:49	38	6th

SEASON 1909-1910
FOOTBALL LEAGUE (DIVISION 1)

1 Sep	Aston Villa	A	L	1-5
4 Sep	Sheffield U	H	D	0-0
11 Sep	Middlesbrough	A	L	2-5
18 Sep	Bolton W	A	L	0-3
25 Sep	Chelsea	H	W	3-2
2 Oct	Blackburn Rov	A	L	0-7
7 Oct	Notts Co	A	L	1-5
9 Oct	Nottingham F	H	L	0-1
16 Oct	Sunderland	A	L	2-6
23 Oct	Everton	H	W	1-0
30 Oct	Manchester U	A	L	0-1
6 Nov	Bradford C	H	L	0-1
13 Nov	Sheffield Wed	A	D	1-1
20 Nov	Bristol C	H	D	2-2
27 Nov	Bury	A	W	2-1
4 Dec	Tottenham H	H	W	1-0
11 Dec	Preston NE	A	W	4-3
18 Dec	Notts Co	H	L	1-2
25 Dec	Newcastle U	H	L	0-3
27 Dec	Liverpool	H	D	1-1
1 Jan	Liverpool	A	L	1-5
8 Jan	Sheffield U	A	L	0-2
22 Jan	Middlesbrough	H	W	3-0
29 Jan	Bolton W	H	W	2-0
12 Feb	Blackburn Rov	H	L	0-1
26 Feb	Sunderland	H	L	1-2
2 Mar	Nottingham F	A	D	1-1
7 Mar	Everton	A	L	0-1
12 Mar	Manchester U	H	D	0-0
19 Mar	Bradford C	A	W	1-0
25 Mar	Newcastle U	A	D	1-1
26 Mar	Sheffield Wed	H	L	0-1
28 Mar	Chelsea	A	W	1-0
2 Apr	Bristol C	A	W	1-0
9 Apr	Bury	H	D	0-0
11 Apr	Aston Villa	H	W	1-0
16 Apr	Tottenham H	A	D	1-1
23 Apr	Preston NE	H	L	1-3

FA Cup

15 Jan	Watford (1)	H	W	3-0
5 Feb	Everton (2)	A	L	0-5

London FA Challenge Cup

20 Sep	Bromley	H	W	4-0
11 Oct	West Ham U	H	L	0-1

London Professional Charity Fund

1 Nov	Tottenham H	A	L	0-3

Foord Flood Relief Fund

25 Nov	Shorncliffe Garrison and District XI (at Folkestone)		W	5-2

Friendlies

22 Sep	Rest of Kent	A	W	3-2
19 Feb	Fulham	H	D	2-2
5 Mar	Millwall	A	D	3-3
28 Apr	Colchester		W	3-2
30 Apr	Ilford		L	2-3

Position in Football League Table

	P	W	L	D	F:A	Pts	
Aston Villa	38	23	8	7	84:42	53	1st
Arsenal	38	11	18	9	37:67	31	18th

SEASON 1910-1911
FOOTBALL LEAGUE (DIVISION 1)

1 Sep	Manchester U	H	L	1-2
3 Sep	Bury	A	D	1-1
10 Sep	Sheffield U	H	D	0-0
17 Sep	Aston Villa	A	L	0-3
24 Sep	Sunderland	H	D	0-0
1 Oct	Oldham Ath	H	D	0-0
8 Oct	Bradford C	A	L	0-3
15 Oct	Blackburn	H	W	4-1
22 Oct	Nottingham F	A	W	3-2
29 Oct	Manchester C	H	L	0-1
5 Nov	Everton	A	L	0-2
12 Nov	Sheffield W	H	W	1-0
19 Nov	Bristol C	A	W	1-0
26 Nov	Newcastle U	H	L	1-2
3 Dec	Tottenham H	A	L	1-3
10 Dec	Middlesbrough	H	L	0-2
17 Dec	Preston NE	A	L	1-4
24 Dec	Notts Co	H	W	2-1
26 Dec	Manchester U	A	L	0-5
31 Dec	Bury	H	W	3-2
7 Jan	Sheffield U	A	L	2-3
28 Jan	Sunderland	A	D	2-2
11 Feb	Bradford C	H	D	0-0
18 Feb	Blackburn Rov	A	L	0-1
25 Feb	Nottingham F	H	W	3-2
4 Mar	Manchester C	A	D	1-1
6 Mar	Oldham Ath	A	L	0-3
11 Mar	Everton	H	W	1-0
15 Mar	Aston Villa	H	D	1-1
18 Mar	Sheffield Wed	A	D	0-0
25 Mar	Bristol C	H	W	3-0
1 Apr	Newcastle U	A	W	1-0
8 Apr	Tottenham H	H	W	2-0
14 Apr	Liverpool	H	D	0-0
15 Apr	Middlesbrough	A	D	1-1
17 Apr	Liverpool	A	D	1-1
22 Apr	Preston NE	H	W	2-0
29 Apr	Notts Co	A	W	2-0

FA Cup

14 Jan	Clapton Orient (1)*			
16 Jan	Clapton Orient (1)	A	W	2-1
4 Feb	Swindon T (2)	A	L	0-1

*match abandoned, fog

London FA Challenge Cup

19 Sep	Q P R	H	W	3-0
10 Oct	Millwall	A	L	0-1

London Professional Charity Fund

26 Sep	Fulham	A	W	3-2

Position in Football League Table

	P	W	L	D	F:A	Pts	
Manchester U	38	22	8	8	72:40	52	1st
Arsenal	38	13	13	12	41:49	38	10th

SEASON 1911-1912
FOOTBALL LEAGUE (DIVISION 1)

2 Sep	Liverpool	H	D	2-2
9 Sep	Aston Villa	A	L	1-4
16 Sep	Newcastle U	H	W	2-0
23 Sep	Sheffield U	A	L	1-2
30 Sep	Oldham Ath	H	D	1-1
7 Oct	Bolton W	A	D	2-2
14 Oct	Bradford C	H	W	2-0
21 Oct	Preston NE	A	W	1-0
28 Oct	Manchester C	A	D	3-3
4 Nov	Everton	H	L	0-1
11 Nov	W B A	A	D	1-1
18 Nov	Sunderland	H	W	3-0
25 Nov	Blackburn Rov	A	L	0-4
2 Dec	Sheffield Wed	H	L	0-2
9 Dec	Bury	A	L	1-3
16 Dec	Middlesbrough	H	W	3-1
23 Dec	Notts Co	A	L	1-3
25 Dec	Tottenham H	A	L	0-5
26 Dec	Tottenham H	H	W	3-1
30 Dec	Liverpool	A	L	1-4
1 Jan	Manchester U	A	L	0-2
6 Jan	Aston Villa	H	D	2-2
20 Jan	Newcastle U	A	W	2-1
27 Jan	Sheffield U	H	W	3-1
10 Feb	Bolton W	H	W	3-0
17 Feb	Bradford C	A	D	1-1
24 Feb	Middlesbrough	A	W	2-0
2 Mar	Manchester C	H	W	7-0
9 Mar	Oldham Ath	A	D	0-0
16 Mar	W B A	H	L	0-2
23 Mar	Sunderland	A	L	0-1
27 Mar	Everton	A	L	0-1
5 Apr	Manchester U	H	W	2-1
5 Apr	Sheffield Wed	A	L	0-3
6 Apr	Preston NE	H	W	4-1
8 Apr	Bury	H	W	1-0
22 Apr	Blackburn Rov	H	W	5-1
27 Apr	Notts Co	H	L	0-3

FA Cup

13 Jan	Bolton W (1)	A	L	0-1

London FA Challenge Cup

18 Sep	Q P R	A	W	2-0
16 Oct	Chelsea	H	L	2-3

London Professional Charity Fund

4 Sep	Chelsea	A	D	2-2
30 Oct	Chelsea	H	W	1-0

Charity Match Titanic Disaster

29 Apr	Tottennham	H	W	3-0

Friendlies

25 Mar	West Ham U	H	W	3-0
20 Apr	Glasgow Rangers	A	D	0-0

On Tour

17 May	Hertha Berlin	W	5-0
12 May	Viktoria Berliner	D	2-2
16 May	Prague Deutscher	W	4-1
19 May	Furth	W	6-0
22 May	Toma Graz	W	6-0
24 May	Tottenham Vienna	W	4-0
26 May	Vienna Rapide	W	8-2
27 May	Wiener Athletic	W	5-0
29 May	Budapest	W	2-1

Position in Football League Table

	P	W	L	D	F:A	Pts	
Blackburn Rov	38	20	9	9	60:43	49	1st
Arsenal	38	15	15	8	55:59	38	10th

SEASON 1912-1913
FOOTBALL LEAGUE (DIVISION 1)

2 Sep	Manchester U	H	D	0-0
7 Sep	Liverpool	A	L	0-3
14 Sep	Bolton W	H	L	1-2
16 Sep	Aston Villa	H	L	0-3
21 Sep	Sheffield U	A	W	3-1
28 Sep	Newcastle U	H	D	1-1
5 Oct	Oldham Ath	A	D	0-0
12 Oct	Chelsea	H	L	0-1
19 Oct	Sunderland	H	L	1-3
26 Oct	Bradford PA	A	L	1-3
2 Nov	Manchester C	H	L	0-4
9 Nov	W B A	A	L	1-2
16 Nov	Everton	H	D	0-0
23 Nov	Sheffield Wed	A	L	0-2
30 Nov	Blackburn Rov	H	L	0-1
7 Dec	Derby Co	A	L	1-4
14 Dec	Tottenham H	L	H	0-3
21 Dec	Middlesbrough	A	L	0-2
25 Dec	Notts Co	H	D	0-0
26 Dec	Notts Co	A	L	1-2
28 Dec	Liverpool	H	D	1-1
1 Jan	Sunderland	A	L	1-4
4 Jan	Bolton W	A	L	1-5
18 Jan	Sheffield U	H	L	1-3
25 Jan	Newcastle U	A	L	1-3
8 Feb	Oldham Ath	H	D	0-0
15 Feb	Chelsea	A	D	1-1
1 Mar	Bradford PA	H	D	1-1
8 Mar	Manchester C	A	W	1-0
15 Mar	W B A	H	W	1-0
21 Mar	Manchester U	A	L	0-2
22 Mar	Everton	A	L	0-3
24 Mar	Aston Villa	A	L	1-4
29 Mar	Sheffield Wed	H	L	2-5
5 Apr	Blackburn	A	D	1-1
12 Apr	Derby Co	H	L	1-2
19 Apr	Tottenham H	A	D	1-1
26 Apr	Middlesbrough	H	D	1-1

FA Cup

11 Jan	Croydon Common (I)	A	D	0-0
15 Jan	Croydon Common (1R)	H	W	2-1
1 Feb	Liverpool (2)	H	L	1-4

London FA Challenge Cup

23 Sep	Clapton Orient	A	L	2-4

London Professional Charity Fund

30 Sep	Chelsea	A	W	3-1

Kent Senior Shield

16 Oct	Crystal Palace	A	L	0-1

Position in Football League Table

	P	W	L	D	F:A	Pts	
Sunderland	38	25	9	4	86:43	54	1st
Arsenal	38	3	23	12	26:74	18	20th

SEASON 1913-1914
FOOTBALL LEAGUE (DIVISION 2)

6 Sep	Leicester C	H	W	2-1
13 Sep	Wolverhampton W	A	W	2-1
15 Sep	Notts Co	H	W	3-0
27 Sep	Barnsley	A	L	0-1
4 Oct	Bury	H	L	0-1
11 Oct	Huddersfield	A	W	2-1
18 Oct	Lincoln C	H	W	3-0
25 Oct	Blackpool	A	D	1-1
1 Nov	Nottingham F	H	W	3-2
8 Nov	Fulham	A	L	1-6
15 Nov	Grimsby T	A	D	1-1
22 Nov	Birmingham	H	W	1-0
29 Nov	Bristol C	A	D	1-1
6 Dec	Leeds C	H	W	1-0
13 Dec	Clapton Orient	A	L	0-1
20 Dec	Glossop	H	W	2-0
25 Dec	Bradford PA	A	W	3-2
26 Dec	Bradford PA	H	W	2-0
27 Dec	Leicester	A	W	2-1
1 Jan	Notts Co	A	L	0-1
3 Jan	Wolverhampton W	H	W	3-1
17 Jan	Hull C	A	W	2-1
24 Jan	Barnsley	H	W	1-0
7 Feb	Bury	A	D	1-1
14 Feb	Huddersfield T	H	L	0-1
21 Feb	Lincoln C	A	L	2-5
28 Feb	Blackpool	H	W	2-1
7 Mar	Nottingham F	A	D	0-0
14 Mar	Fulham	H	W	2-0
28 Mar	Birmingham	A	L	0-2
4 Apr	Bristol C	A	D	1-1
10 Apr	Stockport Co	A	L	0-2
11 Apr	Leeds C	A	D	0-0
13 Apr	Stockport Co	H	W	4-0
18 Apr	Clapton Orient	H	D	2-2
23 Apr	Grimsby T	H	W	2-0
25 Apr	Glossop	A	W	2-0

FA Cup

10 Jan	Bradford PA (1)	A	L	0-2

London FA Challenge Cup

22 Sep	Q P R	H	D	1-1
29 Sep	Q P R	A	W	3-2
20 Oct	Chelsea	A	W	1-0
10 Nov	Tottenham H	A	L	1-2

London Professional Charity Fund

27 Oct	West Ham U	A	L	2-3

Friendly

31 Jan	Everton	H	L	1-2

Position in Football League Table

	P	W	L	D	F:A	Pts	
Notts Co	38	23	8	7	77:36	53	1st
Arsenal	38	20	9	9	54 38	49	3rd

SEASON 1914-1915
FOOTBALL LEAGUE (DIVISION 2)

1 Sep	Glossop	H	W	3-0
5 Sep	Wolverhampton W	A	L	0-1
8 Sep	Glossop	A	W	4-0
12 Sep	Fulham	H	W	3-0
19 Sep	Stockport Co	A	D	1-1
26 Sep	Hull C	H	W	2-1
3 Oct	Leeds C	A	D	2-2
10 Oct	Clapton Orient	H	W	2-1
17 Oct	Blackpool	H	W	2-0
24 Oct	Derby Co	A	L	0-4
31 Oct	Lincoln C	H	D	1-1
7 Nov	Birmingham	A	L	0-3
14 Nov	Grimsby T	H	W	6-0
18 Nov	Nottingham F	A	D	1-1
21 Nov	Huddersfield T	A	L	0-3
28 Nov	Bristol C	H	W	3-0
5 Dec	Bury	A	L	1-3
12 Dec	Preston NE	H	L	1-2
25 Dec	Leicester	A	W	4-1
26 Dec	Leicester	H	W	6-0
1 Jan	Barnsley	A	L	0-1
2 Jan	Wolverhampton W	H	W	5-1
16 Jan	Fulham	A	W	1-0
23 Jan	Stockport Co	H	W	3-1
6 Feb	Leeds C	H	W	2-0
13 Feb	Clapton Orient	A	L	0-1
20 Feb	Blackpool	A	W	2-0
27 Feb	Derby Co	H	L	1-2
6 Mar	Lincoln C	A	L	0-1
13 Mar	Birmingham	H	W	1-0
20 Mar	Grimsby T	A	L	0-1
27 Mar	Huddersfield T	H	L	0-3
2 Apr	Hull C	A	L	0-1
3 Apr	Bristol C	A	D	1-1
5 Apr	Barnsley	H	W	1-0
10 Apr	Bury	H	W	3-1
17 Apr	Preston NE	A	L	0-3
24 Apr	Nottingham F	H	W	7-0

FA Cup

9 Jan	Merthyr T (1)	H*	W	3-0
30 Jan	Chelsea (2)	A	L	0-1

*by arrangement

London FA Challenge Cup

21 Sep	Tufnell Park	H	W	6-0
19 Oct	Q P R	H	W	2-1
9 Nov	Crystal Palace	A	W	2-0
7 Dec	Millwall (Final)	A	L	1-2

London Professional Charity Fund

2 Nov	West Ham U	H	W	1-0

Friendly

19 Dec	Swindon T		L	1-2

Position in Football League Table

	P	W	L	D	F:A	Pts	
Derby Co	38	23	8	7	71:33	53	1st
Arsenal	38	19	14	5	69:41	43	5th

No League football was played throughout the First World War. Competitive football was played, by Arsenal, during the seasons 1915-16 through 1919-1920, in the form of the London Football Combination and other London based friendlies. Arsenal's highest placing in the London Football combination was 3rd for seasons 1915-16 and 1918-19. Arsenal was a Second Division club at the outbreak of the First World War, finishing fifth in the last pre-war season. After the war, the First Division was increased from 20 to 22 clubs, and Arsenal illogically and possibly corruptly, were elected to one of the new places. Since then they have remained a First Division club, and from now on the records are given in more detail.

SEASON 1919-1920
FOOTBALL LEAGUE (DIVISION 1)

30 Aug	Newcastle U	H	L	0-1
1 Sep	Liverpool	A	W	3-2
6 Sep	Newcastle U	A	L	1-3
8 Sep	Liverpool	H	W	1-0
13 Sep	Sunderland	A	D	1-1
20 Sep	Sunderland	H	W	3-2
27 Sep	Blackburn Rov	A	D	2-2
4 Oct	Blackburn Rov	H	L	0-1
11 Oct	Everton	A	W	3-2
18 Oct	Everton	H	D	1-1
25 Oct	Bradford C	H	L	1-2
1 Nov	Bradford C	A	D	1-1
8 Nov	Bolton W	H	D	2-2
15 Nov	Bolton W	A	D	2-2
22 Nov	Notts Co	H	W	3-1
29 Nov	Notts Co	A	D	2-2
6 Dec	Chelsea	H	D	1-1
13 Dec	Chelsea	A	L	1-3
20 Dec	Sheffield Wed	H	W	3-1
25 Dec	Derby Co	A	L	1-2
26 Dec	Derby Co	H	W	1-0
27 Dec	Sheffield Wed	A	W	2-1
3 Jan	Manchester C	H	D	2-2
17 Jan	Manchester C	A	L	1-4
24 Jan	Aston Villa	H	L	0-1
7 Feb	Oldham Ath	H	W	3-2
11 Feb	Aston Villa	A	L	1-2
14 Feb	Oldham Ath	A	L	0-3
21 Feb	Manchester U	H	L	0-3
28 Feb	Manchester U	A	W	1-0
6 Mar	Sheffield U	A	L	0-2
13 Mar	Sheffield U	H	W	3-0
20 Mar	Middlesbrough	A	L	0-1
27 Mar	Middlesbrough	H	W	2-1
3 Apr	Burnley	A	L	1-2
5 Apr	W B A	H	W	1-0
6 Apr	W B A	A	L	0-1
10 Apr	Burnley	H	W	2-0
17 Apr	Preston NE	A	D	1-1
24 Apr	Preston NE	H	D	0-0
28 Apr	Bradford PA	A	D	0-0
1 May	Bradford PA	H	W	3-0

FA Cup

10 Jan	Rochdale (1)	H	W	4-2
31 Jan	Bristol C (2)	A	L	0-1

Appearances (Goals)

Baker A 17 · Blyth W 29 (4) · Bradshaw F 33 (2) · Buckley C 23 (1) · Burgess D 7 (1) · Butler J 21 (1) · Coopland W 1 · Cownley F 4 · Dunn S 16 · Graham J 22 (5) · Greenaway D 3 · Groves F 29 (5) · Hardinge H 13 (3) · Hutchins A 18 · Lewis C 5 (1) · McKinnon A 41 · North F 41 · Pagnam F 25 (13) · Pattison G 1 · Peart J 5 · Rutherford J 36 (3) · Shaw J 33 · Toner J 15 (1) · Voysey C 5 · White H 29 (15) · Whittaker T 1 · Williamson E 26 · Total: 27 players (56)

Position in League Table

	P	W	L	D	F:A	Pts	
W B A	42	28	10	4	104:47	60	1st
Arsenal	42	15	15	12	56:58	42	10th

SEASON 1920-1921
FOOTBALL LEAGUE (DIVISION 1)

28 Aug	Aston Villa	A	L	0-5
30 Aug	Manchester U	H	W	2-0
4 Sep	Aston Villa	H	L	0-1
6 Sep	Manchester U	A	D	1-1
11 Sep	Manchester C	H	W	2-1
18 Sep	Manchester C	A	L	1-3
25 Sep	Middlesbrough	H	D	2-2
2 Oct	Middlesbrough	A	L	1-2
9 Oct	Bolton W	H	D	0-0
16 Oct	Bolton W	A	D	1-1
23 Oct	Derby County	A	D	1-1
30 Oct	Derby County	H	W	2-0
6 Nov	Blackburn R	A	D	2-2
13 Nov	Blackburn R	H	W	2-0
20 Nov	Huddersfield T	A	W	4-0
27 Nov	Huddersfield T	H	W	2-0
4 Dec	Chelsea	A	W	2-1
11 Dec	Chelsea	H	D	1-1
18 Dec	Bradford C	A	L	1-3
25 Dec	Everton	A	W	4-2
27 Dec	Everton	H	D	1-1
1 Jan	Bradford C	H	L	1-2
15 Jan	Tottenham	A	L	1-2
22 Jan	Tottenham	H	W	3-2
29 Jan	Sunderland	H	L	1-2
5 Feb	Sunderland	A	L	1-5
12 Feb	Oldham Ath	A	D	1-1
19 Feb	Oldham Ath	H	D	2-2
26 Feb	Preston N E	A	W	1-0
12 Mar	Burnley	A	L	0-1
19 Mar	Burnley	H	D	1-1
26 Mar	Sheffield U	H	L	2-6
28 Mar	W B A	H	W	2-1
29 Mar	W B A	A	W	4-3
2 Apr	Sheffield U	A	D	1-1
9 Apr	Bradford PA	H	W	2-1
16 Apr	Bradford PA	A	W	1-0
23 Apr	Newcastle U	H	D	1-1
25 Apr	Preston NE	H	W	2-1
30 Apr	Newcastle U	A	L	0-1
2 May	Liverpool	H	D	0-0
7 May	Liverpool	A	L	0-3

FA Cup

8 Jan	Q P R (1)	A	L	0-2

Appearances (Goals)
Baker A 37 (2) · Blyth W 39 (7) · Bradshaw F 21 · Buckley C 4 (1) · Burgess D 4 · Butler J 36 · Cownley F 1 · Dunn S 9 · Graham A 30 (5) · Groves G 13 (1) · Hopkins J 8 (2) · Hutchins A 39 · McKenzie A 5 (1) · McKinnon A 37 (2) · North E 8 2 · Pagnam F 25 (14) · Paterson Dr J 20 · Pattison G 6 · Peart J 1 · Rutherford J 32 (7) · Shaw J 28 · Smith J 10 (1) · Toner J 11 (3) · Walden H 2 (1) · White H 26 (10) · Whittaker T 5 · Willamson E 33 · Total: 27 players (59)

Position in League Table

	P	W	L	D	F:A	Pts	
Burnley	42	23	6	13	79:36	59	1st
Arsenal	42	15	13	14	59:63	44	9th

SEASON 1921-1922
FOOTBALL LEAGUE (DIVISION 1)

27 Aug	Sheffield U	H	L	1-2
29 Aug	Preston NE	A	L	2-3
3 Sep	Sheffield U	A	L	1-4
5 Sep	Preston NE	H	W	1-0
10 Sep	Manchester C	A	L	0-2
17 Sep	Manchester C	H	L	0-1
24 Sep	Everton	A	D	1-1
1 Oct	Everton	H	W	1-0
8 Oct	Sunderland	A	L	0-1
15 Oct	Sunderland	H	L	1-2
22 Oct	Huddersfield T	A	L	0-2
29 Oct	Huddersfield T	H	L	1-3
5 Nov	Birmingham	A	W	1-0
12 Nov	Birmingham	H	W	5-2
19 Nov	Bolton W	A	L	0-1
3 Dec	Blackburn Rov	A	W	1-0
10 Dec	Blackburn Rov	H	D	1-1
12 Dec	Bolton W	H	D	1-1
17 Dec	Oldham Ath	A	L	1-2
24 Dec	Oldham Ath	H	L	0-1
26 Dec	Cardiff C	H	D	0-0
27 Dec	Cardiff C	A	L	3-4
31 Dec	Chelsea	A	W	2-0
14 Jan	Chelsea	H	W	1-0
21 Jan	Burnley	H	D	0-0
4 Feb	Newcastle U	H	W	2-1
11 Feb	Newcastle U	A	L	1-3
20 Feb	Burnley	A	L	0-1
25 Feb	Liverpool	A	L	0-4
11 Mar	Manchester U	A	L	0-1
18 Mar	Aston Villa	A	L	0-2
22 Mar	Liverpool	H	W	1-0
25 Mar	Aston Villa	H	W	2-0
1 Apr	Middlesbrough	H	D	2-2
5 Apr	Manchester U	H	W	3-1
8 Apr	Middlesbrough	A	L	2-4
15 Apr	Tottenham H	A	L	0-2
17 Apr	W B A	A	W	3-0
18 Apr	W B A	H	D	2-2
22 Apr	Tottenham H	H	W	1-0
29 Apr	Bradford C	A	W	2-0
6 May	Bradford C	H	W	1-0

FA Cup

7 Jan	Q P R (1)	H	D	0-0
11 Jan	Q P R (1R)	A	W	2-1
28 Jan	Bradford C (2)	A	W	3-2
18 Feb	Leicester C (3)	H	W	3-0
4 Mar	Preston NE (4)	H	D	1-1
8 Mar	Preston NE (4R)	A	L	1-2

Appearances (Goals)
Baker A 32 (4) · Blyth W 25 (1) · Boreham R 22 (10) · Bradshaw F 32 (2) · Burgess D 2 · Butler J 25 (2) · Cownley F 10 · Creegan W 5 · Dunn S 1 · Earle S 1 · Graham A 21 (3) · Henderson W 5 · Hutchins A 37 · Hopkins J 11 (3) · Maxwell T 1 · Milne W 4 · McKenzie A 3 · McKinnon A 17 · North F 11 (3) · Paterson Dr J 2 · Pattison G 2 · Rutherford J 36 · Shaw J 6 · Toner J 24 (1) · Turnbull R 5 · Voysey C 1 · Whittaker T 36 (1) · White H 35 (14) · Williamson E 41 · Young A 9 (2) · Total: 30 players (47)

Position in League Table

	P	W	L	D	F:A	Pts	
Liverpool	42	22	7	13	63:36	57	1st
Arsenal	42	15	20	7	47:56	37	17th

SEASON 1922-1923
FOOTBALL LEAGUE (DIVISION 1)

26 Aug	Liverpool	A	L	2-5
28 Aug	Burnley	H	D	1-1
2 Sep	Liverpool	H	W	1-0
4 Sep	Burnley	A	L	1-4
9 Sep	Cardiff C	A	L	1-4
16 Sep	Cardiff C	H	W	2-1
23 Sep	Tottenham H	A	W	2-1
30 Sep	Tottenham H	H	L	0-2
2 Oct	Sheffield U	A	L	1-2
7 Oct	W B A	H	W	3-1
14 Oct	W B A	A	L	0-7
21 Oct	Newcastle U	A	D	1-1
28 Oct	Newcastle U	H	L	1-2
4 Nov	Everton	A	L	0-1
11 Nov	Everton	H	L	1-2
18 Nov	Sunderland	A	D	3-3
25 Nov	Sunderland	H	L	2-3
2 Dec	Birmingham	A	L	2-3
9 Dec	Birmingham	H	W	1-0
16 Dec	Huddersfield T	H	D	1-1
23 Dec	Huddersfield T	A	L	0-4
25 Dec	Bolton W	A	L	1-4
26 Dec	Bolton W	H	W	5-0
30 Dec	Stoke C	H	W	3-0
1 Jan	Blackburn Rov	A	W	5-0
6 Jan	Stoke C	A	L	0-1
20 Jan	Manchester C	H	W	1-0
27 Jan	Manchester C	A	D	0-0
3 Feb	Nottingham F	A	L	1-2
10 Feb	Nottingham F	H	W	2-0
17 Feb	Chelsea	A	D	0-0
24 Feb	Chelsea	H	W	3-1
3 Mar	Middlesbrough	A	L	0-2
10 Mar	Middlesbrough	H	W	3-0
17 Mar	Oldham Ath	H	W	2-0
24 Mar	Oldham Ath	A	D	0-0
31 Mar	Aston Villa	H	W	2-0
2 Apr	Blackburn	H	D	1-1
7 Apr	Aston Villa	A	D	1-1
14 Apr	Preston NE	H	D	1-1
21 Apr	Preston NE	A	W	2-1
28 Apr	Sheffield U	H	W	2-0

FA Cup

13 Jan	Liverpool (1)	A	D	0-0
17 Jan	Liverpool (1R)	H	L	1-4

Appearances (Goals)
Baker A 29 (6) · Blyth W 31 (9) · Boreham R 27 (8) · Bradshaw F 17 · Butler J 18 · Clarke J 2 · Dunn S 17 · Earle S 1 (1) · Elvey J 1 · Graham A 17 (1) · Henderson W 2 · Hopkins J 2 (2) · Hutchins A 10 (1) · John R 24 · Kennedy A 24 · McKenzie A 7 (1) · Milne W 31 · Mackie J 23 · Paterson Dr J 27 · Robson J 20 · Roe A 4 (1) · Rutherford J 26 (1) · Toner J 7 · Townrow F 1 · Turnbull R 35 (20) · Voysey C 18 (4) · White H 11 (1) · Whittaker T 13 (1) · Willamson E 5 · Young A 13 (3) · Own goals 1 · Total: 30 players (61)

Position in League Table

	P	W	L	D	F:A	Pts	
Liverpool	42	26	8	8	70:31	60	1st
Arsenal	42	16	16	10	61:62	42	11th

SEASON 1923-1924
FOOTBALL LEAGUE (DIVISION 1)

25 Aug	Newcastle	H	L	1-4
27 Aug	West Ham U	A	L	0-1
1 Sep	Newcastle U	A	L	0-1
8 Sep	W B A	A	L	0-4
10 Sep	West Ham U	H	W	4-1
15 Sep	W B A	H	W	1-0
22 Sep	Birmingham	A	W	2-0
29 Sep	Birmingham	H	D	0-0
6 Oct	Manchester C	A	L	0-1
13 Oct	Manchester C	H	L	1-2
20 Oct	Bolton W	A	W	2-1
27 Oct	Bolton W	H	D	0-0
3 Nov	Middlesbrough	H	W	2-1
10 Nov	Middlesbrough	A	D	0-0
17 Nov	Tottenham H	H	D	1-1
24 Nov	Tottenham H	A	L	0-3
1 Dec	Blackburn Rov	H	D	2-2
8 Dec	Blackburn Rov	A	L	0-2
15 Dec	Huddersfield T	H	L	1-3
22 Dec	Huddersfield T	A	L	1-6
26 Dec	Notts Co	A	W	2-1
27 Dec	Notts Co	H	D	0-0
29 Dec	Chelsea	H	W	1-0
5 Jan	Chelsea	A	D	0-0
19 Jan	Cardiff C	H	L	1-2
26 Jan	Cardiff C	A	L	0-4
9 Feb	Sheffield U	A	L	1-3
16 Feb	Aston Villa	H	L	0-1
25 Feb	Sheffield U	H	L	1-3
1 Mar	Liverpool	H	W	3-1
12 Mar	Aston Villa	A	L	1-2
15 Mar	Nottingham F	A	L	1-2
22 Mar	Nottingham F	H	W	1-0
2 Apr	Liverpool	A	D	0-0
5 Apr	Burnley	H	W	2-0
12 Apr	Sunderland	H	W	2-0
18 Apr	Everton	A	L	1-3
19 Apr	Sunderland	A	D	1-1
21 Apr	Everton	H	L	0-1
26 Apr	Preston NE	A	W	2-0
28 Apr	Burnley	A	L	1-4
3 May	Preston NE	H	L	1-2

FA Cup

12 Jan	Luton (1)	H	W	4-1
2 Feb	Cardiff (2)	A	L	0-1

Appearances (Goals)
Baker A 21 (1) · Blyth W 27 (3) · Boreham R 2 · Butler J 24 · Clarke J 2 · Earle S 2 (2) · Graham A 25 (1) · Haden S 31 (3) · John R 15 · Jones F 2 · Kennedy A 29 Mackie J 31 · Milne W 36 (1) · Neil A 11 (2) · Paterson Dr J 21 · Ramsay J 11 (4) · Robson J 42 · Rutherford J 22 (2) · Toner J 3 · Townrow F 7 (2) · Turnbull R 18 (6) · Voysey C 10 (2) · Wallington E 1 · Whittaker T 8 · Woods H 36 (8) · Young A 25 (2) Own goals 1 · Total: 26 players (40)

Position in League Table

	P	W	L	D	F:A	Pts	
H.field T	42	23	8	11	60:33	57	1st
Arsenal	42	12	21	9	40:63	33	19th

SEASON 1924-1925
FOOTBALL LEAGUE (DIVISION 1)

30 Aug	Nottingham F	A	W	2-0
1 Sep	Manchester C	H	W	1-0
6 Sep	Liverpool	H	W	2-0
13 Sep	Newcastle U	A	D	2-2
17 Sep	Manchester C	A	L	0-2
20 Sep	Sheffield U	H	W	2-0
27 Sep	West Ham U	A	L	0-1
4 Oct	Blackburn Rov	H	W	1-0
11 Oct	Huddersfield T	A	L	0-4
13 Oct	Bury	H	L	0-1
18 Oct	Aston Villa	H	D	1-1
25 Oct	Tottenham H	H	W	1-0
1 Nov	Bolton W	A	L	1-4
8 Nov	Notts Co	H	L	0-1
15 Nov	Everton	A	W	3-2
22 Nov	Sunderland	H	D	0-0
29 Nov	Cardiff C	A	D	1-1
6 Dec	Preston NE	H	W	4-0
13 Dec	Burnley	A	L	0-1
20 Dec	Leeds U	H	W	6-1
25 Dec	Birmingham	A	L	1-2
26 Dec	Birmingham	H	L	0-1
27 Dec	Nottingham F	H	W	2-1
3 Jan	Liverpool	A	L	1-2
17 Jan	Newcastle U	H	L	0-2
24 Jan	Sheffield U	A	L	1-2
7 Feb	Blackburn Rov	A	L	0-1
14 Feb	Huddersfield T	H	L	0-5
28 Feb	Tottenham H	A	L	0-2
7 Mar	Bolton W	H	W	1-0
14 Mar	Notts Co	A	L	1-2
21 Mar	Everton	H	W	3-1
23 Mar	West Ham U	H	L	1-2
28 Mar	Sunderland	A	L	0-2
1 Apr	Aston Villa	A	L	0-4
4 Apr	Cardiff C	H	D	1-1
11 Apr	Preston NE	A	L	0-2
13 Apr	W B A	A	L	0-2
14 Apr	W B A	H	W	2-0
18 Apr	Burnley	H	W	5-0
25 Apr	Leeds U	A	L	0-1
2 May	Bury	A	L	0-2

FA Cup

14 Jan	West Ham U (1)	A	D	0-0
21 Jan	West Ham U (1R)	H	D	2-2
26 Jan	West Ham U (1R)	A	L	0-1

Appearances (Goals)
Baker A 32 (2) · Blyth W 17 (1) · Brain J 28 (12) · Butler J 39 (3) · Clarke J 2 · Cock D 2 · Haden S 15 (1) · Hoar S 19 · Hughes J 1 · John R 39 (2) · Kennedy A 40 · Lewis D 16 · Mackie J 19 · Milne W 32 · Neil A 16 (2) · Ramsey J 30 4 · Robson J 26 · Roe A 1 · Rutherford J 20 2 · Toner J 26 (2) · Turnbull R 1 · Whittaker T 1 · Woods H 32 (13) · Young A 8 (2) · Total: 24 players (46)

Position in League Table

	P	W	L	D	F:A	Pts	
H.field T	42	21	5	16	69:28	58	1st
Arsenal	42	14	23	5	46:58	33	20th

SEASON 1925-1926
FOOTBALL LEAGUE (DIVISION 1)

29 Aug	Tottenham H	H	L	0-1
31 Aug	Leicester	H	D	2-2
5 Sep	Manchester U	A	W	1-0
7 Sep	Leicester C	A	W	1-0
12 Sep	Liverpool	H	D	1-1
19 Sep	Burnley	A	D	2-2
21 Sep	West Ham U	H	W	3-2
26 Sep	Leeds U	H	W	4-1
3 Oct	Newcastle U	A	L	0-7
5 Oct	West Ham U	A	W	4-0
10 Oct	Bolton W	H	L	2-3
17 Oct	Cardiff C	H	W	5-0
24 Oct	Sheffield U	A	L	0-4
31 Oct	Everton	H	W	4-1
7 Nov	Manchester C	A	W	5-2
14 Nov	Bury	H	W	6-1
21 Nov	Blackburn Rov	A	W	3-2
28 Nov	Sunderland	H	W	2-0
5 Dec	Huddersfield T	A	D	2-2
12 Dec	W B A	H	W	1-0
19 Dec	Birmingham	A	L	0-1
25 Dec	Notts Co	H	W	3-0
26 Dec	Notts Co	A	L	1-4
1 Jan	Tottenham H	A	D	1-1
16 Jan	Manchester U	H	W	3-2
23 Jan	Liverpool	A	L	0-3
3 Feb	Burnley	H	L	1-2
6 Feb	Leeds U	A	L	2-4
13 Feb	Newcastle U	H	W	3-0
23 Feb	Cardiff C	A	D	0-0
13 Mar	Everton	A	W	3-2
17 Mar	Sheffield U	H	W	4-0
20 Mar	Manchester C	H	W	1-0
27 Mar	Bury	A	D	2-2
2 Apr	Aston Villa	A	L	0-3
3 Apr	Blackburn Rov	H	W	4-2
5 Apr	Aston Villa	H	W	2-0
10 Apr	Sunderland	A	L	1-2
17 Apr	Huddersfield T	H	W	3-1
24 Apr	W B A	A	L	1-2
28 Apr	Bolton W	A	D	1-1
1 May	Birmingham	H	W	3-0

FA Cup

9 Jan	Wolves (3)	A	D	1-1
13 Jan	Wolves (3R)	H	W	1-0
30 Jan	Blackburn R (4)	H	W	3-1
20 Feb	Aston Villa (5)	A	D	1-1
24 Feb	Aston Villa (5R)	H	W	2-0
6 Mar	Swansea (6)	A	L	1-2

Appearances (Goals)
Baker A 31 (6) · Blyth W 40 (7) · Brain J 41 (33) · Buchan C 39 (19) · Butler J 41 · Cock D 1 · Haden S 25 (2) · Harper W 19 · Hoar S 21 (3) · Hulme J 15 (2) · John R 29 · Kennedy A 16 · Lawson H 13 (2) · Lewis D 14 · Mackie J 35 · Milne W 5 · Neil A 27 (6) · Parker T 7 (3) · Paterson Dr J 1 (1) · Ramsey J 16 · Robson J 9 · Rutherford J 3 · Rutherford J J 1 · Seddon W 1 · Toner J 2 · Voysey C 1 · Woods H 2 · Young A 7 · Own goals 3 · Total: 28 players (87)

Position in League Table

	P	W	L	D	F:A	Pts	
H.field T	42	23	8	11	92:60	57	1st
Arsenal	42	22	12	8	87:63	52	2nd

SEASON 1926-1927
FOOTBALL LEAGUE (DIVISION 1)

28 Aug	Derby Co	H	W	2-1
1 Sep	Bolton W	H	W	2-1
4 Sep	Sheffield U	A	L	0-4
6 Sep	Bolton W	A	D	2-2
11 Sep	Leicester C	H	D	2-2
15 Sep	Manchester U	A	D	2-2
18 Sep	Liverpool	H	W	2-0
25 Sep	Leeds U	A	L	1-4
2 Oct	Newcastle U	H	D	2-2
9 Oct	Burnley	A	L	0-2
16 Oct	West Ham U	H	D	2-2
23 Oct	Sheffield Wed	H	W	6-2
30 Oct	Everton	A	L	1-3
6 Nov	Blackburn Rov	H	D	2-2
13 Nov	Huddersfield T	A	D	3-3
20 Nov	Sunderland	H	L	2-3
27 Nov	W B A	A	W	3-1
4 Dec	Bury	H	W	1-0
11 Dec	Birmingham	A	D	0-0
18 Dec	Tottenham H	H	L	2-4
27 Dec	Cardiff C	A	L	0-2
28 Dec	Manchester U	H	W	1-0
1 Jan	Cardiff C	H	W	3-2
15 Jan	Derby Co	A	W	2-0
22 Jan	Sheffield U	H	D	1-1
5 Feb	Liverpool	A	L	0-3
10 Feb	Leicester C	A	L	1-2
12 Feb	Leeds	H	W	1-0
26 Feb	Burnley	H	W	6-2
7 Mar	West Ham U	A	L	0-7
12 Mar	Sheffield Wed	A	L	2-4
19 Mar	Everton	H	L	1-2
2 Apr	Huddersfield T	H	L	0-2
6 Apr	Newcastle U	A	L	1-6
9 Apr	Sunderland	A	L	1-5
15 Apr	Aston Villa	H	W	2-1
16 Apr	W B A	H	W	4-1
18 Apr	Aston Villa	A	W	3-2
28 Apr	Blackburn Rov	A	W	2-1
30 Apr	Birmingham	H	W	3-0
4 May	Bury	A	L	2-3
7 May	Tottenham H	A	W	4-0

FA Cup

8 Jan	Sheffield U (3)	A	W	3-2
29 Jan	Port Vale (4)	A	D	2-2
2 Feb	Port Vale (4R)	H	W	1-0
19 Feb	Liverpool (5)	H	W	2-0
5 Mar	Wolves (6)	H	W	2-1
26 Mar	Southampton (SF) (at Chelsea)		W	2-1
23 Apr	Cardiff (F) (at Wembley)		L	0-1

Appearances (Goals)
Baker A 23 · Barley J 3 1 · Blyth W 33 3 · Bowen E 1 · Brain J 37 31 · Buchan C 33 14 · Butler J 31 · Cope H 11 · Haden S 17 4 · Harper W 23 · Hoar S 16 2 · Hulme J 37 8 · John R 41 3 · Kennedy A 11 · Lambert J 16 1 · Lee J 7 · Lewis D 17 · Milne W 6 · Moody J 2 · Parker T 42 4 · Peel H 9 · Ramsey J 12 2 · Roberts H 2 · Seddon C 17 · Shaw J 5 1 · Tricker R 4 3 · Young A 6 · Total: 27 players 77

Position in League Table

	P	W	L	D	F:A	Pts	
Newcastle U	42	25	11	6	96:58	56	1st
Arsenal	42	17	16	9	77:86	43	11th

SEASON 1927-1928
FOOTBALL LEAGUE (DIVISION 1)

27 Aug	Bury	A	L	1-5
31 Aug	Burnley	H	W	4-1
3 Sep	Sheffield U	H	W	6-1
5 Sep	Burnley	A	W	2-1
10 Sep	Aston Villa	A	D	2-2
17 Sep	Sunderland	H	W	2-1
24 Sep	Derby Co	A	L	0-4
1 Oct	West Ham U	H	D	2-2
8 Oct	Portsmouth	A	W	3-2
15 Oct	Leicester C	H	D	2-2
22 Oct	Sheffield Wed	A	D	1-1
29 Oct	Bolton W	H	L	1-2
5 Nov	Blackburn Rov	A	L	1-4
12 Nov	Middlesbrough	H	W	3-1
19 Nov	Birmingham	A	D	1-1
3 Dec	Huddersfield	A	L	1-2
10 Dec	Newcastle U	H	W	4-1
17 Dec	Manchester U	A	L	1-4
24 Dec	Everton	H	W	3-2
27 Dec	Liverpool	A	W	2-0
31 Dec	Bury	H	W	3-1
2 Jan	Tottenham H	H	D	1-1
7 Jan	Sheffield U	A	L	4-6
21 Jan	Aston Villa	H	L	0-3
4 Feb	Derby Co	H	L	3-4
11 Feb	West Ham U	A	D	2-2
25 Feb	Leicester C	A	L	2-3
7 Mar	Liverpool	H	W	6-3
10 Mar	Bolton W	A	D	1-1
14 Mar	Sunderland	A	L	1-5
17 Mar	Blackburn Rov	H	W	3-2
28 Mar	Portsmouth	H	L	0-2
31 Mar	Birmingham	H	D	2-2
6 Apr	Cardiff C	H	W	3-0
7 Apr	Tottenham H	A	L	0-2
9 Apr	Cardiff C	A	D	2-2
14 Apr	Huddersfield	H	D	0-0
18 Apr	Middlesbrough	A	D	2-2
21 Apr	Newcastle U	A	D	1-1
28 Apr	Manchester U	H	L	0-1
2 May	Sheffield Wed	H	D	1-1
5 May	Everton	A	D	3-3

FA Cup

14 Jan	W B A (3)	H	W	2-0
28 Jan	Everton (4)	H	W	4-3
18 Feb	Aston Villa (5)	H	W	4-1
3 Mar	Stoke C (6)	H	W	4-1
24 Mar	Blackburn R (SF) (at Leicester)		L	0-1

Appearances (Goals)
Baker A 36 (3) · Barley J 2 · Blyth W 39 (7) · Brain J 39 (25) · Buchan C 30 (16) · Butler J 39 · Clark A 1 · Cope H 24 · Hapgood E 3 · Hoar S 38 (9) · Hulme J 36 (8) · John R 39 (1) · Kennedy A 2 · Lambert J 16 (3) · Lewis D 33 · Moody J 4 · Parker T 42 (4) · Paterson W 5 · Peel H 13 · H 3 · Seddon C 4 · Shaw J 6 (3) · Thompson L 1 · Tricker R 7 (2) · Own goals 1 Total: 24 players (82)

Position in League Table

	P	W	L	D	F:A	Pts	
Everton	42	20	9	13	102:66	53	1st
Arsenal	42	13	14	15	82:86	41	10th

SEASON 1928-1929
FOOTBALL LEAGUE (DIVISION 1)

25 Aug	Sheffield Wed	A	L	2-3
29 Aug	Derby Co	H	L	1-3
1 Sep	Bolton W	H	W	2-0
8 Sep	Portsmouth	A	L	0-2
15 Sep	Birmingham	H	D	0-0
22 Sep	Manchester C	A	L	1-4
26 Sep	Derby Co	A	D	0-0
29 Sep	Huddersfield	H	W	2-0
6 Oct	Everton	A	L	2-4
13 Oct	West Ham U	H	L	2-3
20 Oct	Newcastle U	A	W	3-0
27 Oct	Liverpool	H	D	4-4
3 Nov	Cardiff C	A	D	1-1
10 Nov	Sheffield U	H	W	2-0
17 Nov	Bury	A	L	0-1
24 Nov	Aston Villa	H	L	2-5
1 Dec	Leicester C	A	D	1-1
8 Dec	Manchester U	H	W	3-1
15 Dec	Leeds	A	D	1-1
22 Dec	Burnley	H	W	3-1
25 Dec	Blackburn Rov	A	L	2-5
26 Dec	Sunderland	H	D	1-1
29 Dec	Sheffield Wed	H	D	2-2
1 Jan	Sunderland	A	L	1-5
5 Jan	Bolton W	A	W	2-1
19 Jan	Portsmouth	H	W	4-0
2 Feb	Manchester C	H	D	0-0
9 Feb	Huddersfield	A	W	1-0
23 Feb	West Ham U	A	W	4-3
9 Mar	Liverpool	A	W	4-2
13 Mar	Birmingham	A	D	1-1
16 Mar	Cardiff C	H	W	2-1
23 Mar	Sheffield U	A	D	2-2
29 Mar	Blackburn Rov	H	W	1-0
30 Mar	Bury	H	W	7-1
2 Apr	Newcastle U	H	L	1-2
6 Apr	Aston Villa	A	L	2-4
13 Apr	Leicester C	H	D	1-1
20 Apr	Manchester U	A	L	1-4
22 Apr	Everton	H	W	2-0
27 Apr	Leeds U	H	W	1-0
4 May	Burnley	A	D	3-3

FA Cup

12 Jan	Stoke (3)	H	W	2-1
26 Jan	Mansfield T (4)	H	W	2-0
16 Feb	Swindon T (5)	A	D	0-0
20 Feb	Swindon T (5R)	H	W	1-0
2 Mar	Aston Villa (6)	A	L	0-1

Appearances (Goals)
Baker A 32 · Barley J 3 · Blyth W 20 (1) · Brain J 37 19 · Butler J 22 · Cope H 23 · Hapgood E 17 · Hoar S 6 (1) · Hulme J 41 (6) · Jack D 31 25 · John R 34 (1) · Jones C 39 (6) · Lambert J 6 (1) · Lewis D 32 · Parker T 42 (3) · Parkin R 5 3 · Paterson W 10 · Peel H 24 (5) · Roberts H 20 · Thompson L 17 (5) · Tricker R 1 · Own goals 1 · Total: 21 players (77)

Position in League Table

	P	W	L	D	F:A	Pts	
Sheffield Wed	42	21	11	10	86:62	52	1st
Arsenal	42	16	13	13	77:72	45	9th

SEASON 1929-1930
FOOTBALL LEAGUE (DIVISION 1)

31 Aug	Leeds U	H	W	4-0
4 Sep	Manchester C	A	L	1-3
7 Sep	Sheffield Wed	A	W	2-0
11 Sep	Manchester C	H	W	3-2
14 Sep	Burnley	H	W	6-1
21 Sep	Sunderland	A	W	1-0
25 Sep	Aston Villa	A	L	2-5
28 Sep	Bolton W	H	L	1-2
5 Oct	Everton	A	D	1-1
12 Oct	Derby Co	H	D	1-1
19 Oct	Grimsby T	H	W	4-1
26 Oct	Manchester U	A	L	0-1
2 Nov	West Ham U	H	L	0-1
9 Nov	Birmingham	A	W	3-2
23 Nov	Blackburn Rov	A	D	1-1
27 Nov	Middlesbrough	H	L	1-2
30 Nov	Newcastle U	H	L	0-1
14 Dec	Huddersfield T	H	W	2-0
16 Dec	Sheffield U	A	L	1-4
21 Dec	Liverpool	A	L	0-1
25 Dec	Portsmouth	A	W	1-0
26 Dec	Portsmouth	H	L	1-2
28 Dec	Leeds U	A	L	0-2
4 Jan	Sheffield W	H	L	2-3
18 Jan	Burnley	A	D	2-2
1 Feb	Bolton W	A	D	0-0
8 Feb	Everton	H	W	4-0
19 Feb	Derby Co	A	L	1-4
22 Feb	Grimsby T	A	D	1-1
8 Mar	West Ham U	A	L	2-3
12 Mar	Manchester U	H	W	4-2
15 Mar	Birmingham	H	W	1-0
29 Mar	Blackburn Rov	H	W	4-0
2 Apr	Liverpool	H	L	0-1
5 Apr	Newcastle U	A	D	1-1
9 Apr	Middlesbrough	A	D	1-1
12 Apr	Sheffield U	H	W	8-1
18 Apr	Leicester	H	D	1-1
19 Apr	Huddersfield	A	D	2-2
21 Apr	Leicester C	A	D	6-6
28 Apr	Sunderland	H	L	0-1
3 May	Aston Villa	H	L	2-4

FA Cup

11 Jan	Chelsea (3)	H	W	2-0
25 Jan	Birmingham (4)	H	D	2-2
29 Jan	Birmingham (4R)	A	W	1-0
15 Feb	Middlesbrough (5)	A	W	2-0
1 Mar	West Ham U (6)	A	W	3-0
22 Mar	Hull C (SF) (at Leeds)		D	2-2
26 Mar	Hull C (SFR) (at Aston Villa)		W	1-0
26 Apr	Huddersfield T (F) (at Wembley)		W	2-0

Appearances (Goals)
Baker A 19 · Bastin C 21 (7) · Brain J 6 · Butler J 2 · Cope H 1 · Halliday D 15 (9) · Hapgood E 38 · Haynes A 13 · Hulme J 37 (14) · Humpish E 3 · Jack D 33 (12) · James A 31 (5) · John R 34 · Johnstone W 7 (3) · Jones C 31 (2) Lambert J 20 (19) · Lewis D 30 · Parker T 41 (3) · Peel H 1 · Preedy C 12 · Roberts H 26 · Seddon C 24 · Thompson L 5 (1) · Williams J 12 (3) · Total: 24 players (78)

Position in League Table

	P	W	L	D	F:A	Pts	
Sheffield Wed	42	26	8	8	105:57	60	1st
Arsenal	42	14	17	11	78:66	39	14th

SEASON 1930-1931
FOOTBALL LEAGUE (DIVISION 1)

30 Aug	Blackpool	A	W	4-1
1 Sep	Bolton W	A	W	4-1
6 Sep	Leeds U	H	W	3-1
10 Sep	Blackburn Rov	H	W	3-2
13 Sep	Sunderland	A	W	4-1
15 Sep	Blackburn Rov	A	D	2-2
20 Sep	Leicester C	H	W	4-1
27 Sep	Birmingham	A	W	4-2
4 Oct	Sheffield U	H	D	1-1
11 Oct	Derby Co	A	L	2-4
18 Oct	Manchester U	A	W	2-1
25 Oct	West Ham U	H	D	1-1
1 Nov	Huddersfield T	A	D	1-1
8 Nov	Aston Villa	H	W	5-2
15 Nov	Sheffield Wed	A	W	2-1
22 Nov	Middlesbrough	H	W	5-3
29 Nov	Chelsea	A	W	5-1
13 Dec	Liverpool	A	D	1-1
20 Dec	Newcastle U	H	L	1-2
25 Dec	Manchester C	A	W	4-1
26 Dec	Manchester C	H	W	3-1
27 Dec	Blackpool	H	W	7-1
17 Jan	Sunderland	H	L	1-3
28 Jan	Grimsby T	H	W	9-1
31 Jan	Birmingham	H	D	1-1
5 Feb	Leicester	A	W	7-2
7 Feb	Sheffield U	A	D	1-1
14 Feb	Derby Co	H	W	6-3
21 Feb	Manchester U	H	W	4-1
28 Feb	West Ham U	A	W	4-2
7 Mar	Huddersfield T	H	D	0-0
11 Mar	Leeds U	A	W	2-1
14 Mar	Aston Villa	A	L	1-5
21 Mar	Sheffield W	H	W	2-0
28 Mar	Middlesbrough	A	W	5-2
3 Apr	Portsmouth	A	D	1-1
4 Apr	Chelsea	H	W	2-1
6 Apr	Portsmouth	H	D	1-1
11 Apr	Grimsby T	A	W	1-0
18 Apr	Liverpool	H	W	3-1
25 Apr	Newcastle U	A	W	3-1
2 May	Bolton W	H	W	5-0

FA Cup

10 Jan	Aston Villa (3)	H	D	2-2
14 Jan	Aston Villa (3R)	A	W	3-1
24 Jan	Chelsea (4)	A	L	1-2

FA Charity Shield

8 Oct	Sheffield Wed (at Chelsea)		W	2-1

Appearances (Goals)
Baker A 1 · Bastin C 42 (28) · Brain J 16 (4) · Cope H 1 · Hapgood E 38 · Harper W 19 · Haynes A 2 · Hulme J 32 (14) · Jack D 35 (31) .James A 40 (5) · John R 40 (2) · Johnstone W 2 (1) · Jones C 24 (1) · Keyser G 12 · Lambert J 34 (38) · Male G 3 · Parker T 41 · Preedy C 11 · Roberts H 40 (1) · Seddon C 18 · Thompson L 2 · Williams J 9 (2) · Total: 22 players (127)

Position in League Table

	P	W	L	D	F:A	Pts	
Arsenal	42	28	4	10	127:59	66	1st

SEASON 1931-1932
FOOTBALL LEAGUE (DIVISION 1)

29 Aug	W B A	H	L	0-1
31 Aug	Blackburn Rov	A	D	1-1
5 Sep	Birmingham	A	D	2-2
9 Sep	Portsmouth	H	D	3-3
12 Sep	Sunderland	H	W	2-0
16 Sep	Portsmouth	A	W	3-0
19 Sep	Manchester C	A	W	3-1
26 Sep	Everton	H	W	3-2
3 Oct	Grimsby T	A	L	1-3
10 Oct	Blackpool	A	W	5-1
17 Oct	Bolton W	H	D	1-1
24 Oct	Leicester C	A	W	2-1
31 Oct	Aston Villa	H	D	1-1
7 Nov	Newcastle U	A	L	2-3
14 Nov	West Ham W	H	W	4-1
21 Nov	Chelsea	A	L	1-2
28 Nov	Liverpool	H	W	6-0
5 Dec	Sheffield Wed	A	W	3-1
12 Dec	Huddersfield	H	D	1-1
19 Dec	Middlesbrough	A	W	5-2
25 Dec	Sheffield U	A	L	1-4
26 Dec	Sheffield U	H	L	0-2
2 Jan	W B A	A	L	0-1
16 Jan	Birmingham	H	W	3-0
30 Jan	Manchester C	H	W	4-0
6 Feb	Everton	A	W	3-1
17 Feb	Grimsby	H	W	2-0
20 Feb	Blackpool	H	W	2-0
2 Mar	Bolton W	A	L	0-1
5 Mar	Leicester C	H	W	2-1
19 Mar	Newcastle U	H	W	1-0
25 Mar	Derby Co	H	W	2-1
26 Mar	West Ham U	A	D	1-1
28 Mar	Derby C	A	D	1-1
3 Apr	Chelsea	H	D	1-1
6 Apr	Sunderland	A	L	0-2
9 Apr	Liverpool	A	L	1-2
16 Apr	Sheffield Wed	H	W	3-1
25 Apr	Aston Villa	A	D	1-1
27 Apr	Huddersfield	A	W	2-1
30 Apr	Middlesbrough	H	W	5-0
7 May	Blackburn Rov	H	W	4-0

FA Cup

9 Jan	Darwen (3)	H	W	11-1
23 Jan	Plymouth (4)	H	W	4-2
13 Feb	Portsmouth (5)	A	W	2-0
27 Feb	Huddersfield (6)	A	W	1-0
12 Mar	Manchester C (SF) (at Aston Villa)		W	1-0
23 Apr	Newcastle U (F) (at Wembley)		L	1-2

FA Charity Shield

7 Oct	W B A (at Aston Villa)		W	1-0

Appearances (Goals)
Bastin C 40 (15) · Beasley A 3 · Coleman E 6 (1) · Compton L 4 · Cope H 1 · Hapgood E 41 · Harper W 2 · Haynes A 7 · Hulme J 40 (14) · Jack D 34 (20) · James A 32 (2) · John R 38 (3) · Jones C 37 · Lambert J 36 (22) · Male G 9 · Moss F 27 · Parker T 38 · Parkin R 9 (7) · Preedy C 13 · Roberts H 35 · Seddon C 5 · Stockill R 3 (1) · Thompson L 1 · Williams J 1 · Own goals 5 · Total: 24 players (90)

Position in League Table

	P	W	L	D	F:A	Pts	
Everton	42	26	12	4	116:64	56	1st
Arsenal	42	22	10	10	90:48	54	2nd

SEASON 1932-1933
FOOTBALL LEAGUE (DIVISION 1)

27 Aug	Birmingham	A	W	1-0
31 Aug	W B A	H	L	1-2
3 Sep	Sunderland	H	W	6-1
10 Sep	Manchester C	A	W	3-2
14 Sep	W B A	A	D	1-1
17 Sep	Bolton W	H	W	3-2
24 Sep	Everton	H	W	2-1
1 Oct	Blackpool	A	W	2-1
8 Oct	Derby Co	H	D	3-3
15 Oct	Blackburn Rov	A	W	3-2
22 Oct	Liverpool	A	W	3-2
24 Oct	Leicester C	H	W	8-2
5 Nov	Wolverhampton W	A	W	7-1
12 Nov	Newcastle U	H	W	1-0
19 Nov	Aston Villa	A	L	3-5
26 Nov	Middlesbrough	H	W	4-2
3 Dec	Portsmouth	A	W	3-1
10 Dec	Chelsea	H	W	4-1
17 Dec	Huddersfield	A	W	1-0
24 Dec	Sheffield U	H	W	9-2
26 Dec	Leeds U	H	L	1-2
27 Dec	Leeds U	A	D	0-0
31 Dec	Birmingham	H	W	3-0
2 Jan	Sheffield W	A	L	2-3
7 Jan	Sunderland	A	L	2-3
21 Jan	Manchester C	H	W	2-1
1 Feb	Bolton W	A	W	4-0
4 Feb	Everton	A	D	1-1
11 Feb	Blackpool	H	D	1-1
22 Feb	Derby Co	A	D	2-2
25 Feb	Blackburn Rov	H	W	8-0
4 Mar	Liverpool	H	L	0-1
11 Mar	Leicester C	A	D	1-1
18 Mar	Wolverhampton W	H	L	1-2
25 Mar	Newcastle U	A	L	1-2
1 Apr	Aston Villa	H	W	5-0
8 Apr	Middlesbrough	A	W	4-3
14 Apr	Sheffield Wed	H	W	4-2
15 Apr	Portsmouth	H	W	2-0
22 Apr	Chelsea	A	W	3-1
29 Apr	Huddersfield	H	D	2-2
6 May	Sheffield U	A	L	1-3

FA Cup

14 Jan	Walsall (3)	A	L	0-2

Appearances (Goals)
Bastin C 42 33 · Bowden R 7 2 · Coleman E 27 24 · Compton L 4 · Cope H 4 · Hapgood E 38 · Haynes A 6 · Hill F 26 1 · Hulme J 40 20 · Jack D 34 18 · James A 40 3 · John R 37 · Jones C 16 · Lambert J 12 14 · Male · G Moss F 41 · Parker T 5 · Parkin R 5 · Preedy C 1 · Roberts H 36 · Sidey N 2 · Stockill R 4 3 · Total: 22 players 118

Position in League Table

	P	W	L	D	F:A	Pts	
Arsenal	42	25	9	8	118:61	58	1st

SEASON 1933-1934
FOOTBALL LEAGUE (DIVISION 1)

26 Aug	Birmingham	H	D	1-1
2 Sep	Sheffield W	A	W	2-1
6 Sep	W B A	H	W	3-1
9 Sep	Manchester C	H	D	1-1
13 Sep	W B A	A	L	0-1
16 Sep	Tottenham H	A	D	1-1
23 Sep	Everton	A	L	1-3
30 Sep	Middlesbrough	H	W	6-0
7 Oct	Blackburn Rov	A	D	2-2
14 Oct	Newcastle U	H	W	3-0
21 Oct	Leicester C	H	W	2-0
28 Oct	Aston Villa	A	W	3-2
4 Nov	Portsmouth	H	D	1-1
11 Nov	Wolverhampton W	A	W	1-0
18 Nov	Stoke C	H	W	3-0
25 Nov	Huddersfield T	A	W	1-0
2 Dec	Liverpool	H	W	2-1
9 Dec	Sunderland	A	L	0-3
16 Dec	Chelsea	H	W	2-1
23 Dec	Sheffield U	A	W	3-1
25 Dec	Leeds U	A	W	1-0
26 Dec	Leeds U	H	W	2-0
30 Dec	Birmingham	A	D	0-0
6 Jan	Sheffield W	H	D	1-1
20 Jan	Manchester C	A	L	1-2
31 Jan	Tottenham H	H	L	1-3
3 Feb	Everton	H	L	1-2
10 Feb	Middlesbrough	A	W	2-0
21 Feb	Blackburn	H	W	2-1
24 Feb	Newcastle U	A	W	1-0
8 Mar	Leicester C	A	L	1-4
10 Mar	Aston Villa	H	W	3-2
24 Mar	Wolverhampton W	H	W	3-2
30 Mar	Derby Co	H	W	1-0
31 Mar	Stoke C	A	D	1-1
2 Apr	Derby Co	A	W	4-2
7 Apr	Huddersfield	H	W	3-1
14 Apr	Liverpool	A	W	3-2
18 Apr	Portsmouth	A	L	0-1
21 Apr	Sunderland	H	W	2-1
28 Apr	Chelsea	A	D	2-2
5 May	Sheffield U	H	W	2-0

FA Cup

13 Jan	Luton (3)	A	W	1-0
27 Jan	Crystal Palace (4)	H	W	7-0
17 Feb	Derby Co (5)	H	W	1-0
3 Mar	Aston Villa (6)	H	L	1-2

FA Charity Shield

18 Oct	Everton	A	W	3-0

Appearances (Goals)
Bastin C 38 (13) · Beasley A 23 (10) · Birkett B 15 (5) · Bowden R 32 (13) · Coleman E 12 (1) · Cox G 2 · Dougall P 5 · Drake E 10 (7) · Dunne J 21 (9) · Hapgood E 40 · Haynes A 1 · Hill F 25 Hulme J 8 (5) · Jack D 14 (5) · James A 22 (3) John R 31 (1) · Jones C 29 · Lambert J 3 (1) · Male G 42 · Moss F 37 · Parkin R 5 · Roberts H 30 (1) · Sidey N 12 · Wilson A 5 · Own goals 1 · Total: 24 players (75)

Position in League Table

	P	W	L	D	F:A	Pts	
Arsenal	42	25	8	9	75:47	59	1st

SEASON 1934-1935
FOOTBALL LEAGUE (DIVISION 1)

25 Aug	Portsmouth	A	D	3-3
1 Sep	Liverpool	H	W	8-1
5 Sep	Blackburn Rov	H	W	4-0
8 Sep	Leeds U	A	D	1-1
15 Sep	W B A	H	W	4-3
17 Sep	Blackburn Rov	A	L	0-2
22 Sep	Sheffield Wed	A	D	0-0
29 Sep	Birmingham	H	W	5-1
6 Oct	Stoke C	A	D	2-2
13 Oct	Manchester C	H	W	3-0
20 Oct	Tottenham H	H	W	5-1
27 Oct	Sunderland	A	L	1-2
3 Nov	Everton	H	W	2-0
10 Nov	Grimsby T	A	D	2-2
17 Nov	Aston Villa	H	L	1-2
24 Nov	Chelsea	A	W	5-2
1 Dec	Wolverhampton W	H	W	7-0
8 Dec	Huddersfield T	A	D	1-1
15 Dec	Leicester C	H	W	8-0
22 Dec	Derby Co	A	L	1-3
25 Dec	Preston NE	H	W	5-3
26 Dec	Preston NE	A	L	1-2
29 Dec	Portsmouth	H	D	1-1
5 Jan	Liverpool	A	W	2-0
19 Jan	Leeds U	H	W	3-0
30 Jan	W B A	A	W	3-0
2 Feb	Sheffield W	H	W	4-1
9 Feb	Birmingham	A	L	0-3
20 Feb	Stoke C	H	W	2-0
23 Feb	Manchester C	A	D	1-1
6 Mar	Tottenham H	A	W	6-0
9 Mar	Sunderland	H	D	0-0
16 Mar	Everton	A	W	2-0
23 Mar	Grimsby T	H	D	1-1
30 Mar	Aston Villa	A	W	3-1
6 Apr	Chelsea	H	D	2-2
13 Apr	Wolverhampton W	A	D	1-1
19 Apr	Middlesbrough	H	W	8-0
20 Apr	Huddersfield T	H	W	1-0
22 Apr	Middlesbrough	A	W	1-0
27 Apr	Leicester C	A	W	5-3
4 May	Derby Co	H	L	0-1

FA Cup

12 Jan	Brighton & HA (3)	A	W	2-0
26 Jan	Leicester C (4)	A	W	1-0
16 Feb	Reading (5)	A	W	1-0
2 Mar	Sheffield W (6)	A	L	1-2

FA Charity Shield

28 Nov	Man City	H	W	4-0

Appearances (Goals)
Bastin C 36 (20) · Beasley A 20 (6) · Birkett R 4 (2) · Bowden E 24 (14) · Compton L 5 (1) · Copping W 31 · Crayston J 37 (3) · Davidson R 11 (2) · Dougall P 8 (1) · Drake E 41 (42) · Dunne J 1 · Hapgood E 34 (1) · Hill F 15 (3) · Hulme J 16 (8) · James A 30 (4) · John R 9 · Kirchen A 7 (2) · Male C 39 · Marshall Drj 4 · Moss F 33 (1) · Roberts L 36 · Rogers L 5 (2) · Sidey N 6 · Trim R 1 · Wilson A 9 · Own goals 3 Total: 25 players (115)

Position in League Table

	P	W	L	D	F:A	Pts	
Arsenal	42	23	7	12	115:46	58	1st

SEASON 1935-1936
FOOTBALL LEAGUE (DIVISION 1)

31 Aug	Sunderland	H	W	3-1
3 Sep	Grimsby T	A	L	0-1
7 Sep	Birmingham	A	D	1-1
11 Sep	Grimsby T	H	W	6-0
14 Sep	Sheffield Wed	H	D	2-2
18 Sep	Leeds U	A	D	1-1
21 Sep	Manchester C	H	L	2-3
28 Sep	Stoke C	A	W	3-0
5 Oct	Blackburn Rov	H	W	5-1
12 Oct	Chelsea	A	D	1-1
19 Oct	Portsmouth	A	L	1-2
26 Oct	Preston NE	H	W	2-1
2 Nov	Brentford	A	L	1-2
9 Nov	Derby Co	H	D	1-1
16 Nov	Everton	A	W	2-0
23 Nov	Wolverhampton W	H	W	4-0
30 Nov	Huddersfield T	A	D	0-0
9 Dec	Middlesbrough	H	W	2-0
14 Dec	Aston Villa	A	W	7-1
25 Dec	Liverpool	A	W	1-0
26 Dec	Liverpool	H	L	1-2
28 Dec	Sunderland	A	L	4-5
4 Jan	Birmingham	H	D	1-1
18 Jan	Sheffield Wed	A	L	2-3
1 Feb	Stoke C	H	W	1-0
8 Feb	Blackburn Rov	A	W	1-0
22 Feb	Portsmouth	H	L	2-3
4 Mar	Derby Co	A	W	4-0
7 Mar	Huddersfield T	H	D	1-1
11 Mar	Manchester City	A	L	0-1
14 Mar	Preston NE	A	L	0-1
25 Mar	Everton	H	D	1-1
28 Mar	Wolverhampton W	A	D	2-2
1 Apr	Bolton W	H	D	1-1
4 Apr	Brentford	H	D	1-1
10 Apr	W B A	H	W	4-0
11 Apr	Middlesbrough	A	D	2-2
13 Apr	W B A	A	L	0-1
18 Apr	Aston Villa	H	W	1-0
27 Apr	Chelsea	H	D	1-1
29 Apr	Bolton W	A	L	1-2
2 May	Leeds U	H	D	2-2

FA Cup

11 Jan	Bristol Rov (3)	A	W	5-1
25 Jan	Liverpool (4)	A	W	2-0
15 Feb	Newcastle (5)	A	D	3-3
19 Feb	Newcastle (5R)	H	W	3-0
29 Feb	Bamsley (6)	H	W	4-1
21 Mar	Grimsby T (SF) (at Huddersfield)		W	1-0
25 Apr	Sheffield U (F) (at Wembley)		W	1-0

FA Charity Shield

23 Oct	Sheffield Wed	H	L	0-1

Appearances (Goals)
Bastin C 31 (11) · Beasley A 26 (2) · Bowden R 22 (6) · Cartwright S 5 · Compton L 12 (1) · Copping W 33 · Cox G 5 (1) · Crayston J 36 (5) · Davidson R 13 · Dougall R 8 (3) · Drake E 26 (24) · Dunne J 6 (1) · Hapgood E 33 · Hill F 10 · Hulme J 21 (6) · James A 17 (2) · John R 6 · Joy B 2 · Kirchen A 6 (3) · Male G 35 · Milne J 14 (6) · Moss F 5 · Parkin R 1 (1) · Roberts H 26 (1) · Rogers E 11 (3) · Sidey N 11 · Tuckett E 2 · Westcott R 2 (1) · Wilson A 37 · Own goals 1 · Total: 29 players (78)

Position in League Table

	P	W	L	D	F:A	Pts	
Sunderland	42	25	11	6	109:74	56	1st
Arsenal	42	15	12	15	78:48	45	6th

SEASON 1936-1937
FOOTBALL LEAGUE (DIVISION 1)

29 Aug	Everton	H	W	3-2
3 Sep	Brentford	A	L	0-2
5 Sep	Huddersfield T	A	D	0-0
9 Sep	Brentford	H	D	1-1
12 Sep	Sunderland	H	W	4-1
19 Sep	Wolverhampton W	A	L	2-4
26 Sep	Derby Co	H	D	2-2
3 Oct	Manchester U	A	L	0-2
10 Oct	Sheffield Wed	H	D	1-1
17 Oct	Charlton Ath	A	W	2-0
24 Oct	Grimsby T	H	D	0-0
31 Oct	Liverpool	A	L	1-2
7 Nov	Leeds U	H	W	4-1
14 Nov	Birmingham	A	W	3-1
21 Nov	Middlesbrough	H	W	5-3
28 Nov	W B A	A	W	4-2
5 Dec	Manchester City	H	L	1-3
12 Dec	Portsmouth	A	W	5-1
19 Dec	Chelsea	H	W	4-1
25 Dec	Preston NE	H	W	4-1
26 Dec	Everton	A	D	1-1
28 Dec	Preston NE	A	W	3-1
1 Jan	Bolton W	A	W	5-0
2 Jan	Huddersfield T	H	D	1-1
9 Jan	Sunderland	A	D	1-1
23 Jan	Wolverhampton W	H	W	2-1
3 Feb	Derby Co	A	L	4-5
6 Feb	Manchester U	H	D	1-1
13 Feb	Sheffield Wed	A	D	0-0
24 Feb	Charlton Ath	H	D	1-1
27 Feb	Grimsby T	A	W	3-1
10 Mar	Liverpool	H	W	1-0
13 Mar	Leeds U	A	W	4-3
20 Mar	Birmingham	H	D	1-1
26 Mar	Stoke C	H	D	0-0
27 Mar	Middlesbrough	A	D	1-1
29 Mar	Stoke C	A	D	0-0
3 Apr	W B A	H	W	2-0
10 Apr	Manchester City	A	L	0-2
17 Apr	Portsmouth	H	W	4-0
24 Apr	Chelsea	A	L	0-2
1 May	Bolton W	H	D	0-0

FA Cup

16 Jan	Chesterfield (3)	A	W	5-1
30 Jan	Manchester U (4)	H	W	5-0
20 Feb	Burnley (5)	A	W	7-1
6 Mar	W B A (6)	A	L	1-3

FA Charity Shield

28 Oct	Sunderland	A	L	1-2

Appearances (Goals)
Bastin C 33 (5) · Beasley A 7 (1) · Biggs A 1 · Boulton F 21 · Bowden R 28 (6) · Cartwright S 2 · Compton D 14 (4) · Compton L 15 · Copping W 38 · Crayston J 30 (1) · Davidson R 28 (9) · Drake E 26 (20) · Hapgood E 32 (1) · Hulme J 3 James A 19 (1) · John R 5 · Joy B 6 · Kirchen A 33 (18) · Male G 37 · Milne J 19 (9) · Nelson D 8 (3) · Roberts H 30 (1) · Sidey N 6 Swindin G 19 · Wilson A 2 · Own goals 1 · Total: 25 players (80)

Position in League Table

	P	W	L	D	F:A	Pts	
Manchester C	42	22	7	13	107:61	57	1st
Arsenal	42	18	8	16	80:49	52	3rd

SEASON 1937-1938
FOOTBALL LEAGUE (DIVISION 1)

28 Aug	Everton	A	W	4-1
1 Sep	Huddersfield T	H	W	3-1
4 Sep	Wolverhampton W	H	W	5-0
8 Sep	Huddersfield T	A	L	1-2
11 Sep	Leicester C	A	D	1-1
15 Sep	Bolton W	A	L	0-1
18 Sep	Sunderland	H	W	4-1
25 Sep	Derby Co	A	L	0-2
2 Oct	Manchester C	H	W	2-1
9 Oct	Chelsea	A	D	2-2
16 Oct	Portsmouth	H	D	1-1
23 Oct	Stoke C	A	D	1-1
30 Oct	Middlesbrough	H	L	1-2
6 Nov	Grimsby T	A	L	1-2
13 Nov	W B A	H	D	1-1
20 Nov	Charlton Ath	A	W	3-0
27 Nov	Leeds U	H	W	4-1
4 Dec	Birmingham	A	W	2-1
11 Dec	Preston NE	H	W	2-0
18 Dec	Liverpool	A	L	0-2
25 Dec	Blackpool	A	L	1-2
27 Dec	Blackpool	H	W	2-1
1 Jan	Everton	H	W	2-1
15 Jan	Wolverhampton W	A	L	1-3
29 Jan	Sunderland	A	D	1-1
2 Feb	Leicester C	H	W	3-1
5 Feb	Derby Co	H	W	3-0
16 Feb	Manchester C	A	W	2-1
19 Feb	Chelsea	H	W	2-0
26 Feb	Portsmouth	A	D	0-0
5 Mar	Stoke C	H	W	4-0
12 Mar	Middlesbrough	A	L	1-2
19 Mar	Grimsby	H	W	5-1
26 Mar	W B A	A	D	0-0
2 Apr	Charlton Ath	H	D	2-2
9 Apr	Leeds U	A	W	1-0
15 Apr	Brentford	H	L	0-2
16 Apr	Birmingham	H	D	0-0
18 Apr	Brentford	A	L	0-3
23 Apr	Preston NE	A	W	3-1
30 Apr	Liverpool	H	W	1-0
7 May	Bolton W	H	W	5-0

FA Cup

8 Jan	Bolton W (3)	H	W	3-1
22 Jan	Wolves (4)	A	W	2-1
12 Feb	Preston NE (5)	H	L	0-1

Appearances (Goals)
Bastin C 38 (15) · Biggs A 2 · Boulton F 15 · Bowden R 10 (1) · Bremner G 2 (1) · Carr E 11 7 · Cartwright S 6 (2) · Collett E 5 · Compton D 7 1 · Compton L 9 (1) · Copping W 38 Crayston J 31 (4) · Davidson R 5 (2) · Drake E 27 (17) · Drury G 11 · Griffiths W 9 (5) · Hapgood E 41 · Hulme J 7 (2) · Hunt G 18 (3) · Jones L 28 (3) · Joy B 26 · Kirchen A 19 (6) · Lewis R 4 (2) · Male G 34 · Milne J 16 (4) · Roberts H 13 · Sidey N 3 · Swindin G 17 · Wilson A 10 · Own goals 1 · Total: 29 players (77)

Position in League Table

	P	W	L	D	F:A	Pts	
Arsenal	42	21	11	10	77:44	52	1st

SEASON 1938-1939
FOOTBALL LEAGUE (DIVISION 1)

27 Aug	Portsmouth	H	W	2-0
3 Sep	Huddersfield T	A	D	1-1
8 Sep	Brentford	A	L	0-1
10 Sep	Everton	H	L	1-2
14 Sep	Derby Co	H	L	1-2
17 Sep	Wolverhampton W	A	W	1-0
24 Sep	Aston Villa	H	D	0-0
1 Oct	Sunderland	A	D	0-0
8 Oct	Grimsby T	H	W	2-0
15 Oct	Chelsea	A	L	2-4
22 Oct	Preston NE	H	W	1-0
29 Oct	Bolton W	A	D	1-1
5 Nov	Leeds U	H	L	2-3
12 Nov	Liverpool	A	D	2-2
19 Nov	Leicester C	H	D	0-0
26 Nov	Middlesbrough	A	D	1-1
3 Dec	Birmingham	H	W	3-1
10 Dec	Manchester U	A	L	0-1
17 Dec	Stoke C	H	W	4-1
24 Dec	Portsmouth	A	D	0-0
27 Dec	Charlton Ath	A	L	0-1
31 Dec	Huddersfield T	H	W	1-0
14 Jan	Everton	A	L	0-2
21 Jan	Charlton Ath	H	W	2-0
28 Jan	Aston Villa	A	W	3-1
1 Feb	Wolverhampton W	H	D	0-0
4 Feb	Sunderland	H	W	2-0
18 Feb	Chelsea	H	W	1-0
21 Feb	Grimsby T	A	L	1-2
25 Feb	Preston NE	A	L	1-2
4 Mar	Bolton W	H	W	3-1
11 Mar	Leeds U	A	L	2-4
18 Mar	Liverpool	H	W	2-0
25 Mar	Leicester C	A	W	2-0
1 Apr	Middlesbrough	H	L	1-2
7 Apr	Blackpool	A	L	0-1
8 Apr	Birmingham	A	W	2-1
10 Apr	Blackpool	H	W	2-1
15 Apr	Manchester U	H	W	2-1
22 Apr	Stoke C	A	L	0-1
29 Apr	Derby Co	A	W	2-1
6 May	Brentford	H	W	2-0

FA Cup

7 Jan	Chelsea (3)	A	L	1-2

FA Charity Shield

26 Sep	Preston	H	W	2-1

Appearances (Goals)
Bastin C 23 (3) · Bremner G 13 (3) · Carr E 1 · Cartwright S 3 · Collett R 9 · Compton D 1 · Compton L 18 (2) · Copping W 26 · Crayston J 34 (3) · Cumner R 12 (2) · Curtis G 2 · Drake E 38 (14) · Drury G 23 (3) · Farr A 2 (1) · Fields A 3 · Hapgood E 38 · Jones B 30 (4) · Jones B 30 4 · Jones L 18 · Joy B 39 · Kirchen A 27 (9) · Lewis R 15 (7) · Male G 28 · Marks G 2 · Nelson D 9 (1) · Pryde D 4 · Pugh S 1 · Swindin G 21 · Walsh W 3 · Wilson A 19 · Own goals 3 Total: 29 players (55)

Position in League Table

	P	W	L	D	F:A	Pts	
Everton	42	27	10	5	88:52	59	1st
Arsenal	42	19	14	9	55:41	47	5th

SEASON 1939-1940
FOOTBALL LEAGUE (DIVISION 1)

(Prior to outbreak of War)

26 Aug	Wolverhampton W 2 Arsenal 2
30 Aug	Arsenal 1 Blackburn Rov 0
2 Sep	Arsenal 5 Sunderland 2
21 Aug	Jubilee Match Arsenal 1 Tottenham H 1 (Drury)

Goal Scorers (Football League)

Drake	4
Bastin	1
Drury	1
Lewis	1
Kirchen	1

The Football League was again suspended during the Second World War, the 1939-1940 competition having been cut short after just four matches. During the seven seasons that followed the outbreak of the War, Arsenal played in a variety of competitions: the Regional League South, the London War Cup, the London League, the League Cup (South) and the Football League (South). Arsenal won the Regional League South (A Division) in the season 1939-1940, won the London League in 1942 and retained the title the following year. They won the League Cup (South) in the season 1942-1943 and again in the season 1944-1945. Arsenal finished 11th in the League Table (South), in season 1944-1945. 1944-1945 saw a number of minor, regional competitions with guest players often constituting the teams. The FA Cup, however, was held and Arsenal were knocked out in their first, two-legged game, thus:

5 Jan	West Ham	A	L	0-6
9 Jan	West Ham	H	W	1-0

SEASON 1946-1947
FOOTBALL LEAGUE (DIVISION 1)

31 Aug	Wolverhampton W	A	L	1-6
4 Sep	Blackburn Rov	H	L	1-3
7 Sep	Sunderland	A	D	2-2
11 Sep	Everton	A	L	2-3
14 Sep	Aston Villa	A	W	2-0
17 Sep	Blackburn Rov	A	W	2-1
21 Sep	Derby Co	H	L	0-1
28 Sep	Manchester U	A	L	2-5
5 Oct	Blackpool	A	L	1-2
12 Oct	Brentford	H	D	2-2
19 Oct	Stoke C	H	W	1-0
26 Oct	Chelsea	A	L	1-2
2 Nov	Sheffield U	H	L	2-3
9 Nov	Preston NE	A	L	0-2
16 Nov	Leeds U	H	W	4-2
23 Nov	Liverpool	A	L	2-4
30 Nov	Bolton W	H	D	2-2
7 Dec	Middlesbrough	A	L	0-2

14 Dec	Charlton Ath	H	W	1-0
21 Dec	Grimsby T	A	D	0-0
25 Dec	Portsmouth	H	W	2-1
26 Dec	Portsmouth	A	W	2-0
28 Dec	Wolverhampton W	H	D	1-1
4 Jan	Sunderland	A	W	4-1
18 Jan	Aston Villa	H	L	0-2
1 Feb	Manchester U	H	W	6-2
8 Feb	Blackpool	H	D	1-1
22 Feb	Stoke C	A	L	1-3
1 Mar	Chelsea	H	L	1-2
15 Mar	Preston NE	H	W	4-1
22 Mar	Leeds U	A	D	1-1
4 Apr	Huddersfield T	H	L	1-2
5 Apr	Bolton W	A	W	3-1
7 Apr	Huddersfield T	A	D	0-0
12 Apr	Middlesbrough	H	W	4-0
19 Apr	Charlton Ath	A	D	2-2
26 Apr	Grimsby T	H	W	5-3
10 May	Derby Co	A	W	1-0
24 May	Liverpool	H	L	1-2
26 May	Brentford	A	W	1-0
31 May	Everton	H	W	2-1
7 June	Sheffield U	A	L	1-2

FA Cup

11 Jan	Chelsea (3)	A	D	1-1
15 Jan	Chelsea (3R)	H	D	1-1
20 Jan	Chelsea (3R) (at Tottenham)		L	0-2

Appearances (Goals)

Barnes W 26 · Bastin C 6 · Calverley A 11 · Collett E 6 · Compton D 1 1 · Compton L 36 · Curtis G 11 · Drury G 4 · Fields A 8 · Grant C 2 Gudmundsson A 2 · Hodges C 2 · Jones B 26 1 .Joy B 13 · Lewis R 28 (29) · Logie J 35 (8) · Male G 15 · McPherson L 37 (6) · Mercer J 25 · Morgan S 2 · Nelson D 10 · Dr O'Flanagan K 14 (3) · Platt T 4 · Rooke R 24 (21) · Rudkin T 5 2 · Scott L 28 · Sloan P 30 (1) · Smith A 3 · Swindin G 38 · Wade J 2 · Waller H 8 · Total: 31 players (72)

Position in League Table

	P	W	L	D	F:A	Pts	
Liverpool	42	25	10	7	84:52	57	1st
Arsenal	42	16	17	9	72:70	41	13th

SEASON 1947-1948
FOOTBALL LEAGUE (DIVISION 1)

23 Aug	Sunderland	H	W	3-1
27 Aug	Charlton Ath	A	W	4-2
30 Aug	Sheffield U	A	W	2-1
3 Sep	Charlton Ath	H	W	6-0
6 Sep	Manchester U	H	W	2-1
10 Sep	Bolton W	H	W	2-0
13 Sep	Preston NE	A	D	0-0
20 Sep	Stoke C	H	W	3-0
27 Sep	Burnley	A	W	1-0
4 Oct	Portsmouth	H	D	0-0
11 Oct	Aston Villa	H	W	1-0
18 Oct	Wolverhampton W	A	D	1-1
25 Oct	Everton	H	D	1-1
1 Nov	Chelsea	A	D	0-0
8 Nov	Blackpool	H	W	2-1
15 Nov	Blackburn Rov	A	W	1-0
22 Nov	Huddersfield T	H	W	2-0
29 Nov	Derby Co	A	L	0-1
6 Dec	Manchester C	H	D	1-1
13 Dec	Grimsby T	A	W	4-0
20 Dec	Sunderland	A	D	1-1
25 Dec	Liverpool	A	W	3-1
27 Dec	Liverpool	H	L	1-2
1 Jan	Bolton W	A	W	1-0
3 Jan	Sheffield U	H	W	3-2
17 Jan	Manchester U	A	D	1-1
31 Jan	Preston NE	H	W	3-0
7 Feb	Stoke C	A	D	0-0
14 Feb	Burnley	H	W	3-0
28 Feb	Aston Villa	A	L	2-4
6 Mar	Wolverhampton W	H	W	5-2
13 Mar	Everton	A	W	2-0
20 Mar	Chelsea	H	L	0-2
26 Mar	Middlesbrough	H	W	7-0
27 Mar	Blackpool	A	L	0-3
29 Mar	Middlesbrough	A	D	1-1
3 Apr	Blackburn Rov	H	W	2-0
10 Apr	Huddersfield T	A	D	1-1
17 Apr	Derby Co	H	L	1-2
21 Apr	Portsmouth	A	D	0-0
24 Apr	Manchester C	A	D	0-0
1 May	Grimsby T	H	W	8-0

FA Cup

10 Jan	Bradford Park Ave (3)	H	L	0-1

Appearances (Goals)

Barnes W 35 · Compton D 14 (6) · Compton L 35 · Fields A 6 · Forbes A 11 (2) · Jones B 7 (1) Lewis R 28 (14) · Logie J 39 (8) · Macaulay A 40 · Male G 8 · McPherson L 29 (5) · Mercer J 40 · Rooke R 42 (33) · Roper D 40 (10) · Scott L 39 · Sloan W 3 · Smith L 1 · Swindin G 42 · Wade J 3 · Own goals 2 · Total: 19 players (81)

Position in League Table

	P	W	L	D	F:A	Pts	
Arsenal	42	23	6	13	81:32	59	1st

SEASON 1948-1949
FOOTBALL LEAGUE (DIVISION 1)

21 Aug	Huddersfield T	A	D	1-1
25 Aug	Stoke C	H	W	3-0
28 Aug	Manchester U	H	L	0-1
30 Aug	Stoke C	A	L	0-1
4 Sep	Sheffield U	A	D	1-1
8 Sep	Liverpool	H	D	1-1
11 Sep	Aston Villa	H	W	3-1
15 Sep	Liverpool	A	W	1-0
18 Sep	Sunderland	A	D	1-1
25 Sep	Wolverhampton W	H	W	3-1
2 Oct	Bolton W	A	L	0-1
9 Oct	Burnley	H	W	3-1
16 Oct	Preston NE	A	D	1-1
23 Oct	Everton	H	W	5-0
30 Oct	Chelsea	A	W	1-0
6 Nov	Birmingham C	H	W	2-0
13 Nov	Middlesbrough	A	W	1-0
20 Nov	Newcastle U	H	L	0-1
27 Nov	Portsmouth	A	L	1-4
4 Dec	Manchester C	H	D	1-1
11 Dec	Charlton Ath	A	L	3-4
18 Dec	Huddersfield T	H	W	3-0
25 Dec	Derby Co	H	D	3-3
27 Dec	Derby Co	A	L	1-2
1 Jan	Manchester U	A	L	0-2
15 Jan	Sheffield U	H	W	5-3
22 Jan	Aston Villa	A	L	0-1
5 Feb	Sunderland	H	W	5-0
19 Feb	Wolverhampton W	A	W	3-1
26 Feb	Bolton W	H	W	5-0
5 Mar	Burnley	A	D	1-1
12 Mar	Preston NE	H	D	0-0
19 Mar	Newcastle U	A	L	2-3
2 Apr	Birmingham C	A	D	1-1
9 Apr	Middlesbrough	H	D	1-1
15 Apr	Blackpool	A	D	1-1
16 Apr	Everton	A	D	0-0
18 Apr	Blackpool	H	W	2-0
23 Apr	Chelsea	H	L	1-2
27 Apr	Manchester C	A	W	3-0
4 May	Portsmouth	H	W	3-2
7 May	Chartton Ath	H	W	2-0

FA Cup

8 Jan	Tottenham H (3)	H	W	3-0
29 Jan	Derby Co (4)	A	L	0-1

FA Charity Shield

6 Oct	Manchester U	H	W	4-3

Appearances (Goals)

Barnes W 40 · Compton D 6 (2) · Compton L 40 · Daniel R 1 · Fields A 1 · Forbes A 25 (4) · Jones B 8 1 · Lewis R 25 (16) · Lishman D 23 12 · Logie J 35 (11) · Macaulay A 39 (1) · McPherson L 33 (5) · Mercer J 33 · Platt E 10 · Rooke R 22 (14) · Roper D 31 (5) · Scott L 12 · Smith L 32 · Swindin G 32 · Vallance T 14 (2) · Own goals 1 · Total: players 20 (74)

Position in League Table

	P	W	L	D	F:A	Pts	
Portsmouth	42	25	9	8	84:42	58	1st
Arsenal	42	18	11	13	74:44	49	5th

SEASON 1949-1950
FOOTBALL LEAGUE (DIVISION 1)

20 Aug	Burnley	H	L	0-1
24 Aug	Chelsea	A	W	2-1
27 Aug	Sunderland	A	L	2-4
31 Aug	Chelsea	H	L	2-3
3 Sep	Liverpool	H	L	1-2
7 Sep	W B A	A	W	2-1
10 Sep	Huddersfield T	A	D	2-2
14 Sep	W B A	H	W	4-1
17 Sep	Bolton W	A	D	2-2
24 Sep	Birmingham C	H	W	4-2
1 Oct	Derby Co	A	W	2-1
8 Oct	Everton	H	W	5-2
15 Oct	Middlesbrough	A	D	1-1
22 Oct	Blackpool	H	W	1-0
29 Oct	Newcastle U	A	W	3-0
5 Nov	Fulham	H	W	2-1
12 Nov	Manchester C	A	W	2-0
19 Nov	Charlton Ath	H	L	2-3
26 Nov	Aston Villa	A	D	1-1
3 Dec	Wolverhampton W	H	D	1-1
10 Dec	Portsmouth	A	L	1-2
17 Dec	Burnley	A	D	0-0
24 Dec	Sunderland	H	W	5-0
26 Dec	Manchester U	A	L	0-2
27 Dec	Manchester U	H	D	0-0
31 Dec	Liverpool	A	L	0-2
14 Jan	Huddersfield T	H	W	1-0
21 Jan	Bolton W	H	D	1-1
4 Feb	Birmingham C	A	L	1-2
18 Feb	Derby Co	H	W	1-0
25 Feb	Everton	A	W	1-0
8 Mar	Middlesbrough	H	D	1-1
11 Mar	Charlton Ath	A	D	1-1
25 Mar	Fulham	A	D	2-2
29 Mar	Aston Villa	H	L	1-3
1 Apr	Manchester C	H	W	4-1
8 Apr	Blackpool	A	L	1-2
10 Apr	Stoke C	H	W	6-0
15 Apr	Newcastle U	H	W	4-2
22 Apr	Wolverhampton W	A	L	0-3
3 May	Portsmouth	H	W	2-0
6 May	Stoke C	A	W	5-2

FA Cup

7 Jan	Sheffield W (3)	H	W	1-0
28 Jan	Swansea T (4)	H	W	2-1
11 Feb	Burnley (5)	H	W	2-0
4 Mar	Leeds U (6)	H	W	1-0
18 Mar	Chelsea (SF) (at White Hart Lane)		D	2-2
22 Mar	Chelsea (SFR) (at White Hart Lane)		W	1-0
29 Apr	Liverpool (F) (at Wembley)		W	2-0

Appearances (Goals)

Barnes W 38 (5) · Compton D 11 (1) · Compton L 35 · Cox F 32 (3) · Daniel R 6 · Forbes A 23 (2) · Kelly N 1 · Lewis R 31 (19) · Lishman D 14 (9) · Logie J 34 (7) · Macaulay A 24 · McPherson 27 (3) · Mercer J 35 · Platt E 19 · Roper D 27 (7) · Scott L 15 · Shaw A 5 · Smith L 31 · Swindin G 23 · Vallance T 1 · Wade J 1 · Own goals 2 · Total: 22 players (79)

Position in League Table

	P	W	L	D	F:A	Pts	
Portsmouth	42	22	11	9	74:38	53	1st
Arsenal	42	19	12	11	79:55	49	6th

SEASON 1950-1951
FOOTBALL LEAGUE (DIVISION 1)

19 Aug	Burnley	A	W	1-0
23 Aug	Chelsea	H	D	0-0
26 Aug	Tottenham H	H	D	2-2
30 Aug	Chelsea	A	W	1-0
2 Sep	Sheffield W	H	W	3-0
6 Sep	Everton	H	W	2-1
9 Sep	Middlesbrough	A	L	1-2
13 Sep	Everton	A	D	1-1
16 Sep	Huddersfield T	H	W	6-2
23 Sep	Newcastle U	A	L	1-2
30 Sep	W B A	H	W	3-0
7 Oct	Charlton Ath	A	W	3-1
14 Oct	Manchester U	H	W	3-0
21 Oct	Aston Villa	A	D	1-1
28 Oct	Derby Co	H	W	3-1
4 Nov	Wolverhampton W	A	W	1-0
11 Nov	Sunderland	H	W	5-1
18 Nov	Liverpool	A	W	3-1
25 Nov	Fulham	H	W	5-1
2 Dec	Bolton W	A	L	0-3
9 Dec	Blackpool	H	D	4-4
16 Dec	Burnley	H	L	0-1
23 Dec	Tottenham H	A	L	0-1
25 Dec	Stoke C	H	L	0-3
26 Dec	Stoke C	A	L	0-1
30 Dec	Sheffield W	A	W	2-0
13 Jan	Middlesbrough	H	W	3-1
20 Jan	Huddersfield T	A	D	2-2
3 Feb	Newcastle U	H	D	0-0
17 Feb	W B A	A	L	0-2
24 Feb	Charlton Ath	H	L	2-5
3 Mar	Manchester U	A	L	1-3
10 Mar	Aston Villa	H	W	2-1
17 Mar	Derby Co	A	L	2-4
23 Mar	Portsmouth	H	L	0-1
24 Mar	Wolverhampton W	H	W	2-1
26 Mar	Portsmouth	A	D	1-1
31 Mar	Sunderland	A	W	2-0
7 Apr	Liverpool	H	L	1-2
14 Apr	Fulham	A	L	2-3
21 Apr	Bolton W	H	D	1-1
2 May	Blackpool	A	W	1-0

FA Cup

6 Jan	Carlisle U (3)	H	D	0-0
11 Jan	Carlisle U (3R)	A	W	4-1
27 Jan	Northampton (4)	H	W	3-2
10 Feb	Manchester U (5)	A	L	0-1

Appearances (Goals)

Barnes W 35 (3) · Bowen D 7 · Compton L 36 · Cox F 13 (2) · Daniel R 5 · Fields A 1 · Forbes A 32 (4) · Goring P 34 (15) · Holton C 10 (5) · Kelsey J 4 · Lewis R 14 (8) · Lishman D 26 (17) · Logie J 39 (9) · McPherson L 26 · Marden B 11 (2) · Mercer J 31 · Milton A 1 · Platt E 17 Roper D 34 (7) · Scott L 17 · Shaw A 16 · Smith L 32 · Swindin G 21 · Own goals1 · Total: 23 players (73)

Position in League Table

	P	W	L	D	F:A	Pts	
Tottenham H	42	25	7	10	82:44	60	1st
Arsenal	42	19	14	9	73:56	47	5th

SEASON 1951-1952
FOOTBALL LEAGUE (DIVISION 1)

18 Aug	Huddersfield T	H	D	2-2
22 Aug	Chelsea	A	W	3-1
25 Aug	Wolverhampton W	A	L	1-2
29 Aug	Chelsea	H	W	2-1
1 Sep	Sunderland	H	W	3-0
5 Sep	Liverpool	H	D	0-0
8 Sep	Aston Villa	A	L	0-1
12 Sep	Liverpool	A	D	0-0
15 Sep	Derby Co	H	W	3-1
22 Sep	Manchester C	A	W	2-0
29 Sep	Tottenham H	H	D	1-1
6 Oct	Preston NE	A	L	0-2
13 Oct	Burnley	H	W	1-0
20 Oct	Charlton Ath	A	W	3-1
27 Oct	Fulham	H	W	4-3
3 Nov	Middlesbrough	A	W	3-0
10 Nov	W B A	H	W	6-3
17 Nov	Newcastle U	A	L	0-2
24 Nov	Bolton W	H	W	4-2
1 Dec	Stoke C	A	L	1-2
8 Dec	Manchester U	H	L	1-3
15 Dec	Huddersfield T	A	W	3-2
22 Dec	Wolverhampton W	H	D	2-2
25 Dec	Portsmouth	H	W	4-1
26 Dec	Portsmouth	A	D	1-1
29 Dec	Sunderland	A	L	1-4
5 Jan	Aston Villa	H	W	2-1
19 Jan	Derby Co	A	W	2-1
26 Jan	Manchester C	H	D	2-2
9 Feb	Tottenham H	A	W	2-1
16 Feb	Preston NE	H	D	3-3
1 Mar	Burnley	A	W	1-0
13 Mar	Charlton	H	W	2-1
15 Mar	Fulham	A	D	0-0
22 Mar	Middlesbrough	H	W	3-1
11 Apr	Blackpool	A	D	0-0
12 Apr	Bolton	A	L	1-2
14 Apr	Blackpool	H	W	4-1
16 Apr	Newcastle U	H	D	1-1
19 Apr	Stoke C	H	W	4-1
21 Apr	W B A	A	L	1-3
26 Apr	Manchester U	A	L	1-6

FA Cup

12 Jan	Norwich C (3)	A	W	5-0
2 Feb	Barnsley (4)	H	W	4-0
23 Feb	Leyton Orient (5)	A	W	3-0
8 Mar	Luton T (6)	A	W	3-2
5 Apr	Chelsea (SF) (at Tottenham)		D	1-1
7 Apr	Chelsea (SFR) (at Tottenham)		W	3-0
3 May	Newcastle (F) (at Wembley)		L	0-1

Appearances (Goals)

Barnes W 41 (2) · Bowen D 8 · Chenhall J 3 · Compton L 4 · Cox F 25 (3) · Daniel R 34 · Forbes A 38 (2) · Goring P 16 (4) · Holton C 28 17 · Lewis R 9 (8) · Lishman D 38 (23) · Logie J 34 (4) · Marden R 7 2 · Mercer J 36 · Milton A 20 (5) · Robertson J 1 · Roper D 30 (9) · Scott L 4 · Shaw A 8 · Smith L 28 · Swindin G 42 · Wade J 8 · Own goals 1 · Total: 22 players (80)

Position in League Table

	P	W	L	D	F:A	Pts	
Manchester U	42	23	8	11	95:52	57	1st
Arsenal	42	21	10	11	80:61	53	3rd

SEASON 1952-1953
FOOTBALL LEAGUE (DIVISION 1)

23 Aug	Aston Villa	A	W	2-1
27 Aug	Manchester U	H	W	2-1
30 Aug	Sunderland	H	L	1-2
3 Sep	Manchester U	A	D	0-0
6 Sep	Wolverhampton W	A	D	1-1
10 Sep	Portsmouth	H	W	3-1
13 Sep	Charlton Ath	H	L	3-4
17 Sep	Portsmouth	A	D	2-2
20 Sep	Tottenham H	A	W	3-1
27 Sep	Derby Co	A	L	0-2
4 Oct	Blackpool	H	W	3-1
11 Oct	Sheffield W	H	D	2-2
25 Oct	Newcastle U	H	W	3-0
1 Nov	W B A	A	L	0-2
8 Nov	Middlesbrough	H	W	2-1
15 Nov	Liverpool	A	W	5-1
22 Nov	Manchester C	H	W	3-1
29 Nov	Stoke C	A	D	1-1
13 Dec	Burnley	A	D	1-1
20 Dec	Aston Villa	H	W	3-1
25 Dec	Bolton W	A	W	6-4
3 Jan	Sunderland	A	L	1-3
17 Jan	Wolverhampton W	H	W	5-3
24 Jan	Charlton Ath	A	D	2-2
7 Feb	Tottenham H	H	W	4-0
18 Feb	Derby Co	H	W	6-2
21 Feb	Blackpool	A	L	2-3
2 Mar	Sheffield W	A	W	4-1
7 Mar	Cardiff	H	L	0-1
14 Mar	Newcastle U	A	D	2-2
19 Mar	Preston NE	H	D	1-1
21 Mar	W B A	H	D	2-2
28 Mar	Middlesbrough	A	L	0-2
3 Apr	Chelsea	A	D	1-1
4 Apr	Liverpool	H	W	5-3
6 Apr	Chelsea	H	W	2-0
11 Apr	Manchester C	A	W	4-2
15 Apr	Bolton W	H	W	4-1
18 Apr	Stoke C	H	W	3-1
22 Apr	Cardiff	A	D	0-0
25 Apr	Preston NE	A	L	0-2
1 May	Burnley	H	W	3-2

FA Cup

10 Jan	Doncaster Rov (3)	H	W	4-0
31 Jan	Bury (4)	H	W	6-2
14 Feb	Burnley (5)	A	W	2-0
28 Feb	Blackpool (6)	H	L	1-2

Appearances (Goals)

Bowen D 2 · Chenhall J 13 · Cox F 9 (1) · Daniel R 41 (5) · Dodgin W 1 · Forbes A 33 (1) · Goring P 29 (10) · Holton C 21 (19) · Kelsey J 25 · Lishman D 39 (22) · Logie J 32 (10) · Marden R 8 (4) · Mercer J 28 (2) · Milton A 25 7 · Oakes D 2 (1) · Platt E 3 · Roper D 41 (14) · Shaw A 25 · Smith L 31 · Swindin G 14 · Wade J 40 · Own goals1 · Total: 21 players (97)

Position in League Table

	P	W	L	D	F:A	Pts	
Arsenal	42	21	9	12	97:64	54	1st

SEASON 1953-1954
FOOTBALL LEAGUE (DIVISION 1)

19 Aug	W B A	A	L	0-2
22 Aug	Huddersfield T	H	D	0-0
24 Aug	Sheffield U	A	L	0-1
29 Aug	Aston Villa	A	L	1-2
1 Sep	Sheffield U	H	D	1-1
5 Sep	Wolverhampton W	H	L	2-3
8 Sep	Chelsea	H	L	1-2
12 Sep	Sunderland	A	L	1-7
15 Sep	Chelsea	A	W	2-0
19 Sep	Manchester C	H	D	2-2
26 Sep	Cardiff	A	W	3-0
3 Oct	Preston NE	H	W	3-2
10 Oct	Tottenham H	A	W	4-1
17 Oct	Burnley	H	L	2-5
24 Oct	Charlton Ath	A	W	5-1
31 Oct	Sheffield W	H	W	4-1
7 Nov	Manchester U	A	D	2-2
14 Nov	Bolton W	H	W	4-3
21 Nov	Liverpool	A	W	2-1
28 Nov	Newcastle U	H	W	2-1
5 Dec	Middlesbrough	A	L	0-2
12 Dec	W B A	H	D	2-2
19 Dec	Huddersfield T	A	D	2-2
26 Dec	Blackpool	A	D	2-2
28 Dec	Blackpool	H	D	1-1
16 Jan	Wolverhampton W	A	W	2-0
23 Jan	Sunderland	H	L	1-4
6 Feb	Manchester C	A	D	0-0
13 Feb	Cardiff	H	D	1-1
24 Feb	Preston NE	A	W	1-0
27 Feb	Tottenham H	H	L	0-3
6 Mar	Burnley	A	L	1-2
13 Mar	Charlton Ath	H	D	3-3
20 Mar	Sheffield W	A	L	1-2
27 Mar	Manchester U	H	W	3-1
3 Apr	Bolton W	A	L	1-3
6 Apr	Aston Villa	H	D	1-1
10 Apr	Liverpool	H	W	3-0
16 Apr	Portsmouth	H	W	3-0
17 Apr	Newcastle U	A	L	2-5
19 Apr	Portsmouth	A	D	1-1
24 Apr	Middlesbrough	H	W	3-1

FA Cup

9 Jan	Aston Villa (3)	H	W	5-1
30 Jan	Norwich (4)	H	L	1-2

FA Charity Shield

12 Oct	Blackpool	H	W	3-1

Appearances (Goals)

Barnes W 19 (1) · Bowen D 10 · Dickson W 24 1 · Dodgin W 39 · Evans D 10 · Forbes A 30 (4) Goring P 9 · Holton C 32 (17) · Kelsey J 39 · Lawton T 9 (1) · Lishman D 39 (18) · Logie J 35 (8) · Marden R 9 (3) · Mercer J 19 · Milton A 21 (3) · Roper D 39 (12) · Shaw A 2 · Smith L 7 Sullivan C 1 · Swindin G 2 · Tapscott D 5 (5) · Tilley P 1 · Wade J 18 · Walsh B 10 · Ward G 3 Wills L 30 · Own goals 2 · Total: 26 players (75)

Position in League Table

	P	W	L	D	F:A	Pts	
Wolverhampton W	42	25	10	7	96:56	57	1st
Arsenal	42	15	14	13	75:73	43	12th

SEASON 1954-1955
FOOTBALL LEAGUE (DIVISION 1)

21 Aug	Newcastle U	H	L	1-3
25 Aug	Everton	A	L	0-1
28 Aug	W B A	A	L	1-3
31 Aug	Everton	H	W	2-0
4 Sep	Tottenham H	H	W	2-0
8 Sep	Manchester C	A	L	1-2
11 Sep	Sheffield U	H	W	4-0
14 Sep	Manchester C	H	L	2-3
18 Sep	Preston NE	A	L	1-3
25 Sep	Burnley	H	W	4-0
2 Oct	Leicester C	A	D	3-3
9 Oct	Sheffield W	A	W	2-1
16 Oct	Portsmouth	H	L	0-1
23 Oct	Aston Villa	A	L	1-2
30 Oct	Sunderland	H	L	1-3
6 Nov	Bolton W	A	D	2-2
13 Nov	Huddersfield T	H	L	3-5
20 Nov	Manchester U	A	L	1-2
27 Nov	Wolverhampton W	H	D	1-1
4 Dec	Blackpool	A	D	2-2
11 Dec	Charlton Ath	H	W	3-1
18 Dec	Newcastle U	A	L	1-5
25 Dec	Chelsea	H	W	1-0
27 Dec	Chelsea	A	D	1-1
1 Jan	W B A	H	D	2-2
15 Jan	Tottenham H	A	W	1-0
5 Feb	Preston NE	H	W	2-0
12 Feb	Burnley	A	L	0-3
19 Feb	Leicester C	H	D	1-1
26 Feb	Sheffield W	H	W	3-2
5 Mar	Charlton Ath	A	D	1-1
12 Mar	Aston Villa	H	W	2-0
19 Mar	Sunderland	A	W	1-0
26 Mar	Bolton W	H	W	3-0
2 Apr	Huddersfield T	A	W	1-0
8 Apr	Cardiff	H	W	2-0
9 Apr	Blackpool	H	W	3-0
11 Apr	Cardiff	A	W	2-1
16 Apr	Wolverhampton W	A	L	1-3
18 Apr	Sheffield U	A	D	1-1
23 Apr	Manchester U	H	L	2-3
30 Apr	Portsmouth	A	L	1-2

FA Cup

8 Jan	Cardiff (3)	H	W	1-0
29 Jan	Wolves (4)	A	L	0-1

Appearances (Goals)

Barnes W 25 · Bloomfield J 19 4 · Bowen D 21 Clapton Danny 16 · Dickson W 4 · Dodgin W 3 · Evans D 21 · Forbes A 20 1 Fotheringham J 27 Goring P 41 1 · Guthrie R 2 · Haverty J 6 · Herd D 3 1 · Holton C 8 Kelsey J 38 Lawton T 18 6 · Lishman D 32 19 · Logie J 13 3 · Marden R 7 · Milton A 8 3 · Oakes D 9 · Roper D 35 17 · Shaw A 1 · Sullivan C 2 · Swallow R 1 · Tapscott D 37 13 · Wade J 14 · Walsh J 6 · Wilkinson J 1 · Wills L 24 1 · Total: players 30 (69)

Position in League Table

	P	W	L	D	F:A	Pts	
Chelsea	42	20	10	12	81:57	52	1st
Arsenal	42	17	16	9	69:63	43	9th

SEASON 1955-1956
FOOTBALL LEAGUE (DIVISION 1)

20 Aug	Blackpool	A	L	1-3
23 Aug	Cardiff C	H	W	3-1
27 Aug	Chelsea	H	D	1-1
31 Aug	Manchester C	A	D	2-2
3 Sep	Bolton W	A	L	1-4
6 Sep	Manchester C	H	D	0-0
10 Sep	Tottenham H	A	L	1-3
17 Sep	Portsmouth	H	L	1-3
24 Sep	Sunderland	A	L	1-3
1 Oct	Aston Villa	H	W	1-0
8 Oct	Everton	A	D	1-1
15 Oct	Newcastle U	H	W	1-0
22 Oct	Luton T	A	D	0-0
29 Oct	Charlton Ath	H	L	2-4
5 Nov	Manchester U	A	D	1-1
12 Nov	Sheffield U	H	W	2-1
19 Nov	Preston NE	A	W	1-0
26 Nov	Burnley	H	L	0-1
3 Dec	Birmingham C	A	L	0-4
10 Dec	W B A	H	W	2-0
17 Dec	Blackpool	H	W	4-1
24 Dec	Chelsea	A	L	0-2
26 Dec	Wolverhampton W	A	D	3-3
27 Dec	Wolverhampton W	H	D	2-2
31 Dec	Bolton W	H	W	3-1
14 Jan	Tottenham H	H	L	0-1
21 Jan	Portsmouth	A	L	2-5
4 Feb	Sunderland	H	W	3-1
11 Feb	Aston Villa	A	D	1-1
21 Feb	Everton	H	W	3-2
25 Feb	Newcastle U	A	L	0-2
6 Mar	Preston NE	H	W	3-2
10 Mar	Charlton Ath	A	L	0-2
17 Mar	Manchester U	H	D	1-1
24 Mar	Sheffield U	A	W	2-0
31 Mar	Luton T	H	W	3-0
2 Apr	Huddersfield T	H	W	2-0
3 Apr	Huddersfield T	A	W	1-0
7 Apr	Burnley	A	W	1-0
14 Apr	Birmingham C	H	W	1-0
21 Apr	W B A	A	L	1-2
28 Apr	Cardiff C	A	W	2-1

FA Cup

7 Jan	Bedford Town (3)	H	D	2-2
12 Jan	Bedford Town (3R)	A	W	2-1
28 Jan	Aston Villa (4)	H	W	4-1
18 Feb	Charlton Ath (5)	A	W	2-0
3 Mar	Birmingham C (6)	H	L	1-3

Appearances (Goals)

Barnes W 8 · Bloomfield J 32 (3) · Bowen D 22 · Charlton S 19 · Clapton Danny 39 (2) · Dickson W 1 · Dodgin W 15 · Evans D 42 · Forbes A 5 · Fotheringham J 25 · Goring P 37 · Groves V 15 (8) · Haverty J 8 (2) · Herd D 5 (2) · Holton C 31 (8) · Kelsey J 32 · Lawton T 8 (6) · Lishman D 15 (5) · Nutt G 8 (1) · Roper D 16 (4) Sullivan C 10 · Swallow R 1 (1) · Tapscott D 31 (17) · Tiddy M 21 · Walsh B · 1 · Wills 15 · Own goals 1 · Total: 26 players (60)

Position in League Table

	P	W	L	D	F:A	Pts	
Manchester U	42	25	7	10	83:51	60	1st
Arsenal	42	18	14	10	60:61	46	5th

SEASON 1956-1957
FOOTBALL LEAGUE (DIVISION 1)

18 Aug	Cardiff C	H	D	0-0
21 Aug	Burnley	H	W	2-0
25 Aug	Birmingham C	A	L	2-4
28 Aug	Burnley	A	L	1-3
1 Sep	W B A	H	W	4-1
4 Sep	Preston NE	H	L	1-2
8 Sep	Portsmouth	A	W	3-2
10 Sep	Preston NE	A	L	0-3
15 Sep	Newcastle U	H	L	0-1
22 Sep	Sheffield W	A	W	4-2
29 Sep	Manchester U	H	L	1-2
6 Oct	Manchester C	H	W	7-3
13 Oct	Charlton Ath	A	W	3-1
20 Oct	Tottenham H	H	W	3-1
27 Oct	Everton	A	L	0-4
3 Nov	Aston Villa	H	W	2-1
10 Nov	Wolverhampton W	A	L	2-5
17 Nov	Bolton W	H	W	3-0
24 Nov	Leeds U	A	D	3-3
1 Dec	Sunderland	H	D	1-1
8 Dec	Luton T	A	W	2-1

15 Dec	Cardiff C	A	W	3-2
22 Dec	Birmingham C	H	W	4-0
25 Dec	Chelsea	A	D	1-1
26 Dec	Chelsea	H	W	2-0
29 Dec	W B A	A	W	2-0
12 Jan	Portsmouth	H	D	1-1
19 Jan	Newcastle U	A	L	1-3
2 Feb	Sheffield W	H	W	6-3
9 Feb	Manchester U	A	L	2-6
23 Feb	Everton	H	W	2-0
9 Mar	Luton T	H	L	1-3
13 Mar	Tottenham H	A	W	3-1
16 Mar	Aston Villa	A	D	0-0
20 Mar	Manchester C	A	W	3-2
23 Mar	Wolverhampton W	H	D	0-0
30 Mar	Bolton W	A	L	1-2
6 Apr	Leeds U	H	W	1-0
13 Apr	Sunderland	A	L	0-1
19 Apr	Blackpool	H	D	1-1
20 Apr	Charlton Ath	H	W	3-1
22 Apr	Blackpool	A	W	4-2

FA Cup

5 Jan	Stoke C (3)	H	W	4-2
26 Jan	Newport Co (4)	A	W	2-0
16 Feb	Preston NE (5)	A	D	3-3
19 Feb	Preston NE (5R)	H	W	2-1
2 Mar	W B A (6)	A	D	2-2
5 Mar	W B A (6R)	H	L	1-2

Appearances (Goals)
Barnwell J 1 · Bloomfield J 42 (10) · Bowen D 30 (2) · Charlton S 40 · Clapton Danny 39 (2) · Dodgin W · 41 · Evans D 40 (4) · Goring P 13 · Groves V 5 (2) · Haverty J 28 (8) · Herd D 22 (2) Holton C 39 (10) · Kelsey J 30 · Nutt G 1 · Roper D 4 (3) · Sullivan C 12 · Swallow R 4 · Tapscott D 38 (25) · Tiddy M 15 (6) · Wills L 18 Own goals 1 · Total: 20 players 85

Position in League Table

	P	W	L	D	F:A	Pts	
Manchester U	42	28	6	8	103:54	64	1st
Arsenal	42	21	13	8	85:69	50	5th

SEASON 1957-1958
FOOTBALL LEAGUE (DIVISION 1)

24 Aug	Sunderland	A	W	1-0
27 Aug	W B A	H	D	2-2
31 Aug	Luton T	H	W	2-0
4 Sep	W B A	A	W	2-1
7 Sep	Blackpool	A	L	0-1
10 Sep	Everton	H	L	2-3
14 Sep	Leicester C	H	W	3-1
21 Sep	Manchester U	A	L	2-4
28 Sep	Leeds U	H	W	2-1
2 Oct	Aston Villa	H	W	4-0
5 Oct	Bolton W	A	W	1-0
12 Oct	Tottenham H	A	L	1-3
16 Oct	Everton	A	D	2-2
19 Oct	Birmingham C	H	L	1-3
26 Oct	Chelsea	A	D	0-0
2 Nov	Manchester C	H	W	2-1
9 Nov	Nottingham F	A	L	0-4
16 Nov	Portsmouth	H	W	3-2
23 Nov	Sheffield W	A	L	0-2
30 Nov	Newcastle U	H	L	2-3
7 Dec	Burnley	A	L	1-2
14 Dec	Preston NE	H	W	4-2
21 Dec	Sunderland	H	W	3-0
26 Dec	Aston Villa	A	L	0-3
28 Dec	Luton T	A	L	0-4
11 Jan	Blackpool	H	L	2-3
18 Jan	Leicester C	A	W	1-0
1 Feb	Manchester U	H	L	4-5
18 Feb	Bolton W	H	L	1-2
22 Feb	Tottenham H	H	D	4-4
1 Mar	Birmingham C	A	L	1-4
8 Mar	Chelsea	H	W	5-4
15 Mar	Manchester C	A	W	4-2
19 Mar	Leeds U	A	L	0-2
22 Mar	Sheffield W	H	W	1-0
29 Mar	Portsmouth	A	L	4-5
7 Apr	Wolverhampton W	H	L	0-2
8 Apr	Wolverhampton W	A	W	2-1
12 Apr	Newcastle U	A	D	3-3
19 Apr	Burnley	H	D	0-0
21 Apr	Nottingham F	H	D	1-1
26 Apr	Preston NE	A	L	0-3

FA Cup

4 Jan	Northampton (3)	A	L	1-3

Appearances (Goals)
Biggs A 2 · Bloomfield J 40 (16) · Bowen D 30 · Charlton S 36 · Clapton Danny 28 (5) · Dodgin W 23 · Evans D 32 · Fotheringham J 19 · Goring P 10 · Groves V 30 (10) · Haverty J 15 · Herd D 39 (24) · Holton C 26 (4) · Kelsey J 38 · U Roux D 5 · Nutt G 21 (3) · Petts J 9 · Standen J 1 · Sullivan C 3 · Swallow R 7 (3) · Tapscott D 8 (2) · Tiddy M 12 (2) · Ward G 10 · Wills L 18 (1) Own goals 3 · Total: 24 players (73)

Position in League Table

	P	W	L	D	F:A	Pts	
Wolverhampton W	42	28	6	8	103:47	64	1st
Arsenal	42	16	19	7	73:85	39	12th

SEASON 1958-1959
FOOTBALL LEAGUE (DIVISION 1)

23 Aug	Preston NE	A	L	1-2
26 Aug	Burnley	H	W	3-0
30 Aug	Leicester C	H	W	5-1
2 Sep	Burnley	A	L	1-3
6 Sep	Everton	A	W	6-1
9 Sep	Bolton W	H	W	6-1
13 Sep	Tottenham H	H	W	3-1
17 Sep	Bolton W	A	L	1-2
20 Sep	Manchester C	H	W	4-1
27 Sep	Leeds U	A	L	1-2
4 Oct	W B A	H	W	4-3
11 Oct	Manchester U	A	D	1-1
18 Oct	Wolverhampton W	H	D	1-1
22 Oct	Aston Villa	A	W	2-1
25 Oct	Blackburn Rov	A	L	2-4
1 Nov	Newcastle U	H	W	3-2
8 Nov	West Ham U	A	D	0-0
15 Nov	Nottingham F	H	W	3-1
22 Nov	Chelsea	A	W	3-0
29 Nov	Blackpool	H	L	1-4
6 Dec	Portsmouth	A	W	1-0
13 Dec	Aston Villa	H	L	1-2
20 Dec	Preston NE	H	L	1-2
26 Dec	Luton T	A	L	3-6
27 Dec	Luton T	H	W	1-0
3 Jan	Leicester C	A	W	3-2
17 Jan	Everton	H	W	3-1
31 Jan	Tottenham	A	W	4-1
7 Feb	Manchester C	A	D	0-0
21 Feb	W B A	A	D	1-1
24 Feb	Leeds U	H	W	1-0
28 Feb	Manchester U	H	W	3-2
7 Mar	Wolverhampton W	A	L	1-6
14 Mar	Blackburn Rov	H	D	1-1
21 Mar	Newcastle U	A	L	0-1
28 Mar	West Ham U	H	L	1-2
4 Apr	Nottingham F	A	D	1-1
11 Apr	Chelsea	H	D	1-1
14 Apr	Birmingham C	A	L	1-4
18 Apr	Blackpool	A	W	2-1
25 Apr	Portsmouth	H	W	5-2
4 May	Birmingham C	H	W	2-1

FA Cup

10 Jan	Bury (3)	A	W	1-0
24 Jan	Colchester U (4)	A	D	2-2
28 Jan	Colchester U (4R)	H	W	4-0
14 Feb	Sheffield U (5)	H	D	2-2
18 Feb	Sheffield U (5R)	A	L	0-3

Appearances (Goals)
Barnwell J 16 (3) · Biggs A 2 (1) · Bloomfield J 29 (10) · Bowen D 16 · Charlton S 4 · Clapton Danny 39 (6) · Docherty T 38 (1) · Dodgin W 39 Evans D 37 (5) · Fotheringham J 1 · Goring P 2 Goulden R · 1 · Goy P 2 · Groves V 33 (10) · Haverty J 10 (3) · Henderson J 21 (12) · Herd D 26 (15) · Holton C 3 (3) · Julians L 10 (5) · Kelsey J 27 · McCullough W 10 · Nutt G 16 (6) Petts J 3 · Standen J 13 · Ward G 31 (4) · Wills L 33 (1) · Own goals 3 · Total:26 players (88)

Position in League Table

	P	W	L	D	F:A	Pts	
Wolverhampton W	42	28	9	5	110:49	61	1st
Arsenal	42	21	13	8	88:68	50	3rd

SEASON 1959-1960
FOOTBALL LEAGUE (DIVISION 1)

22 Aug	Sheffield W	H	L	0-1
26 Aug	Nottingham F	A	W	3-0
29 Aug	Wolverhampton W	A	D	3-3
1 Sep	Nottingham F	H	D	1-1
5 Sep	Tottenham H	H	D	1-1
9 Sep	Bolton W	A	W	1-0
12 Sep	Manchester C	H	W	3-1
15 Sep	Bolton W	H	W	2-1
19 Sep	Blackburn Rov	A	D	1-1
26 Sep	Blackpool	H	W	2-1
3 Oct	Everton	A	L	1-3
10 Oct	Manchester U	A	L	2-4
17 Oct	Preston NE	H	L	0-3
24 Oct	Leicester C	A	D	2-2
31 Oct	Birmingham C	H	W	3-0
7 Nov	Leeds U	A	L	2-3
14 Nov	West Ham U	H	L	1-3
21 Nov	Chelsea	A	W	3-1
28 Nov	W B A	H	L	2-4
5 Dec	Newcastle U	A	L	1-4
12 Dec	Burnley	H	L	2-4
19 Dec	Sheffield W	A	L	1-5
26 Dec	Luton T	H	L	0-3
28 Dec	Luton T	A	W	1-0
2 Jan	Wolverhampton W	H	D	4-4
16 Jan	Tottenham H	A	L	0-3
23 Jan	Manchester C	A	W	2-1
6 Feb	Blackburn Rov	H	W	5-2
13 Feb	Blackpool	A	L	1-2
20 Feb	Everton	H	W	2-1
27 Feb	Newcastle U	H	W	1-0
5 Mar	Preston NE	A	W	3-0
15 Mar	Leicester C	H	D	1-1
19 Mar	Burnley	A	L	2-3
26 Mar	Leeds U	H	D	1-1
2 Apr	West Ham U	A	D	0-0
9 Apr	Chelsea	H	L	1-4
15 Apr	Fulham	H	W	2-0
16 Apr	Birmingham C	A	L	0-3
18 Apr	Fulham	A	L	0-3
23 Apr	Manchester U	H	W	5-2
30 Apr	W B A	A	L	0-1

FA Cup

9 Jan	Rotherham U (3)	A	D	2-2
13 Jan	Rotherham U (3R)	H	D	1-1
18 Jan	Rotherham U (3R) (at Sheffield Wed)		L	0-2

Appearances (Goals)
Barnwell J 28 (7) · Bloomfield J 36 (10) · Charles M 20 (8) · Clapton D P (Denis) 3 · Clapton D R (Danny) 23 (7) · Docherty T 24 · Dodgin W 30 · Evans D 7 (1) · Everitt M 5 · Groves V 30 (1) · Haverty J 35 (8) · Henderson J 31 (7) · Herd D 31 (14) · Julians L 8 (2) · Kelsey J 22 · Magill E 17 · MCcullough W 33 · Nutt G 3 · Petts J 7 · Snedden J 1 · Standen J 20 · Ward G 15 1 · Wills L 33 (1) · Own goals 1 Total: 23 players (68)

Position in League Table

	P	W	L	D	F:A	Pts	
Burnley	42	24	11	7	85:61	55	1st
Arsenal	42	15	18	9	68:80	39	13th

SEASON 1960-1961
FOOTBALL LEAGUE (DIVISION 1)

20 Aug	Burnley	A	L	2-3
23 Aug	Preston NE	H	W	1-0
27 Aug	Nottingham F	H	W	3-0
30 Aug	Preston NE	A	L	0-2
3 Sep	Manchester C	A	D	0-0
6 Sep	Birmingham C	H	W	2-0
10 Sep	Tottenham H	H	L	2-3
14 Sep	Birmingham C	A	L	0-2
17 Sep	Newcastle U	H	W	5-0
24 Sep	Cardiff C	A	L	0-1
1 Oct	W B A	H	W	1-0
8 Oct	Leicester C	A	L	1-2
15 Oct	Aston Villa	H	W	2-1
22 Oct	Blackburn Rov	A	W	4-2
29 Oct	Manchester U	H	W	2-1
5 Nov	West Ham U	A	L	0-6
12 Nov	Chelsea	H	L	1-4
19 Nov	Blackpool	A	D	1-1
26 Nov	Everton	H	W	3-2
3 Dec	Wolverhampton W	A	L	3-5
10 Dec	Bolton W	H	W	5-1
17 Dec	Bumley	H	L	2-5
23 Dec	Sheffield W	A	D	1-1
26 Dec	Sheffield W	H	D	1-1
31 Dec	Nottingham F	A	W	5-3
14 Jan	Manchester C	H	W	5-4
21 Jan	Tottenham H	A	L	2-4
4 Feb	Newcastle U	A	D	3-3
11 Feb	Cardiff C	H	L	2-3
18 Feb	W B A	A	W	3-2
25 Feb	Leicester C	H	L	1-3
4 Mar	Aston Villa	A	D	2-2
11 Mar	Blackburn Rov	H	D	0-0
18 Mar	Manchester U	A	D	1-1
25 Mar	West Ham U	H	D	0-0
31 Mar	Fulham	A	D	2-2
1 Apr	Bolton W	A	D	1-1
3 Apr	Fulham	H	W	4-2
8 Apr	Blackpool	H	W	1-0
15 Apr	Chelsea	A	L	1-3
22 Apr	Wolverhampton W	H	L	1-5
29 Apr	Everton	A	L	1-4

FA Cup

7 Jan	Sunderland (3)	A	L	1-2

Appearances (Goals)
Bacuzzi D 13 · Barnwell J 26 (6) · Bloomfield J 12 (1) Charles M 19 3 · Clapton D R (Danny) 18 2 · Clapton D P (Denis) 1 · Docherty T 21 · Eastham G 19 5 · Everitt M 4 (1) · Griffiths A 1 · Groves V 32 · Haverty J 12 (4) · Henderson J 39 10 · Herd D 40 (29) · Kane P 4 (1) · Kelsey J 37 · Magill E 6 · McClelland J 4 · McCullough W 41 · Neill T 14 (1) · O'Neill F 2 · Petts J 1 · Skirton A 16 (3) · Snedden J 23 · Standen J 1 · Strong G 19 (10) · Ward G 9 (1) · Wills L 24 · Young D 4 · Total: 29 players (77)

Position in League Table

	P	W	L	D	F:A	Pts	
Tottenham H	42	31	7	4	115:55	66	1st
Arsenal	42	15	16	11	77:85	41	11th

SEASON 1961-1962
FOOTBALL LEAGUE (DIVISION 1)

19 Aug	Burnley	H	D	2-2
23 Aug	Leicester C	A	W	1-0
26 Aug	Tottenham H	A	L	3-4
29 Aug	Leicester C	H	D	4-4
2 Sep	Bolton W	A	L	1-2
9 Sep	Manchester C	H	W	3-0
16 Sep	W B A	A	L	0-4
20 Sep	Sheffield W	A	D	1-1
23 Sep	Birmingham C	H	D	1-1
30 Sep	Everton	A	L	1-4
7 Oct	Blackpool	H	W	3-0
14 Oct	Blackburn Rov	A	D	0-0
21 Oct	Manchester U	H	W	5-1
28 Oct	Cardiff C	A	D	1-1
4 Nov	Chelsea	H	L	0-3
11 Nov	Aston Villa	A	L	1-3
14 Nov	Sheffield W	H	W	1-0
18 Nov	Nottingham F	H	W	2-1
25 Nov	Wolverhampton W	A	W	3-2
2 Dec	West Ham U	H	D	2-2
9 Dec	Sheffield U	A	L	1-2
16 Dec	Burnley	A	W	2-0
23 Dec	Tottenham H	H	W	2-1
26 Dec	Fulham	H	W	1-0
13 Jan	Bolton W	H	L	1-2
20 Jan	Manchester C	A	L	2-3
3 Feb	W B A	H	L	0-1
10 Feb	Birmingham C	A	L	0-1
24 Feb	Blackpool	A	W	1-0
3 Mar	Blackburn	H	D	0-0
17 Mar	Cardiff C	H	D	1-1
24 Mar	Chelsea	A	W	3-2
31 Mar	Aston Villa	H	L	4-5
7 Apr	Nottingham F	A	L	2-5
11 Apr	Fulham	A	L	2-5
14 Apr	Wolverhampton W	H	W	3-1
16 Apr	Manchester U	A	W	3-2
20 Apr	Ipswich T	A	D	2-2
21 Apr	West Ham U	A	D	3-3
23 Apr	Ipswich T	H	L	0-3
28 Apr	Sheffield U	H	W	2-0
1 May	Everton	H	L	2-3

FA Cup

6 Jan	Bradford C (3)	H	W	3-0
31 Jan	Manchester U (4)	A	L	0-1

Appearances (Goals)
Armstrong G 4 (1) · Bacuzzi D 22 · Barnwell J 14 (3) · Brown L 41 · Charles M 21 (15) · Clamp L 18 · Clapton Danny 5 (1) · Clarke F 1 · Eastham G 38 (6) · Griffiths A 14 (2) · Groves V 16 · Henderson J 12 · Kelsey J 35 · McLeod J 37 (6) · Magill E 21 · McClelland J 4 · McCullough J 40 · McKechnie 13 · Neill T 20 · Petts 12 · Skirton 38 (19) · Snedden 15 · Strong 20 (12) · Ward 11 · Own goals 2 · Total: 24 players (71)

Position in League Table

	P	W	L	D	F:A	Pts	
Ipswich T	42	24	10	8	93:67	56	1st
Arsenal	42	16	15	11	71:72	43	10th

SEASON 1962-1963
FOOTBALL LEAGUE (DIVISION 1)

18 Aug	Leyton Orient	A	W	2-1
21 Aug	Birmingham C	H	W	2-0
25 Aug	Manchester U	H	L	1-3
29 Aug	Birmingham C	A	D	2-2
1 Sep	Burnley	A	L	1-2
4 Sep	Aston Villa	H	L	1-2
8 Sep	Sheffield W	H	L	1-2
10 Sep	Aston Villa	A	L	1-3
15 Sep	Fulham	A	W	3-1
22 Sep	Leicester C	H	D	1-1
29 Sep	Bolton W	A	L	0-3
6 Oct	Tottenham H	A	D	4-4
13 Oct	West Ham U	H	D	1-1
27 Oct	Wolverhampton W	H	W	5-4
3 Nov	Blackburn Rov	A	D	5-5
10 Nov	Sheffield U	H	W	1-0
14 Nov	Liverpool	A	L	1-2
17 Nov	Nottingham F	A	L	0-3
24 Nov	Ipswich T	H	W	3-1
1 Dec	Manchester C	A	W	4-2
8 Dec	Blackpool	H	W	2-0
15 Dec	Leyton Orient	H	W	2-0
9 Feb	Leicester C	A	L	0-2
16 Feb	Bolton W	H	W	3-2
23 Feb	Tottenham H	H	L	2-3
2 Mar	West Ham U	A	W	4-0
9 Mar	Liverpool	H	D	2-2
23 Mar	Blackburn Rov	H	W	3-1
26 Mar	Everton	H	W	4-3
30 Mar	Ipswich T	A	D	1-1
6 Apr	Nottingham F	H	D	0-0
8 Apr	Wolverhampton W	A	L	0-1
12 Apr	W B A	H	W	3-2
13 Apr	Sheffield U	A	D	3-3
15 Apr	W B A	A	W	2-1
20 Apr	Manchester C	H	L	2-3
24 Apr	Everton	A	D	1-1
27 Apr	Blackpool	A	L	2-3
6 May	Manchester U	A	W	3-2
11 May	Burnley	H	L	2-3
14 May	Fulham	H	W	3-0
18 May	Sheffield W	A	W	3-2

FA Cup

30 Jan	Oxford U (3)	H	W	5-1
12 Mar	Sheffield W (4)	H	W	2-0
19 Mar	Liverpool (5)	H	L	1-2

Appearances (Goals)
Anderson T 5 (1) · Armstrong G 16 (2) · Bacuzzi D (6) · Baker J 39 (29) · Barnwell J 34 (2) · Brown L 38 (1) · Clamp E 4 (1) · Clarke F 5 · Court D 6 (3) · Eastham G 33 (4) · Groves V 9 · MacLeod J 33 (9) · Magill E 36 · McClelland J 33 · McCullough W42 3 · McKechnie I (9) · Neill T 17 · Sammels J 2 (1) · Skirton A 28 (10) · Smithson R 2 · Snedden J 27 · Strong G 36 (18) · Ward G 2 · Own goals 2 · Total: 23 players (86)

Position in League Table

	P	W	L	D	F:A	Pts	
Everton	42	25	6	11	84:42	61	1st
Arsenal	42	18	14	10	86:77	46	7th

SEASON 1963-1964
FOOTBALL LEAGUE (DIVISION 1)

24 Aug	Wolverhampton W	H	L	1-3
27 Aug	W B A	H	W	3-2
31 Aug	Leicester C	A	L	2-7
4 Sep	W B A	A	L	0-4
7 Sep	Bolton W	H	W	4-3
10 Sep	Aston Villa	H	W	3-0
14 Sep	Fulham	A	W	4-1
21 Sep	Manchester U	H	W	2-1
28 Sep	Burnley	A	W	3-0
2 Oct	Everton	A	L	1-2
5 Oct	Ipswich	H	W	6-0
9 Oct	Stoke C	A	W	2-1
15 Oct	Tottenham H	H	D	4-4
19 Oct	Aston Villa	A	L	1-2
26 Oct	Nottingham F	H	W	4-2
2 Nov	Sheffield U	A	D	2-2
5 Nov	Birmingham C	H	W	4-1
9 Nov	West Ham U	H	D	3-3
16 Nov	Chelsea	A	L	1-3
23 Nov	Blackpool	H	W	5-3
30 Nov	Blackburn Rov	A	L	1-4
7 Dec	Liverpool	H	D	1-1
10 Dec	Everton	H	W	6-0
14 Dec	Wolverhampton W	A	D	2-2
21 Dec	Leicester C	H	L	0-1
28 Dec	Birmingham C	A	W	4-1
11 Jan	Bolton W	A	D	1-1
18 Jan	Fulham	H	D	2-2
1 Feb	Manchester U	A	L	1-3
8 Feb	Burnley	H	W	3-2
18 Feb	Ipswich	A	W	2-1
22 Feb	Tottenham H	A	L	1-3
29 Feb	Stoke C	H	D	1-1
7 Mar	Nottingham F	A	L	0-2
14 Mar	Chelsea	H	L	2-4
21 Mar	West Ham U	A	D	1-1
24 Mar	Sheffield W	H	D	1-1
28 Mar	Sheffield U	H	L	1-3
30 Mar	Sheffield W	A	W	4-0
4 Apr	Blackpool	A	W	1-0
11 Apr	Blackburn Rov	H	D	0-0
18 Apr	Liverpool	A	L	0-5

FA Cup

4 Jan	Wolves (3)	H	W	2-1
25 Jan	W B A (4)	A	D	3-3
29 Jan	W B A (4R)	H	W	2-0
15 Feb	Liverpool (5)	H	L	0-1

Inter-Cities Fairs Cup

25 Sep	Staevnet (1)	A	W	7-1
22 Oct	Staevnet (1)	H	L	2-3
13 Nov	FC Liege (2)	H	D	1-1
18 Dec	FC Liege (2)	A	L	1-3

Appearances (Goals)
Anderson T 10 (3) · Armstrong G 28 (3) · Bacuzzi D 5 · Baker J 39 (26) · Barnwell J 19 2 Brown L 22 (1) · Clarke F 5 · Court D 8 1 · Eastham G 38 (10). Furnell J 21 · Groves V 15 · MacLeod J 30 (7) · Magill E 35 · McClelland J 5 · McCullough W 40 (1) · McKechnie 11 (1) · Neill T 11 · Radford J 1 · Simpson P 6 · Skirton A 15 7 · Snedden J 14 · Strong G 38 (26) · Urel 41 (1) · Wilson R 5 · Own goals 1 · Total: 24 players (90)

Position in League Table

	P	W	L	D	F:A	Pts	
Liverpool	42	26	11	5	92:45	57	1st
Arsenal	42	17	14	11	90:82	45	8th

SEASON 1964-1965
FOOTBALL LEAGUE (DIVISION 1)

22 Aug	Liverpool	A	L	2-3
25 Aug	Sheffield W	H	D	1-1
29 Aug	Aston Villa	H	W	3-1
2 Sep	Sheffield W	A	L	1-2
5 Sep	Wolverhampton W	A	W	1-0
8 Sep	Blackburn Rov	H	D	1-1
12 Sep	Sunderland	H	W	3-1
16 Sep	Blackburn Rov	A	W	2-1
19 Sep	Leicester C	A	W	3-2
26 Sep	Chelsea	H	L	1-3
6 Oct	Nottingham F	H	L	0-3
10 Oct	Tottenham H	A	L	1-3
17 Oct	Burnley	H	W	3-2
24 Oct	Sheffield U	A	L	0-4
31 Oct	Everton	H	W	3-1
7 Nov	Birmingham C	A	W	3-2
11 Nov	Leeds U	A	L	1-3
14 Nov	West Ham U	H	L	0-3
21 Nov	W B A	A	D	0-0
28 Nov	Manchester U	H	L	2-3
5 Dec	Fulham	A	W	4-3
12 Dec	Liverpool	H	D	0-0
19 Dec	Aston Villa	A	L	1-3
26 Dec	Stoke C	H	W	3-2
28 Dec	Stoke C	A	L	1-4
2 Jan	Wolverhampton W	H	W	4-1
16 Jan	Sunderland	A	W	2-0
23 Jan	Leicester C	H	W	4-3
6 Feb	Chelsea	A	L	1-2
13 Feb	Leeds U	H	L	1-2
20 Feb	Fulham	H	W	2-0
23 Feb	Tottenham H	H	W	3-1
27 Feb	Burnley	A	L	1-2
6 Mar	Sheffield U	H	D	1-1
13 Mar	Nottingham F	A	L	0-3
27 Mar	West Ham U	A	L	1-2
3 Apr	W B A	H	D	1-1
6 Apr	Birmingham C	H	W	3-0
16 Apr	Blackpool	A	D	1-1
19 Apr	Blackpool	H	W	3-1
24 Apr	Everton	A	L	0-1
26 Apr	Manchester U	A	L	1-3

FA Cup

9 Jan	Darlington (3)	A	W	2-0
30 Jan	Peterborough (4)	A	L	1-2

Appearances (Goals)
Anderson T 10 (2) · Armstrong G 40 (4) · Baker J 42 (25) · Baldwin T 1 · Burns A 24 · Clarke F 15 · Court D 33 (3) · Eastham G 42 (10) · Ferry G 11 · Furnell J 18 · Howe D 40 · MacLeod J 1 · Magill E 1 · McCullough W 30 · McLintock F 25 (2) · Neill T 29 (1) · Radford J 13 (7) · Sammels J 17 (5) · Simpson P 6 (2) · Skirton A 22 (3) · Snedden J 3 · Strong G 12 (3) · Tawse B 5 · Urel 22 (1) · Total: 24 players (69)

Position in League Table

	P	W	L	D	F:A	Pts	
Manchester U	42	26	7	9	89:39	61	1st
Arsenal	42	17	18	7	69:75	41	13th

SEASON 1965-1966
FOOTBALL LEAGUE (DIVISION 1)

21 Aug	Stoke C	H	W	2-1
25 Aug	Northampton T	A	D	1-1
28 Aug	Burnley	A	D	2-2
4 Sep	Chelsea	H	L	1-3
7 Sep	Nottingham F	A	W	1-0
11 Sep	Tottenham H	A	D	2-2
14 Sep	Nottingham F	H	W	1-0
18 Sep	Everton	A	L	1-3
25 Sep	Manchester U	H	W	4-2
28 Sep	Northampton T	H	D	1-1
2 Oct	Newcastle U	A	W	1-0
9 Oct	Fulham	H	W	2-1
16 Oct	Blackpool	A	L	3-5
23 Oct	Blackburn Rov	H	D	2-2
30 Oct	Leicester C	A	L	1-3
6 Nov	Sheffield U	H	W	6-2
13 Nov	Leeds U	A	L	0-2
20 Nov	West Ham U	H	W	3-2
4 Dec	Aston Villa	H	D	3-3
11 Dec	Liverpool	A	L	2-4
27 Dec	Sheffield W	A	L	0-4
28 Dec	Sheffield W	H	W	5-2
1 Jan	Fulham	A	L	0-1
8 Jan	Liverpool	H	L	0-1
15 Jan	Blackburn Rov	A	L	1-2
29 Jan	Stoke C	A	W	3-1
5 Feb	Burnley	H	D	1-1
19 Feb	Chelsea	A	D	0-0
5 Mar	Blackpool	H	D	0-0
8 Mar	Tottenham H	H	D	1-1
12 Mar	Everton	H	L	0-1
19 Mar	Manchester U	A	L	1-2
26 Mar	Newcastle U	H	L	1-3
5 Apr	W B A	H	D	1-1
11 Apr	W B A	A	D	4-4
16 Apr	West Ham U	A	L	1-2
20 Apr	Sunderland	A	W	2-0
23 Apr	Sunderland	H	D	1-1
25 Apr	Sheffield U	A	L	0-3
30 Apr	Aston Villa	A	L	0-3
5 May	Leeds U	H	L	0-3
7 May	Leicester C	H	W	1-0

FA Cup

22 Jan	Blackburn (3)	A	L	0-3

Appearances (Goals)
Armstrong G 39 (6) · Baker J 24 (13) · Baldwin T 8 (5) · Burns A 7 · Court D 38 (1) · Eastham G 37 (6) · Furnell J 31 · Howe D 29 (1) · McCullough W 17 · McGill A 2 · McLintock F 36 (2) · Neill T 39 · Neilson G 2 · Pack R 1 · Radford J 32 (8) · Sammels J 32 (6) · Simpson P 8 · Skirton A 24 (9) · Storey P · 28 · Urel 21 · Walley J 9 (1) · Wilson R 4 · Own goals 4 · Total: 22 players (62)

Position in League Table

i	P	W	L	D	F:A	Pts	
Liverpool	42	26	7	9	79:34	61	1st
Arsenal	42	12	17	13	62:75	37	14th

SEASON 1966-1967
FOOTBALL LEAGUE (DIVISION 1)

20 Aug	Sunderland	A	W	3-1
23 Aug	West Ham U	H	W	2-1
27 Aug	Aston Villa	H	W	1-0
29 Aug	West Ham U	A	D	2-2
3 Sep	Tottenham H	A	L	1-3
6 Sep	Sheffield W	H	D	1-1
10 Sep	Manchester C	A	D	1-1
17 Sep	Blackpool	H	D	1-1
24 Sep	Chelsea	A	L	1-3
1 Oct	Leicester C	H	L	2-4
8 Oct	Newcastle U	H	W	2-0
15 Oct	Leeds U	A	L	1-3
22 Oct	W B A	H	L	2-3
29 Oct	Manchester U	A	L	0-1
5 Nov	Leeds U	H	L	0-1
12 Nov	Everton	A	D	0-0
19 Nov	Fulham	H	W	1-0
26 Nov	Nottingham F	A	L	1-2
3 Dec	Burnley	H	D	0-0
10 Dec	Sheffield U	A	D	1-1
17 Dec	Sunderland	H	W	2-0
26 Dec	Southampton	H	W	4-1
27 Dec	Southampton	A	L	1-2
31 Dec	Aston Villa	A	W	1-0
7 Jan	Tottenham H	H	L	0-2
14 Jan	Manchester C	H	W	1-0
21 Jan	Blackpool	A	W	3-0
4 Feb	Chelsea	H	W	2-1
11 Feb	Leicester C	A	L	1-2
25 Feb	Newcastle U	A	L	1-2
3 Mar	Manchester U	H	D	1-1
18 Mar	W B A	A	W	1-0
25 Mar	Sheffield U	H	W	2-0

27 Mar	Liverpool	A	D	0-0
28 Mar	Liverpool	H	D	1-1
1 Apr	Stoke C	A	D	2-2
19 Apr	Fulham	A	D	0-0
22 Apr	Nottingham F	H	D	1-1
25 Apr	Everton	H	W	3-1
29 Apr	Burnley	A	W	4-1
6 May	Stoke C	H	W	3-1
13 May	Sheffield W	A	D	1-1

FA Cup

28 Jan	Bristol Rov (3)	A	W	3-0
18 Feb	Bolton W (4)	A	D	0-0
22 Feb	Bolton W (4R)	H	W	3-0
11 Mar	Birmingham C (5)	A	L	0-1

Football League Cup

13 Sep	Gillingham (2)	H	D	1-1
21 Sep	Gillingham (2R)	A	D	1-1
28 Sep	Gillingham (2R)	H	W	5-0
5 Oct	West Ham U (3)	H	L	1-3

Appearances (Goals)

Armstrong G 40 (7) · Addison C 17 (4) · Baldwin T 8 (2) · Boot M 4 (2) · Coakley T 9 (1) · Court D 13 · Furnell J 42 · Graham G 33 (11) · Howe D 1 · McNab R 26 · McGill J 8 · McLintock F 40 (9) · Neill T 34 · Neilson G 12 2 · Radford J 30 (4) · Sammels J 42 10 · Simpson P 36 (1) · Skirton A 2 2 · Storey P 34 (1) · Urel 37 · Walley J 4 · Woodward J 3 · Own Goals2 · Total: 22 players (58)

Position in League Table

	P	W	L	D	F:A	Pts	
Manchester U	42	24	6	12	84:45	60	1st
Arsenal	42	16	12	14	58:47	46	7th

SEASON 1967-1968
FOOTBALL LEAGUE (DIVISION 1)

19 Aug	Stoke C	H	W	2-0
22 Aug	Liverpool	A	L	0-2
26 Aug	Nottingham F	A	L	0-2
28 Aug	Liverpool	H	W	2-0
2 Sep	Coventry C	H	D	1-1
6 Sep	W B A	A	W	3-1
9 Sep	Sheffield U	A	W	4-2
16 Sep	Tottenham H	H	W	4-0
23 Sep	Manchester C	H	W	1-0
30 Sep	Newcastle U	A	L	1-2
7 Oct	Manchester U	A	L	0-1
14 Oct	Sunderland	H	W	2-1
23 Oct	Wolverhampton W	A	L	2-3
28 Oct	Fulham	H	W	5-3
4 Nov	Leeds U	A	L	1-3
11 Nov	Everton	H	D	2-2
18 Nov	Leicester C	A	D	2-2
25 Nov	West Ham U	H	D	0-0
2 Dec	Burnley	A	L	0-1
16 Dec	Stoke C	A	W	1-0
23 Dec	Nottingham F	H	W	3-0
26 Dec	Chelsea	A	L	1-2
30 Dec	Chelsea	H	D	1-1
6 Jan	Coventry C	A	D	1-1
13 Jan	Sheffield U	H	D	1-1
20 Jan	Tottenham H	A	L	0-1
3 Feb	Manchester C	A	D	1-1
10 Feb	Newcastle U	H	D	0-0
24 Feb	Manchester U	H	L	0-2
16 Mar	Wolverhampton W	H	L	0-2
23 Mar	Fulham	A	W	3-1
29 Mar	West Ham U	A	D	1-1
6 Apr	Everton	A	L	0-2
10 Apr	Southampton	A	L	0-2
13 Apr	Leicester C	H	W	2-1
15 Apr	Southampton	H	L	0-3
20 Apr	Sunderland	A	L	0-2
27 Apr	Burnley	H	W	2-0
30 Apr	Sheffield W	H	W	3-2
4 May	Sheffield W	A	W	2-1
7 May	Leeds U	H	W	4-3
11 May	W B A	H	W	2-1

FA Cup

27 Jan	Shrewsbury T (3)	A	D	1-1
30 Jan	Shrewsbury T (3R)	H	W	2-0
17 Feb	Swansea T (4)	A	W	1-0
9 Mar	Birmingham C (5)	H	D	1-1
12 Mar	Birmingham C (5R)	A	L	1-2

Football League Cup

12 Sep	Coventry C (2)	A	W	2-1
11 Oct	Reading T (3)	H	W	1-0
1 Nov	Blackburn Rov (4)	H	W	2-1
29 Nov	Burnley (5)	A	D	3-3
5 Dec	Burnley (5R)	H	W	2-1
17 Jan	Huddersfield (SF)	H	W	3-2
6 Feb	Huddersfield (SF)	A	W	3-1
2 Mar	Leeds U (F) (at Wembley)		L	0-1

Appearances (Goals)

Addison C 11 (5) · Armstrong G 42 (5) · Court D 16 (3) · Davidson R 1 · Furnell J 29 · Gould R 16 (6) · Graham G 38 (16) · Jenkins D 3 · Johnston G 18 (3) · McLintock F 38 (4) · McNab R 30 · Neill T 38 (2) · Radford J 39 (10) · Rice P 6 · Sammels J 35 (4) · Simpson P 40 · Storey P 39 · Urel 21 · Wilson R 13 · Own goals 2 · Total: 19 players (60)

Position in League Table

	P	W	L	D	F:A	Pts	
Manchester C	42	26	10	6	86:43	58	1st
Arsenal	42	17	15	10	60:56	44	9th

SEASON 1968-1969
FOOTBALL LEAGUE (DIVISION 1)

10 Aug	Tottenham H	A	W	2-1
13 Aug	Leicester C	H	W	3-0
17 Aug	Liverpool	H	D	1-1
21 Aug	Wolverhampton W	A	D	0-0
24 Aug	Ipswich T	A	W	2-1
27 Aug	Manchester C	H	W	4-1
31 Aug	Q P R	H	W	2-1
7 Sep	Southampton A	A	W	2-1
14 Sep	Stoke C	H	W	1-0
21 Sep	Leeds U	A	L	0-2
28 Sep	Sunderland	H	D	0-0
5 Oct	Manchester U	A	D	0-0
9 Oct	Manchester C	A	D	1-1
12 Oct	Coventry C	H	W	2-1
19 Oct	W B A	A	L	0-1
26 Oct	West Ham U	H	D	0-0
9 Nov	Newcastle U	H	D	0-0
16 Nov	Nottingham F	A	W	2-0
23 Nov	Chelsea	H	L	0-1
30 Nov	Burnley	A	W	1-0
7 Dec	Everton	H	W	3-1
14 Dec	Coventry	A	W	1-0
21 Dec	W B A	H	W	2-0
26 Dec	Manchester U	H	W	3-0
11 Jan	Sheffield W	H	W	2-0
18 Jan	Newcastle U	A	L	1-2
1 Feb	Nottingham F	H	D	1-1
15 Feb	Burnley	H	W	2-0
18 Feb	Ipswich T	H	L	0-2
1 Mar	Sheffield W	A	W	5-0
22 Mar	Q P R	A	W	1-0
24 Mar	Tottenham H	H	W	1-0
29 Mar	Southampton	H	D	0-0
31 Mar	Liverpool	A	D	1-1
5 Apr	Sunderland	A	D	0-0
7 Apr	Wolverhampton W	H	W	3-1
8 Apr	Leicester C	A	D	0-0
12 Apr	Leeds U	H	L	1-2
14 Apr	Chelsea	A	L	1-2
19 Apr	Stoke C	A	W	3-1
21 Apr	West Ham U	A	W	2-1
29 Apr	Everton	A	L	0-1

FA Cup

4 Jan	Cardiff (3)	A	D	0-0
7 Jan	Cardiff (3R)	H	W	2-0
25 Jan	Charlton Ath (4)	H	W	2-0
12 Feb	W B A (5)	A	L	0-1

Football League Cup

4 Sep	Sunderland (2)	H	W	1-0
25 Sep	Scunthorpe U (3)	A	W	6-1
15 Oct	Liverpool (4)	H	W	2-1
29 Oct	Blackpool (5)	H	W	5-1
20 Nov	Tottenham H (SF)	H	W	1-0
4 Dec	Tottenham H (SF)	A	D	1-1
15 Mar	Swindon T (F) (at Wembley)		L	1-3*

*aet, 1-1 at 90 mins

Appearances (Goals)

Armstrong G 29 (5) · Court D 40 (6) · Gould R 38 (10) · Graham G 25 (4) · Jenkins D · 14 · (3). Johnston G 3 · McLintock F 37 (1) · McNab R 42 · Neill T 22 (2) · Radford J 34 (15) · Robertson J 19 (3) · Sammels J 36 (4) · Simpson P 34 · Storey P 42 · Urel 23 · Wilson R 42 · Own goals 3 · Total: 16 players (56)

Position in League Table

	P	W	L	D	F:A	Pts	
Leeds	42	27	2	13	66:26	67	1st
Arsenal	42	22	8	12	56:27	56	4th

SEASON 1969-1970
FOOTBALL LEAGUE (DIVISION 1)

9 Aug	Everton	H	L	0-1
13 Aug	Leeds U	A	D	0-0
16 Aug	W B A	A	W	1-0
19 Aug	Leeds U	H	D	1-1
23 Aug	Nottingham F	H	W	2-1
25 Aug	West Ham U	A	D	1-1
30 Aug	Newcastle U	A	L	1-3
6 Sep	Sheffield W	H	D	0-0
13 Sep	Burnley	A	W	1-0
16 Sep	Tottenham H	H	L	2-3
20 Sep	Manchester U	H	D	2-2
27 Sep	Chelsea	A	L	0-3
4 Oct	Coventry C	H	L	0-1
7 Oct	W B A	H	D	1-1
11 Oct	Stoke C	A	D	0-0
18 Oct	Sunderland	A	D	1-1
25 Oct	Ipswich T	H	D	0-0
1 Nov	Crystal Palace	A	W	5-1
8 Nov	Derby Co	H	W	4-0
15 Nov	Wolverhampton W	A	L	0-2
22 Nov	Manchester C	H	D	1-1
29 Nov	Liverpool	A	W	1-0
6 Dec	Southampton	H	D	2-2
13 Dec	Burnley	H	W	3-2
20 Dec	Sheffield W	A	D	1-1
26 Dec	Nottingham F	A	D	1-1
27 Dec	Newcastle U	H	D	0-0
10 Jan	Manchester U	A	L	1-2
17 Jan	Chelsea	H	L	0-3
31 Jan	Coventry C	A	L	0-2
7 Feb	Stoke C	H	D	0-0
14 Feb	Everton	A	D	2-2
18 Feb	Manchester C	A	D	1-1
21 Feb	Derby Co	A	L	2-3
28 Feb	Sunderland	H	W	3-1
14 Mar	Liverpool	H	W	2-1
21 Mar	Southampton	A	W	2-0
28 Mar	Wolverhampton W	H	D	2-2
30 Mar	Crystal Palace	H	W	2-0
31 Mar	Ipswich T	A	L	1-2
4 Apr	West Ham U	H	W	2-1
2 May	Tottenham H	A	L	0-1

FA Cup

3 Jan	Blackpool (3)	H	D	1-1
15 Jan	Blackpool (3R)	A	L	2-3

Football League Cup

2 Sep	Southampton (2)	A	D	1-1
4 Sep	Southampton (2R)	H	W	2-0
24 Sep	Everton (3)	H	D	0-0
1 Oct	Everton (3R)	A	L	0-1

European Fairs Cup

9 Sep	Glentoran (1)	H	W	3-0
29 Sep	Glentoran (1)	A	L	0-1
20 Oct	Sp Cb de Port (2)	A	D	0-0
26 Nov	Sp Cb de Port (2)	H	W	3-0
17 Dec	Rouen (3)	A	D	0-0
13 Jan	Rouen (3)	H	W	1-0
11 Mar	Dinamo Bacau (4)	A	W	2-0
18 Mar	Dinamo Bacau (4)	H	W	7-1
8 Apr	Ajax (SF)	H	W	3-0
15 Apr	Ajax (SF)	A	L	0-1
22 Apr	Anderlecht (F)	A	L	1-3
28 Apr	Anderlecht (F)	H	W	3-0

Appearances (Goals)

Armstrong G 17 3 · Barnett G 11 · Court D 21 · George C 28 (6) · Gould R 11 · Graham G 36 (7) · Kelly E 16 · (2) · Kennedy R 4 (1) · Marinello P 14 (1) · McLintock F 30 · McNab R 37 (2) · Neill T 17 (1) · Nelson S 4 · Radford J 39 (12) · Rice P 7 (1) · Roberts J 11 (1) · Robertson J 27 (4) · Sammels J 36 (8) · Simpson P 39 Storey P 39 1 · Urel 3 · Webster M (3) · Wilson R 28 · Own goals 1 · Total: 23 players (51)

Position in League Table

	P	W	L	D	F:A	Pts	
Everton	42	29	5	8	72:34	66	1st
Arsenal	42	12	12	18	51:49	42	12th

The next 41 years of statistics are presented in greater detail and include a full team listing, with details of goalscorers. They begin with Arsenal's Double winning season 1970–71.

SEASON 1970–71 FOOTBALL LEAGUE (DIVISION 1)

15 Aug	Everton	A	D	2-2	Wilson	Rice	McNab	Kelly	Roberts	McLintock	Armstrong	Storey	Radford	George1	Graham1	Marinello for George
17 Aug	West Ham U	A	D	0-0	..	Storey	..	..	McLintock	Roberts	..	Radford	Kennedy	Marinello	..	
22 Aug	Manchester U	H	W	4-0	..	Rice	..	..	..	..	..	Storey	Radford3	Kennedy	..1	Marinello for Radford
25 Aug	Huddersfield T	H	W	1-0	..	..	..	..	..	..	..	..	..	..1	..	Nelson for Radford
29 Aug	Chelsea	A	L	1-2	..	..	..	..1	..	..	..	..	Nelson	..	..	
1 Sep	Leeds U	H	D	0-0	..	..	..	..	..	..	..	..	Radford	..	..	
5 Sep	Tottenham	H	W	2-0	..	..	..	..	..	..	..2	..	..	..	..	Nelson for McLintock
12 Sep	Burnley	A	W	2-1	..	..	..	..	..	..	..	..	..1	..1	..	
19 Sep	W B A	H	W	6-2	..	..	..	..	..	*opponents*	..1	..	..	..2	..2	
26 Sep	Stoke C	A	L	0-5	..	..	..	..	..	..	..	..	..	..	..	
3 Oct	Nottingham F	H	W	4-0	..	..	..	..	..	..	..1	..	..	..3	..	
10 Oct	Newcastle U	A	D	1-1	..	..	..	..	..	..	..	..	..	..	..1	
17 Oct	Everton	H	W	4-0	..	..	..	..1	..	..	..	..1	..	..2	..	
24 Oct	Coventry C	A	W	3-1	..	..	..	..	..	..	..	..	..1	..1	..1	
31 Oct	Derby Co	H	W	2-0	..	..	..	..1	..	..	..	..	..1	..	..	
7 Nov	Blackpool	A	W	1-0	..	..	..	..	..	..	..	..	..1	..	..	
14 Nov	Crystal Palace	H	D	1-1	..	..	..	..	..	..	..	..	..1	..	..	
21 Nov	Ipswich T	A	W	1-0	..	..	..	..	..	Simpson	..1	..	..	..	Sammels	
28 Nov	Liverpool	H	W	2-0	..	..	..	..	..	..	..	..	..1	..	..	Graham1 for Kelly
5 Dec	Manchester C	A	W	2-0	..	..	..	Graham	..	..	..1	..	..1	..	..	
12 Dec	Wolverhampton W	H	W	2-1	..	..	..	Storey	..	..	..	Sammels	..1	..	Graham1	
19 Dec	Manchester U	A	W	3-1	..	..	..	..	..1	..	..	..	..	..1	..1	
26 Dec	Southampton	H	D	0-0	..	..	..	..	..	..	..	..	..	..	..	
9 Jan	West Ham U	H	W	2-0	..	..	Nelson	..	..	..	..	..	..	..1	..1	
16 Jan	Huddersfield T	A	L	1-2	..	..	McNab	..	..	..	..	..	..	..1	..	
30 Jan	Liverpool	A	L	0-2	..	..	..	..	..	..	..	..	..	..	..	
6 Feb	Manchester C	H	W	1-0	..	..	..	..	..	..	..	..	..1	..	George	
20 Feb	Ipswich	H	W	3-2	..	..	..	..	..1	..	..	..	..1	..	..1	
27 Feb	Derby Co	A	L	0-2	..	..	..	..	..	..	..	..	..	..	..	Graham for Rice
2 Mar	Wolverhampton W	A	W	3-0	..	..	..	..	..	..	..1	..	..1	..1	..	
13 Mar	Crystal Palace	A	W	2-0	..	..	..	..	..	..	..	Graham1	..	..	..	Sammels1 for George
20 Mar	Blackpool	H	W	1-0	..	..	..	..1	..	..	..	..	..	..	..	
3 Apr	Chelsea	H	W	2-0	..	..	..	..	..	..	..	..	..	..2	..	Kelly for Armstrong
6 Apr	Coventry C	H	W	1-0	..	..	..	..	..	..	..	..	..	..1	..	
10 Apr	Southampton	A	W	2-1	..	..	..	..	..1	..	..	..	..1	..	..	
13 Apr	Nottingham F	A	W	3-0	..	..	..	..	..1	..	..	..	..	..1	..1	
17 Apr	Newcastle U	H	W	1-0	..	..	..	..	..	..	..	..	..	..	..1	
20 Apr	Burnley	H	W	1-0	..	..	Roberts	Kelly	..	..	..	..	..	..	..1	
24 Apr	W B A	A	D	2-2	..	..	McNab	Storey	..1	*opponents*	..	..	..	..	..	Sammels for Rice
26 Apr	Leeds U	A	L	0-1	..	..	..	..	..	..	..	..	..	..	..	
1 May	Stoke C	H	W	1-0	..	..	..	..	..	..	..	..	..	..	..	Kelly1 for Storey
3 May	Tottenham H	A	W	1-0	..	..	..	Kelly	..	..	..	..	..	..	..1	..

FA Cup

6 Jan	Yeovil T (3)	A	W	3-0	Wilson	Rice	McNab	Storey	McLintock	Simpson	Armstrong	Sammels	Radford2	Kennedy1	Graham	Kelly for McNab
23 Jan	Portsmouth (4)	A	D	1-1	..	..	..	..1	..	..	..	..	..	..	..	George for Rice
1 Feb	Portsmouth (4R)	H	W	3-2	..	..	..	..1	..	..1	..	..	..	..	George1	
17 Feb	Manchester C (5)	A	W	2-1	..	..	..	..	..	..	..	..	..	..	..2	
6 Mar	Leicester C (6)	A	D	0-0	..	..	..	..	..	..	..	..	..	..	..	
15 Mar	Leicester C (6R)	H	W	1-0	..	..	..	..	..	..	..	Graham	..	..	..1	
27 Mar	Stoke C (SF) (at Sheffield W)		D	2-2	..	..	..	..2	..	..	..	..	..	..	..	Sammels for George
31 Mar	Stoke C (SFR) (at Birmingham)		W	2-0	..	..	..	..	..	..	..	..1	..	..1	..	
8 May	Liverpool (F) (at Wembley)		W	2-1*	..	..	..	..	..	..	..	..	..	..	..1	Kelly1 for Storey

*aet, 0-0 at 90 mins

Football League Cup

8 Sep	Ipswich T (2)	A	D	0-0	Wilson	Rice	McNab	Kelly	McLintock	Roberts	Armstrong	Storey	Nelson	Kennedy	Graham	
28 Sep	Ipswich T (2R)	H	W	4-0	..	..	..	..	..	..1	..	..	Radford1	..2	..	
6 Oct	Luton T (3)	A	W	1-0	..	..	..	..	..	..	..	..	..	..	..1	
28 Oct	Crystal Palace (4)	A	D	0-0	..	..	..	..	..	..	..	..	..	..	..	

9 Nov	Crystal Palace (4R)	H	L	0-2	..	..	..	..	..	..	..	..	..	..	..	

European Fairs Cup

16 Sep	Lazio Roma (1)	A	D	2-2	Wilson	Rice	McNab	Kelly	McLintock	Roberts	Armstrong	Storey	Radford2	Kennedy	Graham	
23 Sep	Lazio Roma (1)	H	W	2-0	..	..	..	..	..	..	..1	..	..1	..	..	Nelson for Graham
21 Oct	Sturm Graz (2)	A	L	0-1	..	..	..	..	..	..	..	..	..	..	..	
4 Nov	Sturm Graz (2)	H	W	2-0	..	..	..	..	..	..	..	..1	..	..1	..	
2 Dec	Beveren Waas (3)	H	W	4-0	..	..	..	Sammels1	..	Simpson	..	..	..	..2	..1	
16 Dec	Beveren Waas (3)	A	D	0-0	..	..	..	Storey	Roberts	..	..	Sammels	..	..	..	Marinello for Armstrong, George for Radford
9 Mar	FC Koln (4)	H	W	2-1	..	..	..	..1	McLintock1	..	..	George	..	..	..	
23 Mar	FC Koln (4)	A	L	0-1	..	..	..	..	..	..	..	Graham	..	..	George	

Appearances (Goals)
Armstrong G 42 (7) · George C 17 (5) · Graham G 38 (11) · Kelly E 23 (4) · Kennedy R 41 (19) · Marinello P 3 · McLintock F 42 (5) · McNab R 40 · Nelson S 4 · Radford J 41 (15) · Rice P 41 · Roberts J 18 · Sammels J 15 (1) · Simpson P 25 · Storey P 40 (2) · Wilson R 42 · Own Goals 2 · **Total: 16 players (71)**

Position in League Table

	P	W	L	D	F:A	Pts	
Arsenal	38	22	6	10	73:36	76	1st

SEASON 1971–72 FOOTBALL LEAGUE (DIVISION 1)

14 Aug	Chelsea	H	W	3-0	Wilson	Rice	McNab	Storey	McLintock1	Simpson	Armstrong	Kelly	Radford1	Kennedy1	Graham	
17 Aug	Huddersfield T	A	W	1-0	..	..	..	..	..	..	..	..	..	..1	..	
20 Aug	Manchester U (Liverpool)	A	L	1-3	..	..	..	..	..1	..	..	..	..	..	..	
24 Aug	Sheffield U	H	L	0-1	..	..	..	..	..	..	..	..	..	..	..	
28 Aug	Stoke C	H	L	0-1	..	..	..	..	..	..	..	..	..	..	..	Roberts for Rice
4 Sep	W B A	A	W	1-0	..	..	..	..	..	Roberts1	..	..	..	..	..	
11 Sep	Leeds U	H	W	2-0	..	..	..	..1	..	..	..	Simpson	..	..	..1	
18 Sep	Everton	A	L	1-2	..	..	..	..	..	..	..	..	..	..1	..	Kelly for McLintock
25 Sep	Leicester C	H	W	3-0	..	..1	Nelson	..	Simpson	..	..	Kelly	..2	..	..	George for Storey
2 Oct	Southampton	A	W	1-0	..	..	..	McLintock	..1	..	..	..	..	..	..	
9 Oct	Newcastle U	H	W	4-2	..	..	..	..	..	George	..1	..1	..	..1	..1	Davis for Radford
16 Oct	Chelsea	A	W	2-1	..	..	..	..	Roberts	..	..	..	..	..2	..	Simpson for Kelly
23 Oct	Derby Co	A	L	1-2	..	..	..	..	..	..	..	..	..	..	..1	Simpson for Kelly
30 Oct	Ipswich T	H	W	2-1	..	..	..	Storey	..	McLintock	*opponents*	George1	..	..	..	
6 Nov	Liverpool	A	L	2-3	..	..	..	..	..	..	*opponents*	..	..	..1	..	
13 Nov	Manchester C	H	L	1-2	..	..	..1	..	..	..	..	..	..	..	..	
20 Nov	Wolverhampton W	A	L	1-5	..	..	..	..	..	..	..	..	..	..1	..	
24 Nov	Tottenham H	A	D	1-1	..	..	McNab	..	..	..	..	Kelly	..	..1	..	
27 Nov	Crystal Palace	H	W	2-1	..	..	..	..	..	..	..	..1	..1	..	..	
4 Dec	West Ham U	A	D	0-0	..	..	..	..	McLintock	Simpson	..	..	..	..	..	
11 Dec	Coventry C	H	W	2-0	..	..	..	..	..	..	..	..	..2	..	..	Marinello for Simpson
18 Dec	W B A	H	W	2-0	..	..	..	..	..	Roberts2	..	..	..	..	..	
27 Dec	Nottingham F	A	D	1-1	..	..	..	Kelly	..	Simpson	..	Ball	..	..	..1	
1 Jan	Everton	H	D	1-1	..	..	..	..	Roberts	..1	..	..	..	..	..	George for Armstrong
8 Jan	Stoke C	A	D	0-0	..	..	..	..	McLintock	..	..	..	..	..	..	
22 Jan	Huddersfield T	H	W	1-0	..	..	Nelson	..	..	..	..1	..	..	..	..	George for Ball
29 Jan	Sheffield U	A	W	5-0	..	..	..	Roberts	..	..1	..	..	George2	..1	..1	
12 Feb	Derby Co	H	W	2-0	..	..	..	Kelly	..	..	..	..	..2	..	..	
19 Feb	Ipswich T	A	W	1-0	..	..	..	..	..	..	..	..	..1	..	..	
4 Mar	Manchester C	A	L	0-2	..	..	..	Storey	..	..	..	..	..	Radford	..	
11 Mar	Newcastle U	A	L	0-2	..	..	..	..	Simpson	Graham	..	..	..	Kennedy	Radford	Batson for George
25 Mar	Leeds U	A	L	0-3	..	..	..	..	McLintock	Simpson	..	..	..	..	Roberts	Marinello for Roberts
28 Mar	Southampton	H	W	1-0	..	..	..	..	..	..	..	..	..	..	Marinello1	
1 Apr	Nottingham F	H	W	3-0	..	..	..	..	Roberts	..	..	..	..1	..1	..	Graham1 for Kennedy
4 Apr	Leicester C	A	D	0-0	..	..	..	..	McLintock	..	..	..	..	Graham	..	
8 Apr	Wolverhampton W	H	W	2-1	..	..	..	..	..	..	Marinello	..	..	Kennedy	Graham2	Armstrong for Marinello
11 Apr	Crystal Palace	A	D	2-2	..	..	..	..	Roberts	..	Armstrong	..1	Radford1	George	..	
22 Apr	West Ham U	H	W	2-1	Barnett	..	McNab	..	McLintock	..	..	..2	..	..	..	Baston for McLintock
25 Apr	Manchester U	H	W	3-0	..	..	..	Roberts	..	..1	..	Nelson	..1	Kennedy1	..	Marinello for Graham
1 May	Coventry C	A	W	1-0	..	..	..	Storey	..1	..	..	Ball	..	George	..	
8 May	Liverpool	H	D	0-0	..	..	Nelson	..	..	..	..	..	..	Kennedy	..	Roberts for Rice
11 May	Tottenham H	H	L	0-2	..	..	McNab	Nelson	..	Roberts	..	Simpson	..	..	..	Marinello for Simpson

FA Cup

15 Jan	Swindon T (3)	A	W	2-0	Wilson	Rice	Nelson	Kelly	McLintock	Simpson	Armstrong1	Ball1	Radford	Kennedy	Graham	
5 Feb	Reading (4)	A	W	2-1	..	..1	..	..	..	*opponents*	..	..	George	..	..	
26 Feb	Derby Co (5)	A	D	2-2	..	..	..	..	..	..	..	..	..2	..	..	Storey for Kelly
29 Feb	Derby Co (5R)	H	D	0-0	..	..	..	Storey	..	..	..	..	..	..	..	Radford for Kennedy
13 Mar	Derby Co (5R) (at Leicester)		W	1-0	..	..	..	..	..	..	..	..	..	..1	..	
18 Mar	Orient (6)	A	W	1-0	..	..	..	..	..	..	..	..1	..	..	..	
15 Apr	Stoke C (SF) (at Villa Park)		D	1-1	Wilson injured Radford in goal	..	McNab	..	..	..	..1	..	Radford	George	..	Kennedy for Wilson
19 Apr	Stoke C (SFR) (at Everton)		W	2-1	Barnett	..	..	..	..	..	..	..	..1	..1	..	
6 May	Leeds U (F) (at Wembley)		L	0-1	..	..	..	..	..	..	..	..	..	..	..	Kennedy for Radford

Football League Cup

8 Sep	Barnsley (2)	H	W	1-0	Wilson	Rice	McNab	Storey	McLintock	Roberts	Marinello	Kelly	Radford	Kennedy1	Graham	
6 Oct	Newcastle U (3)	H	W	4-0	..	..	Nelson	McLintock	Simpson	..	Armstrong	..	..2	..1	..1	
26 Oct	Sheffield U (4)	H	D	0-0	Barnett	..	..	Storey	Roberts	McLintock	..	George	..	..	..	
8 Nov	Sheffield U (4R)	A	L	0-2	Wilson	..	..	Kelly	..	..	..	..	..	..	..	McNab for McLintock

European Cup

15 Sep	St't Drammen (1)	A	W	3-1	Wilson	Rice	Simpson1	McLintock	McNab	Roberts	Kelly1	Marinello1	Graham	Radford	Kennedy	Davies for Marinello
29 Sep	St't Drammen (1)	H	W	4-0	..	..	Nelson	Kelly	Simpson	..	Armstrong1	George	Radford2	Kennedy1	Graham	
20 Oct	Gr'pers Zurich (2)	A	W	2-0	..	..	..	McLintock	Roberts	George	..	Kelly	..	..1	..1	
3 Nov	Gr'pers Zurich (2)	H	W	3-0	..	..	..	Storey	..	McLintock	..	George1	..1	..1	..	Simpson for Roberts, McNab for McLintock
8 Mar	Ajax Ams'dam (3)	A	L	1-2	..	..	..	..	McLintock	Simpson	..	..	..	..1	..	Roberts for Nelson
22 Mar	Ajax Ams'dam (3)	H	L	0-1	..	..	..	..	..	..	..	..	Marinello	..	..	Roberts for Nelson

Appearances (Goals)
Armstrong G 42 (2) · Ball A 18 (3) · Batson B 2 · Barnett G 5 · Davies P 1 · George C 23 (7) · Graham G 40 (8) · Kelly E 23 (2) · Kennedy R 37 (12) · McNab R 20 · McLintock F 37 (3) · Marinello P 8 1 · Nelson S 24 (1) · Radford J 34 (8) · Rice P 42 (1) · Roberts J 23 (3) · Simpson P 34 (4) · Storey P 29 (1) · Wilson R 37 · Own goals 2 · **Total: 19 players (58)**

Position in League Table

	P	W	L	D	F:A	Pts	
Derby Co	42	24	8	10	69:33	58	1st
Arsenal	42	22	12	8	58:40	52	5th

SEASON 1972–73 FOOTBALL LEAGUE (DIVISION 1)

12 Aug	Leicester C	A	W	1-0	Barnett	Rice	McNab	Storey	McLintock	Simpson	Armstrong	Ball1	Radford	Kennedy	Graham	
15 Aug	Wolverhampton W	H	W	5-2	..	..	..1	..	..	..1	..	..	..2	..1	..	Roberts for Simpson
19 Aug	Stoke C	H	W	2-0	..	..	..	..	..	Roberts	..	..	..	..2	..	
22 Aug	Coventry C	A	D	1-1	..	..1	..	..	..	Simpson	..	..	..	..	..	
26 Aug	Manchester U	A	D	0-0	..	..	..	..	..	..	..	..	George	..	..	
29 Aug	West Ham U	H	W	1-0	..	..	..	..	..	..	..	..1	Radford	..	..	George for Armstrong
2 Sep	Chelsea	H	D	1-1	..	..	..	..	..	*opponents*	..	..	..	..	..	George for Armstrong
9 Sep	Newcastle U	A	L	1-2	..	..	..	..	..	Roberts	Marinello	..	..	..1	..	
16 Sep	Liverpool	H	D	0-0	..	..	..	..	..	..	..	..	..	..	..	
23 Sep	Norwich C	A	L	2-3	..	..	..	..1	..	..	..	..	..1	..	..	
26 Sep	Birmingham C	H	W	2-0	..	..	..	..1	..	..	..	..	..	..	George1	
30 Sep	Southampton	H	W	1-0	..	..	..	..	..	..	..	..	..	..	..	Graham1 for Kennedy
7 Oct	Sheffield U	A	L	0-1	..	..	..	..	..	Blockley	..	..	..	Graham	..	
14 Oct	Ipswich T	H	W	1-0	..	..	..	..	..	..	..	..	..	..1	..	

21 Oct	Crystal Palace	A	W	3-2	..	..1	..	..	..	..	..	Kelly	..1	..	..1	Nelson for Kelly
28 Oct	Manchester C	H	D	0-0	..	..	..	..	..	..	..	..	..	George	Graham	
4 Nov	Coventry C	H	L	0-2	..	..	..	..	..	..	..	Ball	..	..	Kelly	Graham for Kelly
17 Nov	Wolverhampton W	A	W	3-1	..	..	..	..	..	..	..1	..	..2	..	..	
18 Nov	Everton	H	W	1-0	..	..	..	..	Simpson	..	..	..	..1	..	..	
25 Nov	Derby Co	A	L	0-5	Wilson	..	..	..	McLintock	Simpson	..	..	..	..	..	Armstrong for Marinello
2 Dec	Leeds U	H	W	2-1	..	..	..	..	Blockley	..	Armstrong	..1	..1	Kennedy	..	
9 Dec	Tottenham H	A	W	2-1	..	..	..	..1	..	..	..	..	..1	..	..	McLintock for Simpson
16 Dec	W B A	H	W	2-1	Barnett	..	..	..	McLintock	*opponents*	..	..	..1	..	..	George for Rice
23 Dec	Birmingham C	A	D	1-1	Wilson	Nelson	..	..	Blockley	..	..	..	..	..	..1	
26 Dec	Norwich C	H	W	2-0	..	..	..	..	..	..	..	..1	..1	..	..	George for Nelson
30 Dec	Stoke C	A	D	0-0	..	Rice	..	..	..	..	..	..	..	..	..	
6 Jan	Manchester U	H	W	3-1	..	..	..	..	..	..	..1	..1	..	..1	..	
20 Jan	Chelsea	A	W	1-0	..	..	..	..	..	..	..	..	..	..1	..	McLintock for Kelly
27 Jan	Newcastle U	H	D	2-2	..	..	..	..	..	..	..	..1	..	..1	..	George for Armstrong
10 Feb	Liverpool	A	W	2-0	..	..	..	..	..	..	..	..1	..1	..	..	George for Radford
17 Feb	Leicester C	H	W	1-0	..	..	..	..	..	McLintock	*opponents*	..	..	..	..	George for Blockley
28 Feb	W B A	A	L	0-1	..	..	..	Batson	McLintock	George	..	..	..	..	..	
3 Mar	Sheffield U	H	W	3-2	..	..	..	George2	..	Batson	..	..1	..	..	..	Nelson for Batson
10 Mar	Ipswich T	A	W	2-1	..	..	..	Storey	..	Simpson	..	..1	..1	..	..	
24 Mar	Manchester C	A	W	2-1	..	..	..	..	..	..	..	..	George1	..1	..	Nelson for Kelly
26 Mar	Crystal Palace	H	W	1-0	..	..	..	..	..	..	..	..1	..	..	..	
31 Mar	Derby Co	H	L	0-1	..	..	..	..	..	..	..	..	..	..	..	Nelson for McLintock
14 Apr	Tottenham H	H	D	1-1	Wilson	Rice	McNab	Storey1	Blockley	Simpson	Armstrong	Ball	Radford	Kennedy	Kelly	George for Kelly
21 Apr	Everton	A	D	0-0	..	..	..	..	..	..	..	..	..	..	..	George for Blockley
23 Apr	Southampton	A	D	2-2	..	..	..	..	Kelly	..	..	..	..1	George1	Kennedy	
28 Apr	West Ham U	A	W	2-1	..	..	..	..	..	..	..	..	..1	Kennedy1	George	
9 May	Leeds U	A	L	1-6	..	Batson	..	..	Blockley	..	..1	..	..	..	Hornsby	Price for Hornsby

FA Cup

13 Jan	Leichester C (3)	H	D	2-2	Wilson	Rice	McNab	Storey	Blockley	Simpson	Armstrong1	Ball	Radford	Kennedy1	Kelly	
17 Jan	Leicester C (3R)	A	W	2-1	..	..	..	..	..	..	..	..	..1	..	..1	
3 Feb	Bradford C (4)	H	W	2-0	..	..	..	..	..	..	..	..1	George1	..	..	Marinello for George
24 Feb	Carlisle U (5)	A	W	2-1	Barnett	..	..	..	McLintock1	..	..	..1	Radford	..	..	Nelson for Storey
17 Mar	Chelsea (6)	A	D	2-2	Wilson	..	..	..	..	..	..	..1	George1	..	..	
20 Mar	Chelsea (6R)	H	W	2-1	..	..	..	..	..	..	..	..1	..	..1	..	
7 Apr	Sunderland (SF) (at Sheffield W)	A	L	1-2	..	..	..	..	Blockley	..	..	..	..1	..	..	Radford for Blockley

Football League Cup

Sep	Everton (2)	H	W	1-0	Barnett	Rice	McNab	Storey1	McLintock	Simpson	Marinello	Ball	Radford	Kennedy	Graham	
3 Oct	Rotherham U (3)	H	W	5-0	..	..	Nelson	..1	..	Roberts	..1	..	..2	Graham	George1	
31 Oct	Sheffield U (4)	A	W	2-1	..	..	McNab	..	..	Simpson	..	Kelly	..1	..	..1	
21 Nov	Norwich C (5)	H	L	0-3	..	..	..	..	..	..	..	Ball	..	George	Kelly	

Appearances (Goals)
Armstrong G 30 (2) · Ball A 40 (10) · Barnett G 20 · Batson B 3 · Blockley J 20 · George C 27 (6) · Graham G 16 (2) · Hornsby B 1 · Kelly E 27 (1) · McLintock F 29 · McNab R 42 (1) · Marinello P 13 1 · Nelson S 6 · Price D 1 · Radford J 38 (15) · Rice P 39 (2) · Roberts J 7 · Simpson P 27 (1) · Storey P 40 (4) · Wilson R 22 · Own goals 3 · **Total: 21 players (57)**

Position in League Table

	P	W	L	D	F:A	Pts	
Liverpool	42	25	7	10	72:42	60	1st
Arsenal	42	23	8	11	57:43	57	2nd

SEASON 1973–74 FOOTBALL LEAGUE (DIVISION 1)

25 Aug	Manchester U	H	W	3-0	Wilson	Rice	McNab	Price	Blockley	Simpson	Armstrong	Ball1	Radford1	Kennedy1	George	Hornsby for Radford
28 Aug	Leeds U	H	L	1-2	..	..	..	Storey	..1	..	..	..	..	..	..	Price for Simpson
1 Sep	Newcastle U	A	D	1-1	..	..	..	Price	..	Storey	..	..	Kelly	..	..1	
4 Sep	Sheffield U	A	L	0-5	..	..	..	Batson	..	..	..	..	..	..	..	
8 Sep	Leicester C	H	L	0-2	..	..	..	Storey	..	Simpson	Kelly	..	Radford	..	..	Armstrong for Kelly
11 Sep	Sheffield U	H	W	1-0	..	..	..	..	..	..	Armstrong	..	..	..1	Kelly	
15 Sep	Norwich C	A	W	4-0	..	..	..1	..	..	George1	..	..1	..	..1	..	
22 Sep	Stoke C	H	W	2-1	..	..	..	..	..	Simpson	..	..1	..1	..	George	Kelly for George
29 Sep	Everton	A	L	0-1	..	..	..	..	..	..	..	..	..	..	..	Kelly for George
6 Oct	Birmingham C	H	W	1-0	..	..	..	..	..	..	..	Chambers	..	..1	Kelly	Brady for Blockley
13 Oct	Tottenham H	A	L	0-2	..	..	..	..	Simpson	Kelly	..	George	..	..	Brady	Batson for Radford
20 Oct	Ipswich T	H	D	1-1	..	..	..	..	..1	..	..	..	Batson	..	Price	
27 Oct	Q P R	A	L	0-2	..	..	..	..	..	..	..	..	..	..	Powling	
3 Nov	Liverpool	H	L	0-2	..	..	..	..	..	Powling	..	..	Radford	..	Kelly	Batson for Kelly
10 Nov	Manchester C	A	W	2-1	..	..	..	..	..	Kelly1	Ball	..	Hornsby1	..	Armstrong	
17 Nov	Chelsea	H	D	0-0	..	..	..	..	..	..	..	..	..	..	..	
24 Nov	West Ham U	A	W	3-1	..	..	..	..	..	..	..2	..1	..	..	..	
1 Dec	Coventry C	H	D	2-2	..	..	..	..	..	..	..	..	..1	..	..	Nelson1 for Kelly
4 Dec	Wolverhampton W	H	D	2-2	..	..	..	..	..	..	..	..1	Radford	..	..	Hornsby1 for George
8 Dec	Derby Co	A	D	1-1	..	..	..	..	..	*opponents*	..	Blockley	..	..	..	
15 Dec	Burnley	A	L	1-2	..	..	Nelson	..	..	..	..	..	..1	..	..	
22 Dec	Everton	H	W	1-0	..	..	McNab	..	Blockley	Simpson	Armstrong	Ball1	Hornsby	..	Kelly	
26 Dec	Southampton	A	D	1-1	..	..	Nelson	..	..	..	..	..1	Radford	..	..	Hornsby for Kelly
29 Dec	Leicester C	A	L	0-2	..	..	..	..	..	..	..	..	..	..	Hornsby	
1 Jan	Newcastle U	H	L	0-1	..	..	..	..	..	..	..	..	..	..	Kelly	
12 Jan	Norwich C	H	W	2-0	..	..	Storey	Kelly	..	..	..	..2	..	..	Brady	
19 Jan	Manchester U	A	D	1-1	..	..	McNab	Storey	..	..	..	..	..	..1	Kelly	
2 Feb	Burnley	H	D	1-1	..	..	Storey	Kelly	..	..	..	..1	..	..	Brady	
5 Feb	Leeds U	A	L	1-3	..	..	Nelson	Storey	..	..	..	..1	..	..	..	
16 Feb	Tottenham H	H	L	0-1	..	..	..	..	Simpson	Kelly	..	..	..	..	..	
23 Feb	Birmingham C	A	L	1-3	..	..	..	..	..	..	George	..	..	..1	..	
2 Mar	Southampton	H	W	1-0	..	..	..	..	..	..	..	..1	..	..	Armstrong	
16 Mar	Ipswich T	A	D	2-2	..	McNab	..	..	..1	..	..	Brady	..	..1	..	
23 Mar	Manchester C	H	W	2-0	..	Rice	..	..	..	..	..	Ball	..2	..	..	
30 Mar	Stoke C	A	D	0-0	..	..	..	..	Blockley	..	Armstrong	..	..	..	George	Simpson for Kelly
6 Apr	West Ham U	H	D	0-0	..	..	..	..	..	..	..	..	..	..	..	
13 Apr	Chelsea	A	W	3-1	..	..	..	..	..	..	..	..	..1	..2	..	Simpson for Kelly
15 Apr	Wolverhampton W	A	L	1-3	..	..	..	..	..	Simpson	..	..	..	..1	..	Brady for Radford
20 Apr	Derby Co	H	W	2-0	..	..	..	..	..	Kelly	..	..1	George1	..	Brady	Simpson for George
24 Apr	Liverpool	A	W	1-0	Rimmer	..	..	..	..	..	..	..	Radford	..1	..	Simpson for Blockley
27 Apr	Coventry	A	D	3-3	Wilson	..1	..	..	Simpson	..	..	..	..1	..1	George	
30 Apr	Q P R	H	D	1-1	..	..	..	..	..	..	..	..	..	..	..	Brady1 for Ball

FA Cup

5 Jan	Norwich C (3)	A	W	1-0	Wilson	Rice	McNab	Storey	Blockley	Simpson	Kelly1	Ball	Radford	Kennedy	Armstrong	
26 Jan	Aston Villa (4)	H	D	1-1	..	..	..	..	..	..	Armstrong	..	..	..1	Kelly	
30 Jan	Aston Villa (4R)	A	L	0-2	..	..	..	..	..	..	..	..	..	..	..	Brady for McNab

Football League Cup

2 Oct	Tranmere Rov (2)	H	L	0-1	Wilson	Rice	McNab	Storey	Blockley	Simpson	Armstrong	Ball	Radford	Kennedy	Kelly	Chambers for Ball

FA Cup (1972-73) Third Place Play-off

18 Aug	Wolverhampton	H	L	1-3	Wilson	Batson	McNab	Price	Blockley	Simpson	Chambers	Ball	Radford	Kennedy	Hornsby1	

Appearances (Goals)
Armstrong G 41 · Ball A 36 (13) · Batson B 5 · Blockley J 26 (1) · Brady L 13 (1) · Chambers B 1 · George C 28 (5) · Hornsby B 9 (3) · Kelly E 37 (1) · Kennedy R 2 (12) · McNab R 23 (1) · Nelson S 19 (1) · Powling R 2 · Price D 4 · Radford J 32 (7) · Rice P 41 (1) · Rimmer J 1 · Simpson P 38 (2) · Storey P 41 · Wilson R 41 · Own goals 1 · **Total: 20 players (49)**

Position in League Table

	P	W	L	D	F:A	Pts	
Leeds U	42	24	4	14	66:31	62	1st
Arsenal	42	14	14	14	49:51	42	10th

SEASON 1974–75 FOOTBALL LEAGUE (DIVISION 1)

17 Aug	Leicester C	A	W	1-0	Rimmer	Matthews	Nelson	Storey	Simpson	Kelly	Armstrong	Brady	Radford	George	Kidd1	Price for Kelly
20 Aug	Ipswich T	H	L	0-1	..	Storey	..	Kelly	..	Matthews	..	Hornsby	..	Kidd	Brady	
24 Aug	Manchester C	H	W	4-0	..	Rice	..	..	..	Storey	Matthews	George	..2	..2	..	Armstrong for Simpson
27 Aug	Ipswich T	A	L	0-3	..	..	..	..	..	Matthews	Brady	..	..	..	Storey	
31 Aug	Everton	A	L	1-2	..	..	..	Storey	..	Kelly	Blockley	Brady	..	George	Kidd1	Powling for Kelly
7 Sep	Burnley	H	L	0-1	..	..	..	..	Blockley	Matthews	Armstrong	..	..	..	..	Simpson for Rice
14 Sep	Chelsea	A	D	0-0	..	Kelly	Simpson	..	..	..	..	George	..	Kidd	Brady	
21 Sep	Luton T	H	D	2-2	..	Simpson	Nelson	..	..	..	..	Kelly	..	..2	..	
28 Sep	Birmingham C	A	L	1-3	..	Storey	Simpson	Kelly	..	..	George1	Ball	..	..	..	
5 Oct	Leeds U	A	L	0-2	..	..	..	..	..	..	Armstrong	..	..	..	..	Powling for Blockley
12 Oct	Q P R	H	D	2-2	..	..	..	..	Powling	..	..	..	..1	..1	..	
16 Oct	Manchester C	A	L	1-2	..	..	..	Nelson	..	Kelly	Ball	Brady	..1	..	Armstrong	
19 Oct	Tottenham H	A	L	0-2	..	..	Nelson	Kelly	..	Simpson	Armstrong	Ball	..	Brady	Kidd	
26 Oct	West Ham U	H	W	3-0	..	..	McNab	..	Mancini	..	Rice	..	..1	..1	..1	Armstrong for Rice
2 Nov	Wolverhampton W	H	D	0-0	..	..	..	..	..	..	..	..	..	..	..	
9 Nov	Liverpool	A	W	3-1	..	Rice	..	..	..	..	Storey	..2	..	Kidd	Brady1	
16 Nov	Derby Co	H	W	3-1	..	..	..	..	..	..	..	..2	..	..1	..	
23 Nov	Coventry C	A	L	0-3	..	..	..	..	Simpson	Powling	Armstrong	..	..	..	..	George for Brady
30 Nov	Middlesbrough	H	W	2-0	..	..	..	..	..	..	George	..1	..	..	..1	
7 Dec	Carlisle U	A	L	1-2	..	..	..	..	..	Mancini	Storey	..	..	..1	Cropley	
14 Dec	Leicester C	H	D	0-0	..	..	..	..	Mancini	Simpson	..	..	..	..	..	
21 Dec	Stoke C	A	W	2-0	..	..	..	..	..	..	..	..	..	..2	..	
26 Dec	Chelsea	H	L	1-2	..	..	..	..	..	..	..	..1	..	..	..	
28 Dec	Sheffield U	A	D	1-1	..	..	..	..	..	..	..	..	George1	..	..	Armstrong for Kelly
11 Jan	Carlisle U	H	W	2-1	..	..	..	..	..	..	Armstrong	..	Radford1	..	..1	
18 Jan	Middlesbrough	A	D	0-0	..	..	..	..	..	..	..	..	Storey	..	..	
1 Feb	Liverpool	H	W	2-0	..	..	..	Matthews	..	..	..	..2	Brady	..	Storey	Ross for Ball
8 Feb	Wolverhampton W	A	L	0-1	..	..	..	Ross	..	..	..	Brady	Radford	..	..	
22 Feb	Derby Co	A	L	1-2	..	..	..	Storey	..	..	..	Ball	..1	..	Brady	
1 Mar	Everton	H	L	0-2	..	..	..	..	..	..	..	..	..	..	..	
15 Mar	Birmingham C	H	D	1-1	..	..	Nelson	..	..	..	Matthews	..	..	..1	..	
18 Mar	Newcastle U	H	W	3-0	..	..	..	Rostron1	..	..	..	..1	Hornsby	..1	..	
22 Mar	Burnley	A	D	3-3	..	..	..	Matthews	..	..	Rostron1	..	..2	..	..	Powling for Matthews
25 Mar	Luton T	A	L	0-2	..	..	..	Storey	..	..	..	..	Radford	Hornsby	..	
29 Mar	Stoke C	H	D	1-1	..	..	McNab	..	Kelly1	..	Matthews	..	Stapleton	Rostron	Hornsby	Brady for Stapleton
31 Mar	Sheffield U	H	W	1-0	..	..	Nelson	..	Mancini	..	..	Kelly	Hornsby	Kidd1	Armstrong	
8 Apr	Coventry C	H	W	2-0	..	..	..	..	..	..	..	..	..	..2	..	
12 Apr	Leeds U	H	L	1-2	..	..	..	..	..	..	..	..	..	..1	..	Brady for Nelson
19 Apr	Q P R	A	D	0-0	..	..	..	..	..	..	Ball	..	..	..	..	
23 Apr	Newcastle U	A	L	1-3	..	..	Matthews	..	..	Brady	..	..	..1	..	Rostron	Nelson for Kelly
26 Apr	Tottenham H	H	W	1-0	Barnett	..	Nelson	..	..	Simpson	..	Brady	..	..1	Armstrong	
28 Apr	West Ham U	A	L	0-1	..	Storey	..	Kelly	..	Matthews	..	..	..	..	Rostron	

FA Cup

4 Jan	York C (3)	H	D	1-1	Rimmer	Rice	McNab	Kelly1	Mancini	Powling	Storey	Ball	Armstrong	Kidd	Cropley	
7 Jan	York C (3R)	A	W	3-1	..	..	..	..	Simpson	Mancini	Armstrong	..	Radford	..3	..	
25 Jan	Coventry (4)	A	D	1-1	..	..	..	Storey	Mancini	Simpson	..	..1	..	..	George	Matthews for George
29 Jan	Coventry (4R)	H	W	3-0	..	..	..	Matthews1	..	..	..2	..	..	..	Storey	Brady for Radford
15 Feb	Leicester C (5)	H	D	0-0	..	..	..	Storey	..	..	..	..	..	..	Brady	
19 Feb	Leicester C (5R)	A	D	1-1	..	..	..	..	..	..	..	..	..1	..	Matthews	Brady for Matthews
24 Feb	Leicester C (5R)	A	W	1-0	..	..	..	..	..	..	..	..	..1	..	..	Brady for Matthews
8 Mar	West Ham (6)	H	L	0-2	..	..	..	..	..	..	Matthews	..	..	..	Brady	Armstrong for Radford

Football League Cup

10 Sep	Leicester C (2)	H	D	1-1	Rimmer	Kelly	Simpson	Storey	Blockley	Mathews	Armstrong	George	Radford	Kidd1	Brady	
18 Sep	Leicester C (2R)	A	L	1-2	..	Simpson	Nelson	..	..	..	..	Kelly	..	..	..1	

Appearances (Goals)
Armstrong G 24 – Ball A 30 (9) – Barnett G 2 – Blockley J 6 – Brady L 32 (3) – Cropley A 7 (1) – George C 10 (2) – Hornsby B 12 (3) – Kelly E 32 (1) – Kidd B 40 (19) – Mancini T 26 – McNab R 18 – Matthews J 20 – Nelson S 20 – Powling R 8 – Price D 1 – Radford J 29 (7) – Rice P 32 – Rimmer J 40 – Ross T 2 Rostron W 6 2 – Simpson P 40 – Stapleton F 1 – Storey P 37 – Total 24 players (47)

Position in League Table

	P	W	L	D	F:A	Pts	
Derby	42	21	10	11	67:49	53	1st
Arsenal	42	13	18	11	47:49	37	16th

SEASON 1975–76 FOOTBALL LEAGUE (DIVISION 1)

16 Aug	Burnley	A	D	0-0	Rimmer	Rice	Nelson	Kelly	Mancini	O'Leary	Armstrong	Cropley	Hornsby	Kidd	Brady	
19 Aug	Sheffield U	A	W	3-1	..	..1	..	..	..	..	..	..	..	..1	..1	
23 Aug	Stoke C	H	L	0-1	..	..	..	..	..	..	..	..	..	..	..	
26 Aug	Norwich C	H	W	2-1	..	..	Storey	..1	..	..	..	..	Ball1	..	..	
30 Aug	Wolverhampton W	A	D	0-0	..	..	Nelson	..	..	..	Ball	..	Radford	..	..	
6 Sep	Leicester C	H	D	1-1	..	..	..	..	..	..	..	..	Stapleton1	..	..	
13 Sep	Aston Villa	A	L	0-2	..	..	..	..	..	..	..	..	..	..	..	
20 Sep	Everton	H	D	2-2	..	..	..	..	..	..	..	..	..1	..1	..	
27 Sep	Tottenham H	A	D	0-0	..	..	..	..	..	..	..	..	..	..	Rostron	Brady for Rostron
4 Oct	Manchester C	H	L	2-3	..	..	..	..	Simpson	..	..1	..1	..	..	Brady	Rostron for Kelly
11 Oct	Coventry C	H	W	5-0	..	..	..	Powling	..	..	..1	..2	..	..2	..	Rostron for Cropley
18 Oct	Manchester U	A	L	1-3	..	..	..	Kelly1	O'Leary	Simpson	..	..	..	..	..	
25 Oct	Middlesbrough	H	W	2-1	..	..	..	..	..	..	..	..1	..1	..	..	Powling for Kelly
1 Nov	Newcastle U	A	L	0-2	..	..	..	..	..	..	..	Powling	..	..	..	
8 Nov	Derby Co	H	L	0-1	..	..	Storey	..	..	Powling	..	Cropley	..	Hornsby	..	
15 Nov	Birmingham C	A	L	1-3	..	..	..	..	..	..	..1	..	..	Kidd	..	Matthews for Cropley
22 Nov	Manchester U	H	W	3-1	..	..	..	Nelson	..	*opponents*	..1	Armstrong1	..	..	..	
29 Nov	West Ham U	A	L	0-1	..	..	Nelson	Storey	..	..	..	..	..	..	..	
2 Dec	Liverpool	A	D	2-2	..	..	Storey	Nelson	..	..	..1	..	..	..1	..	
6 Dec	Leeds U	H	L	1-2	..	..	Nelson	Storey	..	..	Armstrong	Ball	..	..	..1	
13 Dec	Stoke C	A	L	1-2	Barnett	..	..	..	..	..	..1	..	..	..	..	Simpson for Nelson
20 Dec	Burnley	H	W	1-0	Rimmer	..	Simpson	Kelly	Mancini	..	..	..	Radford1	..	..	Stapleton for Brady
26 Dec	Ipswich	A	L	0-2	..	..	Kelly	Storey	O'Leary	..	..	..	..	..	..	
27 Dec	Q P R	H	W	2-0	..	..	Nelson	..	..	..	..	..1	Stapleton	..1	..	
10 Jan	Aston Villa	H	D	0-0	..	..	..	Powling	..	Mancini	..	..	..	..	..	
17 Jan	Leicester C	A	L	1-2	..	..	..	Ross1	..	..	..	..	..	..	..	
31 Jan	Sheffield U	H	W	1-0	..	..	..	..	Mancini	Powling	..	..	..	..	..1	Rostron for Nelson
7 Feb	Norwich C	A	L	1-3	..	..	Storey	..	..	Simpson	..	..	..	..1	..	
18 Feb	Derby Co	A	L	0-2	..	..	Nelson	..	..	Powling	..	..	Radford	..	..	
21 Feb	Birmingham C	H	W	1-0	..	..	..	..	..	..	..	..	..	..	..1	Simpson for Brady
24 Feb	Liverpool	H	W	1-0	..	..	..	..	..	..	..	..	..1	..	..	
28 Feb	Middlesbrough	A	W	1-0	..	..	..	..	..	..	..	..	..1	..	..	
13 Mar	Coventry C	A	D	1-1	..	..	..	..	..	..1	..	..	..	..	..	
16 Mar	Newcastle U	H	D	0-0	..	..	..	..	..	..	..	..	..	..	..	
20 Mar	West Ham U	H	W	6-1	..	..	..	..	..	..	..1	..2	..	..3	..	Stapleton for Rice
27 Mar	Leeds U	A	L	0-3	..	..	..	..	..	..	..	..	..	..	..	
3 Apr	Tottenham H	H	L	0-2	..	..	..	..	..	..	..	..	..	..	..	
10 Apr	Everton	A	D	0-0	..	..	..	..	..	..	..	..	..	Cropley	..	
13 Apr	Wolverhampton W	H	W	2-1	..	..	..	..	..1	..	..	..	..	..1	..	
17 Apr	Ipswich T	H	L	1-2	..	..	..	..	O'Leary	..	Rostron	..	Stapleton1	..	..	
19 Apr	Q P R	A	L	1-2	..	..	..	..	..	..	Kidd1	..	Radford	..	..	Armstrong for Radford
24 Apr	Manchester C	A	L	1-3	..	..	..	..	Mancini	..	Armstrong1	..	Stapleton	..	..	

FA Cup

3 Jan	Wolves (3)	A	L	0-3	Rimmer	Rice	Nelson	Storey	O'Leary	Powling	Armstrong	Ball	Stapleton	Kidd	Brady	

Football League Cup

9 Sep	Everton (2)	A	D	2-2	Rimmer	Rice	Nelson	Kelly	Mancini	O'Leary	Ball	Cropley1	Radford	Kidd	Brady	Stapleton1 for Mancini
23 Sep	Everton (2R)	H	L	0-1	..	..	..	..	..	..	..	..	Stapleton	..	Rostron	

Appearances (Goals)
Armstrong G 29 (4) – Ball A 39 (9) – Barnett J 1 – Brady L 42 (5) – Cropley A 20 (4) – Hornsby B 4 – Kelly E 17 (2) – Kidd B 37 (11) – Mancini T 26 (1) – Matthews J 1 – Nelson S 36 – O'Leary D 27 – Powling R 29 (1) – Radford J 15 (3) – Rice P 42 (1) – Rimmer J 41 – Ross T 17 (1) – Rostron W 5 – Simpson P 9 Stapleton F 25 – 4 Storey P 11 – Own goals 1 – Total 21 players (47)

Position in League Table

	P	W	L	D	F:A	Pts	
Liverpool	42	23	5	14	66:31	60	1st
Arsenal	42	13	19	10	47:53	36	17th

SEASON 1976–77 FOOTBALL LEAGUE (DIVISION 1)

Date	Opponent	V	Res	Score	Notes
21 Aug	Bristol C	H	L	0-1	
25 Aug	Norwich C	A	W	3-1	Storey for Cropley
28 Aug	Sunderland	A	D	2-2	Brady
4 Sep	Manchester C	H	D	0-0	
11 Sep	West Ham U	A	W	2-0	Armstrong / Cropley for Stapleton
18 Sep	Everton	H	W	3-1	Storey for O'Leary
25 Sep	Ipswich T	A	L	1-3	
2 Oct	QPR	H	W	3-2	
16 Oct	Stoke C	H	W	2-0	Storey for Nelson
20 Oct	Aston Villa	A	L	1-5	Radford for Stapleton
23 Oct	Leicester C	A	L	1-4	
30 Oct	Leeds U	A	L	1-2	
6 Nov	Birmingham C	H	W	4-0	
20 Nov	Liverpool	H	D	1-1	Storey for O'Leary
27 Nov	Coventry C	A	W	2-1	
4 Dec	Newcastle U	H	W	5-3	
15 Dec	Derby Co	A	D	0-0	Matthews for Rice
18 Dec	Manchester U	H	W	3-1	
27 Dec	Tottenham H	A	D	2-2	Rostron for Stapleton
3 Jan	Leeds U	H	D	1-1	
15 Jan	Norwich C	H	W	1-0	
18 Jan	Birmingham C	A	D	3-3	
22 Jan	Bristol C	A	L	0-2	Rostron
5 Feb	Sunderland	H	D	0-0	
12 Feb	Manchester C	A	L	0-1	
15 Feb	Middlesbrough	A	L	0-3	Matthews for O'Leary
19 Feb	West Ham U	H	L	2-3	Powling for Howard
1 Mar	Everton	A	L	1-2	
5 Mar	Ipswich T	H	L	1-4	Nelson for Matthews
8 Mar	WBA	H	L	1-2	Price for Hudson
12 Mar	QPR	A	L	1-2	
23 Mar	Stoke C	A	D	1-1	
2 Apr	Leicester C	H	W	3-0	Matthews for Powling
9 Apr	WBA	A	W	2-0	
11 Apr	Tottenham H	H	W	1-0	Brady for Rix
16 Apr	Liverpool	A	L	0-2	Rix for Ross
23 Apr	Coventry C	H	W	2-0	Rix for Ross
25 Apr	Aston Villa	H	W	3-0	
30 Apr	Newcastle U	A	W	2-0	Howard for O'Leary
3 May	Derby Co	H	D	0-0	Rix for Young
7 May	Middlesbrough	H	D	1-1	Price for Matthews
14 May	Manchester U	A	L	2-3	Rix for Young

FA Cup

Date	Opponent	V	Res	Score	Notes
8 Jan	Notts Co (3)	A	W	1-0	
29 Jan	Coventry C (4)	H	W	3-1	Storey for Macdonald
26 Feb	Middlesbrough (5)	A	L	1-4	Matthews for O'Leary

Football League Cup

Date	Opponent	V	Res	Score	Notes
31 Aug	Carlisle U (2)	H	W	3-2	
21 Sep	Blackpool (3)	A	D	1-1	
28 Sep	Blackpool (3R)	H	D	0-0	Storey for Nelson
5 Oct	Blackpool (3R)	H	W	2-0	
26 Oct	Chelsea (4)	H	W	2-1	
1 Dec	QPR (5)	A	L	1-2	

Appearances (Goals)
Armstrong G 37 (2) – Ball A 14 (1) – Brady L 38 (5) – Cropley A 3 – Howard P 16 – Hudson A 19 – Macdonald M 41 (25) – Matthews J 17 (2) – Nelson S 32 (3) – O'Leary D 33 (2) – Powling R 12 – Price D 8 (1) – Radford J 2 – Rice P 42 (3) – Rimmer J 42 – Rix G 7 (1) – Ross T 29 (4) – Rostron W 5 – Simpson P 19 – Stapleton F 40 (13) – Storey P 11 – Young W 14 (1) – Own goals 1 – Total 22 players (64)

Position in League Table

	P	W	L	D	F:A	Pts	
Liverpool	42	23	8	11	62:33	57	1st
Arsenal	42	16	15	11	64:59	43	8th

SEASON 1977–78 FOOTBALL LEAGUE (DIVISION 1)

Date	Opponent	V	Res	Score	Notes
20 Aug	Ipswich T	A	L	0-1	Price for Brady
23 Aug	Everton	H	W	1-0	
27 Aug	Wolverhampton W	A	D	1-1	
3 Sep	Nottingham F	H	W	3-0	
10 Sep	Aston Villa	A	L	0-1	
17 Sep	Leicester C	H	W	2-1	
24 Sep	Norwich C	A	L	0-1	Walford for Matthews
1 Oct	West Ham U	H	W	3-0	
4 Oct	Liverpool	H	D	0-0	Matthews for Ross
8 Oct	Manchester C	A	L	1-2	
15 Oct	QPR	H	W	1-0	
22 Oct	Bristol C	A	W	2-0	
29 Oct	Birmingham C	H	D	1-1	Heeley for Price
5 Nov	Manchester U	A	W	2-1	
12 Nov	Coventry C	H	D	1-1	
19 Nov	Newcastle U	A	W	2-1	
26 Nov	Derby Co	H	L	1-3	
3 Dec	Middlesbrough	A	W	1-0	
10 Dec	Leeds U	H	D	1-1	
17 Dec	Coventry C	A	W	2-1	
26 Dec	Chelsea	H	W	3-0	Simpson for Stapleton
27 Dec	WBA	A	W	3-1	Simpson for Macdonald
31 Dec	Everton	A	L	0-2	Simpson for Heeley
2 Jan	Ipswich T	H	W	1-0	
14 Jan	Wolverhampton W	H	W	3-1	
21 Jan	Nottingham F	A	L	0-2	
4 Feb	Aston Villa	H	L	0-1	
11 Feb	Leicester C	A	D	1-1	
25 Feb	West Ham U	A	D	2-2	Walford for Rix
28 Feb	Norwich C	H	D	0-0	Heeley for Macdonald
4 Mar	Manchester C	H	W	3-0	Walford for Price
18 Mar	Bristol C	H	W	4-1	Rix for Sunderland
21 Mar	Birmingham C	A	D	1-1	
25 Mar	WBA	H	W	4-0	Rix for Sunderland
27 Mar	Chelsea	A	D	0-0	
1 Apr	Manchester U	H	W	3-1	
11 Apr	QPR	A	L	1-2	Matthews for Young
15 Apr	Newcastle U	H	W	2-1	
22 Apr	Leeds U	A	W	3-1	
25 Apr	Liverpool	A	L	0-1	Matthews for Brady
29 Apr	Middlesbrough	H	W	1-0	
9 May	Derby Co	A	L	0-3	

FA Cup

Date	Opponent				1	2	3	4	5	6	7	8	9	10	11	Notes
7 Jan	Sheffield U (3)	A	W	5-0	Jennings	Rice	Nelson	Price	O'Leary1	Young	Brady	Sunderland	Macdonald2	Stapleton2	Rix	
28 Jan	Wolves (4)	H	W	2-1	..	..	..	..	..	..	..	..1	..1	Hudson	..	
18 Feb	Walsall (5)	H	W	4-1	..	..	..	..	..	..	..	..1	..1	Stapleton2	..	
11 Mar	Wrexham (6)	A	W	3-2	..	..	..	..	..	..1	..	..1	..1	..1	Hudson	
8 Apr	Orient (SF) (at Chelsea)	A	W	3-0	..	..	..	..	..	..	..	Rix1	..2	..	..	
6 May	Ipswich (F) (at Wembley)	A	L	0-1	..	..	..	..	..	..	..	Sunderland	..	..	..	Rix for Brady

Football League Cup

Date	Opponent				1	2	3	4	5	6	7	8	9	10	11	Notes
30 Aug	Manchester U (2)	H	W	3-2	Jennings	Rice	Nelson	Powling	O'Leary	Young	Brady1	Ross	Macdonald2	Stapleton	Rix	
25 Oct	Southampton (3)	H	W	2-0	..	..	..	Price	Young	Simpson	..1	Hudson	..	..1	..	Simpson for O'Leary
29 Nov	Hull C (4)	H	W	5-1	..	..	..	..	O'Leary	Young	..1	Matthews2	..1	..1	..	
18 Jan	Manchester C (5)	A	D	0-0	..	..	..	..	..	..	..	..	..	..	..	
24 Jan	Manchester C (5R)	H	W	1-0	..	..	..	..	..	..	..1	Hudson	..	..1	..	Hudson for Matthews
7 Feb	Liverpool (SF)	A	L	1-2	..	..	..	..	..	..	..	Hudson	..	..	..	
14 Feb	Liverpool (SF)	H	D	0-0	..	..	..	..	..	..	..	..	..1	..	..	

Appearances (Goals)
Brady L 39 (9) – Devine J 3 – Harvey J 1 – Heeley M 4 – Hudson A 17 – Jennings P 42 – Macdonald M 39 (15) – Matthews J 5 – Nelson S 41 (1) – O'Leary D 41 (1) – Powling R 4 (2) – Price D 39 (5) – Rice P 38 (2) – Rix G 39 (2) – Ross T 10 – Simpson P 9 – Stapleton F 39 (13) – Sunderland A 23 (4) – Walford S 5 – Young W 35 (3) – Own goals 3 – Total: 20 players (60)

Position in League Table

	P	W	L	D	F:A	Pts	
Nottingham F	42	25	3	14	69:24	64	1st
Arsenal	42	21	11	10	60:37	52	5th

SEASON 1978–79 FOOTBALL LEAGUE (DIVISION 1)

Date	Opponent				1	2	3	4	5	6	7	8	9	10	11	Notes
19 Aug	Leeds U	H	D	2-2	Jennings	Devine	Nelson	Price	O'Leary	Young	Brady2	Sunderland	Macdonald	Stapleton	Harvey	Kosmina for Price
22 Aug	Manchester C	A	D	1-1	Barron	Rice	..	..	..	..	Devine	..	..1	..	Walford	Walford for Devine
26 Aug	Everton	A	L	0-1	..	..	..	..	..	..	Brady	..	..	..	Devine	Walford for Devine
2 Sep	Q P R	H	W	5-1	Jennings	..	..	..	..	..	..1	..	Walford	..2	Rix2	
9 Sep	Nottingham F	A	L	1-2	..	..	..	..	..	..	..1	..	..	Stapleton1	Heeley	Harvey for O'Leary
16 Sep	Bolton W	H	W	1-0	..	..	..	..	Walford	..	..	..	..	Heeley	Walford	Heeley for Walford
23 Sep	Manchester U	H	D	1-1	..	..	..	..1	O'Leary	..	..	..	..	Walford	Devine	Walford1 for Devine
30 Sep	Middlesbrough	A	W	3-2	..	..	..	..1	..1	..	..	..	..1	Walford	..	
7 Oct	Aston Villa	H	D	1-1	..	..	..	..	..	..	..	..	..	..	..	Stead for Sunderland
14 Oct	Wolverhampton W	A	L	0-1	..	..	..	Stead	Gatting	..	..1	Heeley	..	Heeley	..	
21 Oct	Southampton	H	W	1-0	..	..	..	Price	O'Leary	..	..2	Gatting	..	Gatting	..	Walford for O'Leary
28 Oct	Bristol C	A	W	3-1	..	..	..1	..	..	..	..	Sunderland	..3	Heeley	..	
4 Nov	Ipswich T	H	W	4-1	..	..	..	..	..	..	..2	..	..	..1	..	
11 Nov	Leeds U	A	W	1-0	..	..	..	..	..	..	..	..	..	..	..	
18 Nov	Everton	H	D	2-2	..	..	..	..	..	..	..	..	..	Walford	..	Heeley for Price
25 Nov	Coventry C	A	D	1-1	..	..	..1	..	..	..	..	..	..	Gatting	..	
2 Dec	Liverpool	H	W	1-0	..	..	..	..	..	..	..	..	..	..	..	Walford for Nelson
9 Dec	Norwich C	A	D	0-0	..	..	Walford	..	..	..	..	..	..1	..	..	
16 Dec	Derby Co	H	W	2-0	..	..	Walford	..1	..	..	..	..	..1	..	..	
23 Dec	Tottenham H	A	W	5-0	..	..	..	..	..	..	..1	..3	..1	..	..	
26 Dec	W B A	H	L	1-2	..	..1	..	..	..	..	..1	..	..	..	..	
30 Dec	Birmingham C	H	W	3-1	..	..1	..	..	..	..	..1	..	..1	Price1	..	
13 Jan	Nottingham F	H	W	2-1	..	Walford	Nelson	Talbot	..	..	..1	..	..1	..	..	
3 Feb	Manchester U	A	W	2-0	..	Rice	..	..	..	..	..2	..	..	..	..	
10 Feb	Middlesbrough	H	D	0-0	..	..	..	..	..	..	..	..	..	..	..	
13 Feb	Q P R	A	W	2-1	..	..	..	..	..	..	..1	..	..1	..	..	Walford for Young
24 Feb	Wolverhampton W	H	L	0-1	..	..	Gatting	..	Walford	..	..	..	..	..	..	Heeley for Gatting
3 Mar	Southampton	A	L	0-2	..	..	Nelson	..	..	..	Gatting	..1	..	..1		McDermott for Heeley
10 Mar	Bristol C	H	W	2-0	..	..	..	..	..	..	Heeley	..	..	..	..	Gatting for Price
17 Mar	Ipswich T	A	L	0-2	..	..	..	..	..	..	Sunderland	..	..	..		McDermot for Young
24 Mar	Manchester C	H	D	1-1	..	..	..	..	Young	Heeley	..1	..	..1	..		Heeley1 for Talbot
26 Mar	Bolton W	A	L	2-4	..	..	..	..	Walford	Gatting	..	..	Heeley	..		Walford for Heeley
3 Apr	Coventry C	A	L	0-3	..	..	Walford	..	Young	..	..	..	Price	..		Brignall for Stapleton
7 Apr	Liverpool	H	W	1-0	..	..	..	..	..	..	Brady	..	..1	..		
10 Apr	Tottenham H	A	D	1-1	..	..	Nelson	..	Walford	..	..1	..	..	..		Gatting for Rix
14 Apr	W B A	H	W	5-2	..	..	..	..	..1	..	..	..1	..2	..1		
16 Apr	Chelsea	H	W	5-2	..	..	Walford	..	Gatting	Young	..1		..	..		
21 Apr	Derby Co	A	L	0-2	..	..		..		Devine		..	..1			
25 Apr	Aston Villa	A	L	1-5	..	..		..		Walford1		..				
28 Apr	Norwich C	H	D	1-1	..	Devine	Nelson	..	..	Young	O'Leary	..				Walford for Barron-Price in goal
5 May	Birmingham C	A	D	0-0	Barron	Rice	..	..	O'Leary	Young	..	Vaessen	Macdonald1	Devine		
14 May	Chelsea	A	D	1-1	Jennings	..	..	..	..	..	..					

FA Cup

Date	Opponent				1	2	3	4	5	6	7	8	9	10	11	Notes
6 Jan	Sheffield W (3)	A	D	1-1	Jennings	Rice	Walford	Price	O'Leary	Young	Brady	Sunderland1	Stapleton	Gatting	Rix	
9 Jan	Sheffield W (3R)	H	D	1-1	..	..	Nelson	..	..	..	..1	..	..	..	..	
15 Jan	Sheffield W (3R) (at Leicester)		D	2-2												
17 Jan	Sheffield W (3R) (at Leicester)		D	3-3	Jennings	Rice	Nelson	Price	O'Leary	Young1	Brady	Sunderland	Stapleton2	Gatting	Rix	
22 Jan	Sheffield W (3R) (at Leicester)		W	2-0	..	..	..	..	..	..	..	..	..1	..1	..	Walford for Nelson
27 Jan	Notts County (4)	H	W	2-0	..	..	..	Talbot1	..1	..	..	..	..	Price	..	
26 Feb	Nottingham F (5)	A	W	1-0	..	..	..	..	Walford	..	..	..	..	..1	..	Walford for Price
19 Mar	Southampton (6)	A	D	1-1	..	..	..	..	Young	..	..	..	..2	..1	..	Walford for Brady
21 Mar	Southampton (6R)	H	W	2-0	..	..	..	..	..	..	..	..	..	..	..	
31 Mar	Wolves (SF) (at Aston Villa)		W	2-0	..	..	..	..	..	Gatting	..	..1	..	..	..	
12 May	Manchester U (F) (at Wembley)		W	3-2	..	..	..	..	..	..	Brady	..1	..1	..	..	Walford for Price

Football League Cup

Date	Opponent				1	2	3	4	5	6	7	8	9	10	11	Notes
29 Aug	Rotherham U (2)	A	L	1-3	Jennings	Rice	Nelson	Price	O'Leary	Young	Brady	Sunderland	Macdonald	Stapleton1	Rix	

UEFA Cup

Date	Opponent				1	2	3	4	5	6	7	8	9	10	11	Notes
13 Sep	L'motive Leipzig (1)	H	W	3-0	Jennings	Rice	Nelson	Price	Walford	Young	Brady	Sunderland1	Stapleton2	Harvey	Rix	Gatting for Brady, Heeley for Harvey
27 Sep	L'motive Leipzig (1)	A	W	4-1	..	..	..	..	O'Leary	..	..1	..	..2	Devine	..	Vaessen for Price, Walford for Young
18 Oct	Hajduk Split (2)	A	L	1-2	..	..	..	..	..	..	..1	Heeley	..	Kosmina	..	
1 Nov	Hajduk Split (2)	H	W	1-0	..	..	..	..	..	..1	..	Gatting	..	Heeley	..	Kosmina for Heeley, Vaessen for Kosmina
22 Nov	Red Star B'grade (3)	A	L	0-1	..	..	..	..	..	..	Heeley	Sunderland	..	Walford	..	
6 Dec	Red Star B'grade (3)	H	D	1-1	..	..	..	..	..	..	..	..	..1	..	Gatting	Kosmina for Heeley, Macdonald for Rix

Appearances (Goals)
Barron P 3 – Brady L 37 (13) – Brignall S 1 – Devine J 7 – Gatting S 21 (1) – Harvey J 1 – Heeley M 10 (1) – Jennings P 39 – Kosmina A 1 – McDermott B 2 – Macdonald M 4 (2) – Nelson S 33 (2) – O'Leary D 37 (2) – Price D 39 (8) – Rice P 39 (1) – Rix G 39 (3) – Stapleton F 41 (17) – Stead K 2 – Sunderland A 37 (9) – Talbot B 20 – Vaessen P 1 – Walford S 33 (2) – Young W 33 – **Total: 23 players (61)**

Position in League Table

	P	W	L	D	F:A	Pts	
Liverpool	42	30	4	8	85:16	68	1st
Arsenal	42	17	11	14	61:48	48	7th

SEASON 1979–80 FOOTBALL LEAGUE (DIVISION 1)

Date	Opponent				1	2	3	4	5	6	7	8	9	10	11	Notes
18 Aug	Brighton & HA	A	W	4-0	Jennings	Rice	Nelson	Talbot	O'Leary	Young	Brady1	Sunderland2	Stapleton1	Price	Rix	Hollins for Brady
21 Aug	Ipswich T	H	L	0-2	..	..	..	..	..	..	..	..	..	..	..	Hollins for Price
25 Aug	Manchester U	H	D	0-0	..	..	..	..	..	..	Gatting	..	..	Hollins	..	Walford for Gatting
1 Sep	Leeds U	A	D	1-1	..	..	..1	..	..	..	..	..	..	..	..	
8 Sep	Derby Co	A	L	2-3	..	..	..	..	..	..	Brady	..1	..1	..	..	
15 Sep	Middlesbrough	H	W	2-0	..	..	..	..	..	..	..	..	..	..1	..1	
22 Sep	Aston Villa	A	D	0-0	Barron	..	..	..	..	..	..	..	..	..	..	

29 Sep	Wolverhampton W	H	L	2-3	Jennings	..	..	..	Walford	..	..	..	..1	..1	..	Price for Talbot
6 Oct	Manchester C	H	D	0-0	..	..	..	..	O'Leary	..	..	..	..	..	..	
9 Oct	Ipswich T	A	W	2-1	..	Walford	..	..	..	..	..	..1	..	..	..1	
13 Oct	Bolton W	A	D	0-0	..	Rice	..	..	..	..	..	..	..	..	..	
20 Oct	Stoke C	H	D	0-0	..	..	..	..	..	..	..	..	..	..	..	
27 Oct	Bristol C	A	W	1-0	..	..	..	..	..	..	..	..1	..	..	..	
3 Nov	Brighton & HA	H	W	3-0	..	Devine	..	..	..	..	..1	..1	..	..	..1	Gatting for Sunderland
10 Nov	Crystal Palace	A	L	0-1	..	..	..	..	..	..	..	Gatting	..	Price	..	Walford for Devine
17 Nov	Everton	H	W	2-0	..	..	..	..	..	..	..	Vaessen	..2	..	..	Gatting for Brady
24 Nov	Liverpool	H	D	0-0	..	..	..	..	..	..	Gatting	Sunderland	..	..	..	
1 Dec	Nottingham F	A	D	1-1	..	..	..	..	..	Walford	..	..	..1	..	..	
8 Dec	Coventry C	H	W	3-1	..	..	..	..	..1	..	Brady	..1	..1	Hollins	..	Gatting for Nelson
15 Dec	W B A	A	D	2-2	..	..	..1	..	..	..	..	..	..1	..	..	
21 Dec	Norwich C	H	D	1-1	..	..	..	..	..	..	..	..	..1	..	..	McDermott for Nelson
26 Dec	Tottenham H	H	W	1-0	..	..	Rice	..	..	Young	..	..1	..	..	..	
29 Dec	Manchester U	A	L	0-3	..	..	..	..	..	..	..	..	..	..	..	Walford for O'Leary
1 Jan	Southampton	A	W	1-0	..	..	..	..	Walford	..1	Gatting	..	..	..	..	
12 Jan	Leeds U	H	L	0-1	..	Rice	Nelson	..	..	..	Brady	..	..	..	..	
19 Jan	Derby Co	H	W	2-0	..	..	..	..	..	..1	..1	..	..	Price	..	
9 Feb	Aston Villa	H	W	3-1	..	..	..	..	O'Leary	..	..	..2	..	..	..1	
23 Feb	Bolton W	H	W	2-0	..	..	..	..	..	..1	..	..	..1	..	..	Vaessen for Rice
1 Mar	Stoke C	A	W	3-2	..	Devine	..	..	..	..	..1	..1	..	..1	..	
11 Mar	Bristol C	H	D	0-0	..	..	..	..	..	..	..	Vaessen	..	..	..	
15 Mar	Manchester C	A	W	3-0	..	..	..	..	..	..	..2	..	..1	..	..	Gatting for Stapleton
22 Mar	Crystal Palace	H	D	1-1	..	..	..	..	..	..	..1	Sunderland	..	..	..	
28 Mar	Everton	A	W	1-0	Barron	Rice	..	..	..	..	Gatting1	..	Vaessen	..	..	
2 Apr	Norwich C	A	D	1-2	Jennings	Devine	..	..	..	..	Brady	..	Stapleton	..	..1	Vaessen for Nelson
5 Apr	Southampton	H	D	1-1	..	..	Walford	..	..	..	..	..1	..	..	..	Vaessen for Price
7 Apr	Tottenham H	A	W	2-1	Barron	Rice	..	..	..	..	..	Devine	Vaessen1	Hollins	Davis	Sunderland1 for Brady
19 Apr	Liverpool	A	D	1-1	Jennings	..	..	..1	..	..	Gatting	Sunderland	Stapleton	Price	Hollins	Vaessen for Stapleton
26 Apr	W B A	H	D	1-1	Barron	..	Devine	..	Walford	..	Brady	..	..1	Hollins	Vaessen	Gatting for Young
3 May	Coventry C	A	W	1-0	..	..	Nelson	..	..	..	Gatting	..	Vaessen1	Price	Hollins	Davis for Price
5 May	Nottingham F	H	D	0-0	Jennings	Devine	..	..	O'Leary	..	Brady	Vaessen	Stapleton	..	Rix	Hollins for Stapleton
16 May	Wolverhampton W	A	W	2-1	..	Rice	..	..	Walford1	..	..	Sunderland	..1	..	..	Vaessen for Price
19 May	Middlesbrough	A	L	0-5	..	..	..	..	..	..	..	..	..	..	..	Vaessen for Walford

FA Cup

5 Jan	Cardiff C (3)	A	D	0-0	Jennings	Rice	Devine	Talbot	Walford	Young	Gatting	Sunderland	Stapleton	Hollins	Rix	
8 Jan	Cardiff C (3R)	H	W	2-1	..	..	Nelson	..	..	..	..	..2	..	..	..	
26 Jan	Brighton & HA (4)	H	W	2-0	..	..	..1	..1	O'Leary	..	Brady	..	..	Price	..	
5 Feb	Bolton W (5)	A	D	1-1	..	..	..	..	..	..	..	..	..1	..	..	
19 Feb	Bolton W (5R)	H	W	3-0	..	..	..	..	..	..	..	..2	..1	..	..	
8 Mar	Watford (6)	A	W	2-1	..	Devine	..	..	..	..	..	..	..2	..	..	Gatting for Sunderland
12 Apr	Liverpool (SF) (at Sheffield W)		D	0-0	..	Rice	..	..	..	..	..	..	..	..	..	Walford for Nelson
16 Apr	Liverpool (SFR) (at Aston Villa)		D	1-1	..	..	Walford	..	..	..	..	..1	..	..	..	
28 Apr	Liverpool (SFR) (at Aston Villa)		D	1-1	..	..	Devine	..	..	..	..	..1	..	..	..	
1 May	Liverpool (SFR) (at Coventry)		W	1-0	..	..	..	..1	..	..	..	..	..	..	..	
10 May	West Ham U (F) (at Wembley)		L	0-1	..	..	..	..	..	..	..	..	..	..	..	Nelson for Devine

Football League Cup

29 Aug	Leeds (2)	A	D	1-1	Jennings	Rice	Nelson	Talbot	O'Leary	Young	Brady	Sunderland	Stapleton1	Hollins	Rix	
4 Sep	Leeds (2R)	H	W	7-0	..	..	..1	..	..	..	..2	..3	..1	..	..	
25 Sep	Southampton (3)	H	W	2-1	..	..	..	..	Walford	..	..1	..	..1	..	..	
30 Oct	Brighton & HA (4)	A	D	0-0	..	..	..	..	O'Leary	..	..	..	..	..	..	Gatting for Rice
13 Nov	Brighton & HA (4R)	H	W	4-0	..	Devine	..	..	..	..	..	Vaessen2	..2	Price	..	
4 Dec	Swindon T (5)	H	D	1-1	..	..	..	..	..	Walford	Gatting	Sunderland1	..	..	..	Hollins for Price
11 Dec	Swindon T (5R)	A	L	3-4	..	..	Walford	..1	..	Young	Brady2	..	..	Hollins	..	

FA Charity Shield

11 Aug	Liverpool (at Wembley)		L	1-3	Jennings	Rice	Nelson	Talbot	O'Leary	Walford	Brady	Sunderland1	Stapleton	Price	Rix	Young for Nelson, Hollins for Price

European Cup-Winners Cup

19 Sep	Fenerbahce (1)	H	W	2-0	Jennings	Rice	Nelson	Talbot	O'Leary	Young1	Brady	Sunderland1	Stapleton	Hollins	Rix	
3 Oct	Fenerbahce (1)	A	D	0-0	..	..	..	..	..	..	..	..	..	..	..	
24 Oct	Magdeburg (2)	H	W	2-1	..	..	..	..	..	..1	..	..1	..	..	..	
7 Nov	Magdeburg (2)	A	D	2-2	..	Devine	..	..	..	..	..1	Gatting	..	..	..	Price1 for Hollins, Walford for Nelson
5 Mar	IFK Gothenburg (3)	H	W	5-1	..	..	..	..	..	..1	..1	Sunderland2	..	Price1	..	Hollins for Brady, McDermott for Sunderland
19 Mar	IFK Gothenburg (3)	A	D	0-0	..	..	..	..	..	..	..	Vaessen	..	..	..	
9 Apr	Juventus (SF)	H	D	1-1	..	..	Walford	..	*opponents*	..	..	Sunderland	..	..	..	Vaessen for Devine, Rice for O'Leary
23 Apr	Juventus (SF)	A	W	1-0	..	Rice	Devine	..	..	..	..	..	..	..	..	Vaessen1 for Price, Hollins for Talbot
14 May	Valencia (F) (at Brussels)		D	0-0*	..	..	Nelson	..	..	..	..	..	..	..	..	Hollins for Price

*lost 4-5 on penalties

Appearances (Goals)

Barron P 5 – Brady L 34 (7) – Davis P 2 – Devine J 20 – Gatting S 14 (1) – Hollins J 26 (1) – Jennings P 37 – McDermott B 1 – Nelson S 35 (2) – O'Leary D 34 (1) – Price D 22 (1) – Rice P 26 – Rix G 38 (4) – Stapleton F 39 (14) – Sunderland A 37 (14) – Talbot B 42 (1) – Vaessen P 14 (2) – Walford S 19 (1) – Young W 38 (3) – **Total 19 players 52**

Position in League Table

	P	W	L	D	F:A	Pts	
Liverpool	42	25	7	10	81:30	60	1st
Arsenal	42	18	7	17	52:36	52	4th

SEASON 1980–81 FOOTBALL LEAGUE (DIVISION 1)

16 Aug	W B A	A	W	1-0	Jennings	Devine	Sansom	Talbot	O'Leary	Young	Vaessen	Price	Stapleton1	Hollins	Rix	
19 Aug	Southampton	H	D	1-1	..	..	..	..	..	..	Hollins	Vaessen	Price	Stapleton1	..	McDermott for Talbot
23 Aug	Coventry C	A	L	1-3	..	..	..	..	..	..	..	Sunderland	Stapleton1	Price	..	Rice for Price
30 Aug	Tottenham H	H	W	2-0	..	..	..	..	..	..	..	..	..1	..1	..	
6 Sep	Manchester C	A	D	1-1	..	..	..	..	..	..1	..	..	..	..	..	
13 Sep	Stoke C	H	W	2-0	..	..	..1	..	..	..	..1	..	..	..	..	
20 Sep	Middlesbrough	A	L	1-2	Wood	..	..	..	..	..	..	..	..	..	..1	
27 Sep	Nottingham F	H	W	1-0	..	..	..	..	..	..	..	..	..	Gatting	..1	
4 Oct	Leicester C	H	W	1-0	..	..	..	..	Walford	..	..	..	..1	..	..	
7 Oct	Birmingham C	A	L	1-3	..	..	..	..	..	..	..	..1	..	..	..	
11 Oct	Manchester U	A	D	0-0	..	..	..	..	..	..	..	..	..	..	..	
18 Oct	Sunderland	H	D	2-2	..	..	..	..	..	..1	..	..	..	..1	..	McDermott for Talbot
21 Oct	Norwich C	H	W	3-1	..	..	..1	..1	..	..	..	..	..	..	..	McDermott1 for Hollins
25 Oct	Liverpool	A	D	1-1	..	..	..	..	..	..	..	..1	..	Price	..	Rice for Price
1 Nov	Brighton & HA	H	W	2-0	..	..	..	..	..	..	..	..	..	McDermott1	..1	
8 Nov	Leeds U	A	W	5-0	..	..	..	..1	..	..	..2	..1	Gatting1	..	..	
11 Nov	Southampton	A	L	1-3	..	..	..	..	..	..	..	..	McDermott	Gatting	..1	Price for Gatting
15 Nov	W B A	H	D	2-2	Jennings	..	..	..	O'Leary	..	*opponents*	..1	Stapleton	..	..	
22 Nov	Everton	H	W	2-1	..	..	..	..	..	Walford	..	..	..1	McDermott1	..	Gatting for Sanson
29 Nov	Aston Villa	A	D	1-1	..	..	..	..1	Walford	Young	..	..	..	Gatting	..	
6 Dec	Wolverhampton W	H	D	1-1	..	..	..	..	..	..	..	McDermott	..1	..	..	Vaessen for Hollins
13 Dec	Sunderland	A	L	0-2	..	..	..	..	..	..	Price	..	..	..	Davis	Vaessen for Gatting
20 Dec	Manchester U	H	W	2-1	..	..	..	..	..	..	Vaessen1	..	..	..	Rix1	
26 Dec	Crystal Palace	A	D	2-2	..	..	..	..	..	..	Hollins	Vaessen	..1	McDermott1	..	
27 Dec	Ipswich T	H	D	1-1	..	..	..	..	..	..	..	Sunderland1	..	Gatting	..	
10 Jan	Everton	A	W	2-1	..	..	..	Davis	..	..	..	Vaessen1	..	..1	McDermott	Price for Hollins
17 Jan	Tottenham H	A	L	0-2	..	..	..	McDermott	..	..	..	Sunderland	..	..	Rix	
31 Jan	Coventry C	H	D	2-2	..	Hollins	..	Talbot1	..	..	McDermott	..	..1	..	..	
7 Feb	Stoke C	A	D	1-1	..	..	..	..	O'Leary	..	..	..	..1	..	..	

Date	Opponent	V	R	Score											Notes
21 Feb	Nottingham F	A	L	1-3	..		Devine		..1		..		Hollins	..1	..1	..	Devine for Gatting
24 Feb	Manchester C	H	W	2-0	..							Walford	..1		..1		McDermott for Sunderland
28 Feb	Middlesbrough	H	D	2-2							Young			..		Price for Hollins
7 Mar	Leicester C	A	L	0-1					..1				Nicholas		McDermott	..	
21 Mar	Norwich C	A	D	1-1								Hollins	..1		Nicholas		
28 Mar	Liverpool	H	W	1-0						..1		Davis		..1			Davis for Hollins
31 Mar	Birmingham C	H	W	2-1											Hollins1		McDermott for Devine
4 Apr	Brighton & HA	A	W	1-0								Hollins			Nicholas	Davis	McDermott for Hollins
11 Apr	Leeds U	H	D	0-0				..1							..1		
18 Apr	Ipswich T	A	W	2-0						..1						..1	McDermott for Sunderland
20 Apr	Crystal Palace	H	W	3-2				..1		..1							
25 Apr	Wolverhampton W	A	W	2-1								opponents	McDermott	..1			
2 May	Aston Villa	H	W	2-0			Hollins			..1		McDermott1	Sunderland	..			Nelson for Talbot

FA Cup

3 Jan	Everton (3)	A	L	0-2	Jennings	Devine	Sansom	Talbot	O'Leary	Young	Hollins	Sunderland	Stapleton	Gatting	Rix	McDermott for Talbot

Football League Cup

26 Aug	Swansea (2)	A	D	1-1	Jennings	Devine	Sansom	Talbot	O'Leary	Young	Hollins	Sunderland	Stapleton1	Price	Rix	
2 Sep	Swansea (2R)	H	W	3-1	..				Walford1		..1	..1				
22 Sep	Stockport Co (3)	A	W	3-1	Wood				O'Leary		..1	..1				
4 Nov	Tottenham H (4)	A	L	0-1	..				Walford					Gatting		McDermott for Hollins

Appearances (Goals)
Davis P 10 (1) — Devine J 43 — Gatting S 24 (3) — Hollins J 44 (8) — Jennings P 38 — McDermott B 29 (6) — Meade 2 (1) — Nelson S 1 — Nicholas P 12 (1) — O'Leary D 31 (1) — Price D 14 (1) — Rice P 2 — Rix G 41 (6) — Sansom K 51 (3) — Stapleton F 45 (15) — Sunderland A 43 (9) — Talbot B 49 (8) — Vaessen P 9 (2) — Walford S 22 — Whyte 2 — Wood G 13 — Young W 48 (4) — Own goals 2 — **Total 22 players (61)**

Position in League Table

	P	W	L	D	F:A	Pts	
Aston Villa	42	26	8	8	72:40	60	1st
Arsenal	42	19	8	15	61:45	53	3rd

SEASON 1981–82 FOOTBALL LEAGUE (DIVISION 1)

Date	Opponent	V	R	Score											Notes
29 Aug	Stoke C	H	L	0-1	Jennings	Devine	Sansom	Talbot	O'Leary	Young	Davis	Sunderland	McDermott	Nicholas	Rix	Vaessen for Devine
2 Sep	WBA	A	W	2-0	..			..1				..1				Davis for Nicholas
5 Sep	Liverpool	A	L	0-2							Hollins					
12 Sep	Sunderland	H	D	1-1		Hollins					Davis	..1				
19 Sep	Leeds U	A	D	0-0												Devine for Nicholas
22 Sep	Birmingham C	H	W	1-0		Devine		..1						Hollins		
26 Sep	Manchester U	H	D	0-0							Hollins		Hawley	Nicholas	Davis	
3 Oct	Notts Co	A	L	1-2		Hollins					Davis		..1		Rix	McDermott for Hawley
10 Oct	Swansea C	A	L	0-2		Devine									Hollins	
17 Oct	Manchester C	H	W	1-0		Hollins				Whyte	McDermott		Meade1		Rix	
24 Oct	Ipswich T	A	L	1-2						Young	Davis	..1				
31 Oct	Coventry C	H	W	1-0					opponents	Whyte	McDermott	Vaessen	Hawley			
7 Nov	Aston Villa	A	W	2-0		Devine		..1			Hollins		Davis		..1	
21 Nov	Nottingham F	A	W	2-1				..1				Sunderland1				
28 Nov	Everton	H	W	1-0												McDermott for Devine
5 Dec	West Ham U	A	W	2-1	..	Robson				..1	..1					
20 Jan	Stoke C	A	W	1-0	Wood							..1				
23 Jan	Southampton	A	L	1-3					..1		McDermott					McDermott for O'Leary
26 Jan	Brighton & HA	H	D	0-0					Hollins		McDermott					Meade for Davis
30 Jan	Leeds U	H	W	1-0		Hollins			O'Leary		Vaessen1					
2 Feb	Wolverhampton W	H	W	2-1							..1				..1	Hawley for Sunderland
6 Feb	Sunderland	A	D	0-0												
13 Feb	Notts Co	H	W	1-0												Meade1 for Nicholas
16 Feb	Middlesbrough	H	D	1-1											..1	Meade for Nicholas
20 Feb	Manchester U	A	D	0-0												Meade for Vaessen
27 Feb	Swansea C	H	L	0-2												Meade for Vaessen
6 Mar	Manchester C	A	D	0-0							Gorman			Robson		
13 Mar	Ipswich T	H	W	1-0										..1		
16 Mar	WBA	H	D	2-2								..1				Meade1 for Gorman
20 Mar	Coventry C	A	L	0-1					Devine							Meade for Gorman
27 Mar	Aston Villa	H	W	4-3					O'Leary		Meade1	..1			..2	
29 Mar	Tottenham H	A	D	2-2								..2				Nicholas for Davis
3 Apr	Wolverhampton W	A	D	1-1									..1			Hawley for Meade
10 Apr	Brighton & HA	A	L	1-2				..1							Nicholas	
12 Apr	Tottenham H	H	L	1-3								Hawley1	Nicholas		Rix	McDermott for Robson
17 Apr	Nottingham F	H	W	2-0				..1					Davis		..1	
24 Apr	Everton	A	L	1-2							Hawley	Sunderland			..1	Nicholas for Hollins
1 May	West Ham U	H	W	2-0											..1	
4 May	Birmingham C	H	W	1-0						..1						
8 May	Middlesbrough	A	W	3-1				..1					..1		..1	Nicholas for Davis
11 May	Liverpool	H	D	1-1							Nicholas	..1	Hawley			Meade for Hawley
15 May	Southampton	H	W	4-1							Davis2			..1		

FA Cup

2 Jan	Tottenham Hotspur (3)	A	L	0-1	Jennings	Robson	Sansom	Talbot	O'Leary	Whyte	Hollins	Sunderland	Rix	Nicholas	Davis	

League Cup

6 Oct	Sheffield United (2)	A	L	0-1	Jennings	Devine	Sansom	Talbot	O'Leary	Young	Rix	Sunderland	Hawley	Nicholas	Davis	
27 Oct	Sheffield United (2R)	H	W	2-1	Jennings	Hollins	Sansom	Talbot	O'Leary	Young 1	McDermott	Sunderland 1	Meade	Nicholas	Rix	
10 Nov	Norwich City (3)	H	W	1-0	Jennings	Hollins	Sansom	Talbot	O'Leary	Whyte	McDermott	Sunderland	Davis	Nicholas	Rix	
1 Dec	Liverpool (4)	H	D	0-0	Jennings	Hollins	Sansom	Talbot	O'Leary	Whyte	McDermott	Sunderland	Davis	Nicholas	Rix	Hankin for McDermott
8 Dec	Liverpool (4R)	A	L	0-3	Woods	Robson	Sansom	Talbot	O'Leary	Whyte	Hollins	Sunderland	Davis	Nicholas	Rix	Hankin for Nicholas

UEFA Cup

16 Sep	Panathinaikos (1)	A	W	2-0	Jennings	Hollins	Sansom	Talbot	O'Leary	Young	Davis	Vaessen	McDermott1	Nicholas	Rix	Meade1 for Vaessen
30 Sep	Panathinaikos (1)	H	W	1-0	..	Devine		..1			Hollins	Sunderland				Whyte for O'Leary
20 Oct	KFC Winterslag (2)	A	L	0-1	..								Meade			McDermott for Meade
3 Nov	KFC Winterslag (2)	H	W	2-1						Whyte	McDermott	Vaessen			..1	Davis for Vaessen

Appearances (Goals)
Davis P 38 (4) — Devine J 11 — Gorman P 4 — Hawley J 14 (3) — Hollins J 40 (1) — Jennings P 16 — McDermott 13 (1) — Meade R 16 (4) — Nicholas P 31 — O'Leary D 40 (1) — Rix G 39 (9) — Robson S 20 (2) — Sansom K 42 — Sunderland A 38 (11) — Talbot B 42 (7) — Vaessen P 10 (2) — Whyte C 32 (2) — Wood G 26 — Young W 10 — Own goals 1 — **Total 19 players (48)**

Position in League Table

	P	W	L	D	F:A	Pts	
Liverpool	42	26	7	9	80:32	87	1st
Arsenal	42	20	11	11	48:37	71	5th

SEASON 1982–83 FOOTBALL LEAGUE (DIVISION 1)

Date	Opponent	V	R	Score											Notes
28 Aug	Stoke C	A	L	1-2	Wood	Hollins	Sansom	Talbot	O'Leary	Whyte	Robson	Sunderland1	Chapman	Woodcock	Rix	Davis for Sunderland
31 Aug	Norwich C	H	D	1-1	..				Davis					..1		Devine for Sansom
4 Sep	Liverpool	H	L	0-2			Devine		O'Leary			Davis				
7 Sep	Brighton & HA	A	L	0-1												Hawley for Talbot
11 Sep	Coventry C	A	W	2-0			Sansom				Davis	Robson	..1	..1		
18 Sep	Notts Co	H	W	2-0			..1						..1		..1	
25 Sep	Manchester U	A	D	0-0												
2 Oct	West Ham U	H	L	2-3				..1				Sunderland				
9 Oct	Ipswich T	A	W	1-0									Robson	..1		Hawley for Hollins
16 Oct	WBA	A	W	2-1		Devine						..1		..1		
23 Oct	Nottingham F	A	L	0-3		Hollins										Chapman for Robson
30 Oct	Birmingham C	H	D	0-0		O'Shea										Chapman for Woodcock
6 Nov	Luton T	A	D	2-2				..1							..1	
13 Nov	Everton	H	D	1-1	Jennings							Chapman				McDermott1 for O'Leary
20 Nov	Swansea C	A	W	2-1	Wood							Sunderland		..1		Chapman1 for Woodcock
27 Nov	Watford	H	L	2-4				..1						..1		

Date	Opponent	V	R	Score											Notes
4 Dec	Manchester C	A	L	1-2	..	..	..	..	..	..	..	Chapman	Robson	..	McDermott1 for O'Shea
7 Dec	Aston Villa	H	W	2-1	Jennings	Hollins	..	..	..	..1	..	..	Robson	Woodcock1	..
18 Dec	Sunderland	A	L	0-3	..	..	..	..	..	..	..	..	..	..	Chapman for Davis
27 Dec	Tottenham H	H	W	2-0	..	..	..	Robson	..	..	..1	Nicholas	..1	..	
28 Dec	Southampton	A	D	2-2	..	..	..	..	..	..1	Petrovic	..1	..		Chapman1 for Woodcock
1 Jan	Swansea C	H	W	2-1	..	..	..	..	..	Nicholas	Chapman	..	..1		Chapman for Sunderland
3 Jan	Liverpool	A	L	1-3	..	..1	..	..1	..						
15 Jan	Stoke C	H	W	3-0	..1	..	Whyte	..	Nicholas	Davis	Sunderland	..1	..	..1	Talbot for O'Leary
22 Jan	Notts Co	A	L	0-1	Robson										Talbot for Davis
5 Feb	Brighton & HA	H	W	3-1	..	..	..	..	..	Talbot	Meade2	..	Davis	..1	
26 Feb	W B A	A	D	0-0	Key	..	Whyte	..	Devine	Davis	Meade	Woodcock	..		Talbot for Rix
5 Mar	Nottingham F	H	D	0-0	Hollins	..	..	Talbot	Sunderland						Meade for Sunderland
15 Mar	Birmingham C	A	L	1-2	..	..	Petrovic	..1							Talbot for Petrovic
19 Mar	Luton T	H	W	4-1	O'Leary	..	Talbot	..1	..	..3					Meade for O'Leary
22 Mar	Ipswich T	H	D	2-2	Wood	Hollins	..	Devine	..1	..	..1	..	..1		
26 Mar	Everton	A	W	3-2	Robson1	..	Whyte	O'Leary	..	..1	..	..1			
2 Apr	Southampton	H	D	0-0	Kay	..									
4 Apr	Tottenham H	A	L	0-5	Robson	..									
9 Apr	Coventry C	H	W	2-1	..	Kay	..	Petrovic	..						Petrovic for Whyte; Chapman for Nicholas
20 Apr	Norwich C	A	L	1-3	Kay	..	Talbot	O'Leary	Whyte	McDermott	Hill	Davis1	Chapman		Hollins for Rix
23 Apr	Manchester C	H	W	3-0	Jennings	..	Whyte	..	Nicholas	Talbot3	Davis	McDermott	Woodcock	Hill	Hawley for Woodcock
30 Apr	Watford	A	L	1-2	..	..1	Hawley								Petrovic for Hawley
2 May	Manchester U	H	W	3-0	Devine	..	..1	..	..2						Petrovic for Hawley
7 May	Sunderland	H	L	0-1	..	..	Petrovic	McDermott	..						Hawley for Devine
10 May	West Ham U	A	W	3-1	Kay	..1	..	..1	..						
14 May	Aston Villa	A	L	1-2	Devine	..1	..	McDermott	Petrovic	..					

FA Cup

Date	Opponent	V	R	Score											Notes
8 Jan	Bolton W (3)	H	W	2-1	Jennings	Hollins	Sansom	Talbot	O'Leary	Robson	Davis1	Sunderland	Nicholas	Woodcock	Rix1
29 Jan	Leeds U (4)	H	D	1-1	Robson	..	..	Nicholas	Talbot	..1	Petrovic				
2 Feb	Leeds U (4R)	A	D	1-1	..	..	..	..	..1						Davis for Sunderland
9 Feb	Leeds U (4R)	H	W	2-1	..	..	..	Meade	..	..1					
19 Feb	Middlesbrough (5)	A	D	1-1	..	Whyte	..	Davis	..1						
28 Feb	Middlesbrough (5R)	H	W	3-2	..	..	..	..1	..1	Sunderland	..1				
12 Mar	Aston Villa (6)	H	W	2-0	Petrovic1	..	..								
16 Apr	Manchester U (SF) (at Aston Villa)		L	1-2	Wood	Robson	..	Whyte	O'Leary	Hollins	..	Petrovic	..1		Chapman for Robson

Milk Cup

Date	Opponent	V	R	Score											Notes
5 Oct	Cardiff C (2)	H	W	2-1	Wood	Hollins1	Sansom	Talbot	O'Leary	Whyte	Davis1	Sunderland	Robson	Woodcock	Rix
26 Oct	Cardiff C (2)	A	W	3-1	..	..	..1	..1	..1						
9 Nov	Everton (3)	A	D	1-1	Jennings	O'Shea	..	..1							Chapman for Sunderland
23 Nov	Everton (3R)	H	W	3-0	Wood	..	..3	..							Chapman for Sunderland
30 Nov	Huddersfield T (4)	H	W	1-0	..	..									
18 Jan	Sheffield W (5)	H	W	1-0	Jennings	Hollins	Nicholas	Robson	Petrovic	..1					
15 Feb	Manchester U (SF)	H	L	2-4	Robson	..	Nicholas1	Talbot	Meade	..1					Davis for O'Leary
23 Feb	Manchester U (SF)	A	L	1-2	Whyte	..1									Davis for Hollins

UEFA Cup

Date	Opponent	V	R	Score											Notes
14 Sep	Spartak Moscow (1)	A	L	2-3	Wood	Hollins	Sansom	Talbot	O'Leary	Whyte	Davis	Robson1	Chapman1	Woodcock	Rix
29 Sep	Spartak Moscow (1)	H	L	2-5	..	..	..	*opponents*	..	..	..1	..	..	Sunderland for Hollins, McDermott for Davis

Appearances (Goals)
Chapman L 19 (3) – Davis P 41 (4) – Devine J 9 – Hawley J 6 – Hill C 7 – Hollins J 23 (2) – Jennings P 19 – Kay J 7 – McDermott B 9 (4) – Meade R 4 (2) – Nicholas P 21 – O'Leary D 36 (1) – O'Shea D 6 – Petrovic V 13 (2) – Rix G 36 (6) – Robson S 31 (2) – Sansom K 40 – Sunderland A 25 (6) – Talbot B 42 (9) – Whyte C 36 3 – Wood G 23 – Woodcock A 34 (14) – **Total 22 players (58)**

Position in League Table

	P	W	L	D	F:A	Pts	
Liverpool	42	24	8	10	87:37	82	1st
Arsenal	42	16	16	10	58:56	58	10th

SEASON 1983–84 FOOTBALL LEAGUE (DIVISION 1)

Date	Opponent	V	R	Score											Notes
27 Aug	Luton T	H	W	2-1	Jennings	Robson	Sansom	Talbot	O'Leary	Hill	McDermott1	Davis	Woodcock1	Nicholas	Rix
29 Aug	Wolverhampton W	A	W	2-1	..	..	..	..	..	..	..	..	..2	..	
3 Sep	Southampton	A	L	0-1	..	..	..	..	..	..	..	..			Whyte for McDermott
6 Sep	Manchester U	H	L	2-3	..	..	..1	..	..	..	..1				Sunderland for McDermott
10 Sep	Liverpool	H	L	0-2	..	..	..	..	..	Sunderland					
17 Sep	Notts Co	A	W	4-0	Whyte	..	*opponents*	..1	..	..1	Talbot1 for Nicholas
24 Sep	Norwich C	H	W	3-0	..	..	..	..2	Chapman1	..					McDermott for Nicholas
1 Oct	Q P R	A	L	0-2	..										
15 Oct	Coventry C	H	L	0-1											McDermott for Whyte
22 Oct	Nottingham F	H	W	4-1	..1	..	..1	..	Woodcock2	..					McDermott for Nicholas
29 Oct	Aston Villa	A	W	6-2	..	..1	..5	..							McDermott for Robson
5 Nov	Sunderland	H	L	1-2	Adams	..	Talbot	..1	..						McDermott for Sunderland
12 Nov	Ipswich T	A	L	0-1	O'Leary	Davis									Gorman for Sunderland
19 Nov	Everton	H	W	2-1	..1	..	..1	Gorman	McDermott	..					Meade for Sunderland
26 Nov	Leicester C	A	L	0-3	Kay	Davis	Woodcock								Chapman for Rix
3 Dec	W B A	H	L	0-1	Caton	Adams	Hill	Madden	..	..	Allinson	Meade for Robson
10 Dec	West Ham U	A	L	1-3	Hill	Kay	Whyte1	Caton	..						Meade for Hill
17 Dec	Watford	H	W	3-1	Cork	Meade3	..	..							Cork for Robson
26 Dec	Tottenham H	A	W	4-2	Robson	O'Leary	..2	..2							McDermott for Caton
27 Dec	Birmingham C	H	D	1-1	Cork	Whyte	..1								
31 Dec	Southampton	H	D	2-2	..1	O'Leary	..1								
2 Jan	Norwich C	A	D	1-1	..1										
14 Jan	Luton T	A	W	2-1	..	Kay	..1	Talbot	..1	Rix					
21 Jan	Notts Co	H	D	1-1	Adams	..1									McDermott for Adams
28 Jan	Stoke C	A	L	0-1	O'Leary	McDermott	Meade	..							Cork for Meade
4 Feb	Q P R	H	L	0-2											
11 Feb	Liverpool	A	L	1-2	Jennings	Hill	Sansom	Talbot	O'Leary	Caton	Cork	Davis	Woodcock	Nicolas	Rix1	Allinson for Cork
18 Feb	Aston Villa	H	D	1-1	..	Davis	Nicholas	Mariner	Woodcock	..1					
25 Feb	Nottingham F	A	W	1-0	..	..	..1								
3 Mar	Sunderland	A	D	2-2	..1	..1									
10 Mar	Ipswich T	H	W	4-1	..1	..2	..1								Allinson for Rix
17 Mar	Manchester U	A	L	0-4	Robson										
24 Mar	Wolverhampton W	A	W	4-1	..1	..1	..1	..							
31 Mar	Coventry C	A	W	4-1	Sparrow	..1	..	Whyte1	..1	..1	..				Kay for Jennings (Robson in goal)
7 Apr	Stoke C	H	W	3-1	Lukic	Caton	..1	Caton	..1	..					Meade for Nicholas
9 Apr	Everton	A	D	0-0	Sansom										
21 Apr	Tottenham H	H	W	3-2	..1	..1									Davis for Rix
23 Apr	Birmingham C	A	D	1-1	..	..									Davis
28 Apr	Leicester C	H	W	2-1	Jennings	..1	..	Rix	Davis1 for Talbot
5 May	W B A	A	W	3-1	..1	..1									Davis for Robson
7 May	West Ham U	H	D	3-3	..1	..1									Davis for Rix
12 May	Wartford	A	L	1-2	..1	Davis	Meade								

FA Cup

Date	Opponent	V	R	Score											Notes
7 Jan	Middlesbrough (3)	A	L	2-3	Jennings	Hill	Sansom	Cork	O'Leary	Caton	Meade	Davis	Woodcock1	Nicholas1	Rix	Talbot for Cork

Milk Cup

Date	Opponent	V	R	Score											Notes
4 Oct	Plymouth Arg (2)	A	D	1-1	Jennings	Robson	Sansom	Whyte	O'Leary	Hill	Sunderland	Davis	Woodcock	Nicholas	Rix1	Talbot for Woodcock
25 Oct	Plymouth Arg (2)	H	W	1-0	..	..	..	..1	..						
9 Nov	Tottenham H (3)	A	W	2-1	..	..	..	..	..1						
29 Nov	Walsall (4)	H	L	1-2	..1	..	..	Allinson							

Appearances (Goals)
Adams T 3 – Allinson J 9 – Caton T 26 – Chapman L 4 (1) – Cork D 7 (1) – Davis P 35 (1) – Gorman P 2 – Hill C 37 (1) – Jennings P 38 – Kay J 7 – Lukic J 4 – Madden D 2 – Mariner P 15 (7) – Meade R 13 (5) – McDermott B 13 (2) – Nicholas C 41 (11) – O'Leary D 36 – Rix G 34 (4) – Robson S 28 (6) – Sansom K 40 – Sparrow B 2 – Sunderland A 12 (4) – Talbot B 27 (6) – Whyte C 15 (2) – Woodcock A 37 (21) – Own goals 1 – **Total 25 players (74)**

Position in League Table

	P	W	L	D	F:A	Pts	
Liverpool	42	22	6	14	73:32	80	1st
Arsenal	42	18	15	9	74:60	63	6th

SEASON 1984–85 FOOTBALL LEAGUE (DIVISION 1)

Date	Opponent	V	Res	Score	GK	2	3	4	5	6	7	8	9	10	11	Substitutions
25 Aug	Chelsea	H	D	1-1	Jennings	Anderson	Sansom	Talbot	O'Leary	Caton	Robson	Davis	Mariner1	Woodcock	Allison	Allison for Talbot
29 Aug	Nottingham F	A	L	0-2	..	..	..	.1	..	..	..	Nicholas	Davis	.1	Nicholas2	
1 Sep	Watford	A	W	4-3	..	..	.1	.1	..	..	..	Davis	..	.1		
4 Sep	Newcastle U	H	W	2-0	..	..	..	.2	..	..	..	..	..	.1	..	
8 Sep	Liverpool	H	W	3-1	..	..	..	..	..	..	..	Rix	..	..	..	
15 Sep	Ipswich T	A	L	1-2	..	..	.1	..	..	..	..	..	.1	.2	.1	
22 Sep	Stoke C	H	W	4-0	..	..	..	..	..	..	..	..	.1	.1	.1	
29 Sep	Coventry C	A	W	2-1	..	..	.1	..	..	..	..	..	Allison	..	..	Davis for Talbot
6 Oct	Everton	H	W	1-0	..	..	.1	.2	..	..	..	..	..	Davis	..	
13 Oct	Leicester C	H	W	4-1	..	..	.1	.1	..	Hill	..	..	.1	Woodcock1	..	Davis for Woodcock
20 Oct	Sunderland	H	W	3-2	Lukic	..	..	..	..	Coton	Davis	..	.1	..	..	Adams for Rix
27 Oct	West Ham U	A	L	1-3	Jennings	..	..	..	..	Adams	Robson	Davis	Mariner1	.1	..	Allison for Caton
2 Nov	Manchester U	A	L	2-4	..	..	..	..	..	..	..	..	Allison	..	..	Allison for O'Leary
10 Nov	Aston Villa	H	D	1-1	..	O'Leary	Hill	..	Adams	Caton	..	Nicholas	Mariner	.1	..	
17 Nov	Q P R	H	W	1-0	Lukic	Anderson	Sansom	..	O'Leary	Adams	..	Caton	..	.1	Allison1	Meade for Allison
25 Nov	Sheffield W	A	L	1-2	..	..	..	.1	Adams	Caton	..	Nicholas2	..	..	.2	Nicholas for Allison
1 Dec	Luton T	H	W	3-1	..	Anderson	Sansom	Caton	..	..	..	Allison	.1	Nicholas	.1	Williams for Nicholas
8 Dec	Southampton	A	L	0-1	..	..	Sansom	..	Caton	..	Davis	Willams	.1	Meade1	Allison1	Nicholas for Caton
15 Dec	W B A	H	W	4-0	..	..	..	Williams	..	Caton	..	Davis	..	Woodcock	Nicholas	Talbot for Davis
22 Dec	Watford	H	D	1-1	..	..	..	..	..	..	..	.1	..	.1	..	
26 Dec	Norwich C	A	L	0-1	..	..	..	Talbot	..	..	Talbot	..	..	..	..	Meade for Woodcock
29 Dec	Newcastle U	A	W	3-1	..	..	..	Williams1	Adams	..	Robson1	Rix	..	Meade1	..	Talbot for Nicholas
1 Jan	Tottenham H	H	L	1-2	..	..	..	..	O'Leary	..	..	Rix	..	.1	.1	Talbot for Davis
19 Jan	Chelsea	A	D	1-1	..	..	..	..	..	..	Talbot	..	..	Talbot	..	Talbot for Robson
2 Feb	Coventry C	H	W	2-1	..	..	..	..	..	..	Robson1	..	Allison1	..	.1	Allison for Meade
12 Feb	Liverpool	A	L	0-3	..	..	..	..	..	..	..	..	.1	.1	.1	Allison for Mariner
23 Feb	Manchester U	H	L	0-1	..	..	..	..	Adams	..	..	.1	..	.1	.1	Mariner for O'Leary
2 Mar	West Ham U	H	W	2-1	..	..	..	..	O'Leary	..	Mariner1	..	Allison	.1	.1	Mariner for Adams
9 Mar	Sunderland	A	D	0-0	..	..	..	Talbot	..	..	..	..	..	Allison	.1	Allison for Robson
13 Mar	Aston Villa	A	D	0-0	..	..	..	..	..	Davis	..	..	..	Allison	..	Davis for Caton
16 Mar	Leicester C	H	W	2-0	..	..	..	Williams1	Adams	..	..	..	..	Davis	..	Allison1 for Nicholas
19 Mar	Ipswich T	H	D	1-1	..	..	..	..	O'Leary	..	..	..	..	opponents	..	

FA Cup

Date	Opponent	V	Res	Score	GK	2	3	4	5	6	7	8	9	10	11	Substitutions
5 Jan	Hereford (3)	A	D	1-1	Lukic	Anderson	Caton	Talbot	O'Leary	Adams	Robson	Willams	Mariner	Woodcock1	Nicholas	Allison for Nicholas
22 Jan	Hereford (3R)	H	W	7-2	..	.1	Sansom	.2	..	Caton	..	..	.2	.1	.1	
26 Jan	York C (4)	A	L	0-1	..	..	..	..	..	..	..	..	..	..	..	Allison for Nicholas

Milk Cup

Date	Opponent	V	Res	Score	GK	2	3	4	5	6	7	8	9	10	11	Substitutions
25 Sep	Bristol R (2)	H	W	4-0	Jennings	Anderson1	Sansom	Talbot	O'Leary	Caton	Robson	Rix	Mariner	Woodcock1	Nicholas2	
9 Oct	Bristol R (2)	A	D	1-1	..	..	..	..	..	..	..	..	..	..	..	
31 Oct	Oxford U (3)	A	L	2-3	..	..	..	..	..	..	..	.1	..	Allison1	..	Adams for Robson

Appearances (Goals)

Adams T 16 – Allinson I 27 (10) – Caton T 35 (1) – Davis P 24 (1) – Hill C 2 – Jennings P 15 – Lukic J 27 – Mariner P 36 (7) – Meade R 8 (3) – Nicholas C 38 (9) – O'Leary D 36 – Rix G 18 (2) – Robson S 40 (2) – Sansom K 39 (1) – Talbot B 41 (10) – Williams S 15 (1) – Woodcock T 27 (10) – Own goals 1 – **Total 18 players (61)**

Position in League Table

	P	W	L	D	F:A	Pts	
Everton	42	28	8	6	88:43	90	1st
Arsenal	42	19	14	9	60:47	66	7th

SEASON 1985–86 FOOTBALL LEAGUE (DIVISION 1)

Date	Opponent	V	Res	Score	GK	2	3	4	5	6	7	8	9	10	11	Substitutions
17 Aug	Liverpool	A	L	0-2	Lukic	Anderson	Sansom	Williams	O'Leary	Caton	Robson	Allison	Nicholas	Woodcock	Rix	
20 Aug	Southampton	H	W	3-2	..	..	..	..	..	.1	.1	..	..	.1	..	
24 Aug	Manchester U	H	L	1-2	..	..	..	..	..	..	..	.1	..	..	..	Davis for Williams
27 Aug	Luton T	A	D	2-2	..	..	..	Davis	..	..	..	opponents	..	..	.1	Mariner for O'Leary
31 Aug	Leicester C	H	W	1-0	..	..	..	..	Mariner	..	..	.1	..	.1	..	
3 Sep	Q P R	A	W	1-0	..	..	..	..	O'Leary	..	..	.1	..	..	..	
7 Sep	Coventry C	A	W	2-0	..	..	..	..	..	..	..	..	.1	.1	..	
14 Sep	Sheffield W	H	W	1-0	..	..	..	..	..	..	..	.1	..	..	..	
21 Sep	Chelsea	A	L	1-2	..	..	..	..	..	..	..	.1	..	..	..	
28 Sep	Newcastle U	H	D	0-0	..	..	..	..	..	..	Rocastle	..	..	..	..	
5 Oct	Aston Villa	H	W	3-2	..	..	.1	..	..	..	Whyte1	..	..	.1	..	Rocastle for O'Leary
12 Oct	West Ham U	A	D	0-0	..	..	..	..	..	..	..	..	..	..	..	Rocastle for Nicholas
19 Oct	Ipswich T	H	W	1-0	..	..	..	.1	..	..	..	..	..	..	..	Rocastle for Allison
26 Oct	Nottingham F	A	L	2-3	..	..	..	.1	..	..	..	..	..	..	.1	Rocastle for Allison
2 Nov	Manchester C	H	W	1-0	..	..	..	.1	..	..	Williams	..	..	..	..	Whyte for Allison
9 Nov	Everton	A	L	1-6	..	..	..	..	..	..	..	..	.1	..	..	Allison for Woodcock
16 Nov	Oxford U	H	W	2-1	..	..	..	.1	..	..	Robson	..	..	.1	Hayes	Allison for Hayes
23 Nov	W B A	A	D	0-0	..	..	..	..	Keown	..	..	..	..	..	..	Whyte for Hayes
30 Nov	Birmingham C	H	D	0-0	..	..	..	..	O'Leary	..	..	..	..	..	..	Allison for Williams
7 Dec	Southampton	A	L	0-3	..	..	..	..	..	..	..	..	..	..	..	Allison for Hayes
14 Dec	Liverpool	H	W	2-0	..	..	..	..	Keown	Allison	..	..	.1	Quinn1	Rix	
21 Dec	Manchester U	A	W	1-0	..	Caesar	..	..	..	..	..	..	.1	..	..	
28 Dec	Q P R	H	W	3-1	..	Anderson	..	..	..	..	Robson1	.1	.1	..	..	Woodcock1 for Robson
1 Jan	Tottenham H	H	D	0-0	..	..	..	..	..	..	..	.1	.1	..	..	
18 Jan	Leicester C	A	D	2-2	..	..	..	Rocastle	..	..	.1	Allison1	..	.1	..	
1 Feb	Luton T	H	W	2-1	..	..	..	Williams	..	..	Allison	Rocastle	Nicholas	Woodcock	Rix	Mariner for Woodcock
1 Mar	Newcastle U	A	L	0-1	Lukic	Anderson	Sansom	Williams	O'Leary	Keown	Allison	Rocastle	Nicholas	Woodcock	Rix	Mariner for Woodcock
8 Mar	Aston Villa	A	W	4-1	Wilmot	..	..	..	opponents	..	Hayes1	.1	.1	..	..	Mariner for O'Leary
11 Mar	Ipswich T	A	W	2-1	Lukic	..	..	..	..	..	..	..	.1	..	..	
15 Mar	West Ham U	H	W	1-0	..	..	..	..	opponents	..	..	..	.1	..	..	
22 Mar	Coventry C	H	W	3-0	..	Adams	..	..	..	..	.1	..	.1	..	..	
29 Mar	Tottenham H	A	L	0-1	..	Anderson	..	..	..	..	..	..	Quinn	..	..	Mariner for Quinn
31 Mar	Watford	H	L	0-2	..	..	..	..	..	..	..	..	Mariner	..	..	Robson for Hayes
1 Apr	Watford	A	L	0-3	..	..	..	..	Adams	..	Robson	..	Woodcock	..	..	Allinson for Williams
5 Apr	Manchester C	A	W	1-0	..	..	..	Allinson	..	..	.1	..	Quinn	..	..	Mariner for Quinn
8 Apr	Nottingham F	H	D	0-1	..	..	..	.1	..	..	..	..	Quinn	..	..	Mariner for Rocastle
12 Apr	Everton	H	L	0-1	..	..	..	..	..	..	Davis	..	..	..	..	
16 Apr	Sheffield W	A	L	0-2	..	..	..	..	..	..	..	..	Woodcock	..	..	
26 Apr	W B A	H	D	2-2	..	..	..	.1	O'Leary	Adams	.1	..	Hayes	..	..	Quinn for Woodcock
29 Apr	Chelsea	H	W	2-0	..	.1	..	Keown	..	..	..	..	Nicholas1	..	..	Quinn for Rix
3 May	Birmingham C	A	W	1-0	..	..	..	..	..	..	..	..	..	.1	..	
5 May	Oxford U	A	L	0-3	..	..	..	..	..	..	..	..	..	..	..	Allison for O'Leary

FA Cup

Date	Opponent	V	Res	Score	GK	2	3	4	5	6	7	8	9	10	11	Substitutions
4 Jan	Grimsby T (3)	A	W	4-3	Lukic	Anderson	Sansom	Davis	O'Leary	Keown	Allison	Rocastle	Nicholas3	Quinn	Rix1	Woodcock for Robson
25 Jan	Rotherham U (4)	H	W	5-1	..	..	..	Rocastle	..	..	.2	Robson1	.1	..	.1	Mariner for Nicholas
15 Feb	Luton T (5)	A	D	2-2	..	..	..	Williams	..	..	.1	Rocastle1	..	Woodcock	..	
3 Mar	Luton T Extra Time (5R)	H	D	0-0	..	..	..	..	..	..	..	..	..	Mariner	..	
5 Mar	Luton T (5 2nd Rep)	A	L	0-3	..	..	..	..	..	..	..	..	..	..	Hayes	Quinn for Hayes

Milk Cup

25 Sep	Hereford U (2)	A	D	0-0	Lukic	Anderson	Sansom	Davis	O'Leary	Caton	Robson	Allinson	Nicholas	Woodcock	Rix	Mariner for Robson
8 Oct	Hereford U (2 extra time)	H	W	2-1	..	..1	..	..	..	..	Whyte	..	..1	..	..	Rocastle for Davis
30 Oct	Manchester C (3)	A	W	2-1	..	..	..	..	..	..	Williams	..1	..1	..	..	
19 Nov	Southampton (4)	H	D	0-0	..	..	..	..	..	..	..	Robson	..	..	Hayes	Allinson for Hayes
26 Nov	Southampton (4R)	A	W	3-1	..	..	..	..	..	..	..	..1	..1	..	..1	
22 Jan	Aston Villa (5)	A	D	1-1	Wilmot	..	..	Rocastle	..	..	Allinson	..	..1	Quinn	Rix	Woodcock for Robson
4 Feb	Aston Villa (5R)	H	L	1-2	Lukic	..	..	..	..	..	..	Mariner1	..	..	..	Woodcock for Allinson

Appearances (Goals)
Adams T 10 – Allinson I 33 (6) – Anderson V 39 (2) – Ceasar G 20 (1) – Caton T 20 (1) – Davis P 29 (4) – Hayes M 11 (2) – Keown M 22 – Lukic J 40 – Mariner P 9 – Nicholas C 41 (10) – O'Leary D 35 – Quinn N 12 (1) – Rix G 38 (3) – Robson S 27 (4) – Rocastle D 16 (1) – Sansom K 42 – Whyte C 7 (1) – Williams S 17 – Wilmot R 2 – Woodcock T 33 (11) – Own goals 3 – **Total 21 players 49**

Position in League Table

	P	W	L	D	F:A	Pts	
Liverpool	42	26	6	10	89:37	88	1st
Arsenal	42	20	13	9	49:47	69	7th

SEASON 1986–87 FOOTBALL LEAGUE (DIVISION 1)

23 Aug	Manchester U	H	W	1-0	Lukic	Anderson	Sansom	Robson	O'Leary	Adams	Rocastle	Davis	Quinn	Nicholas1	Rix	Hayes for Rocastle
26 Aug	Coventry C	A	L	1-2	..	..1	..	..	..	..	..	..	..	..	..	Hayes for Rix
30 Aug	Liverpool	A	L	1-2	..	..	..	..	..	..1	..	..	..	..	..	Williams for Robson
2 Sep	Sheffield W	H	W	2-0	..	..	..	..	..	..1	..	..	..1	..	..	Hayes for Rocastle
6 Sep	Tottenham H	H	D	0-0	..	..	..	..	..	..	..	..	..	..	..	Hayes for Rocastle
13 Sep	Luton T	A	D	0-0	..	..	..	Williams	..	..	..	..	..	..	..	Groves for Rix
20 Sep	Oxford U	H	D	0-0	..	..	..	..	..	..	..	..	..	..	..	Groves for Rix
27 Sep	Nottingham F	A	L	0-1	..	..	..	..	..	..	..	..	..	..	Groves	Allinson for Nicholas
4 Oct	Everton	A	W	1-0	..	..	..	..1	..	..	..	..	..	Allinson	..	Caesar for Groves
11 Oct	Watford	H	W	3-1	..	..	..	..	..	..	..	..	..1	Groves1	Hayes1	Allinson for O'Leary
18 Oct	Newcastle U	A	W	2-1	..	..1	..	..1	..	..	..	..	..	..	..	Caesar for Quinn
25 Oct	Chelsea	H	W	3-1	..	..	..	..	..	..	..1	..	..	..	..2	Allinson for Quinn
1 Nov	Charlton A	A	W	2-0	..	..	..	..	..	..1	..	..	..	..	..1	Caesar for Groves
8 Nov	West Ham U	H	D	0-0	..	..	..	..	..	..	..	..	..	..	..	
15 Nov	Southampton	A	W	4-0	..	..1	..	..	..	..	..	..	..1	..1	..1	Caesar for Rocastle
22 Nov	Manchester C	H	W	3-0	..	..1	..	..	..	..1	..	..	..1	Allinson	..	Merson for Hayes
29 Nov	Aston Villa	A	W	4-0	..	..	*opponents*	..	..	..	..1	..	..	Groves1	..1	
6 Dec	Q P R	H	W	3-1	..	..	..	..	..	..	..	..	..1	..	..2	Nicholas for Groves
13 Dec	Norwich C	A	D	1-1	..	..	..	..	..	..	..	..	..	..	..1	Caesar for Groves
20 Dec	Luton T	H	W	3-0	..	..	..	..	..	..1	..	..	..1	..	..1	Nicholas for Groves
26 Dec	Leicester C	A	D	1-1	..	..	..	..	..	..	..	..	..	..	..1	Caesar for Groves
27 Dec	Southampton	H	W	1-0	..	..	..	..	..	..	..	..	..1	Nicholas	..	Allinson for Hayes
1 Jan	Wimbledon	H	W	3-1	..	..	..	..	..	..	..	..	..	..2	..1	Allinson for Rocastle
4 Jan	Tottenham H	A	W	2-1	..	..	..	..	..	..1	..	..1	..	..	..	Rix for Quinn
18 Jan	Coventry C	H	D	0-0	..	..	..	..	..	..	..	..	..	..	..	Rix for Hayes
24 Jan	Manchester U	A	L	0-2	..	..	..	..	..	..	..	..	..	..	..	Caesar for Nicholas
14 Feb	Sheffield W	A	D	1-1	..	Thomas	..	..	..	..	Groves	..	..1	Rix	..	Allinson for Williams
25 Feb	Oxford U	A	D	0-0	..	Anderson	..	Thomas	..	..	Rocastle	..	..	Groves	..	Nicholas for Groves
7 Mar	Chelsea	A	L	0-1	..	..	..	..	..	..	..	Caesar	..	Allinson	..	Merson for Hayes
10 Mar	Liverpool	H	L	0-1	..	..	..	..	..	..	..	Groves	..	..	..	Caesar for Hayes
17 Mar	Nottingham F	H	D	0-0	..	..	..	Williams	Caesar	..	..	..	..	Nicholas	Thomas	Allinson for Groves
21 Mar	Watford	A	L	0-2	..	Caesar	..	Thomas	O'Leary	..	Allinson	Davis	..	..	Hayes	Rix for Quinn
28 Mar	Everton	H	L	0-1	..	Anderson	..	Williams	..	..	Rocastle	..	..	..	..	Groves for Hayes
8 Apr	West Ham U	A	L	1-3	Wilmot	..	Thomas	..	..	..	..	..	Groves	..	..1	Rix for Hayes
11 Apr	Charlton A	H	W	2-1	Lukic	..	Sansom	..	..	..	..	..1	Quinn	..	..1	Groves for Quinn
14 Apr	Newcastle U	H	L	0-1	..	..	Thomas	..	..	..	..	..	Groves	..	..	Rix for Rocastle
18 Apr	Wimbledon	A	W	2-1	..	..	Caesar	..	..	..	..	..1	Merson1	..	Rix	Allinson for Rocastle
20 Apr	Leicester C	H	W	4-1	Wilmot	..	Sansom	..	..	..	Hayes2	..1	..	..1	..	Caesar for O'Leary
25 Apr	Manchester C	A	L	0-3	..	..	Thomas	..	Caesar	..	..	..	..	..	..	Allinson for Merson
2 May	Aston Villa	H	W	2-1	..	..	..	..	O'Leary	..	Rocastle	..	Quinn	..	Hayes2	Groves for Quinn
4 May	Q P R	A	W	4-1	..	..	..	..	Caesar	..	Rix2	..	Merson1	..	..1	
9 May	Norwich C	H	L	1-2	..	..	..	..	O'Leary	..	..	..	..1	..	..	Groves for Anderson

FA Cup

10 Jan	Reading (3)	A	W	3-1	Lukic	Anderson	Sansom	Williams	O'Leary	Adams	Rocastle	Davis	Quinn	Nicholas2	Hayes1	
31 Jan	Plymouth A (4)	H	W	6-1	..	..2	..	..	..	..	..1	..1	..1	..1	..	Groves for Hayes/Caesar for Groves
21 Feb	Barnsley (5)	H	W	2-0	..	..	..	Allinson	..	..	..	..	..	Groves	..1	Nicholas1 for Quinn/Thomas for Hayes
14 Mar	Watford (QF)	H	L	1-3	..	..	..	Williams	..	..	..	Groves	..	Allinson1	..	Nicholas for Allinson/Thomas for Hayes

Football League (Littlewoods) Cup

23 Sep	Huddersfield T (2)	H	W	2-0	Lukic	Anderson	Sansom	Williams	O'Leary	Adams	Rocastle	Davis1	Quinn1	Nicholas	Rix	Groves for Quinn
7 Oct	Huddersfield T (2)	A	D	1-1	..	..	..	..	..	..	..	..	..	Allinson	Groves	Hayes1 for Allinson
28 Oct	Manchester C (3)	H	W	3-1	..	..	..	..	..	..	..1	..1	..	Groves	Hayes1	Allinson for Quinn
18 Nov	Charlton A (4)	H	W	2-0	..	..	..	*opponents*	..	..	..	..	..1	..	..	Allinson for Groves
21 Jan	Nottingham F (QF)	H	W	2-0	..	..	..	..	..	..	..	..	..	Nicholas1	..1	Rix for Quinn
8 Feb	Tottenham H (SF1)	H	L	0-1	..	Caesar	..	..	..	..	Groves	..	..	..	..	Thomas for Caesar/Rix for Nicholas
1 Mar	Tottenham H (SF2)	A	W	2-1	..	Anderson1	..	Thomas	..	..	Rocastle	..	..1	..	..	Allinson for Nicholas
4 Mar	Tottenham H (SFR)	A	W	2-1	..	..	..	..	..	..	..1	..	..	..	..	Allinson1 for Thomas
5 Apr	Liverpool (F) (at Wembley)		W	2-1	..	..	..	Williams	..	..	..	..	..	..2	..	Groves for Quinn/Thomas for Hayes

Appearances (Goals)
Adams T 42 (6) – Allinson I 14 – Anderson V 40 (4) – Caesar G 15 – Davis P 39 (4) – Groves P 25 (3) – Hayes M 35 (19) – Lukic J 36 – Merson P 7 (3) – Nicholas C 28 (4) – O'Leary D 39 – Quinn N 35 (8) – Rix G 18 (2) – Robson S 5 – Rocastle D 36 (2) – Sansom K 35 – Thomas M 11 – Williams S 34 (2) – Wilmot R 6 – Own goals 1 – **Total 19 players (58)**

Position in League Table

	P	W	L	D	F:A	Pts	
Everton	42	26	8	8	76:31	86	1st
Arsenal	42	20	12	10	58:35	70	4th

SEASON 1987–88 FOOTBALL LEAGUE (DIVISION 1)

15 Aug	Liverpool	H	L	1-2	Lukic	Thomas	Sansom	Williams	O'Leary	Adams	Rocastle	Davis1	Smith	Nicholas	Hayes	Groves for Rocastle
19 Aug	Manchester U	A	D	0-0	..	..	..	..	..	..	..	..	..	..	..	Groves for Nicholas
22 Aug	Q P R	A	L	0-2	..	..	..	..	..	..	..	..	..	..	..	Rix for Rocastle
29 Aug	Portsmouth	H	W	6-0	..	..	..	..	..	..1	..1	..1	..3	Groves	Rix	Merson for Groves/Richardson for Rix
31 Aug	Luton T	A	D	1-1	..	..	..	..	..	..	..	..1	..	..	..	
12 Sep	Nottingham F	A	W	1-0	..	..	..	..	..	..	..	..	..1	..	..	Hayes for Rocastle
19 Sep	Wimbledon	H	W	3-0	..	..1	..	..	..	..	..1	..	..1	..	..	Merson and Richardson for Groves and Williams
26 Sep	West Ham U	H	W	1-0	..	..	..1	..	..	..	..	..	..	..	..	Hayes for Rocastle
3 Oct	Charlton A	A	W	3-0	..	..1	..	..	..	..1	..	..	..	..1	..	Hayes for Rocastle
10 Oct	Oxford U	H	W	2-0	..	..	..	..1	..	..	..	..1	..	..	Richardson	Hayes and Caesar for Rocastle and Smith
18 Oct	Tottenham H	A	W	2-1	..	..1	..	..	..	..	..	..	..1	..	..	Hayes for Groves
24 Oct	Derby C	H	W	2-1	..	..1	..	..	..	..	..	..	..	..	..1	Merson for Groves
31 Oct	Newcastle U	A	W	1-0	..	..	..	..	..	..	..	..	..1	..	..	Caesar and Hayes for Williams and Adams
3 Nov	Chelsea	H	W	3-1	..	..	..o.g.	..	..	..	..	..	..	..	..2	
14 Nov	Norwich C	A	W	4-2	..	..1	..	..	..	..	..2	..	..	..1	..	Caesar for Adams
21 Nov	Southampton	H	L	0-1	..	..	..	..	..	..	..	..	..	..	..	Quinn for Groves, Winterburn for Quinn
28 Nov	Watford	A	L	0-2	..	..	..	..	..	..	..	..	..	..	..	Hayes for Richardson
5 Dec	Sheffield W	H	W	3-1	..	..	..	..	..	..	..	..	..	..1	..1	Merson1 for Davis
13 Dec	Coventry C	A	D	0-0	..	..	..	..	..	..	..	Hayes	..	..	..	Merson for Hayes
19 Dec	Everton	H	D	1-1	..	..	..	..	..	..	..1	Davis	..	..	..	Merson for Richardson
26 Dec	Nottingham F	H	L	0-2	..	..	..	..	..	..	..	Merson	Quinn	..	..	Smith and Caesar for Merson and O'Leary
28 Dec	Wimbledon	A	L	1-3	..	..	..	..	Caesar	..	..	Hayes	..1	..	..	Smith for Hayes
1 Jan	Portsmouth	A	D	1-1	..	..	Winterburn	..	..	..	..	..	..	..	..	Smith1 and Merson for Quinn and Groves
2 Jan	Q P R	H	D	0-0	..	Winterburn	Sansom	..	..	..	..	..	Smith	Merson	..	Groves for Merson
16 Jan	Liverpool	A	L	0-2	..	..	..	..	..	..	..	..	..	Quinn	..	Thomas and Groves for Caesar and Rocastle
24 Jan	Manchester U	H	L	1-2	..	Thomas	Winterburn	..	O'Leary	..	..	Rix	..	..1	..	Groves for Rix
13 Feb	Luton T	H	W	2-1	..	Dixon	..	Thomas1	..	..	..1	Hayes	..	..	..	Caesar for Adams
27 Feb	Charlton A	H	W	4-0	..	Winterburn	Sansom	..1	Caesar	..	..	..	..1	Merson2	..	Davis and Quinn for Merson and Richardson

6 Mar	Tottenham H	H	W	2-1	..	..	..	..	..	..	..	..	..1	Groves1	..	
19 Mar	Newcastle U	H	D	1-1	..	Dixon	Winterburn	..	..	..	..	Davis	..	..1	Hayes	Quinn for Smith
26 Mar	Derby Co	A	D	0-0	..	..	..	..	..	..	..	..	..	..	..	Richards and Quinn for Rocastle and Smith
30 Mar	Oxford U	A	D	0-0	..	Winterburn	Sansom	..	..	..	..	..	..	..	Marwood	Merson and Quinn for Rocastle and Marwood
2 Apr	Chelsea	A	D	1-1	..	Dixon	Winterburn	Williams	..	..	..o.g.	..	Quinn	..	Hayes	
4 Apr	Norwich C	H	W	2-0	..	Winterburn	Sansom	..	..	..	..	..	Smith1	..1	..	
9 Apr	Southampton	A	L	2-4	..	..	..	..	..	Thomas	..	..1	..	..o.g.	..	Merson for Groves
12 Apr	West Ham U	A	W	1-0	..	..	..	Thomas1	..	Adams	..	..	..	Merson	Richardson	Rix for Richardson
15 Apr	Watford	H	L	0-1	..	..	..	..	..	..	..	..	..	..	..	Hayes for Richardson
30 Apr	Sheffield W	A	D	3-3	..	..	..	..	..	..	..	..	..1	..2	Marwood	Richardson and Hayes for Davis and Winterburn
2 May	Coventry C	H	D	1-1	..	Dixon	..	..	..	..	..	..	..	..	..1	Hayes and Groves for Merson and Richardson
7 May	Everton	A	W	2-1	..	..	..	..1	..	..	..	..	..	Hayes1	..	Rix and Campbell for Caesar and Hayes

FA Cup

9 Jan	Millwall (3)	H	W	2-0	Lukic	Winterburn	Sansom	Williams	O'Leary	Adams	Rocastle1	Hayes1	Smith	Merson	Richardson	Groves for Merson
30 Jan	Brighton (4)	A	W	2-1	..	..	..	..	..	..	..	Rix	Groves1	Quinn	..1	Hayes for Rix
20 Feb	Manchester U (5)	H	W	2-1	..	..	..	Thomas	..	..o.g.	..	Hayes	Smith1	Groves	..	Rix for O'Leary
12 Mar	Nottingham F (6)	H	L	1-2	..	..	..	..	..	..	..1	..	..	..	..	Davis and Quinn for O'Leary and Hayes

Football League (Littlewoods) Cup

23 Sep	Doncaster (2)	A	W	3-0	Lukic	Thomas	Sansom	Williams1	O'Leary	Adams	Rocastle	Davis	Smith1	Groves1	Rix	Richardson and Quinn for Groves and Rix
6 Oct	Doncaster (2)	H	W	1-0	..	..	..	..	Caesar	..	..	..	..	..	Hayes	
27 Oct	Bournemouth (3)	H	W	3-0	..	..1	..	..	O'Leary	..	..	..	..1	..	Richardson1	Merson for Groves
17 Nov	Stoke C (4)	H	W	3-0	..	..	..	..	..1	..	..1	..	..	..	..1	Hayes for Groves
20 Jan	Sheffield W (5)	A	W	1-0	..	Winterburn1	..	..	..	..	..	Rix	..	Quinn	..	Groves for Quinn
7 Feb	Everton (SF)	A	W	1-0	..	..	..	Thomas	..	..	..	Hayes	..	Groves1	..	Caesar and Quinn for Rocastle and Smith
24 Feb	Everton (SF)	H	W	3-1	..	..	..	..1	..	..	..1	..	..1	..	..	Davis for O'Leary
24 Apr	Luton (F) (at Wembley)		L	2-3	..	..	..	..	Caesar	..	..	Davis	..1	..	..	Hayes1 for Groves

Appearances League only (Goals)
Lukic 40 – Rocastle 40 (7) – Adams 39 (2) – Smith 39 (11) – Thomas 37 (9) – Groves 34 (6) – Sansom 34 (1) – Richardson 29 (4) – Williams 29 (1) – Davis 29 (5) Hayes 27 (1) – O'Leary 23 – Caesar 22 – Winterburn 17 – Merson 15 (5) – Quinn 11 (2) – Rix 10 – Dixon 6 – Marwood 4 (1) – Nicholas 3 – Campbell 1 – Own goals 3 – **Total 21 players (58)**

Position in League Table

	P	W	L	D	F:A	Pts	
Liverpool	40	26	2	12	87:24	90	1st
Arsenal	40	18	10	12	58:39	66	6th

SEASON 1988–89 FOOTBALL LEAGUE (DIVISION 1)

27 Aug	Wimbledon	A	W	5-1	Lukic	Dixon	Winterburn	Thomas	Bould	Adams	Rocastle	Davis	Smith3	Merson1	Marwood1	-
3 Sep	Aston Villa	H	L	2-3	..	..	..	..	O'Leary	..	..	..	..1	..	..1	Groves for Rocastle
10 Sep	Tottenham H	A	W	3-2	..	..	..1	..	..	..	..	..	..1	..	..1	Groves/Richardson for Rocastle/Marwood
17 Sep	Southampton	H	D	2-2	..	..	..	..	..	..	..	..	..1	..	..1	Hayes/Richardson for Davis/Merson
24 Sep	Sheffield W	A	L	1-2	..	..	..	..	..	..	..	..	..1	..	..	Groves for Merson
1 Oct	West Ham U	A	W	4-1	..	..	..	..1	Bould	..	..1	..	..2	Groves	..	Hayes for Groves
22 Oct	Q P R	H	W	2-1	..	..	..	..	..	..1	..	Richardson	..1	Merson	..	Groves for Merson
25 Oct	Luton T	A	D	1-1	..	..	..	..	..	..	..	..	..1	..	..	
29 Oct	Coventry C	H	W	2-0	..	..	..	..1	..	..1	..	..	..	..	..	Groves/Hayes for Rocastle/Merson
6 Nov	Nottingham F	A	W	4-1	..	..	..	..	..1	..1	..	..	..1	..	..1	Hayes for Merson
12 Nov	Newcastle U	A	W	1-0	..	..	..	..	..1	..	..	..	..	Hayes	..	Merson for Rocastle
19 Nov	Middlesbrough	H	W	3-0	..	..	..	..	..	..	..1	..	..	Merson2	..	Hayes for Marwood
26 Nov	Derby Co	A	L	1-2	..	..	..	..1	..	..	..	..	..	..	Hayes	Groves for Richardson
4 Dec	Liverpool	H	D	1-1	..	..	..	..	..	..	..	..	..1	..	Marwood	Hayes for Marwood
10 Dec	Norwich C	A	D	0-0	..	..	..	..	..	..	..	..	..	..	..	Hayes for Marwood
17 Dec	Manchester U	H	W	2-1	..	..	..	..1	..	..	..	..	..	..1	..	
26 Dec	Charlton A	A	W	3-2	..	O'Leary	..	..	..	..	..	..	..	..1	..2	
31 Dec	Aston Villa	A	W	3-0	..	..	..	..	..	..	..1	..	..1	..	..	Groves1 for Merson
2 Jan	Tottenham H	H	W	2-0	..	..	..	..1	..	..	..	..	..	..1	..	Davis/Groves for Richardson/Marwood
14 Jan	Everton	A	W	3-1	..	Dixon	..	Davis	O'Leary	Caesar	..	..1	..1	..1	..	Groves/Thomas for Merson/Marwood
21 Jan	Sheffield W	H	D	1-1	..	..	..	..	..	..	..	..	..	..1	..	Groves/Thomas for Caesar/Rocastle
4 Feb	West Ham U	H	W	2-1	..	..	..	Thomas	..	Adams	..	..	..1	..	Groves1	Bould/Hayes for O'Leary/Merson
11 Feb	Millwall	A	W	2-1	..	..	..	..	..	..	..	..	..1	..	Marwood1	Bould for O'Leary
18 Feb	Q P R	A	D	0-0	..	..	..	..	..	..	..	..	..	..	..	Bould/Hayes for Dixon/Merson
21 Feb	Coventry C	A	L	0-1	..	Bould	..	..	..	..	..	..	..	..	..	Hayes for Marwood
25 Feb	Luton T	H	W	2-0	..	..	..	..	..	..	..	..	..1	Groves1	..	Merson for Rocastle
28 Feb	Millwall	H	D	0-0	..	..	..	..	..	..	..	..	..	..	..	Merson/Dixon for Rocastle/Richardson
11 Mar	Nottingham F	H	L	1-3	..	..	..	..	..	..	..	..	..1	..	..	Merson/Dixon for Bould/Groves
21 Mar	Charlton A	H	D	2-2	..	Dixon	..	Davis1	..	..	..1	..	..	Merson	..	Groves/Thomas for Richardson/Merson
25 Mar	Southampton	A	W	3-1	..	..	..	..	..	..	..1	..	..	Groves1	..	Merson1 for Groves
2 Apr	Manchester U	A	D	1-1	..	..	..	..	..	..1	..	..	..	Bould	..	Thomas/Merson for Davis/Marwood
8 Apr	Everton	H	W	2-0	..	..1	..	Thomas	..	..	..	..	Quinn1	..	..	Merson for Marwood
15 Apr	Newcastle U	H	W	1-0	..	..	..	..	..	..	..	..	..	..	..1	Merson/Groves for O'Leary/Rocastle
1 May	Norwich C	H	W	5-0	..	..	..1	..1	..	..	..1	..	Smith2	..	Merson	Quinn/Hayes for Bould/Merson
6 May	Middlesbrough	A	W	1-0	..	..	..	..	..	..	..	..	..	..	..	Hayes1 for Merson
13 May	Derby Co	H	L	1-2	..	..	..	..	..	..	..	..	..1	..	..	Hayes/Groves for Bould/Merson
17 May	Wimbledon	H	D	2-2	..	..	..1	..	..	..	..	..	..1	..		Groves/Hayes for Bould/Merson
26 May	Liverpool	A	W	2-0	..	..	..	..1	..	..	..	..	..1	..	..	Groves/Hayes for Bould/Merson

FA Cup

8 Jan	West Ham U (3)	A	D	2-2	Lukic	O'Leary	Winterburn	Thomas	Bould	Adams	Rocastle	Richardson	Smith	Merson2	Marwood	Davis and Groves for Bould and Marwood
11 Jan	West Ham U (3R)	H	L	0-1	..	Dixon	..	..	O'Leary	..	..	..	..	..	..	Davis and Groves for Rocastle and Marwood

Football League (Littlewoods) Cup

28 Sep	Hull C (2)	A	W	2-1	Lukic	Dixon	Winterburn1	Thomas	Bould	Adams	Rocastle	Davis	Smith	Groves	Marwood1	Hayes and Richardson for Groves and Rocastle
12 Oct	Hull C (2)	H	W	3-0	..	..	..	..	..	..	..	..	..2	Merson1	..	Hayes and Richardson for Davis and Marwood
2 Nov	Liverpool (3)	A	D	1-1	..	..	..	..	..	..	..1	Richardson	..	..	..	Groves for Merson
9 Nov	Liverpool (3R)	H	D	0-0	..	..	..	..	..	..	..	..	..	..	..	Hayes for Merson
23 Nov	Liverpool (3R2)	A	L	1-2	..	..	..	..	..	..	..	..	..	..1	..	Hayes for Marwood

Appearances League Only (Goals)
Lukic 38 – Rocastle 38 (6) – Winterburn 38 (3) – Thomas 37 (7) – Merson 37 (9) – Adams 36 (4) – Smith 36 (24) – Richardson 34 (1) – Dixon 33 (1) – Marwood 31 (9) – Bould 30 (2) – O'Leary 26 – Groves 21 (4) – Hayes 17 (1) – Davis 12 (1) – Quinn 3 (1) – Caesar 2 – **Total 17 players (73)**

Position in League Table

	P	W	L	D	F:A	Pts	
Arsenal	38	22	6	10	73:36	76	1st

SEASON 1989–90 FOOTBALL LEAGUE (DIVISION 1)

19 Aug	Manchester U	A	L	1-4	Lukic	Dixon	Winterburn	Thomas	O'Leary	Adams	Rocastle1	Richardson	Smith	Merson	Marwood	Caesar/Groves for Adams/Merson
22 Aug	Coventry C	H	W	2-0	..	..	..	..1	..	..	..	..	..	..	..1	Groves for Rocastle
26 Aug	Wimbledon	H	D	0-0	..	..	..	..	..	..	..	..	..	..	..	Groves for Merson
09 Sep	Sheffield W	H	W	5-0	..	..	..	..1	..	..1	..	..	..1	..1	..1	
16 Sep	Nottingham F	A	W	2-1	..	..	..	..	..	..	..	..	..	..1	..1	Groves for Merson
23 Sep	Charlton A	H	W	1-0	..	..	..	..	..	..	..	..	..	..	..1p	Groves for Rocastle
30 Sep	Chelsea	A	D	0-0	..	..	..	..	..	..	..	..	..	Groves	Hayes	Merson for Rocastle
14 Oct	Manchester C	H	W	4-0	..	..	..	..1	..	..	..	..	..	..2	Marwood	Jonsson/Merson1 for Richardson/Marwood
18 Oct	Tottenham H	A	L	1-2	..	..	..	..1	..	..	..	..	..	..	Hayes	Jonsson/Merson for Richardson/Smith
21 Oct	Everton	A	L	0-3	..	..	..	..	..	..	..	..	Quinn	Merson	..	Smith for Hayes
28 Oct	Derby Co	H	D	1-1	..	..	..	..	..	..	..	..	Smith1	Quinn	Merson	Jonsson/Campbell for Winterburn/Quinn
4 Nov	Norwich C	H	W	4-3	..	..2.1p	..	..	..1	..	..	..	..	..1	..	Groves for Merson
11 Nov	Millwall	A	W	2-1	..	..	..	..1	..	..	..	..	..	..1	Marwood	Groves for Quinn
18 Nov	Q P R	H	W	3-0	..	..1p	..	..	..	..	..	..	..1	..	..	Groves/Jonsson1 for Rocastle/Marwood
26 Nov	Liverpool	A	L	1-2	..	..	..	..	..	..	..	..	..1	..	Groves	Hayes/Jonsson for Quinn/O'Leary
3 Dec	Manchester U	H	W	1-0	..	..	..	..	..	..	..	..	..	Groves1	Marwood	Merson for Marwood
9 Dec	Coventry C	A	W	1-0	..	..	..	..	..	..	..	..	..	..	..	Merson1 for Marwood
16 Dec	Luton T	H	W	3-2	..	..	..	..	..	..	..	..	..1	..	..1	Merson1/Jonsson for Smith/Groves
26 Dec	Southampton	A	L	0-1	..	..	..	..	..	..	..	..	..	Merson	..	Davis/Groves for Marwood/Merson

30 Dec	Aston Villa	A	L	1-2	..	..	..	..	..1	Groves	..	..	Bould	Merson	..	Rocastle for Bould
1 Jan	Crystal Palace	H	W	4-1	..	..1	..	..	..	..1	..	..	..2	..	..	Rocastle/Davis for Smith/Winterburn
13 Jan	Wimbledon	A	L	0-1	..	..	..	Davis	..	..	..	..	..	..	..	Caesar/Rocastle for O'Leary/Smith
20 Jan	Tottenham H	H	W	1-0	..	..	Davis	Thomas	..	..1	Rocastle	..	..	..	Groves	
17 Feb	Sheffield W	A	L	0-1	..	..	Pates	Davis	..	..	..	..	..	..	Merson	Caesar/Campbell for Pates/Richardson
27 Feb	Charlton A	A	D	0-0	..	..	Winterburn	Thomas	Bould	..	..	..	..	Merson	Marwood	Campbell for Marwood
3 Mar	Q P R	A	L	0-2	..	..	..	..	..	..	..	..	..	..	Groves	O'Leary/Campbell for Thomas/Smith
7 Mar	Nottingham F	H	W	3-0	..	..	..	..	..	..1	..	..	..	..	..1	Campbell1/O'Leary for Merson/Groves
10 Mar	Manchester C	A	D	1-1	..	..	..	..	..	..	..	..	..	Campbell	Marwood1	Hayes for Rocastle
17 Mar	Chelsea	H	L	0-1	..	..	..	..	..	..	..	..	..	..	Groves	Hayes/O'Leary for Rocastle/Campbell
24 Mar	Derby Co	A	W	3-1	..	..	..	..	..	..	Hayes2	..	..	..1	..	O'Leary/Ampadu for Bould/Campbell
31 Mar	Everton	H	W	1-0	..	..	..	..	..	..	..	..	..1	..	..	O'Leary/Ampadu for Richardson/Campbell
11 Apr	Aston Villa	H	L	0-1	..	..	..	..	..	..	..	O'Leary	..	..	..	Merson for Hayes
14 Apr	Crystal Palace	A	D	1-1	..	..	..	..	..	..	..1	..	..	..	..	Davis/Merson for Bould/Campbell
18 Apr	Liverpool	H	D	1-1	..	..	..	..	..	..	Davis	..	..	Merson1	..	Campbell/Pates for Groves/Bould
21 Apr	Luton T	A	L	0-2	..	..	..	..	..	..	..	..	..	..	Campbell	Hayes/Rocastle for O'Leary/Merson
28 Apr	Millwall	H	W	2-0	..	..	..	..	..	..	Rocastle	Davis1	..	..1	Marwood	Campbell/Richardson for Marwood/Thomas
2 May	Southampton	H	W	2-1	..	..1p	..	..	..	..	Richardson	..	..	..	..	Rocastle1/Groves for Richardson/Marwood
5 May	Norwich C	A	D	2-2	..	..	..	Hayes	..	..	Rocastle	..	..2	Campbell	Groves	O'Leary/Thomas for Bould/Davis

FA Cup

6 Jan	Stoke C (3)	A	W	1-0	Lukic	Dixon	Davis	Thomas	O'Leary	Adams	Quinn1	Richardson	Groves	Bould	Merson	Jonsson/Rocastle for Thomas/Merson
27 Jan	Q P R (4)	H	D	0-0	..	..	Winterburn	Davis	..	..	Rocastle	..	Smith	..	Groves	Thomas/Merson for Davis/Bould
31 Jan	Q P R (4R)	A	L	0-2	..	..	..	Thomas	..	..	..	..	..	..	..	Merson for Groves

Football League (Littlewoods) Cup

19 Sep	Plymouth (2)	H	W	2-0	Lukic	Dixon og	Winterburn	Thomas	O'Leary	Adams	Rocastle	Richardson	Smith1	Bould	Groves	Merson for Groves
3 Oct	Plymouth (2)	A	W	6-1	..	*opponents*	..	..3	..	..	..	..	..1	Groves1	Hayes	Caesar/Merson for Dixon/Groves
25 Oct	Liverpool (3)	H	W	1-0	..	..	..	..	..	..	..	..	Quinn	Merson	..	Smith1 for Hayes
22 Nov	Oldham A (4)	A	L	1-3	..	..	..	..	..	..	..	..	Smith	Quinn1	Jonsson	Groves for Jonsson

FA Charity Shield

12 Aug	Liverpool (at Wembley)		L	0-1	Lukic	Dixon	Winterburn	Thomas	O'Leary	Adams	Rocastle	Richardson	Smith	Caesar	Merson	Marwood/Quinn for Caesar/Smith

Appearances (Goals)

Lukic 38 – Dixon 38 (5) – Adams 38 (5) – Smith 38 (10) – Winterburn 36 – Thomas 36 (5) – O'Leary 34 (1) – Richardson 33 – Rocastle 33 (2) – Groves 30 (4) – Merson 29 (7) – Bould 19 – Marwood 17 (6) – Campbell 15 (2) – Hayes 12 (3) – Davis 11 (1) – Quinn 6 (2) – Jonsson 6 (1) – Caesar 3 – Pates (2) – **Total 19 players (54)**

Position in League Table

	P	W	D	L	F:A	Pts	
Liverpool	38	23	10	5	78:37	79	1st
Arsenal	38	18	8	12	54:38	62	4th

SEASON 1990–91 FOOTBALL LEAGUE (DIVISION 1)

25 Aug	Wimbledon	A	W	3-0	Seaman	Dixon	Winterburn	Thomas	Bould	Adams	Rocastle	Davis	Smith1	Merson1	Limpar	Groves1 for Limpar
29 Aug	Luton T	H	W	2-1	..	..	..	..1	..	..	..	..	..	..1	..	Groves for Limpar
1 Sep	Tottenham H	H	D	0-0	..	..	..	..	..	..	..	..	..	..	..	Groves for Merson
8 Sep	Everton	A	D	1-1	..	..	..	..	..	..	..	..	..	..	..	Groves1 for Smith
15 Sep	Chelsea	H	W	4-1	..	..1p	..	..	..	..	..1	..	Groves	..1	..1	Campbell/Linighan for Groves/Bould
22 Sep	Nottingham F	A	W	2-0	..	..	..	..	..	..	..1	..	..	..	..1	Smith for Rocastle
29 Sep	Leeds U	A	D	2-2	..	..	..	Jonsson	..	..	..	..	Smith	..	..2	Hillier/Groves for Winterburn/Merson
6 Oct	Norwich C	H	W	2-0	..	..	..	..	..	..	..	..2	..	..	..	Hillier/Groves for Limpar/Merson
20 Oct	Manchester U	A	W	1-0	..	..	..	Thomas	..	..	..	..	..	..	..1	Groves for Rocastle
27 Oct	Sunderland	H	W	1-0	..	..1p	..	..	..	..	..	..	..	..	..	Groves for Rocastle
3 Nov	Coventry C	A	W	2-0	..	..	..	..	..	..	Groves	..	..	..	..2	Campbell/O'Leary for Smith/Groves
10 Nov	Crystal Palace	A	D	0-0	..	..	..	..	..	..	O'Leary	..	Campbell	..	..	Groves/Smith for Merson/Limpar
17 Nov	Southampton	H	W	4-0	..	..	..	..	..	..	Groves	..	Smith2	..1	..1	O'Leary/Campbell for Dixon/Groves
24 Nov	Q P R	A	W	3-1	..	..	..	..	..	..	..	..	..1	..1	..	Campbell1/O'Leary for Groves/Adams
2 Dec	Liverpool	H	W	3-0	..	..1p	..	..	..	..	O'Leary	..	..1	..1	..	
8 Dec	Luton T	A	D	1-1	..	..	..	..	..	..	..	..	..1	..	..	Groves for Limpar
15 Dec	Wimbledon	H	D	2-2	..	..	..	..	..	..1	Groves	..	..	..1	..	O'Leary for Winterburn
23 Dec	Aston Villa	A	D	0-0	..	..	..	..	..	Linighan	..	..	..	..	..	Rocastle for Limpar
26 Dec	Derby Co	H	W	3-0	..	..	..	..	..	..	Rocastle	..	..2	..1	..	Campbell/O'Leary for Rocastle/Limpar
29 Dec	Sheffield U	H	W	4-1	..	..1p	..	..1	..	..	Groves	..	..2	..	..	Cole/O'Leary for Groves/Winterburn
1 Jan	Manchester C	A	W	1-0	..	..	..	..	..	..	O'Leary	..	..1	..	..	Hillier/Groves for O'Leary/Limpar
12 Jan	Tottenham H	A	D	0-0	..	..	..	..	..	..	..	..	..	..	..	Hillier/Groves for Davis/Merson
19 Jan	Everton	H	W	1-0	..	..	..	..	..	Groves	..	..	..	..1	..	Campbell/Hillier for Limpar/Bould
2 Feb	Chelsea	A	L	1-2	..	..	..	..	..	Linighan	Groves	..	..1	..	..	Hillier/Campbell for Bould/Limpar
23 Feb	Crystal Palace	H	W	4-0	..	..	..	..	..	..	O'Leary1	..	..1	..1	Campbell1	Pates/Rocastle for Linighan/Merson
3 Mar	Liverpool	A	W	1-0	..	..	..	..	..	Adams	..	Hillier	..	..1	..	Rocastle/Davis for Campbell/Adams
17 Mar	Leeds U	H	W	2-0	..	..	..	..	..	..	..	..	..	..	..2	
20 Mar	Nottingham F	H	D	1-1	..	..	..	..	..	..	..	Davis	..	..	..1	Groves/Limpar for Davis/Merson
23 Mar	Norwich C	A	D	0-0	..	..	..	Rocastle	..	..	..	..	..	Campbell	Limpar	Groves/Linighan for Limpar/Rocastle
30 Mar	Derby Co	A	W	2-0	..	..	..	Campbell	..	..	Rocastle	..	..2	Merson	..	Groves/Hillier for Limpar/Rocastle
3 Apr	Aston Villa	H	W	5-0	..	..	..	Hillier	..	..	Campbell2	..1	..2	..	..	Thomas/Groves for Hillier/Merson
6 Apr	Sheffield U	A	W	2-0	..	..	..	..	..	..	..1	..	..1	..	..	Groves/Thomas for Merson/Limpar
9 Apr	Southampton	A	D	1-1	..	*opponents*	..	..	..	..	..	..	..	Groves	..	Thomas/Merson for Hillier/Limpar
17 Apr	Manchester C	H	D	2-2	..	..	..	Thomas	..	..	..1	..	..	..	Merson1	Limpar/O'Leary for Merson/Dixon
23 Apr	Q P R	H	W	2-0	..	..1p	..	Hillier	..	..	..	..	..	..1	Limpar	O'Leary/Groves for Merson/Limpar
4 May	Sunderland	A	D	0-0	..	..	..	..	..	..	..	..	..	..	Groves	O'Leary for Groves
6 May	Manchester U	H	W	3-1	..	..	..	..	..	..	..	..	..3.1p	..	Limpar	Thomas/O'Leary for Hillier/Limpar
11 May	Coventry C	H	W	6-1	..	*opponents*	..	..	..	..	..	..	..1	..	..3	Linighan/Groves1 for Merson/Campbell

FA Cup

5 Jan	Sunderland (3)	H	W	2-1	Seaman	Dixon	Winterburn	Thomas	Bould	Linighan	Groves	Davis	Smith1	Merson	Limpar1	O'Leary for Limpar
27 Jan	Leeds U (4)	H	D	0-0	..	..	..	..	..	Groves	O'Leary	..	..	..	..	Hillier/Campbell for O'Leary/Limpar
30 Jan	Leeds U (4R)	A	D	1-1*	..	..	..	..	..	Linighan	Hillier	..	..	..	..1	
13 Feb	Leeds U (4R/2)	H	D	0-0*	..	..	..	..	..	Groves	O'Leary	..	..	..	..	Campbell/Linighan for Groves/Limpar
16 Feb	Leeds U (4R/3)	A	W	2-1	..	..1	..	..	..	Linighan	..	..	..	..1	Campbell	
27 Feb	Shrewsbury T (5)	A	W	1-0	..	..	..	..1	..	Adams	..	Hillier	..	..	..	Rocastle for Merson
9 Mar	Cambridge U (6)	H	W	2-1	..	..	..	..	..	..1	..	..	..	..	..1	Davis for Hillier
14 Apr	Tottenham H (S/F) (at Wembley)		L	1-3	..	..	..	..	..	..	Campbell	Davis	..1	..	Limpar	Groves for Limpar

*after extra time

Football League (Rumblelows) Cup

25 Sep	Chester (2)	A	W	1-0	Seaman	Dixon	Winterburn	Hillier	Bould	Adams	Rocastle	Davis	Smith	Merson1	Groves	Cambell for Rocastle
9 Oct	Chester (2)	H	W	5-0	..	..	..	..	..	..1	..	..	..1	..1	..2	Campbell/O'Leary for Rocastle/Bould
30 Oct	Manchester C (3)	A	W	2-1	..	..	..	Thomas	..	..1	Groves1	..	..	..	Limpar	Campbell for Limpar
28 Nov	Manchester U (4)	H	L	2-6	..	..	..	..	..	..	..	..	..2	..	..	Campbell for Limpar

Appearances (Goals)

Bould 38 (5) – Dixon 38 (5) – Seaman 38 – Winterburn 38 – Davis 37 (13) – Merson 37 (13) – Smith 37 (22) – Limpar 34 (11) – Groves 32 (3) – Thomas 31 (2) – Adams 30 (1) – Campbell 22 (9) – O'Leary 21 (1) – Rocastle 16 (2) – Hillier 16 – Linighan 10 – Jonsson 2 – Cole 1 – Pates 1 – Own goals 2 – **Total 19 players (86)**

Position in League Table

	P	W	D	L	F:A	Pts	
Arsenal	38	24	13	1	74:18	83**	1st

**two points deducted

SEASON 1991–92 FOOTBALL LEAGUE (DIVISION 1)

17 Aug	Q P R	H	D	1-1	Seaman	Dixon	Winterburn	Hillier	O'Leary	Adams	Campbell	Davis	Smith	Merson1	Limpar	Rocastle/Groves for O'Leary/Campbell
20 Aug	Everton	A	L	1-3	..	..	..1	..	..	..	Rocastle	..	..	..	..	Groves/Linighan for Limpar/Hillier
24 Aug	Aston Villa	A	L	1-3	..	..	..	Linighan	..	..	..	..	..1	..	..	Groves/Thomas for O'Leary/Rocastle
27 Aug	Luton T	H	W	2-0	..	..	..	Thomas	Linighan	..	..	..	..1	..1	..	
31 Aug	Manchester C	H	W	2-1	..	..	..	..	..	..	..	..	..1	..	..1	Campbell/Pates for Rocastle/Limpar
3 Sep	Leeds U	A	D	2-2	..	..	..	..	..	..	O'Leary	..	..2	..	Campbell	Rocastle for Thomas
7 Sep	Coventry C	H	L	1-2	..	..	..	Campbell	..	..1	Rocastle	..	..	..	Limpar	O'Leary/Thomas for Limpar/Davis

14 Sep	Crystal Palace	A	W	4-1	..	..	..	Hillier	..	..	..	Groves	..1	..	Campbell2	Thomas1/O'Leary for Groves/Hillier
21 Sep	Sheffield U	H	W	5-2	..	..1	..	Campbell1	..	..	..1	Davis	..1	..	Groves1	O'Leary/Thomas for Winterburn/Groves
28 Sep	Southampton	A	W	4-0	..	..	..	Thomas	..	..	..1	Wright3	..	..	Limpar	Campbell for Merson
5 Oct	Chelsea	H	W	3-2	..	..1p	..	..	..	Pates	..	..1	..	Campbell1	..	Merson/O'Leary for Limpar/Wright
19 Oct	Manchester U	A	D	1-1	..	..	..	Davis	Pates	Adams	..1	..	..	Merson	Campbell	
26 Oct	Notts Co	H	W	2-0	..	..	..	..	..	..	..	..1	..1	..	..	Limpar for Campbell
2 Nov	West Ham	H	L	0-1	..	..	..	Thomas	..	Linighan	..	..	..	..	Limpar	Groves for Thomas
16 Nov	Oldham A	A	D	1-1	..	..	..	Hillier	Bould	..	..	..1	..	..	Pates	O'Leary/Groves for Bould/Pates
23 Nov	Sheffield W	A	D	1-1	..	..	..	..	..1	..	..	..	..	..	..	O'Leary for Hillier
1 Dec	Tottenham H	H	W	2-0	..	..	..	..	..	..	..	..1	..	..	Campbell1	Limpar/O'Leary for Wright/Rocastle
8 Dec	Nottingham F	A	L	2-3	..	..	..	..	..	..	..	Campbell	..1	..1	Limpar	Carter/O'Leary for Limpar/Bould
21 Dec	Everton	H	W	4-2	..	..	..	..	..	Adams	..	Wright4	..	..	..	O'Leary/Campbell for Rocastle/Merson
26 Dec	Luton T	A	L	0-1	..	..	..	O'Leary	..	..	..	..	..	..	..	Campbell for Limpar
28 Dec	Manchester C	A	L	0-1	..	..	..	..	..	..	..	..	..	..	Davis	Linighan/Groves for Bould/O'Leary
1 Jan	Wimbledon	H	D	1-1	..	..	..	Hillier	Linighan	..	..	..	..	..1	Carter	Campbell for Wright
11 Jan	Aston Villa	H	D	0-0	..	..	..	..	O'Leary	..	..	Campbell	..	..	..	Groves for Merson
18 Jan	Q P R	A	D	0-0	..	..	..	Davis	..	..	..	Wright	..	..	..	
29 Jan	Liverpool	A	L	0-2	..	..	..	Parlour	..	..	..	..	..	..	..	Bould/Groves for O'Leary/Parlour
1 Feb	Manchester U	H	D	1-1	..	..	..	Hillier	Bould	..	..1	..	..	..	..	Pates/Limpar for Rocastle/Carter
8 Feb	Notts Co	A	W	1-0	..	..	..	..	..	..	Pates	..	..1	..	Groves	Parlour/Campbell for Winterburn/Groves
11 Feb	Norwich C	H	D	1-1	..	..	..	..	..	..	..	..	..	..1	Limpar	Campbell/Parlour for Limpar/Winterburn
15 Feb	Sheffield W	H	W	7-1	..	..	..	..	..	..	Rocastle	..1	..1	..1	..2	Campbell2 for Smith
22 Feb	Tottenham H	A	D	1-1	..	..	..	..	..	Pates	..	..1	..	..	Campbell	O'Leary/Limpar for Hillier/Rocastle
10 Mar	Oldham A	H	W	2-1	..	..	..	..	..	Adams	..	..1	..	..1	Limpar	O'Leary for Limpar
14 Mar	West Ham U	A	W	2-0	..	..	..	..	..	..	..	..2	..	..	Groves	Campbell/O'Leary for Smith/Groves
22 Mar	Leeds U	H	D	1-1	..	..	..	..	..	..	..	..	O'Leary	..1	Campbell	Parlour/Limpar for Hillier/Rocastle
28 Mar	Wimbledon	A	W	3-1	..	..	..	..	..	..	Parlour1	..1	Campbell1	..	Groves	Limpar/Lydersen for Groves/Merson
31 Mar	Nottingham F	H	D	3-3	..	..1p	..	..	..	..1	Rocastle	..	..	..1	Limpar	Lydersen/Smith for Rocastle/Wright
4 Apr	Coventry C	A	W	1-0	..	..	..	..	..	..	Lydersen	..	..1	..	..	Rocastle/Smith for Winterburn/Limpar
8 Apr	Norwich C	A	W	3-1	..	O'Leary	Lydersen	..	..	..	Rocastle	..2.1p	..1	..	..	Morrow/Smith for O'Leary/Limpar
11 Apr	Crystal Palace	H	W	4-1	..	Lydersen	Winterburn	..	..	..	..	..	..1	..3	..	Smith/Morrow for Limpar/Winterburn
18 Apr	Sheffield U	A	D	1-1	..	..	..	..	..	..	..	Campbell1	Smith	..	..	Heaney for Limpar
20 Apr	Liverpool	H	W	4-0	..	..	..	..1	..	..	..	Wright2	Campbell	..	..1	O'Leary for Lydersen
25 Apr	Chelsea	A	D	1-1	..	Dixon1	..	..	..	..	..	..	..	..	..	Smith/Merson for Limpar/O'Leary
2 May	Southampton	H	W	5-1	..	..	..	..	..	..	..	..3.1p	..1	..	..	Smith1/Parlour for Limpar/Merson

FA Cup

4 Jan	Wrexham (3)	A	L	1-2	Seaman	Dixon	Winterburn	Hillier	O'Leary	Adams	Rocastle	Campbell	Smith1	Merson	Carter	Groves for Campbell

Football League (Rumbelows) Cup

25 Sep	Leicester C (2)	A	D	1-1	Seaman	Dixon	Thomas	Campbell	Linighan	Adams	Rocastle	Davis	Wright1	Merson	Groves	O'Leary for Linighan
8 Oct	Leicester C (2)	H	W	2-0	..	..	Winterburn	Thomas	Pates	..	..	Wright1	Smith	..1	Campbell	Groves for Writht
30 Oct	Coventry C (3)	A	L	0-1	..	..	..	Davis	..	..	..	..	..	..	Limpar	Groves/Linighan for Limpar/Pates

FA Charity Shield

18 Aug	Tottenham H	D	0-0	Seaman (at Wembley)	Dixon	Winterburn	Hillier	O'Leary	Adams	Rocastle	Davis	Smith	Merson	Campbell	Thomas/Cole for Rocastle/Campbell

European Cup

18 Sept	FK Austria (1)	H	W	6-1	Seaman	Dixon	Winterburn	Campbell	Linighan1	Adams	Rocastle	Davis	Smith4	Merson	Limpar1	Groves for Limpar
2 Oct	FK Austria (1)	A	L	0-1	..	..	..	Thomas	..	..	..	Campbell	..	..	O'Leary	Groves for Merson
23 Oct	Benfica (2)	A	D	1-1	..	..	..	Davis	Pates	..	..	..1	..	..	Limpar	Groves/Thomas for Campbell/Limpar
6 Nov	Benifica (2)	H	L	1-3*	..	..	..	..	..1	..	..	..	..	..	..	

*after extra time

Appearances (Goals)

Seaman 42 – Merson 42 (12) – Winterburn 41 (1) – Rocastle 39 (4) – Smith 39 (2) – Dixon 38 (4) – Adams 35 (2) – Campbell 31 (13) – Wright 30 (24) – Limpar 29 (4) – Hillier 27 (1) – Bould 25 (1) – O'Leary 25 – Linighan 17 – Groves 13 (1) – Davis 12 – Pates 11 – Thomas 10 (1) – Carter 6 – Parlour 6 (1) – Morrow (2) – Heaney 1 – **Total 22 players (71)**

Position in League Table

	P	W	D	L	F:A	Pts	
Leeds U	42	22	16	4	74:37	82	1st
Arsenal	42	19	15	8	81:46	72	4th

SEASON 1992–93 FA PREMIER LEAGUE

15 Aug	Norwich C	H	L	2-4	Seaman	Dixon	Winterburn	Hiller	Bould1	Adams	Jensen	Smith	Campbell1	Merson	Limpar	Wright for Merson
18 Aug	Blackburn Rov	A	L	0-1	..	..	..	..	..	..	..	..	..	Carter	..	Pates/Groves for Jensen/Limpar
23 Aug	Liverpool	A	W	2-0	..	..	..	..	Pates	..	..	Wright1	..	Parlour	..1	Merson for Limpar
26 Aug	Oldham	H	W	2-0	..	..	..1	..	Bould	..	Parlour	..1	..	Merson	Morrow	Pates/Smith for Merson/Wright
29 Aug	Sheffield W	H	W	2-1	..	..	..	..	..	..	Jensen	..	..	..1	Parlour1	Smith for Merson
2 Sep	Q P R	A	D	0-0	..	..	..	..	..	..	..	..	..	..	..	Pates/Smith for Hillier/Merson
5 Sep	Wimbledon	A	L	2-3	..	..	..	Pates	..	..	..	..2	..	..	..	O'Leary/Smith for Jensen/Adams
12 Sep	Blackburn Rov	H	L	0-1	..	..	..	Selley	..	..	..	..	Smith	..	..	Campbell/Morrow for Parlour/Jensen
19 Sep	Sheffield U	A	D	1-1	..	..	..	Parlour	..	..	..	..1	..	..	Limpar	Linighan/Flatts for Merson/Limpar
28 Sep	Manchester C	H	W	1-0	..	..	..	Hillier	..	..	..	..1	..	..	Campbell	Limpar for Smith
3 Oct	Chelsea	H	W	2-1	..	..	..	..	..	..	..	..1	..	..1	..	Limpar for Merson
17 Oct	Nottingham F	A	W	1-0	..	..	..	..	..	..	..	..	..	..1	..	Limpar/Pates for Wright/Jensen
24 Oct	Everton	H	W	2-0	..	..	..	..	..	..	..	..	..1	..	..	Pates/Limpar1 for Dixon/Wright
2 Nov	Crystal P	A	W	2-1	..	..	Morrow	..	..	..	..	..1	..	..1	..	Limpar for Wright
7 Nov	Coventry C	H	W	3-0	..	..	..	..	..	..	..	..1	..1	..	..1	Limpar for Campbell
21 Nov	Leeds U	A	L	0-3	..	..	..	..	..	..	..	..	Campbell	..	Limpar	Parlour/Miller for Hillier/Seaman
28 Nov	Manchester U	H	L	0-1	..	..	..	..	..	..	..	..	..	..	..	Parlour/Flatts for Jensen/Limpar
5 Dec	Southampton	A	L	0-2	..	..	..	..	..	..	Parlour	..	..	..	Flatts	Jensen/Limpar for Dixon/Flatts
12 Dec	Tottenham H	A	L	0-1	..	Lydersen	Winterburn	..	..	..	Jensen	..	..	..	Parlour	Limpar for Jensen
19 Dec	Middlesbrough	H	D	1-1	..	..	..	..	Linighan	..	Flatts	..1	Smith	..	..	Jensen/Campbell for Merson/Parlour
26 Dec	Ipswich T	H	D	0-0	..	..	..	..	Bould	Linighan	Jensen	..	..	Campbell	Flatts	O'Leary Limpar for Jensen/Campbell
28 Dec	Aston Villa	A	L	0-1	..	..	..	..	..	..	O'Leary	..	..	..	Parlour	Flatts/Limpar for Parlour/Hillier
9 Jan	Sheffield U	H	D	1-1	..	Dixon	..	..1	Linighan	Adams	Jensen	..	..	Merson	Limpar	O'Leary for Merson
16 Jan	Manchester C	A	W	1-0	..	..	..	..	Bould	..	..	Campbell	..	..1	Flatts	
31 Jan	Liverpool	H	L	0-1	..	..	..	..	Linighan	..	Carter	..	..	..	Parlour	O'Leary/Heaney for Hiller/O'Leary
10 Feb	Wimbledon	H	L	0-1	..	Keown	..	..	..	..	Selley	Wright	..	..	Campbell	Carter/Morrow for Merson/Smith
20 Feb	Oldham A	A	W	1-0	..	..	Morrow	..	..1	..	Jensen	Selley	Campbell	..	Limpar	Carter for Limpar
24 Feb	Leeds U	H	D	0-0	..	..	Winterburn	..	..	..	Selley	Wright	Smith	..	..	Campbell for Limpar
1 Mar	Chelsea	A	L	0-1	..	Dixon	Morrow	..	..	Keown	Jensen	Campbell	..	..	Flatts	Lydersen/Carter for Hillier/Campbell
3 Mar	Norwich C	A	D	1-1	..	..	Winterburn	Davis	..	..	..	Wright1	Parlour	Carter	Limpar	Campbell for Limpar
13 Mar	Coventry C	A	W	2-0	..	..	Keown	..	..	Adams	Parlour	..1	Campbell1	Merson	Morrow	Limpar/Hillier for Wright/Merson
20 Mar	Southampton	H	W	4-3	..	Keown	Winterburn	..	..1	..	Carter2	Morrow	..	..1	Limpar	Hillier/Dickov for Davis/Limpar
24 Mar	Manchester U	A	D	0-0	..	Dixon	Keown	Morrow	..	..	Jensen	Wright	..	..	Carter	Parlour/Hillier for Carter/Adams
6 Apr	Middlesbrough	A	L	0-1	..	O'Leary	Winterburn	Hillier	..	..	..	..	Smith	Carter	Limpar	Morrow/Keown for Hillier/O'Leary
10 Apr	Ipswich T	A	W	2-1	..	..	..	Morrow	..	Keown	..	Campbell	..1	Merson1	Carter	Adams/Parlour for O'Leary/Jensen
12 Apr	Aston Villa	H	L	0-1	..	Dixon	..	Selley	Keown	Adams	Morrow	Wright	..	..	Campbell	Parlour/Linighan for Wright/Campbell
21 Apr	Nottingham F	H	D	1-1	..	..	..	..	Linighan	Keown	Jensen	..1	..	Parlour	Carter	Adams/Campbell for Winterburn/Parlour
1 May	Everton	A	D	0-0	..	O'Leary	Lydersen	Davis	..	Bould	Keown	Selley	..	Campbell	..	Jensen/Heaney for Lydersen/Carter
4 May	Q P R	H	D	0-0	Miller	Dixon	Keown	..	..	Adams	Jensen	Campbell	..	Merson	Heaney	Carter for Merson
6 May	Sheffield W	A	L	0-1	..	Lydersen	..	Marshall	O'Leary	Bould	..	Selley	..	Heaney	Carter	McGowan/Flatts for Jensen/Lydersen
8 May	Crystal P	H	W	3-0	Seaman	Dixon	Winterburn	Davis	Linighan	Adams	Carter	Wright1	Campbell1	Merson	Parlour	Dickov1/O'Leary for Carter/Wright
11 May	Tottenham H	H	L	1-3	Miller	Lydersen	Keown	Marshall	O'Leary	Bould	Flatts	Selley	Smith	Dickov1	Heaney	McGowan/Carter for Lydersen/Flatts

FA Cup

2 Jan	Yeovil T (3)	A	W	3-1	Seaman	Dixon	Winterburn	Hillier	Bould	Adams	O'Leary	Wright3	Smith	Merson	Limpar	
25 Jan	Leeds U (4)	H	D	2-2	..	..	..	..	Linighan	..	Jensen	Campbell	..	..1	Parlour1	Carter for Jensen
3 Feb	Leeds U (4R)	A	W	3-2*	..	..	..	Selley	..	..	Morrow	Wright2	..1	..	..	Campbell/O'Leary for Parlour/Winterburn
13 Feb	Nottingham F (5)	H	W	2-0	..	..	..	Hillier	..	..	Jensen	..2	Selley	..	Limpar	Campbell/Morrow for Wright/Limpar
6 Mar	Ipswich T (6)	A	W	4-2	..	*Opponents*	..	Davis	..	..1	Carter	..1p	Smith	..	Morrow	Hillier/Campbell1 for Carter/Smith
4 Apr	Tottenham H (SF) (at Wembley)		W	1-0	..	..	..	Hillier	..	..1	Parlour	..	Campbell	..	Selley	Smith/Morrow for Wright/Campbell
15 May	Sheffield W (F) (at Wembley)		D	1-1*	..	..	..	Davis	..	..	Jensen	..1	..	..	Parlour	Smith/O'Leary for Parlour/Wright
20 May	Sheffield W (FR) (at Wembley)		W	2-1*	..	..	..	..	..1	..	..	..1	Smith	..	Campbell	O'Leary for Wright

*after extra time

Football League (Coca-Cola) Cup

22 Sep	Millwall (2)	H	D	1-1	Seaman	Dixon	Winterburn	Hillier	Bould	Adams	Parlour	Wright	Smith	Merson	Limpar	Campbell1 for Limpar
7 Oct	Millwall (2)	A	D	1-1*	..	..	..	..	..	..	Jensen	..	..	..	Campbell1	Parlour for Merson
	*(won 3-1 on penalties)															
28 Oct	Derby Co (3)	A	D	1-1	..	Lydersen	Morrow	..	..	..	..	Campbell1	..	..	Limpar	
1 Dec	Derby Co (3R)	H	W	2-1	..	Dixon	..	..	..	..	Parlour	Wright1	Campbell1	..	Flatts	
6 Jan	Scarborough (4)	A	W	1-0	..	..	Winterburn1	..	..	..	O'Leary	..	Smith	..	Limpar	Campbell for Merson
12 Jan	Nottingham F (5)	H	W	2-0	..	..	..	..	Linighan	..	Jensen	..2	..	..	..	Campbell for Limpar
7 Feb	Crystal P (SF)	A	W	3-1	..	..	..	..	..	..	Selley	..1p	..2	..	Campbell	Morrow for Wright
10 Mar	Crystal P (SF)	H	W	2-0	..	..	..	Davis	..1	..	Carter	..1	..	..	Morrow	Hillier/Campbell for Winterburn/Smith
18 Apr	Sheffield W (f) (at Wembley)		W	2-1	..	O'Leary	..	Morrow1	..	..	Campbell	..	Davis	..1	Parlour	

Appearances (Goals)

Seaman 39 – Campbell 37 (4) – Adams 35 – Merson 33 (6) – Jensen 32 – Wright 31 (15) – Smith 31 (3) – Hillier 30 (1) – Dixon 29 – Winterburn 29 (1) – Bould 24 (1) – Limpar 23 (2) – Linighan 21 (2) – Parlour 21 (1) – Morrow 16 – Carter 16 (2) – Keown 16 – O'Leary 11 – Flatts 10 – Selley 9 – Lydersen 8 – Pates 7 – Davis 6 – Heaney 5 – Miller 4 – Dickov 3 (2) – Marshall 2 – McGowan 2 – Groves 1 – **Total 29 players (40)**

Position in League Table

	P	W	D	L	F:A	Pts	
Manchester U	42	24	12	6	67:31	84	1st
Arsenal	42	15	11	16	40:38	56	10th

SEASON 1993–94 FA PREMIER LEAGUE

14 Aug	Coventry C	H	L	0-3	Seaman	Dixon	Winterburn	Davis	Linighan	Adams	Jensen	Wright	Campbell	Merson	Limpar	McGoldrick/Keown for Jensen/Dixon
16 Aug	Tottenham H	A	W	1-0	..	Keown	..	..	..	..	..	..1	..	McGoldrick	Parlour	
21 Aug	Sheffield W	A	W	1-0	..	..	..	..	..	..	..	..1	..	..	..	Merson for Parlour
24 Aug	Leeds U	H	W	2-1	..	*opponents*	..	..	..	Selley	Merson1	..	..	..	..	Hillier for Davis
28 Aug	Everton	H	W	2-0	..	..	..	Hillier	..	Adams	Jensen	..2	..	..	..	Merson for Hillier
1 Sep	Blackburn Rov	A	D	1-1	..	..	..	Merson	..	..	..	..	..1	..	..	Selley for Merson
11 Sep	Ipswich T	H	W	4-0	..	..	..	Davis	..	..	..	..1	..3	Merson	McGoldrick	Hillier/Limpar for Jensen/Merson
19 Sep	Manchester U	A	L	0-1	..	..	..	Hillier	..	..	..	..	..	..	..	Davis/Smith for Hillier/Merson
25 Sep	Southampton	H	W	1-0	..	..	..	Davis	..	..	..	..	..	..1	..	Hillier for Davis
2 Oct	Liverpool	A	D	0-0	..	Dixon	..	..	..	..	..	..	..	..	..	
16 Oct	Manchester C	H	D	0-0	..	..	..	..	..	..	Heaney	..	Smith	Parlour	..	Campbell for Heaney
23 Oct	Oldham A	A	D	0-0	..	..	..	..	..	..	Hillier	..	..	Merson	..	Campbell for Hillier
30 Oct	Norwich C	H	D	0-0	..	..	..	..	Bould	..	Jensen	..	..	..	Limpar	Keown/Campbell for Winterburn/Smith
6 Nov	Aston Villa	H	L	1-2	..	..	..	Selley	Keown	..	..	..1	Campbell	Merson	..	
20 Nov	Chelsea	A	W	2-0	..	..	..	Davis	Linighan	Bould	Keown	..1p	Smith1	..	Selley	Morrow for Winterburn
24 Nov	West Ham U	A	D	0-0	..	..	..	Keown	..	..	Morrow	..	..	..	Limpar	Campbell/Miller for Limpar/Wright
27 Nov	Newcastle	H	W	2-1	..	..	..	Morrow	Keown	..	Jensen	..1	..1	..	McGoldrick	
4 Dec	Coventry C	A	L	0-1	..	..	..	Davis	..	Adams	Selley	..	..	..	..	Bould/Campbell for Adams/McGoldrick
6 Dec	Tottenham H	H	D	1-1	..	..	Keown	Selley	Bould	..	Jensen	..1	..	..	Limpar	Campbell for Smith
12 Dec	Sheffield W	H	W	1-0	Miller	..	Morrow	..	Keown	..	..	..1	..	..	..	Bould/Campbell for Keown/Merson
18 Dec	Leeds U	A	L	1-2	Seaman	..	Winterburn	..	Bould	..	..	..	..	Campbell1	..	Parlour/Morrow for Smith/Dixon
27 Dec	Swindon T	A	W	4-0	..	..	..	Parlour	..	..	..	..1	Campbell3	Hillier	McGoldrick	Merson/Keown for Parlour/Adams
29 Dec	Sheffield U	H	W	3-0	..	..	..	..	..	..	..	..1	..2	..	..	Merson/Keown for Wright/Parlour
1 Jan	Wimbledon	A	W	3-0	..	..	..	..1	..	..	..	..1	..1	..	..	Keown/Merson for Dixon/Jensen
3 Jan	Q P R	H	D	0-0	..	..	..	..	..	..	..	..	..	..	..	Keown for Jensen
15 Jan	Manchester C	A	D	0-0	..	..	..	..	..	..	..	..	..	..	..	Merson/Keown for McGoldrick/Jensen
22 Jan	Oldham A	H	D	1-1	..	..	..	..	..	..	..	..1p	..	..	..	Merson/Keown for McGoldrick/Jensen
13 Feb	Norwich C	A	D	1-1	..	..	Davis	..	..	..	Campbell1	Smith	Merson	Parlour		
19 Feb	Everton	A	D	1-1	..	..	..	..	..	..	..	..	..	..1	..	Keown/Hillier for Adams/Jensen
26 Feb	Blackburn Rov	H	W	1-0	..	..	..	..	..	..	..	..	..	..1	..	
5 Mar	Ipswich T	A	W	5-1	..	*opponents*	..	Selley	..	..	Parlour1	Wright3.1p	..	Hillier	Limpar	Merson/Keown for Limpar/Hillier
19 Mar	Southampton	A	W	4-0	..	..	..	Keown	Linighan	..	..	..3.1p	Campbell1	Selley	..	Smith for Limpar
22 Mar	Manchester U	H	D	2-2	..	*opponents*	..	Davis	Bould	..	Jensen	..	Smith	Merson1	Selley	Campbell for Davis
26 Mar	Liverpool	H	W	1-0	..	..	Keown	Parlour	..	Linighan	..	..	Campbell	..1	..	Morrow/Smith for Jensen/Wright
2 Apr	Swindon T	H	D	1-1	..	..	..	Davis	Linighan	Adams	..	..	Smith1	..	Parlour	Campbell/McGoldrick for Merson/Jensen
4 Apr	Sheffield U	A	D	1-1	..	Keown	Winterburn	Parlour	Bould	..	Campbell1	..	..	Selley	McGoldrick	Dixon/Merson for Keown/McGoldrick
16 Apr	Chelsea	H	W	1-0	..	Dixon	Morrow	Hillier	Keown	..	Selley	..1	Campbell	Parlour	..	Smith for Hillier
19 Apr	Wimbeldon	H	D	1-1	..	..	Keown	Davis	Bould1	..	Campbell	..	Smith	..	Selley	Flatts for Davis
23 Apr	Aston Villa	A	W	2-1	..	..	..	..	..	Linighan	..	..2.1p	..	Morrow	Flatts	Parlour for Davis
27 Apr	Q P R	A	D	1-1	..	..	..	Morrow	Linighan	Adams	Flatts	..	..	Merson1	Parlour	Selley/McGoldrick for Flatts/Keown
30 Apr	West Ham U	H	L	0-2	Millier	McGoldrick	Winterburn	Davis	Bould	Linighan	Parlour	..	Campbell	..	Selley	Morrow/Dickov for McGoldrick/Merson
7 May	Newcastle	A	L	0-2	..	Dixon	..	..	..	Adams	McGoldrick	..	Smith	Morrow	Selley	Parlour/Linighan for Davis/Dixon

FA Cup

10 Jan	Millwall (3)	A	W	1-0	Seaman	Dixon	Winterburn	Parlour	Bould	Adams1	Keown	Wright	Campbell	Hillier	McGoldrick	Merson/Jensen for Wright/Hillier
31 Jan	Bolton W (4)*	A	D	2-2	..	..	..	..	..	..1	..	..1	..	..	Merson	Smith for Parlour
9 Feb	Bolton W (4R)	H	L	1-3*	..	..	..	Hillier	..	..	Campbell	..	Smith1	Merson	Parlour	Keown/McGoldrick for Hillier/Wright

Football League (Coca-Cola) Cup

21 Sep	Huddersfield T (2)	A	W	5-0	Seaman	Keown	Winterburn	Davis	Linighan	Adams	Jensen	Wright3	Campbell1	Merson1	McGoldrick	Hillier/Smith for Jensen/Merson
5 Oct	Huddersfield (2)	H	D	1-1	..	Dixon	..	Parlour	..	Bould	..	Smith1	..	Limpar	..	Selley/Heaney for Jensen/McGoldrick
26 Oct	Norwich C (3)	H	D	1-1	..	..	..	..	..	Adams	..	Wright1	Smith	Merson	..	Campbell/Davis for Merson/McGoldrick
10 Nov	Norwich C (3R)	A	W	3-0	..	..	Keown	Selley	..	Bould	..	..2	..	..1	Limpar	
30 Nov	Aston Villa (4)	H	L	0-1	..	..	Winterburn	Morrow	Keown	..	..	..	..	..	McGoldrick	Campbell/Davis for Jensen/Dixon

FA Charity Shield

7 Aug	Manchester U (at Wembley)		D	1-1	Seaman	Dixon	Winterburn	Davis	Linighan	Adams	Jensen	Wright1	Campbell	Merson	Limpar	Keown/McGoldrick for Dixon/Limpar

European Cup Winners' Cup

15 Sep	Odense (1)	A	W	2-1	Seaman	Selley	Winterburn	Davis	Linighan	Keown	Jensen	Wright1	Campbell	Merson1	McGoldrick	Smith for Wright
29 Sep	Odense (1)	H	D	1-1	..	Dixon	..	..	Keown	Adams	..	..	..1	..	..	Smith for Wright
20 Oct	Standard Liege (2)	H	W	3-0	..	..	..	..	..	..	..	..2	Smith	..1	..	Campbell/Linighan for Wright/Keown
3 Nov	Standard Liege (2)	A	W	7-0	..	..	..	..	..	..1	..	Selley1	..1	..1	Campbell2	McGoldrick 1/Bould for Smith/Keown
2 Mar	Torino (3)	A	D	0-0	..	..	..	..	Bould	..	..	Campbell	..	..	Hillier	Selley for Davis
15 Mar	Torino (3)	H	W	1-0	..	..	..	..	..	..1	..	Wright	..	..	..	Selley/Keown for Hillier/Jensen
29 Mar	Paris St-German (SF)	A	D	1-1	..	..	..	..	..	..	..	..1	..	..	Selley	Keown/Campbell for Davis/Smith
12 Apr	Paris St-German (SF)	H	W	1-0	..	..	..	..	..	..	..	..	..	Campbell1	Selley	Hillier/Keown for Davis/Winterburn
4 May	Parma (F) (at Copenhagen)		W	1-0	..	..	..	..	..	..	Campbell	Morrow	..1	Merson	..	McGoldrick for Merson

Appearances (Goals)

Seaman 39 – Wright 39 (23) – Campbell 37 (14) – Adams 35 – Winterburn 34 – Dixon 33 – Keown 33 – Merson 33 (7) – Jensen 27 – Parlour 27 (2) – McGoldrick 26 – Bould 25 (1) – Smith 25 (3) – Davis 22 – Linighan 21 – Selley 18 – Hillier 15 – Morrow 11 – Limpar 10 – Miller 4 – Flatts 3 – Dickov 1 – Heaney 1 – Own goals 3 – **Total 23 players (51)**

Position in League Table

	P	W	D	L	F:A	Pts	
Manchester U	42	27	11	4	80:38	92	1st
Arsenal	42	18	17	7	53:28	71	4th

SEASON 1994–95 FA PREMIER LEAGUE

20 Aug	Manchester C	H	W	3-0*	Seaman	Dixon	Winterburn	Jensen	Bould	Adams	Campbell1	Wright1	Smith	Merson	Schwarz	Keown/Dickov for Adams/Merson
23 Aug	Leeds U	A	L	0-1	..	..	..	..	..	..	..	..	..	..	..	Keown for Bould
28 Aug	Liverpool	A	L	0-3	..	..	..	..	Keown	..	..	..	..	..	..	Linighan/Davis for Jensen/Merson
31 Aug	Blackburn Rov	H	D	0-0	..	..	..	..	..	..	..	..	..	..	..	Dickov/Linighan for Merson/Adams
10 Sep	Norwich C	A	D	0-0	..	..	..	Selley	..	..	Parlour	..	..	Campbell	McGoldrick	Smith for McGoldrick
18 Sep	Newcastle U	H	L	2-3	..	..	..	Jensen	..	..1	..	..1	Smith	Merson	..	Selley/Campbell for Jensen/Parlour
25 Sep	West Ham U	A	W	2-0	..	..	..	Davis	..	..1	Selley	..1	..	..	..	Linighan for Keown
1 Oct	Crystal P	H	L	1-2	..	..	..	..	Linighan	..	..	..1	..	..	..	Campbell for Davis
8 Oct	Wimbledon	A	W	3-1	..	..	..	Jensen	Bould	..	Parlour	..1	..1	Campbell1	..	Hillier for Schwarz
15 Oct	Chelsea	H	W	3-1	..	..	..	..	..	..	..	..2	..	..1	..	Selley/Keown for Jensen/Adams
23 Oct	Coventry C	H	W	2-1	..	..	..	Selley	..	Keown	Campbell	..2	..	Schwarz	Parlour	McGoldrick for Wright
29 Oct	Everton	A	D	1-1	..	McGoldrick	..	Jensen	Keown	Adams	Parlour	Campbell	..	Merson	Schwarz1	Selley/Linighan for Winterburn/Merson
6 Nov	Sheffield W	H	D	0-0	..	Keown	..	Selley	Bould	..	..	Dickov	..	Schwarz	McGoldrick	Campbell for Smith
19 Nov	Southampton	A	L	0-1	..	Dixon	..	..	..	..	Keown	..	Campbell	McGoldrick	Schwarz	Carter for McGoldrick
23 Nov	Leicester C	A	L	1-2	..	..	..	..	..	Linighan	..	Wright1p	Dickov	Carter	..	Campbell/Morrow for Linighan/Selley

26 Nov	Manchester U	H	D	0-0	..	..	..	Jensen	..	Adams	Morrow	..	Smith	McGoldrick	Carter	Dickov/Keown for Carter/Jensen
3 Dec	Nottingham F	A	D	2-2	Bartram	..	..	Davis1	..	Keown1	Parlour	Hillier	Campbell	Flatts	Schwarz	Shaw for Flatts
12 Dec	Manchester C	A	W	2-1	..	..	..	Morrow	..	..	Jensen	Campbell	Smith1	Parlour	..1	
17 Dec	Leeds U	H	L	1-3	..	..	..	..	..	..	..	..	..	..	..	Flatts/Linighan1 for Smith/Jensen
26 Dec	Aston Villa	H	D	0-0	..	..	..	..	..	..	Hughes	Dickov	Campbell	..	..	Flatts for Hughes
28 Dec	Ipswich T	A	W	2-0	..	..	..	Jensen	..	..	Campbell1	Wright1	Smith	..	..	Linighan/Dickov for Smith/Wright
31 Dec	Q P R	H	L	1-3	..	..	..1	..	..	..	..	..	..	..	..	Clarke for Smith
2 Jan	Tottenham H	A	L	0-1	Seaman	..	..	..	..	Linighan	Selley	..	Campbell	..	..	Smith for Selley
14 Jan	Everton	H	D	1-1	..	..	..	..	Keown	..	Hillier	..1	Hartson	..	..	Kiwomya/Morrow for Parlour/Jensen
21 Jan	Coventry C	A	W	1-0	..	..	Morrow	Keown	Bould	..	Campbell	..	..1	Hillier	..	Parlour/Kiwomya for Hillier/Wright
24 Jan	Southampton	H	D	1-1	..	..	..	..	..	..	Jensen	..	..1	Parlour	..	Hillier/Kiwomya for Keown/Parlour
4 Feb	Sheffield Wed	A	L	1-3	..	..	Winterburn	Jensen	Linighan1	Adams	Selley	Campbell	..	Merson	Kiwomya	Keown/Parlour for Jensen/Selley
11 Feb	Leicester C	H	D	1-1	..	..	..	..	..	..	McGoldrick	Selley	..	..1	..	Keown/Parlour for Selley/Jensen
21 Feb	Nottingham F	H	W	1-0	..	..	..	..	Bould	Linighan	..	Merson	Kiwomya1	Schwarz	Helder	
25 Feb	Crystal P	A	W	3-0	..	..	..	..	..	..	..	..1	..2	..	..	Morrow for Winterburn, then Parlour for Morrow
5 Mar	West Ham U	H	L	0-1	Bartram	..	..	..	..	..	Parlour	Wright	Helder	Merson	Schwarz	Morrow/Kiwomya for Jensen/Helder
8 Mar	Blackburn Rov	A	L	1-3	..	..	..	Morrow1	Linighan	Adams	..	Helder	Hartson	..	..	Wright/Bould for Hartson/Linighan
19 Mar	Newcastle U	A	L	0-1	..	..	..	Jensen	Bould	..	Morrow	Wright	..	..	Helder	Parlour/McGoldrick for Helder/Hartson
22 Mar	Manchester U	A	L	0-3	..	..	..	Morrow	..	Adams	Keown	..	Kiwomya	Merson	Parlour	Helder for Parlour
1 Apr	Norwich C	H	W	5-1	..	..1	..	..	..	*opponents*	Hillier	..	Hartson2	..1	Helder	Keown/Kiwomya for Morrow/Hartson
8 Apr	Q P R	A	L	1-3	Seaman	..	..	Schwarz	..	Adams1	Morrow	..	..	..	..	Hillier/Kiwomya for Morrow/Hartson
12 Apr	Liverpool	H	L	0-1	..	Keown	..	..	..	..	Hillier	..	McGoldrick	..	..	Parlour/Hartson for Merson/Helder
15 Apr	Ipswich T	H	W	4-1	..	Dixon	..	..	..	..	Keown	..3	Hartson	..1	..	Parlour/Kiwomya for Winterburn/Wright
17 Apr	Aston Villa	A	W	4-0	..	..	..	..	..	..	..	..2.1p	..2	..	Parlour	Hillier/Kiwomya for Parlour/Wright
29 Apr	Tottenham H	H	D	1-1	..	..	..	..	..	..	..	..1p	..	..	Helder	Parlour for Helder
4 May	Wimbledon	H	D	0-0	..	..	..	Jensen	Linighan	..	Parlour	..	..	..	..	Kiwomya for Hartson
14 May	Chelsea	A	L	1-2	..	..	McGowan	..	Bould	..	..	..	..1	..	..	Linighan/Dickov for McGowan/Helder

*including an own goal

FA Cup

7 Jan	Millwall (3)	A	D	0-0	Seaman	Dixon	Winterburn	Jensen	Bould	Linighan	Hillier	Wright	Smith	Parlour	Schwarz	Keown/Campbell for Jensen/Smith
18 Jan	Millwall (3R)	H	L	0-2	..	..	..	..	Keown	..	..	..	Campbell	..	Morrow	Adams/Flatts for Keown/Jensen

Football League (Coca-Cola) Cup

21 Sep	Hartlepool U (2)	A	W	5-0	Seaman	Dixon	Keown	Davis	Linighan	Adams1	Parlour	Wright2	Smith1	Merson1	Selley	McGoldrick for Smith
5 Oct	Hartlepool U (2)	H	W	2-0	..	..	Winterburn	..	Bould	Keown	..	Dickov1	Campbell1	Hillier	McGoldrick	
26 Oct	Oldham A(3)	A	D	0-0	..	..	..	Selley	..	Adams	..	Campbell	Smith	Merson	Schwarz	Keown/McGoldrick for Dixon/Campbell
9 Nov	Oldham A (3R)	H	W	2-0	..	Keown	..	..	..	..	..	Dickov2	Campbell	McGoldrick	..	Jensen for Selley
30 Nov	Sheffield W (4)	H	W	2-0	..	Dixon	..	Morrow1	..	..	Campbell	Wright1	Smith	..	..	Bartram/Dickov/ Keown for Seaman/ Morrow/McGoldrick
11 Jan	Liverpool (QF)	A	L	0-1	..	..	..	Jensen	..	Linighan	Hillier	..	Campbell	Parlour	..	Morrow/Dickov for Bould/Parlour

European Cup Winners' Cup

15 Sep	Omonia Nicosia (1)	A	W	3-1	Seaman	Dixon	Winterburn	Schwarz	Linighan	Keown	Jensen	Wright1	Smith	Merson2	Parlour	Morrow for Schwarz
29 Sep	Omonia Nicosia (1)	H	W	3-0	..	..	..	..1	..	Adams	..	..2	..	..	..	Hillier/Campbell for Jensen/Merson
20 Oct	Brondby (2)	A	W	2-1	..	..	..	..	Bould	..	..	..1	..1	Campbell	..	
3 Nov	Brondby (2)	H	D	2-2	..	..	..	Selley1	Keown	..	..	..1p	..	Merson	..	Campbell/Bould for Wright/Dixon
2 Mar	Auxerre (3)	H	D	1-1	..	..	..	Schwarz	Bould	..	..	..1p	Kiwomya	..	McGoldrick	Hartson/Parlour for McGoldrick/Kiwomya
16 Mar	Auxerre (3)	A	W	1-0	..	..	..	..	..	..	Keown	..1	Hartson	..	Parlour	Morrow for Hartson
6 Apr	Sampdoria (SF)	H	W	3-2	..	..	..	..	..2	..	Hillier	..1	..	..	..	Kiwomya/Morrow for Wright/Merson
20 Apr	Sampdoria (SF)	A	L	2-3*	..	..	..	..1	..	..	Keown	..1	..	..	Hillier	McGoldrick/Kiwomya for Hillier/Wright
	*Arsenal won 3-2 on penalties after extra time															
10 May	Real Zaragoza (F)		L	1-2*	..	..	..	..	Linighan	..	..	..	..1	..	Parlour	Morrow/Hillier for Winterburn/Keown
	(at Paris) *after extra time															

Appearances (Goals)

Winterburn 39 – Dixon 39 (1) – Schwarz 34 (2) – Bould 31 – Wright 31 (18) – Seaman 31 – Keown 31 (1) – Parlour 30 – Adams 27 (3) – Merson 24 (4) – Jensen 24 (1) – Campbell 23 (4) – Linighan 20 (2) – Smith 19 (2) – Hartson 15 (7) – Morrow 15 (1) – Kiwomya 14 (3) – Selley 13 – Helder 13 – Bartram 11 – McGoldrick 11 – Hillier 9 – Dickov 9 – Davis 4 (1) – Carter 3 – Flatts 3 – Hughes 1 – Shaw 1 – Clarke 1 – McGowan 1 – own goals 2 – **Total 30 players (50)**

Position in League Table

	P	W	D	L	F:A	Pts	
Blackburn R	42	27	8	7	80:39	89	1st
Arsenal	42	13	12	17	52:49	51	12th

SEASON 1995–96 FA PREMIER LEAGUE

20 Aug	Middlesbrough	H	D	1-1	Seaman	Dixon	Winterburn	Keown	Bould	Adams	Platt	Wright1	Merson	Bergkamp	Parlour	Helder for Parlour
23 Aug	Everton	A	W	2-0	..	..	..	..	..	..	..1	..1	..	..	..	Jensenw for Keown
26 Aug	Coventry C	A	D	0-0	..	..	..	..	..	..	..	..	..	..	..	Jensen/Helder for Dixon/Parlour
29 Aug	Nottm F	H	D	1-1	..	..	..	..	..	..	..1	..	..	..	..	Helder for Parlour
10 Sept	Manchester C	A	W	1-0	..	..	..	..	..	..	Jensen	..1	..	..	..	McGoldrick for Parlour
16 Sept	West Ham U	H	W	1-0	..	Dixon	..	Jensen	..	..	Parlour	..1p	..	..	Helder	
23 Sept	Southampton	H	W	4-2	..	..	..	Keown	..	..1	..	..1	..	..2	..	
30 Sept	Chelsea	A	L	0-1	..	..	..	..	..	..	..	..	..	..	Jensen	Helder/Linighan for Jensen/Keown
14 Oct	Leeds U	A	W	3-0	..	..	..	..	..	..	..	..1	..1	..1	Helder	
21 Oct	Aston Villa	H	W	2-0	..	..	..	..	..	..	..	..1	..1	..	..	
30 Oct	Bolton W	A	L	0-1	..	..	..	..	..	..	..	..	..	..	..	Platt for Keown
4 Nov	Manchester U	H	W	1-0	..	..	..	..	..	..	Platt	..	..	..1	..	Hartson for Wright
18 Nov	Tottenham H	A	L	1-2	..	..	..	..	..	..	..	Hartson	..	..1	..	Hillier for Helder
21 Nov	Sheffield W	H	W	4-2	..	..	..1	..	..	..	..	..1	..	..1	..	Dickov1 for Helder
26 Nov	Blackburn R	H	D	0-0	..	..	..	..	..	..	..	..	..	..	Hillier	Helder/Dickov for Keown/Hartson
2 Dec	Aston Villa	A	D	1-1	..	..	..	Jensen	..	..	..1	Wright	..	Hartson	Helder	Morrow/Dickov for Helder/Hartson
9 Dec	Southampton	A	D	0-0	..	..	..	Keown	..	..	..	..	..	..	Jensen	Clarke for Hartson
16 Dec	Chelsea	H	D	1-1	..	..1	..	..	..	..	..	..	..	..	..	Helder for Jensen
23 Dec	Liverpool	A	L	1-3	..	..	..	Jensen	Keown	Linighan	..	..1p	..	Parlour	..	Marshall/Hartson for Parlour/Helder
26 Dec	Q P R	H	W	3-0	..	..	..	..	..	Adams	..	..1	..2	Dickov	Clarke	
30 Dec	Wimbledon	H	L	1-3	..	..	..	..	..	Linighan	..	..1	..	Bergkamp	..	Parlour/Dickov for Clarke/Jensen
2 Jan	Newcastle U	A	L	0-2	..	..	..	Keown	Bould	Adams	..	..	..	..	Parlour	Dickov/Clarke for Bould/Parlour
13 Jan	Middlesbrough	A	W	3-2	..	..	McGowan	Jensen	Keown	Adams	..1	..	..1	..	Helder1	
20 Jan	Everton	H	L	1-2	..	..	Winterburn	..	Linighan	Marshall	Clarke	..1	..	..	..	Dickov for Clarke
3 Feb	Coventry	H	D	1-1	..	..	..	..	..	..	..	..	..	..1	..	Hughes for Jensen
10 Feb	Nottm F	A	W	1-0	..	..	..	..	..	Keown	Hillier	..	..	..1	..	
24 Feb	West Ham U	A	W	1-0	..	..	..	Morrow	..	..	..	Hartson1	..	..	Parlour	Platt for Hillier
2 Mar	Q P R	A	D	1-1	..	..	..	..	..	..	Platt	..	..	..1	..	Rose for Morrow
5 Mar	Manchester C	H	W	3-1	..	..1	..	Rose	..	..	..	..2	..	..	..	
16 Mar	Wimbledon	A	W	3-0	..	..	..1	Marshall	..	..	..1	Wright	..	..1	Hartson	
20 Mar	Manchester U	A	L	0-1	..	..	..	..	..	..	..	..	..	..	..	Hillier/Helder for Bergkamp/Merson
23 Mar	Newcastle U	H	W	2-0	..	..	..	..1	..	..	..	..1	..	..	..	Parlour/Helder for Wright/Winterburn
6 April	Leeds U	H	W	2-1	..	..	..	..	..	..	..	..2	..	..	..	
8 April	Sheffield W	A	L	0-1	..	..	Helder	..	..	..	..	..	..	..	..	Rose/Shaw for Helder/Hartson
15 April	Tottenham H	H	D	0-0	..	..	Winterburn	..	..	..	..	..	..	..	..	Helder for Merson
27 April	Blackburn R	A	D	1-1	..	..	..	Morrow	..	..	..	..1p	..	..	..	Rose/Shaw/Hartson for Morrow/ Linighan/Wright
1 May	Liverpool	H	D	0-0	..	..	..	Marshall	..	..	..	Hartson	..	..	..	
5 May	Bolton	H	W	2-1	..	..	..	..	..	..	..1	Wright	..	..1	..	Shaw/Hartson for Marshall/Wright

FA Cup

6 Jan	Sheffield U (3)	H	D	1-1	Seaman	Dixon	Winterburn	Jensen	Keown	Adams	Clarke	Wright1	Merson	Hartson	Helder	
17 Jan	Sheffield U (3R)	A	L	0-1	..	..	McGowan	..	..	....	Platt	..	..	Bergkamp	..	Linighan/Clarke for Dixon/Jensen

Football League (Coca Cola) Cup

19 Sept	Hartlepool (2)	A	W	3-0	Seaman	Dixon	Winterburn	Jensen	Bould	Adams2	Parlour	Wright1	Merson	Bergkamp	Helder	
3 Oct	Hartlepool (2)	H	W	5-0	..	..	..	Keown	..	..	..	..3	..	..2	Jensen	Helder/Hartson for Merson/Bergkamp
24 Oct	Barnsley (3)	A	W	3-0	Seaman	..	..	..1	..	..	Jensen	..	..	..1	Helder	Hughes/Hartson for Jensen/Wright
29 Nov	Sheffield W (4)	H	W	2-1	..	..	..	Jensen	..	..	Platt	..1p	..	..	Hartson1	Helder for Bergkamp
10 Jan	Newcastle U (5)	H	W	2-0	..	..	..	Keown	..	..	..	..2	Merson	..	Helder	Jensen for Bould
14 Feb	Aston Villa (SF)	H	D	2-2	..	..	..	Jensen	Linighan	Keown	Hillier	..	..	..2	..	Parlour for Helder
21 Feb	Aston Villa (SF)	A	D	0-0	(aet)	..	..	..	Morrow	..	..	Hillier	..	..	Parlour	Platt for Winterburn

Appearances (Goals)

Seaman 38 – Dixon 38 (2) – Merson 38 (5) – Winterburn 36 (2) – Keown 34 – Bergkamp 33 (11) – Wright 31 (15) – Platt 29 (5) – Helder – 24 (1) – Parlour 22 – Adams 21 (1) – Bould 19 – Hartson 19 (4) – Linighan 18 – Jensen 15 – Marshall 11 (1) – Dickov 7 (1) – Clarke 6 – Hillier 5 – Morrow 4 – Rose 4 – Shaw 3 – McGowan 1 – McGoldrick 1 – Hughes 1 – **Total 25 players (48)**

Position in League Table

	P	W	D	L	F:A	Pts	
Manchester U	38	25	7	6	73:35	82	1st
Arsenal	38	17	12	9	49:32	63	5th

SEASON 1996–97 FA PREMIER LEAGUE

17 Aug	West Ham U	H	W	2-0	Seaman	Dixon	Winterburn	..	Bould	Linighan	Parlour	Morrow	Merson	Bergkamp1p	Hartson1	Wright/Dickov for Hartson/Bergkamp
19 Aug	Liverpool	A	L	0-2	..	..	..	..	..	..	..	..	..	..	..	Wright/Helder/Hillier for Bergkamp/Hartson/Morrow
24 Aug	Leicester C	A	W	2-0	..	..	..	..	..	..	..	..	..	.. 1p	..	Wright1/Hillier for Bergkamp/Hartson
4 Sept	Chelsea	H	D	3-3	Lukic	..	..	..1	..	..	..	..	..1	..	..	Platt/Wright1 for Bould/Hartson
7 Sept	Aston Villa	A	D	2-2	..	..	..	..	Morrow	..1	Platt	Wright	..1	..	Parlour	Hartson/Helder for Morrow/Bergkamp
16 Sept	Sheffield W	H	W	4-1	Seaman	..	..	..	Bould	..	..1	..3.1p	..	Parlour	Hartson	Vieira for Platt
21 Sept	Middlesbrough	A	W	2-0	..	..	..	..	..	..	..	..1	..	Vieira	..1	Adams for Dixon
28 Sept	Sunderland	H	W	2-0	..	..	..	..	..	Adams	..	..	..	..	..1	Parlour1/Shaw for Vieira/Winterburn
12 Oct	Blackburn Rov	A	W	2-0	..	..	..	..	..	..	..	..2	..	..	..	Parlour for Hartson
19 Oct	Coventry C	H	D	0-0	..	..	..	..	..	..	..	..	..	..	..	Bergkamp for Hartson
26 Oct	Leeds U	H	W	3-0	..	..1	..	..	..	..	..	..1	..	Bergkamp1	Vieira	Morrow/Garde for Winterburn/Wright
2 Nov	Wimbledon	A	D	0-0	..	..	..	..	..	..	..	..1	..1	..	..	Garde for Bergkamp
16 Nov	Manchester U	A	L	0-1	..	..	..	..	..	..	..	..	..	..	..	
24 Nov	Tottenham H	H	W	3-1	Lukic	..	..	..	..	..1	..	..1p	..	..1	..	Hartson/Parlour for Platt/Bergkamp
30 Nov	Newcastle U	A	W	2-1	..	..1	..	..	..	..	..	..1	..	Hartson	..	Linighan/Morrow/Parlour for Keown/Hartson/..
4 Dec	Southampton	H	W	3-1	Lukic	..	..	Linighan	..	..	..	..1p	..1	..	..	Shaw1/Parlour for Platt/Hartson
7 Dec	Derby Co	H	D	2-2	..	..	..	Linighan	..	..1	..	..	..	..	..1	Shaw for Linighan
21 Dec	Nottingham F	A	L	1-2	..	McGowan	..	Keown	..	Linighan	..	..1	..	Bergkamp	Garde	Hartson/Parlour/Morrow for McGowan/Garde/Bergkamp
26 Dec	Sheffield W	A	D	0-0	..	Parlour	..	..	..	Adams	..	..	..	..	..	Shaw/Marshall for Keown/Platt
28 Dec	Aston Villa	H	D	2-2	..	..	..	..	..	..	Garde	..1	..1	..	Vieira	Morrow for Garde
1 Jan	Middlesbrough	H	W	2-0	..	..	..	..	..	..	..	..1	..	..1	..	Hartson/Morrow/Shaw for Garde/../Bergkamp
11 Jan	Sunderland	A	L	0-1	Seaman	..	..	..	..	..	Platt	Hartson	..	..	..	Hughes for ..
19 Jan	Everton	H	W	3-1	..	..	..	..	..	..	..	Wright	..1	..1	..1	Dixon/Hughes for Platt/Wright
29 Jan	West Ham U	A	W	2-1	..	Dixon	..	Rose	..	..	Parlour1	..1	..	Hughes	..	Hartson/Marshall/Morrow for Rose/Wright/Hughes
1 Feb	Leeds U	A	D	0-0	..	..	..	Marshall	..	..	..	Hartson	..	..	..	Wright for Hartson
15 Feb	Tottenham H	A	D	0-0	Lukic	..	..	Keown	..	..	..	Wright	..	Bergkamp	..	Hughes for ..
19 Feb	Manchester U	H	L	1-2	..	..	..	..	..	..	..	..	..	..1	..	Hughes for Adams
23 Feb	Wimbledon	H	L	0-1	..	..	..	Garde	..	Marshall	..	..	..	..	..	Hughes/Morrow/Shaw for Garde/Bould/ Parlour
1 Mar	Everton	A	W	2-0	..	..	..	Keown	Garde	..	Platt	..1	Hughes	..1	..	Morrow for Garde
8 Mar	Nottingham F	H	W	2-0	..	..	..	..	Marshall	Adams	..	Hughes	Merson	..2.1p	..	Morrow for Hughes
15 Mar	Southampton	A	W	2-0	Harper	Parlour	..	..	..	..	..	Shaw1	Hughes1	..	..	Garde for Shaw
24 Mar	Liverpool	H	L	1-2	Seaman	Dixon	..	..	..	..	..	Wright1	..	..	..	Parlour/Garde/Shaw for Dixon/Marshall/Hughes
5 Apr	Chelsea	A	W	3-0	..	..	..	..	Bould	Garde	..1	..1	..	..1	..	Parlour/Anelka/Selley for Wright/Hughes/Vieira
12 Apr	Leicester C	H	W	2-0	Seaman	..	..	..	..	Adams1	..1	..	..	..	..	Parlour for Hughes
19 Apr	Blackburn Rov	H	D	1-1	..	..	..	..	..	..	..1	..	..	..	..	Parlour for Hughes
21 Apr	Coventry C	A	D	1-1	..	..	..	..	..	..	..	.. 1p	Merson	..	..	Parlour/Anelka for Dixon/Merson
3 May	Newcastle U	H	L	0-1	..	..	..	..	..	..	..	..	..	..	..	Parlour/Anelka for Adams/Platt
11 May	Derby Co	A	W	3-1	..	..	..	..	..	..	..	.. 2	..	..1	..	Anelka/Parlour for Merson/Vieira

Football League (Coca-Cola) Cup

23 Oct	Stoke City (3)	A	D	1-1	Seaman	Dixon	Winterburn	Keown	Bould	Adams	Platt	Wright1	Merson	Bergkamp	Vieira	Hartson for Bergkamp
13 Nov	Stoke City (3R)	H	W	5-2	..	..	..	..	..	..	..1	..2.1p	..1	..1	..	Hartson/Morrow for Vieira/Bergkamp
27 Nov	Liverpool (4R)	A	L	2-4	Lukic	..	..	..	..	..	..	.. 2p	..	Hartson	..	Parlour/Morrow for Merson/Winterburn

FA Cup

4 Jan	Sunderland (3)	H	D	1-1	Lukic	Parlour	Winterburn	Keown	Bould	Adams	Morrow	Hartson1	Merson	Bergkamp	Vieira	Shaw for Morrow
15 Jan	Sunderland (3R)	A	W	2-0	Seaman	..	..	..	..	..	Platt	Hughes1	..	..1	..	
4 Feb	Leeds U (4)	H	L	0-1	..	Dixon	Morrow	..	..	..	Parlour	Wright	..	Hughes	..	Hartson for Hughes

UEFA Cup

10 Sep	Moenchengladbach	H	L	2-3	Seaman	Dixon	Winterburn	Keown	Linighan	Parlour	Platt	Wright1	Merson1	Bergkamp	Hartson	Helder/Bould for Parlour/Bergkamp
25 Sep	Moenchengladbach	A	L	2-3	..	Linighan	..	..	Bould	Adams	..	..1	..1	Vieira	..	Parlour/Helder for Linighan/Adams

Appearances (Goals)

Winterburn 38 – Wright 35 (23) – Bould 33 – Keown 33 (1) – Dixon 32 (2) – Merson 32 (6) – Vieira 31 (2) – Parlour 30 (2) – Bergkamp 29 (12) – Adams 28 (3) – Platt 28 (4) – Seaman 22 – Hartson 19 (3) – Lukic 15 – Hughes 14 (1) – Linighan 11 (1) – Garde 11 – Marshall 8 – Morrow 14 – Shaw 8 (2) – Anelka 4 – Helder 2 – Hillier 2 – Dickov 1 – Harper 1 – McGowan 1 – Rose 1 – Selley 1 – **Total 28 players (62 goals)**

Position in League Table

	P	W	D	L	F:A	Pts	
Manchester U	38	21	12	5	76:44	75	1st
Arsenal	38	19	11	8	62:32	68	3rd

SEASON 1997–98 FA PREMIER LEAGUE

9 Aug	Leeds United	A	D	1-1	Seaman	Garde	Bould	Grimandi	Winterburn	Parlour	Vieira	Petit	Overmars	Wright1	Bergkamp	Platt/Hughes for Vieira/Overmars
11 Aug	Coventry City	H	W	2-0	..	..	Marshall	..	..	..	..	..	..	..2	..	Platt/Hughes for Petit/Overmars
23 Aug	Southampton	A	W	3-1	..	..	Bould	..	..	..	..	..	..1	..	..2	Platt/Marshall/Boa Morte for Grimandi/Petit/Overmars
27 Aug	Leicester City	A	D	3-3	..	Dixon	..	..	..	..	..	..	..	..	..3	Anelka/Platt/Hughes for Parlour/Overmars/Wright
30 Aug	Tottenham Hotspur	H	D	0-0	..	..	..	..	..	..	..	..	..	..	..	Platt/Anelka for Parlour/Petit
13 Sep	Bolton Wanderers	H	W	4-1	..	..	..	..	..	..1	..	..	..	..3	..	Platt/Boa Morte/Anelka for Parlour/Overmars/Wright
21 Sep	Chelsea	A	W	3-2	..	..	..	Adams	..1	..	..	..	..	..	..2	Boa Morte/Grimandi for Parlour/Overmars
24 Sep	West Ham United	H	W	4-0	..	..	..	..	..	..	..	..	..2	..1p	..1	Grimandi/Platt/Anelka for Dixon/Winterburn/Wright
27 Sep	Everton	A	D	2-2	..	Grimandi	..	..	..	..	..	..	..1	..1	..	Boa Morte/Platt/Garde for Parlour/Vieira/Wright
4 Oct	Barnsley	H	W	5-0	..	Dixon	..	..	..	..1	..	..	..	..1	..2	Platt1/Anelka/Boa Morte for Parlour/Overmars/Wright
18 Oct	Crystal Palace	A	D	0-0	..	Grimandi	..	..	..	..	..	..	Boa Morte	..	..	Platt/Mendez for Parlour/Boa Morte
26 Oct	Aston Villa	H	D	0-0	..	Dixon	..	..	..	..	..	..	..	..	..	Platt/Anelka for Parlour/Boa Morte
1 Nov	Derby County	A	L	0-3	..	..	..	..	..	..	..	..	Platt	..	Anelka	Boa Morte/Wreh for Winterburn/Anelka
9 Nov	Manchester United	H	W	3-2	..	..	Grimandi	..	..	..	..1	Platt1	Overmars	..	..1	Bould/Wreh for Vieira/Anelka
22 Nov	Sheffield Wednesday	A	L	0-2	..	..	Keown	..	..	..	Platt	Grimandi	..	..	Mendez	Hughes/Marshall/Wreh for Parlour/Grimandi/Mendez
30 Nov	Liverpool	H	L	0-1	..	..	..	..	..	Hughes	..	Petit	..	..	Bergkamp	Wreh/Grimandi for Hughes/Petit
6 Dec	Newcastle United	A	W	1-0	..	..	..	..	..	Parlour	..	..	..	..1	..	
13 Dec	Blackburn Rovers	H	L	1-3	..	..	..	..	..	..	..	..	..1	..	..	Vieira/Boa Morte for Parlour/Platt
26 Dec	Leicester City	H	W	2-1*	..	..	Gould	Keown	..	..	Vieira	Platt1	..	..	..	Hughes/Anelka for Platt/Wright - own goal
28 Dec	Tottenham Hotspur	A	D	1-1	..	..	..	..	..	..1	..	Petit	..	Anelka	..	Grimandi/Hughes/Rankin for Dixon/Anelka/Bergkamp
10 Jan	Leeds United	H	W	2-1	..	..	..	..	..	..	..	..	..2	Wright	..	
17 Jan	Coventry City	A	D	2-2	..	..	..	..	..	..	..	..	Upson	Anelka1	..1	Grimandi/Boa Morte for Keown/Anelka
31 Jan	Southampton	H	W	3-0	Manninger	Grimandi	..	Adams1	..	..	Hughes	..	Overmars	..1	..1	Platt/Wreh for Hughes/Anelka
8 Feb	Chelsea	H	W	2-0	..	..	..	..	..	..	..2	..	..	..	..	Dixon/Wright/Platt for Grimandi/Overmars/Anelka
21 Feb	Crystal Palace	H	W	1-0	..	Dixon	Keown	Grimandi1	Upson	Venazza	Vieira	Hughes	Boa Morte	Platt	..	McGowan for Vernazza
2 Mar	West Ham United	A	D	0-0	..	..	..	Adams	..	Hughes	..	Petit	Overmars	..	..	Winterburn/Boa Morte for Upson/Platt
11 Mar	Wimbledon	A	W	1-0	..	..	..	..	Winterburn	Parlour	..	..	..	Wreh1	..	Garde/Hughes/Boa Morte for Parlour/Overmars/Wreb
14 Mar	Manchester United	A	W	1-0	..	..	..	..	..	..	..	..	..1	..	..	Anelka/Garde for Wreh/Parlour
28 Mar	Sheffield Wednesday	H	W	1-0	..	..	..	..	..	..	..	Hughes	..	..	..1	Garde/Anelka/Grimandi for Dixon/Parlour/Wreh
31 Mar	Bolton Wanderers	A	W	1-0	..	Grimandi	..	..	..	..	..	Petit	..	..1	Anelka	Hughes/Bould/Platt for Overmars/Wreh/Anelka
11 Apr	Newcastle United	H	W	3-1	..	Garde	Gould	..	..	..	..1	..	..	Anelka2	Wreh	Platt/Hughes/Boa Morte for Overmars/Anelka/Wreh
13 Apr	Blackburn Rovers	A	W	4-1	..	..	..	..	..	..2	..	..	..	..1	Bergkamp1	Platt/Hughes for Overmars/Anelka
18 Apr	Wimbledon	H	W	5-0	..	..	Upson	..1	..	..	..	..1	..1	..	..1	Dixon/Wreh1/Platt for Garde/Vieira/Anelka
25 Apr	Barnsley	A	W	2-0	..	Dixon	Keown	..	..	Platt	..	..	..1	..	..1	Wreh forAnelka
29 Apr	Derby County	H	W	1-0	..	..	..	..	..	Parlour	..	..1	..	..	..	Wreh/Platt for Bergkamp/Anelka
3 May	Everton	H	W	4-0*	..	..	..	..1	..	..	..	..	..2	..	Wreh	Wright/Bould for Anelka/Wreh - own goal
6 May	Liverpool	A	L	0-4	Manninger	..	Bould	Upson	Grimandi	..	Platt	Hughes	Boa Morte	Wright	..	Vieira/Mendez/Anelka for Parlour/Wreh/Wright
10 May	Aston Villa	A	L	0-1	Seaman	Grimandi	Keown	Adams	..	..	Vieira	Petit	Overmars	..	Anelka	Platt/Wreh for Parlour/Wright

FA Cup

3 Jan	Port Vale (3)	H	D	0-0	Seaman	Grimandi	Keown	Bould	Winterburn	Parlour	Vieira	Petit	Overmars	Anelka	Bergkamp	Hughes/Boa Morte/Wreh for Parlour/Petit/Anelka
24 Jan	Port Vale (3R)	A	D	1-1 *	..	Dixon	Bould	Keown	..	..	..	Hughes	..	Wright	..1	Grimandi/Anelka/Boa Morte for Vieira/Overmars/Wright
24 Jan	Middlesbrough (4)	A	W	2-1	Manninger	..	..	Adams	..	..1	..	Petit	..1	Anelka	..	Grimandi for Dixon
15 Feb	Crystal Palace (5)	H	D	0-0	..	..	..	Grimandi	..	..	Hughes	..	..	..	..	Vieira/Platt/Wreh for Bould/Hughes/Anelka
25 Feb	Crystal Palace (5R)	A	W	2-1	..	..	Keown	Adams	Upson	Boa Morte	Vieira	Platt	Hughes	..1	..1	Overmars/Crowe for Upson/Bergkamp

8 Mar	West Ham (6)	H	D	1-1	..	..	..	..	Winterburn	Parlour	Vieira	Petit	Overmars	..	..1	Wreh for Anelka
17 Mar	West Ham (6R)	A	D	1-1*	..	..	..	..	..	Garde	..	..	..	..	..1p	Hughes/Wreh/Boa Morte for Petit/Overmars/Anelka
	*Arsenal won on penalties after extra time															
5 Apr	Wolverhampton (SF) at Aston Villa		W	1-0	Seaman	Grimandi	..	..	..	Parlour	..	..	..	Wreh1	..	Bould/Hughes/Platt for Keown/Wreh/Anelka
16 May	Newcastle United (F) at Wembley		W	2-0	..	Dixon	..	..	..	..	..	..	..1	..	..1	Platt for Wreh

Football League (Coca-Cola) Cup

14 Oct	Birmingham City (3) (a.e.t)	H	W	4-1	Manninger	Dixon	Marshall	Grimandi	Upson	Mendez1	Platt1	Vernazza	Hughes	Wreh	Boa Morte2	Crowe/Muntasser for Dixon/Boa Morte
18 Nov	Coventry City (4) (a.e.t)	H	W	1-0	..	..	Bould	Keown	..	Parlour	..	Mendez	..	Anelka	Bergkamp1	Wreh/ Marshall for Mendez/Anelka
6 Jan	West Ham (QF)	A	W	2-1	Seaman	Grimandi	Keown	Bould	Winterburn	..	Vieira	Petit	Overmars1	Wright1	..	Wreh/Hughes for Overmars/Wright
28 Jan	Chelsea (SF)	H	W	2-1	Manninger	..	Bould	Adams	..	..	Hughes1	..	..1	Anelka	..	Platt for Grimandi
18 Feb	Chelsea (SF)	A	L	1-3		Dixon	Grimandi1	..	..	..	Vieira	..	..	..	..	Platt/Hughes fo Winterburn/Parlour

UEFA Cup

16 Sep	PAOK Salonika (1)	A	L	0-1	Seaman	Dixon	Bould	Adams	Winterburn	Parlour	Vieira	Petit	Overmars	Wright	Anelka	Platt/Boa Morte/Wreh for Parlour/Overmars/Anelka
30 Sep	PAOK Salonika (1)	H	W	1-1	..	..	..	..	..	..	..	..	..	..	Bergkamp1	Platt/Anelka for Parlour/Overmars

League Appearances (Goals in brackets)
Winterburn 36 (1) – Parlour 34 (5) – Petit 32 (2) – Overmars 32 (12) – Vieira 33 (2) – Seaman 31 – Bergkamp 28 (16) – Dixon 28 – Adams 26 (3) – Wright 24 (11) – Bould 24 – Keown 18 – Anelka 26 (6) – Grimandi 22 (1) – Platt 31 (3) – Hughes 17 (2) – Wreh 16 (3) – Manninger 7 – Garde 10 – Upson 5 – Boa Morte 15 – Marshall 3 – Mendez 3 – Vernazza 1 – Rankin 1 – McGowan 1 – Own goals 2 – **Total 26 players (68)**

Position in League Table

	P	W	L	D	F:A	Pts	
Arsenal	38	23	6	9	68:33	78	1st

SEASON 1998–99 FA PREMIER LEAGUE

17 Aug	Nottingham Forest	H	W	2-1	Seaman	Dixon	Keown	Adams	Winterburn	Parlour	Vieira	Petit1	Overmars1	Anelka	Bergkamp	
22 Aug	Liverpool	A	D	0-0	..	..	..	Bould	..	..	..	..	..	..	..	Vivas for Vieira
29 Aug	Charlton	H	D	0-0	..	..	..	Adams	..	..	..	..	..	..	..	Vivas/Wreh/Hughes for Dixon/Anelka/Vieira
9 Sep	Chelsea	A	D	0-0	..	..	..	..	..	..	..	..	..	..	..	Garde/Hughes/Wreh for Overmars/Anelka/Bergkamp
12 Sep	Leicester	A	D	1-1	..	..	..	Bould	..	..	..	Hughes1	..	Wreh	..	Anelka/Garde/Vivas for Wreh/Vieira/Dixon
20 Sep	Manchester United	H	W	3-0	..	..	..	Adams1	..	..	..	..	..	Anelka1	..	Ljungberg1 for Anelka
26 Sep	Sheffield Wednesday	A	L	0-1	Manninger	Vivas	..	..	..	..	..	Petit	..	..	..	Bould/Hughes/Ljungberg for Parlour/Petit/Overmars
4 Oct	Newcastle	H	W	3-0	Seaman	Dixon	..	..	..	Ljungberg	..	..	..	..1	..2(1p)	Bould/Hughes/Mendez for Keown/Petit/Ljungberg
17 Oct	Southampton	H	D	1-1	..	..	..	..	..	Parlour	..	Hughes	..	..1	..	Wreh for Parlour
25 Oct	Blackburn	A	W	2-1	..	..	..	Bould	..	Ljungberg	..	Petit1	..	..1	..	
31 Oct	Coventry	A	W	1-0	..	..	..	..	..	Parlour	..	..	..	..1	Ljungberg	Boa Morte/Hughes for Ljungberg/Overmars
8 Nov	Everton	H	W	1-0	..	..	..	Grimandi	..	..	..	..	..	..1	..	
14 Nov	Tottenham	H	D	0-0	..	..	..	Adams	..	..	..	..	..	..	..	Wreh/Boa Morte for Anelka/Ljungberg
21 Nov	Wimbledon	A	L	0-1	..	..	..	..	..	..	..	..	..	..	Bergkamp	Hughes/Wreh/Ljungberg for Overmars/Bergkamp/Vieira
29 Nov	Middlesbrough	H	D	1-1	..	..	..	Bould	..	..	Garde	Ljungberg	..	..1	Wreh	Vivas/Boa Morte/Caballero for Winterburn/Ljungberg/Wreh
5 Dec	Derby	A	D	0-0	..	..	..	..	Vivas	..	..	Grimandi	..	..	..	Ljungberg/Boa Morte for Garde/Wreh
13 Dec	Aston Villa	A	L	2-3	..	..	..	..	..	..	Vieira	Ljungberg	..	..	Bergkamp2	Grimandi/Boa Morte for Parlour/Ljungberg
20 Dec	Leeds	H	W	3-1	Manninger	..	..	..	..	Ljungberg	..1	Petit1	..	..	..	Grimandi/Wreh for Ljungberg1/Overmars
26 Dec	West Ham	H	W	1-0	..	..	..	..	..	Parlour	..	..	..1	..	..	Wreh/Grimandi for Anelka/Vivas
28 Dec	Charlton	A	W	1-0	..	..	..	..	Winterburn	..	..	..	..1p	Boa Morte	..	Vivas/Wreh/Grimandi for Winterburn/Boa Morte/Bergkamp
9 Jan	Liverpool	H	D	0-0	..	..	..	..	Grondin	..	..	..	..	Anelka	Boa Morte	Upson/Garde/Wreh for Bould/Overmars/Anelka
16 Jan	Nottingham Forest	A	W	1-0	..	..	..1	Adams	Winterburn	..	Garde	..	..	..	Bergkamp	Vivas/Upson for Overmars/Anelka
31 Jan	Chelsea	H	W	1-0	Seaman	..	..	..	..	..	..	..	..	..	..1	Upson/Vivas/Diawara for Anelka/Overmars/Bergkamp
6 Feb	West Ham	A	W	4-0	..	..	..	..	..	..1	Vieira	..	..1	..1	..1	
17 Feb	Manchester United	A	D	1-1	..	..	Bould	..	..	..	..	Hughes	..	..1	Kanu	Garde/Vivas/Diawara for Overmars/Winterburn/Kanu
20 Feb	Leicester	H	W	5-0	..	..	Grimandi	..	Vivas	..2	..	Garde	..	..3	Bergkamp	Diawara/Kanu/Hughes for Overmars/Anelka/Vieira
28 Feb	Newcastle	A	D	1-1	..	..	Keown	..	Winterburn	..	..	..	..	..1	..	Hughes/Upson for Garde/Overmars
9 Mar	Sheffield Wednesday	H	W	3-0	..	..	..	..	Vivas	..	..	Ljungberg	..	..	..2	Diawara/Kanu1/Petit for Anelka/Parlour/Ljungberg
13 Mar	Everton	A	W	2-0	..	..	..	..	Winterburn	..1	..	Petit	..	..	..1(p)	Vivas/Upson for Overmars/Anelka
20 Mar	Coventry	H	W	2-0	..	..	..	..	..	..1	..	..	..1	..	..	Ljungberg/Diawara/Kanu for Dixon/Anelka/Overmars
3 Apr	Southampton	A	D	0-0	..	..	..	..	..	..	..	Ljungberg	Diawara	..	Kanu	Boa Morte/Vivas/Bould for Ljungberg/Diawara/Keown
6 Apr	Blackburn	H	W	1-0	..	..	..	..	..	..	..	Vivas	Overmars	Diawara	Bergkamp1	Kanu/Bould for Diawara/Overmars
19 Apr	Wimbledon	H	W	5-1*	..	Vivas	..	..	..	..1	..1	Petit	..	Kanu1	..1	Diawara/Bould for Bergkamp/Keown - own goal
24 Apr	Middlesbrough	A	W	6-1	..	Dixon	Bould	..	..	..	..1	..	..1	Anelka2	Kanu2	Diawara/Vivas/Hughes for Kanu/Overmars/Petit
2 May	Derby	H	W	1-0	..	..	..	..	..	..	..	..	..	..1	..	Bergkamp/Hughes/Diawara for Anelka/Overmars/Kanu
5 May	Tottenham	A	W	3-1	..	..	Keown	..	..	..	..	..1	..	..1	Bergkamp	Vivas/Kanu1/Grimandi for Parlour/Bergkamp/Overmars
11 May	Leeds	A	L	0-1	..	..	..	..	..	..	..	..	..	..	..	Kanu/Diawara/Vivas for Overmars/Parlour/Winterburn
16 May	Aston Villa	H	W	1-0	..	..	..	..	Vivas	..	..	..	..	..	..	Ljungberg/Kanu1/Diawara for Vivas/Anelka/Overmars

League Appearances (Goals in brackets)
Overmars 36 (6) – Dixon 35 – Parlour 34 (6) – Anelka 34 (17) – Keown 33 (1) – Vieira 33 (3) – Seaman 31 – Winterburn 30 – Bergkamp 28 (12) – Petit 26 (4) – Adams 25 (1) – Vivas 22 – Bould 19 – Ljungberg 15 (1) – Hughes 14 (1) – Wreh 12 – Kanu 11 (5) – Diawara 11 – Garde 10 – Grimandi 8 – Boa Morte 8 – Upson 5 – Grondin 1 – Mendez 1 – Caballero 1 – Own goals 2 - **Total 25 players (59)**

Position in League Table

	P	W	L	D	F:A	Pts	
Manchester U	38	22	3	13	80:37	79	1st
Arsenal	38	22	4	12	59:17	78	2nd

Charity Shield

9 Aug	Manchester United (at Wembley)		W	3-0	Seaman	Dixon	Keown	Adams	Winterburn	Parlour	Vieira	Petit	Overmars1	Anelka1	Wreh	Wreh1/Hughes/Boa Morte/Bould/Grimandi for Bergkamp/Overmars/Petit/Adams/Vieira

FA Cup

4 Jan	Preston (3)	A	W	4-2	Manninger	Dixon	Keown	Bould	Vivas	Parlour	Vieira	Petit2	Overmars1	Mendez	Boa Morte1	Caballero/Garde for Mendez/Overmars
24 Jan	Wolverhampton (4)	A	W	2-1	..	..	Upson	Adams	Winterburn	..	Garde	..	..1	Anelka	Bergkamp1	Vivas/Grimandi/Hughes for Garde/Anelka/Overmars
13 Feb	Sheffield United (5)	H	W	2-1	Seaman	Vivas	Grimandi	Bould	..	..	Vieira1	Garde	..1	Diawara	..	Hughes/Kanu for Garde/Diawara
(THE RESULT OF THIS MATCH WAS DECLARED VOID, BUT ARSENAL STILL INCLUDE IT IN THEIR STATISTICS)																
23 Feb	Sheffield United (5)	H	W	2-1	..	..	Bould	Adams	..	..	..	Hughes	..1	Anelka	..1	Kanu/Garde/Diawara for Anelka/Bergkamp/Overmars
6 Mar	Derby	H	W	1-0	..	Dixon	Keown	..	..	..	Hughes	Ljungberg	..	..	..	Vivas/Kanu1/Diawara for Ljungberg/Hughes/Overmars
11 Apr	Manchester United (S/F) (at Villa Park)		D	0-0	..	..	..	..	..	..	Vieira	Vivas	..	..	..	Ljungberg/Kanu for Overmars/Anelka
14 Apr	Manchester United (S/F-R) (at Villa Park)		L	1-2	..	..	..	..	..	..	..	Petit	Ljungberg	..	..1	Overmars/Kanu/Bould for Ljungberg/Parlour/Petit

League (Worthington) Cup

28 Oct	Derby (3)	A	W	2-1	Manninger	Vivas1	Grimandi	Upson	Grondin	Ljungberg	Garde	Mendez	Hughes	Wreh	Boa Morte	Crowe/Riza for Upson/Wreh - own goal
11 Nov	Chelsea (4)	H	L	0-5	..	..	..	..	..	..	..	Hughes	Boa Morte	..	Bergkamp	Mendez/Caballero for Garde/Bergkamp

Champions League (Group matches – all home games played at Wembley))

16 Sep	Lens	A	D	1-1	Seaman	Dixon	Keown	Adams	Winterburn	Parlour	Vieira	Petit	Overmars1	Anelka	Bergkamp	Hughes/Garde for Petit/Bergkamp
30 Sep	Panathinaikos	H	W	2-1	..	..	..1	..1	..	Garde	..	..	..	..	..	Vivas for Garde
21 Oct	Dynamo Kiev	H	D	1-1	..	..	..	..	..	Parlour	Garde	Hughes	..	..	..1	Vivas for Anelka
4 Nov	Dynamo Kiev	A	L	1-3	..	..	..	Bould	..	..	Vieira	Petit	Vivas	Wreh	Boa Morte	Grimandi/Hughes1/Garde for Bould/Vivas/Boa Morte
25 Nov	Lens	H	L	0-1	..	..	..	Adams	..	..	Garde	Hughes	Overmars	Anelka	Wreh	Bould/Vivas/Boa Morte for Adams/Garde/Wreh
9 Dec	Panathinaikos	A	W	3-1	..	Vivas	Upson	Bould	Grondin	Grimandi	Vernazza	Mendez1	Boa Morte1	..1	..	M.Black for Mendez

SEASON 1999–2000 FA PREMIER LEAGUE

7 Aug	Leicester	H	W	2-1	Manninger	Dixon	Keown	Grimandi	Winterburn	Parlour	Vieira	Petit	Ljungberg	Kanu	Bergkamp1	Henry/Overmars/Silvinho for Ljungberg/Parlour/Bergkamp [Frank Sinclair own goal]
10 Aug	Derby	A	W	2-1	..	..	..	Upson	..	..	..	..1	Henry	..	..1	Silvinho/Luzhny/Boa Morte forParlour/Kanu/Henry
14 Aug	Sunderland	A	D	0-0	..	..	..	..	Silvinho	..	..	..	..	..	..	Ljungberg/Boa Morte for Petit/Bergkamp
22 Aug	Manchester Utd	H	L	1-2	..	..	..	..	..	..	..	Ljungberg1	..	..	..	Overmars/Suker for Kanu/Henry
25 Aug	Bradford City	H	W	2-0	..	Vivas	..	Grimandi	..	..	..1	..	..	..1p	..	Overmars/Suker/Upson forHenry/Bergkamp/Kanu
28 Aug	Liverpool	A	L	0-2	..	Dixon	..	Adams	Winterburn	..	..	..	Overmars	Henry	..	Suker/Silvinho for Overmars/Parlour
11 Sept	Aston Villa	H	W	3-1	..	..	..	..	..	..	..	Grimandi	..	Suker2	..	Silvinho/Kanu1/Henry for Suker/Bergkamp/Overmars
18 Sept	Southampton	A	W	1-0	..	..	..	..	..	Ljungberg	..	..	..	Kanu	..	Parlour/Henry1/Luzhny for Ljungberg/Kanu/Overmars
25 Sept	Watford	H	W	1-0	..	Luzhny	..	..	Silvinho	Parlour	..	Ljungberg	..	..1	Henry	Suker/Bergkamp/Vivas for Ljungberg/Henry/Kanu
3 Oct	West Ham	A	L	1-2	Seaman	..	..	..	..	Ljungberg	..	Grimandi	Henry	Suker1	Bergkamp	Overmars/Kanu for Luzhny/Henry

16 Oct	Everton	H	W	4-1	..	Dixon1	..	..	Winterburn	Parlour	..	..	Overmars	..2	..	Silvinho/Kanu1/Ljungberg for Overmars/Bergkamp/Parlour
23 Oct	Chelsea	H	W	3-2	..	..	..	..	Silvinho	..	Ljungberg	Petit	..	Kanu3	Suker	Henry/Vivas/Vernazza for Ljungberg/Petit/Overmars
30 Oct	Newcastle	H	D	0-0	..	Luzhny	..	..	Winterburn	Ljungberg	Vieira	Grimandi	Silvinho	Henry	..	Bergkamp/Overmars/Upson for Henry/Silvinho/Keown
7 Nov	Tottenham	A	L	1-2	..	Dixon	..	..	..	..	..1	Petit	Overmars	Kanu	Bergkamp	Suker/Grimandi for Kanu/Petit
20 Nov	Middlesbrough	H	W	5-1	..	..	Grimandi	..	..	Parlour	Ljungberg	..	..3	..	..2	Upson/Vivas/Suker for Grimandi/Dixon/Bergkamp
28 Nov	Derby	H	W	2-1	Manninger	Luzhny	Upson	..	..	..	Grimandi	..	..	Henry2	Bergkamp	Kanu/Suker/Malz for Bergkamp/Henry/Overmars
4 Dec	Leicester	A	W	3-0	..	Dixon1	..	..	..	Silvinho	..1	..	..1	..	Kanu	Vivas/Hughes/Barrett for Upson/Silvinho/Henry
18 Dec	Wimbledon	H	D	1-1	..	..	Luzhny	Grimandi	..	..	Ljungberg	..	..	..1	..	Suker for Winterburn
26 Dec	Coventry	A	L	2-3	Seaman	..	Keown	Adams	..	Ljungberg1	Grimandi	..	..	..	..	Suker1 for Grimandi
28 Dec	Leeds	H	W	2-0	..	Luzhny	Grimandi	..	Silvinho	..1	Vieira	..	..	..1	..	Suker/Winterburn for Henry/Petit
3 Jan	Sheffield Wed	A	D	1-1	..	..	..	..	..	..	..	..1	..	..	Kanu	Winterburn/Suker for Overmars/Kanu
15 Jan	Sunderland	H	W	4-1	..	Dixon	Keown	Luzhny	..	Parlour	..	..	Ljungberg	..2	Suker2	Malz/Barrett for Ljungberg/Henry
24 Jan	Manchester Utd	A	D	1-1	..	..	..	Grimandi	..	..	..	..	..1	Hughes	Henry	Winterburn/Malz for Silvinho/Hughes
5 Feb	Bradford City	A	L	1-2	..	..	..	..	Winterburn	..	Ljungberg	..	Malz	Henry1	Suker	Bergkamp for Malz
13 Feb	Liverpool	H	L	0-1	..	..	..	..	Silvinho	..	Vieira	..	Ljungberg	..	Bergkamp	Overmars/Suker/Luzhny for Petit/Bergkamp/Ljungberg
26 Feb	Southampton	H	W	3-1	..	..	..	Adams	..	..	..	..	..2	Bergkamp1	Kanu	Overmars for Bergkamp
5 Mar	Aston Villa	A	D	1-1	..	..1	..	Grimandi	..	..	..	..	Henry	Kanu	Bergkamp	Overmars/Luzhny/Winterburn for Bergkamp/Grimandi/Petit
12 Mar	Middlesbrough	A	L	1-2	..	Luzhny	Winterburn	..	..	..	..	..	Ljungberg	Henry	Kanu	Manninger/Bergkamp1/Suker for Seaman/Ljungberg/Parlour
19 Mar	Tottenham	H	W	2-1	Manninger	Dixon	Luzhny	Adams	..	..	..	Grimandi	Overmars	..1	..	Ljungberg/Winterburn for Henry/Overmars - own goal
26 Mar	Coventry	H	W	3-0	Seaman	..	..	..1	Winterburn	..	..	Petit	..	..1	Bergkamp	Kanu1/Ljungberg/Suker for Bergkamp/Henry/Overmars
1 Apr	Wimbledon	A	W	3-1	..	..	Keown	Luzhny	Silvinho	..	..	Grimandi	..	Kanu2	..	Petit/Henry1/Winterburn for Overmars/Kanu/Bergkamp
16 Apr	Leeds	A	W	4-0	..	..	..1	Adams	..	..	..	Petit	Ljungberg	Henry1	..	Kanu1/Overmars1/Winterburn for Bergkamp/Henry/Petit
23 Apr	Watford	A	W	3-2	..	Luzhny	..	Grimandi	Winterburn	..1	..	..	Overmars	..2	..	Silvinho for Overmars
29 Apr	Everton	A	W	1-0	..	Dixon	..	Adams	Silvinho	..	Grimandi	..	..1	Kanu	..	Vieira/Winterburn/Black for Bergkamp/Overmars/Petit
2 May	WestHam	H	W	2-1	..	..	Luzhny	..	..	..	Vieira	Grimandi	..1	..	..	Petit1 for Dixon
6 May	Chelsea	H	W	2-1	..	..	Grimandi	..	..	..	..	Petit	..	Henry2	..	Winterburn/Kanu/Luzhny for Overmars/Bergkamp/Petit
9 May	Sheffield Wed	H	D	3-3	..	..1	Keown	Luzhny	Winterburn	..	Grimandi	Vieira	..	Kanu	Henry1	Bergkamp/Silvinho1 for Parlour/Winterburn
17 May	Newcastle	A	L	2-4	Manninger	Luzhny	..	Weston	Cole	..	Vernazza	Malz1	Winterburn	..1	Suker	Silvinho/McGovern/Gray for Parlour/Weston/Kanu

League Appearances (Goals in brackets)
Henry 31 (17)–Overmars 31 (7)–Kanu 31 (12)–Silvinho 31 (1)–Vieira 31 (2)–Parlour 30 (1)–Dixon 28 (4) Bergkamp 28 (6)–Grimandi 28 (2)–Winterburn 28–Keown 27 (1)–Petit 26 (3)–Ljungberg 26 (6)–Seaman 24–Suker 22 (8)–Adams 21–Luzhny 21–Manninger 15–Upson 8–Vivas 5–Malz 5 (1)–Hughes 2–Boa Morte 2–Barrett 2–Vernazza 2–Black 1–Cole 1–Weston 1–Gray 1–McGovern 1–own goals (2) – **Total 30 players (73)**

Position in League Table

	P	W	L	D	F:A	Pts	
Manchester U	38	28	7	3	97:45	91	1st
Arsenal	38	22	9	7	73:43	73	2nd

Charity Shield

31 Jul	Manchester Utd (at Wembley)		W	2-1	Manninger	Dixon	Winterburn	Keown	Grimandi	Silvinho	Parlour1	Vieira	Petit	Ljungberg	Kanu1p	Boa Morte for Ljungberg/ Luzhny for Dixon

FA Cup**

13 Dec	Blackpool (3)	H	W	3-1	Manninger	Dixon	Luzhny	Adams1	Silvinho	Ljungberg	Grimandi1	Petit	Overmars1	Suker	Henry	Kanu/Hughes for Suker/Ljungberg
9 Jan	Leicester (4)	H	D	0-0	Seaman	..	Keown	Grimandi	..	..	Vieira	..	Malz	..	..	Kanu for Malz
19 Jan	Leicester (4R)	A	D	0-0*	..	..	..	..	..	Parlour	..	..	..	..	..	Hughes for Malz

*Arsenal lost 6-5 on penalties after extra time
** Manchester United did not enter

Worthington Cup

12 Oct	Preston (3)	H	W	2-1	Seaman	Luzhny	Grimandi	Upson	Winterburn	Parlour	Vernazza	Malz1	Silvinho	Kanu1	Henry	Overmars/Wreh for Vernazza/Kanu
30 Nov	Middlesbrough (4)	A	D	2-2*	Manninger	Vivas	Luzhny	..	Silvinho	..	..	..	Black	Suker1	..1	Weston/Pennant/Cole for Luzhny/Black/Parlour

*Arsenal lost 3-1 on penalties after extra time

Champions League

14 Sep	Fiorentina	A	D	0-0	Manninger	Luzhny	Keown	Adams	Winterburn	Ljungberg	Vieira	Grimandi	Overmars	Suker	Bergkamp	Kanu/Henry for Suker/Bergkamp
22 Sep	AIK Solna	H	W	3-1	..	..	..	..	..	..1	..	..	..	..1	..	Silvinho/Kanu/Henry1 for Grimandi/Overmars/Ljungberg
29 Sep	Barcelona	A	D	1-1	..	..	..	..	..	Parlour	..	..	..	Kanu1	..	Suker/Henry/Ljungberg for Bergkamp/Parlour/Overmars
19 Oct	Barcelona	H	L	2-4	Seaman	..	..	..	..	Ljungberg	..	Parlour	..1	..	..1	Upson/Suker/Henry for Keown/Kanu/Ljungberg
27 Oct	Fiorentina	H	L	0-1	..	..	..	..	..	Parlour	..	Petit	..	..	..	Ljungberg/Vivas/Suker for Parlour/Petit/Dixon
2 Nov	AIK Solna	A	W	3-2	Manninger	..	Luzhny	Upson	..	Ljungberg	..	..	..2	..	Suker1	Vivas/Malz/Hughes for Luzhny/Petit/Suker

(all home games played at Wembley)

UEFA Cup

25 Nov	Nantes	H	W	3-0	Seaman	Vivas	Grimandi	Adams	Winterburn1	Ljungberg	Vieira	Petit	Overmars1p	Kanu	Bergkamp1	Parlour/Suker/Henry for Petit/Ljungberg/Kanu
9 Dec	Nantes	A	D	3-3	Manninger	Dixon	..1	..	..	..	..	..	..1	..	Henry1	Silvinho/Vivas/Suker for Overmars/Ljungberg/Henry
2 Mar	La Coruna	H	W	5-1	Seaman	..1	Keown	Luzhny	Silvinho	..	Grimandi	..	Overmars	Henry2	Bergkamp1	Kanu1/Suker/Parlour for Overmars/Henry/Bergkamp
9 Mar	La Coruna	A	L	1-2	..	..	Luzhny	Winterburn	..	Parlour	Vieira	Petit	Ljungberg	Henry1	..	Suker/Malz/Vernazza for Henry/Kanu/Winterburn
16 Mar	Werder Bremen	H	W	2-0	..	..	..	Adams	..	..	..	Grimandi	..1	..1	Bergkamp	Kanu/Overmars/Suker for Parlour/Bergkamp/Henry
23 Mar	Werder Bremen	A	W	4-2	Manninger	..	..	..	..	..3	..	..	..	..1	Kanu	Petit/Overmars/Winterburn for Adams/Kanu/Vieira
6 Apr	Lens (SF)	H	W	1-0	Seaman	..	Keown	Grimandi	..	..	..	Petit	Overmars	Kanu	Bergkamp1	Ljungberg/Suker for Overmars/Bergkamp
20 Apr	Lens (SF)	A	W	2-1	..	..	..	Adams	..	..	..	..	Ljungberg	Henry1	..	Kanu1/Overmars/Grimandi for Bergkamp/Ljungberg/Henry
17 May	Galatasaray (F) (at Copenhagen)			0-0*	..	..	..	..	..	..	..	Overmars	..	..	..	Kanu/Suker for Bergkamp/Overmars

*lost 4-1 on penalties after extra time

SEASON 2000–01 FA PREMIER LEAGUE

19 Aug	Sunderland	A	L	0-1	Seaman	Dixon	Keown	Adams	Silvinho	Parlour	Grimandi	Vieira	Ljungberg	Henry	Kanu	Pires/Bergkamp/Lauren for Ljungberg/Grimandi/Dixon
21 Aug	Liverpool	H	W	2-0	..	Luzhny	..	..	..	Lauren1	..	..	Pires	..1	Bergkamp	Kanu for Bergkamp
26 Aug	Charlton	H	W	5-3	..	Dixon	..	..	..1	..	..	..2	..	..2	Kanu	Bergkamp for Lauren
6 Sept	Chelsea	A	D	2-2	..	..	..	Luzhny	..1	..	..	Parlour	..	..1	..	Bergkamp/Wiltord/Ljungberg for Dixon/Parlour/Pires
9 Sept	Bradford	A	D	1-1	..	..	..	..	Cole1	Parlour	..	Ljungberg	..	..	Wiltord	Kanu for Wiltord
16 Sept	Coventry	H	W	2-1	..	Luzhny	..	Adams	Silvinho	..	..	..	..	Bergkamp	..1	Henry/Vernazza1/Kanu for Wiltord/Parlour/Bergkamp
23 Sept	Ipswich	A	D	1-1	..	Vivas	..	Luzhny	..	..	..	..	Bergkamp1	Henry	..	Kanu/Vernazza for Wiltord/Grimandi
1 Oct	Manchester Utd	H	W	1-0	..	Luzhny	..	Adams	..	..	..	..	..	..1	Kanu	Vivas/Wiltord for Kanu/Bergkamp
14 Oct	Aston Villa	H	W	1-0	..	Dixon	Grimandi	..	..	Lauren	Parlour	Vieira	Pires	Bergkamp	Henry1	Wiltord/Kanu/Luzhny forHenry/Pires/Bergkamp
21 Oct	West Ham	A	W	2-1	..	Lauren	Keown	Luzhny	..	Ljungberg	Grimandi	..	..1	..	Wiltord	Parlour/Henry/Kanu for Ljungberg/Wiltord/Bergkamp (own goal)
28 Oct	Manchester City	H	W	5-0	Lukic	Luzhny	..	Adams	Cole1	Parlour	..	..	..	..1	Henry2	Ljungberg/Wiltord1/Dixon for Pires/Parlour/Luzhny
4 Nov	Middlesbrough	A	W	1-0	..	Dixon	..	..	Silvinho	..	..	..	Ljungberg	..	..1	Lauren for Bergkamp
11 Nov	Derby	H	D	0-0	..	Luzhny	..	Grimandi	..	Ljungberg	Parlour	..	Bergkamp	Henry	Wiltord	Dixon/Kanu for Grimandi/Ljungberg
18 Nov	Everton	A	L	0-2	Manninger	Dixon	..	Luzhny	Cole	..	Pires	Parlour	..	Kanu	..	Upson for Dixon
26 Nov	Leeds	A	L	0-1	..	Luzhny	..	Adams	Silvinho	Lauren	Parlour	Vieira	Pires	Henry	..	Kanu for Lauren
2 Dec	Southampton	A	W	1-0	..	..	..	..	..	Ljungberg	Grimandi	..	..	Bergkamp	..	Dixon/Henry/Kanu for Silvinho/Wiltord/Pires (own goal)
9 Dec	Newcastle	H	W	5-0	..	Dixon	..	..	Vivas	..	..	Parlour3	..	Henry1	Kanu1	Lauren/Bergkamp/Luzhny for Grimandi/Kanu/Ljungberg
18 Dec	Tottenham	A	D	1-1	..	..	..	..	Silvinho	..	..	..	..	..	..	Vieira1/Bergkamp/Wiltord fo Grimandi/Pires/Kanu
23 Dec	Liverpool	A	L	0-4	..	..	..	Luzhny	..	Parlour	..	Vieira	Ljungberg	..	Bergkamp	Pires/Wiltord/Kanu for Luzhny/Ljungberg/Bergkamp
26 Dec	Leicester	H	W	6-1	..	..	Stepanovs	Adams1	..	..	..	..1	Pires	..3	Kanu	Ljungberg1/Vivas/Cole for Kanu/Grimandi/Pires
30 Dec	Sunderland	H	D	2-2	..	..1	..	..	..	Ljungberg	..	..1	..	..	..	Parlour/Danilevicius for Kanu/Henry
1 Jan	Charlton	A	L	0-1	..	..	..	Grimandi	..	Parlour	Vivas	..	..	Ljungberg	..	Danilevicius/Cole/Malz for Pires/Silvinho/Grimandi
13 Jan	Chelsea	H	D	1-1	Seaman	..	Stepanovs	Keown	..	Ljungberg	Parlour	..	..1	Henry	Wiltord	Vivas for Ljungberg
20 Jan	Leicester	A	D	0-0	..	..	Keown	Adams	..	..	..	..	..	..	..	Edu/Bergkamp forLjungberg/Edu
30 Jan	Bradford	H	W	2-0	..	..	Stepanovs	..	Cole	Lauren1	..1	..	..	..	Bergkamp	Grimandi/Kanu for Lauren/Bergkamp
3 Feb	Coventry	A	W	1-0	..	..	..	..	..	..	..	..	..	Wiltord	..1	Grimandi/Vivas for Lauren/Pires
10 Feb	Ipswich	H	W	1-0	..	..	..	..	..	Lauren	..	Grimandi	..	..	..	Henry1/Ljungberg for Lauren/Wiltord
25 Feb	Manchester Utd	A	L	1-6	..	Luzhny	..	Grimandi	..	Silvinho	..	Vieira	..	Henry1	Wiltord	Ljungberg/Vivas for Cole/Parlour
3 Mar	West Ham	H	W	3-0	..	Dixon	Grimandi	Adams	..	Ljungberg	Lauren	..	..	Wiltord3	Bergkamp	Vivas/Henry/Edu for Cole/Wiltord/Pires
18 Mar	Aston Villa	A	D	0-0	Manninger	..	..	Luzhny	Silvinho	..	..	..	..	..	..	Pires/Henry/Vivas for Ljungberg/Wiltord/Parlour
31 Mar	Tottenham	H	W	2-0	Seaman	..	Keown	Adams	Cole	Lauren	Parlour	..	..1	Henry1	Wiltord	Kanu/Luzhny for Lauren/Dixon
11 Apr	Manchester City	A	W	4-0	..	Luzhny	Stepanovs	Keown	..	..	..	Edu	Ljungberg2	Wiltord1	Kanu1	Vieira/Henry/Vivas for Edu/ Wiltord/Parlour
14 Apr	Middlesbrough	H	L	0-3	..	Dixon	Keown	Adams	Silvinho	Ljungberg	Edu	Vieira	Pires	Henry	..	Wiltord/Parlour for Edu/Ljungberg
21 Apr	Everton	H	W	4-1	..	..	..	..	Cole	..1	Grimandi1	..	..	..1	Wiltord1	Vivas/Silvinho for Grimandi/Pires
28 Apr	Derby	A	W	2-1	..	..	..	..	..	Lauren	..	..	Ljungberg	Wiltord	Kanu1	Henry/Pires1/Parlour for Lauren/Ljungberg/Kanu
5 May	Leeds	H	W	2-1	..	..	..	..	..	Ljungberg1	..	..	Pires	Henry	Wiltord1	Parlour for Wiltord
15 May	Newcastle	A	D	0-0	..	Dixon	..	..	..	Lauren	Parlour	..	..	Bergkamp	Henry	Kanu for Bergkamp
19 May	Southampton	A	L	2-3	Manninger	Grimandi	..	..	..1	Parlour	Vieira	Ljungberg1	..	..	..	Kanu/Edu/Upson for Bergkamp/Ljungberg/Pires

League Appearances (Goals in brackets)
Henry 35 (17) – Pires 33 (4) – Parlour 33 (4) – Vieira 30 (5) – Ljungberg 30 (6) – Grimandi 29 (1) – Dixon 29 (1) – Keown 28 – Wiltord 27 (8) – Kanu 27 (3) – Adams 26 (1) – Bergkamp 25 (3) – Seaman 24 – Silvinho 24 (2) – Luzhny 19 – Lauren 18 (2) – Cole 17 (3) – Manninger 11 – Vivas 11 – Stepanovs 9 – Edu 5 – Lukic 3 – Vernazza 2 (1) – Upson 2 – Danilevicius 2 – Malz 1. Own goals (2)

Position in League Table

	P	W	L	D	F:A	Pts	
Manchester U	38	24	8	6	79:31	80	1st
Arsenal	38	20	8	10	68:38	70	2nd

Worthington (League) Cup

1 Nov	Ipswich (3)	H	L	1-2	Taylor	Weston	Stepanovs1	Upson	Cole	Vivas	Pennant	Vernazza	Barrett	Wiltord	Volz	Mendez/Wreh/Canoville for Pennant/Volz/Weston

FA Cup

6 Jan	Carlisle (3)	A	W	1-0	Manninger	Dixon	Stepanovs	Vivas	Cole	Ljungberg	Vieira	Parlour	Pires	Bergkamp	Wiltord1	Silvinho, Danilevicius, Malz for Ljungberg/Wiltord/Cole
27 Jan	QPR (4)	A	W	6-0	Seaman	..	..	Adams	..	Lauren	..	..	..1	..1	..2	Grimandi/Malz/Vivas for Lauren/Pires/Vieira (2 own goals)
18 Feb	Chelsea (5)	H	W	3-1	..	..	..	Luzhny	..	..	Vieira	Ljungberg	..	Henry1	Bergkamp	Wiltord2/Vivas for Pires/Bergkamp
10 Mar	Blackburn (6)	H	W	3-0	..	..	Luzhny	Adams1	..	..	Grimandi	..	..1	Bergkamp	Wiltord1	Silvinho/Vieira/Henry for Ljungberg/Pires/Bergkamp
8 Apr	Tottenham (SF)		W	2-1	..	..	Keown	..	Silvinho	..	Vieira1	Parlour	..1	Henry	..	Ljungberg/Cole for Pires/Wiltord
12 May	Liverpool (Final) at the Millennium stadium, Cardiff		L	1-2	..	..	..	..	Cole	Ljungberg1	Grimandi	Vieira	..	..	..	Parlour/Kanu/Bergkamp for Wiltord/Ljungberg/Dixon

European Champions' League

12 Sept	Sparta Prague	A	W	1-0	Seaman	Dixon	Keown	Luzhny	Silvinho1	Ljungberg	Vieira	Grimandi	Pires	Henry	Kanu	Wiltord/Vivas forHenry/Ljungberg
20 Sept	Shakhtar Donetsk	H	W	3-2	..	..	..2	..	..	..	..	..	..	..	..	Wiltord1/Bergkamp for Pires/Ljungberg
27 Sept	Lazio	H	W	2-0	..	Luzhny	..	Adams	..	..2	..	Parlour	Bergkamp	..	..	Vivas/Wiltord for Bergkamp/Henry
17 Oct	Lazio	A	D	1-1	Lukic	Dixon	..	Luzhny	..	..	..	Grimandi	Parlour	..	..	Pires1/Lauren/Wiltord for Parlour/Grimandi/Ljungberg
25 Oct	Sparta Prague	H	W	4-2	Seaman	..1	Vivas	..	..	Lauren1	..	Parlour1	Pires	..	..1	Cole/Bergkamp/Wiltord for Silvinho/Pires/Henry
7 Nov	Shakhtar Donetsk	A	L	0-3	Taylor	..	Keown	Upson	Cole	..	Vivas	..	Wiltord	..	..	Ljungberg/Vernazza for Henry/Parlour
22 Nov	Spartak Moscow	A	L	1-4	Manninger	Luzhny	..	Adams	Silvinho1	Ljungberg	..	..	Pires	..	..	Wiltord/Lauren for Kanu/Pires
5 Dec	Bayern Munich	H	D	2-2	..	..	..	..	Cole	..	Vieira	Grimandi	..	..1	..1	Wiltord/Lauren for Pires/Luzhny
13 Feb	Lyon	A	W	1-0	Seaman	Dixon	Grimandi	..	..	Lauren	..	Parlour	..	..1	..	Ljungberg/Vivas for Pires/Kanu
21 Feb	Lyon	H	D	1-1	..	..	..	Luzhny	..	Ljungberg	..	..	..	..	Bergkamp1	Wiltord/Lauren/Kanu for Bergkamp/Pires/Henry
6 Mar	Spartak Moscow	H	W	1-0	..	..	..	Adams	..	..	..	Lauren	..	..1	..	Wiltord/Kanu/Vivas for Pires/Bergkamp/Henry
14 Mar	Bayern Munich	A	L	0-1	..	..	..	..	..	..	..	..	..	..	Kanu	Wiltord/Parlour/Silvinho for Kanu/Ljungberg/Pires
4 Apr	Valencia (QF)	H	W	2-1	..	..	Keown	..	..	..	..	Parlour1	..	..1	..	Wiltord/Lauren for Ljungberg/Kanu
17 Apr	Valencia (QF)	A	L	0-1	..	..	..	..	..	Lauren	..	..	..	..	Wiltord	Ljungberg/Kanu for Parlour/Pires

SEASON 2001–02 FA PREMIER LEAGUE

18 Aug	Middlesbrough	A	W	4-0	Seaman	Lauren	Campbell	Adams	Cole	Parlour	Pires1p	Vieira	Ljungberg	Henry1	Wiltord	Bergkamp2/Grimandi/Van Bronckhorst for Henry/Ljungberg/Wiltord
21 Aug	Leeds	H	L	1-2	..	..	..	..	..	..	..	..	..	..	..1	Bergkamp/Jeffers/Van Bronckhorst for Parlour/Ljungberg/Wiltord
25 Aug	Leicester	H	W	4-0	..	..	..	..	..	Ljungberg1	Vieira	Van Bronckhorst	Pires	Bergkamp	..1	Grimandi/Henry1/Kanu1 for Ljungberg/Wiltord/Bergkamp
8 Sept	Chelsea	A	D	1-1	..	..	Keown	..	..	Wiltord	Grimandi	..	..	..	Henry1	Kanu/Ljungberg/Campbell for Bergkamp/Wiltord/Adams
15 Sept	Fulham	A	W	3-1	..	..	Campbell	Keown	..	Parlour	Pires	Vieira	Ljungberg1	Henry1	Jeffers	Bergkamp1/Wiltord/Grimandi for Jeffers/Parlour/Henry
22 Sept	Bolton	H	D	1-1	..	Luzhny	Grimandi	Adams	..	..	Vieira	Van Bronckhorst	Bergkamp	..	Wiltord	Upson/Jeffers1/Pires for Grimandi/Van Bronckhorst/Parlour
29 Sept	Derby	A	W	2-0	Wright	Lauren	Upson	Keown	..	Ljungberg	..	..	Pires	..2,1p	Jeffers	Kanu/Luzhny/Grimandi for Jeffers/Ljungberg/Henry
13 Oct	Southampton	A	W	2-0	..	..	Campbell	Upson	..	..	..	..	..1	..1	Wiltord	Bergkamp/Parlour/Grimandi for Wiltord/ Ljungberg/Van Bronckhorst
20 Oct	Blackburn	H	D	3-3	..	..	Keown	..	Van Bronckhorst	Parlour	..	Grimandi	..1	..1	Bergkamp1	Wiltord/Kanu for Pires/Parlour
27 Oct	Sunderland	A	D	1-1	..	..	Campbell	Keown	Upson	..	..	Van Bronckhorst	Ljungberg	Kanu1	Wiltord	Henry/Bergkamp for Wiltord/Kanu
4 Nov	Charlton	H	L	2-4	..	..	Keown	Grimandi	Cole	Ljungberg	..	..	Pires	Henry2,1p	Bergkamp	Wiltord for Cole
17 Nov	Tottenham	A	D	1-1	..	..	Campbell	Keown	..	Parlour	..	Grimandi	..1	Bergkamp	Wiltord	Kanu for Bergkamp
25 Nov	Manchester Utd	H	W	3-1	Taylor	..	..	Upson	..	..	..	Pires	Ljungberg1	Henry2	Kanu	Bergkamp/Grimandi for Kanu/Pires
1 Dec	Ipswich	A	W	2-0	..	..	..	..	..	..	..	..	..1	..1p	..	Bergkamp/Van Bronckhorst/Edu for Kanu/Pires/Ljungberg
9 Dec	Aston Villa	H	W	3-2	..	..	..	..	..	..	..	..	..	..2	Bergkamp	Keown/Wiltord1/Kanu for Upson/Ljungberg/Bergkamp
15 Dec	West Ham	A	D	1-1	..	..	..	Keown	..1	Grimandi	..	..	Bergkamp	..	Wiltord	Edu/Kanu for Wiltord/Pires
18 Dec	Newcastle	H	L	1-3	..	..	..	..	..	Parlour	..	..1	Kanu	..	..	Van Bronckhorst/Bergkamp for Kanu/Wiltord
23 Dec	Liverpool	A	W	2-1	..	..	..	..	..	..	Pires	Van Bronckhorst	Ljungberg1	..1p	Kanu	Upson/Luzhny/Wiltord for Pires/Kanu/Henry
26 Dec	Chelsea	H	W	2-1	..	..	..1	..	..	..	Vieira	Pires	..	..	..	Van Bronckhorst/Wiltord1/Bergkamp for Parlour/Ljungberg/Kanu
29 Dec	Middlesbrough	H	W	2-1	..	Luzhny	..	..	..1	Ljungberg	..	Van Bronckhorst	Pires1	..	..	Bergkamp/Wiltord/Grimandi for Kanu/Ljungberg/Henry
13 Jan	Liverpool	H	D	1-1	..	..	..	..	Upson	..1	..	Grimandi	..	..	..	Bergkamp/Wiltord/Dixon for Kanu/Pires/Luzhny
20 Jan	Leeds	A	D	1-1	Wright	..	..	..	Cole	Parlour	..	Pires1	Ljungberg	..	Bergkamp	Van Bronckhorst/Wiltord/Dixon for Ljungberg/Bergkamp/Luzhny
23 Jan	Leicester	A	W	3-1	..	..	..	..	..	..	..	Van Bronckhorst1	Pires	..1	..	Grimandi/Upson/Wiltord1 for Parlour/Van Bronckhorst/Bergkamp
30 Jan	Blackburn	A	W	3-2	..	..	..	..	..	..	..	Pires	Wiltord	..1	..2	Van Bronckhorst/Upson/Grimandi for Wiltord/Keown/Pires
2 Feb	Southampton	H	D	1-1	..	..	..	Upson	..	..	..	..	..1	..	..	Van Bronckhorst/Grimandi/Edu for Vieira/Cole/Bergkamp
10 Feb	Everton	A	W	1-0	..	..	..	Stepanovs	Upson	..	..	Grimandi	Van Bronckhorst	..	Wiltord1	Dixon for Upson
23 Feb	Fulham	H	W	4-1	Seaman	..	..	..	Van Bronckhorst	..	..1	Pires	Lauren1	..2	..	Dixon/Grimandi/Aladiere for Van Bronckhorst/Pires/Henry
2 Mar	Newcastle	A	W	2-0	..	Dixon	..1	..	Luzhny	Lauren	..	Grimandi	Pires	Bergkamp1	..	Kanu/Edu for Bergkamp/Wiltord
5 Mar	Derby	H	W	1-0	..	Lauren	..	..	..	Parlour	..	Pires1	Wiltord	Henry	Bergkamp	Dixon/Edu for Luzhny/Wiltord
17 Mar	Aston Villa	A	W	2-1	..	..	..	..	..	Ljungberg	..	Edu1	Pires1	Bergkamp	Wiltord	Dixon/Grimandi/Kanu for Stepanovs/Ljungberg/Bergkamp
30 Mar	Sunderland	H	W	3-0	..	Luzhny	..	Adams	Cole	Wiltord1	..	..	Ljungberg	..1	Henry1	Grimandi/Jeffers/KanuforWiltord/Ljungberg/Bergkamp
1 Apr	Charlton	A	W	3-0	..	Dixon	..	Keown	..	..	..	Grimandi	..1	..	..2	Luzhny/Edu for Cole/Bergkamp
6 Apr	Tottenham	H	W	2-1	..	Lauren1p	..	Adams	Luzhny	..	..	Edu	..1	..	..	Dixon/Parlour/Kanu/Dixon for Bergkamp/Edu/Wiltord
21 Apr	Ipswich	H	W	2-0	..	..	Keown	..	Cole	Parlour	..	..	..2	..	..	Kanu/Grimandi for Edu/Bergkamp
24 Apr	West Ham	H	W	2-0	..	..	..	..	..	..	..	..	..1	..	..	Kanu1/Grimandi/Dixon for Edu/Bergkamp/Lungberg
29 Apr	Bolton	A	W	2-0	..	..	..	..	..	..	..	..	..1	..	Wiltord1	Dixon/Kanu/Campbell for Edu/Bergkamp/Wiltord
8 May	Manchester Utd	A	W	1-0	..	..	Campbell	Keown	..	..	..	..	..	Kanu	..1	Dixon for Kanu
11 May	Everton	H	W	4-3	Wright	Dixon	Stepanovs	Luzhny	..	..	Grimandi	..	Wiltord	Bergkamp1	Henry2	Jeffers1/Vieira/Taylor for Wiltord/Parlour/Wright

League Appearances (Goals in brackets)
Vieira 36 (2) – Henry 33 (24) – Wiltord 33 (10) – Bergkamp 33 (9) – Campbell 31 (2) – Cole 29 – Pires 28 (9) – Lauren 27 (2) – Parlour 27 – Grimandi 26 – Ljungberg 25 (12) – Kanu 23 (3) – Keown 22 – Van Bronckhorst 21 (1) – Luzhny 18 – Seaman 17 – Edu 14 (1) – Upson 14 – Dixon 13 – Wright 12 – Adams 10 – Taylor 10 – Stepanovs 6 – Jeffers 6(1) -–Aladiere 1

Position in League Table

	P	W	L	D	F:A	Pts	
Arsenal	38	26	3	9	79:36	87	1st

FA Cup

5 Jan	Watford (3)	A	W	4-2	Taylor	Luzhny	Campbell	Keown	Cole	Ljungberg1	Vieira	Van Bronckhorst	Pires	Henry1	Kanu1	Wiltord/Bergkamp1 for Henry/Kanu
27 Jan	Liverpool (4)	H	W	1-0	Wright	..	..	..	..	Wiltord	..	..	..	..	Bergkamp1	Parlour/Upson/Grimandi for Pires/Wiltord/Van Bronckhorst
18 Feb	Gillingham (5)	H	W	5-2	..	Dixon	..	Adams1	Juan	Parlour1	..	Edu	Wiltord2	Jeffers	Kanu	Henry/Pires/Grimandi for Jeffers/Edu/Kanu
9 Mar	Newcastle (6)	A	D	1-1	..	..	..	Stepanovs	Lauren	Ljungberg	..	Grimandi	Edu1	Wiltord	..	Pires/Bergkamp for Ljungberg/Edu
23 Mar	Newcastle (6R)	H	W	3-0	..	Luzhny	..1	Adams	Cole	..	..	Edu	Pires1	Bergkamp1	Wiltord	Grimandi/Jeffers/Dixon for Pires/Edu/Wiltord
14 Apr	Middlesbrough (S-F) Old Trafford	N	W	1-0*	..	Lauren	..	Keown	Luzhny	Wiltord	..	..	Ljungberg	..	Henry	Dixon/Parlour/Kanu for Luzhny/Campbell/Bergkamp
4 May	Chelsea (Final) Cardiff	N	W	2-0	Seaman	..	..	Adams	Cole	..	Parlour1	Vieira	..1	..	..	Edu/Kanu/Keown for Bergkamp/Henry/Wiltord

Worthington (League) Cup

5 Nov	Manchester Utd(3)	H	W	4-0	Wright	Luzhny	Tavlaridis	Stepanovs	Van Bronckhorst	Parlour	Grimandi	Edu	Pennant	Kanu1p	Wiltord3,1p	Halls/Ricketts/Itonga for Van Bronckhorst/Pennant/Grimandi
27 Nov	Grimsby (4)	H	W	2-0	Taylor	Tavlaridis	Keown	..	Juan	Inamoto	Van Bronckhorst	..1	..	Bergkamp	..1	Svart/Aliadiere/Halls for Pennant/Van Bronckhorst/Inamoto
11 Dec	Blackburn (5)	A	L	0-4	..	..	..	Upson	Van Bronckhorst	..	Grimandi	..	..	Kanu	..	Stepanovs/Aliadiere/Halls for Inamoto/Pennant/Tavlaridis

Champions League

First Group Phase

11 Sept	Mallorca	A	L	0-1	Seaman	Lauren	Campbell	Keown	Cole	Ljungberg	Vieira	Van Bronckhorst	Pires	Henry	Wiltord	Kanu/Jeffers/Parlour for Ljungberg/Wiltord/Pires
19 Sept	Schalke	H	W	3-2	..	..	Grimandi	..	Van Bronckhorst	Parlour	..	Pires	Ljungberg1	..2,1p	..	Bergkamp/Inamoto/Upson for Wiltord/Pires/Henry
26 Sept	Panathinaikos	A	L	0-1	..	..	Keown	Upson	Cole	..	..	..	..	..	..	Van Bronckhorst/Jeffers/Kanu for Parlour/Wiltord/Ljungberg
16 Oct	Panathinaikos	H	W	2-1	Wright	..	Campbell	..	..	Ljungberg	..	Van Bronckhorst	Pires	..2,1p	..	Parlour/Bergkamp/Grimandi for Pires/Wiltord/Henry
24 Oct	Mallorca	H	W	3-1	..	..	..	Keown	Van Bronckhorst	..	..	Grimandi	..1	..1	Bergkamp1	Wiltord/Kanu/Parlour for Bergkamp/Ljungberg/Grimandi
30 Oct	Schalke	A	L	1-3	..	Luzhny	..	Upson	Cole	..	..	Van Bronckhorst	..	Kanu	Wiltord1	Stepanovs/Keown/Pennant for Upson/Campbell/Kanu

Second Group Phase

21 Nov	Deportivo	A	L	0-2	Wright	Lauren	Campbell	Upson	Cole	Parlour	Vieira	Pires	Ljungberg	Henry	Wiltord	Taylor/Kanu/Edu for Wright/Wiltord/Van Bronckhorst
4 Dec	Juventus	H	W	3-1	Taylor	..	..	..	..	..	..	..	..2	..1	Kanu	Bergkamp/Grimandi/Keown for Kanu/Henry/Cole
19 Feb	Bayer Leverkusen	A	D	1-1	Seaman	..	..	Stepanovs	Van Bronckhorst	..	..	..1	Kanu	..	Wiltord	Grimandi/Edu for Wiltord/Kanu
27 Feb	Bayer Leverkusen	H	W	4-1	..	Dixon	..	..	Lauren	Grimandi	..1	..1	Wiltord	..1	Bergkamp1	Edu/Inamoto/Pennant for Grimandi/Lauren/Wiltord
12 Mar	Deportivo	H	L	0-2	..	Lauren	..	..	Luzhny	Wiltord	..	Grimandi	Pires	Bergkamp	Henry	Kanu/Ljungberg for Wiltord/Grimandi
20 Mar	Juventus	A	L	0-1	..	Dixon	..	Luzhny	Lauren	Ljungberg	..	Edu	..	Kanu	..	Wiltord/Cole for Lauren/Kanu

SEASON 2002–03 FA PREMIER LEAGUE

18 Aug	Birmingham City	H	W	2-0	Seaman	Lauren	Keown	Campbell	Cole	Parlour	Vieira	Edu	Wiltord1	Bergkamp	Henry1	Gilberto/Toure/Aliadiere for Bergkamp/Edu/Wiltord
24 Aug	West Ham United	A	D	2-2	..	..	..	..	..	..	..	..	..1	..	..1	Toure/Pennant/Kanu for Lauren/Parlour/Bergkamp
27 Aug	West Brom Albion	H	W	5-2	..	..1	..	..	..1	Gilberto	..	..	..2	Kanu	..	Parlour/Toure/Aliadiere1 for Kanu/Vieira/Wiltord
1 Sep	Chelsea	A	D	1-1	..	..	..	..	..	Parlour	..	..	..	..	Gilberto	Cygan/Toure1/Aliadiere for Kanu/Edu/Wiltord
10 Sep	Manchester City	H	W	2-1	..	Luzhny	..	..	..	Wiltord1	..	..	Bergkamp	Gilberto	Henry1	Toure for Edu

14 Sep	Charlton Athletic	A	W	3-0	..	..	..	..	..	Toure	..	Gilberto	..	Wiltord1	..1	Cygan/Edu1/Kanu for Wiltord/Toure/Bergkamp
21 Sep	Bolton Wanderers	H	W	2-1	..	Lauren	..	..	..	Ljungberg	Parlour	..	Wiltord	Kanu1	..1	Toure/Bergkamp/Jeffers for Lauren/Ljungberg/Wiltord
28 Sep	Leeds United	A	W	4-1	..	..	Cygan	..	..	Toure1	Vieira	..	..	..2	Henry1	Luzhny/Pennant/Jeffers for Toure/Wiltord/Kanu
6 Oct	Sunderland	H	W	3-1	..	..	..	..	..	Ljungberg	..1	..	..	..2	..	Edu/Toure/Jeffers for Wiltord/Ljungberg/Henry
19 Oct	Everton	A	L	1-2	..	..	..	..	..	..1	..	..	Toure	..	..	Edu/Wiltord/Jeffers for Ljungberg/Toure/Kanu
26 Oct	Blackburn Rovers	H	L	1-2	..	..	..	..	..	..	Edu1	..	Wiltord	..	..	Toure/Pires/Bergkamp for Cole/Edu/Kanu
3 Nov	Fulham	A	W	*1-0	..	..	..	..	..	..	..	..	..	Bergkamp	..	Luzhny/Toure/Kanu for Lauren/Wiltord/Bergkamp
9 Nov	Newcastle United	H	W	1-0	..	Luzhny	..	..	..	..	Vieira	..	..1	..	..	Edu/Pires for Wiltord/Bergkamp
16 Nov	Tottenham Hotspur	H	W	3-0	Shaaban	..	..	..	..	..1	..	..	..1	..	..1	Van Bronckhorst/Pires/Jeffers for Vieira/Bergkamp/Henry
23 Nov	Southampton	A	L	2-3	Seaman	..	..	..	..	..	..	Edu	..	..	..	Toure/Pires/Jeffers for Edu/Bergkamp/Ljungberg
30 Nov	Aston Villa	H	W	3-1	Shaaban	..	..	..	Van Bronckhorst	Toure	..	Gilberto	Pires1	..	..2	Keown/Ljungberg/Wiltord for Toure/Pires/Bergkamp
7 Dec	Manchester United	A	L	0-2	..	..	..	Keown	Cole	Ljungberg	..	..	..	Wiltord	..	Taylor/Toure/Bergkamp for Shaaban/Pires/Wiltord
15 Dec	Tottenham Hotspur	A	D	1-1	Seaman	Lauren	Campbell	..	..	..	Parlour	..	..1	Bergkamp	..	Van Bronckhorst/Toure/Wiltord for Pires/Ljungberg/Bergkamp
21 Dec	Middlesbrough	H	W	2-0	..	..	..1	..	..	..	Van Bronckhorst	..	..1	Wiltord	..	
26 Dec	West Brom Albion	A	W	2-1	..	..	..	..	..	Wiltord	Vieira	..	Van Bronckhorst	Jeffers1	..1	Pires/Kanu for Van Bronckhorst/Jeffers
29 Dec	Liverpool	H	D	1-1	..	..	..	..	..	..	..	..	Pires	Kanu	..1	Van Bronckhorst/Bergkamp/Jeffers for Pires/Kanu/Wiltord
1 Jan	Chelsea	H	W	*3-2	..	Luzhny	..	..	..	..	..	..	..	Bergkamp	..1	Lauren/Toure/Van Bronckhorst1 for Wiltord/Bergkamp/Pires
12 Jan	Birmingham City	A	W	4-0	..	Lauren1	..	..	..	..	Edu	..	..1	..	..2	Van Bronckhorst/Toure/Jeffers for Edu/Pires/Bergkamp
19 Jan	West Ham United	H	W	3-1	..	..	..	..	Van Bronckhorst	..	..	..	..	..	..3	Luzhny/Parlour/Jeffers for Wiltord/Edu/Bergkamp
29 Jan	Liverpool	A	D	2-2	..	..	..	Cygan	Cole	Parlour	Vieira	..	..1	..1	..	Luzhny for Bergkamp
1 Feb	Fulham	H	W	2-1	..	..	..	Keown	..	Wiltord	..	..	..2	..	..	Toure/Van Bronckhorst/Jeffers for Lauren/Gilberto/Wiltord
9 Feb	Newcastle United	A	D	1-1	..	..	..	..	..	..	..	..	..	..	..1	Van Bronckhorst/Parlour/Jeffers for Wiltord/Gilberto/Bergkamp
22 Feb	Manchester City	A	W	5-1	Taylor	..	..	..1	Van Bronckhorst	..	..1	..	..1	..1	..1	Edu/Parlour/Jeffers for Pires/Bergkamp/Wiltord
2 Mar	Charlton Athletic	H	W	2-0	Seaman	Toure	..	..	..	Edu	Ljungberg	Parlour	..1	Jeffers1	..	Gilberto/Wiltord for Pires/Ljungberg
15 Mar	Blackburn Rovers	A	L	0-2	Taylor	Lauren	Cygan	..	..	..	..	..	..	Bergkamp	..	Gilberto/Wiltord/Jeffers for Keown/Pires/Edu
23 Mar	Everton	H	W	2-1	..	..	..1	Campbell	..	Gilberto	..	Vieira1	..	..	..	Toure/Parlour for Bergkamp/Pires
5 Apr	Aston Villa	A	D	1-1	..	..	..	..	Toure	..	..1	..	Parlour	..	..	Cole/Wiltord/Jeffers for Toure/Parlour/Bergkamp
16 Apr	Manchester United	H	D	2-2	..	..	Keown	..	Cole	..	..	..	Pires	..	..2	Edu/Wiltord/Kanu for Vieira/Bergkamp/Pires
19 Apr	Middlesbrough	A	W	2-0	..	..	Cygan	..	..	..	..	Parlour	..1	Wiltord1	..	Luzhny/Van Bronckhorst/Bergkamp for Cole/Pires/Henry
26 Apr	Bolton Wanderers	A	D	2-2	Seaman	..	..	..	..	..	..	..	..	..1	..1	Keown/Luzhny/Van Bronckhorst for Cygan/Ljungberg/Lauren
4 May	Leeds United	H	L	2-3	Seaman	Toure	Keown	Luzhny	..	..	Wiltord	..	..	Bergkamp1	..1	Van Bronckhorst/Pennant/Kanu for Pires/Wiltord/Toure
7 May	Southampton	H	W	6-1	Taylor	..	Stepanovs	..	Garry	Van Bronckhorst	Pennant3	..	..3	Kanu	..	Tavlaridis/Hoyte/Bergkamp for Luzhny/Pennant/Pires
11 May	Sunderland	A	W	4-0	Seaman	..	..	..	Cole	Gilberto	Ljungberg3	..	..	Bergkamp	..	Van Bronckhorst/Pennant/Kanu for Parlour/Pires/Bergkamp

League Appearances (Goals in brackets)
Henry 37 (24) – Gilberto 35 (0) – Wiltord 34 (10) – Campbell 33 (2) – Cole 31 (1) – Bergkamp 29 (4) – Seaman 28 – Lauren 27 (1) – Pires 26 (14) – Toure 26 (2) – Vieira 24 (3) – Keown 24 – Ljungberg 20 (6) – Van Bronckhorst 20 (1) – Parlour 19 – Cygan 18 (1) – Edu 18 (2) – Luzhny 17 – Jeffers 16 (2) – Kanu 16 (5) – Taylor 8 – Pennant 5 (3) – Aliadiere 3 (1) – Shaaban 3 – Stepanovs 2 – Garry 1 – Hoyte 1 – Tavlaridis 1

Position in League Table

	P	W	L	D	F:A	Pts	
Manchester U	38	25	5	8	74:34	83	1st
Arsenal	38	23	6	9	85:42	78	2nd

FA Community Shield

11 Aug	Liverpool	N*	W	2-0	Seaman	Lauren	Keown	Campbell	Cole	Parlour	Vieira	Edu	Wiltord	Bergkamp	Henry	Gilberto1/Toure for Edu/Bergkamp

* played at Millennium Stadium

FA Cup sponsored by AXA

4 Jan	Oxford Utd (3)	H	W	*2-0	Seaman	Luzhny	Keown	Upson	Van Bronckhorst	Toure	Edu	Svard	Pires	Bergkamp1	Jeffers	Gilberto/Bentley for Svard/Toure
25 Jan	Farnborough Tn (4)	A*	W	5-1	Taylor	Lauren1	Cygan	Campbell1	..	..	Parlour	Vieira	..	Kanu	..2	Edu/Bergkamp1/Wiltord for Kannu/Pires/Toure
15 Feb	Manchester Utd (5)	A	W	2-0	Seaman	..	Keown	..	Cole	Edu1	..	..	..	Wiltord1	..	Van Bronckhorst/Toure/Henry for Pires/Wiltord/Jeffers
8 Mar	Chelsea (6)	H	D	2-2	..	..	..	..	Van Bronckhorst	..	..	..	Ljungberg	Henry1	..1	Toure/Pires for Henry/Ljungberg
25 Mar	Chelsea (6R)	A	W	*3-1	Taylor	..1	Cygan	..	Toure	..	..	..	Pires	Wiltord1	..	Van Bronckhorst/Ljungberg/Henry for Jeffers/Pires/Wiltord
13 Apr	Sheffield Utd (S-F)	N+	W	1-0	Seaman	Lauren	Keown	..	Cole	..	..	..	Ljungberg1	..	..	Gilberto/Bergkamp/Henry for Vieira/Wiltord/Jeffers
17 May	FA Cup Final	N~	W	1-0	..	..	..	Luzhny	..	Gilberto	..	Pires1	..	Bergkamp	Henry	Wiltord for Bergkamp

* played at Highbury
+ played at Old Trafford
~ played at Millennium Stadium

Worthington Cup

6 Nov	Sunderland	H	L	2-3	Taylor	Luzhny	Stepanovs	Tavlaridis	Svard	Pennant	Pires1	Van Bronckhorst	Toure	Kanu	Jeffers1	Garry/Volz for Svard/Pennant

Champions League

17 Sep	Borussia Dortmund	H	W	2-0	Seaman	Luzhny	Keown	Campbell	Cole	Ljungberg1	Gilberto	Vieira	Wiltord	Bergkamp1	Henry	Cygan/Lauren/Toure for Ljungberg/Luzhny/Wiltord
25 Sep	PSV Eindhoven	A	W	4-0	..	Lauren	..	..	..	..1	..1	..	..	..	..2	Cygan/Toure/Kanu for Keown/Ljungberg/Bergkamp
2 Oct	Auxerre	A	W	1-0	..	..	Cygan	..	..	Toure	..1	..	..	Kanu	..	Luzhny/Edu/Pennant for Wiltord/Toure/Henry
22 Oct	Auxerre	H	L	1-2	..	..	..	..	..	Ljungberg	..	..	..	..1	..	Pires/Toure for Gilberto/Lauren
30 Oct	Borussia Dortmund	A	L	1-2	..	..	..	..	..	..	..	..	..	Pires	..1	Edu/Toure/Kanu for Gilbert/Pires/Wiltord
12 Nov	PSV Eindhoven	H	D	0-0	Shaaban	Luzhny	..	Stepanovs	Toure	Van Bronckhorst	Edu	..	Jeffers	..	..	Gilberto/Bergkamp/Wiltord for Vieira/Henry/Jeffers
27 Nov	Roma	A	W	3-1	..	..	..	Campbell	Cole	Ljungberg	Gilberto	..	Wiltord	..	..3	Keown/Edu/Van Bronckhorst for Wiltord/Ljungberg/Pires
10 Dec	Valencia	H	D	0-0	Seaman	Lauren	..	..	..	..	..	..	Bergkamp	..	..	Parlour/Kanu/Wiltord for Vieira/Pires/Ljungberg
18 Feb	Ajax	H	D	1-1	..	..	..	..	..	Wiltord1	..	..	..	..	..	Taylor/Kanu/Jeffers for Seaman/Bergkamp/Gilberto
26 Feb	Ajax	A	D	0-0	..	..	Keown	..	..	..	..	..	..	..	..	Parlour/Van Bronckhorst/Jeffers for Wiltord/Pires/Bergkamp
11 Mar	Roma	H	D	1-1	..	..	..	Cygan	Van Bronckhorst	..	..	..1	..	..	..	Ljungberg/Kanu/Jeffers for Wiltord/Lauren/Bergkamp
19 Mar	Valencia	A	L	1-2	Taylor	..	Campbell	..	Toure	..	..	..	Ljungberg	..	..1	Kanu/Jeffers for Toure/Wiltord

SEASON 2003–04 FA PREMIER LEAGUE

16 Aug	Everton	H	W	2-1	Lehmann	Lauren	Campbell	Toure	Cole	Ljungberg	Gilberto	Vieira	Pires1	Henry1p	Wiltord	Keown/Parlour for Wiltord/Pires
24 Aug	Middlesbrough	A	W	4-0	..	..	..	..	..	..	..1	..	..	..1	..2	Parlour/Edu/Bergkamp for Ljungberg/Pires/Wiltord
27 Aug	Aston Villa	H	W	2-0	..	..	..1	..	..	..	..	..	..	..1	..	Bergkamp/Parlour for Wiltord/Ljungberg
31 Aug	Manchester City	A	W	2-1	..	..	Keown	..	..	..1	..	..	..	..	..1	Parlour/Bergkamp/Edu for Ljungberg/Wiltord/Pires
13 Sept	Portsmouth	H	D	1-1	..	..	Campbell	..	..	Parlour	Edu	..	Pires	..1p	Bergkamp	Ljungberg/Wiltord for Edu/Bergkamp
21 Sept	Manchester Utd	A	D	0-0	..	..	Keown	..	..	..	Gilberto	..	Ljungberg	..	..	Edu for Bergkamp
26 Sept	Newcastle Utd	H	W	3-2	..	..	..	..	..	..	..1	..	..	..2,1p	Wiltord	Edu/Cygan/Pires for Vieira/Cole/Parlour
4 Oct	Liverpool	A	W	2-1	..	..	Campbell	..	..	..	..	Edu	Pires1	..	Aliadiere	Wiltord for Aliadiere
18 Oct	Chelsea	H	W	2-1	..	..	..	..	..	..	..	..1	..	..1	Wiltord	Bergkamp/Kanu/Cygan for Wiltord/Pires/Parlour
26 Oct	Charlton Athletic	A	D	1-1	..	..	..	..	..	Ljungberg	..	Parlour	..	..1	Bergkamp	Kanu/Wiltord for Ljungberg/Bergkamp
1 Nov	Leeds United	A	W	4-1	..	..	..	..	..	..	..1	..	..1	..2	..	Edu/Aliadiere for Ljungberg/Bergkamp
8 Nov	Tottenham Hotspur	H	W	2-1	..	..	..	..	..	..1	..	..	..1	..	Kanu	Bergkamp/Cygan/Edu for Gilberto/Kanu/Lauren
22 Nov	Birmingham City	A	W	3-0	..	Toure	..	Cygan	..	..1	Clichy	Edu	1	..	Bergkamp1	Kanu/Hoyte/Aliadiere for Clichy/Pires/Bergkamp
30 Nov	Fulham	H	D	0-0	..	..	..	..	..	..	Gilberto	..	..	..	..	Kanu/Aliadiere for Gilberto/Ljungberg
6 Dec	Leicester City	A	D	1-1	..	..	..	..	..	..	..1	..	..	Aliadiere	..	Wiltord/Clichy/Keown for Aliadiere/Bergkamp/Ljungberg
14 Dec	Blackburn Rovers	H	W	1-0	..	..	..	..	..	..	..	Vieira	..	Henry	..1	Parlour/Edu for Bergkamp/Ljungberg
20 Dec	Bolton Wanderers	A	D	1-1	..	..	..	..	Clichy	..	..	..	..1	..	..	Parlour for Bergkamp
26 Dec	Wolverhampton W	H	W	3-0	..	..	..	..	..	..	Parlour	..	..	..2	..	Edu/Aliadiere for Ljungberg/Pires
29 Dec	Southampton	A	W	1-0	..	..	..	..	..	..	..	..	..1	..	..	Edu/Kanu/Lauren for Ljungberg/Bergkamp/Pires
7 Jan	Everton	A	D	1-1	..	..	..	..	Cole	..	..	..	..	..	Kanu1	Lauren/Edu/Gilberto for Toure/Kanu/Ljungberg
10 Jan	Middlesbrough	H	W	4-1	..	Lauren	..	..	..	..1	Gilberto	..	..1	..1p	Aliadiere	Kanu/Edu/Parlour for Aliadiere/Pires/Ljungberg
18 Jan	Aston Villa	A	W	2-0	..	..	..	Cygan	..	..	..	Vieira	..	..2,1p	Kanu	Edu/Toure/Parlour for Pires/Kanu/Ljungberg
1 Feb	Manchester City	H	W	2-1	..	..	..	Toure	..	..	..	Parlour	..	..1	Bergkamp	Edu/Reyes/Cygan for Ljungberg/Bergkamp/Pires
7 Feb	Wolverhampton W	A	W	3-1	..	..	..	..	..	Edu	..	Vieira	..	..1	..1	Reyes for Bergkamp
10 Feb	Southampton	H	W	2-0	..	..	..	..	..	Parlour	..	..	..	..2	Reyes	Clichy for Reyes
21 Feb	Chelsea	A	W	2-1	..	..	..	..	Clichy	Edu1	..	..1	..	..	Bergkamp	Ljungberg for Bergkamp
28 Feb	Charlton Athletic	H	W	2-1	..	..	..	..	Cole	Ljungberg	Edu	..	..1	..1	..	Reyes/Gilberto/Cygan for Bergkamp/Ljungberg/Pires
13 Mar	Blackburn Rovers	A	W	2-0	..	..	..	..	..	Edu	Gilbert	..	..1	..1	Reyes	Clichy/Cygan forReyes/Pires
20 Mar	Bolton Wanderers	H	W	2-1	..	..	..	..	..	..	..	..	..1	..	Bergkamp1	Ljungberg/Cygan for Gilberto/Pires
28 Mar	Manchester Utd	H	D	1-1	..	..	..	..	Clichy	Ljungberg	Edu	..	..	..1	Reyes	Gilberto/Cygan/Bergkamp for Reyes/Ljungberg/Pires
9 Apr	Liverpool	H	W	4-2	..	..	..	..	Cole	..	Gilberto	..	..1	..3	Bergkamp	Edu/Keown for Pires/Ljungberg
11 Apr	Newcastle Utd	A	D	0-0	..	..	..	..	..	Wiltord	..	..	Edu	..	Reyes	Bergkamp/Pires/Clichy for Reyes/Wiltord/Cole
16 Apr	Leeds Utd	H	W	5-0	..	..	..	..	Clichy	..	..	..	Pires1	..4	Bergkamp	Edu/Parlour/Reyes for Gilberto/Pires/Bergkamp
25 Apr	Tottenham Hotspur	A	D	2-2	..	..	..	..	Cole	Parlour	..	..1	..1	..	..	Edu/Reyes for Parlour/Bergkamp
1 May	Birmingham City	H	D	0-0	..	..	..	..	..	Ljungberg	..	..	Reyes	..	..	Pires/Aliadiere/Keown for Ljungberg/Reyes/Bergkamp
4 May	Portsmouth	A	D	1-1	..	..	..	..	..	..	Campbell	..	Bentley	..	Reyes1	Kanu/Aliadiere/Keown for Bentley Ljungberg/Reyes
9 May	Fulham	A	W	1-0	..	..	..	..	..	..	Parlour	..	Pires	..	Reyes1	Aliadiere/Clichy/Keown for Reyes/Pires/Ljungberg
15 May	Leicester City	H	W	2-1	..	..	..	..	..	..	Gilberto	..1	..	..1p	Bergkamp	Edu/Reyes/Keown for Pires/Bergkamp/Ljungberg

League Appearances (Goals in brackets)
Lehmann 38 – Henry 37 (30) – Toure 37 (1) – Campbell 35 (1) – Pires 36 (14) – Cole 32 – Lauren 32 – Gilberto 32 (4) – Vieira 29 (3) – Ljungberg 30 (4) – Bergkamp 28 (4) – Parlour 25 – Edu 30 (2) – Cygan 18 – Wiltord 12 (3) – Reyes 13 (2) – Clichy 12 – Kanu 10 (1) – Aliadiere 10 – Keown 10 – Bentley 1 – Hoyte 1

FA Premier League

	P	W	L	D	F:A	Pts	
Arsenal	38	26	0	12	73:26	90	1st

UEFA Champions League

17 Sept	Inter Milan	H	L	0-3	Lehman	Lauren	Campbell	Toure	Cole	Ljungberg	Gilberto	Vieira	Pires	Henry	Wiltord	Kanu/Bergkamp/Parlour for Gilberto/Pires/Wiltord
30 Sept	Lokomotiv Moscow	A	D	0-0	..	..	Keown	..	..	Parlour	..	Edu	..	..	..	
21 Oct	Dynamo Kyiv	A	L	1-2	..	..	Campbell	..	..	..	..	..	..	..1	..	Vieira/Kanu/Ljungberg for Edu/Gilberto/Parlour
5 Nov	Dynamo Kyiv	H	W	1-0	..	..	..	..	..1	Ljungberg	..	Parlour	..	..	Bergkamp	Wiltord/Kanu/Edu for Ljungberg/Parlour/Bergkamp
25 Nov	Inter Milan	A	W	5-1	..	Toure	..	Cygan	..	..1	Parlour	Edu1	..1	..2	Kanu	Gilberto/Aliadiere for Kanu/Henry
10 Dec	Lokomotiv Moscow	H	W	2-0	..	..	..	..	..	..1	Gilberto	Vieira	..1	..	Bergkamp	Kanu for Bergkamp
24 Feb	Celta Vigo	A	W	3-2	..	Lauren	..	Toure	Clichy	..	Edu2	..	..1	..	..	
10 Mar	Celta Vigo	H	W	2-0	..	..	..	..	Cole	..	..	..	..	..2	..	Reyes/Gilberto/Kanu for Pirews/Edu/Bergkamp
24 Mar	Chelsea	A	D	1-1	..	..	..	..	..	..	..	..	..1	..	..	Gilberto/Reyes for Bergkamp/Ljungberg
6 Apr	Chelsea	H	L	1-2	..	..	..	..	..	..	..	..	..	..	Reyes 1	Bergkamp for Henry

The FA Cup

4 Jan	Leeds Utd (3)	A	W	4-1	Lehmann	Lauren	Campbell	Keown	Cole	Ljungberg	Gilberto	Vieira	Edu1	Henry 1	Kanu	Pires 1/Toure 1/Parlour for Edu/Ljungberg/Kanu
24 Jan	Middlesbrough (4)	H	W	4-1	..	..	..	Toure	..	..2	Parlour	..	..	Pires	Bergkamp1	Clichy/Bentley 1 for Vieira/Bergkamp
15 Feb	Chelsea (5)	H	W	2-1	..	..	..	..	..	Parlour	Gilberto	..	Pires	Reyes 2	..	Edu/Clichy for Parlour/Reyes
6 Mar	Portsmouth (6)	A	W	5-1	..	..	..	..1	..	Ljungberg2	..	..	Edu	Henry 2	Reyes	Clicht/Bentley/Kanu for Vieira/Ljungberg/Henry
3 Apr	Manchester Utd	N	L	0-1	..	..	..	..	Clichy	..	Edu	..	Pires	Aliadiere	Bergkamp	Reyes/Henry/Kanu for Aliadiere/Pires/Edu
	(at Villa Park) (S-F)															

The FA Community Shield

10 Aug	Manchester Utd	N	D	1-1	Lehmann	Lauren	Campbell	Toure	Cole	Parlour	Vieira	Gilberto	Ljungberg	Bergkamp	Henry1	Wiltord/Pires/Edu/Jeffers/Van Bronckhorst for Henry/Parlour/Gilberto/Bergkamp/Ljungberg

The Carling Cup

28 Oct	Rotherham United	H	W	1-1	Stack	Hoyte	Tavlaridis	Cygan	Clichy	Fabregas	Edu	Thomas	Wiltord	Kanu	Aliadiere1	Smith/Owusu-Abeyle/Spicer for Thomas/Fabregas/Hoyte
	(Arsenal won 9-8 on penalties)															
2 Dec	Wolverhampton W	H	W	5-1	..	..	..	Simek	Clichy	..1	Vieira	Bentley	Wiltord 1	Kanu 1	..2	Skulason/Smith/Papadopulos for Hoyte/Bentley/Aliadiere
16 Dec	West Brom	A	W	2-0	..	Lauren	..	Keown	Clichy	Parlour	Edu	..	Wiltord	Kanu 1	..1	Fabregas/Thomas/Thomas for Aliadiere/Bentley
20 Jan	Middlesbrough	H	L	0-1	..	Toure	Keown	Cygan	Clichy	Gilberto	..	..	Parlour	Kanu	Owusu-Abeyle	Thomas/Smith for Owusu-Abeyle/Bentley
3 Feb	Middlesbrough	A	L	1-2	..	..	..	..	Cole	Parlour	..1	Vieira	Clichy	Reyes	Bentley	Owusu-Abeyle for Clichy

SEASON 2004–05 FA PREMIER LEAGUE

15 Aug	Everton	A	W	4-1	Lehmann	Lauren	Toure	Cygan	Cole	Ljungberg1	Gilberto	Fabregas	Reyes1	Bergkamp1	Henry	Pennant/Pires1/Flamini for Ljungberg/Reyes/Gilberto
22 Aug	Middlesbrough	H	W	5-3	..	..	..	..	..	..	..	..	..1	..1	..2	Pires1/Flamini for Ljungberg/Reyes
25 Aug	Blackburn Rovers	H	W	3-0	..	..	..	..	..	Pennant	..	..1	Pires	..	..1	Reyes1/Ljungberg/Flamini for Bergkamp/Pennant/Fabregas
28 Aug	Norwich City	A	W	4-1	..	..	..	Hoyte	..	Ljungberg	..	..	..1	Reyes1	..1	Bergkamp1/Edu/Clichy for Reyes/Fabregas/Pires
11 Sept	Fulham	A	W	*3-0	..	..	..	Cygan	..	..1	..	Vieira	..	Bergkamp	..	Reyes1/Pennant/Fabregas for Pires/Ljungberg/Vieira
18 Sept	Bolton Wanderers	H	D	2-2	..	..	..	..	..	..	..	..	..1	Reyes	..1	Edu/Bergkamp/Clichy for Gilberto/Reyes/Pires
25 Sept	Manchester City	A	W	1-0	..	..	..	Campbell	..1	..	Edu	..	Reyes	Bergkamp	..	Clichy/Fabregas/van Persie for Reyes/Ljungberg/Bergkamp
2 Oct	Charlton Athletic	H	W	4-0	..	..	..	..	Clichy	..1	Fabregas	..	..1	..	..2	Pennant/van Persie/Flamini for Ljungberg/Henry/Fabregas
16 Oct	Aston Villa	H	W	3-1	..	..	..	..	Cole	Pires2(1p)	..	..	..	..	..1	Pennant/Flamini/van Persie for Reyes/Vieira/Pires
24 Oct	Manchester Utd	A	L	0-2	..	..	..	..	..	Ljungberg	Edu	..	..	..	..	Pires for Reyes
30 Oct	Southampton	H	D	2-2	..	..	..	Cygan	..	..	..	..	..	..	..1	Pires/Fabregas/van Persie1 for Reyes/Edu/Ljungberg
6 Nov	Crystal Palace	A	D	1-1	..	..	..	..	..	..	Fabregas	..	Pires	Reyes	..1	Bergkamp/van Persie/Flamini for Ljungberg/Pires/Fabregas
13 Nov	Tottenham Hotspur	A	W	5-4	..	..1(p)	..	..	..	..1	..	..1	Reyes	Bergkamp	..1	Pires1/van Persie for Reyes/Bergkamp
20 Nov	West Brom Albion	H	D	1-1	..	..	..	..	..	..	..	..	Pires1	..	..	Reyes/van Persie for Fabregas/Bergkamp
28 Nov	Liverpool	A	L	1-2	..	..	..	Campbell	..	..	..	..1	..	Reyes	..	van Persie for Reyes
4 Dec	Birmingham City	H	W	3-0	Almunia	..	..	..	..	..	..	..	..1	..	..2	Clichy/Flamini for Reyes/Fabregas
12 Dec	Chelsea	H	D	2-2	..	..	..	..	..	Pires	..	Flamini	Reyes	Bergkamp	..2	van Persie/Clichy for Bergkamp/Reyes
19 Dec	Portsmouth	A	W	1-0	..	..	..	..1	..	..	Flamini	Vieira	Clichy	van Persie	..	Bergkamp for van Persie
26 Dec	Fulham	H	W	2-0	..	..	..	..	Clichy	Ljungberg	Fabregas	..	Pires1	Bergkamp	..1	Flamini/van Persie for Ljungberg/Bergkamp
29 Dec	Newcastle Utd	A	W	1-0	..	..	..	..	Cole	..	Flamini	..1	..	van Persie	..	Clichy for van Persie
1 Jan	Charlton Athletic	A	W	3-1	..	Hoyte	..	..	..	..2	Fabregas	..	Clichy	..1	..	Pires/Senderos/Pennant for van Persie/Campbell/Ljungberg
4 Jan	Manchester City	H	D	1-1	..	..	..	Senderos	..	..1	..	..	Pires	..	..	Pennant for Fabregas
15 Jan	Bolton Wanderers	A	L	0-1	..	..	..	Campbell	..	..	..	..	..	..	..	Reyes/Bergkamp for Fabregas/van Persie
23 Jan	Newcastle Utd	H	W	1-0	..	Lauren	..	..	..	Pires	Flamini	..	Reyes	Bergkamp1	..	Fabregas for Reyes
1 Feb	Manchester Utd	H	L	2-4	..	..	Cygan	..	..	Ljungberg	..	..1	Pires	..1	..	Reyes/Hoyte/Fabregas for Flamini/Campbell/Lauren
5 Feb	Aston Villa	A	W	3-1	Lehmann	..	..	Senderos	..1	..1	Edu	..	Reyes	..	..1	Flamini/Pires/Fabregas for Edu/Bergkamp/Reyes
14 Feb	Crystal Palace	H	W	5-1	..	..	Toure	Cygan	Clichy	Pires	..	..1	..1	..1	..2	Flamini/van Persie/Fabregas for Edu/Bergkamp/Pires
26 Feb	Southampton	A	D	1-1	..	Toure	Senderos	..	Cole	Ljungberg1	Flamini	..	Pires	van Persie	..	Clichy/Eboue for Pires/Toure
5 Mar	Portsmouth	H	W	3-0	..	..	..	..	Clichy	Fabregas	..	..	Cole	Owusu-Abeyie	Henry3	Lauren/van Persie/Ljungberg for Cygan/Owusu-Abeyie/Fabregas
19 Mar	Blackburn Rovers	A	W	1-0	..	Lauren	Toure	Senderos	..	..	..	..	..	Reyes	van Persie1	
2 Apr	Norwich City	H	W	4-1	..	..	..	Cygan	Cole	Ljungberg1	..	Gilberto	Pires	..	Henry3	Fabregas/van Persie/Clichy for Flamini/Reyes/Pires
9 Apr	Middlesbrough	A	W	1-0	..	..	..	Senderos	..	Fabregas	Gilberto	Vieira	..1	..	..	Bergkamp for Reyes
20 Apr	Chelsea	A	D	0-0	..	..	..	..	..	..	..	..	..	Bergkamp	Reyes	van Persie/Aliadiere for Bergkamp/Fabregas
25 Apr	Tottenham Hotspur	H	W	1-0	..	..	..	..	..	..	..	..	..	van Persie	..1	Bergkamp/Edu/Aliadiere for van Persie/Fabregas/Reyes
2 May	West Brom Albion	A	W	2-0	..	..	..	..	..	..	..	..	..	..1	..	Bergkamp/Edu1 for van Persie/Fabregas
8 May	Liverpool	H	W	3-1	..	..	..	..	..	..1	..	..	..1	..	..1	Bergkamp/Edu/Aliadiere for van Persie/Pires/Reyes
11 May	Everton	H	W	7-0	..	..	Campbell	..	..	Pires2	Vieira1	Edu1	Reyes	Bergkamp1	van Persie1	Henry/Flamini1/Fabregas for van Persie/Vieira/Pires
15 May	Birmingham City	A	L	1-2	..	Toure	..	..	..	Fabregas	Gilberto	Vieira	Ljungberg	..1	van Persie	Edu/Aliadiere/Flamini for Ljungberg/van Persie/Fabregas

League Appearances (Goals in brackets)
Cole 35 (2) – Toure 35 – Lauren 33 (1) – Pires 33 (14) – Fabregas 33 (2) – Vieira 32 (6) – Henry 32 (25) – Reyes 30 (9) – Bergkamp 29 (8) – Ljungberg 26 (10) – van Persie 26 (5) – Flamini 21 (1) – Campbell 16 – Cygan 15 – Clichy 15 – Gilberto 13 – Senderos 13 – Edu 12 (2) – Almunia 10 – Hoyte 5 – Aliadiere 4 – Owusu-Abeyie 1 – Eboue 1

FA Premier League

	P	W	L	D	F:A	Pts	
Chelsea	38	29	8	1	72:15	95	1st
Arsenal	38	25	5	8	87:36	83	2nd

The FA Community Shield

8 Aug	Manchester Utd	N	W	*3-1	Lehmann	Lauren	Toure	Cygan	Cole	Pennant	Gilberto1	Fabregas	Reyes1	Bergkamp	Henry	van Persie/Aliadiere/Clichy/Hoyte/Svard for Henry/Bergkamp/Aliadiere/Reyes/Fabregas
	(played at Millennium Stadium Cardiff)															

The FA Cup

9 Jan	Stoke City (3)	H	W	2-1	Lehmann	Eboue	Toure	Senderos	Clichy	Pennant	Fabregas	Vieira	Pires	Reyes1	van Persie1	Hoyte for Eboue
29 Jan	Wolverhampton W (4)	H	W	2-0	..	..	Cygan	Campbell	..	Ljungberg1	Flamini	..1(p)	Reyes	van Persie	Henry	Pires/Fabregas/Owusu-Abeyie for Reyes/van Persie/Ljungberg
19 Feb	Sheffield Utd (5)	H	D	1-1	Almunia	..	Toure	Senderos	..	..	..	Fabregas	..	..	Bergkamp	Pires1/Cygan for van Persie/Reyes
1 Mar	Sheffield Utd (5R)	A	D	0-0	..	Lauren	Cygan	..	..	Fabregas	..	Vieira	Cole	Ljungberg	Lupoli	Owusu-Abeyie/Toure/Aliadiere for Lupoli/Fabregas/Flamini
	(Arsenal won 4-2 on penalties after extra time in this replay)															
12 Mar	Bolton Wdrs (6)	A	W	1-0	Lehmann	..	Toure	..	..	Ljungberg1	..	..	Pires	Reyes	Bergkamp	
16 Apr	Blackburn Rvrs (S-F)	N	W	3-0	..	..	..	..	Cole	..	Gilberto	..	..1	..	..	Fabregas/van Persie2/Aliadiere for Ljungberg/Bergkamp/Reyes
21 May	Manchester Utd	N	D	0-0	..	..	..	..	..	Fabregas	..	..	..	..	..	Ljungberg/van Persie/Edu for Bergkamp/Fabregas/Pires
	(Played at Millennium Stadium, Cardiff)															
	(Arsenal won 5-4 on penalties after extra time)															

The Carling Cup

27 Oct	Manchester City	A	W	2-1	Almunia	Hoyte	Senderos	Cygan	Larsson	Pennant	Fabregas	Flamini	Smith	Lupoli	van Persie1	Owusu-Abeyie/Karbassiyoon1/Djourou for Smith/Lupoli/Pennant
9 Nov	Everton	H	W	3-1	..	..	..	Djourou	Karbassiyoon	..	Edu	..	..	..2	..	Owusu-Abeyie1/Larsson/Cregg for Smith/Edu/Lupoli
1 Dec	Manchester Utd	A	L	0-1	..	..	..	..	Clichy	..	Larsson	..	Owusu-Abeyie	..	..	Smith/Cregg/Karbassiyoon fo Lupoli/Larsson/Clichy

UEFA Champions League

14 Sept	PSV Eindhoven	H	W	1-0	Lehmann	Lauren	Toure	Cygan	Cole	Pires	Gilberto	Vieira	Reyes	Bergkamp	Henry	Edu for Reyes
29 Sept	Rosenborg	A	D	1-1	..	..	..	Campbell	..	Ljungberg1	Edu	..	..	Pires	..	van Persie for Pires
20 Oct	Panathinaikos	A	D	2-2	..	..	..	..	..	..1	..	Fabregas	..	..	..1	
2 Nov	Panathinaikos	H	D	1-1	..	..	..	Cygan	..	..	Fabregas	..	Pires	Bergkamp	..1(p)	Reyes/van Persie for Bergkamp/Ljungberg
24 Nov	PSV Eindhoven	A	D	1-1	..	..	..	Campbell	..	..	..	..	..	Reyes	Henry1	van Persie/Hoyte/Flamini for Reyes/Pires/van Persie
7 Dec	Rosenborg	H	W	5-1	Almunia	Hoyte	..	..	..	Pires1(p)	..1	Flamini	Reyes1	Bergkamp	..1	Clichy/van Persie1/Owusu-Abeyie for Bergkamp/Cole/Pires
22 Feb	Bayern Munich	A	L	1-3	Lehmann	Lauren	..1	Cygan	Clichy	..	Edu	Vieira	..	Ljungberg	..	Flamini/van Persie/Cole for Edu/Ljungberg/Clichy
9 Mar	Bayern Munich	H	W	1-0	..	..	..	Senderos	Cole	Ljungberg	Flamini	..	..	Bergkamp	..1	Fabregas/Pires/van Persie for Flamini/Reyes/Ljungberg

SEASON 2005–06 FA PREMIER LEAGUE

14 Aug	Newcastle United	H	W	2-0	Lehmann	Lauren	Cole	Senderos	Toure	Ljungberg	Fabregas	Gilberto	Hleb	Pires	Henry1p	Hleb/van Persie1/Flamini for Fabregas/Bergkamp/Pires
21 Aug	Cheslea	A	L	0-1	..	..	..	..	..	..	..	..	Hleb	Pires	..	van Persie/Flamini for Ljungberg/Fabregas
24 Aug	Fulham	H	W	4-1	..	..	..	Cygan2	..	Hleb		..	..	Reyes	Bergkamp2	Flamini/Clichy for Reyes/Hleb
10 Sep	Middlesbrough	A	L	1-2	..	..	..	..	..	..	Flamini	..	Pires	..	Reyes1	Fabregas/van Persie for Flamini/Pires
19 Sep	Everton	H	W	2-0	..	..	..	Campbell2	..	Ljungberg	Fabregas	..	..	van Persie	..	Hleb/Bergkamp/Song for Pires/Van Persie/Reyes
24 Sep	West Ham United	A	D	0-0	..	..	..	..	..	..	..	..	Hleb	..	..	Flamini/Owusu-Abeyie/Clichy for Gilberto/Reyes/van Persie
2 Oct	Birmingham City	H	W	1-0	..	..	..	..	..	Hleb	..	..	Pires	Ljungbergog		Bergkamp/van Persie/Flamini for Hleb/Pires/Ljungberg
15 Oct	WBA	A	L	1-2	..	..	Clichy	Senderos1	..	Ljungberg	..	Flamini	..	Bergkamp	..	Eboue/Owusu-Abeyie for Ljungberg/Flamini
22 Oct	Manchester City	H	W	1-0	..	..	..	Cygan	..	Fabregas	Flamini	Gilberto	..1p	..	Henry	
29 Oct	Tottenham Hotspur	A	D	1-1	..	..	..	Campbell	..	..	..	..	Ljungberg	..	Reyes	Pires1/van Persie/Cygan for Flamini/Ljungberg/Cygan
5 Nov	Sunderland	H	W	3-1	..	..	..	..	..	Pires	Fabregas	..	Reyes	van Persie1	Henry2	Eboue/Bergkamp for Reyes/van Persie
19 Nov	Wigan Athletic	A	W	3-2	..	..	..	..	..	Ljungberg	..	Gilberto	..	..1	..2	Flamini/Bergkamp/Senderos for Pires/van Persie/Fabregas
26 Nov	Blackburn Rovers	H	W	3-0	..	..	..	..	..	Pires	..1	..	Reyes	Bergkamp	..1	Ljungberg/Flamini/van Persie1 for Reyes/Pires/Bergkamp
3 Dec	Bolton Wanderers	A	L	0-2	..	..	..	..	..	Ljungberg	..	..	Pires	van Persie	..	Reyes/Bergkamp/Eboue for Fabregas/vanPersie/Lauren
10 Dec	Newcastle United	A	L	0-1	..	Toure	Lauren	..	Senderos	..	..	..	Hleb	..	..	Flamini/Pires/Owusu/Abeyie for Hleb/van Persie/Fabregas
18 Dec	Chelsea	H	L	0-2	..	..	..	..	..	..	..	Flamini	..	..	..	Bergkamp/Pires/Owusu/Abeyie for Ljungberg/Hleb/van Persie
26 Dec	Charlton Athletic	A	W	1-0	..	Lauren	Cygan	..	Toure	..	..	Gilberto	..	Reyes1	..	Pires/Flamini for Hleb/Reyes
28 Dec	Portsmouth	H	W	4-0	..	..	..	..	..	Pires	Flamini	..	Reyes1	Bergkamp1	Henry 2(1p)	Eboue/Fabregas for Reyes/Gilberto
31 Dec	Aston Villa	A	D	0-0	..	..	..	..	..	Ljungberg	Fabregas	Flamini	Hleb	van Persie	..	Bergkamp/Reyes/Pires for van Persie/Hleb/Ljungberg
3 Jan	Manchester United	H	D	0-0	..	..	..	..	..	Pires	..	Gilberto	..	Reyes	..	Bergkamp/Flamini/Eboue for Hleb/Fabregas/Reyes
14 Jan	Middlesbrough	H	W	7-0	..	..	..	Djourou	Senderos1	Ljungberg	..	..1	Pires1	..	..3	Cole/Flamini/Hleb1 for Cygan/Gilberto/Pires
21 Jan	Everton	A	L	0-1	..	Gilbert	Lauren	Campbell	..	..	..	..	..	..	..	Hleb/Diaby for Gilbert/Pires
1 Feb	West HamUnited	H	L	2-3	..	..	Senderos	..	Djourou	..	Diaby	..	..1	van Persie	..1	Flamini/Larsson/Bergkamp for Gilbert/Campbell/Diaby
4 Feb	Birmingham City	A	W	2-0	..	Flamini	Larsson	Djourou	Senderos	Fabregas	..	..	Reyes	Adebayor1	Henry1	Hleb for Reyes
11 Feb	Bolton Wanderers	H	D	1-1	..	..	..	..	..	..	..	..1	..	..	..	Pires/Ljungberg/Bergkamp for Reyes/Diaby/Larsson
14 Feb	Liverpool	A	L	0-1	..	Eboue	Flamini	Senderos	Toure	Ljungberg	Fabregas	..	Pires	..	..	Hleb for Pires
25 Feb	Blackburn Rovers	A	L	0-1	..	..	..	..	..	Fabregas	Diaby	..	Reyes	..	..	Pires/Hleb/Lupoli for Reyes/Diaby/Gilberto
4 Mar	Fulham	A	W	4-0	..	..	..	..	..	Ljungberg	..	..	Hleb	..1	..2	Bergkamp/Fabregas1/Reyes for Adebayor/Hleb/Henry
12 Mar	Liverpool	H	W	2-1	..	..	..	..	..	..	Fabregas	..	..	..	..2	Pires/Bergkamp for Ljungberg/Adebayor
18 Mar	Charlton Athletic	H	W	3-0	..	..	..	..	..	Hleb1	..	..	Pires1	..1	..	Bergkamp/van Persie/Song for Hleb/Adebayor/Fabregas
1 Apr	Aston Villa	H	W	5-0	..	..	..	..	..	Pires	..	..	Reyes	..1	..2	Diaby1/van Persie1/Djourou for Fabregas/Henry/Eboue
9 Apr	Manchester United	A	L	0-2	..	..	..	..	..	..	..	..	Hleb	..	van Persie	Henry/Diaby/Ljungberg for van Persie/Fabregas/Hleb
12 Apr	Portsmouth	A	D	1-1	..	Djourou	..	Campbell	..	Ljungberg	Diaby	Song	Reyes	..	Henry1	van Persie/Hleb/Eboue for Adebayor/Reyes/Campbell
15 Apr	WBA	H	W	3-1	..	Eboue	..	Senderos	..	Hleb1	..	Gilberto	..	van Persie	..	Adebayor/Pires1/Bergkamp1 for Henry/Hleb/van Persie
22 Apr	Tottenham Hotspur	H	D	1-1	..	Djourou	..	..	..	Pires	..	..	..	Adebayor	van Persie	Eboue/Fabregas/Henry1 for Senderos/Diaby/van Persie
1 May	Sunderland	A	W	3-0	og	Eboue	Clichy	Campbell	..	Fabregas1	..	Song	Pires	..	Henry1	Cole/van Persie/Bergkamp for Pires/Adebayor/Henry
4 May	Manchester City	A	W	3-1	..	..	Cole	..	..	Ljungberg1	Song	Gilberto	Hleb	van Persie	..	Fabregas/Pires/Reyes2 for Song/Hleb/van Persie
7 May	Wigan Athletic	H	W	4-2	..	..	..	..	..	Pires1	Fabregas	..	..	Reyes	..3	Ljngberg/van Persie/Bergkamp for Pires/Reyes/Hleb

League Appearances (Goals in brackets)
Adebayor 13 (4) – Cole 11 – Bergkamp 24 (2) – Campbell 20 (2) – Clichy 7 – Cygan 12 (2) – Diaby 12 (1) – Djourou 7 – Eboue 18 – Fabregas 35 (3) – Flamini 31 – Gilbert 2 – Henry 32 (27) – Hleb 25 (3) – Larsson 3 – Lauren 22 – Lehmann 38 – Ljungberg 25 (1) – Lupoli 1 – Owusu-Abeyie 4 - Pires 33 (7) – Reyes 26 (5) – Senderos 20 (2) – Gilberto Silva 33 (2) – Song Billong 5 – Toure 33 – van Persie 24 (5)

FA Premier League

	P	W	L	D	F:A	Pts	
Chelsea	38	29	5	4	72:22	91	1st
Arsenal	38	25	8	7	57:25	82	3rd

UEFA Champions League

14 Sep	FC Thun	H	W	2-1	Almunia	Lauren	Campbell	Toure	Cole	Ljungberg	Fabregas	Gilberto1	Pires	van Persie	Reyes	Bergkamp1/Hleb/Owusu-Abeyie for Fabregas/Ljungberg/Reyes
27 Sep	Ajax	A	W	2-1	..	..	..	..	..	Hleb	..	Flamini	..1p	Ljungberg1	..	Owusu-Abeyie/Clichy/Cygan for Reyes/Pires/Hleb
18 Oct	Sparta Prague	A	W	2-0	Lehmann	..	Cygan	..	Clichy	Fabregas	Flamini	Gilberto	..	van Persie	..	Henry2/Eboue/Owusu-Abeyie for Reyes/van Persie/Fabregas
2 Nov	Sparta Prague	H	W	3-0	Almunia	..	Campbell	..	..	Pires	..	..	Reyes	Bergkamp	Henry1	van Persie2/Fabregas/Eboue for Henry/Pires.Reyes
22 Nov	FC Thun	A	W	1-0	..	Eboue	..	Senderos	Cygan	Ljungberg	..	Song	..	van Persie	..	Fabregas/Lauren/Pires1p for Song/Cygan/Henry
7 Dec	Ajax	H	D	0-0	..	..	Senderos	Toure	Lauren	Hleb	..	Larsson	Owusu-Abeyie	Reyes	..	Fabregas/van/Persie/Gilbert for Hleb/Reyes/Lauren
21 Feb	Real Madrid	A	W	1-0	Lehmann	..	..	..	Flamini	Ljungberg	Fabregas	Gilberto	Hleb	..	..1	Pires/Diaby/Song for Hleb/Reyes/Ljungberg
8 Mar	Real Madrid	H	D	0-0	..	..	..	..	..	..	..	..	..	..	..	Pires/Bergkamp for Reyes/Hleb
28 Mar	Juventus	H	W	2-0	..	..	..	..	..	..	1	..	..	..1	..	van Persie for Reyes
5 Apr	Juventus	A	D	0-0	..	..	..	..	..	..	..	..	..	..	..	Pires/Diaby for Reyes/Hleb
19 Apr	Villarreal CF	H	W	1-0	..	..	..	..1	..	..	..	..	..	Pires	Henry	van Persie/Bergkamp for Ljungberg/Hleb
25 Apr	Villarreal CF	A	D	0-0	..	..	Campbell	..	..	..	..	..	..	Reyes	..	Clichy/Pires for Flamini/Reyes
17 May	Barcelona	N	L	1-2	..	..	..1	..	Cole	..	..	..	..	Pires	..	Almunia/Flamini/Reyes for Pires/Fabregas/Hleb

The FA Cup

7 Jan	Cardiff City (3)	H	W	2-1	Almunia	Gilbert	Senderos	Djourou	Lauren	Pires2	Flamini	Gilberto	Reyes	van Persie	Bergkamp	Owusu-Abeyie/Larsson for Reyes/van Persie
28 Jan	Bolton Wdrs (4)	A	L	0-1	..	..	Campbell	..	Senderos	Hleb	..	Diaby	Ljungberg	..	Reyes	

The FA Community Shield

7 Aug	Chelsea	N	L	1-2	Lehmann	Lauren	Toure	Senderos	Cole	Flamini	Pires	Ljungberg	Fabregas1	Bergkamp	Henry	Hleb/Gilberto/van Persie/Reyes/Cygan/Hoyte for Flamini/Pires/Bergkamp/Ljungberg/Senderos/Lauren

The Carling (League) Cup

25 Oct	Sunderland (3)	A	W	3-0	Almunia	Eboue1	Campbell	Senderos	Cygan	Muamba	Song	Larsson	Owusu-Abeyie	van Persie2(1p)	Lupoli	Cregg/Stokes/Bendtner for Larsson/Lupoli/Owusu-Abeyie
29 Nov	Reading (4)	H	W	3-0	..	..	Djourou	..	Gilbert	..	Flamini	..	..	..1	Reyes1	Lupoli1/Cygan/Bendtner for van Persie/Reyes/Owusu-Abeyie
21 Dec	Doncaster Rvrs (5) (Arsenal won 3-1 on penalties)	A	W	2-2	..	..	..	..	Cygan	Gilberto1	Song	Hleb	..1	..	Lupoli	Bendtner/Larsson/Gilbert for vanPersie/Owusu-Abeyie/Lupoli
10 Jan	Wigan Athletic (SF)	A	L	0-1	..	Gilbert	..	..	..	..	Flamini	..	Ljungberg	Owusu-Abeyie	Reyes	Lupoli/Fabregas/Larsson for Owusu-Abeyie/Reyes/Gilbert
24 Jan	Wigan Athletic (SF)	H	W	2-1	(aet)	..	Campbell	..	Lauren	..	Diaby	..	Reyes	Bergkamp	Henry1	Flamini/Pires/van Persie1 for Diaby/Hleb/Henry

SEASON 2006–07 FA PREMIER LEAGUE

19 Aug	Aston Villa	H	D	1-1	Lehmann	Eboue	Hoyte	Toure	Djourou	Hleb	Fabregas	Gilberto1	Ljungberg	Adebayor	Henry	van Persie/Walcott/Flamini for Adebayor/Ljungberg/Hoyte
26 Aug	Manchester City	A	L	0-1	..	..	..	..	..	..	..	..	Rosicky	van Persie	..	Walcott/Adebayor/Flamini for Rosicky/Hleb/Eboue
9 Sep	Middlesbrough	H	D	1-1	..	..	Gallas	..	..	..	..	..	Ljungberg	..	..1p	Rosicky/Adebayor/Baptista for Ljungberg/van Persie/Gilberto
17 Sep	Manchester United	A	W	1-0	..	..	..	..	..	..	..	..	..	Rosicky	Adebayor1	Baptista/Flamini for Hleb/Adebayor
23 Sep	Sheffield United	H	W	3-0	og	..	..1	..	..	Rosicky	..	..	..	Adebayor	Henry1	van Persie/Hleb/Baptista for Adebayor/Rosicky/Ljungberg
30 Sep	Charlton Athletic	A	W	2-1	..	..	Hoyte	..	Gallas	Hleb	..	..	..	van Persie2	Henry	Rosicky/Djourou for van Persie/Hleb
14 Oct	Watford	H	W	3-0	og	Hoyte	Gallas	..	Djourou	Walcott	..	..	Rosicky	Adebayor1	..1	Hleb/van Persie/Clichy forWalcot/Rosicky/Gallas
22 Oct	Reading	A	W	4-0	..	..	..	..	..	Hleb1	..	..	..	van Persie1	Henry 2(1p)	Walcott/Adebayor/Song for van Persie/Hleb/Rosicky
28 Oct	Everton	H	D	1-1	..	..	..	..	..	..	..	..	..	..1	..	Flamini/Walcott/Aliadiere for Hoyte/Djourou/Hleb
5 Nov	West Ham	A	L	0-1	..	..	Clichy	..	Gallas	..	..	..	..	..	..	Adebayor/Eboue/Flamini forvan Persie/Hleb/Hoyte
12 Nov	Liverpool	H	W	3-0	Almunia	Eboue	..	..1	..1	..	..	..	..1	..	..	Adebayor for van Persie
18 Nov	Newcastle	H	D	1-1	Lehmann	Eboue	..	..	..	..	..	Baptista	..	..	Adebayor	Henry1/Walcott for van Persie/Baptista
25 Nov	Bolton	A	L	1-3	..	..	..	..	Senderos	Ljungberg	..	Gilberto1	..	Walcott	Adebayor	Baptista/Hleb for Flamini/Ljungberg
29 Nov	Fulham	A	L	1-2	..	Hoyte	Flamini	..	..	Hleb	Song	..	Rosicky	van Persie1	Henry	Fabregas/Walcott/Djourou forSong/Rosicky/Hleb
2 Dec	Tottenham Hotspur	H	W	3-0	..	Eboue	Clichy	..	Djourou	Ljungberg	Fabregas	Gilberto2(1p)	Rosicky	van Persie	Adebayor1	Hleb/Baptista/Walcott for Rosicky/van Persie/Adebayor
10 Dec	Chelsea	A	D	1-1	..	..	..	Senderos	..	Hleb	..	..	Flamini1	..	..	Ljungberg/van Persie
13 Dec	Wigan Athletic	A	W	1-0	..	..	..	Toure	..	Ljungberg	Baptista	..	..	Walcott	..1	Fabregas/van Persie/Hoyte for Flamini/Baptsita/Walcott
16 Dec	Portsmouth	H	D	2-2	..	..	..	..	..	Hleb	Fabregas	..1	Ljungberg	van Persie	Aliadiere	Walcott/Adebayor/Flamini for Ljungberg/Aliadiere/Eboue
23 Dec	Blackburn	H	W	6-2	..	Hoyte	..	..	..	..1	..	..1	Rosicky	..2	..1p	Flamini1/Walcott/Baptista for Rosicky/Hleb/Adebayor
26 Dec	Watford	A	W	2-1	..	..	..	..	..	..	..	..1	..	..1	..	Senderos/Walcott/Baptista for Djourou/Hleb/Rosicky
30 Dec	Sheffield United	A	L	0-1	..	..	..	..	Senderos	Rosicky	Flamini	..	Baptista	..	Aliadiere	Fabregas/Denilson for Hoyte/Rosicky
2 Jan	Charlton Athletic	H	W	4-0	..	..1	..	..	..	Hleb	Fabregas	..	Rosicky	van Persie2(1p)	Henry1p	Flamini/Aliadiere/Denilson for Gilberto/Rosicky/Fabregas
13 Jan	Blackburn Rovers	A	W	2-0	..	..	..	..1	..	..	..	..	..	..	..1	Flamini/Adebayor/Djourou for van Persie/Henry/Fabregas
21 Jan	Manchester United	H	W	2-1	..	Eboue	..	..	..	..	..	Flamini	..	Adebayor	..1	van Persie1/Baptista/Hoyte forHleb/Flamini/Eboue
3 Feb	Middlesbrough	A	D	1-1	..	Hoyte	..	..	..	Flamini	..	Gilberto	..	..	..1	Denilson/Aliadiere for Hoyte/Adebayor
11 Feb	Wigan Athletic	H	W	2-1	og	..	..	..	Djourou	Walcott	..	..	..1	Baptista	..	Adebayor/Aliadiere/Flamini forDjourou/Walcott/Hoyte
3 Mar	Reading	H	W	2-1	..	Djourou	..	Gilberto1p	Gallas	Hleb	..	Denilson	Ljungberg	..1	Walcott	Diaby/Aliadiere/Senderos for Ljungberg/Walcott/Hleb
14 Mar	Aston Villa	A	W	1-0	..	..	Hoyte	..	..	Ljungberg	..	..	Diaby1	..	Aliadiere	Rosicky/Flamini/Senderos for Diaby/Baptista/Aliadiere
18 Mar	Everton	A	L	0-1	..	Toure	..	..	..	..	..	Diaby	Rosicky	..	..	Hleb/Walcott/Denilson for Rosicky/Aliadiere/Baptista
31 Mar	Liverpool	A	L	1-4	..	Eboue	Clichy	Toure	..1	Hleb	..	..	Denilson	..	Adebayor	Ljungberg/Rosicky/Hoyte forBaptista/Diaby/Eboue
7 Apr	West Ham United	H	L	0-1	..	..	..	..	..	..	..	Gilberto	Rosicky	Ljungberg	..	Aliadiere/Baptista/Diaby forHleb/Ljungberg/Gilberto
9 Apr	Newcastle United	A	D	0-0	..	..	..	..	..	..	..	..	Diaby	..	..	Baptista/Aliadiere forHleb/Adebayor
14 Apr	Bolton Wanderers	H	W	2-1	..	..	..	..	..	..	..1	..	Rosicky1	..	..	Diaby/Baptista for Ljungberg/Hleb
17 Apr	Manchester City	H	W	3-1	..	..	..	..	..	..	..1	..	..1	Diaby	..	Baptista1/Denilson/Senderos forDiaby/Fabregas/Rosicky
21 Apr	Tottenham Hotspur	A	D	2-2	..	..	..	..1	..	..	Diaby	..	..	Ljungberg	..1	Fabregas/Baptista/Senderos for Ljungber/Rosicky/Hleb
29 Apr	Fulham	H	W	3-1	..	..	..	..	..	..	Fabregas	..1p	Diaby	Baptista1	..1	Denilson for Baptista

6 May	Chelsea	H	D	1-1	..	..	..	..	..	Denilson	..	..1p	..	..	..	Hleb/Hoyte for Denilson/Diaby
13 May	Portsmouth	A	D	0-0	Poom	..	..	..	Hoyte	Djourou	Senderos	Fabregas	..	..	Hleb	

League Appearances (Goals in brackets)
Adebayor 29 (8) – Aliadiere 11 – Almunia 1 – Clichy 27 – Denilson 10 – Diaby 12 (1) – Djourou 21 – Eboue 24 – Fabregas 38 (2) – Flamini 20 (3) – Gallas 21 (3) – Henry 17 (10) – Hleb 33 (2) – Baptista 24 (3) – Hoyte 22 (1) – Lehmann 36 – Ljungberg 18 – Poom 1- Rosicky 26 (3) – Senderos 14 – Gilberto Silva 34 (10) – Song Billong 2 – Toure 35 (3) – van Persie 22 (11) – Walcott 16

FA Premier League

	P	W	L	D	F:A	Pts	
Manchester U	38	28	5	5	83:27	89	1st
Arsenal	38	19	8	11	63:35	68	4th

UEFA Champions League

8 Aug	Dinamo Zagreb	A	W	3-0	Almunia	Eboue	Toure	Djourou	Hoyte	Hleb	Fabregas2	Gilberto	Rosicky	van Persie1	Adebayor	Flamini/Aliadiere for Rosicky/Adebayor
23 Aug	Dinamo Zagreb	H	W	2-1	..	..	..	..	..	..	..	Flamini1	Ljungberg1	..	..	Henry/Gilberto/Walcott for Adebayor/Hleb/van Persie
13 Sep	Hamburg	A	W	2-1	Lehmann	..	..	..	Gallas	..	..	Gilberto1p	Rosicky1	..	..	Hoyte/Flamini/Baptista for Toure/Hleb/van Persie
26 Sep	Porto	H	W	2-0	..	..	..	Gallas	Hoyte	..1	..	..	..	..	Henry1	Ljungberg/Walcott/Song for van Persie/Hleb/Gallas
17 Oct	CSKA Moscow	A	L	0-1	..	Hoyte	..	Djourou	Gallas	..	..	..	..	..	..	Adebayor/Clichy/Walcott for van Persie/Hleb/Rosicky
1 Nov	CSKA Moscow	H	D	0-0	..	..	..	Gallas	Clichy	..	..	..	..	..	..	Walcott/Aliadiere/Flamini for Hleb/van Persie/Fabregas
21 Nov	Hamburg	H	W	3-1	..	Eboue1	..	Senderos	..	..	..	Flamini	Ljungberg	..1	..	Adebayor/Walcott/Baptista for van Persie/Ljungberg/Hleb
6 Dec	Porto	A	D	0-0	..	..	..	Djourou	..	..	..	Gilberto	Flamini	Ljungberg	Adebayor	van Persie forAdebayor
20 Feb	PSV Eindhoven	A	L	0-1	..	Gallas	..	Senderos	..	..	..	..	Rosicky	Adebayor	Henry	Baptista for Hleb
7 Mar	PSV Eindhoven	H	D	1-1	..	Toure	Gallas	Gilberto	..	..	..	Denilson	Ljungberg	..	Baptista	Henry/Diaby/Walcott for Baptista/Ljungberg/Clichy

The FA Cup

6 Jan	Liverpool (3)	A	W	3-1	Almunia	Eboue	Clichy	Senderos	Toure	Hleb	Flamini	Gilberto	Rosicky2	van Persie	Henry1	Hoyte/Baptista/Walcott forEboue/van Persie/Henry
28 Jan	Bolton (4)	H	D	1-1	..	Hoyte	..	..	..1	Walcott	..	Fabregas	..	Adebayor	..	Baptista/Aliadiere for Hoyte/Walcott
14 Feb	Bolton (4R)	A	W	3-1	..	Djourou	..	Gilberto	..	Hleb	Diaby	Denilson	..	..2	Baptista	Ljungberg1/Aliadiere/Hoyte for Hleb/Rosicky/Djourou
17 Feb	Blackburn Rvrs (5)	H	D	0-0	..	Hoyte	Gallas	Senderos	..	Walcott	Flamini	Fabregas	Ljungberg	Aliadiere	Henry	Clichy/Adebayor/Rosicky for Gallas/Walcott/Ljungberg
28 Feb	Blackburn Rvrs (5R)	A	L	0-1	..	Eboue	Traore	..	Gallas	Hleb	Denilson	Gilberto	..	..	Baptista	Walcott/Clichy forEboue/Traore

The Carling (League) Cup

24 Oct	WBA (3)	A	W	2-0	Almunia	Connolly	Senderos	Djourou	Clichy	Walcott	Song	Flamini	Denilson	Aliadiere2(1p)	Adebayor	Traore/Randall for Adebayor/Denilson
8 Nov	Everton (4)	A	W	1-0	..	Eboue	..	..	Traore	..	..	..	..	..	..1	Poom/Randall for Almunia/Denilson
9 Jan	Liverpool (5)	A	W	6-3	..	Hoyte	Toure	..	..	..	..1	Fabregas	..	..1	Baptista4	Diaby/Connolly for Walcott/Traore
24 Jan	Tottenham (SF)	A	D	2-2	..	..	..	Senderos	..	..	Diaby	..	..	..	..2	Hleb/Eboue/Flamini for Diaby/Aliadiere/Hleb
31 Jan	Tottenham (SF)	H	W3-1(aet)		og	..	..	..	..	..	..	Gilberto	..	..1	Adebayor1	Rosicky/Clichy/Fabregas forWalcott/Traore/Diaby
25 Feb	Chelsea (F)	N	L1-2(aet)		..	..	..	..	..	..1	..	Fabregas	..	..	Baptista	Eboue/Hleb/Adebayor for Traore/Diaby/Aliadiere

SEASON 2007–08 FA PREMIER LEAGUE

12 Aug	Fulham	H	W	2-1	Lehmann	Sagna	Toure	Gallas	Clichy	Eboue	Fabregas	Flamini	Rosicky	Hleb1	van Persie1	Walcott/Bendtner for Eboue/Rosicky
19 Aug	Blackburn Rovers	A	D	1-1	..	..	..	..	..	Walcott	Flamini	Fabregas	Hleb	Eduardo	..1	Senderos/Bendtner/Denilson for Gallas/Walcott/Eduardo
25 Aug	Manchester City	H	W	1-0	Almunia	..	Gilberto	Toure	..	Hleb	Fabregas1	Flamini	Rosicky	Adebayor	..	Denilson/Eduardo/Song for Sagna/Adebayor/van Persie
2 Sep	Portsmouth	H	W	3-1	..	Toure	Senderos	Gilberto	..	Rosicky1	..1	..	Hleb	van Persie	Adebayor1	Denilson/Diaby/Eduardo for Hleb/van Persie/Adebayor
15 Sep	Tottenham Hotspur	A	W	3-1	..	Sagna	Toure	..	..	Hleb	..1	Diaby	Flamini	Adebayor2	van Persie	Song/Rosicky/Denilson for Hleb/Diaby/van Persie
22 Sep	Derby County	H	W	5-0	..	..	..	Senderos	..	Walcott	..1	Flamini	Diaby1	Eduardo	Adebayor3	Diarra/Denilson/Song for Walcott/Fabregas/Flamini
29 Sep	West Ham United	A	W	1-0	..	..	..	..	..	Hleb	..	..	..	Adebayor	van Persie1	Eboue/Gilberto/Bendtner for Hleb/Adebayor/van Persie
7 Oct	Sunderland	H	W	3-2	..	..	..	..1	..	..	..	..	..	..	..2	Eboue/Walcott/Gilberto for Sagna/Diaby/van Persie
20 Oct	Bolton Wanderers	H	W	2-0	..	..	..1	Gallas	..	Eboue	..	..	Hleb	Eduardo	Adebayor	Rosicky1/Diaby/Walcott for Eboue/Hleb/Eduardo
28 Oct	Liverpool	A	D	1-1	..	..	..	..	..	..	..1	..	..	Rosicky	..	Gilberto/Bendtner/Walcott for Clichy/Eboue/Rosicky
3 Nov	Manchester United	H	D	2-2	..	..	..	..1*	..	..	..1	..	Rosicky	Hleb	..	Walcott/Eduardo/Gilberto for Eboue/Rosicky/Hleb
12 Nov	Reading	A	W	3-1	..	..	..	..	..	..	..	..1	..	..1	..1	Walcott/Diarra/Bendtner for Rosicky/Hleb/Adebayor
24 Nov	Wigan Athletic	H	W	2-0	..	..	..	..1	..	..	Denilson	Diarra	..1	Adebayor	Walcott	Eduardo/Bendtner for Eboue/Walcott
1 Dec	Aston Villa	A	W	2-1	..	..	..	..	..	..	Diarra	Flamini1	..	Hleb	Adebayor1	Gilberto/Walcott/Bendtner for Rosicky/Hleb/Adebayor
5 Dec	Newcastle United	A	D	1-1	..	..	..	..	..	..	..	Gilberto	..	Adebayor1	Eduardo	Bendtner for Eduardo
9 Dec	Middlesbrough	A	L	1-2	..	..	..	..	..	..	..	..	..1	Eduardo	Adebayor	Walcott/Denilson/Bendtner for Eboue/Diarra/Eduardo
16 Dec	Chelsea	H	W	1-0	..	..	..	..1	..	..	Flamini	Fabregas	..	Hleb	..	van Persie/Gilberto for Eboue/Hleb
22 Dec	Tottenham Hotspur	H	W	2-1	..	..	..	..	..	..	Fabregas	Flamini	..	..	..1	Bendtner1/Gilberto for Eboue/Hleb
26 Dec	Portsmouth	A	D	0-0	..	..	..	..	..	..	Flamini	Fabregas	Hleb	Rosicky	..	Diaby/Bendtner for Eboue/Hleb
29 Dec	Everton	A	W	4-1	..	..	..	..	..	Hleb	Fabregas	Flamini	Diaby	Bendtner	Eduardo2	Diarra/Rosicky1/Adebayor1 for Hleb/Fabregas/Eduardo
1 Jan	West Ham United	H	W	2-0	..	Hoyte	..	..	..	Eboue	..	..	Rosicky	Eduardo1	Adebayor1	Hleb/Diaby/Walcott for Eboue/Rosicky/Eduardo
12 Jan	Birmingham City	H	D	1-1	..	Sagna	Senderos	..	..	Walcott	..	..	Hleb	..	..1(p)	Diaby/Bendtner for Sagna/Walcott
19 Jan	Fulham	A	W	3-0	..	..	..	..	..	Hleb	Flamini	Fabregas	Rosicky1	Adebayor2	Eduardo	
29 Jan	Newcastle United	H	W	3-0	..	..	Gallas	Senderos	..	Diaby	Fabregas1	Flamini1	Hleb	..1	..	Gilberto/Walcott/Bendtner for Diaby/Adebayor/Eduardo
2 Feb	Manchester City	A	W	3-1	Lehmann	..	..	..	..	Hleb	..	..	Diaby	..2	..1	Hoyte for Hleb
11 Feb	Blackburn Rovers	H	W	2-0	..	..	..	..1	..	Fabregas	Flamini	Gilberto	Hleb	..1	..	
23 Feb	Birmingham City	A	D	2-2	Almunia	..	..	..	..	Walcott2	Fabregas	Flamini	..	Eduardo	Adebayor	Denilson/Gilberto/Bendtner for Walcott/Hleb/Eduardo
1 Mar	Aston Villa	H	D	1-1	..	..	..	..	..	Hleb	..	..	Diaby	Adebayor	Walcott	Denilson/Gilberto/Bendtner1 for Senderos/Flamini/Diaby
9 Mar	Wigan Athletic	A	D	0-0	..	..	Senderos	Gallas	..	Fabregas	Flamini	Gilberto	Hleb	..	Bendtner	Toure/van Persie for Gilberto/Bendtner
15 Mar	Middlesbrough	H	D	1-1	..	..	Toure1	..	..	Eboue	Fabregas	Flamini	..	..	van Persie	Bendtner/Senderos/Walcott for Sagna/Clichy/van Persie
23 Mar	Chelsea	A	L	1-2	..	..1	..	..	..	..	..	..	..	..	..	Diaby/Bendtner/Walcott for Sagna/Flamini/van Persie
29 Mar	Bolton Wanderers	A	W	3-2*	..	Toure	Senderos	..1	..	Hleb	Flamini	Fabregas	Diaby	Bendtner	..1	Walcott/Adebayor/Hoyte for Senderos/Bendtner/van Persie
5 Apr	Liverpool	H	D	1-1	..	Hoyte	Gallas	Toure	Traore	Eboue	Fabregas	Gilberto	Flamini	..1	Walcott	Adebayor/Clichy/Hleb for Hoyte/Traore/Flamini
13 Apr	Manchester United	A	L	2-1	Lehmann	Toure	..	Song	Clichy	..	..	..	Hleb	van Persie	Adebayor1	Hoyte/Walcott/Bendtner for Toure/Eboue/Van Persie
19 Apr	Reading	H	W	2-0	..	..	..	..	..	Walcott	..	..1	..	..	..1	Eboue/Denilson/Bendtner for Toure/Hleb/Adebayor
28 Apr	Derby County	A	W	6-2	Fabianski	..	..	..	..	Eboue	..	Denilson	Walcott1	..1	Bendtner1	Djourou/Gilberto/Adebayor3 for Toure/Denilson/van Persie
4 May	Everton	H	W	1-0	..	..	..	..	..	..	Gilberto	..	..	Adebayor	..1	Lehmann/Traore/Senderos for Fabianski/Toure/Adebayor
11 May	Sunderland	A	W	1-0	..	Song	Senderos	Djourou	..	..	Denilson	Gilberto	..1	..	..	Randall/Traore for Eboue/Bendtner

League Appearances (Goals in brackets)
Clichy 38 (0) – Adebayor 36 (24) – Gallas 31 (4) – Fabregas 32 (7) – Hleb 31 (2) – Flamini 30 (3) – Toure 30 (2) – Almunia 29 – Sagna 29 (1) – Bendtner 27 (5) – Walcott 25 (4) – Eboue 23 – Gilberto 23 (1) Rosicky 18 (6) – Eduardo 17 (4) – Senderos 17 (2) – van Persie 15 (7) – Diaby 15 (1) – Denilson 13 – Song 9 – Lehmann 7 – Hoyte 5 – Fabianski 3 – Traore 3 – Djourou 2 – Randall 1

FA Premier League

	P	W	L	D	F:A	Pts	
Manchester U	38	27	6	5	80:22	87	1st
Arsenal	38	24	11	3	74:31	83	3rd

UEFA Champions League

15 Aug	Sparta Prague	A	W	2-0	Lehmann	Sagna	Toure	Gallas	Clichy	Eboue	Flamini	Fabregas1	Rosicky	Hleb 1	van Persie	Song for Rosicky
29 Aug	Sparta Prague	H	W	3-0	Almunia	Hoyte	..	Senderos	..	Diaby	Gilberto	Rosicky1	Walcott	Eduardo1	..	Adebayor/Denilson/Fabregas1 for Diaby/Rosicky/van Persie
19 Sep	Sevilla	H	W	3-0	..	Clichy	Sagna	..	Toure	Fabregas1	Flamini	Hleb	Rosicky	Adebayor	..	Diaby/Eduardo1/Diarra for Rosicky/Adebayor/van Persie
2 Oct	Steaua Bucharest	A	W	1-0	..	Sagna	Toure	..	Clichy	Hleb	Fabregas	Flamini	Eboue	Adebayor	..1	Gilberto for Eboue
23 Oct	Slavia Prague	H	W	7-0*	..	..	..	Gallas	..	Eboue2	..1	..	Hleb1	..	Walcott2	Gilberto/Rosicky/Bendtner1 for Flamini/Hleb/Adebayor
7 Nov	Slavia Prague	A	D	0-0	Almunia	Diarra	Gallas	Song	..	Walcott	Gilberto	Denilson	Diaby	Bendtner	Eduardo	Eboue/Adebayor for Eduardo/Bendtner
27 Nov	Sevilla	A	L	3-1	..	Hoyte	Toure	Senderos	Traore	Eboue	Fabregas	Gilberto	Denilson	Eduardo1	Bendtner	Sagna/Rosicky/Walcott for Justin Hoyte/Fabregas/Eduardo
12 Dec	Steaua Bucharest	H	W	2-1	Lehmann	Sagna	Gallas	..	..	Walcott	Song	Denilson	Diaby1	van Persie	Bendtner1	Diarra/Eboue/Eduardo for Sagna/Diaby/van Persie
20 Feb	AC Milan	H	D	0-0	..	..	Toure	Gallas	Clichy	Eboue	Flamini	Fabregas	Hleb	Adebayor	Eduardo	Senderos/Walcott/Bendtner for Toure/Eboue/Eduardo
4 Mar	AC Milan	A	W	2-0	Almunia	Clichy	Senderos	..	Sagna	Diaby	Fabregas1	Flamini	Eboue	Hleb	Adebayor1	Walcott/Gilberto for Eboue/Hleb
2 Apr	Liverpool	H	D	1-1	..	Toure	Gallas	Senderos	Clichy	Eboue	Flamini	Fabregas	Hleb	van Persie	..1	Bendtner/Walcott for Eboue/van Persie
8 Apr	Liverpool	A	L	4-2	..	..	..	..	..	..	..	..	Diaby1	Hleb	..1	Walcott/Gilberto/van Persie for Eboue/Flamini/Diaby

The FA Cup

6 Jan	Burnley (3)	A	W	2-0	Lehmann	Sagna	Toure	Senderos	Traore	Eboue	Gilberto	Denilson	Diaby	Bendtner1	Eduardo1	Hoyte for Traore
26 Jan	Newcastle Utd (4)	H	W	3-0*	..	Hoyte	Senderos	Gallas	Clichy	Diaby	Flamini	Fabregas	Rosicky	Walcott	Adebayor2	Gilberto/Eduardo/Hleb for Diaby/Rosicky/Walcott
16 Feb	Manchester Utd (5)	A	L	0-4	..	..	Gallas	Toure	Traore	Eboue	Fabregas	Gilberto	Hleb	Eduardo	Bendtner	Flamini/Adebayor/Senderos for Fabregas/Hleb/Eduardo

The Carling (League) Cup

25 Sep	Newcastle Utd (3)	H	W	2-0	Fabianski	Hoyte	Eboue	Senderos	Traore	Diarra	Denilson1	Song	Walcott	Bendtner1	Eduardo	Diaby for Eboue
31 Oct	Sheffield Utd (4)	A	W	3-0	..	..	Song	Diarra	Gibbs	Diaby	..	Gilberto1	..	..	Eduardo2	Perez/Lansbury/Barazite for Diaby/Walcott/Eduardo
18 Dec	Blackburn Rvrs (5)	A	W3-2(aet)		..	..	Senderos	Song	Traore	Randall	Diaby1	Denilson	Diarra	Eduardo2	Bendtner	Barazite/Merida/Gibbs for Randall/Barazite/Eduardo
9 Jan	Tottenham (SF)	H	D	1-1	..	..	Djourou	Senderos	..	Walcott1	Denilson	Gilberto	Diaby	van Persie	..	Sagna/Eduardo for Djourou/van Persie
22 Jan	Tottenham (SF)	A	L	1-5	..	Sagna	Hoyte	Gallas	..	Hleb	..	..	..	Walcott	..	Eduardo/ Fabregas/Adebayor for Traore/Denilson/Walcott

SEASON 2008–09 FA PREMIER LEAGUE

16 Aug	West Brom Albion	H	W	1-0	Almunia	Sagna	Djourou	Gallas	Clichy	Walcott	Eboue	Denilson	Nasri1	Bendtner	Adebayor	van Persie/Toure for Bendtner/Walcott
23 Aug	Fulham	A	L	0-1	..	..	Toure	..	..	..	..	..	..	van Persie	..	Bendtner/Song for Walcott/Toure
30 Aug	Newcastle United	H	W	3-0	..	..	..	..	..	Eboue	Fabregas	Denilson1	..	..2,1p	..	Vela/Song/Walcott for van Persie/Denilson/Eboue
13 Sept	Blackburn Rovers	A	W	4-0	..	..	..	..	..	..	..	..	Walcott	..1	..3,1p	Song/Ramsey/Wilshere for Walcott/Eboue/van Persie

20 Sept	Bolton Wanderers	A	W	3-1	..	..	..	..	..	..1	..	Song	Denilson1	Bendtner1	..	Djourou/Walcott/Ramsey for Clichy/Bendtner/Eboue
27 Sept	Hull City	H	L	2-1	..	..	..	..	..	..	..1	Denilson	Walcott	van Persie	..	Bendtner/Vela for Eboue/Walcott
4 Oct	Sunderland	A	D	1-1	..	..	..	..	..	Song	..1	..	..	..	..	Bendtner/Nasri/Vela for Walcott/Denilson/Song
18 Oct	Everton	H	W	3-1	..	Song	..	Silvestre	..	Eboue	..	..	Nasri1	..1	..	Walcott1/Diaby for Toure/Nasri
26 Oct	West Ham United	A	W	2-0	..	Eboue	Silvestre	Gallas	..	Walcott	..	Song	..	..	Bendtner	Adebayor1/Diaby/Sagna for Walcott/Nasri/van Persie
29 Oct	Tottenham Hotspur	H	D	4-4	..	Sagna	..1	..1	..	..	..	Denilson	..	..1	Adebayor1	Eboue/Diaby/Song for Walcott/van Persie/Nasri
1 Nov	Stoke City	A	L	2-1	..	..	Toure	Silvestre	..1	Denilson	..	Song	Diaby	Bendtner	..	Walcott/van Persie/Vela for Sagna/Denilson/Adebayor
8 Nov	Manchester United	H	W	2-1	..	..	Gallas	Clichy	Walcott	Fabregas	Denilson	Nasri2	..	..	..	Song/Fabianski/Toure for Walcott/Almunia/Diaby
15 Nov	Aston Villa	H	L	2-0	..	..	Silvestre	Gallas	Clichy	Walcott	Fabregas	Denilson	Nasri	Diaby	Bendtner	Adebayor/Vela/Toure for Diaby/Bendtner/Sagna
22 Nov	Manchester City	A	L	3-0	..	Hoyte	..	Djourou	..	Denilson	Song	Diaby	..	van Persie	..	Ramsey/Vela/ for Hoyte/Diaby
30 Nov	Chelsea	A	W	2-1	..	Sagna	Djourou	Gallas	..	..	Fabregas	Song	..	..2	Abebayor	Bendtner for Adebayor
6 Dec	Wigan Athletic	H	W	1-0	..	..	Toure	Djourou	..	..	..	..	..	..	..1	Eboue/Silvestre for Nasri/Eboue
13 Dec	Middlesbrough	A	D	1-1	..	..	Djourou	Gallas	..	..	..	..	Diaby	..	..1	Bendtner for Diaby
21 Dec	Liverpool	H	D	1-1	..	..	..	..	..	..	..	..	Nasri	..1	..	Diaby/Eboue for Fabregas/Nasri
26 Dec	Aston Villa	A	D	2-2	..	..	Toure	..	Silvestre	Eboue	Denilson1	..	..	Diaby1	van Persie	Ramsey/Clichy for Song/Nasri
28 Dec	Portsmouth	H	W	1-0	..	..	Silvestre	..1	Clichy	..	..	Diaby	..	Bendtner	Adebayor	Vela/Ramsey for Eboue/Diaby
10 Jan	Bolton Wanderers	H	W	1-0	..	..	Toure	Djourou	..	..	..	..	..	van Persie	..	Vela/Bendtner1/Ramsey for Diaby/Eboue/Adebayor
17 Jan	Hull City	A	W	3-1	..	..	..	..	..	..	..	..	..1	..	..1	Bendtner1/Song for Eboue/Adebayor
28 Jan	Everton	A	D	1-1	..	..	Djourou	Gallas	..	Song	..	..	..	..1	..	Bendtner/Eboue for Song/Sagna
31 Jan	West Ham United	H	D	0-0	..	..	Toure	..	..	Eboue	..	..	..	Bendtner	..	Vela/van Persie/Song for Eboue/Bendtner/Diaby
8 Feb	Tottenham Hotspur	A	D	0-0	..	..	..	..	..	..	..	Song	..	van Persie	..	Bendtner/Gibbs for Adebayor/Clichy
21 Feb	Sunderland	H	D	0-0	..	..	Gallas	Toure	..	Nasri	..	..	Arshavin	Bendtner	van Persie	Vela/Eboue/Gibbs for Arshavin/Song/Clichy
28 Feb	Fulham	H	D	0-0	..	..	Toure	Gallas	..	Arshavin	..	Diaby	Nasri	van Persie	Vela	Bendtner/Eboue for Vela/Sagna
3 Mar	West Brom Albion	A	W	3-1	..	..	..1	Djourou	..	Eboue	Song	Denilson	..	Bendtner2	Arshavin	Diaby/Ramsey/Merida for Toure/Eboue/Nasri
14 Mar	Blackburn Rovers	H	W	4-0	..	..	..	..	..	Walcott	..	..	Arshavin1	Nasri	Bendtner	Diaby/Vela/Eboue2,1p for Walcott/Bendtner/Nasri
21 Mar	Newcastle United	A	W	3-1	..	..	Gallas	Toure	..	Arshavin	Denilson	Diaby1	Nasri1	van Persie	..1	Song/Eboue for Arshavin/Bendtner
4 Apr	Manchester City	H	W	2-0	..	..	Toure	Gallas	..	Fabregas	Song	Denilson	Walcott	Adebayor2	Arshavin	Eboue/Bendtner/Ramsey for Walcott/Adebayor/Fabregas
11 Apr	Wigan Athletic	A	W	4-1	Fabianski	..	..	Djourou	Gibbs	Walcott1	Denilson	Song1	Arshavin1	Fabregas	Bendtner	Silvestre1/van Persie/Adebayor for Djourou/Denilson/Walcott
21 Apr	Liverpool	A	D	4-4	..	..	..	Silvestre	..	Arshavin4	Song	Fabregas	Denilson	Nasri	..	Walcott/Diaby for Denilson/Bendtner
26 Apr	Middlesbrough	H	W	2-0	Almunia	Eboue	..	..	..	Walcott	Denilson	..2	Nasri	Arshavin	..	Djourou/Diaby/Adebayor for Silvestre/Walcott/Fabregas
2 May	Portsmouth	A	W	3-0	Fabianski	Sagna	Song	Djourou	Eboue	..	..	Ramsey	Arshavin	Bendtner2,1p	Vela1	Bischoff/Merida/Randall for Walcott/Bendtner/Ramsey
10 May	Chelsea	H	L	4-1	..	..	Toure	Silvestre	Gibbs	..	Nasri	Song	Diaby	Fabregas	van Persie	Bendtner1/Denilson/Adebayor for Diaby/Song/Walcott
16 May	Manchester United	A	D	0-0	..	..	..	Song	..	Nasri	Denilson	Diaby	Fabregas	Arshavin	..	Walcott/Bendtner/Eboue for Arshavin/Nasri/Gibbs
24 May	Stoke City	H	W	4-1	Mannone	..	..	..	..	Diaby1	Fabregas	Denilson	Arshavin	van Persie2,1p	Walcott	Bendtner/Eboue/Vela for Walcott/Sagna/Arshavin

League Appearances (Goals in brackets)
Denilson 37 (3) – Bacary Sagna 35 – Manuel Almunia 32 – Nicklas Bendtner 32 (9) – Gael Clichy 31 (1) – Alex Song 31 (1) – Samir Nasri 29 (6) – Kolo Toure 29 (1) – Emmanuel Eboue 28 (3) – Robin van Persie 28 (11) – Emmanuel Adebayor 26 (10) – Abou Diaby 24 (3) – Theo Walcott 24 (2) – William Gallas 23 (2) – Cesc Fabregas 22 (3) – Johan Djourou 15 – Mikael Silvestre 14 (2) – Carlos Vela 14 (1) Andrey Arshavin 12 (6) – Aaron Ramsey 9 – Kieran Gibbs 8 – Lukaz Fabianski 6 – Fran Merida 2 – Amaury Bischoff 1 – Gavin Hoyte 1 – Vito Mannone 1 – Mark Randall 1 – Jack Wilshere 1

FA Premier League

	P	W	L	D	F:A	Pts	
Manchester U	38	28	4	6	68:24	90	1st
Arsenal	38	20	6	12	68:37	72	4th

UEFA Champions League

13 Aug	FC Twente	A	W	2-0	Almunia	Sagna	Djourou	Gallas1	Clichy	Eboue	Ramsey	Denilson	Walcott	Adebayor1	van Persie	Randall/Bendtner for Walcott/van Persie
27 Aug	FC Twente	H	W	4-0	..	..	Gallas1	Djourou	..	Walcott1	Fabregas	..	Nasri1	van Persie	Bendtner1	Eboue/Adebayor/Song for Nasri/van Persie/Fabregas
17 Sep	tDynamo Kiev	A	D	1-1	..	Toure	Song	Clichy	Sagna	Gallas1	..	Walcott	Denilson	Adebayor	van Persie	Bendtner/Eboue/Vela for Song/Sagna/van Persie
30 Sept	FC Porto	H	W	4-0	..	Sagna	Toure	Gallas	Clichy	Walcott	..	Denilson	Nasri	van Persie2	Adebayor2,1p	Eboue/Bendtner/Vela for van Persie/Nasri/Walcott
21 Oct	Fenerbahce	A	W	5-2	..	Eboue	Song1	Silvestre	..	..1	..	Diaby1	Denilson	Nasri	..1	Ramsey1/Djourou/Vela for Diaby/Walcott/Adebayor
5 Nov	Fenerbahce	H	D	0-0	Fabianski	Toure	Djourou	..	..	Ramsey	..	Denilson	Nasri	Bendtner	van Persie	Vela/Diaby/Song for Bendtner/Ramsey/Silvestre
25 Nov	Dynamo Kiev	H	W	1-0	Almunia	Djourou	Gallas	..	..	Denilson	..	Song	Ramsey	Vela	..	Bendtner1/Wilshere for Ramsey/Vela
10 Dec	FC Porto	A	L	2-0	..	Eboue	..	..	Djourou	Ramsey	Diaby	..	Denilson	..	Bendtner	Wilshere/Gibbs/Randall for Ramsey/Diaby/Song
24 Feb	AS Roma	H	W	1-0	..	Sagna	Toure	Gallas	Clichy	Eboue	Denilson	Diaby	Nasri	van Persie1p	..	Song/Vela /Ramsey for Diaby/Bendtner/Eboue
11 Mar	AS Roma	A	L	1-0	..	..	..	..	..	Diaby	..	Eboue	..	Bendtner	van Persie	Walcott/Eduardo for Eboue/Bendtner
	(Arsenal won 7-6 on penalties)															
7 Apr	Villarreal	A	D	1-1	..	..	..	..	..	Denilson	Song	Walcott	Fabregas	Nasri	Adebayor1	Fabianski/Djourou/Eboue for Almunia/Gallas/Walcott
15 Apr	Villarreal	H	W	3-0	Fabianski	Eboue	..	Silvestre	Gibbs	Walcott1	..	Fabregas	Nasri	Adebayor1	van Persie1p	Diaby/Denilson/Bendtner for van Persie/Walcott/Adebayor
29 Apr	Manchester United	A	L	1-0	Almunia	Sagna	..	..	..	Song	Diaby	Walcott	Fabregas	Nasri	Adebayor	Bendtner/Eduardo for Walcott/Adebayor
5 May	Manchester United	H	L	3-1	..	..	..	Djourou	..	Walcott	Fabregas	Song	Nasri	van Persie1p	..	Eboue/Bendtner/Vela for Gibbs/Walcott /van Persie

The FA Cup

3 Jan	Plymouth Argyle	H	W	3-1	Fabianski	Sagna	Gallas	Djourou	Silvestre	Eboue	Diaby	Nasri	Ramsey	van Persie2	Bendtner1	Gibbs/Vela/Wilshere for Silvestre/Eboue/Bendtner
25 Jan	Cardiff City	A	D	0-0	..	..	Toure	..	Gibbs	Nasri	Ramsey	Song	Eboue	..	..	Diaby/Adebayor/Wilshere for Ramsey/Eboue/Bendtner
16 Feb	Cardiff City	H	W	4-0	..	..	..	Gallas	..	..	Denilson	..	Vela	Eduardo2,1p	..1	Ramsey/van Persie1/Bischoff for Nasri/Eduardo/Vela
8 Mar	Burnley	H	W	3-0	..	..	Djourou	..	..	Eduardo1	Song	Diaby	..1	Eboue1	Arshavin	van Persie/Walcott/Ramsey for Vela/Diaby/Eduardo
17 Mar	Hull City	H	W	2-1	..	..	Gallas1	Djourou	..	Walcott	..	..	..	van Persie1	..	Nasri/Bendtner/Eboue for Vela/Song/Walcott
18 Apr	Chelsea	N	L	2-1	..	Eboue	Toure	Silvestre	..	..1	Fabregas	..	Denilson	..	Adebayor	Arshavin/Bendtner/Nasri for van Persie/Adebayor/Denilson

The Carling (League) Cup

23 Sep	Sheffield United	H	W	6-0	..	Hoyte	Djourou	Song	Gibbs	Randall	Ramsey	Merida	Wilshere1	Bendtner2	Vela3	Lansbury/Coquelin/Simpson for Song/Merida/Bendtner
11 Nov	Wigan Athletic	H	W	3-0	..	..	Song	Djourou	..	Wilshere	..	Ramsey	Merida	Simpson2	..1	Bischoff/Lansbury/Fonte for Wilshere/Simpson/Vela
2 Dec	Burnley	A	L	2-0	..	..	Silvestre	Ramsey	..	Rodgers	..	Merida	Wilshere	Bendtner	..	Lansbury/Simpson/Bischoff fo Rodgers/Wilshere/Randall

SEASON 2009–10 FA PREMIER LEAGUE

15 Aug	Everton	A	W	6-1	Almunia	Sagna	Gallas1	Vermaelen1	Clichy	Fabregas2	Song	Denilson1	Bendtner	van Persie	Arshavin	Eduardo1/Eboue/Ramsey for Fabregas/Bendtner/vanPersie
22 Aug	Portsmouth	H	W	4-1	..	Eboue	..1	..	Gibbs	Diaby2	Fabregas	..	Arshavin	..	Eduardo	Ramsey1/Merida/Bendtner for Fabregas/Arshavin/Eduardo
29 Aug	Manchester United	A	L	2-1	..	Vermaelen	Clichy	Sagna	Gallas	Arshavin1	Eboue	Song	Denilson	Diaby	van Persie	Ramsey/Bendtner/Eduardo for Arshavin/Eboue/Denilson
12 Sept	Manchester City	A	L	4-2	..	..	..	..	..	Fabregas	Song	Denilson	Diaby	van Persie1	Bendtner	Eboue/Eduardo/Rosicky1 for Sagna/Song/Denilson
19 Sept	Wigan	H	W	4-0	Mannone	..2	..	..	..	..1	Eboue1	Song	..	..	Eduardo	Bendtner/Ramsey/Rosicky for Diaby/Eboue/Eduardo
26 Sept	Fulham	A	W	1-0	..	..	..	..	..	Arshavin	Fabregas	..	..	..1	Bendtner	Rosicky/Eboue for Arshavin/van Persie
4 Oct	Blackburn Rovers	H	W	6-2	..	..1	..	..	..	..1	..1	..	..	Rosicky	van Persie1	Bendtner1/Ramsey/Walcott1 for Arshavin/Fabregas/Rosicky
17 Oct	Birmingham City	H	W	3-1	..	..	Gibbs	Gallas	Fabregas	Eboue	Walcott	..	..1	..	..1	Wilshere/Arshavin1/Sagna for Eboue/Walcott/Rosicky
25 Oct	West Ham	A	D	2-2	..	..	Clichy	Sagna	Gallas1	Arshavin	Fabregas	Eboue	Song	Diaby	..1	Bendtner/Eduardo for Eboue/Diaby
31 Oct	Tottenham Hotspur	H	W	3-0	Almunia	..	..	..	..	..	..1	Song	Diaby	van Persie2	Bendtner	Eboue/Ramsey/Eduardo for Arshavin/van Persie/Bendtner
7 Nov	Wolves	A	W	4-1	..	..	Sagna	Gibbs	..	..1	..1	Diaby	Ramsey	..	Eduardo	Nasri/Song/Rosicky for Arshavin/Diaby/Eduardo
21 Nov	Sunderland	A	L	1-0	..	..	Traore	Sagna	..	Fabregas	Song	Nasri	..	Rosicky	..	Ramsey/Rosicky/Eduardo
29 Nov	Chelsea	H	L	3-0	..	..	..	..	..	Arshavin	Fabregas	Song	Denilson	Nasri	..	Walcott/Rosicky/Vela for Song/Nasri/Eduardo
5 Dec	Stoke	H	W	2-0	..	..	..	..	..	..1	..	Eboue	..	..	Rosicky	Silvestre/Ramsey1/Vela for Traore/Eboue/Rosicky
13 Dec	Liverpool	A	W	2-1	..	..	..	..	..	..1	..	Walcott	Song	Denilson	Nasri	Silvestre/Ramsey/Diaby for Traore/Arshavin/Walcott
16 Dec	Burnley	A	D	1-1	..	..	Silvestre	..	..	..	..1	..	..	Nasri	Diaby	Ramsey/Eduardo for Fabregas/Walcott
19 Dec	Hull City	H	W	3-0	..	..	..	Gallas	Arshavin	Eboue	Song	Denilson1	Nasri	Diaby1	Eduardo1	Vela/Ramsey/Walcott for Arshavin/Nasri/Eduardo
27 Dec	Aston Villa	H	W	3-0	..	..	Traore	Sagna	Gallas	Arshavin	..	..	..	..1	..	Fabregas2/Walcott/Ramsey for Denilson/Eduardo/Fabregas
30 Dec	Portsmouth	A	W	4-1	..	..	..	..	..	..	..1	Nasri1	Diaby	Ramsey1	..1	Vela/Eastmond/Rosicky for Arshavin/Nasri/Eduardo
9 Jan	Everton	H	W	2-1	..	..	..	..	..	..	Denilson1	..	..	..	..	Merida/Rosicky1/Vela for Denilson/Ramsey/Eduardo
17 Jan	Bolton	A	W	2-0	..	..	..	..	..	..	Fabregas1	Diaby	Eastmond	Rosicky	..	Merida1/Clichy/Vela for Eastmond/Rosicky/Eduardo
20 Jan	Bolton	H	W	4-2	..	..1	Clichy	..	..	..1	..1	Denilson	Diaby	..1	..	Eastmond/Vela/Walcott for Diaby/Rosicky/Eduardo
27 Jan	Aston Villa	A	D	0-0	..	..	..	..	..	..	..	..	Ramsey	..	..	Campbell/Nasri/Bendtner for Vermaelen/Rosicky/Eduardo
31 Jan	Manchester United	H	L	3-1	..	..1	..	..	..	..	..	Song	Denilson	Nasri	Rosicky	Eboue/Walcott/Bendtner for Sagna/Denilson/Rosicky
7 Feb	Chelsea	A	L	2-0	..	..	..	..	..	..	..	Walcott	Song	..	Diaby	Eboue/Bendtner/Rosicky for Sagna/Walcott/Diaby
10 Feb	Liverpool	H	W	1-0	..	..	..	Gallas	Arshavin	Fabregas	Eboue	Song	Nasri	Diaby1	Bendtner	Walcott/Rosicky/Sagna for Arshavin/Nasri/Bendtner
20 Feb	Sunderland	H	W	2-0	..	..	..	Silvestre	Fabregas1	Eboue	Walcott	..	..	Ramsey	..1	Denilson/Sagna/Rosicky for Eboue/Walcott/Nasri
27 Feb	Stoke City	A	W	3-1	..	..1	..	Campbell	Sagna	Fabregas1	Eboue	..	..	..	..1	Walcott/Eduardo/Ramsey for Eboue/Nasri/Rosicky
6 Mar	Burnley	H	W	3-0	..	..	..	Silvestre	Fabregas1	Eboue	Walcott1	Denilson	..	Rosicky	..	Diaby/Arshavin1/Eduardo for Fabregas/Rosicky/Bendtner
13 Mar	Hull City	A	W	2-1	..	..	..	Campbell	Sagna	Arshavin1	Eboue	..	..	Diaby	..1	Walcott/Eduardo for Eboue/Nasri
20 Mar	West Ham United	H	W	2-0	..	..	..	..	Arshavin	Fabregas1p	..	Song	Denilson1	Nasri	..	Eduardo/Sagna/Diaby for Arshavin/Nasri/Bendtner
27 Mar	Birmingham City	A	D	1-1	..	Clichy	Campbell	Sagna	Fabregas	Walcott	Song	Denilson	Diaby	Rosicky	..	Nasri1/Arshavin for Walcott/Rosicky
3 Apr	Wolves	H	W	1-0	..	Vermaelen	Silvestre	Campbell	Sagna	Eboue	Walcott	Song	Denilson	..	Eduardo	Bendtner1/Nasri/Vela for Eboue/Walcott/Eduardo
14 Apr	Tottenham	A	L	2-1	..	..	Clichy	..	..	..	Denilson	Nasri	Diaby	..	Bendtner1	Silvestre/Walcott/van Persie for Vermaelen/Sagna/Denilson
18 Apr	Wigan Athletic	A	L	3-2	Fabianski	Clichy	Silvestre1	..	..	Walcott1	Nasri	Diaby	Eastmond	..	..	Eboue/van Persie/Merida for Walcott/Eastmond/Rosicky
24 Apr	Manchester City	H	D	0-0	..	..	..	..	..	..	Song	Nasri	Diaby	..	van Persie	Eboue/Bendtner for Walcott/Rosicky
3 May	Blackburn Rovers	A	L	2-1	..	Silvestre	Campbell	Traore	..	Eboue	Walcott	..	..	van Persie1	Vela	Eduardo/Arshavin for Eboue/Vela

League Appearances (Goals in brackets)
Thomas Vermaelen 40 (7) – Bacary Sagna 35 (0) – Arshavin 30 (10) – Manuel Alumnia 29 (0) – Abou Diaby 29 (6) – Cesc Fabregas 27 (15) – William Gallas 26 (3) – Alex Song 26 (1) – Gael Clichy 24 (0) – Samir Nasri 26 (2) – Emmanuel Eboue 25 (1) – Tomas Rosicky 25 (3) – Nicklas Bendtner 23 (6) – Denilson 20 (4) – Robin van Persie 16 (9) – Eduardo 24(3) – Theo Walcott 23 (3) – Sol Campbell 11 (0) Mikael Silvestre 12 (1) – Armand Traore 9 (0) – Aaron Ramsey 18 (3) – Vito Mannone 5 (0) – Lukasz Fabianski 4 (0) – Fran Merida (4) – Kieran Gibbs 3 (0) – Craig Eastmond 4 (0) – Carlos Vela 11 (1) – Jack Wilshere 1 – Johan Djourou 1 – Henri Lansbury 1

FA Premier League

	P	W	L	D	F:A	Pts	
Chelsea	38	27	6	5	103:32	86	1st
Arsenal	38	23	9	6	41:42	75	3rd

UEFA Champions League

18 Aug	Celtic	A	W	2-1	Almunia	Sagna	Vermaelen	Gallas1	Clichy	Song	Fabregas	Denilson	van Persie	Arshavin	Bendtner [og]	Diaby for Arshavin
26 Aug	Celtic	H	W	3-1	..	..	Gallas	Vermaelen	..	Eboue	Song	..	Diaby	Eduardo	..	Wilshere/Ramsey/Arshavin for Eboue/Diaby/Eduardo
16 Sept	Standard Liège	A	W	3-2	Mannone	Vermaelen1	Clichy	Gallas	Fabregas		..	Diaby	Rosicky	Bendtner1	Eduardo1	Sagna/Ramsey/Wilshere for Eboue/Rosicky/Eduardo
29 Sept	Olympiakos	H	W	2-0	..	..	..	..	Arshavin1	Fabregas	Eboue	Song	Diaby	Rosicky	van Persie1	Vela/Eduardo/Ramsey for Diaby/Rosicky/van Persie
20 Oct	AZ Alkmaar	A	D	1-1	..	..	..	Sagna	Gallas	Arshavin	Fabregas1	Eboue	Song	Diaby	..	Ramsey/Vela for Eboue/van Persie
4 Nov	AZ Alkmaar	H	W	4-1	Almunia	..	Gibbs	Gallas	Arshavin	Fabregas2	Eboue	Song	Nasri1	..1	..	Rosicky/Eduardo/Ramsey for Arshavin/Fabregas/van Persie
24 Nov	Standard Liège	H	W	2-0	..	..	..	..		..	..	..	Denilson1	Nasri1	Vela	Silvestre/Rosicky/Walcott for Gallas/Denilson/Nasri
9 Dec	Olympiakos	A	L	1-0	Fabianski	Silvestre	Gilbert	Cruise	Bartley	Walcott	Song	Merida	Ramsey	Wilshere	..	Sunu for Wilshere
17 Feb	Porto	A	L	2-1	..	Vermaelen	Clichy	Campbell1	Sagna	Fabregas	Denilson	Nasri	Diaby	Rosicky	Bendtner	Eboue/Walcott/Vela for Nasri/Rosicky/Bendtner
9 Mar	Porto	H	W	5-0	Almunia	..	..	..	..	Arshavin	Song	..1	..	..	..3	Walcott/Denilson/Eboue for Arshavin/Nasri/Rosicky
31 Mar	Barcelona	H	D	2-2	..	..	..	Sagna	Gallas	..	Fabregas1	Song	Nasri	Diaby	..	Walcott1/Denilson/Eboue for Sagna/Gallas/Arshavin
6 Apr	Barcelona	A	L	4-1	..	..	..	Silvestre	Sagna	Walcott	Denilson	Nasri	Diaby	Rosicky	..1	Eboue/Eduardo for Silvestre/Rosicky

The FA Cup

3 Jan	West Ham United		W	1-2	Fabianski	Vermaelen	Silvestre	Sagna	Gallas	Song	Merida	Ramsey1	Wilshere	Vela	Eduardo1	Nasri/Diaby for Merida/Wilshere
24 Jan	Stoke City		L	3-1	..	Silvestre	Campbell	Traore	Eastmond	Fabregas	Walcott	Denilson1	Coquelin	Emmanuel-Thomas	Vela	Arshavin/Eduardo/Ramsey for Walcott/Coquelin/Emmanuel-Thomas

The Carling (League) Cup

22 Sept	West Brom	H	W	2-0	Szczesny	Senderos	Silvestre	..	Gilbert	Gibbs	Ramsey	Wilshere	..	Sunu	Watt1	Barazite/Vela1/Randall for Traore/Coquelin/Sunu
28 Oct	Liverpool	H	W	2-1	Fabianski	..	..	Gilbert	Gibbs	Eastmond	Nasri	Merida1	Ramsey	Bendtner1	Eduardo	Randall/Coquelin/Watt for Eastmond/Merida/Bendtner
2 Dec	Manchester City	A	L	3-0	..	Eboue	Song	Silvestre	Traore	..	Merida	Ramsey	Rosicky	Wilshere	Vela	Watt for Eastmond

SEASON 2010–11 FA PREMIER LEAGUE

15 Aug	Liverpool	A	D	1-1*	Almunia	Sagna	Koscielny	Vermaelen	Clichy	Eboue	Wilshere	Diaby	Nasri	Arshavin	Chamakh	Rosicky/Walcott/van Persie for Eboue/Wilshere/Diaby
21 Aug	Blackpool	H	W	6-0	..	..	Song	..	..	Rosicky	..	..1	Walcott3	..1p	..1	Fabregas/Vela/van Persie for Diaby/Arshavin/Walcott
28 Aug	Blackburn Rovers	A	W	2-1	..	..	Koscielny	..	..	Fabregas	Song	..	..1	..1	van Persie	Chamakh/Rosicky/Wilshere for van Persie/Fabregas/Arshavin
11 Sep	Bolton Wanderers	H	W	4-1	..	Eboue	..1	Squillaci	Gibbs	..	..1	Wilshere	Rosicky	..	Chamakh1	Diaby/Denilson/Vela1 for Wilshere/Diaby/Chamakh
18 Sep	Sunderland	A	D	1-1	..	Sagna	..	..	Clichy	..1	..	..	Nasri	..	..	Rosicky/Denilson for Fabregas/Arshavin
25 Sep	West Brom Albion	H	L	2-3	..	..	..	..	..	Diaby	..	Eboue	..2	..	..	Wilshere/Rosicky/Vela for Eboue/Diaby/Koscielny
3 Oct	Chelsea	A	L	0-2	Fabianski	..	..	..	..	..	..	Wilshere	..	..	..	Rosicky/Emmanuel-Thomas/Vela for Diaby/Wilshere/Arshavin
16 Oct	Birmingham City	H	W	2-1	..	Eboue	Djourou	..	..	..	..	..	..1p	..	..1	Rosicky/Bendtner for Arshavin/Chamakh
24 Oct	Manchester City	A	W	3-0	..	Sagna	..	..	..	Fabregas	..1	Denilson	..1	..	..	Rosicky/Bendtner1/Walcott for Arshavin/Chamakh/Fabregas
30 Oct	West Ham United	H	W	1-0	..	..	Koscielny	..	..	..	..1	..	..	..	..	Walcott/Bendtner/Eboue for Denilson/Arshavin/Chamakh
7 Nov	Newcastle United	H	L	0-1	..	..	..	..	..	..	..	Wilshere	..	Walcott	..	Arshavin/van Persie/Bendtner for Nasri/Chamakh/Wilshere
10 Nov	Wolves	A	W	2-0	..	..	Djourou	..	..	..	..	..	Rosicky	Arshavin	..2	Denilson/Nasri/Bendtner for Wilshere/Arshavin/Chamakh
14 Nov	Everton	A	W	2-1	..	..1	..	..	...	..1	..	..	Nasri	..	..	Denilson/Rosicky/Eboue for Wilshere/Arshavin/Chamakh
20 Nov	Tottenham Hotspur	H	L	2-3	..	..	Koscielny	..	...	..	...	Denilson	..1	..	..1	van Persie/Rosicky/Walcott for Chamakh/Arshavin/Nasri
27 Nov	Aston Villa	A	W	4-2	..	..	..	..	..	Rosicky	..	Wilshere1	..1	..1	..1	Denilson/Gibbs/Djourou for Rosicky/Arshavin/Rosicky
4 Dec	Fulham	H	W	2-1	..	..	..	..	..	..	..	..	..2	..	..	Djourou/van Persie/Walcott for Koscielny/Rosicky/Wilshere
13 Dec	Manchester United	A	L	0-1	Szczesny	..	..	..	..	..	..	..	...	..	..	Fabregas/van Persie/Walcott for Wilshere/Rosicky/Arshavin
27 Dec	Chelsea	H	W	3-1	Fabianski	..	..	Djourou	..	Fabregas1	..1	..	..	Walcott1	van Persie	Diaby/Chamakh/Rosicky for Walcott/van Persie/Fabregas
29 Dec	Wigan Athletic	A	D	2-2	..	..	..	Squillaci	Eboue	Diaby	Denilson	Rosicky	Bendtner1	Arshavin1	Chamakh	Wilshere/Nasri/Walcott for Diaby/Arshavin/Wilshere
1 Jan	Birmingham City	A	W	3-0*	..	..	..	Djourou	Clichy	Fabregas	Song	Wilshere	Nasri1	Walcott	van Persie1	Arshavin/Denilson for Walcott/Wilshere
5 Jan	Manchester City	H	D	0-0	..	..	..	..	..	..	..	..	..	..	..	Arshavin/Bendtner for Walcott/Wilshere
15 Jan	West Ham United	A	W	3-0	Szczesny	Eboue	..	..	..	..	..	..	..	..1	..2(1p)	Denilson/Arshavin/Gibbs for Fabregas/Walcott/Nasri
22 Jan	Wigan Athletic	H	W	3-0	..	Sagna	..	..	..	..	..	..	..	..	..3	Arshavin/Chamakh/Denilson for Nasri/van Persie/Fabregas
1 Feb	Everton	H	W	2-1	..	..	..1	..	..	..	..	..	Rosicky	..	..	Diaby/Arshavin1/Bendtner for Song/Rosicky/Wilshere
5 Feb	Newcastle United	A	D	4-4	..	..	..	..1	..	..	Diaby	..	Arshavin	..1	..2	Squillaci/Rosicky/Eboue for Djourou/Arshavin/Walcott
12 Feb	Wolves	H	W	2-0	..	..	..	..	..	..	Song	..	..	Walcott	..2	Chamakh/Bendtner/Denilson for van Persie/Arshavin/Wilshere
23 Feb	Stoke City	H	W	1-0	..	..	Squillaci1	..	..	..	..	..	Nasri	..	Bendtner	Arshavin/Denilson/Chamakh for Fabregas/Walcott/Bendtner
5 Mar	Sunderland	H	D	0-0	..	..	Koscielny	..	..	Diaby	Denilson	..	..	Arshavin	..	Chamakh/Rosicky for Denilson/Diaby
19 Mar	West Brom Albion	A	D	2-2	Almunia	..	..	Squillaci	..	Ramsey	..	..	..	..1	..1	Chamakh/Bendtner for Denilson/Ramsey
2 Apr	Blackburn Rovers	H	D	0-0	..	..	..	..	..	Nasri	Song	..	Walcott	..	van Persie	Fabregas/Chamakh/Bendtner for Arshavin/Walcott/Nasri
10 Apr	Blackpool	A	W	3-1	Lehmann	Eboue1	..	..	..	Fabregas	Diaby1	..	Nasri	..	..1	Walcott/Gibbs/Ramsey for Arshavin/Nasri/Fabregas
17 Apr	Liverpool	H	D	1-1	Szczesny	..	..	Djourou	..	..	..	..	..	Walcott	..1p	Arshavin/Bendtner/Song for Walcott/Wilshere/Diaby
20 Apr	Tottenham Hotspur	A	D	3-3	..	Sagna	..	..	..	..	..	Song	..1	..1	..1	Wilshere/Arshavin/Bendtner for Diaby/Nasri/Walcott
24 Apr	Bolton Wanderers	A	L	1-2	..	..	..	..	..	..	Song	Wilshere	..	..	..1	Arshavin/Ramsey/Chamakh for Walcott/Wilshere/Song
1 May	Manchester United	H	W	1-0	..	..	..	..	..	Ramsey1	..	..	..	..	..	Arshavin/Squillaci/Eboue for Nasri/Djourou/Walcott
7 May	Stoke City	A	L	1-3	..	..	..	..	Gibbs	..	..	..	Arshavin	..	..1	Bendtner/Chamakh/Rosicky for Arshavin/Ramsey/Song
14 May	Aston Villa	H	L	1-2	..	..	Vermaelen	Squillaci	..	..	..	..	..	..	..1	Chamakh/Bendtner for Squillaci/Arshavin
22 May	Fulham	A	D	2-2	..	..	..	Djourou	..	..	Diaby	..	Nasri	Chamakh	..1	Arshavin/Eboue/Walcott1 for Diaby/Gibbs/Ramsey

League Appearances (Goals in brackets)
Andrey Arshavin 37 (6) – Jack Wilshere 35 (1) – Gael Clichy 33 (0) – Bacary Sagna 33 (1) – Samir Nasri 31 (1) – Alex Song (4) – Laurent Koscielny 30 (2) – Marouane Chamakh 29 (7) – Theo Walcott 28 (9) – Cesc Fabregas 25 (3) – Robin van Persie 25 (18) – Johan Djourou 22 (1) – Sebastien Squillaci 22 (1) – Tomas Rosicky 21 (0) – Nicklas Bendtner 17 (2) – Denilson 16 (0) –Abou Diaby 16 (2) – Wojciech Szczesny 15 (0) – Lukaz Fabianski 14 (0) – Emmanuel Eboue 13 (1) – Manuel Almunia 8 (0) – Kieran Gibbs 7 (0) – Aaron Ramsey 7 (1) – Thomas Vermaelen 5 (0) – Carlos Vela 4 (1) – Jay Emmanuel-Thomas 1 – Jens Lehmann 1 (0)

Position in League Table

	P	W	L	D	F:A	Pts	
Manchester U	38	23	4	11	78:37	80	1st
Arsenal	38	19	8	11	72:43	68	4th

Uefa Champions League

15 Sep	Braga	H	W	6-0	Almunia	Sagna	Koscielny	Squillaci	Clichy	Fabregas2(1p)	Song	Wilshere	Nasri	Arshavin1	Chamakh1	Denilson/Vela2/Eboue for Song/Chamakh/Arshavin
28 Sep	Partizan Belgrade	A	W	3-1	Fabianski	..	Djourou	..1	Gibbs	Denilson	..	..	Rosicky	..1	..1	Nasri/Vela/Clichy for Wilshere/Chamakh/Arshavin
19 Oct	Shakhtar Donetsk	H	W	5-1	..	Eboue	..	..	Clichy	Fabregas1(p)	..1	..1	..	Nasri1	..1	Denilson/Walcott/Arshavin for Fabregas/Nasri/Chamakh
3 Nov	Shakhtar Donetsk	A	L	1-2	..	..	..	..	..	Rosicky	Eastmond	..	Walcott1	..	...	Vela/Chamakh/Emmanuel-Thomas for Eastmond/Bendtner/Walcott
23 Nov	Braga	A	L	0-2	..	..	..	..	Gibbs	Fabregas	Denilson	..	..	Rosicky	Bendtner	Nasri/Chamakh/Vela for Fabregas/Bendtner/Walcott
8 Dec	Partizan Belgrade	H	W	3-1	..	Sagna	Koscielny	..	..	Nasri1	Song	Denilson	Arshavin	van Persie1(p)	Chamakh	Eboue/Walcott1/Bendtner for Gibbs/Arshavin/Chamakh
16 Feb	Barcelona	H	W	2-1	Szczesny	Eboue	..	Djourou	Clichy	Fabregas	..	Wilshere	Nasri	Walcott	van Persie1	Bendtner/Arshavin1 for Song/Walcott
8 Mar	Barcelona	A	L	1-3*	..	Sagna	..	..	..	..	Diaby	..	..	Rosicky	..	Almunia/Arshavin/Bendtner for Szczesny/Rosicky/Fabregas

The FA Cup

8 Jan	Leeds	H	D	1-1	Szczesny	Eboue	Djourou	Squillaci	Gibbs	Rosicky	Song	Denilson	Bendtner	Arshavin	Chamakh	Fabregas1(p)/Walcott/Vela for Song/Chamakh/Rosicky
19 Jan	Leeds	A	W	3-1	..	Sagna1	..	Koscielny	..	Nasri1	..	..	..	..	..	Fabregas/van Persie1/Clichy for Arshavin/Chamakh/Nasri
30 Jan	Huddersfield Town	H	W	2-1	Almunia	Eboue	Squillaci	..	..	..	Diaby	..	..1	..	..	Rosicky/Song/Fabregas1 for Nasri/Chamakh/Diaby
20 Feb	Leyton Orient	A	D	1-1	..	Sagna	..	Miquel	..	Rosicky1	Song	..	..	..	..	
2 Mar	Leyton Orient	H	W	5-0	..	Eboue	..	..	..	Diaby	Henderson	..	..3(1p)	Rosicky	..1	Nasri/Wilshere/Clichy1 for Rosicky/Diaby/Bendtner
12 Mar	Manchester Uunited	A	L	0-2	..	Sagna	Koscielny	Djourou	..	..	Wilshere	..	Nasri	Arshavin	van Persie	Chamakh/Rosicky/Ramsey for Denilson/Diaby/Arshavin

The Carling (League) Cup

21 Sep	Tottenham Hotspur	A	W	4-1	Fabianski	Eboue	Koscielny	Djourou	Gibbs	Wilshere	Denilson	Lansbury1	Rosicky	Nasri2(p)	Vela	Chamakh/Arshavin1/Clichy for Vela/Rosicky/Gibbs
27 Oct	Newcastle United	A	W	4-0*	Szczesny	..	..	..	..	Eastmond	..	Rosicky	Walcott2	Vela	Bendtner1	Sagna/Fabregas/Emmanuel-Thomas for Gibbs/Vela/Bendtner
30 Nov	Wigan Athletic	H	W	2-0*	..	..	..	..	..	Wilshere	..	van Persie	..	..	Bendtner1	Nasri/Eastmond/Emmanuel-Thomas for Wilshere/van Persie/Bendtner
12 Jan	Ipswich Town	A	L	0-1	..	..	..	...	..	..	..	Fabregas	..	Arshavin	..	Song/Chamakh/Vela for Wilshere/Bendtner/Arshavin
25 Jan	Ipswich Town	H	W	3-0	..	Sagna	..1	..	Clichy	..	..	..1	Bendtner1	..	van Persie	Eboue/Nasri/Walcott for Sagna/Arshavin/van Persie
27 Feb	Birmingham City	N	L	1-2	..	..	..	..	..	..	Song	Rosicky	Nasri	..	..1	Bendtner/Chamakh for van Persie/Arshavin

ARSENAL HONOURS

CHAMPIONS

1931, 1933, 1934, 1935, 1938, 1948, 1953, 1971, 1989, 1991, 1998, 2002, 2004

FA CUP WINNERS

1930
Arsenal 2   Huddersfield T 0
James 17
Lambert 83

1936
Arsenal 1   Sheffield U 0
Drake 74

1950
Arsenal 2   Liverpool 0
Lewis 17, 63

1971 (a.e.t.)
Arsenal 2   Liverpool 1
Kelly 101   Heighway 92
George 111

1979
Arsenal 3   Manchester U 2
Talbot 13   McQueen 87
Stapleton 44   McIlroy 89
Sunderland 89

1993 (a.e.t.)
Arsenal 2   Sheffield Wed 1
Wright 33   Waddle 66
Linighan 119
(replay after Arsenal 1 (Wright 23)
Sheffield Wed 1 (Hirst 68)

1998
Arsenal 2   Newcastle U 0
Overmars 23
Anelka 69

2002
Arsenal 2   Chelsea 0
Parlour 70
Ljungberg 80

2003
Arsenal 1   Southampton 0
Pires 38

2005 (a.e.t.)
Arsenal 0   Manchester U 0
(Arsenal won 5–4 on penalties)

LEAGUE CUP WINNERS

1987
Arsenal 2   Liverpool 1
C. Nicholas 44, 83   Rush 23

1993
Arsenal 2   Sheffield Wed 1
Merson 20   Harkes 8
Morrow 68

FAIRS CUP WINNERS

1970: 1st leg
Anderlecht 3   Arsenal 1
Devrindt 25   Kennedy 82
Muller 30, 76

1970: 2nd leg
Arsenal 3   Anderlecht 0
Kelly 26
Radford 71
Sammels 73

EUROPEAN CUP WINNERS' CUP WINNERS

1994
Arsenal 1   Parma 0
Smith 19

ARSENAL HISTORY

Formed: 1886
Turned Professional: 1891
Grounds: 1886, Plumstead Common; 1887, Sportsman Ground; 1888, Manor Ground; 1890 Invicta Ground; 1893, Manor Ground; 1913, Highbury; 2006, Emirates Stadium

CLUB RECORDS

Biggest league win:
12-0 v Loughborough T, Division 2, 12 March, 1900

Biggest league defeat:
8-0 v Loughborough T, Division 2, 12 December, 1896

Record points total (2 pts for a win):
66 from 42 matches, Division 1, 1931

Record points total (3 pts for a win):
90 from 38 matches, Premiership, 2004

Most goals scored:
127 in 42 matches, Division 1, 1931

Least goals conceded:
17 in 38 matches, Premiership, 1999

Most appearances (League, FA Cup, League Cup, Europe and Charity Shield):
722 by David O'Leary, 1975–93

Most goals:
214 by Thierry Henry, 1999–2007

Most League goals:
164 by Thierry Henry, 1999–2007

Most League goals in a season:
42 by Ted Drake, 1935

Most League goals in a match:
7 by Ted Drake, v Aston Villa (away) on 14 December, 1935

Most European goals:
41 by Thierry Henry, 1999–2007

Most international appearances:
77 by Kenny Sansom for England (from a total of 86 from 1979–88), 1980–88

Record attendance (at Highbury):
73,295 v Sunderland League, Division 1, 9 March, 1935

Record attendance (at Wembley):
73,707 v RC Lens, UEFA Champions League, 25 November, 1998

Record attendance (at Emirates):
60,161 v Manchester United, 3 November 2007

PLAYERS WHO HAVE SCORED MORE THAN 100 GOALS FOR ARSENAL

1. Thierry Henry	214
2. Ian Wright	185
3. Cliff Bastin	178
4. John Radford	149
5. Jimmy Brain	139
5=. Ted Drake	139
7. Doug Lishman	137
8. Joe Hulme	125
9. David Jack	124
10. Dennis Bergkamp	121
11. Reg Lewis	118
12. Alan Smith	115
13. Jack Lambert	109
14. Frank Stapleton	108
15. David Herd	107
16. Joe Baker	100

ARSENAL MANAGERS

1894–97:	Sam Hollis
1897–98:	Thomas Brown Mitchell
1898–99:	George Elcoat
1899–1904:	Harry Bradshaw
1904–08:	Phil Kelso
1908–15:	George Morrell
1919–25:	Leslie Knighton
1925–34:	Herbert Chapman
1934–47:	George Allison
1947–56:	Tom Whittaker
1956–58:	Jack Crayston
1958–62:	George Swindin
1962–66:	Billy Wright
1966–76:	Bertie Mee
1976–83:	Terry Neill
1984–86:	Don Howe
1986–95:	George Graham
1995 and 1996:	Stewart Houston
1995–96:	Bruce Rioch
1996–:	Arsène Wenger

ARSENAL IN EUROPE

Fairs Cup:
1963–64, 1969–70 (winners), 1970–71.

European Cup/Champions League:
1971–72, 1991–92, 1998–99, 1999–2000, 2000–01, 2001–02, 2002–03, 2003–04, 2004–05, 2005–06 (runners up), 2006–07, 2007–08, 2008–09, 2009–10, 2010–11.

UEFA Cup:
1978–79, 1981–82, 1982–83, 1996–97, 1997–98, 1999–2000 (runners up).

European Cup Winners' Cup:
1979–80 (runners up), 1993–94 (winners), 1994–95 (runners up).

ARSENAL TIMELINE

1886 Workers at the Royal Arsenal in Woolwich form a football team. Initially, the team is called 'Dial Square', taking its name from one of the arsenal's workshops. The team is given a set of red shirts by Nottingham Forest and becomes known as the Woolwich Reds before establishing themselves in local football as 'Royal Arsenal'.

1891 Arsenal take the bold decision to go professional after a proposal from committee member John Humble is passed at the club's AGM. Humble had grown tired of seeing the club's better players lured away by professional clubs. However, it is a move that is greeted with disapproval from the London FA who ban Arsenal from their competitions.

1893 Ostracised by the London FA, the Gunners – who are by now called Woolwich Arsenal – become the first Southern team to join the Football League. Their first League match ends in a 2–2 draw against Newcastle United at the Manor Ground. In order to raise enough money to finance the move to the Manor Ground, Arsenal form a limited liability company. The new company is established with a nominal capital of 4,000 £1 shares but only 860 people subscribed for 1,552 shares, with the remainder left unissued.

1894 Sam Hollis becomes the club's first manager.

1897 Former Blackburn manager Tom Mitchell takes charge but stays for just one season.

1898 George Elcoat becomes Arsenal's third manager in little over a year. He stays for just 15 months and is replaced by Harry Bradshaw for the 1899–1900 season.

1904 Bradshaw leads Arsenal to promotion in his fifth season in charge. Before the club can take its place in the First Division, he leaves to become Fulham manager. Former Hibernian boss Phil Kelso takes charge.

1908 Scotsman George Morrell is appointed manager. He guides his new team to sixth place in the First Division – the highest League finish in the club's history to date.

1913 Arsenal are relegated after winning just three of their 38 games during the 1912–13 season. Arsenal move from south London to Highbury.

Tom Parker (left) leads Arsenal out for the 1930 FA Cup final against Huddersfield.

1919 Leslie Knighton takes over as manager. However, of more significance is Arsenal's election back to the First Division, which is engineered by the club's charismatic chairman, Sir Henry Norris.

1925 Herbert Chapman arrives at Highbury, becoming the club's eighth manager in 31 years. He has previously enjoyed a successful spell in charge at Huddersfield Town.

1930 Arsenal win their first major trophy by beating Huddersfield 2–0 in the FA Cup final at Wembley. The match becomes known as the Graf Zeppelin final after the famous German airship that flies over the stadium while the match is in progress.

1931 Chapman's Arsenal are crowned League Champions for the first time, collecting a record points total of 66 to become the first Southern club to win the trophy.

1932 Gillespie Road underground station is renamed 'Arsenal' at the behest of Chapman.

1933 Arsenal are crowned Champions again, though this time they collect eight fewer points than in 1931.

1934 Herbert Chapman dies unexpectedly, with his team en route to their third League triumph. The Arsenal manager had caught a heavy cold while on scouting missions in Bury and Sheffield, and had ignored doctor's advice to stay at home and rest. Instead he went to watch Arsenal's third team on a bitterly cold day in Guildford and his cold turned into pneumonia. Thirty-six hours later he was dead.

1934 Arsenal director George Allison is appointed Chapman's successor. Allison relies heavily on backroom staff like Joe Shaw and Tom Whittaker to compensate for his lack of managerial experience as he seeks to maintain the momentum of the Chapman era.

1935 Allison leads Arsenal to a third successive title.

1936 Arsenal win the FA Cup for the second time, defeating Sheffield United 1–0 with a goal from Ted Drake at Wembley.

1937 Arsenal become the first football team in the world to be seen on television when BBC cameras film a practice game between the reserves and the first team at Highbury.

1938 Arsenal collect their seventh major honour of the 1930s by pipping Wolves and Brentford to the Championship.

1947 Tom Whittaker succeeds Allison as manager for the second season of postwar football and immediately makes his mark, guiding Arsenal to the League Championship in his first season in charge.

1950 Arsenal don unfamiliar gold jerseys for the 1950 FA Cup final against Liverpool. Despite their kit, Arsenal triumph over the Merseysiders, with Reg Lewis scoring both of the game's goals.

1953 Whittaker's Arsenal win the Championship on goal average from Preston after Jimmy Logie's strike at Highbury on 1 May gives Arsenal a vital 3–2 victory over Burnley.

Billy Wright was the world's most capped footballer prior to taking charge at Highbury.

1956 Whittaker dies of a heart attack in October. His assistant Jack Crayston takes over as manager.

1958 Crayston's managerial tenure comes to an end after a disagreement with directors over money for new players. Former Arsenal goalkeeper George Swindin is appointed as his successor.

1962 Ex-England captain Billy Wright takes over from the outgoing George Swindin as manager. Wright, who had enjoyed a glittering playing career with Wolves, has no managerial experience.

1966 Arsenal win the FA Youth Cup for the first time. The Arsenal board announce that physiotherapist Bertie Mee is to be the club's new manager.

1969 Mee's team lose out to Swindon Town in the League Cup final, having lost the previous year's final to Leeds United.

1970 Seventeen trophyless years come to an end when Arsenal overturn a two-goal first leg deficit against Anderlecht at Highbury to clinch the European Fairs Cup. Eddie Kelly, Jon Sammels and John Radford are the scorers in a memorable 3–0 victory.

1971 Mee's Arsenal become only the second team to claim a League and FA Cup Double in the 20th century. Mee is named Manager of the Year and celebrates by bringing World Cup winning midfielder Alan Ball to the club for a British record transfer fee.

1976 Erstwhile Tottenham manager Terry Neill is given the job of succeeding Bertie Mee, who becomes general manager.

1979 Arsenal beat Manchester United 3–2 in an epic FA Cup final at Wembley with a late goal from Alan Sunderland. Of the three successive Cup finals under Neill, this was to be the Club's only win.

1980 Neill's team lose out to Valencia in a penalty shoot-out after the European Cup Winners' Cup final ends in a goalless draw in Brussels.

1983 Former player and coach Don Howe takes over from Terry Neill in December. He is initially appointed as caretaker-manager but his position is made permanent in June 1984.

Michael Thomas holds the League Championship trophy aloft at Anfield in 1989.

1986 George Graham becomes Arsenal's 17th manager and leads the club to League Cup success in his first season in charge.

1989 Arsenal win the League Championship for the first time in 18 years, pipping Liverpool to the title with a 2–0 victory at Anfield in the final match of the season.

1991 Arsenal lose just one game and concede a mere 18 goals en route to their second League title success under Graham.

1993 Graham's team win a unique cup Double with victories over Sheffield Wednesday in both the FA Cup and League Cup finals at Wembley.

1994 Arsenal claim their second major European trophy when Alan Smith's goal in Copenhagen earns them a victory over Parma in the final of the Cup Winners' Cup. Arsenal reach the final of the same competition a year later, losing out to Spanish side Real Zaragoza.

1995 Stewart Houston takes charge as caretaker-manager either side of Bruce Rioch's one-season reign as Arsenal manager in 1995–96. Houston's first spell in the hotseat comes in the wake of Graham's departure in early 1995.

1996 Frenchman Arsène Wenger is appointed Arsenal manager.

1998 Wenger's team complete a Premiership and FA Cup double by beating Newcastle United in the Cup final at Wembley with goals from Nicolas Anelka and Marc Overmars.

2002 After three seasons as runners-up, Arsenal reclaim the Premiership with 87 points, thereby setting a new club record. Victory over Chelsea, courtesy of goals from Ray Parlour and Freddie Ljungberg in the FA Cup final see Arsenal complete the Double for the third time.

2003 A goal from Robert Pires at the Millennium Stadium is enough to beat Southampton and earn Arsenal a ninth FA Cup success.

2004 Arsenal go through an entire League season without defeat, the first club to do so since Preston North End more than 120 years before. Off the pitch, Emirates Airline signed the biggest sponsorship deal in English football with the Club, worth about £100m.

2005 Arsenal win the FA Cup for the tenth time, beating Manchester United 5–4 on penalties at Cardiff's Millennium Stadium after the game finished 0–0 after extra time.

2006 Club leaves Highbury and begins a new era at the Emirates Stadium.

2011 Arsenal celebrate the 125th anniversary of the Club.

Patrick Vieira with the 2003–04 Barclaycard Premiership trophy.

INDEX